The Development

— OF —

Economic Thought

GREAT ECONOMISTS
IN PERSPECTIVE

A WILEY PUBLICATION
IN ECONOMICS

Kenneth E. Boulding
Consultant in Economics

The Development

OF

Economic Thought

GREAT ECONOMISTS
IN PERSPECTIVE

Edited by

HENRY WILLIAM SPIEGEL

Professor of Economics
The Catholic University of America

JOHN WILEY & SONS, INC., NEW YORK
CHAPMAN & HALL, LIMITED, LONDON

To

WILLIAM EBENSTEIN

Foreword

I began Professor Spiegel's collection with skepticism, and finished it with enthusiasm. It must not be dismissed as a scissors-and-paste job, designed to make a quick dollar or impress a dean. It is a careful and scholarly collection, bringing to the attention of the English-language reader a wide selection of articles from many languages, dealing with a group of economists representative of the whole field of Western economic thought. The device of seeking out the verdict of economists on the economists is well adapted to bringing out the intimate and organic nature of economic thought. Indeed, this is a good tonic for those who are overly depressed about the state of the science. It is not only that the economists write well—indeed, when writing about each other they seem to develop a felicity of style which is not always observable when they are writing about economics. In writing about each other the economists also reveal that they are writing about a growing body of understanding regarding the complex problems of society. There emerges from this collection of essays a sense of the progress through time of a true science, a sense not always obtained even from formal histories.

The value of a work of this kind to the teacher and the student of the history of economic thought is immediately apparent, and the collection will no doubt find its greatest use in that field. It should not, however, be neglected by the general reader of economic literature. It can hardly fail to bring to his attention ideas that he has overlooked in the general course of his reading. It will refresh his interest in his intellectual heritage. And it will almost certainly make him want to read further in the living corpus of economic discussion. Professor Spiegel's tidbits are hors d'oeuvres and serve to whet the appetite for more reading in the many fields of interest of which he allows us brief tastes.

KENNETH BOULDING

Editor's Preface

Many great economists have shown a profound interest in the history of their discipline, and have left behind a legacy of appraisals of the work of their fellow-economists. A number of such studies have been assembled in this volume, together with kindred essays by contemporary writers of distinction. The studies are arranged in chronological order, enabling the reader to obtain a first-hand view of the development of economics as seen through the eyes of the great economists themselves. This double perspective in which the various figures and phases of the history of economics are presented will bring to light many new facets of a subject which, in Paul Samuelson's words, "is a game only worth playing if it is played very well indeed." Nobody surely could play it better than the great men, from Aristotle down to the present, who are here acting out the story of which they themselves are the heroes, telling us what they think about each other.

The work is international in scope and representative of a multiplicity of points of view. The reader will find, displayed at the market place, as it were, the great ideas that have inspired economic thought throughout the ages. The very profusion of ideas, it is hoped, will prove a challenge to the critical mind, and a wholesome antidote against any narrow dogmatism of the Keynesian or other variety.

How did I go about the work of collection? It was my aim to assemble outstanding essays by great economists about other great economists. There were a few articles whose very fame seemed to make their inclusion mandatory. With a few other articles I had to take what was available in order to round out the story. Most often, however, an article was selected as the result of a process of sifting, calling for discretion and judgment. It goes without saying that in this task I had no axe to grind; that I had what seemed to me sound reasons for inclusions and rejections; and that the opinions expressed by my authors are not necessarily my own. The justification of each selection would make a long story, too long and too tedious to be told here. Suffice it to say that it was my intention to steer clear of obituaries, to include only one article by any one author, and to concentrate on appraisals of individuals rather than of schools of thought. These self-imposed rules have, with very few exceptions, been obeyed.

It is in the nature of a work such as the present that its contents will not be overly technical, that is, mathematical, but rather illustrative of the "literary" variety of economics. I considered it my duty, however, to include at least one example that would display the sustained reasoning power of mathematical economics, and with this aim in mind I was fortunate enough to secure the cooperation of Professor Ragnar Frisch, whose essay on Wicksell is published here for the first time.

Other appraisals that have not been published before include J. M. Clark's essay on his father, and Colin Clark's study of Pigou. The essays by Perlman on Commons and by Burns on Mitchell contain elaborations or modifications of previously published material. A number of appraisals have been translated by me, and are now for the first time available in English. These include the essays by Einaudi on Galiani, Marx on the physiocrats, Halévy on Sismondi, Schmoller on Roscher, Walras on Gossen, Hayek on Wieser, Schumpeter on Böhm-Bawerk, and Demaria on Pareto.

I am indebted to the contributors of the original articles and to publishers and authors for permission to reprint or translate. Specific credits are indicated at the proper places. I also owe a great debt of gratitude to many friends and colleagues who have helped with moral support and friendly advice: first of all, to William Ebenstein and Fritz Machlup, who never failed with aid and encouragement; then, to James Washington Bell, Kenneth Boulding, F. A. Hayek, E. A. G. Robinson, Paul Samuelson, and Jacob Viner, who took a sustained interest in the project; and, finally, to Sir Ernest Barker, Marian Bowley, Harry Gunnison Brown, George R. Geiger, Paul F. Gemmill, Sir Alexander Gray, Werner Jaeger, M. L. W. Laistner, A. E. Monroe, Joseph E. Morton, Gunnar Myrdal, and Edgar Salin, who gave expert advice on specific points. Last, but not least, my wife gave much help with the translations, and if these have turned out faithful as well as beautiful, this is largely due to her efforts.

HENRY WILLIAM SPIEGEL

Washington, D. C.
January, 1952

Contents

THE DAWN OF ECONOMIC SCIENCE 1

Aristotle on Plato 3
Tawney on Medieval Economic Thought 16
Heckscher on Mercantilism 31
Jevons on Cantillon 42
Einaudi on Galiani 61
Smith on the Physiocrats 83
Marx on the Physiocrats 100

THE CLASSICAL SCHOOL 111

Douglas on Smith 113
Bonar, Fay, and Keynes on Malthus 144
McCulloch on Ricardo 158
Marshall on Ricardo 173
Mill on Bentham 184
Viner on Bentham and Mill 201
Cairnes on Bastiat 226
List on Say 241

SOCIALISTS AND REFORMERS 251

Halévy on Sismondi 253
Foxwell on Ricardian Socialists 269
Cole on Owen 297
Veblen on Marx 313
Hobson on George 329
Tawney on the Webbs 341

HISTORICAL AND INSTITUTIONAL APPROACHES . . 361

Schmoller on Roscher 363
Mitchell on Veblen 378
Perlman on Commons 403
Burns on Mitchell 413

THE RISE OF MARGINALISM 443

Schneider on Thünen 445
Fisher on Cournot 458
Walras on Gossen 470
Keynes on Jevons 489
Hayek on Menger 526
Hayek on Wieser 554
Schumpeter on Böhm-Bawerk 568
Hicks on Walras 580
J. M. Clark on J. B. Clark 592

THE GROWTH OF MODERN ECONOMICS 613

Bowley on Edgeworth 615
Demaria on Pareto 628
Frisch on Wicksell 652
Robbins on Wicksteed 700
Viner on Marshall 718
Haberler on Schumpeter 734
Samuelson on Keynes 763
Colin Clark on Pigou 779

INDEX 795

The Dawn of
Economic Science

Aristotle
on
Plato

Social thought, in the western world, begins with the Greek philosophers. With them there was born the spirit of critical enquiry, which never tires of examining human institutions, appraising them in the light of moral and political ideals. In the writings of the Greek philosophers economic arguments are developed only incidentally, and they are fused with ethical and political considerations.

The unity of Greek thought is symbolized by the student-teacher relation which links Plato (427–347 B.C.) with Socrates, and Aristotle (384–322 B.C.) with Plato. Plato's ideal state, as conceived in the *Republic,* is no inspiration for democrats, but as a grandiose piece of art it has fascinated the ages. In the *Laws* this romantic dream of the youthful Plato gives way to a less extreme conception.

Aristotle frequently expressed criticism of Plato's ideas. The chapters from his *Politics* that are reprinted here are devoted to a critical appraisal of Plato's thought on economic matters. They contain what is probably still the most cogent common-sense defense of private property. Aristotle's ideas on economic justice and on interest, as developed in his *Ethics,* were to exert a profound influence during the Middle Ages, when the doctrines of "The Philosopher" were accepted as unquestioned authority.

I

OUR PURPOSE is to consider what form of political community is best of all for those who are most able to realize their ideal of life. We must therefore examine not only this but other constitutions, both such as actually exist in well-governed states, and any theoretical forms which are held in esteem; that what is good and useful may be brought to light. And let no one suppose that in seeking for something beyond them we are anxious to make a sophistical display at any cost; we only undertake this inquiry because all the constitutions with which we are acquainted are faulty.

We will begin with the natural beginning of the subject. Three alternatives are conceivable: The members of a state must either have (1) all things or (2) nothing in common, or (3) some things in common and some not. That they should have nothing in common is clearly impossible, for the constitution is a community, and must at any rate have a common place—one city will be in one place, and the citizens are those who share in that one city. But should a well-ordered state have all things, as far as may be, in common, or some only and not others? For the citizens might conceivably have wives and children and property in common, as Socrates proposes in the *Republic* of Plato. Which is better, our present condition, or the proposed new order of society?

II

There are many difficulties in the community of women. And the principle on which Socrates rests the necessity of such an institution evidently is not established by his arguments. Further, as a means to the end which he ascribes to the state, the scheme, taken literally, is impracticable, and how we are to interpret it is nowhere precisely stated. I am speaking of the premiss from which the argument of Socrates proceeds, "that the greater the unity of the state the better." Is it not

[Aristotle, *Politics*, Bk. II, Chaps. 1–6. Reprinted by permission from Jowett's translation, published in the Oxford Translation Series, with introduction, analysis, and index by H. W. C. Davis, Clarendon Press, 1905.]

obvious that a state may at length attain such a degree of unity as to
be no longer a state?—since the nature of a state is to be a plurality,
and in tending to greater unity, from being a state, it becomes a family,
and from being a family, an individual; for the family may be said to
be more than the state, and the individual than the family. So that
we ought not to attain this greatest unity even if we could, for it would
be the destruction of the state. Again, a state is not made up only of
so many men, but of different kinds of men; for similars do not constitute a state. It is not like a military alliance. The usefulness of the
latter depends upon its quantity even where there is no difference in
quality (for mutual protection is the end aimed at), just as a greater
weight of anything is more useful than a less (in like manner, a state
differs from a nation, when the nation has not its population organized
in villages, but lives an Arcadian sort of life); but the elements out of
which a unity is to be formed differ in kind. Wherefore the principle
of compensation, as I have already remarked in the *Ethics,* is the salvation of states. Even among freemen and equals this is a principle which
must be maintained, for they cannot all rule together, but must change
at the end of a year or some other period of time or in some order
of succession. The result is that upon this plan they all govern; just
as if shoemakers and carpenters were to exchange their occupations,
and the same persons did not always continue shoemakers and carpenters. And since it is better that this should be so in politics as well,
it is clear that while there should be continuance of the same persons in
power where this is possible, yet where this is not possible by reason of
the natural equality of the citizens, and at the same time it is just that
all should share in the government (whether to govern be a good thing
or a bad), an approximation to this is that equals should in turn retire
from office and should, apart from official position, be treated alike.
Thus the one party rule and the others are ruled in turn, as if they were
no longer the same persons. In like manner when they hold office there
is a variety in the offices held. Hence it is evident that a city is not by
nature one in that sense which some persons affirm; and that what is
said to be the greatest good of cities is in reality their destruction; but
surely the good of things must be that which preserves them. Again, in
another point of view, this extreme unification of the state is clearly
not good; for a family is more self-sufficing than an individual, and a
city than a family, and a city only comes into being when the community is large enough to be self-sufficing. If then self-sufficiency is to
be desired, the lesser degree of unity is more desirable than the greater.

III

But, even supposing that it were best for the community to have the greatest degree of unity, this unity is by no means proved to follow from the fact "of all men saying 'mine' and 'not mine' at the same instant of time," which, according to Socrates, is the sign of perfect unity in a state. For the word "all" is ambiguous. If the meaning be that every individual says "mine" and "not mine" at the same time, then perhaps the result at which Socrates aims may be in some degree accomplished; each man will call the same person his own son and the same person his own wife, and so of his property and of all that falls to his lot. This, however, is not the way in which people would speak who had their wives and children in common; they would say "all" but not "each." In like manner their property would be described as belonging to them, not severally but collectively. There is an obvious fallacy in the term "all": like some other words, "both," "odd," "even," it is ambiguous, and even in abstract argument becomes a source of logical puzzles. That all persons call the same thing mine in the sense in which each does so may be a fine thing, but it is impracticable; or if the words are taken in the other sense, such a unity in no way conduces to harmony. And there is another objection to the proposal. For that which is common to the greatest number has the least care bestowed upon it. Every one thinks chiefly of his own, hardly at all of the common interest; and only when he is himself concerned as an individual. For besides other considerations, everybody is more inclined to neglect the duty which he expects another to fulfil; as in families many attendants are often less useful than a few. Each citizen will have a thousand sons who will not be his sons individually, but anybody will be equally the son of anybody, and will therefore be neglected by all alike. Further, upon this principle, every one will use the word "mine" of one who is prospering or the reverse, however small a fraction he may himself be of the whole number; the same boy will be "my son," "so and so's son," the son of each of the thousand, or whatever be the number of the citizens; and even about this he will not be positive; for it is impossible to know who chanced to have a child, or whether, if one came into existence, it has survived. But which is better—for each to say "mine" in this way, making a man the same relation to two thousand or ten thousand citizens, or to use the word "mine" in the ordinary and more restricted sense? For usually the same person is called by one man his own son whom another calls his own brother or cousin or kinsman—blood relation or connexion by marriage either of himself or of some relation of his, and yet another his clansman or tribesman; and how much better is it to be the real cousin of somebody than to be a son after Plato's fashion! Nor is there any way of preventing brothers and children and fathers and mothers from sometimes recognizing one another; for children are born like their parents, and they will necessarily be finding indications of their relationship to one another. Geographers declare such to be the fact; they say that in part of Upper Libya, where the women are common, nevertheless the children who are born are assigned to their respective fathers on the ground of their likeness. And some women, like the females of other animals—for example, mares and cows—have a strong tendency to produce offspring resembling their parents, as was the case with the Pharsalian mare called Honest.

IV

Others evils, against which it is not easy for the authors of such a community to guard, will be assaults and homicides, voluntary as well as involuntary, quarrels and slanders, all which are most unholy acts when committed against fathers and mothers and near relations, but not equally unholy when there is no relationship. Moreover, they are much more likely to occur if the relationship is unknown, and, when they have occurred, the customary expiations of them cannot be made. Again, how strange it is that Socrates, after having made the children common, should hinder lovers from carnal intercourse only, but should permit love and familiarities between father and son or between brother and brother, than which nothing can be more unseemly, since even without them love of this sort is improper. How strange, too, to forbid intercourse for no other reason than the violence of the pleasure, as though the relationship of father and son or of brothers with one another made no difference.

This community of wives and children seems better suited to the husbandmen than to the guardians, for if they have wives and children in common, they will be bound to one another by weaker ties, as a subject class should be, and they will remain obedient and not rebel. In a word, the result of such a law would be just the opposite of that which good laws ought to have, and the intention of Socrates in making these regulations about women and children would defeat itself. For friendship we believe to be the greatest good of states and the preservative of them against revolutions; neither is there anything which Socrates so greatly lauds as the unity of the state which he and all the world declare to be created by friendship. But the unity which he commends would be like that of the lovers in the *Symposium,* who, as Aristophanes says, desire to grow together in the excess of their affection, and from being two to become one, in which case one or both would certainly perish. Whereas in a state having women and children common, love will be watery; and the father will certainly not say "my son," or the son "my father." As a little sweet wine mingled with a great deal of water is imperceptible in the mixture, so, in this sort of community, the idea of relationship which is based upon these names will be lost; there is no reason why the so-called father should care about the son, or the son about the father, or brothers about one another. Of the two qualities which chiefly inspire regard and affection—that a thing is your own and that it is your only one—neither can exist in such a state as this.

Again, the transfer of children as soon as they are born from the rank of husbandmen or of artisans to that of guardians, and from the rank of guardians into a lower rank, will be very difficult to arrange; the givers or transferrers cannot but know whom they are giving and transferring, and to whom. And the previously mentioned evils, such as assaults, unlawful loves, homicides, will happen more often amongst those who are transferred to the lower classes, or who have a place assigned to them among the guardians; for they will no longer call the members of the class they have left brothers, and children, and fathers, and mothers, and will not, therefore, be afraid of committing any crimes by reason of consanguinity. Touching the community of wives and children, let this be our conclusion.

V

Next let us consider what should be our arrangements about property: should the citizens of the perfect state have their possessions in common or not? This question may be discussed separately from the enactments about women and children. Even supposing that the women and children belong to individuals, according to the custom which is at present universal, may there not be an advantage in having and using possessions in common? Three cases are possible: (1) the soil may be appropriated, but the produce may be thrown for consumption into the common stock; and this is the practice of some nations. Or (2), the soil may be common, and may be cultivated in common, but the produce divided among individuals for their private use; this is a form of common property which is said to exist among certain barbarians. Or (3), the soil and the produce may be alike common.

When the husbandmen are not the owners, the case will be different and easier to deal with; but when they till the ground for themselves the question of ownership will give a world of trouble. If they do not share equally in enjoyments and toils, those who labour much and get little will necessarily complain of those who labour little and receive or consume much. But indeed there is always a difficulty in men living together and having all human relations in common, but especially in their having common property. The partnerships of fellow-travellers are an example to the point; for they generally fall out over everyday matters and quarrel about any trifle which turns up. So with servants: we are most liable to take offense at those with whom we most frequently come into contact in daily life.

These are only some of the disadvantages which attend the community of property; the present arrangement, if improved as it might be by good customs and laws, would be far better, and would have the advantages of both systems. Property should be in a certain sense common, but, as a general rule, private; for, when every one has a distinct interest, men will not complain of one another, and they will make more progress, because every one will be attending to his own business. And yet by reason of goodness, and in respect of use, "Friends," as the proverb says, "will have all things common." Even now there are traces of such a principle, showing that it is not impracticable, but, in well-ordered states, exists already to a certain extent and may be carried further. For, although every man has his own property, some things he will place at the disposal of his friends, while of others he shares the use with them. The Lacedaemonians, for example, use one another's slaves, and horses, and dogs, as if they were their own; and when they lack provisions on a journey, they appropriate what they find in the fields throughout the country. It is clearly better that property should be private, but the use of it common; and the special business of the legislator is to create in men this benevolent disposition. Again, how immeasurably greater is the pleasure, when a man feels a thing to be his own; for surely the love of self is a feeling implanted by nature and not given in vain, although selfishness is rightly censured; this, however, is not the mere love of self, but the love of self in excess, like the miser's love of money; for all, or almost all, men love money and other such objects in a measure. And further, there is the greatest pleasure in doing a kindness or service to friends or guests or companions, which can only be rendered when a man has private property. These advantages are lost by excessive unification of the state. The exhibition of two virtues, besides, is visibly annihilated in such a state: first, temperance towards women (for it is an honourable action to abstain from another's wife for temperance sake); secondly, liberality in the matter of property. No one, when men have all things in common, will any longer set an example of liberality or do any liberal action; for liberality consists in the use which is made of property.

Such legislation may have a specious appearance of benevolence; men readily listen to it, and are easily induced to believe that in some wonderful manner everybody will become everybody's friend, especially when some one is heard denouncing the evils now existing in states, suits about contracts, convictions for perjury, flatteries of rich men and the like, which are said to arise out of the possession of private property. These evils, however, are due to a very different cause—the wickedness of human nature. Indeed, we see that there is much more quarrelling among those who have all things in common, though there are not many of them when compared with the vast numbers who have private property.

Again, we ought to reckon, not only the evils from which the citizens will be saved, but also the advantages which they will lose. The life which they are to lead appears to be quite impracticable. The error of Socrates must be attributed to the false notion of unity from which he starts. Unity there should be, both of the family and of the state, but in some respects only. For there is a point at which a state may attain such a degree of unity as to be no longer a state, or at which, without actually ceasing to exist, it will become an inferior state, like harmony passing into unison, or rhythm which has been reduced to a single foot. The state, as I was saying, is a plurality, which should be united and made into a community by education; and it is strange that the author of a system of education which he thinks will make the state virtuous, should expect to improve his citizens by regulations of this sort, and not by philosophy or by customs and laws, like those which prevail at Sparta and Crete respecting common meals, whereby the legislator has made property common. Let us remember that we should not disregard the experience of ages; in the multitude of years these things, if they were good, would certainly not have been unknown; for almost everything has been found out, although sometimes they are not put together; in other cases men do not use the knowledge which they have. Great light would be thrown on this subject if we could see such a form of government in the actual process of construction; for the legislator could not form a state at all without distributing and dividing its constituents into associations for common meals, and into phratries and tribes. But all this legislation ends only in forbidding agriculture to the guardians, a prohibition which the Lacedaemonians try to enforce already.

But, indeed, Socrates has not said, nor is it easy to decide, what in such a community will be the general form of the state. The citizens who are not guardians are the majority, and about them nothing has been determined: are the husbandmen, too, to have their property in common? Or is each individual to have his own? and are the wives and children to be individual or common? If, like the guardians, they are to have all things in common, in what do they differ from them, or what will they gain by submitting to their government? Or, upon what principle would they submit, unless indeed the governing class adopt the ingenious policy of the Cretans, who give their slaves the same institutions as their own, but forbid them gymnastic exercises and the possession of arms. If, on the other hand, the inferior classes are to be like other cities in respect of marriage and property, what will be the form of the community? Must it not contain two states in one, each hostile to the other? He makes the guardians into a mere occupying garrison, while the husbandmen and artisans and the rest are the real citizens. But if so the suits and quarrels, and all the evils which Socrates affirms to exist in other states, will exist equally among them. He says indeed that, having so good an education, the citizens will not need many laws, for example laws about the city or about the markets; but then he confines his education to the guardians. Again, he makes the husbandmen owners of the property upon condition of their paying a tribute. But in that case they are likely to be much more unmanageable and conceited than the Helots, or Penestae, or slaves in general. And whether community of wives and property be necessary for the lower equally with the higher class or not, and the questions akin to this, what will be the education, form of government, laws of the lower class, Socrates has nowhere determined: neither is it easy to discover this, nor is their character of small importance if the common life of the guardians is to be maintained.

Again, if Socrates makes the women common, and retains private property, the men will see to the fields, but who will see to the house? And who will do so if the agricultural class have both their property and their wives in common? Once more: it is absurd to argue, from the analogy of the animals, that men and women should follow the same pursuits, for animals have not to manage a household. The government, too, as constituted by Socrates, contains elements of danger; for he makes the same persons always rule. And if this is often a cause of disturbance among the meaner sort, how much more among high-spirited warriors? But that the persons whom he makes rulers must be the same is evident; for the gold which the God mingles in the souls of men is not at one time given to one, at another time to another, but always to the same: as he says, "God mingles gold in some, and silver in others, from their very birth; but brass and iron in those who are meant to be artisans and husbandmen." Again, he deprives the guardians even of happiness, and says that the legislator ought to make the whole state happy. But the whole cannot be happy unless most, or all, or some of its parts enjoy happiness. In this respect happiness is not like the even principle in numbers, which may exist only in the whole, but in neither of the parts; not so happiness. And if the guardians are not happy, who are? Surely not the artisans, or the common people. The Republic of which Socrates discourses has all these difficulties, and others quite as great.

VI

The same, or nearly the same, objections apply to Plato's later work, the *Laws,* and therefore we had better examine briefly the constitution which is therein described. In the *Republic,* Socrates has definitely settled in all a few questions only; such as the community of women and children, the community of property, and the constitution of the state. The population is divided into two classes—one of husbandmen, and the other of warriors; from this latter is taken a third class of counsellors and rulers of the state. But Socrates has not determined whether the husbandmen and artisans are to have a share in the government, and whether they, too, are to carry arms and share in military service, or not. He certainly thinks that the women ought to share in the education of the guardians, and to fight by their side. The remainder of the work is filled up with digressions foreign to the main subject, and with discussions about the education of the guardians. In the *Laws* there is hardly anything but laws; not much is said about the constitution. This, which he had intended to make more of the ordinary type, he gradually brings round to the other or ideal form. For with the exception of the community of women and property, he supposes everything to be the same in both states; there is to be the same education; the citizens of both are to live free from servile occupations, and there are to be common meals in both. The only difference is that in the *Laws,* the common meals are extended to women, and the warriors number 5000, but in the *Republic* only 1000.

The discourses of Socrates are never commonplace; they always exhibit grace and originality and thought; but perfection in everything can hardly be expected. We must not overlook the fact that the number of 5000 citizens, just now mentioned, will require a territory as large as Babylon, or some other huge site, if so many persons are to be supported in idleness, together with their women and attendants, who will be a multitude many times as great. In framing an ideal we may assume what we wish, but should avoid impossibilities.

It is said that the legislator ought to have his eye directed to two points—the people and the country. But neighbouring countries also must not be forgotten by him, firstly because the state for which he legislates is to have a political and not an isolated life. For a state must have such a military force as will be serviceable against her neighbours, and not merely useful at home. Even if the life of action is not admitted to be the best, either for individuals or states, still a city should be formidable to enemies, whether invading or retreating.

There is another point: Should not the amount of property be defined in some way which differs from this by being clearer? For Socrates says that a man should have so much property as will enable him to live temperately, which is only a way of saying "to live well"; this is too general a conception. Further, a man may live temperately and yet miserably. A better definition would be that a man must have so much property as will enable him to live not only temperately but liberally; if the two are parted, liberality will combine with luxury; temperance will be associated with toil. For liberality and temperance are the only eligible qualities which have to do with the use of property. A man cannot use property with mildness or courage, but temperately and liberally he may; and therefore the practice of these virtues is inseparable from property. There is an inconsistency, too, in equalizing the property and not regulating the number of the citizens; the population is to remain unlimited, and he thinks that it will be sufficiently equalized by a certain number of marriages being unfruitful, however many are born to others, because he finds this to be the case in existing states. But greater care will be required than now; for among ourselves, whatever may be the number of citizens, the property is always distributed among them, and therefore no one is in want; but, if the property were incapable of division as in the *Laws,* the supernumeraries, whether few or many, would get nothing. One would have thought that it was even more necessary to limit population than property; and that the limit should be fixed by calculating the chances of mortality in the children, and of sterility in married persons. The neglect of this subject, which in existing states is so common, is a never-failing cause of poverty among the citizens; and poverty is the parent of revolution and crime. Pheidon the Corinthian, who was one of the most ancient legislators, thought that the families and the number of citizens ought to remain the same, although originally all the lots may have been of different sizes: but in the *Laws* the opposite principle is maintained.

What in our opinion is the right arrangement will have to be explained hereafter.

There is another omission in the *Laws:* Socrates does not tell us how the rulers differ from their subjects; he only says that they should be related as the warp and the woof, which are made out of different wools. He allows that a man's whole property may be increased fivefold, but why should not his land also increase to a certain extent? Again, will the good management of a household be promoted by his arrangement of homesteads? For he assigns to each individual two homesteads in separate places, and it is difficult to live in two houses.

The whole system of government tends to be neither democracy nor oligarchy, but something in a mean between them, which is usually called a polity, and is composed of the heavy-armed soldiers. Now, if he intended to frame a constitution which would suit the greatest number of states, he was very likely right, but not if he meant to say that this constitutional form came nearest to his first or ideal state; for many would prefer the Lacedaemonian, or, possibly, some other more aristocratic government. Some, indeed, say that the best constitution is a combination of all existing forms, and they praise the Lacedaemonian because it is made up of oligarchy, monarchy, and democracy, the king forming the monarchy, and the council of elders the oligarchy, while the democratic element is represented by the Ephors; for the Ephors are selected from the people. Others, however, declare the Ephoralty to be a tyranny, and find the element of democracy in the common meals and in the habits of daily life. In the *Laws* it is maintained that the best constitution is made up of democracy and tyranny, which are either not constitutions at all, or are the worst of all. But they are nearer the truth who combine many forms; for the constitution is better which is made up of more numerous elements. The constitution proposed in the Laws has no element of monarchy at all; it is nothing but oligarchy and democracy, leaning rather to oligarchy. This is seen in the mode of appointing magistrates; for although the appointment of them by lot from among those who have been already selected combines both elements, the way in which the rich are compelled by law to attend the assembly and vote for magistrates or discharge other political duties, while the rest may do as they like, and the endeavour to have the greater number of the magistrates appointed out of the richer classes and the highest officers selected from those who have the greatest incomes, both these are oligarchical features. The oligarchical principle prevails also in the choice of the council, for all are compelled to choose, but the compulsion extends only to the choice out of the first class, and of an equal number out of the second class and out of the third class, but not in this latter case to all the voters but to those of the first three classes; and the selection of candidates out of the fourth class is only compulsory on the first and second. Then, from the persons so chosen, he says that there ought to be an equal number of each class selected. Thus a preponderance will be given to the better sort of people, who have the larger incomes, because many of the lower classes, not being compelled, will not vote. These considerations, and others which will be adduced when the time comes for examining similar polities, tend to show that states like Plato's should not be composed of democracy and monarchy. There is also a danger in electing the magistrates out of a body who are themselves elected; for, if but a small number choose to combine, the elections will always go as they desire. Such is the constitution which is described in the *Laws*.

Tawney

on

Medieval Economic Thought

Medieval economic thought is inspired by ethics, and reflects the doctrines of Aristotle as well as the Hebrew-Christian tradition as set forth in the Scriptures and in the teachings of the Fathers of the Church. It has found its most perfect expression in the writings of Saint Thomas Aquinas (c. 1225–1274), the "prince of scholasticism." His great *Summa Theologica,* an encyclopedic work of numerous volumes, has secured him a leading position in medieval thought.

Richard H. Tawney (1880–   ) is a profound interpreter of economic history. His best-known work, *Religion and the Rise of Capitalism* (1926), of which a selection is reproduced here, traces the influence of religious ideas on social thought and institutions.

Tawney, who was educated at Oxford, held the chair of economic history at the University of London from 1931 to his retirement in 1949. After becoming a member of the British Labour Party at an early age, he took a vigorous interest in the political developments of his time, serving as a member of various public bodies. He has made a name for himself as a brilliant critic of social institutions and attitudes with his two books, *The Acquisitive Society* (1921), and *Equality* (1931).

THE ECONOMIC doctrines elaborated in the *Summae* of the School-men have not infrequently been dismissed as the fanciful extravagances of writers disqualified from throwing light on the affairs of this world by their morbid preoccupation with those of the next. In reality, whatever may be thought of their conclusions, both the occasion and the purpose of scholastic speculations upon economic questions were eminently practical. The movement which prompted them was the growth of trade, of town life, and of a commercial economy, in a world whose social categories were still those of the self-sufficing village and the feudal hierarchy. The object of their authors was to solve the problems to which such developments gave rise. It was to reconcile the new contractual relations, which sprang from economic expansion, with the traditional morality expounded by the Church. Viewed by posterity as reactionaries, who damned the currents of economic enterprise with an irrelevant appeal to Scripture and to the Fathers, in their own age they were the pioneers of a liberal intellectual movement. By lifting the weight of antiquated formulae they cleared a space within the stiff framework of religious authority for new and mobile economic interests, and thus supplied an intellectual justification for developments which earlier generations would have condemned.

The mercantilist thought of later centuries owed a considerable debt to scholastic discussions of money, prices, and interest. But the specific contributions of medieval writers to the technique of economic theory were less significant than their premises. Their fundamental assumptions, both of which were to leave a deep imprint on the social thought of the sixteenth and seventeenth centuries, were two: that economic interests are subordinate to the real business of life, which is salvation, and that economic conduct is one aspect of personal conduct, upon which, as on other parts of it, the rules of morality are binding. Material riches are necessary; they have a secondary importance, since without them men cannot support themselves and help one another; the wise ruler, as St. Thomas said,[1] will consider in founding his State the natural resources of the country. But economic motives are suspect. Because they are powerful appetites, men fear them, but they are not mean enough to applaud them. Like other strong passions, what they need, it is thought, is not a clear field, but repression. There is no place in medieval theory for economic activity which is not related to a moral end, and to found a science of society upon the assumption that the appetite for economic gain is a constant and measurable force, to be accepted, like other natural forces, as an inevitable and self-evident *datum* would have appeared to the medieval thinker as hardly less irrational or less immoral than to make the premise of social philosophy the unrestrained operation of such necessary human attributes as pugnacity or the sexual instinct. The outer is ordained for the sake of the inner; economic goods are instrumental—*sicut quaedam adminicula, quibus adjuvamur ad tendendum in beatitudinem.* "It is lawful to desire temporal blessings, not putting them in the first place, as though setting up our rest in them, but regarding them as aids to blessedness, inasmuch as they support our corporal life and serve as instruments for acts of virtue." [2] Riches, as St. Antonino says, exist for man, not man for riches.

At every turn, therefore, there are limits, restrictions, warnings against allowing economic interests to interfere with serious affairs. It is right for a man to seek such wealth as is necessary for a livelihood in his station. To seek more is not enterprise, but avarice, and avarice is a deadly sin. Trade is legitimate; the different resources of different countries show that it was intended by Providence. But it is a dangerous business. A man must be sure that he carries it on for the public benefit, and that the profits which he takes are no more than the wages of his labor. Private property is a necessary institution, at least in a fallen world; men work more and dispute less when goods are private than when they are common. But it is to be tolerated as a concession to human frailty, not applauded as desirable in itself. "Communis enim," wrote Gratian in his *Decretum,* "usus omnium, quae sunt in hoc mundo, omnibus hominibus esse debuit." [3] At best, indeed, the estate is somewhat encumbered. It must be legitimately acquired.

[1] Aquinas, *De Regimine Principium,* lib. ii, cap. i–vii, where the economic foundations of a State are discussed.

[2] Aquinas, *Summa Theol.,* 2ª 2ᵃᵉ, Q. lxxxiii, art. vi. For St. Antonino's remarks to the same purpose, see Jarrett, *St. Antonino and Mediæval Economics,* p. 59.

[3] Gratian, *Decretum,* pt. ii, causa xii, Q. i, c. ii, § 1.

It must be in the largest possible number of hands. It must provide for the support of the poor. Its use must as far as practicable be common. Its owners must be ready to share it with those who need, even if they are not in actual destitution. Such were the conditions which commended themselves to an archbishop of the business capital of fifteenth-century Europe.[4] There have been ages in which they would have been described, not as a justification of property, but as a revolutionary assault on it. For to defend the property of the peasant and small master is necessarily to attack that of the monopolist and usurer, which grows by devouring it.

The assumption on which all this body of doctrine rested was simple. It was that the danger of economic interests increased in direct proportion to the prominence of the pecuniary motives associated with them. Labor—the common lot of mankind—is necessary and honorable; trade is necessary, but perilous to the soul; finance, if not immoral, is at best sordid and at worst disreputable. This curious inversion of the social values of more enlightened ages is best revealed in medieval discussions of the ethics of commerce. The severely qualified tolerance extended to the trader was partly, no doubt, a literary convention derived from classical models; it was natural that Aquinas should laud the State which had small need of merchants because it could meet its needs from the produce of its own soil; had not the Philosopher himself praised αὐταρκεία? But it was a convention which coincided with a vital element in medieval social theory, and struck a responsive note in wide sections of medieval society. It is not disputed, of course, that trade is indispensable; the merchant supplements the deficiencies of one country with the abundance of another. If there were no private traders, argued Duns Scotus, whose indulgence was less carefully guarded, the governor would have to engage them. Their profits, therefore, are legitimate, and they may include, not only the livelihood appropriate to the trader's status, but payment for labor, skill, and risks.[5]

The defence, if adequate, was somewhat embarrassing. For why should a defence be required? The insistence that trade is not positively sinful conveys a hint that the practices of traders may be, at

---

[4] A good account of St. Antonino's theory of property is given by Ilgner, *Die volkswirthschaftlichen Anschauungen Antonins von Florenz,* chap. x.

[5] "Sed si esset bonus legislator in patria indigente, deberet locare pro pretio magno huiusmodi mercatores . . . et non tantum eis et familiæ sustentationem necessarium invenire, sed etiam industriam, peritiam, et pericula omnia locare; ergo etiam hoc possunt ipsi in vendendo" (quoted Schreiber, *Die volkswirthschaftlichen Anschauungen der Scholastik seit Thomas v. Aquin,* p. 154).

least, of dubious propriety.   And so, in the eyes of most medieval thinkers, they are.   *Summe periculosa est venditionis et emptionis negotiatio.*[6]   The explanation of that attitude lay partly in the facts of contemporary economic organization.   The economy of the medieval borough—consider only its treatment of food supplies and prices— was one in which consumption held somewhat the same primacy in the public mind, as the undisputed arbiter of economic effort, as the nineteenth century attached to profits.   The merchant pure and simple, though convenient to the Crown, for whom he collected taxes and provided loans, and to great establishments such as monasteries, whose wool he bought in bulk, enjoyed the double unpopularity of an alien and a parasite.   The best practical commentary on the tepid indulgence extended by theorists to the trader is the network of restrictions with which medieval policy surrounded his activities, the recurrent storms of public indignation against him, and the ruthlessness with which boroughs suppressed the middleman who intervened between consumer and producer.

Apart, however, from the color which it took from its environment, medieval social theory had reasons of its own for holding that business, as distinct from labor, required some special justification.   The suspicion of economic motives had been one of the earliest elements in the social teaching of the Church, and was to survive till Calvinism endowed the life of economic enterprise with a new sanctification.   In medieval philosophy the ascetic tradition, which condemned all commerce as the sphere of iniquity, was softened by a recognition of practical necessities, but it was not obliterated; and, if reluctant to condemn, it was insistent to warn.   For it was of the essence of trade to drag into a position of solitary prominence the acquisitive appetites; and towards those appetites, which to most modern thinkers have seemed the one sure social dynamic, the attitude of the medieval theorist was that of one who holds a wolf by the ears.   The craftsman labors for his living; he seeks what is sufficient to support him, and no more.   The merchant aims, not merely at livelihood, but at profit. The traditional distinction was expressed in the words of Gratian: "Whosoever buys a thing, not that he may sell it whole and unchanged, but that it may be a material for fashioning something, he is no merchant.   But the man who buys it in order that he may gain by selling it again unchanged and as he bought it, that man is of the buyers and sellers who are cast forth from God's temple."[7]   By very definition a man who "buys in order that he may sell dearer," the trader is

[6] Henry of Ghent, *Aurea Quodlibeta*, p. 42*b* (quoted Schreiber, *op. cit.*, p. 135).
[7] Gratian, *Decretum*, pt. 1, dist. lxxxviii, cap. xi.

moved by an inhuman concentration on his own pecuniary interest, unsoftened by any tincture of public spirit or private charity. He turns what should be a means into an end, and his occupation, therefore, "is justly condemned, since, regarded in itself, it serves the lust of gain." [8]

The dilemma presented by a form of enterprise at once perilous to the soul and essential to society was revealed in the solution most commonly propounded for it. It was to treat profits as a particular case of wages, with the qualification that gains in excess of a reasonable remuneration for the merchant's labor were, though not illegal, reprehensible as *turpe lucrum*. The condition of the trader's exoneration is that "he seeks gain, not as an end, but as the wages of his labor." [9] Theoretically convenient, the doctrine was difficult of application, for evidently it implied the acceptance of what the sedate irony of Adam Smith was later to describe as "an affectation not very common among merchants." But the motives which prompted it were characteristic. The medieval theorist condemned as a sin precisely that effort to achieve a continuous and unlimited increase in material wealth which modern societies applaud as a quality, and the vices for which he reserved his most merciless denunciations were the more refined and subtle of the economic virtues. "He who has enough to satisfy his wants," wrote a Schoolman of the fourteenth century, "and nevertheless ceaselessly labors to acquire riches, either in order to obtain a higher social position, or that subsequently he may have enough to live without labor, or that his sons may become men of wealth and importance —all such are incited by a damnable avarice, sensuality, or pride." [10] Two and a half centuries later, in the midst of a revolution in the economic and spiritual environment, Luther, in even more unmeasured language, was to say the same.[11] The essence of the argument was that payment may properly be demanded by the craftsmen who make the goods, or by the merchants who transport them, for both labor in their vocation and serve the common need. The unpardonable sin is that of the speculator or the middleman, who snatches private gain by the exploitation of public necessities. The true descendant of the doctrines of Aquinas is the labor theory of value. The last of the Schoolmen was Karl Marx.

[8] Aquinas, *Summa Theol.*, 2ᵃ 2ᵃᵉ, Q. lxxvii, art. iv.

[9] *Ibid.* Trade is unobjectionable, "cum aliquis negotiationi intendit propter publicam utilitatem, ne scilicet res necessariæ ad vitam patriæ desint, et lucrum expetit, non quasi finem, sed quasi stipendium laboris."

[10] Henry of Langenstein, *Tractatus bipartitus de contractibus emptionis et venditionis*, i, 12 (quoted Schreiber, *op. cit.*, p. 197).

[11] See Tawney, *Religion and the Rise of Capitalism*, chap. II, § ii.

THE SIN OF AVARICE

If such ideas were to be more than generalities, they required to be translated into terms of the particular transactions by which trade is conducted and property acquired. Their practical expression was the body of economic casuistry, in which the best-known elements are the teaching with regard to the just price and the prohibition of usury. These doctrines sprang as much from the popular consciousness of the plain facts of the economic situation as from the theorists who expounded them. The innumerable fables of the usurer who was prematurely carried to hell, or whose money turned to withered leaves in his strong box, or who (as the scrupulous recorder remarks), "about the year 1240," on entering a church to be married, was crushed by a stone figure falling from the porch, which proved by the grace of God to be a carving of another usurer and his money-bags being carried off by the devil, are more illuminating than the refinements of lawyers.[12]

On these matters, as the practice of borough and manor, as well as of national governments, shows, the Church was preaching to the converted, and to dismiss its teaching on economic ethics as the pious rhetoric of professional moralists is to ignore the fact that precisely similar ideas were accepted in circles which could not be suspected of any unnatural squeamishness as to the arts by which men grow rich. The best commentary on ecclesiastical doctrines as to usury and prices is the secular legislation on similar subjects, for, down at least to the middle of the sixteenth century, their leading ideas were reflected in it. Plain men might curse the chicanery of ecclesiastical lawyers, and gilds and boroughs might forbid their members to plead before ecclesiastical courts; but the rules which they themselves made for the conduct of business had more than a flavor of the canon law. Florence was the financial capital of medieval Europe; but even at Florence the secular authorities fined bankers right and left for usury in the middle of the fourteenth century, and, fifty years later, first prohibited credit transactions altogether, and then imported Jews to conduct a business forbidden to Christians.[13] Cologne was one of the greatest of commercial entrepôts; but, when its successful business man came to make

[12] Examples of these stories are printed by Coulton, *A Mediæval Garner*, 1910, pp. 212–15, 298, and *Social Life in England from the Conquest to the Reformation*, 1919, p. 346.

[13] The facts are given by Arturo Segre, *Storia del Commercio*, vol. i, p. 223. For a fuller account of credit and money-lending in Florence, see Doren, *Studien aus der Florentiner Wirthschaftsgeschichte*, vol. i, pp. 173–209.

his will, he remembered that trade was perilous to the soul and avarice a deadly sin, and offered what atonement he could by directing his sons to make restitution and to follow some less dangerous occupation than that of the merchant.[14] The burgesses of Coventry fought the Prior over a question of common rights for the best part of a century; but the Court Leet of that thriving business city put usury on a par with adultery and fornication, and decreed that no usurer could become mayor, councillor, or master of the gild.[15] It was not that laymen were unnaturally righteous; it was not that the Church was all-powerful, though its teaching wound into men's minds through a hundred channels, and survived as a sentiment long after it was repudiated as a command. It was that the facts of the economic situation imposed themselves irresistibly on both. In reality, there was no sharp collision between the doctrine of the Church and the public policy of the world of business—its individual practice was, of course, another matter—because both were formed by the same environment, and accepted the same broad assumptions as to social expediency.

The economic background of it all was very simple. The medieval consumer—we can sympathize with him today more easily than in 1914—is like a traveller condemned to spend his life at a station hotel. He occupies a tied house and is at the mercy of the local baker and brewer. Monopoly is inevitable. Indeed, a great part of medieval industry is a system of organized monopolies, endowed with a public status, which must be watched with jealous eyes to see that they do not abuse their powers. It is a society of small masters and peasant farmers. Wages are not a burning question, for, except in the great industrial centers of Italy and Flanders, the permanent wage-earning class is small. Usury is, as it is today in similar circumstances. For loans are made largely for consumption, not for production. The farmer whose harvest fails or whose beasts die, or the artisan who loses money, must have credit, seed-corn, cattle, raw materials, and his distress is the money-lender's opportunity. Naturally, there is a passionate popular sentiment against the engrosser who holds a town to ransom, the monopolist who brings the livings of many into the hands of one, the money-lender who takes advantage of his neighbors' necessities to get a lien on their land and foreclose. "The usurer would not loan to men these goods, but if he hoped winning, that he loves more than

[14] Bruno Kuske, *Quellen zur Geschichte des Kölner Handels und Verkehrs im Mittelalter,* vol. iii, 1923, pp. 197–8.

[15] Early English Text Society, *The Coventry Leet Book,* ed. M. D. Harris, 1907–13, p. 544.

charity. Many other sins be more than this usury, but for this men curse and hate it more than other sin." [16]

No one who examines the cases actually heard by the courts in the later Middle Ages will think that resentment surprising, for they throw a lurid light on the possibilities of commercial immorality.[17] Among the peasants and small masters who composed the mass of the population in medieval England, borrowing and lending were common, and it was with reference to their petty transactions, not to the world of high finance, that the traditional attitude towards the money-lender had been crystallized. It was natural that "Juetta [who] is a usuress and sells at a dearer rate for accommodation," and John the Chaplain, *qui est usurarius maximus,*[18] should be regarded as figures at once too scandalous to be tolerated by their neighbors and too convenient to be altogether suppressed. The Church accepts this popular sentiment, gives it a religious significance, and crystallizes it in a system, in which economic morality is preached from the pulpit, emphasized in the confessional, and enforced, in the last resource, through the courts.

The philosophical basis of it is the conception of natural law. "Every law framed by man bears the character of a law exactly to that extent to which it is derived from the law of nature. But if on any point it is in conflict with the law of nature, it at once ceases to be a law; it is a mere perversion of law." [19] The plausible doctrine of compensations, of the long run, of the self-correcting mechanism, has not yet been invented. The idea of a law of nature—of natural justice which ought to find expression in positive law, but which is not exhausted in it—supplies an ideal standard by which the equity of particular relations can be measured. The most fundamental difference between medieval and modern economic thought consists, indeed, in the fact that, whereas the latter normally refers to economic expediency, however it may be interpreted, for the justification of any particular action, policy, or system of organization, the former starts from the position that there is a moral authority to which considerations of economic expediency must be subordinated. The practical application of this conception is the

[16] Wyclif, *On the Seven Deadly Sins,* chap. xxiv (*Works of Wyclif,* ed. T. Arnold, vol. iii, pp. 154–5). The word rendered "loan" is "leeve" [? leene] in the text.

[17] For examples of such cases see *Early Chancery Proceedings,* Bdle. lxiv, nos. 291 and 1089; Bdle. xxxvii, no. 38; Bdle. xlvi, no. 307. They are discussed in some detail in my introduction to Thomas Wilson's *Discourse upon Usury,* 1925, pp. 28–9.

[18] *Hist. MSS. Com., of Marquis of Lothian,* p. 27; Selden Society, *Leet Jurisdiction in the City of Norwich,* p. 35.

[19] Aquinas, *Summa Theol.,* 1a 2æ, Q. xcv, art. ii.

attempt to try every transaction by a rule of right, which is largely, though not wholly, independent of the fortuitous combinations of economic circumstances. No man must ask more than the price fixed, either by public authorities, or, failing that, by common estimation. True, prices even so will vary with scarcity; for, with all their rigor, theologians are not so impracticable as to rule out the effect of changing supplies. But they will not vary with individual necessity or individual opportunity. The bugbear is the man who uses, or even creates, a temporary shortage, the man who makes money out of the turn of the market, the man who, as Wyclif says, *must* be wicked, or he could not have been poor yesterday and rich today.[20]

The formal theory of the just price went, it is true, through a considerable development. The dominant conception of Aquinas—that prices, though they will vary with the varying conditions of different markets, should correspond with the labor and costs of the producer, as the proper basis of the *communis estimatio,* conformity with which was the safeguard against extortion—was qualified by subsequent writers. Several Schoolmen of the fourteenth century emphasized the subjective element in the common estimation, insisted that the essence of value was utility, and drew the conclusion that a fair price was most likely to be reached under freedom of contract, since the mere fact that a bargain had been struck showed that both parties were satisfied.[21] In the fifteenth century St. Antonino, who wrote with a highly developed commercial civilization beneath his eyes, endeavored to effect a synthesis, in which the principle of the traditional doctrine should be observed, while the necessary play should be left to economic motives. After a subtle analysis of the conditions affecting value, he concluded that the fairness of a price could at best be a matter only of "probability and conjecture," since it would vary with places, periods and persons.

[20] *On the Seven Deadly Sins,* chap. xxiv (*Works of Wyclif,* ed. T. Arnold, vol. iii, p. 153): "Bot men of lawe and marchauntis and chapmen and vitelers synnen more in avarice then done pore laboreres. And this token hereof; for now ben thei pore, ond now ben thei ful riche, for wronges that thei done."

[21] *E.g., Ægidius Lessinus, De Usuris,* cap. ix, pt. i: "Tantum res estimatur juste, quantum ad utilitatem possidentis refertur, et tantum juste valet, quantum sine fraude vendi potest . . . Omnis translatio facta libera voluntate dominorum juste fit"; Johannes Buridanus, *Quæstiones super decem libros Ethicorum Aristotelis,* v, 23: "Si igitur rem suam sic alienat, ipse secundum suam estimationem non damnificatur, sed lucratur; igitur non injustum patitur." Both writers are discussed by Schreiber (*op. cit.,* pp. 161–71 and 177–91). The theory of Buridanus appears extraordinarily modern; but he is careful to emphasize that prices should be fixed "secundum utilitatem et necessitatem totius communitatis," not "penes necessitatem ementis vel vendentis."

His practical contribution was to introduce a new elasticity into the whole conception by distinguishing three grades of prices—a *gradus pius, discretus,* and *rigidus.* A seller who exceeded the price fixed by more than 50 per cent. was bound, he argued, to make restitution, and even a smaller departure from it, if deliberate, required atonement in the shape of alms. But accidental lapses were venial, and there was a debatable ground within which prices might move without involving sin.[22]

This conclusion, with its recognition of the impersonal forces of the market, was the natural outcome of the intense economic activity of the later Middle Ages, and evidently contained the seeds of an intellectual revolution. The fact that it should have begun to be expounded as early as the middle of the fourteenth century is a reminder that the economic thought of Schoolmen contained elements much more various and much more modern than is sometimes suggested. But the characteristic doctrine was different. It was that which insisted on the just price as the safeguard against extortion. "To leave the prices of goods at the discretion of the sellers is to give rein to the cupidity which goads almost all of them to seek excessive gain." Prices must be such, and no more than such, as will enable each man to "have the necessaries of life suitable for his station." The most desirable course is that they should be fixed by public officials, after making an enquiry into the supplies available and framing an estimate of the requirements of different classes. Failing that, the individual must fix prices for himself, guided by a consideration of "what he must charge in order to maintain his position, and nourish himself suitably in it, and by a reasonable estimate of his expenditure and labor." [23] If the latter recommendation was a counsel of perfection, the former was almost a platitude. It was no more than an energetic mayor would carry out before breakfast.

No man, again, may charge money for a loan. He may, of course, take the profits of partnership, provided that he takes the partner's risks. He may buy a rent-charge; for the fruits of the earth are produced by nature, not wrung from man. He may demand compensation

---

[22] St. Antonino, *Summa Theologica,* pars ii, tit. i, cap. viii, § i, and cap. xvi, § iii. An account of St. Antonino's theory of prices is given by Ilgner, *Die volkswirthschaftlichen Anschauungen Antonins von Florenz,* chap. iv; Jarrett, *St. Antonino and Mediæval Economics;* and Schreiber, *op. cit.,* pp. 217–23. Its interest consists in the attempts to maintain the principle of the just price, while making allowance for practical necessities.

[23] Henry of Langenstein, *Tarctatus bipartitus de contractibus emptionis et venditionis,* i, 11, 12 (quoted Schreiber, *op. cit.,* pp. 198–200).

—*interesse*—if he is not repaid the principal at the time stipulated. He may ask payment corresponding to any loss he incurs or gain he foregoes. He may purchase an annuity, for the payment is contingent and speculative, not certain. It is no usury when John Deveneys, who has borrowed £19 16s., binds himself to pay a penalty of £40 in the event of failure to restore the principal, for this is compensation for damages incurred; or when Geoffrey de Eston grants William de Burwode three marks of silver in return for an annual rent of six shillings, for this is the purchase of a rent-charge, not a loan; or when James le Reve of London advances £100 to Robert de Bree of Dublin, merchant, with which to trade for two years in Ireland, for this is a partnership; or when the priority of Worcester sells annuities for a capital sum paid down.[24] What remained to the end unlawful was that which appears in modern economic text-books as "pure interest" —interest as a fixed payment stipulated in advance for a loan of money or wares without risk to the lender. "Usura est ex mutuo lucrum pacto debitum vel exactum . . . quidquid sorti accedit, subaudi per pactum vel exactionem, usura est, quodcunque nomen sibi imponat."[25] The emphasis was on *pactum*. The essence of usury was that it was certain, and that, whether the borrower gained or lost, the usurer took his pound of flesh. Medieval opinion, which has no objection to rent or profits, provided that they are reasonable—for is not every one in a small way a profit-maker?—has no mercy for the debenture-holder. His crime is that he takes a payment for money which is fixed and certain, and such a payment is usury.

The doctrine was, of course, more complex and more subtle than a bald summary suggests. With the growth of the habit of investment, of a market for capital, and of new forms of economic enterprise such as insurance and exchange business, theory became steadily more elaborate and schools more sharply divided. The precise meaning and scope of the indulgence extended to the purchase of rent-charges pro-

[24] For these examples see *Cal. of Early Mayor's Court Rolls of the City of London*, ed. A. H. Thomas, pp. 259–60; *Records of the City of Norwich*, ed. W. Hudson and J. C. Tingey, vol. i, 1906, p. 227; *Cal. of Early Mayor's Court Rolls*, p. 132; J. M. Wilson, *The Worcester Liber Albus*, 1920, pp. 199–200, 212–13. The question of the legitimacy of rent-charges and of the profits of partnership has been fully discussed by Max Neumann, *Geschichte des Wuchers in Deutschland* (1865), and by Ashley, *Economic History*. See also G. O'Brien, *An Essay on Mediæval Economic Teaching* (1920), and G. G. Coulton, *An Episode in Canon Law* (in *History*, July 1921), where the difficult question raised by the Decretal *Naviganti* is discussed.

[25] *Bernardi Papiensis Summa Decretalium* (ed. E. A. D. Laspeyres, 1860); lib. v, tit. xv.

duced one controversy, the foreign exchanges another, the development of *Monts de Piété* a third. Even before the end of the fourteenth century there had been writers who argued that interest was the remuneration of the services rendered by the lender, and who pointed out (though apparently they did not draw the modern corollary) that present are more valuable than future goods.[26] But on the iniquity of payment merely for the act of lending, theological opinion, whether liberal or conservative, was unanimous, and its modern interpreter,[27] who sees in its indulgence to *interesse* the condonation of interest, would have created a scandal in theological circles in any age before that of Calvin. To take usury is contrary to Scripture; it is contrary to Aristotle; it is contrary to nature, for it is to live without labor; it is to sell time, which belongs to God, for the advantage of wicked men; it is to rob those who use the money lent, and to whom, since they make it profitable, the profits should belong; it is unjust in itself, for the benefit of the loan to the borrower cannot exceed the value of the principal sum lent him; it is in defiance of sound juristic principles, for when a loan of money is made, the property in the thing lent passes to the borrower, and why should the creditor demand payment from a man who is merely using what is now his own?

The part played by authority in all this is obvious. There were the texts in Exodus and Leviticus; there was Luke vi. 35—apparently a mistranslation; there was a passage in the *Politics,* which some now say was mistranslated also.[28] But practical considerations contributed more to the doctrine than is sometimes supposed. Its character had been given it in an age in which most loans were not part of a credit system, but an exceptional expedient, and in which it could be said that "he who borrows is always under stress of necessity." If usury were general, it was argued, "men would not give thought to the cultivation of their land, except when they could do nought else, and so there would be so great a famine that all the poor would die of hunger; for even if they could get land to cultivate, they would not be able to get the beasts and implements for cultivating it, since the poor themselves would not have them, and the rich, for the sake both of profit and of security, would put their money into usury rather than into smaller

[26] *E.g.,* Ægidius Lessinus, *De Usuris,* chap. ix, pt. ii: "Etiam res futhræ per tempora non sunt tantæ estimationis, sicut eædem collectæ in instanti, nec tantam utilitatem inferunt possibentibus, propter quod oportet, quod sint minoris estimationis secundum justitiam."

[27] O'Brien (*op. cit.*) appears, unless I misunderstand him, to take this view.

[28] *Politics,* I, iii, *ad fin.* 1258b. See "Who said 'Barren Metal'?" by E. Cannan, W. D. Ross, etc., in *Economica,* June 1922, pp. 105–7.

and more risky investments." [29]   The man who used these arguments was not an academic dreamer.   He was Innocent IV, a consummate man of business, a believer, even to excess, in *Realpolitik,* and one of the ablest statemen of his day.

True, the Church could not dispense with commercial wickedness in high places.   It was too convenient.   The distinction between pawn-broking, which is disreputable, and high finance, which is eminently honorable, was as familiar in the Age of Faith as in the twentieth century; and no reasonable judgment of the medieval denunciation of usury is possible, unless it is remembered that whole ranges of financial business escaped from it almost altogether.   It was rarely applied to the large-scale transactions of kings, feudal magnates, bishops and abbots. Their subjects, squeezed to pay a foreign money-lender, might grumble or rebel, but, if an Edward III or a Count of Champagne was in the hands of financiers, who could bring either debtor or creditor to book? It was even more rarely applied to the Papacy itself; Popes regularly employed the international banking houses of the day, with a singular indifference, as was frequently complained, to the morality of their business methods, took them under their special protection, and sometimes enforced the payment of debts by the threat of excommunication. As a rule, in spite of some qualms, the international money-market escaped from it; in the fourteenth century Italy was full of banking-houses doing foreign exchange business in every commercial center from Constantinople to London, and in the great fairs, such as those of Champagne, a special period was regularly set aside for the negotiation of loans and the settlement of debts.[30]

It was not that transactions of this type were expressly excepted; on the contrary, each of them from time to time evoked the protests of moralists.   Nor was it mere hypocrisy which caused the traditional doctrine to be repeated by writers who were perfectly well aware that neither commerce nor government could be carried on without credit. It was that the whole body of intellectual assumptions and practical interests, on which the prohibition of usury was based, had reference to a quite different order of economic activities from that represented by loans from great banking-houses to the merchants and potentates who were their clients.   Its object was simple and direct—to prevent the well-to-do money-lender from exploiting the necessities of the peasant or the craftsman; its categories, which were quite appropriate

[29] Innocent IV, *Apparatus,* lib. v, *De Usuris.*

[30] For Italy, see Arturo Segre, *Storia del Commercio,* vol. i, pp. 179–91, and for France, P. Boissonade, *Le Travail dans l'Europe chrétienne au Moyen Age,* 1921, pp. 206–9, 212–13.   Both emphasize the financial relations of the Papacy.

to that type of transaction, were those of personal morality. It was in
these commonplace dealings among small men that oppression was
easiest and its results most pitiable. It was for them that the Church's
scheme of economic ethics had been worked out, and with reference
to them, though set at naught in high places, it was meant to be enforced, for it was part of Christian charity.

Heckscher

—————————————————————————— on ——————————————

Mercantilism

Beginning with the sixteenth and seventeenth centuries, the number of writers on economic questions increased rapidly, in England as well as in parts of the continent of Europe. They became known as bullionists, mercantilists, or cameralists, designations which indicate the principal emphasis of their work: treasure, trade, and the power of the prince. These writers developed the rudiments of an economic system in which foreign trade was to be the means for the accumulation of treasure which in turn was to enhance the power of the prince.

Eli F. Heckscher (1879–   ) is an outstanding economic historian and the highest authority on the mercantilist period. He was educated at the University of Upsala in Sweden and has held the chair of economic history at the University of Stockholm for many years. A bibliography of his works, published in 1950, lists some 1100 items. Among these, his two-volume treatise on *Mercantilism* (English translation 1935) stands out. Heckscher also has done distinguished work in the field of economic theory and its history.

MERCANTILISM, ORIGINALLY a term of opprobrium, lacks the clear cut meaning of an expression coined for purely scientific purposes. Used sporadically by the French physiocrats, the term was brought into general currency through Adam Smith, who devoted about one fourth of *The Wealth of Nations* to a relentless criticism of what he termed "the commercial or mercantile system." His attack started with the views of money which he attributed to the mercantilist writers; but the greater part of his discussion referred to commercial policy and consequently treated mercantilism as a system of protection. More than a century later in 1884 a greatly different use of the word was introduced by Gustav Schmoller in his essay, *Das Merkantilsystem in seiner historischen Bedeutung.* In Schmoller's opinion mercantilism was essentially a policy of economic unity—to a large extent independent of particular economic tenets—expressing the efforts of territorial princes, German in the first place, to overcome the disruption caused by mediaeval conditions. In England at about the same time William Cunningham in *The Growth of English Industry and Commerce* (1882) viewed mercantilism still differently as the expression of a striving after economic power for political purposes manifesting itself particularly in England. The discordance between these views was principally due to a confusion between the ends and means of economic policy; each of them pointed to something of fundamental importance in the development of economic activities and ideas in the period between the Middle Ages and the industrial revolution.

If one considers mercantilism first as a system of national economic unity, it is quite clear that there was an enormous task awaiting the rulers of most continental states at the end of the Middle Ages. Under feudalism independent petty rulers and even quite ordinary private landowners had usurped the powers of the state, harassing and impeding trade and industry and laying both under contribution for their own benefit. Among the numerous manifestations of this tendency the most important was perhaps the almost endless confusion caused

[From Edwin R. A. Seligman, ed., *Encyclopaedia of the Social Sciences.* Copyright 1933 by The Macmillan Company. Used with permission.]

throughout Europe by tolls on rivers and highways as well as by the impediments placed on trade between different provinces. An English chronicler, William Wykes, speaking of conditions in the late thirteenth century, referred to *furiosa teutonicorum insania,* "the wild madness of the Germans"; but the condition was quite as widespread in France. On all the great rivers there were separate tolls for each ten or at most fifteen kilometers, which the trader had to pay in succession. The work of unification necessitated the doing away with all this and the creation of national customs systems.

In England, where very little of this confusion had ever existed, unification was achieved in the course of the thirteenth century; but on the continent progress was slow and very little was accomplished before the nineteenth century. By far the most important success was scored by Colbert in France through his tariff of 1664. This tariff did away with most of the duties separating from one another the provinces constituting the so-called *cinq grosses fermes;* something like three eighths of the French monarchy was thus made into a single customs territory. But this was in respect only of interprovincial customs. With regard to river and highway tolls Colbert was able to achieve very little; and the customs boundaries between the rest of the provinces he left entirely untouched, with the result that areas conquered about the middle of the sixteenth century were treated as foreign territory from a customs point of view until the French Revolution. Nevertheless, the French tariff of 1664 was almost the only important measure in the direction of customs unification carried out under mercantilism, although Colbert for one was quite aware of the connection between the work of unification and mercantilist aims in the fields of money, foreign trade and colonization.

Throughout this period the towns had a well thought out and surprisingly consistent policy, which also tended to split up the unity of a state's territory. Each town attempted to subject the adjacent countryside to its contol and to hamper in every possible way the trade of competing towns. Mercantilist policy involved the substitution of a scheme which would give the whole territory the benefits that each town had tried to arrogate to itself. The direction of town policy need not necessarily be changed, but its scope must be enlarged from a municipal to a national field.

One such victory of national policy is to be recorded in the famous act of Queen Elizabeth of England—or of her minister William Cecil, Lord Burghley—the Statute of Artificers . . . and Apprentices (1562). Besides Colbert's unifying tariff of 1664 it is perhaps the only successful achievement of mercantilism in the field of economic unity. Based upon legislation which went back to the Black Death, it created a consistent national system of regulation of internal trade and industry in town and country alike, which lasted on paper until the early nineteenth century (1813–14). The positive importance of this measure consisted in its national scope. There was nothing in it favoring the towns at the expense of the countryside, and it did nothing to perpetuate the craft guilds, the typical products of town policy and economy. The guilds were thus prevented from becoming a component part of the trade regulatory system, a circumstance which contributed to weakening the hold of the mediaeval order. Otherwise the factors working for economic change had little relation to mercantilist measures, in England as in other countries. The statesmen of later Tudor and earlier Stuart times made unusually successful attempts to revive the old system of regulation, but that very fact worked in the direction of undermining it when the parliamentary party became victorious.

The importance of this development becomes clear when the French parallel is studied. For in France mercantilism accepted and tried to nationalize the mediaeval system. By the edicts of 1581, 1597 and 1673 the guilds were made compulsory throughout the country even outside the towns; and although these measures came far from achieving their purpose, the whole mediaeval system of regulation was given through them a new and wider lease of life. At the same time the craft guilds remained as exclusively local as they had ever been, so that labor and industry were prevented from flowing freely between the different parts of the country. This was probably one of the reasons why the industrial revolution began in England instead of France. French mercantilism saw the rise of a very extensive civil service engaged in industrial as well as other types of supervision, while England had not even the semblance of such a body. The famous *règlements*, issued at an ever increasing rate from the time of Colbert onward, all perpetuated the mediaeval treatment of industry. A great deal was thus achieved in the perfecting of production on the old lines; but the development of the characteristic aspect of modern industry, mass production for mass consumption, was hampered rather than furthered through the most effective and consistent forms of mercantilist regulation.

The situation was somewhat different in the field of international trade and business organization in general. On the double foundation of private partnerships, mostly of Italian origin, and mediaeval merchant guilds there arose a network of new business corporations, of which the English were more important for later developments, although the Dutch were at one time more powerful. The distinguishing feature of the so-called regulated companies in England which proved so remarkably successful in Atlantic, Mediterranean and Baltic trade was that each merchant traded for himself, although under the rules of the company and with the use of its organization. These chartered companies paved the way for the joint stock company, the direct ancestor of the most important of all modern forms of business organization, the corporation. For the history of mercantilism the important question is to what extent these developments were due to mercantilist policy. In Portugal, Spain and France the chartered companies and the organization of foreign trade and colonization in general were the outcome of state initiative; but in Holland and England, the two important countries in this field, the trading companies were created by private merchants. The state confined itself to giving them more or less extensive privileges, for which they often had to pay dearly, one of which was the preventing of others from use of the more advanced joint stock form of organization. In 1719 the English Parliament passed the Bubble Act, which was intended to check a general growth of company organization and may have achieved at least part of its object. Altogether it is far from clear that the remarkable development of company organization was to any great extent due to mercantilist policy in those countries where it was most important.

The results of mercantilist activity in overcoming the disruption caused by mediaeval conditions were thus rather limited. The laissez faire era may even be considered its executor in this respect. Through the influence of the French Revolution in other countries as well as in France and through the rise of new ideas in the field of economic policy the end of the eighteenth and the first half of the nineteenth century saw changes introduced without much difficulty for which mercantilist statesmen had been striving in vain for several hundred years.

But efforts in the direction of economic unity were only the frame of mercantilist policy. The next question must be, for what purposes mercantilist statesmen wanted to use the resources of a unified state. The answer is, principally for strengthening the powers of the state in its competition with other states. While the mediaeval conception of the object of human effort was the salvation of human souls and while economic liberalism, or laissez faire, aimed at the temporal welfare of individuals, mercantilist statesmen and writers saw in the subjects of the state means to an end, and the end was the power of the state itself. The foremost exponent of this aspect of mercantilism was Colbert; but he had counterparts everywhere. The British navigation laws as well as the old colonial system were its most lasting results. Combined with a static view of economic life this doctrine was responsible for the perpetual commercial wars of the later seventeenth and the eighteenth century, culminating in Napoleon's Continental System and the British Orders in Council of 1807. For if power was the object of economic policy and if the total fund of economic power was given once for all, the only method of benefiting one's own country was to take something away from someone else. Nobody has pointed this out with greater logical incisiveness than Colbert; and, conversely, David Hume in his criticism of mercantilism turned against just this "jealousy of trade."

It soon becomes clear, however, that the characteristic features of this policy resulted less from the striving after power in itself than from the views of its exponents as to the proper means for attaining power or prosperity. Only at this point do we reach the real economic import of mercantilism, what constitutes it an economic tenet and what reveals the fundamental differences between mercantilists and their predecessors as well as their successors. Adam Smith, for example, was entirely in accord with mercantilist aims when he wrote that "defence is of much greater importance than opulence"; the only difference was that he laid much less stress than earlier writers upon that aspect of the problem. The extent to which mercantilists and laissez faire economists were in agreement with regard to ends is suggested by a comparison of the title of Adam Smith's famous work with that of the most important book belonging to German mercantilistic literature, the *Politischer Discurs von den eigentlichen Ursachen des Auf- und Abnehmens der Städt, Länder und Republicken,* by Johann Joachim Becher (Frankfort 1668, 2nd ed. 1673). Only slight shades of meaning distinguish this title from that of the bible of laissez faire. But in their view of the relations between means and ends two books could hardly be more unlike. There lies the most distinctive feature of mercantilism.

The mercantilist conception of what was to a country's advantage centered on two closely allied aspects of economic life—the supply of commodities and of money. These doctrines are best considered separately.

It was possible to regard commodities in a purely neutral way as something to be bought or sold and neither in preference. This was the merchant's point of view; as a German author (Laspeyres) has well said with regard to the Dutch: "The merchant was a free trader in every direction; he wanted no limitation of exports, in order to send out large quantities of goods; no obstacles to imports, in order to take in large quantities; finally no hampering of transit trade, in order both to import and export large quantities." This was what might be called the staple policy of the mediaeval towns, developed first in Italy and Germany, that of drawing trade in both directions to the town itself and away from all competitors. A late but important outcome of this was the old colonial system making the metropolis an *entrepôt* of colonial trade, an idea which culminated in the British Orders in Council of 1807. Important as this tendency was during many centuries of European history it could, however, never triumph completely as it appealed only to a small minority in every community. Instead two other and entirely opposing views came in succession to dominate commercial policy.

The prevalent mediaeval idea had been that a community should aim at the securing of plenty, as Francis Bacon pointed out in his *History of Henry VII* in saying that that monarch was "bowing the ancient policy of this estate from the consideration of plenty to the consideration of power." The result was the setting up of obstacles to exports and the facilitating of imports. Throughout the Middle Ages export prohibitions were innumerable in most countries, while import prohibitions were very scarce. Commercial treaties aimed at securing imports, exports being granted as a favor; in one case it was even required that goods manufactured from raw materials set free for export should be sent back.

It was in criticisms of the prevalence of export prohibitions that the new attitude which was to become typical of mercantilism first found utterance. In *A Discourse of the Common Weal of Thys Realm of England* (1581; ed. by E. Lammond, Cambridge, Eng. 1893), probably written in 1549 by John Hales, one of the most intelligent of mercantilist writers, it was shown at some length and quite clearly how the prevention of exports counteracts its own aim through hampering the production of the commodities in question, while free exports would result in increased production. Mercantilist thought here showed an advance over mediaeval ideas in its ability to take a long view and to disprove the belief that consumers profit by everything which creates momentary plenty. The same trend of thought appears in a well known sentence by Thomas Mun, in *England's Treasure by Forraign Trade* (reprinted Oxford 1928), written about the end of the 1620's and published posthumously in 1664. Referring to export of bullion he writes: "For if we only behold the actions of the husbandman in the seed-time, when he casteth away much good corn into the ground, we will rather accompt him a mad man than a husbandman; but when we consider his labours in the harvest, which is the end of his endeavours, we find the worth and plentiful encrease of his actions." This view of economic life reappeared in the nineteenth century in the teachings of Friedrich List as well as in the "infant industry argument" of John Stuart Mill.

But it did not in itself mean a changed attitude toward the supply of commodities. Mercantilists went much further, however, turning against "a dead stock called plenty," not only for the moment but for the long run period. They came to look upon a plentiful supply of commodities within a country with as great disfavor as mediaeval statesmen had regarded a depletion of commodities. The great object became to *décharger le royaume de ses marchandises,* stimulating exports and hampering imports by every conceivable means. Only thus was a country believed to become "rich"; Sir William Petty characteristically wrote in 1662, and Sir Josiah Child repeated a few years later, that Ireland, "exporting more than it imports, doth yet grow poorer to a paradox"—the opposite result was considered the only natural one. According to this view production must be stimulated to the utmost, but products kept out and sent away. The most difficult problem was the relative treatment of the different factors of production. A natural solution was to retain goods in accordance with their importance to production or with their character as raw materials; but these points of view were very largely discordant and a consistent policy was therefore impossible. On the other hand, it was possible to find a solution with regard to one of the prerequisites of production; namely, labor, as that was not "produced." The result was encouragement of population increase, of child labor and of low wages as a method of stimulating production and increasing the competing power of a country.

It goes without saying that the mercantilist treatment of the supply of commodities was not the outcome of theoretical speculation, although such speculation later developed. How far back the policy of hampering imports went it is difficult to say, but the first known traces of the new policy date from the beginning of the thirteenth century in the towns of north Italy, especially Venice. It passed to the Netherlands about the middle of the following century and to France and England a century later, Edward IV being perhaps the first English ruler wholeheartedly to embrace protection.

Mercantilism in the sense of a policy and doctrine of protection represents the most original contribution of the period in question to economic policy and the one which has retained more sway over men's minds than any other. Various causes contributed to this great change from mediaeval ideas; the most influential apparently was the growing importance of money economy. So long as commodities were mostly exchanged against one another, it was clear to the meanest capacities that nothing could be gained by receiving little in exchange for what you gave away but quite the reverse. When, however, all exchange transactions were overlaid by the cloak of money, the workings of economic life became infinitely more difficult to understand; and then it was easy to believe that commodities were a nuisance and a danger, especially as a cause of unemployment. Although this view was first held with regard to manufactures it spread over the whole economic field, in England coming from a comparatively early date to embrace even food products. As a money economy still survives, it is natural that the mercantilist view of commodities should also have survived when the rest of mercantilism lost its influence, although the ruthless consistency of laissez faire obliterated this too for a short time from men's minds.

So far no mention has been made of the mercantilist views of money. In the opinion of Adam Smith and his followers, however, the real gist of mercantilist doctrine was expressed in the statement "that wealth consists in money, or in gold and silver." From this point of view mercantilist insistence upon an excess of exports over imports—the flow of bullion and money omitted from consideration—was explained as inability to distinguish between money and wealth. It is easy to find in mercantilist literature and state papers an almost unlimited number of utterances supporting that interpretation. But the fact that in recent times the policy of protection has retained or regained its sway, although little is now heard about the necessity for an inflow of precious metals, indicates that protection is the more fundamental tenet. In the mercantilistic period, however, the two cooperated harmoniously.

The differences between an earlier and a later policy with regard to exports of money have led to the drawing of a distinction between bullionists and mercantilists proper. The former wanted to prohibit the outflow of bullion, while the latter brought forward a theory of the balance of trade and saw in an excess of exports over imports of commodities the only possible means of increasing the monetary stock of a country without mines of precious metals. The distinction was certainly important not only for economic policy but perhaps even more as an expression of a general concept of society; but it is also true that both schools were in agreement as to the benefits of a large stock of money. Such a view is indeed very old; what mercantilism did was to bring the rest of economic policy into harmony with it and to elaborate many ingenious although usually mistaken theories to fortify it. The mercantilist theory of money was elaborated principally by a host of English writers in the seventeenth century, foremost among whom were Thomas Mun, Sir William Petty, Sir Josiah Child, John Locke and Charles Davenant; outside England there were few besides Bernardo Davanzati, Antonio Serra and Jean Bodin, the German writers contributing little of an original character in this field.

It is of course a travesty of the real opinion of these writers to say with Adam Smith that they identified wealth—an income—with money; but they very often expressed themselves as if they did so, and that also is of importance. Otherwise their reasoning is as a rule easy to follow, which does not mean that it is correct. Believing that consumption in itself was of no value they came by easy strides to the conclusion that only an excess of income over expenditure increased the riches of a country and that such an excess could consist only in an inflow of precious metals from abroad. Locke is perhaps more suggestive than any other writer on that point. From this followed naturally insistence upon an increased stock of money even by writers who could not explain to what use the money should be put or those who, like Petty, even believed in the possibility of a superabundance of money.

Most mercantilist writers and statesmen, however, insisted in the first place upon the use of money in circulation; this was in harmony with their general eagerness for trade and commerce, movement and exchange. Although the old ideal of cheapness, which was closely allied to that of plenty, held sway for a long time and perhaps never entirely lost its influence, most mercantilists were at heart inflationists. So far their eagerness for increased circulation was a foregone conclusion; for some form of the quantity theory of money was very widely held. One writer, Samuel Fortrey, found a happy expression for this aspect of mercantilism when he said in 1663: "It might be wished, nothing were cheap amongst us but onely money." This view paved the way for the plausible theories of John Law (1705) and for paper money mercantilism generally. That new departure was in strict accordance with the fundamental tenets of the school but unexpected in its results, since under a paper money regime the precious metals would lose their specific importance and much of the theoretical foundation of mercantilist commercial policy disappear. Belief in the benefits of a rapid circulation was strengthened by arguments to the effect that countries with low prices would have to "sell cheap and buy dear." In the hands of Law, who in this as in other respects could fall back upon Locke, this was elaborated into the doctrine that a plentiful supply of money within a country created a favorable rate of exchange. Almost the only writer showing a clear conception of the fact that rapid circulation by increasing prices became an obstacle to exports was Mun; but he did not follow out the conclusions, which would of course have been subversive of the whole body of mercantilist doctrine.

Lastly, mercantilism implied a general view of society, a fact which is often overlooked. This general attitude was closely akin to that of the successors of the mercantilists, the laissez faire philosophers, in almost all other respects their opposites. Both followed the general trend of modern opinion, replacing religious and moral considerations by belief in unalterable laws of social causation—a rationalism often accompanied by a strictly non-moral and non-humanitarian view of social life. The mercantilists were in agreement with laissez faire philosophers not only in basing their reasoning upon natural law; there are many likenesses as well as marked dissimilarities between the views of the two schools as to general social psychology, for example, between Petty and Hobbes on one side and Bentham on the other.

It is especially noticeable that mercantilist statesmen and writers believed in what was called "freedom of trade," or "free trade"; the utterances of Colbert to that effect are innumerable and in most cases quite seriously meant; sometimes it was even said that all interference with economic life should be avoided. How could mercantilists arrive at their practical measures from such premises? Certainly there is much inconsistency to be accounted for, but their fundamental view is quite clear. Unlike the laissez faire economists they did not base their advocacy of free trade and non-interference with economic life on the existence of a preestablished self-operating harmony. What they meant was that interference should aim at changing causes and not effects, that it was useless to punish unavoidable results without removing their causes. As a paradoxical but very typical mercantilist, Bernard Mandeville, wrote in 1714: "Private vices, by the dextrous management of a skilful politician may be turned into public benefits." The contempt of the mercantilists for religion and ethics, their desire to subject individuals to the state, their belief in a somewhat mechanical social causation without belief in a preestablished harmony, made them even more ruthless in their insistence upon setting aside all sorts of time honored customs and human needs and presented a strong contrast to the fundamentally humanitarian attitudes which followed. Moreover, in this respect as in most others the ability of mercantilist statesmen to achieve what was required by their programs was very limited; and their attempts at directing economic life without violence remained mostly on paper. In practise they had recourse to almost all the time honored methods of coercion.

Generally it may be said that mercantilism is of greater interest for what it attempted than for what it achieved. It certainly paved the way for its successors, and the discussions which went on throughout the seventeenth and the early eighteenth century eventually bore fruit, although chiefly through the criticisms they called forth. Great change in the society which mercantilist statesmen had taken over from the Middle Ages did not occur; that was reserved for their successors.

Jevons

---

on

Cantillon

A few solitary figures rank in that period of economic thought which lies between mercantilism and physiocracy. Cantillon and Galiani are its most outstanding representatives. Richard Cantillon (c. 1685–c. 1734) is considered by at least one student of the history of economics as "the greatest economist before Adam Smith" (A. E. Monroe). Cantillon's work had been all but forgotten when Stanley Jevons resuscitated him from oblivion by publishing, in 1881, a famous article of which portions are reprinted here. Since then, Cantillon's position in the history of economic thought has become more widely recognized. To him is due, among other matters, the clear formulation of the concept of "entrepreneur," who purchases goods "at a certain price to sell them again at an uncertain price, because he cannot foresee the extent of the demand."

Cantillon's *Essai sur la nature du commerce en général*, written between 1730 and 1734, was first published in 1755, after the death of its author. The latest edition of this work, with an English translation and other material by Henry Higgs, was published in 1931 by the Royal Economic Society. A few additional data on Cantillon may be found there, including some corrections of Jevons' material. Many details of Cantillon's life and work are still unknown.

(On Jevons, see pp. 489 ff.)

DILIGENT READERS of the *Wealth of Nations* will probably remember that Adam Smith once in a way quotes a certain Mr Cantillon. Hereby hangs a tale, and a tale full of errors, mysteries, and enigmas. Adam Smith quoted so few previous authors that to be mentioned in his pages ensures a kind of immortality. Nevertheless Cantillon has been very unfortunate. Not only was his life prematurely ended by fire and knife, but a series of adverse literary accidents has almost entirely obscured his name and fame.

If, wishing to know more about Cantillon, we turn to that useful but often inaccurate work, M'Culloch's *Literature of Political Economy,* we find (p. 52) some description of a book called *"The Analysis of Trade, Commerce, Bullion, etc.* By Philip Cantillon, late of the City of London, Merchant" (1 vol. 8vo, London, 1759). M'Culloch goes on to remark of this book that "the author adopts several of the views of Hume, whose *Political Essays* were published in 1752. His principles are for the most part liberal, and some of his speculations display considerable ingenuity." Here the filiation of ideas seems to be evident. Cantillon adopted the views of Hume, whose essays, according to his biographer Burton, form the *Cradle of Political Economy.* "Much as that science," says Burton, "has been investigated and expounded in later times, these earliest, shortest, and simplest developments of its principles are still read with delight even by those who are masters of all the literature of this great subject." I am far from denying that "a master of all the literature of political economy," if such a wonderful creature can be imagined, might read the essays of Hume with delight, and he might also possibly agree with Professor Huxley that Hume was in political economy, as in philosophy, "an original, a daring, and a fertile innovator." But he could not possibly allow that Hume's *Essays* of 1752 are "the earliest, shortest, and simplest developments of its principles"; nor could he fall into M'Culloch's blunder of supposing that the Cantillon quoted by Smith owed anything to Hume.

M'Culloch is much to be blamed in this matter, for, had he examined the title-page of the so-called *Analysis of Trade,* he would have seen

[Reprinted in abridged form from *Contemporary Review,* January 1881.]

that the contents of the book purport to be "Taken chiefly from a Manuscript of a very ingenious Gentleman deceas'd, and adapted to the present Situation of our Trade and Commerce." As this book was published in 1759, and Hume's *Essays* in 1752, seven years hardly make a sufficient interval to enable Philip Cantillon to adopt the views of Hume, to write the manuscript, to become deceased, and after all to need adapting "to the present situation of our trade," etc. Had M'Culloch glanced into some ordinary bibliographical or biographical works of reference, he might have been saved from blundering.[1] The great French biographical works (both the *Biographie Universelle,* Paris, 1843, vol. VI, p. 584, and Didot's *Nouvelle Biographie Générale,* vol. VIII, pp. 528–9) contain particulars of "Philip" Cantillon's life, stating that he died in 1733 (more accurately 1734). This fact of course disperses the notion that he could have borrowed from Hume. We learn also from these and other books to be presently quoted that Cantillon's work was first printed in the French language in the year 1755, under the title *"Essai sur la Nature du Commerce en Général.* Traduit de l'Anglois. Londres."

The briefest examination of this latter volume at once shows that the English version of 1759 is so horribly garbled as to give no idea of the merits of the original work. The so-called *Analysis of Trade* is a loose translation of portions of the real *Essai,* omitting usually the best parts of the chapters in order to allow of the insertion of extracts from Hume's *Essays,* rodomontades about Oliver Cromwell, and other wholly irrelevant matter. The book is said to be "Printed for the Author," but this author must have been a wretched literary hack, and in saying that the book was "taken chiefly from a manuscript of a very ingenious gentleman deceased" he diverged considerably from the line of strict veracity.

The original *Essai* is thus described on its title-page: *"Essai sur la Nature du Commerce en Général.* Traduit de l'Anglois. A Londres, chez Fletcher Gyles, dans Holborn. MDCCLV." The book consists of half-title, title, 430 pages, and 6 pages of contents; 12mo, sheets A to T ii. The date is erroneously given as 1752 in the French *Dictionnaire de l'Économie Politique,* and in Mr Macleod's *Dictionary.*

Before turning to analyse the contents of this *Essai,* it will be well to learn what we can about the book and its author from extrinsic sources. It appears that the so-called Philippe de Cantillon was a clever merchant, of an Irish family towards the end of the seventeenth

---

[1] M'Culloch's erroneous account of Cantillon has been unfortunately copied by Allibone in his *Dictionary of English Literature.*

century. At first he carried on business as a merchant in London, but afterwards removed to Paris, and established a banking-house. "Joining to immense credit," as the *Biographie Universelle* says, "amiable manners and much wit, he was sought after in the best society and lived in intimacy with persons of the first distinction." He was a friend of Lord Bolingbroke, and it is even asserted that he stood well with the Princesse d'Auvergne. Such, indeed, was his success, financial and social, that the great John Law, then in the midst of his financial combinations, grew jealous of him. Summoning his fellow-countryman to his presence, there ensued a conversation which must be true because, as a French author would say, it is so simple. " 'Si nous étions en Angleterre [said Law] il faudrait traiter ensemble, et nous arranger; mais, comme nous sommes en France, je puis vous envoyer ce soir à la Bastille, si vous ne me donnez votre parole de sortir du Royaume dans les vingt-quatre heures.' Cantillon se mit à rêver un moment et lui dit: 'Tenez; je ne m'en irai pas, et je ferai réussir votre système.' " Accordingly Cantillon took from Law an immense quantity of the new-fangled paper, which through the hands of his numerous commercial friends and agents, and by the force of his immense credit, he was able to place upon the market to great advantage. He thus, if the accounts can be trusted, made a fortune of several millions in a few days, but still, distrusting Law, prudently retired to Holland, whence he subsequently removed to London. Here he was murdered by a *valet-de-chambre* (more correctly a cook), who then decamped with his most valuable and portable property.

If Cantillon were really murdered in London, the newspapers of the time would probably contain some account of the event. Without much difficulty I met with the following particulars. *The Country Journal, or The Craftsman,* of Saturday, 18th May 1734, says:

Tuesday morning about three o'clock a fire happened in the house of Mr Chantillon, a rich French merchant in Albemarle Street, which in a short space destroyed the said house, together with the Lord Viscount St John's adjoining, and also greatly damaged another house. When the flames were first discovered, Mr Chantillon's footman broke into his master's chamber (whom he had about twelve the night before left in his bedchamber reading with a candle), and found him dead in his bed, and with his head almost burnt off.

A paragraph, more important for our purposes, is contained in *Read's Weekly Journal, or British Gazetteer,* of Saturday, 1st June 1734, No. 480. It states that it had been represented to the King, that Richard Cantillon, Esq., was, on Tuesday, 14th May, between three and four in the morning, robbed and murdered in his house in Albemarle Street, and his said house afterwards villainously burnt to the ground. A free pardon is therefore offered by the Government to any accomplices in the deed. And, as a further encouragement, Mr Philip Cantillon, a merchant of this city, has promised a reward of £200 to any one of the criminals, excepting the actual murderer.

It does not appear that the real culprit was ever captured, but according to an entry in the *Gentleman's Magazine,* under the date 7th December 1734 (vol. IV, p. 702), Isaac Burridge, Roger Arnold, and Elizabeth Pembroke were tried for the murder of their master, Mr Cantillon, and for firing his house, and were found not guilty. See also the same volume, p. 273.

The important fact which we gather from the above contemporary records is that there were really two Cantillons, and that the rich French merchant was not Philip Cantillon at all, but Richard Cantillon.

It seems necessary to suppose that the real name of the great economist and financier was lost, and is only now for the first time attached to his work. As the garbled translation of 1759 speaks of Philip as late of the City of London, and the newspapers bear out this statement, while calling Richard a rich French merchant, it is impossible to suppose that Philip was the author and rival of Law, and Richard the London merchant. As a mere surmise we may suppose that Richard and Philip were brothers, and carried on their merchant's and banker's business in close correspondence. But I do not know how to explain the fact that literary reputation became attached to the name Philip Cantillon.

I have been able to meet with few other facts relating to the personality of Cantillon. He was descended from the family of that name belonging to Ballyheige or Ballyhigue, in County Kerry, Ireland, whose armorial bearings are given in Burke's *General Armoury* and other works thus: "az. a lion, rampant, or, between two arrows, or, feathered and barbed, of the second." That this family had connections in France is apparent from the fact that Antoine Sylvain de Cantillon, Baron de Ballyheige, and in France Lieutenant-Colonel Chevalier of the Order of St Louis, bore the same arms. In the *Gentleman's Magazine* for 1743, vol. XIII, p. 389, we read that the Earl of Stafford was married to a Miss Cantillon, so that some of the aristocracy both of England and France are probably descended from the first economist.

The name of course is an essentially Spanish one, and it is well known that many Spanish merchants settled on the west coast of Ireland. Their houses of distinctly Spanish architecture may be seen in Galway to the present day.

Turning now to this remarkable *Essai sur la Nature du Commerce en Général,* we find that it purports, according to the title-page, to be published "à Londres, chez Fletcher Gyles, dans Holborn." This, however, is certainly false. There was indeed in the early part of the eighteenth century a popular bookseller of the name Fletcher Gyles, who had a shop near Middle Row in Holborn, "over against Gray's Inn." Many particulars about him may be gathered from Nichol's *Literary Anecdotes* (see Index, vol. VII, p. 165), and it appears that he did publish various works there mentioned. But then in 1736 the firm is given as Gyles and Wilkinson, and since Fletcher Gyles himself died of apoplexy in 1741, it is unlikely that his sole name would be put upon a title-page in 1755. Moreover, no books are mentioned as published at the Holborn shop after 1737 (*Lit. Anec.,* vol. II, p. 116). As regards type, paper, and general appearance the book is certainly not English, and was probably executed at Paris, as two bibliographical experts of the British Museum assure me. The binding of my copy is also of the contemporary French style. All these facts go to show that, although purporting to be translated from the English, and published by an English bookseller, there was really no connection with London.

The book itself is divided into three parts, containing respectively seventeen, ten, and eight chapters. The first part is to some extent a general introduction to Political Economy, beginning with a definition of wealth, and then discussing the association of people in societies, in villages, towns, cities, and capital cities; the wages of labour; the theory of value; the par between labour and land; the dependence of all classes upon landed proprietors; the multiplication of population; and the use of gold and silver. The second part takes up the subjects of barter, prices, circulation of money, interest, etc., and is a complete little treatise on currency, probably more profound than anything of the same size since published on the subject. The third part treats of foreign commerce, the foreign exchanges, banking, and "refinements of credit." Judged by the knowledge and experience of the time, this third part especially is almost beyond praise, and shows that Richard Cantillon had a sound and pretty complete comprehension of many questions about which pamphleteers are still wrangling and blundering, and perplexing themselves and other people. The *Essai* is far more than a mere essay or even collection of disconnected essays like those of Hume. It is a systematic and connected treatise, going over in a concise manner nearly the whole field of economics, with the exception of taxation. It is thus, more than any other book I know, *the first treatise on economics.* Sir William Petty's *Political Arithmetic* and his *Treatise of Taxes and Contributions* are wonderful books in their way, and at their time, but, compared with Cantillon's *Essai,* they are mere collections of casual hints. There were earlier English works of great merit, such as those of Vaughan, Locke, Child, Mun, etc., but these were either occasional essays and pamphlets, or else fragmentary treatises. Cantillon's essay is, more emphatically than any other single work, "the Cradle of Political Economy."

The opening sentence of the first chapter, "De la Richesse," is especially remarkable, and is as follows: "La Terre est la source ou la matière d'où l'on tire la Richesse; le travail de l'Homme est la forme qui la produit: et la Richesse en elle-même n'est autre chose que la nourriture, les commodités et les agrémens de la vie."

This sentence strikes the keynote, or rather the leading chord of the science of economics. It reminds us at once of the phrase "land and labour of the country" upon which Adam Smith is so frequently harping. Yet it holds the balance between the elements of production more evenly than almost any subsequent treatise. Quesnay, as we shall see, attributed undue weight to some other remarks of Cantillon, and produced an entirely one-sided system of economics depending on land alone; Smith struck off rather on the other track, and took "the annual labour of every nation" as the fund which supplies it with all the necessaries and conveniences of life. Properly interpreted Cantillon's statement is probably the truest which has yet been given.

If, indeed, we are to trace out the filiation of ideas to the utmost, we get back to Sir W. Petty, who, in his *Treatise of Taxes,* chap. X (of Penalties), Article 10 (1st ed. 1662, p. 49), speaks of "our opinion that labour is the father and active principle of wealth, as lands are the mother."

Chapters VII and VIII are interesting because we here find the germ of Adam Smith's important doctrine concerning wages in different employments, as stated in the first part of the tenth chapter of the *Wealth of Nations.* Smith so greatly developed the doctrine and illustrated it so admirably as quite to make it his own; still here in this forgotten *Essai* are the leading ideas, as in the following extracts:

Those who employ artisans and skilled workmen must necessarily pay for their labour more highly than for that of a common labourer; and this labour will necessarily be more dear in proportion to the time lost in learning the trade, and the expense and risk which are required in perfecting the knowledge (p. 24). The arts and trades which are accompanied by risks and dangers, such as those of founders, mariners, silver miners, etc., ought to be paid in proportion to the risks. When, in addition to danger, skill is required, they ought to be still better paid, as in the case of pilots, divers, engineers, etc. When, moreover, capacity and trustworthiness are needed, labour is paid still more highly, as in the case of jewellers, book-keepers, cashiers, and others (pp. 26–27).

It is impossible not to recognise here the agreeableness or disagree-ableness, the easiness and cheapness, the difficulty and expense of learn-ing a trade, and the small or great trust which must be reposed in those who exercise them, three out of the five circumstances enumerated by Smith as causing inequalities in wages.

In Chapter IX Cantillon argues quite in the style of a recent disciple of Ricardo that there is no use in trying to increase the number of artisans in any trade by charity schools or special methods of educa-tion. He thinks there will never be a want of artisans in a State, if there be sufficient employment for them.

Then follows in Chapter X an ingenious theory of value, superior in some respects to the theories of many recent economists. The argu-ment given in the few small pages devoted to the subject is so closely knit, that many large pages would be needed to do justice to the theory. Cantillon's meaning, however, is that certain things, such as Brussels lace, or the balance-spring of an English watch, depend for their value upon the labour involved in their production. The hay from a meadow, the timber from a wood, on the other hand, are governed in value by the matter contained therein, or by the area of land required for its production, regard being had to the goodness of the land. The price of Seine water, as another instance, is not the price of the water itself, of which the quantity is immense, but the price of carrying it into the streets of Paris. He thus arrives at the following conclusion: "By these inductions and examples, I think we can understand that the price or the intrinsic value of a thing is the measure of the quantity of land and of labour which enter into its production, regard being had to the good-ness or productiveness of the land, and to the quality of the labour."

But Cantillon at once proceeds to explain that commodities will not always sell at their "intrinsic value." If a nobleman spends much money in making a beautiful garden, and the garden be brought to the hammer, it may bring only the half of what it has cost; in other cir-cumstances it may bring the double. Corn, again, sells above or below its intrinsic value according to the abundance of the harvests. A per-petual flux and reflux of prices arises from the impossibility of propor-tioning the supply to the demand. In short, these few pages contain not only the whole doctrine of market value as contrasted to cost value, or, as the late Professor Cairnes called it, normal value, but there are allusions to difficulties which Ricardo, Mill and many others have ignored.

We cannot exhaust here, however, the intricacies of the theory of value, and must pass on to Chapter XI, which is interesting, as being the one quoted by Adam Smith. It contains the curious doctrine "of the par or relation of the value of land to the value of labour." Cantillon points out that the labour of the lowest kind of adult slave, must at least equal the quantity of land that the proprietor is obliged to employ for his subsistence, together with double the quantity of land required to bring up a child to the labouring age, remembering that, according to the calculations of the celebrated Dr Halley, half the number of children die before reaching seventeen years of age. The doctrine is carefully guarded by Cantillon, with various qualifications and explanations, which we have not space to consider. Now, Smith refers to this theory in the eighth chapter of the first book of the *Wealth of Nations* (Thorold Rogers's edition, vol. I, p. 71), saying: "Mr Cantillon seems, upon this account, to suppose that the lowest species of common labourers must everywhere earn at least double their own maintenance, in order that, one with another, they may be enabled to bring up two children; the labour of the wife, on account of her necessary attendance on the children, being supposed no more than sufficient to provide for herself. But one-half the children born, it is computed, die before the age of manhood." I believe that Smith must have derived his quotation from the French *Essai;* for he adverts to the fact that the labour of the wife, on account of her necessary attendance on the children, is supposed to be no more than sufficient to provide for herself. This is a point carefully noted by Cantillon (p. 43), but missed out, like most other essential points, in the base English version, which says, vaguely and slightingly, "allowance must be made for females" (p. 24).

It is quite of a piece with the whole history of Cantillon's book, that Smith, in thus quoting Cantillon approvingly, has erred. This chapter, the only one explicitly quoted by Smith, is the only one which Cantillon explicitly assigns to a previous writer—namely, Sir William Petty. Cantillon terminates the chapter thus (pp. 54–55): "Monsieur le Chevalier Petty, in a little manuscript of the year 1685, regards this *par,* or (*en,* in original) equation of land and labour, as the most important consideration in Political Arithmetic; but the research which he has made into it in passing, is only bizarre, and remote from the rules of nature, because he is attached not to causes and principles, but only to effects; as Messieurs Locke and D'Avenant, and all the other English authors who have written anything of this matter, have done after him."

Now, in Sir W. Petty's very remarkable *Treatise of Taxes and Contributions,*[2] of which the first edition was published in 1662, we find the following passage (p. 26):

All things ought to be valued by two natural denominations, which is land and labour; that is, we ought to say, a ship or garment is worth such a measure of land, with such another measure of labour; forasmuch as both ships and garments were the creatures of lands and men's labours thereupon. This being true, we should be glad to find out a natural Par between Land and Labour, so as we might express the value of either of them alone as well or better than by both and reduce one into the other as easily and certainly as we reduce pence into pounds.

Here is a clear forecast, both of Cantillon's theory of value, and of the doctrine of a *par*.

Returning to Cantillon, we find in Chapter XII the germ of the Physiocratic doctrines: "Tous les ordres et tous les hommes d'un état subsistent ou s'enrichissent aux dépens des propriétaires des Terres." As we shall see further on, Quesnay himself, as well as his editors, frankly refers the origin of the great school of French Economists to this *Essai,* though it may be safely said that Cantillon avoids the one-sidedness of Physiocracy.

Hardly do we leave the elements of Physiocracy than we fall, in Chapter XV, into an almost complete anticipation of the Malthusian theory of population. Cantillon says (p. 87):

In a word, we can multiply all sorts of animals in such numbers that we could have them even to infinity, if we could find lands to infinity proper to nourish them; and the multiplication of animals has no other bounds than the greater or less means remaining for their subsistence.

Men multiply like mice in a barn, if they have the means of subsistence without limit; and the English in the colonies become proportionally more numerous in three generations, than they would in England in thirty; because in the colonies they find new lands to cultivate, from which they drive the savages (p. 110).

There are many interesting allusions to the varying standard of living in different states of society; to the prevalence of famines in China and elsewhere; to celibacy, libertinage, and other points of the population question. The chapter is simply Malthus's celebrated Essay, condensed by anticipation into twenty-seven pages. But I am not aware that Malthus ever saw the book, and should think it very unlikely that he

---

[2] *"Tracts relating chiefly to Ireland.* By the late Sir William Petty. Dublin, 1769," p. 31.

knew anything about it. Cantillon winds up the subject prophetically by suggesting that it is a question whether it is better for a kingdom to be filled with a multitude of very poor inhabitants, or with a less considerable number of better maintained persons. Here is a forecast of the most recent hedonic speculations of Mr F. Y. Edgeworth. It should be added that Cantillon, in treating population, refers to the calculations and statistics of Halley, Petty, D'Avenant, and King, all English authorities.

The first part of the Essay is completed by a chapter "On Metals and Money, and particularly of gold and silver," in which the author displays the most precise ideas about the need and nature of a common measure of value, the suitability of different commodities to serve in this capacity: grain, wine, cloth, precious stones, iron, lead, tin, copper, etc., are all compared as to their suitability for currency, just as in various recent works on money; and the author concludes that "gold and silver alone are of small volume, of equal goodness, easy of transport, divisible without loss, easily guarded, beautiful and brilliant, and durable almost to eternity."

We can notice only a few points in the second division of the Essay; for instance, the admirable explanation (pp. 199–203) of the fact that the prices of commodities and the cost of living are higher in cities, especially in capital cities, than in the country. This Cantillon attributes to the fact that a balance of payments is almost always due from the country to the cities, and the capital of the country; and that the commodities with which this balance is practically discharged, incur the cost and risk of conveyance. The same theory is applied (p. 209) to the relations of foreign countries, and Cantillon concludes that any State which sells manufactures to neighbouring States in such quantity as to draw a balance of specie towards itself, will eventually raise its own scale of prices. There is no taint of the Mercantile Fallacy whatever in this theory.

One of the most marvellous things in the book is the manner in which Cantillon (pp. 215–225) explains the successive effects of a discovery of gold or silver mines on the rates of wages and prices of commodities. The proprietors, undertakers, and employees of the mines first profit by the abundance and soon increase their expenditure, which increases the demand for the produce of artisans and other work people. These latter soon acquire increased rates of wages, and gradually the influence of the new money spreads from trade to trade, and from country to country. This is exactly the theory which was brought before the British Association in 1858 by the late Professor Cairnes, and which will be found beautifully expounded in his *Essays in Political Economy: Theoretical and Applied,* Essays I and II (Macmillan, 1873).

It is not too much to say that the subject of the foreign exchanges has never, not even in Mr Goschen's well-known book, been treated with more perspicuity and scientific accuracy than in Cantillon's Essay. It is quite astonishing, for instance, to find in the third part of the Essay (pp. 342–4) an explanation of speculations in the exchanges, which might be mistaken for an extract from Mr Goschen's admirable treatise. Cantillon says:

> If an English banker foresees in January, owing to the consignment of an unusual quantity of merchandise to Holland, that Holland will be indebted considerably to England at the time of the sales and remittances in March, he can, in the month of January, instead of remitting the fifty thousand ecus or ounces that are owing in this month to Holland, furnish his bills of exchange upon his correspondent at Amsterdam, payable at two months' usance. By this means he can profit by the exchanges which were in January above par, and which will be in March below par; thus he can gain thereby without sending a single sol to Holland.

But Cantillon is careful to add (p. 343) that though the speculation and credit of bankers may sometimes retard the transport of bullion from one city or State to another, it is always necessary in the end to discharge a debt and remit the balance of commerce in specie to the place where it is due.

Condillac, who in his profound and original work, *Le Commerce et le Gouvernement,* hardly quotes any writers or acknowledges any obligations, goes quite out of his usual course as regards Cantillon. He states in a footnote (chap. XVI, *Œuvres Complètes,* t. VI, Paris, 1803, p. 141) that he has derived from the *Essai* the basis of his chapter on the circulation of money, besides several observations made use of in other chapters. "It is on this matter," says Condillac, "one of the best works which I know; but I do not know them all, by any means."

There is, perhaps, needed only one further proof of Cantillon's comprehension of monetary and financial questions, and that is furnished by his treatment of bimetallism, as it has since been called by M. Cernuschi. The fourth chapter of the third part contains a luminous discussion of the subject, beginning with an historical review of the variations in the relative values of gold and silver, and ending with most interesting remarks on the motives which actuated Sir Isaac Newton in settling the English guinea at 21*s.* Cantillon's general argument is to the effect that the precious metals must conform in value to the course of the market (p. 371).

It is the market price which decides the proportion of the value of gold to that of silver. On this is based the proportion which we give to pieces of gold and silver money. If the market price varies considerably, it is necessary to alter the proportion of the coins. If we neglect to do this, the circulation is thrown into confusion and disorder, and people will take the pieces of one or other metal at a higher price than that fixed by the Mint. An infinite number of examples of this are to be found in antiquity, but we have a quite recent one in England in the laws made for the Tower of London. The ounce of silver, eleven ounces fine, is there worth 5s. 2d. sterling; since the proportion of gold to silver (which had been fixed in imitation of Spain as 1 to 16) is fallen to 1 to 15 or 1 to 14½, the ounce of silver sold at 5s. 6d., while the gold guinea continued to have currency always at 21s. 6d. That caused people to carry away from England all the silver crowns, shillings, and sixpences which were not worn by circulation. Silver money became so scarce in 1728 (mil sept cent vingt huit), because there remained only the most worn pieces, that people were obliged to change a guinea at a loss of nearly 5 per cent. The embarrassment and confusion which that produced in commerce and the circulation, obliged the Treasury to request the celebrated Sir Isaac Newton, Master of the Mint at the Tower, to make a report on the means which he believed to be the most suitable for remedying this disorder.

There was nothing so easy to do; it was only necessary to follow in the fabrication of silver coins at the Mint the market price of silver. In place of the proportion of gold to silver, which had for a long time been according to the laws and rules of the Mint at the Tower as 1 to 15¾, it was only necessary to make the silver pieces lighter in the proportion of the market price, which had fallen below that of 1 to 15, and to go beyond the variation which the gold of Brazil annually causes in the proportion of the two metals. They might have established the money on the footing of 1 to 14½, as was done in 1725 in France, and as it will be necessary to do in England itself sooner or later.

Here is a distinct prophecy of that which was carried into effect in 1815 at Lord Liverpool's recommendation, and which is still, and probably always will be, the fundamental point in the regulation of our metallic money. Cantillon goes on to explain that Newton took the opposite course, and Parliament followed his advice—namely, in diminishing the nominal value of the gold piece. This, he allows, equally adjusts the relative values of the pieces to the market price, but it is, notwithstanding, a less natural and advantageous method. He pointed out to Newton that by this measure England incurred a loss of £110,741 upon every £5,000,000 of capital which it owed to foreigners, and Newton's reply is given thus (p. 377): "Monsieur Newton m'a dit pour réponse à cette objection, que suivant les loix fondamentales du Roïaume, l'argent blanc étoit la vraie et seule monnoie, et que comme telle, il ne la falloit pas altérer." After giving some other refined arguments, Cantillon finally delivers his opinion against the double standard, saying (p. 380):

Il n'y a que le prix du Marché qui puisse trouver la proportion de la valeur de l'or à l'argent, de même que toutes les proportions des valeurs. La réduction de M. Newton de la quinée à vingt-un schellings n'a été calculée que pour empêcher qu'on n'enlevât les espèces d'ardent foibles et usées qui restent dans la circulation; elle n'étoit pas calculée pour fixer dans les monnoies d'or et d'argent la véritable proportion de leur prix, je veux dire par leur véritable proportion, celle qui est fixée par les prix du Marché. Ce prix est toujours la pierre de touche dans ces matières; les variations en sont assez lentes, pour donner le tems de régler les monnoies et empêcher les désordres dans la circulation.

If I read this remarkable passage aright, it not only reaffirms Cantillon's opinion that it is futile to attempt to fix the proportion of gold and silver perpetually, but that Newton had himself no idea of attempting the impossibility. His reduction of the guinea was only "calculated" to prevent the removal of the worn pieces which still remained in circulation—that is, to effect a matter of immediate practical importance. The bi-metallists having quoted Newton as on their side, Mr Inglis Palgrave and other English economists have been anxious to know the real motives of Newton, which are not easy to gather from his official report. But in these remarks of Cantillon we actually seem to have the statement of an acquaintance of Newton, and a master of currency and finance, that he had discussed the subject with Newton, and that Newton's intention was "not to fix in gold and silver moneys the veritable proportion of their price." I take this to be a distinct disclaimer of bi-metallism.

It must not be supposed that I have at all exhausted the valuable points of his Essay. Every here and there we find a pregnant little paragraph which, when carefully studied, displays an insight into questions still novel, or but half settled after long discussion. Mr Macleod should study p. 291, where it is clearly explained that debts, including State debts, cannot be counted as part of the wealth of the country. In pp. 186, 187 there is a wonderfully clear explanation how much trade goes on between correspondents by book credit, with only occasional payment of balances. This method, which Cantillon aptly calls "troc par évaluation," is the germ of what I have described in my book on *Money and the Mechanism of Exchange* as the cheque and clearing system (chap. XX). I there said: "The banking organisation effects what I have heard Mr W. Langton describe as a *restoration of barter.*"

This is what Cantillon describes in the most precise manner as *barter by valuation.*

In spite of the undeveloped state of the art of banking at the time when Cantillon wrote, his views on this subject are sound as far as they go, and although he is said to have made a fortune of several millions in a few days by speculation in Law's paper-money, he thus summarily dispatches the currency-mongers (p. 413): "An abundance of fictitious and imaginary money causes the same disadvantages as an augmentation of the real money in circulation, by raising the price of land and labour, or by making works and manufacture more expensive at the risk of subsequent loss. But this occult abundance vanishes at the first shock to credit, and precipitates disorder."

In spite of comparisons being odious, I should have liked, had space allowed, to institute a careful comparison between Cantillon's *Essai* and Hume's celebrated *Political Essays.* As regards the value of gold and silver, Eugène Daire has made a comparison of the kind, and decides in favour of Cantillon, Hume's view being, he thinks, subject to certain errors (*Physiocrates, Quesnay,* etc. Paris, 1846, p. 74). It is most instructive to compare Hume's fifth Essay, on the balance of trade, with the seventh chapter of the second part of Cantillon. Both authors imagine the money in a country to be suddenly increased or decreased; but, whereas Hume discusses the matter with vague literary elegance, Cantillon analyses the effects on prices with the scientific precision of a Cairnes or a Cournot.

It is not too much to say of this *Essai* in the words of M. Léonce de Lavergne, that "all the theories of (the) Economists are contained by anticipation in this book, although it has only the extent of a moderate duodecimo volume." Nor is there wanting positive evidence that Quesnay, the founder of the great school of French Economists, actually did draw his leading principle from the *Essai.* Eugène Daire, the editor of the collected works of the Physiocrates, than whom there can be no better authority, expressly points out that Quesnay's fundamental doctrine "la terre est l'unique source des richesses" appears to be borrowed from the opening chapter of Cantillon's *Essai.* The same is the case, he remarks, with the idea that the net produce of the land is the fund on which all non-agriculturists live, the subject, as already stated, of the twelfth chapter. As to this latter point we do not rest on conjecture, because in one of his earliest printed writings, the article on "Grains" in the celebrated *Encyclopédie Méthodique,* of Diderot and D'Alembert, Quesnay actually quotes Cantillon. After saying that land must not only nourish those who cultivate it, but must furnish to the State the

greater part of the revenue, the tithes of the clergy, the income of proprietors, the profits of farmers, the gains of those who are employed in
cultivation, and that it is these revenues, which are expended in payments to the other classes and all the other professions, he goes on:

An author has recognised these fundamental truths when he says that
the assemblage of several rich proprietors who reside on the same spot,
suffices to form what we call a city, where merchants, manufacturers,
artisans, labourers, and servants assemble in proportion to the revenues
which the proprietors there expend, so that the grandeur of a city is naturally proportional to the number of landed proprietors, or rather to the
produce of the land belonging to them.

Quesnay adds a footnote referring to this extract as follows: "Cantillon, *Essai sur le Commerce,* chaps. V, VI." On referring to the
original edition of the *Encyclopédie* (Paris, 1757, folio), I find the
quotation given in this manner in the seventh volume, p. 821. Curiously enough, the quotation is not an accurate verbatim one, as the
inverted commas would make us suppose, but is gathered together from
different parts of the chapters named. In any case we have here the
unquestionable fact that the acknowledged founder of the Physiocratic
school expressly attributes in his earliest writings the fundamental point
of his system to the *Essai.* Moreover, only two years after its publication, he joins the title of the *Essai* with the name of its supposed author,
and no one could do this with greater authority than Quesnay.

There are not wanting some indications that English economic writers
were also indebted to Cantillon, though they did not acknowledge their
debt with Quesnay's candour. It is with regret that I find the earlier
sections of Harris's *Essay upon Money and Coins,* published in London
in 1757 and 1758, to be obviously borrowed from Cantillon. This
work is so excellent as regards its main topic, money, that he need not
have pillaged a contemporary French publication. Not only is there no
reference to Cantillon, but in the Preface we are told that "in order to
clear the way, and for the better settling of things upon their first and
true principles, it hath been thought necessary to take a general view of
wealth and commerce, which is the subject of the first chapter." But
unfortunately this chapter is little more than a selection of passages
from Cantillon. "Land and labour together are the sources of all
wealth." There is the doctrine of three rents, from p. 56 of the *Essai.*
There is the example of the watch-spring already alluded to. In Section
8 the theory of the par of land and labour afterwards quoted by Smith
appears. The difference of wages are explained in Section 10, as depending upon risk, skill, trust required, almost in the words of Cantillon.

Another contemporary writer of some importance in his time, namely Malachy Postlethwayt, had the coolness to embody certain portions of Cantillon's Essay in his book called *Great Britain's True System, etc.,* published in London in 1757. From p. 148 to p. 153, we find a slightly abbreviated translation of Cantillon's eleventh chapter on the par of land and labour, winding up with a reference to Sir W. Petty's MS. of the year 1685, introduced in such a way that we might suppose Postlethwayt to be quoting from it. Then follow other extracts from Cantillon, including the doctrine of three rents, the watch-spring, and water illustrations, and other matters, and Postlethwayt sums up thus his, *i.e.* Cantillon's, theory of value: "From these examples and explanations I believe it will appear that the price of anything intrinsically is the measure of the land and labour that enters into its production."

There still remains the interesting question, Who really did write this most remarkable Essay, the true "Cradle of Political Economy"? The antecedent probabilities are altogether against the idea that a book published in Paris in the middle of the eighteenth century was really written by the man to whom it was attributed. The despotic character of the Government seems to have given rise to a habit of falsifying title-pages to an extraordinary extent, and thus falsifying literary history. In the one year, 1755, in which the Essay was published, no less than ninety books issued in France are attributed on the title-pages to the presses of Amsterdam, London, Brussels, Venice, Berlin, Vienna, Cologne, or other cities.[3]

It was also the practice to conceal the authorship by various devices. Forbonnais wrote under the assumed name of Leclerc, M. du T. . . . , etc. An author often put forward obnoxious opinions in the form of a free translation of some English work, as in the case of Forbonnais's *Le Négociant Anglais,* founded on King's *British Merchant.*

What then would be more probable than that this *Essai sur la Nature du Commerce en Général,* might be the work of some ingenious contemporary French economist, merely attributed by rumour to the popular name of Cantillon, the *manière anglaise* being adopted because it was then much in favour in France.

There is much too in the style of the book, here and there, which raises suspicions as to its being really the finished work of a busy financier. The opening sentence of the book has a metaphysical ring about it: "The land is the matter of riches; labour is the form which produces it." Here is the precise distinction between the material cause

[3] See Émil Weller's *Dictionnaire des Ouvrages Français, portant de fausses indications des lieux d'impression,* Leipzig, 1864, vol. II, p. 141.

and the formal cause, in the Aristotelian philosophy. There is something very scholastic, again, about the footnote on p. 377, the only one in the whole volume, where, in regard to Newton's remark about silver being the true and sole money, it is added, "Ici M. Newton sacrifia le fond à la forme." Even supposing that there were in existence some manuscripts of the real Richard Cantillon, may not one of the numerous and clever economists of the period of Quesnay have worked these materials up into a consistent treatise, and put the whole off upon Cantillon and Fletcher Gyles.

There are, however, many reasons in favour of believing the *Essai* to be really the work of Richard Cantillon. I have not been able to discover in the book any allusion or other intrinsic evidence of any part of the book having been written later than 1725 or thereabouts, when Cantillon was still living. There is here and there a local colouring drawn from London life. On p. 274 we are told that the London brewers were in the habit of advancing barrels of beer to their publicans at an interest of 500 per cent. per annum, and it is said that they could grow rich even though half their publican creditors became bankrupt. On the next page some facts about the fish-women of Billingsgate (Revendeuses) are introduced. But there is also plenty of local French colouring. The authors cited are mostly English, namely Sir W. Petty, D'Avenant, Locke, Halley, Gregory King, Newton. The only French economist whom I remember as being referred to by name is Vauban, whose *Projet d'une Dîme Royale,* published in 1707, is condemned on p. 210. A certain M. Boizard is, however, referred to on p. 137, and an unnamed French author on p. 248.

The best proof, however, of the work being really written by a skilful financier, and not by a literary economist like those who issued such a multitude of small treatises in the time of Quesnay, is found in the intimate acquaintance with the working of commerce displayed throughout the Essay. It is next to impossible that the latter part of the book, especially the third part, could be supposititious. I am not quite so sure about the first part, containing the principles adopted by Quesnay. But the book is so consistent and well knit together that if it were a compound and supposititious work, it would be difficult to admire too much the skill of the economic forger.

And now, if Cantillon's *Essai* be the veritable cradle of Political Economy, what is the nationality of the bantling science? "La Chimie," says M. Wurtz, "est une science française." Lavoisier's immortal "Traité Élémentaire de Chimie" was its cradle. What like conclusion can we draw as to the nationality of economic science? If my careful and laborious inquiries have led to a correct result, I should formulate it thus: The first systematic Treatise on Economics was probably written by a banker of Spanish name, born from an Irish family of the County Kerry, bred we know not where, carrying on business in Paris, but clearly murdered in Albemarle Street. The Treatise was written either in English or French, it is not known which; was first printed in Paris in the guise of a French translation, purporting to be published by Fletcher Gyles over against Gray's Inn in Holborn; was damned in England by a base garbled English retranslation, erroneously attributed to a merchant late of the City of London, perhaps the brother of the author. Except that it was once mistakenly quoted by Adam Smith, it has remained to the present day unknown or entirely misinterpreted in England, while in France it has been explicitly acknowledged to be the source of the leading ideas of the great French school. That French school is known to have formed to a considerable degree the basis of the *Wealth of Nations,* and may yet be destined to be recognised, in regard to many of its doctrines, as the true scientific school of economics. The reader can now readily decide in his own mind the question—What is the Nationality of Political Economy?

Einaudi

——————————————————— on ———

Galiani

The abbot Ferdinando Galiani (1728–1787) is often cited as a precursor of modern economic ideas. His work on money (*Della moneta,* 1750) and his *Dialogues sur le commerce des blés* (1770) mark him as an original thinker, who anticipated a number of concepts that have become current only since the advent of marginal-utility economics. Neither Galiani's works nor an adequate appraisal of them have as yet been available in English translations. Einaudi's essay, which is reproduced here in part, thus fills an important gap.

Luigi Einaudi (1874–   ) is a distinguished Italian statesman and economist. As student and teacher he was associated with the University of Turin for a period of nearly 60 years. His main interests in economics are in the fields of public finance, economic history, and history of economics. Einaudi served as editor of the *Riforma sociale* from 1903 to 1935, and after the suppression of this outstanding periodical he founded the *Rivista di storia economica.* Having been active in the political life of Italy, he was in 1948 elected President of the Republic of Italy, the first economics professor to become the titular head of a state. Einaudi's farewell address before the University of Turin, "Economic Science and Economists at the Present Day," is available in an English translation in UNESCO, *International Social Science Bulletin,* Summer 1950.

FERDINANDO GALIANI had a unique fate. Although a native of Naples, the history of civilization considers him a typical representative of the French *esprit* of his time—the time when Voltaire and the Encyclopedists dominated French culture and when the distinguished men of the whole world met in the *salons* of Paris. At the time of the publication of Galiani's *Dialogues on the Grain Trade* in 1770, Voltaire wrote in a letter: "It seems as if Plato and Molière had joined forces to write this book. . . . Nobody has ever developed his argument better or more pleasantly," and this judgment he confirmed in the *Philosophical Dictionary:* Galiani "has discovered the secret of making the *Dialogues* as amusing as our best novels, and as instructive as our best serious books." Grimm and the *salons* of Madames d'Epinay, Necker, Geoffrin, and of Baron Holbach spread over the whole of Europe the fame of the "little man, born at the foot of Mount Vesuvius," of the new Plato "with the verve and the gestures of Harlequin."

We Italians are proud of Galiani's two masterworks—the *Dialogues on the Grain Trade* and the *Correspondence* with Madame d'Epinay—which he has contributed to the great French century of Voltaire, Rousseau, and the Encyclopedists. We claim his thought for Italy. Benedetto Croce and Fausto Nicolini have demonstrated how profoundly the intellectual development of our youthful author was influenced by the ideas of the greatest thinker produced by Italy at the turn from the seventeenth to the eighteenth century—the ideas of Giambattista Vico, author of the *New Science*. Nowhere in his writings does Galiani mention Vico. But Vician is his opinion that such matters as money, economic structure, and concrete problems, relating, for example, to the grain trade, are neither purely speculative abstractions nor purposive conventions but historical formations, eternal facts of the mind; and Vician is his aversion against all naive, idealized views of a natural status, and his notion of the "ferocity," the "ferocious

[Translated in abridged form from *Schweizerische Zeitschrift für Volkswirtschaft und Statistik,* Vol. 81, No. 1, 1945. By permission.]

status," of primitive man, and of the perpetual struggle which man must carry on to master a hostile nature.

In Italy, Galiani's book *On Money* is more widely read than his *Dialogues* and the *Correspondence*. The work *On Money* had the misfortune of never having been published in a foreign language, and therefore was read only by the few economists who are familiar with Italian. Hence the author of a recently published study of Galiani is right when he characterizes Galiani in the title of his work as a "neglected" economist.[1] Many know the acrimonious critic of the physiocrats from his *Dialogues,* and the man of brilliant intellect from his *Correspondence* as well as from many anecdotes about his marvellous repartee, from his polemic replies and arguments. But outside of Italy there are only a few who know the youthful, 23-year-old author of the treatise *On Money*.

As Ganzoni has pointed out, Galiani opposed the physiocrats but nevertheless was neither a mercantilist nor a foe of free trade; he did not produce a complete system of economics but contributed many new ideas; his theories of value, price, money, and interest contain new thoughts which were to bear fruit only a century later. Furthermore, at the time when the "economists"—this was the name given to the members of the physiocratic school—demanded the reduction of government intervention in economic life to a minimum, Galiani had seen that the problem involved the correct drawing of a boundary line: while government should abstain from interventions which harm private initiative, it should be ready under specific circumstances to remove the obstacles which a temporary emergency or the conflict of interests places in the way of the free play of economic principles. Galiani is in part an exponent of mercantilist ideas, to the extent to which he attaches much significance to the growth of population. But he does not share the monetary prejudices of the mercantilists. To him, the possession of gold is only a means to obtain for a country the consumer and producer goods desired by man.

Galiani was not the founder of the new economic science. But, ahead of Adam Smith, he pointed out the error in the physiocratic theory of the net product. He was lacking in confidence in himself and in his ideas. Being a man of *esprit,* he disseminated an abundance of ideas among his contemporaries. But he failed to follow up a single one, and did not assemble them in an orderly system of thought. While he attracted neither disciples nor followers, there were many

[1] Eduard Ganzoni, *Ferdinando Galiani. Ein verkannter Nationalökonom des 18. Jahrhunderts,* Zurich, H. Girsberger Verlag, 1938.

elegant ladies, serious men of science, and famous politicians who hung on his lips—to pluck the flower of the most powerful intellect living in Paris between 1760 and 1770. Yet, being attached to leisure, he soon tired of writing, lacking the obstinacy of work with which alone a school can be founded. Anyone who today reads Gossen, Jevons, Menger, or Marshall is bound to recall Galiani's penetrating views regarding money; anyone who turns to the pages of Roscher, Hildebrand, and Knies is bound to recall Galiani's *Dialogues on the Grain Trade,* where he insists that those who develop theories should keep in mind the specific circumstances of time and place. Galiani does not mark an epoch. Neither does he represent an intermediary position between the declining mercantilism and the rising liberalism. From a certain point of view he was a forerunner of the next century; but he also was a true representative of his own time. If I were to compare Galiani with another author, I would place him next to Cantillon. In neither case is there much point in raising the question whether he was a mercantilist, a liberal, or a physiocrat. If we raise such a question, we do so by force of scholarly habit, impelled by an inclination aiming at classification and at finding a proper place for everybody in an orderly pattern. But if we answer this question, we really have not said anything which would impart significant information about Cantillon or Galiani.

Professor von Hayek, in his preface to the German edition of Cantillon's little book, has pointed out the characteristic features of this author's work.[2] Cantillon was the first to place the "entrepreneur" in the centre of scientific discussion. A long time, 150 years, was to pass until the entrepreneur again came to the fore of the economic scene, to supersede that bastardly mongrel—the "capitalist" of Smith, Ricardo, and Marx. In the meantime, Cantillon had fallen into oblivion, though not everywhere and surely not in Italy, to be resurrected only by Jevons' rediscovery. Furthermore, Cantillon was the first to establish the purely economic way of argumentation. Instead of giving recipes and practical advice, he used the steel-trap logic of pure economics: such are the assumptions, such are the conclusions. It makes little difference that the great methodological discovery of Cantillon was forgotten until Ricardo. It remains; and anyone who reads the *Essai sur la Nature du Commerce en Général* is bound to derive much pleasure from these unpretentious and brilliant pages.

[2] Richard Cantillon, *Abhandlung über die Natur des Handels im allgemeinen,* German ed. by F. A. Hayek, Jena, Gustav Fischer, 1931.

A similar pleasure is in store for the reader of Galiani. If he is an Italian, he has still another and very special reason for being amazed and delighted. Every once in a while, the exalted and lucid style of the 23-year-old author provides opportunities for vivid expressions and turns of phrases of such splendor and vigor that they recall Machiavelli and Leopardi. If the beauty, the vivacity, and the force-fulness of Galiani's style will appeal especially to Italians—the sub-stance of Galiani's ideas has a general appeal. What does he have to say to us today? Which of his thoughts are still alive? Which are the truths that, stated by him, have continued to live, in improved and modified form, among the fundamental principles of economic science?

GALIANI'S METHOD

In order to present the thoughts and ideas of Galiani in an orderly fashion, I shall organize them systematically. Galiani had no love for systematization and classification. He developed his argument with the help of isolated cases and by means of bold contrasts. To bring some order into his ideas, we may first state that Galiani clearly recog-nized the methodological mistake of considering arbitrarily one of the many data of reality as a cause—thereby turning all other data into effects. In contrast with this, he developed the notion of interdepend-ence of political and economic facts:

In the immense machinery of society, everything hangs together, is con-nected, and linked. Nothing must disturb the equilibrium lest the whole mechanism overturn. That is why I recommend nothing more strongly than the avoidance of shocks and sudden moves. The shocks break the contacts and springs, and the mechanism is destroyed.[3]

In an earlier passage he had cautioned "against confusing cause and effect."

This mistake is made by everybody. To avoid it, it must be recognized that things which are always found together are necessarily connected, and that one is the cause, and, at the same time, the effect, of the other.[4]

Galiani's concept of interdependence and equilibrium is not static. To him, the economic and social equilibrium changes all the time. If the government decides to interfere, it must see to it that it does not come too late and that it does not consider measures which it believes

---

[3] *Dialogues sur le commerce des blés,* London, 1770, p. 279.
[4] *Ibid.,* p. 114.

to have instantaneous effects, while actually circumstances have changed when the effect takes place.

Nature, if left alone, will lead to equilibrium, the natural state of affairs and the most pleasing to man. When this order of necessity is obstructed, it would establish itself and could be regained with ease, were it not for the fact that man always does violence to it and bars it with the help of a thousand inventions. Three fundamental principles—nature, liberty, and equilibrium—could bring about happiness. How true—but also how false! Nature, if left free, tends toward equilibrium. What a lucid truth in the mind of a metaphysician—a truth because one can see the causes and the effects. But one fails to take into account the duration of time required for the return to equilibrium, one is inclined to balance the inequalities with compensations, and one uses average notions which exist only in the mind. . . . Nothing is more true than that the prices of grain, if left alone, will be in equilibrium. Nothing is more true than that commerce, if left free, will distribute grain everywhere where there are consumers and money. Nothing is more true in theory, because all the people run after the grain, and this was to be proved. But in practice care must be taken not to neglect the period of time required for posting letters to dispatch the news of the local grain shortage to a country where grain can be had. Another period of time must pass before the grain arrives. If this period is 15 days, and if there are provisions for just one week, the town remains without bread for 8 days, and the people die from hunger.[5]

Galiani anticipates here the sceptical attitude of modern economists to the solution of economic problems on the assumption *"rebus sic stantibus."* This assumption contradicts reality because it neglects the passage of time. There are at least two variables which must be taken into account in the study of any economic problem. One is the basis of the problem itself, the other the passage of time. As Galiani puts it, it is not only the shortage of grain which is important as determinant of human action. If human action could bring about its effects instantly, grain would move from surplus regions with low prices to regions where there is a grain shortage and where grain prices are high. But time must pass until the news of the famine has spread, until the merchants have transacted their purchases and carried out their shipments, and until the grain arrives at the place of consumption. Meanwhile the famished may have died.

Galiani posed this theoretical problem on the occasion of a concrete issue: Should the government establish storage houses for grain and thus restrict trade, or should the grain trade be left free, as proposed by the physiocrats, with the traders being put in the position to accu-

[5] *Ibid.,* pp. 236 f.

mulate reserves? Galiani, however, sees more than the concrete question. He recognizes the fundamental methodological problem, the contrast between the great principle of tentative approximation and the modification to which it must submit if it is to encompass other factors than those in which the theorist, treating of general and static equilibrium, is interested. Surely, the words which he uses differ from those common today, but he understands the nature of the general issue. If special factors of relevance are neglected, "the theory gets on well, and the problem very badly." Nevertheless, knowledge of the natural, general, abstract laws is by no means useless:

Should we then leave it to nature to take care of our rubbish? Nature is too great a lady for that. Let us leave in her care the great movements, the great revolutions of empires, the long run—just as she takes care of the movements of the stars and elements. Politics is only the science of preventing and averting the sudden movements which come about as the result of extraordinary causes, and it does not go beyond this. The great revolutions are entirely the work of nature. Human effort cannot accomplish anything here; far from originating them, man is only their principal instrument and tool.[6]

But man is not merely a passive subject of the so-called natural laws. Even though he cannot oppose the fundamental forces which exist independently from him, even though he must follow them, he nevertheless is capable of dominating them and of deriving benefit from them:

No doubt, nature restores everything to equilibrium; we only have to wait for the return to equilibrium. We are very small. In the face of nature, time, space, and movement mean nothing. But we cannot wait. We could not enter into an alliance with nature; the disproportion would be too great. Our task down here is to fight. Look around at the cultivated fields, the foreign plants which have become habituated to our climate, the ships, the wagons, the domesticated animals, the houses, the streets, the ports, the dikes, the highways. These are the bastions from which we carry on the fight. All comforts of life, and almost our very existence itself, are the price of victory. With our imperfect ability, and with our God-given intellect, we accept the challenge of nature, often succeeding in defeating and mastering her by using her own forces against her.[7]

When Galiani wrote this, he came closer to the physiocrats than he and the physiocrats themselves believed. The meaning of the

[6] *Ibid.,* p. 237.
[7] *Ibid.,* p. 235.

physiocratic "natural and substantive order of society" still remains to be analyzed on the basis of the original texts. It is my impression that this order must not be identified with the order which some fanciful dreamers attribute to an imaginary, happy state of nature. Rather, it is the status to which society tends and to which it returns after artificial means and accidental happenings have moved it away. The physiocrats were opposed to the arbitrary character of laws which impose dangerous restraints on human activities, and they insisted that above the written law there stands natural law, which needs only to be proclaimed and carried out by the prince. To them, natural law implied a law facilitating the growth and prosperity of society. They had in mind historical and concrete laws, adjusted to place and time and to the basic character of man.[8]

But it happened only too often that the physiocrats, in their writings and in their polemics, forgot about the fundamental principles of their method. Only too often did they fail to correct the belief that they aimed at a complete change of the economic structure of the society in which they lived. Only too often did they create the impression of being abstract, unrealistic theorists. It is because of this that Galiani, with his acute sense of realism, appears to oppose them. In reality, however, Galiani, while using different words, confirmed the physiocratic idea that the true order of society enables man to regulate and modify natural forces in a manner best suited for the maintenance and progress of society itself. Galiani follows Giambattista Vico when he draws attention to the manifestations of perpetual warfare between the blind forces of nature and the human desire for domination and change. He emphasizes the special and accidental, whereas the physiocrats aim at the essential, the lasting, the general. Different in their points of departure, they have the same goal in mind: an enduring, progressive order of human society. Ahead of Adam Smith, and better than he, the physiocrats subjected the economic mechanism to a penetrating analysis, and studied the manner in which its different parts are joined together. Most important, ahead of the other economists, they investigated the continuity of the economic order and the relationship between the various elements of an order which is integrated as well as complex. The *Tableau économique* has meaning only when it is interpreted as an attempt at explaining the relations of the different parts of a whole—of the economic order—and at showing

---

[8] For evidence of the historism of the physiocrats in questions of taxation, see my article, "The Physiocratic Theory of Taxation," in *Economic Essays in Honour of Gustav Cassel,* London, 1933, pp. 129–142.

that production and distribution of goods and services is a continuous process, renewing itself without pause and carrying in itself the factors making for repetition and continuity. But, like the modern schemes of general equilibrium of Walras and Pareto, this portrayal remained a schematic presentation in broad outline, without shadows and contrasts. Apart from the picture of the whole, which describes the permanent, the lasting, and the self-renewing, apart from the equations of general equilibrium, which refer to the state of rest and to the final destination, we are interested also in the explanation of the frictions, the crises, the obstacles to be surmounted, the path toward the goal— that quiet port at which nobody ever arrives. Galiani had in his possession the indispensable tool of analysis. Although he did not call it "method of successive approximation," he knew how to handle it in a masterly fashion.

The method of models, or simplified schemes, enables the investigator to reduce highly complex concrete facts to those elements which appear essential to him. On the basis of such a model he develops his argument and draws the first logical conclusions. Subsequently he introduces a factor neglected before and watches for the changes which must be imposed on the law of first approximation with which he had at first been satisfied. Then he introduces again another factor of variation and makes the necessary corrections; and so forth, until in his opinion he has arrived at a law which adequately reflects full reality. This method of model-construction, which gradually moves from the abstract to the concrete, has been applied by Galiani in an accomplished manner. His treatise *On Money,* Book ii, Chapter 1, may serve as an example.[9] It carries the title "Discussion of the Nature of Money and of its Use." It is customary in Italian seminar courses to read and discuss this chapter with the students. Galiani's model relates to the question whether social life is possible. As the discussion progresses, it becomes more and more complicated.

First step: In a small society, for example, in a religious order composed of select, virtuous men, everybody does work and everybody deposits the products of his labor in a common storehouse. Everybody draws "according to his discretion" from the storehouse "what he needs." The system can endure, and the men can live happily in this community of the few, the select, and the virtuous.

Second step: In a large community the system would not be possible because

9 *Della Moneta* (first published 1750), ed. by Fausto Nicolini, Bari, Laterza, 1915, pp. 79–84.

the idler, who deprives the community of his work, would live unjustly from the labor of others. Moreover, it would be impossible to become rich or to become poor. Hence, the industrious person, with no hope for gain, would work less hard; the lazy person, relying on the work of others, would do little or nothing; and in the end even the virtuous persons would want to live in greater splendor than they deserve in the light of their ability.

To avoid such malproportions, Galiani proposes that every member of such a community should receive, upon delivery of his products to the storage house, a certificate stating:

The person named herein has delivered to the public storage house a certain quantity of a good—say, for example, 100 pairs of shoes. In return he receives a claim, equal in value to his contribution, against the community.

The certificate must state the quality and quantity of the goods which the depositor may claim, for example, 1000 lbs. of bread.

Third step: The system suffers from imperfection because the shoemaker does not live from bread alone. It must be completed with the help of two provisions:

a. The certificates are freely exchangeable against goods from all storage houses;

b. The prince should fix the value of every good since it is not feasible to include in each certificate a list of all goods, their quality and their quantity, which may be claimed.

Hence, the prince should fix all values,

or he should use a common denominator for determining the value of every good, stating, for example, that a hundredweight of grain is equivalent to so-and-so much wine, meat, oil, clothing, cheese, etc. On the basis of this tariff everybody would know how much he can claim for his deliveries, and at which time his claim is exhausted.

Fourth step: But the system could still not endure. Wherefrom should "the persons who serve the entire community," for example, the judges, officials, and soldiers, derive the means for their living? Another provision must thus be added to the model of society constructed by Galiani, the duty

for all citizens to deliver free of charge, that is, without receiving a certificate, a quantity of goods to the storage house equal to the amount fixed by the prince for distribution among the servants of the community.

Fifth step: This society, constructed, as it is, in the mind of the theorist, would be perfect—if all men were always honest. But, who will prevent the supervisors of the storage houses from doing a service to their friends and acquaintances by granting them a claim to 1000 lbs. of bread even though the latter delivered only 10, not 100, pairs of shoes? The stocks would then seem much larger than they really are. Soon they would be depleted, to the disadvantage of the late claimants. To meet these difficulties, Galiani assumes that only the prince is entitled to sign certificates, and that these are all for equal quantities, so that a person delivering 1 lb. of bread receives 1 certificate, a person delivering 2 lbs. of bread, 2 certificates, and so forth.

When Galiani "had arrived in his deliberations at this result," it seemed to him that "society could be ruled and maintained with the help of these institutions." But suddenly, "as if a veil would fall before his eyes," he became aware "that he had entered the world of reality and was walking on native ground, from which he had believed himself so far away." That is, to speak without metaphor, he noticed that his model construction corresponded to the reality which he desired to explain. The "certificates" are coins which are exchanged for goods and services. The constructed communistic society, which cannot exist on the basis of the principles of virtue and love alone—inadequate principles in the case of whole nations—is put alongside of the "very happy" actual "form of society, in which everybody thinks and works for himself, the form which we have maintained for the sake of private interest and public convenience." Instead of common storage houses there are private stores; the certificates, that is, the coins, are neither issued nor received by the supervisors of public storage houses;

instead, everybody takes care of his own affairs—to stock up goods in his store, he pays out the coins with whose help he trades, and he takes them in again when he sells goods. In this manner neither virtue nor honesty is required of the supervisors of storage houses, nor watchful control by the prince, to prevent waste of certificates. Everybody is economical in spending since he spends only his own money, and when he spends it he parts with the products of his own industry.

Virtue suffices to maintain happily "a select, closed society, into which men are not born but admitted as adults." In the great nations there is added to virtue "the worldly interest, whose power in the human souls, including the corrupt ones, is always irresistible." The certificates, which in the ideal society are turned over to the prince free of charge, are the equivalent of the duties and taxes paid by the citizens to the government. The coins are unlike the certificates, which are made from paper or leather, and which the prince "could print in unduly large quantities"—already the least doubt would suffice to reduce confidence and to slow down circulation. Coins, instead, are made from gold or silver, that is, from a material whose quantity

God alone can augment. For, if it were to be mined, or imported from abroad, its cost would be equal to its value, and no gain would result from the increase in quantity.

The method of constructing ideal models which approximate reality is called "analytical" by Galiani. By using this method, he amazingly anticipates the procedure applied by Enrico Barone with modern strength in his famous article on the "Minister of Production," [10] where Barone points out the substantive identity of the solutions to the problems of production by the minister of a collectivist society and under the assumptions of pure competition.

Historically inclined, as he was, Galiani always sees the special side by side with the general; the abstract, the imagined, and the ideal side by side with the concrete, the factual, and the real. In his method, there is no contrast between the book *On Money* and the *Dialogues*. Before Rousseau's *Social Contract* of 1762, Galiani, in 1751, ridiculed

those who insist that all men had once come to an agreement, making a contract providing for the use, as money, of the *per se* useless metals, thus attaching value to them. Where did these conventions of all mankind take place, and where were the agreements concluded? In which century? At which place? Who were the deputies with whose help the Spaniards and Chinese, the Goths and the Africans made an agreement so lasting that during the many centuries which have passed the opinion never was changed? Obviously, if all people have a certain disposition in common, and act upon it during the course of many centuries, this is by no means the result of congresses in which they joined at the foot of the Tower of Babel or when departing from Noah's Arc. It is the disposition of our mind, and the intrinsic organization of matters which really are always the same, and which have always remained the same at all times.[11]

Galiani, being aware, as a true scholar, of the limits of abstract argumentation, possesses a historical mind. He knows that the validity of economic laws, which are true *sub specie aeternitatis* within the limits of their assumptions, cannot be expanded beyond the field delineated by these assumptions. He calls "basic" the assumptions which arise from man's proper nature, and derives certain principles from these. But he corrects and reformulates them in order to take

    [10] *Giornale degli Economisti,* 1908. English translation in F. A. Hayek, ed., *Collectivist Economic Planning,* London, 1932.
    [11] *Della Moneta,* pp. 58 f.

into account the changing circumstances of time and place. His first appeal is directed to reason. Reason is our principal guide in the solution of urgent problems:

Our reason belongs to us; we have only one. Let us not borrow that of our fathers or that of our neighbors. Rather, let us use our own. Good sense is a sovereign court, and the only one which is always in attendance. Let us establish principles which are derived from the nature of things itself. What is man? What is the relationship between man and his food? Let us apply then these principles to time, place, and circumstance. Which is the kingdom with which we are concerned? What is its situation? What are the mores, the opinions, the opportunities which are open, the risks which are to be avoided? Knowing all this, we may arrive at a decision.[12]

The statesmen, when they make up their mind, must not place exclusive reliance on abstract principles, developed with the help of a simplified model. Galiani, in his example of the communal storage house, demonstrates his ability to construct abstract models. But he does not fail to be aware of the need for approximating reality. To be sure, not the reality of concrete cases uniquely conditioned by specific circumstances, but a reality constructed by reason. In order to solve the problems of grain supply, he wants to address an inquiry to the "experts." Since he does not rely on the theoretical economist alone, he wants them to obtain information from the teamsters, the merchants, and the bakers, in order to be able to adjust the general principles to the requirements of time and place. But the teamsters, merchants, and bakers give the right answer only when they are asked the right questions—by somebody who knows the substance and type of the problem which is to be solved:

Remember that the greatest fool can reply when asked; but only the great man can interrogate.[13]

This sentence of Galiani deserves to be placed as a motto over the many volumes of economic and social investigations and statistics which overflow the desks of the economists, and whose greater part is without meaning and use because the investigations and statistics are not guided by a fruitful idea. Reason—this is Galiani's warning, which is still valid today for the pure historists and institutionalists— reason must indicate the aims of the investigation and the activities resulting therefrom.

[12] *Dialogues*, p. 22.   [13] *Ibid.*, p. 172.

THEORY OF VALUE

Galiani's work in the field of methodology is amazing, but he is no less outstanding as pure theorist. This is how he develops some of the fundamental theorems of economic science:

a. There is interdependence between the price and the quantity consumed:

A good whose price falls is used in preference. In this manner the price, which arises from scarcity, regulates consumption. Conversely, consumption regulates the price. For example, if a country with a production and consumption of 50,000 barrels of wine were suddenly invaded by an army, the price of wine would increase because more would wish to drink it.[14]

This is no "Gordian Knot," no "vicious circle." One only has to investigate what in the specific case is the cause of the change, whether it relates to the demand for goods, that is, to their utility, or to the supply. In the latter case the ratio of cost and price of reproducible goods may have changed, because of increasing pain of labor or because of circumstances beyond human control, changes of the season, wars, and the like. It may be impossible to maintain that the demand (utility) or the scarcity (supply) is the only "cause" of the value of things. But it nevertheless is possible to ascertain specifically for every case which circumstance changed, thereby providing the occasion for the change in value or in the estimation of things. Value is no intrinsic characteristic of goods. It is a "calculation," a ratio, or, as Galiani expressed it, "a sort of relationship between the possession of one good and that of another in the human mind." Man always compares one good with another, and since he "always takes care not to lose his highest satisfactions, he exchanges one good for another" only when the equivalence of the exchanged goods is obvious.

b. In the case of different goods there are different reactions to changes in the quantities supplied and demanded:

I often hear it said by people who consider themselves intelligent that one does not need to worry about grain more than about leather for shoemaking; although no police ordinance controls the shoes, nobody has to go barefoot.

Admittedly, even though the need for grain and for shoes may be equally great, that for shoes is less urgent. This explains the ambiguity. Admittedly, there is great need for shoes. But somebody who is accustomed to throw them away when he considers them used, can wear them

[14] *Della Moneta*, p. 42.

eight or more days longer if his shoemaker happens to have no leather and cannot supply new ones. Can one in the same manner stretch a pound of bread to make it last for eight days? Surely not. A piece of bread does not render a succession of services but is used up in one act, and the need for it arises again. . . . Man applies all his malice, and exhausts all his astuteness, for the sake of so urgent a need, and, certain to derive a huge profit from it, he tries to create unrest by ideas of scarcity. He does not at all employ as much astuteness in the leather trade, because he would be a fool doing so. In this manner, any other trade moves along by itself, because there is always some time period allowed to pass, which suffices to restore equilibrium. But the supply of bread is urgent; it must be watched. If the equilibrium is established too late, the people die from hunger.[15]

Galiani wrote his book for the entertainment of the intellectual ladies of Paris. For several months it was exhibited nicely on the little tables in their *salons*. If instead he had written an academic treatise, one would have to admit that he put on paper—not the theory but the fact of "elasticity of demand." The demand for shoes is highly elastic when price rises; the elasticity of demand for bread is very low. To be sure, it cannot be claimed that Galiani developed the theory of demand elasticity ahead of Marshall. But he recognized the fact, not accidentally but in full awareness, and held on to it perseveringly.

c. There exists a relationship between the price of a good and the desire for it, and between these and the purchasing power of money.

If "the principles from which value is to be derived are certain, constant, and generally valid, and based on the order and nature of the things of this world," and if "also their variation is based on orderly, exact, and immutable rules," [16] then these principles must account for the circumstances which affect different people's ideas of the relative advantage of one good or another:

Since men possess unequal wealth, a different bracket of wealth always corresponds to the purchase of certain conveniences. If these become cheaper, they are purchased also by those in the lower bracket; if they become more expensive, those who consumed them before begin to forego them.[17]

Here the general statement that the quantity consumed falls with rising price and rises with falling price is supplemented by the recognition of the social cause of this phenomenon: the unequal distribution

---

[15] *Dialogues*, pp. 182 f.   [17] *Ibid.*, p. 43.
[16] *Della Moneta*, p. 40.

of wealth. A price fall makes available to the poorer classes of consumers a good formerly not obtainable by them. An increase in price restricts the consumption of the wealthier groups. The effect of the unequal distribution of wealth on prices makes itself felt in different ways—in the most peculiar way, as Galiani points out, as the result of fashion. Fashion is referred to as "an ailment of the brain, characteristic of European nations, which is responsible for a reduction of the value of many goods that are not considered novelties." The incidence of the disease is not the same on all persons, because most people, when they select goods for purchase, neither have the opportunity nor the time to worry about their greater or lesser novelty. It especially affects the wealthiest and showiest groups, and, of nations, those which excel in wealth and power. If one really

wishes to find a justification for this affliction of the mind which dominates over so many matters, one would have to say that the change of taste mainly is based on the imitation of the customs of the ruling nations.[18]

Galiani thus came near to the threshold of the discovery which so profoundly affected the prestige of economic science in the middle of the nineteenth century. He came to it not on account of an ingenious inspiration but as the result of purposive meditation over the laws of price, and in clear recognition of the significance of the principles developed by him. Until the time of Lloyd, Gossen, and, later, of Jevons, Menger, and Marshall, scholars had in vain struggled with the paradox of price—which may be low in the case of goods of great objective utility (air and water, for example) and high in the case of goods of small objective utility (pearls, diamonds, gold, etc.). Galiani had taken a few steps toward the solution of this puzzle, by demonstrating that the price is not an inherent characteristic of goods—like volume, weight, or color—but an idea, a concept, formed in the human mind, concerning the advantage of the acquisition of one good compared with another, an idea that varies with the taste and the purchasing power of individuals and social groups.

d. *The utility of successive doses of a good diminishes, and the diminution may be such as to cause total utility to become zero or negative.*

The nature of this paradox, which tormented generations of economists down to Gossen, has been clearly recognized by Galiani:

It is obvious that air and water, which are very useful for human life, have no value because they are not scarce. On the other hand, a bag of

18 *Ibid.,* p. 41.

sand from the shores of Japan would be an extremely rare thing—yet, unless it has a certain utility, it is without value. I can easily see, however, why some people will be sceptical about the great utility of many goods which have an extremely high price. . . .[19]

Most people argue with Bernardo Davanzati: "A living calf is nobler than a golden calf, but how much less is its price!" Others say: "A pound of bread is more useful than a pound of gold." [20]

At an age of 23 years, and in 1751, Galiani formulates the following reply:

This is a wrong and foolish conclusion. It is based on neglect of the fact that "useful" and "less useful" are relative concepts, which depend on the specific circumstances. If somebody is in want of bread and of gold, bread surely is more useful for him. This agrees with the facts of life, because nobody would forego bread, take gold, and die from hunger. People who mine gold never forget to eat and to sleep. But somebody who has eaten his fill will consider bread the least useful of goods. He will then want to satisfy other needs. This goes to show that the precious metals are companions of luxury, that is, of a status in which the elemental needs are taken care of. Davanzati maintains that a single egg, priced at ½ grain of gold, would have had the value of protecting the starving Count Ugolino from death at his tenth day in gaol—a value in excess of that of all the gold in the world. But this confuses awkwardly the price paid by a person unafraid to die from hunger without the egg, and the needs of Count Ugolino. How can Davanzati be sure that the Count would not have paid 1,000 grains of gold for the egg? Davanzati obviously has made a mistake here, and, although he is not aware of it, his further remarks indicate that he knows better. He says: What an awful thing is a rat. But when Casilino was under siege, prices went up so much that a rat fetched 200 guilders—and this price still was not expensive because the seller died from hunger and the buyer could save himself.[21]

This is the classical section which is always read in Italian seminars when a telling illustration of the principle of diminishing utility is to be given. Here one can read:

1. Of a person, satiated with bread, who attaches no utility to additional quantities of bread which might be offered to him (principle of diminishing utility of successive doses of a good);

[19] *Ibid.*, p. 28.

[20] *Ibid.*, p. 32. [Bernardo Davanzati (1529–1606), an Italian who combined business with writing, is remembered for his contributions to the theory of foreign exchanges and of money.—Ed.]

[21] *Ibid.*, pp. 32 f.

2. Of a person, satiated with bread, who turns to the satisfaction of other desires, that is, acquires other goods (principle of equality of the weighted marginal utilities of acquired goods);

3. Of a person, living under normal conditions, who has other food at his disposal and who pays only ½ grain of gold for an egg (principle of ranking of goods);

4. Of Count Ugolino, who, starving, would have been ready to pay as much as 1,000 grains of gold for the same egg (same principle);

5. Of a person who under conditions of siege paid 200 guilders for a rat and thus saved his life (same principle);

6. Of the living calf, which has very little value if there are many calves and if many other foodstuffs are available—whereas a golden calf fetches a very high price. But the opposite is true when there are only a few living calves and when there are no other foodstuffs (principle of substitution of goods).

All these ideas can be found in the section referred to. They were developed in a polemic with Davanzati and other writers who are not mentioned by name. Galiani did not arrive at their formulation as the result of a felicitous, ingenious inspiration but in full awareness of their importance. Such awareness of the importance of newly found and defended truth is the proper characteristic of scientific discovery. We are thus justified in concluding that this section of Galiani's book contains the germs of Gossen's theories of the ranking of goods, of their substitution, of the diminishing utility of additional doses of the same good, and of the equality of the weighted marginal utilities of acquired goods. Germs, but not mature formulations. But the year was 1751, and Galiani had meditated over these insights between his 21st and 23rd year!

e. The rate of exchange and the rate of interest are not in the nature of an agio but are means to accomplish equality in exchange.

Science—promoted by the terror with which accident and fate have haunted mankind during the centuries of ignorance—has

discovered that so-called accidents readily submit to a calculus; that their variation demonstrates immutable order and rational regularity; and that a relation can be established between the certain present and the uncertain future. It has become recognized that the real value of a good varies with the degree of probability controlling the possibility or impossibility of its use: 100 ducats, obtainable with difficulty in the future, are equal in value to 90 present ducats. This is their valuation in every gambling or exchange contract if there is a probability of 90 degrees that they will not be lost, and of 10 degrees that they will be lost. From this arises the rate of exchange and the rate of interest—brother and sister. The former equalizes the present and the spatially distant money. It operates with the help of an apparent agio, which is added sometimes to the present, and at other times to the distant money, in order to equate the real value of the one to that of the other, one being reduced because of lesser convenience or greater risk. Interest equalizes present and future money. Here the effect of time is the same as that of spatial distance in the case of the rate of exchange. The basis of either contract is the equality of the real value. This is so true that on occasion present money is valued less than distant money. This is known as "exchange below par." The bills of exchange, which represent money and which really are nothing but future money, often have more value than cash, the excess being known as "agio." . . . It was a mistake to speak of "gain" or "profit" of money with reference to what only is an offset to a deficit, required for equalization. Where there is equality, there is no gain; where the real price is lessened by risk and inconvenience, the offset is no gain.[22]

If properly interpreted, these propositions contain the germ of the following principles:

1. The rate of exchange and the rate of interest are means used by the contracting parties with the view of equalizing values which numerically are equal but which are separated by time or place.

2. There are two causes of the inequality of the prices of such values: risk and convenience.

3. A risk premium is not in the nature of profit, and it often varies

because the degree of probability of loss shows extreme variations. This sometimes is very high, as in the case of maritime loans; at other times it is as low as zero, as in the case of banks and of the commercial companies of the Republics; and at still other times it is less than zero, assuming a negative value, as was true in France at the time of John Law's system.[23]

A creditor who is afraid that the principal might not be repaid will suffer from palpitations of the heart. But

if somebody suffers all the time from palpitations of the heart, this is painful; it is only proper to pay for it. What is known as reward for pain, is— if it is just—nothing but the price for palpitations of the heart.

Equally, compensation for "convenience"—as seen from the debtor —or for "inconvenience"—as seen from the creditor—is not profit.

[22] *Ibid.*, pp. 291 f.
[23] *Ibid.*, pp. 293 f. This is also the source of the three quotations which follow in the text.

The meaning of "convenience" is elucidated by remarks which follow upon Galiani's definition of a "loan," which, in substance, is "the surrender of a good, with the proviso that an equivalent good is to be returned, not more." What is "equivalent"? The usual definitions relate equivalence to material, objective circumstances, for example, to "weight, or similarity of form"; hence to the identity of the good which is to be surrendered and returned (number of units of money, etc.). But those who adopt such definitions "understand little of human activities." One should recall the basic principles of economic science. Value is not an objective characteristic of goods; rather it is the relationship of goods to our needs. Goods are equivalent when they provide equal convenience to the person with reference to whom they are considered as equivalent.

This is all which Galiani says about this matter. But what he says suffices to explain the thesis that the rate of interest is an instrument for making subjectively equal certain values which numerically are different but separated by time. To the debtor, the convenience derived from the receipt of 100 units of money today is equal to the inconvenience incurred by the repayment of 105 units in a year. To the creditor, the inconvenience caused by the surrender of 100 units today is equal to the convenience derived from receiving 105 units in a year. When the two contracting parties agree on the subjective valuation of the two items, the exchange between the present and the future is accomplished. Nobody derives a profit from the exchange since it is one of subjectively equal goods.

Galiani does not apply here his theory of diminishing utility, and he does not add that, if there is equality at the margin, there nevertheless may be intramarginal exchangers who derive a psychological gain—a gain in pleasure, as Galiani would say—from the exchange between the present and the future. For example, if the market rate of interest is 5 per cent, a person who would be satisfied if at the end of a year he receives 104 or 103 units of money, or perhaps only 100 or 99, in exchange for the present 100 units, derives a differential gain, a saver's rent. It is Galiani's extraordinary merit to have anticipated the theories of the Austrian and other schools, which regard interest as an instrument for the equalization of present and future values. Also, Galiani had not failed to notice that interest, although usually positive, might be negative.

CONTRIBUTIONS TO APPLIED ECONOMICS

Galiani's contributions to applied economics are varied and rich. The historian of war economics surely will recall Galiani's emphasis on grain "as a veritable ammunition of war." [24]   From this point of view he divides the various countries into very small ones, which are almost without any agriculture, into medium-sized ones, which have a commercial establishment, into medium-sized, agricultural countries, into large, agricultural countries which are backward, and into large, agricultural, and industrial countries.   Countries of different type should pursue different agricultural policies, aiming always at the provision of adequate supplies in order to prevent domestic unrest or to be prepared for wartime difficulties.

All students of economic policy should remember Galiani's reply to those who want the government to promote all branches of production, agricultural and industrial: "He who stimulates everything, stimulates nothing.   Stimulation—that is differentiation." [25]   Those who long for artificial stimulation of domestic agriculture—"battles of grain"—and mourn for the past, being envious of countries which produce abundant quantities of grain—they should recall Galiani's comparison of the France of his time, which sometimes had to import grain from abroad, with the France of the good old days, which was a grain-exporter:

Manufacturing trade increases as a result of efficient work; trade in food-stuffs diminishes as a result of efficient work.[26]

Population may grow to such an extent

that one has to turn to the sparsely populated countries for purchases of foodstuffs necessary to maintain the surplus population, exporting manufactured articles in return.   This would be the masterpiece of good government—to compel nature to work such a miracle that on limited ground more people can live than the ground can nourish.

Those who yearn for the past, really yearn

for the beautiful privilege of being underpopulated and of having staple foods for sale abroad.   They long for the allegedly beautiful era of Sully— when France was destroyed by 40 years of murderous civil war—and for the still older time of the wars in Italy and Flanders, the most sanguinary

[24] *Dialogues*, p. 50.

[25] *Ibid.*, p. 122.

[26] *Ibid.*, pp. 150 f.   This is also the source of the two quotations which follow in the text.

wars ever fought by France; for the time when France lost still larger numbers of her population through emigration . . . All that time the Kingdom, badly cultivated as it was, enjoyed the sinister advantage of deriving a surplus of grain from ordinary harvests. Indeed, to the shame of the century, there was then export trade of foodstuffs. Now this is gone, but nobody should be sorry for it. Let us leave such glory to Turkey, Egypt, Algiers, Morocco, Poland, and other poor, underpopulated, and unfortunate countries. If we need grain, they will sell it to us in good time. In the whole world, only the underpopulated countries carry on continuously a huge grain export trade.

For the moment, Galiani seems to have forgotten that grain is an "ammunition of war." In his thoughts he has placed himself in a peaceful world, which is undisturbed by the unrest of war. He has the vision of an epoch in which, thanks to the division of labor, the production of grain becomes the specialty of new countries with sparse population and fertile soil suitable for the production of staple foods. It is a fleeting vision, from which Galiani soon returns to the contemplation of hard reality—which compels every country to turn to the unprofitable production of grain in order to avert the danger of wartime famine.[27]

[27] [The concluding sections of Einaudi's article, which are omitted in this translation, treat of Galiani's discussion of monetary problems.—Ed.]

Smith
on
the Physiocrats

The physiocrats are a group of French writers, including François Quesnay (1694–1774) and Robert-Jacques Turgot (1727–1781), whose name is derived from their emphasis on the rule of true natural laws as contrasted with the despotic rule of man. The physiocrats, also known as *économistes,* were the first to develop a system of economics on the basis of circular-flow analysis, with Quesnay's *tableau économique* serving as model of the circular flow of the national income. Emphasizing the role of agriculture, the physiocrats were inclined to deny the productivity of other economic activities. It was their view that only agriculture turned out a "net product" over and above its cost of production, with the agricultural surplus serving to maintain the "sterile" class of manufacturers and traders. Since only land was recognized as productive by the physiocrats, taxation of land was considered by them as the only proper method of taxation.

Adam Smith traveled widely in France, and he became well acquainted with the members of this school of thought. Of his appraisal of the physiocrats, reprinted here, a modern writer has said: "On Quesnay and his school I have not read any book which gave more than Adam Smith's treatment" (M. Beer).

(On Smith, see pp. 113 ff., below. For another appraisal of the physiocrats, by Marx, see pp. 100 ff., below.)

THAT SYSTEM which represents the produce of land as the sole source of the revenue and wealth of every country has, so far as I know, never been adopted by any nation, and it at present exists only in the speculations of a few men of great learning and ingenuity in France. It would not, surely, be worth while to examine at great length the errors of a system which never has done, and probably never will do, any harm in any part of the world. I shall endeavour to explain, however, as distinctly as I can, the great outlines of this very ingenious system.

Mr. Colbert, the famous minister of Louis XIV., was a man of probity, of great industry and knowledge of detail, of great experience and acuteness in the examination of public accounts, and of abilities, in short, every way fitted for introducing method and good order into the collection and expenditure of the public revenue. That minister had unfortunately embraced all the prejudices of the mercantile system, in its nature and essence a system of restraint and regulation, and such as could scarce fail to be agreeable to a laborious and plodding man of business, who had been accustomed to regulate the different departments of public offices, and to establish the necessary checks and controls for confining each to its proper sphere. The industry and commerce of a great country he endeavoured to regulate upon the same model as the departments of a public office; and instead of allowing every man to pursue his own interest in his own way, upon the liberal plan of equality, liberty, and justice, he bestowed upon certain branches of industry extraordinary privileges, while he laid others under as extraordinary restraints. He was not only disposed, like other European ministers, to encourage more the industry of the towns than that of the country; but, in order to support the industry of the towns, he was willing even to depress and keep down that of the country. In order to render provisions cheap to the inhabitants of the towns, and thereby to encourage manufactures and foreign commerce, he prohibited altogether the exportation of corn, and thus excluded the inhabitants of the country from every foreign market for by far the most important part of the produce of their industry. This prohibition, joined to the re-

[From *The Wealth of Nations,* 1776, Bk. IV, Chap. 9.]

straints imposed by the ancient provincial laws of France upon the transportation of corn from one province to another, and to the arbitrary and degrading taxes which are levied upon the cultivators in almost all the provinces, discouraged and kept down the agriculture of that country very much below the state to which it would naturally have risen in so very fertile a soil and so very happy a climate. This state of discouragement and depression was felt more or less in every different part of the country, and many different inquiries were set on foot concerning the causes of it. One of those causes appeared to be the preference given, by the institutions of Mr. Colbert, to the industry of the towns above that of the country.

If the rod be bent too much one way, says the proverb, in order to make it straight you must bend it as much the other. The French philosophers, who have proposed the system which represents agriculture as the sole source of the revenue and wealth of every country, seem to have adopted this proverbial maxim; and as in the plan of Mr. Colbert the industry of the towns was certainly over-valued in comparison with that of the country; so in their system it seems to be as certainly undervalued.

The different orders of people who have ever been supposed to contribute in any respect towards the annual produce of the land and labour of the country, they divide into three classes. The first is the class of the proprietors of land. The second is the class of the cultivators, of farmers and country labourers, whom they honour with the peculiar appellation of the productive class. The third is the class of artificers, manufacturers, and merchants, whom they endeavour to degrade by the humiliating appellation of the barren or unproductive class.

The class of proprietors contributes to the annual produce by the expense which they may occasionally lay out upon the improvement of the land, upon the buildings, drains, enclosures, and other ameliorations, which they may either make or maintain upon it, and by means of which the cultivators are enabled, with the same capital, to raise a greater produce, and consequently to pay a greater rent. This advanced rent may be considered as the interest or profit due to the proprietor upon the expense or capital which he thus employs in the improvement of his land. Such expenses are in this system called ground expenses (*dépenses foncières*).

The cultivators or farmers contribute to the annual produce by what are in this system called the original and annual expenses (*dépenses primitives et dépenses annuelles*) which they lay out upon the cultivation of the land. The original expenses consist in the instruments of husbandry, in the stock of cattle, in the seed, and in the maintenance of the farmer's family, servants, and cattle during at least a great part of the first year of his occupancy, or till he can receive some return from the land. The annual expenses consist in the seed, in the wear and tear of the instruments of husbandry, and in the annual maintenance of the farmer's servants and cattle, and of his family too, so far as any part of them can be considered as servants employed in cultivation. That part of the produce of the land which remains to him after paying the rent ought to be sufficient, first, to replace to him within a reasonable time, at least during the term of his occupancy, the whole of his original expenses, together with the ordinary profits of stock; and, secondly, to replace to him annually the whole of his annual expenses, together likewise with the ordinary profits of stock. Those two sorts of expenses are two capitals which the farmer employs in cultivation; and unless they are regularly restored to him, together with a reasonable profit, he cannot carry on his employment upon a level with other employments; but, from a regard to his own interest, must desert it as soon as possible and seek some other. That part of the produce of the land which is thus necessary for enabling the farmer to continue his business ought to be considered as a fund sacred to cultivation, which, if the landlord violates, he necessarily reduces the produce of his own land, and in a few years not only disables the farmer from paying this racked rent, but from paying the reasonable rent which he might otherwise have got for his land. The rent which properly belongs to the landlord is no more than the net produce which remains after paying in the completest manner all the necessary expenses which must be previously laid out in order to raise the gross or the whole produce. It is because the labour of the cultivators, over and above paying completely all those necessary expenses, affords a net produce of this kind that this class of people are in this system peculiarly distinguished by the honourable appellation of the productive class. Their original and annual expenses are for the same reason called, in this system, productive expenses, because, over and above replacing their own value, they occasion the annual reproduction of this net produce.

The ground expenses, as they are called, or what the landlord lays out upon the improvement of his land, are in this system, too, honoured with the appellation of productive expenses. Till the whole of those expenses, together with the ordinary profits of stock, have been completely repaid to him by the advanced rent which he gets from his land, that advanced rent ought to be regarded as sacred and inviolable, both by the church and by the king; ought to be subject neither to tithe nor to taxation. If it is otherwise, by discouraging the improvement of land the church discourages the future increase of her own tithes, and the king the future increase of his own taxes. As in a well-ordered state of things, therefore, those ground expenses, over and above reproducing in the completest manner their own value, occasion likewise after a certain time a reproduction of a net produce, they are in this system considered as productive expenses.

The ground expenses of the landlord, however, together with the original and the annual expenses of the farmer, are the only three sorts of expenses which in this system are considered as productive. All other expenses and all other orders of people, even those who in the common apprehensions of men are regarded as the most productive, are in this account of things represented as altogether barren and unproductive.

Artificers and manufacturers in particular, whose industry, in the common apprehensions of men, increases so much the value of the rude produce of land, are in this system represented as a class of people altogether barren and unproductive. Their labour, it is said, replaces only the stock which employs them, together with its ordinary profits. That stock consists in the materials, tools, and wages advanced to them by their employer; and is the fund destined for their employment and maintenance. Its profits are the fund destined for the maintenance of their employer. Their employer, as he advances to them the stock of materials, tools, and wages necessary for their employment, so he advances to himself what is necessary for his own maintenance, and this maintenance he generally proportions to the profit which he expects to make by the price of their work. Unless its price repays to him the maintenance which he advances to himself, as well as the materials, tools, and wages which he advances to his workmen, it evidently does not repay to him the whole expense which he lays out upon it. The profits of manufacturing stock therefore are not, like the rent of land, a net produce which remains after completely repaying the whole expense which must be laid out in order to obtain them. The stock of the farmer yields him a profit as well as that of the master manufacturer; and it yields a rent likewise to another person, which that of the master manufacturer does not. The expense, therefore, laid out in employing and maintaining artificers and manufacturers does no more than continue, if one may say so, the existence of its own value, and does not produce any new value. It is therefore altogether a barren and unproductive expense. The expense, on the contrary, laid out in employing farmers and country labourers, over and above continuing the existence of its own value, produces a new value, the rent of the landlord. It is therefore a productive expense.

Mercantile stock is equally barren and unproductive with manufacturing stock. It only continues the existence of its own value, without producing any new value. Its profits are only the repayment of the maintenance which its employer advances to himself during the time that he employs it, or till he receives the returns of it. They are only the repayment of a part of the expense which must be laid out in employing it.

The labour of artificers and manufacturers never adds anything to the value of the whole annual amount of the rude produce of the land. It adds, indeed, greatly to the value of some particular parts of it. But the consumption which in the meantime it occasions of other parts is precisely equal to the value which it adds to those parts; so that the value of the whole amount is not, at any one moment of time, in the least augmented by it. The person who works the lace of a pair of fine ruffles, for example, will sometimes raise the value of perhaps a pennyworth of flax to thirty pounds sterling. But though at first sight he appears thereby to multiply the value of a part of the rude produce about seven thousand and two hundred times, he in reality adds nothing to the value of the whole annual amount of the rude produce. The working of that lace costs him perhaps two years' labour. The thirty pounds which he gets for it when it is finished is no more than the repayment of the subsistence which he advances to himself during the two years that he is employed about it. The value which, by every day's, month's, or year's labour, he adds to the flax does no more than replace the value of his own consumption during that day, month, or year. At no moment of time, therefore, does he add anything to the value of the whole annual amount of the rude produce of the land: the portion of that produce which he is continually consuming being always equal to the value which he is continually producing. The extreme poverty of the greater part of the persons employed in this expensive though trifling manufacture may satisfy us that the price of their work does not in ordinary cases exceed the value of their subsistence. It is otherwise with the work of farmers and country labourers. The rent of the landlord is a value which, in ordinary cases, it is continually producing, over and above replacing, in the most complete manner, the whole consumption, the whole expense laid out upon the employment and maintenance both of the workmen and of their employer.

Artificers, manufacturers, and merchants can augment the revenue and wealth of their society by parsimony only; or, as it is expressed in this system, by privation, that is, by depriving themselves of a part of the funds destined for their own subsistence. They annually reproduce nothing but those funds. Unless, therefore, they annually save some part of them, unless they annually deprive themselves of the enjoyment of some part of them, the revenue and wealth of their society can never be in the smallest degree augmented by means of their industry. Farmers and country labourers, on the contrary, may enjoy completely the whole funds destined for their own subsistence, and yet augment at the same time the revenue and wealth of their society. Over and above what is destined for their own subsistence, their industry annually affords a net produce, of which the augmentation necessarily augments the revenue and wealth of their society. Nations therefore which, like France or England, consist in a great measure of proprietors and cultivators can be enriched by industry and enjoyment. Nations, on the contrary, which, like Holland and Hamburg, are composed chiefly of merchants, artificers, and manufacturers can grow rich only through parsimony and privation. As the interest of nations so differently circumstanced is very different, so is likewise the common character of the people: in those of the former kind, liberality, frankness, and good fellowship naturally make a part of that common character: in the latter, narrowness, meanness, and a selfish disposition, averse to all social pleasure and enjoyment.

The unproductive class, that of merchants, artificers, and manufacturers, is maintained and employed altogether at the expense of the two other classes, of that of proprietors, and of that of cultivators. They furnish it both with the materials of its work and with the fund of its subsistence, with the corn and cattle which it consumes while it is employed about that work. The proprietors and cultivators finally pay both the wages of all the workmen of the unproductive class, and of the profits of all their employers. Those workmen and their employers are properly the servants of the proprietors and cultivators. They are only servants who work without doors, as menial servants work within. Both the one and the other, however, are equally maintained at the expense of the same masters. The labour of both is equally unproductive. It adds nothing to the value of the sum total of the rude produce of the land. Instead of increasing the value of that sum total, it is a charge and expense which must be paid out of it.

The unproductive class, however, is not only useful, but greatly useful to the other two classes. By means of the industry of merchants, artificers, and manufacturers, the proprietors and cultivators can purchase both the foreign goods and the manufactured produce of their own country which they have occasion for with the produce of a much smaller quantity of their own labour than what they would be obliged to employ if they were to attempt, in an awkward and unskilful manner, either to import the one or to make the other for their own use. By means of the unproductive class, the cultivators are delivered from many cares which would otherwise distract their attention from the cultivation of land. The superiority of produce, which, in consequence of this undivided attention, they are enabled to raise, is fully sufficient to pay the whole expense which the maintenance and employment of the unproductive class costs either the proprietors or themselves. The industry of merchants, artificers, and manufacturers, though in its own nature altogether unproductive, yet contributes in this manner indirectly to increase the produce of the land. It increases the productive powers of productive labour by leaving it at liberty to confine itself to its proper employment, the cultivation of land; and the plough goes frequently the easier and the better by means of the labour of the man whose business is most remote from the plough.

It can never be the interest of the proprietors and cultivators to restrain or to discourage in any respect the industry of merchants, artificers, and manufacturers. The greater the liberty which this unproductive class enjoys, the greater will be the competition in all the different trades which compose it, and the cheaper will the other two classes be supplied, both with foreign goods and with the manufactured produce of their own country.

It can never be the interest of the unproductive class to oppress the other two classes. It is the surplus produce of the land, or what remains after deducting the maintenance, first, of the cultivators, and afterwards of the proprietors, that maintains and employs the unproductive class. The greater this surplus the greater must likewise be the maintenance and employment of that class. The establishment of perfect justice, of perfect liberty, and of perfect equality is the very simple secret which most effectually secures the highest degree of prosperity to all the three classes.

The merchants, artificers, and manufacturers of those mercantile states which, like Holland and Hamburg, consist chiefly of this unproductive class, are in the same manner maintained and employed altogether at the expense of the proprietors and cultivators of land. The only difference is, that those proprietors and cultivators are, the greater part of them, placed at a most inconvenient distance from the merchants, artificers, and manufacturers whom they supply with the materials of their work and the fund of their subsistence,—the inhabitants of other countries and the subjects of other governments.

Such mercantile states, however, are not only useful, but greatly useful to the inhabitants of those other countries. They fill up, in some measure, a very important void, and supply the place of the merchants, artificers, and manufacturers whom the inhabitants of those countries ought to find at home, but whom, from some defect in their policy, they do not find at home.

It can never be the interest of those landed nations, if I may call them so, to discourage or distress the industry of such mercantile states by imposing high duties upon their trade or upon the commodities which they furnish. Such duties, by rendering those commodities dearer, could serve only to sink the real value of the surplus produce of their own land, with which, or, what comes to the same thing, with the price of which those commodities are purchased. Such duties could serve only to discourage the increase of that surplus produce, and consequently the improvement and cultivation of their own land. The most effectual expedient, on the contrary, for raising the value of that surplus produce, for encouraging its increase, and consequently the improvement and cultivation of their own land, would be to allow the most perfect freedom to the trade of all such mercantile nations.

This perfect freedom of trade would even be the most effectual expedient for supplying them, in due time, with all the artificers, manufacturers, and merchants whom they wanted at home, and for filling up in the properest and most advantageous manner that very important void which they felt there.

The continual increase of the surplus produce of their land would, in due time, create a greater capital than what could be employed with the ordinary rate of profit in the improvement and cultivation of land; and the surplus part of it would naturally turn itself to the employment of artificers and manufacturers at home. But those artificers and manufacturers, finding at home both the materials of their work and the fund of their subsistence, might immediately even with much less art and skill be able to work as cheap as the like artificers and manufacturers of such mercantile states who had both to bring from a great distance. Even though, from want of art and skill, they might not for some time be able to work as cheap, yet, finding a market at home, they might be able to sell their work there as cheap as that of the artificers and manufacturers of such mercantile states, which could not be brought to that market but from so great a distance; and as their art and skill improved, they would soon be able to sell it cheaper. The artificers and manufacturers of such mercantile states, therefore, would immediately be rivalled in the market of those landed nations, and soon after undersold and jostled out of it altogether. The cheapness of the manufactures of those landed nations, in consequence of the gradual improvements of art and skill, would, in due time, extend their sale beyond the home market, and carry them to many foreign markets, from which they would in the same manner gradually jostle out many of the manufactures of such mercantile nations.

This continual increase both of the rude and manufactured produce of those landed nations would in due time create a greater capital than could, with the ordinary rate of profit, be employed either in agriculture or in manufactures. The surplus of this capital would naturally turn itself to foreign trade, and be employed in exporting to foreign countries such parts of the rude and manufactured produce of its own country as exceeded the demand of the home market. In the exportation of the produce of their own country, the merchants of a landed nation would have an advantage of the same kind over those of mercantile nations which its artificers and manufacturers had over the artificers and manufacturers of such nations; the advantage of finding at home that cargo and those stores and provisions which the others were obliged to seek for at a distance. With inferior art and skill in navigation, therefore, they would be able to sell that cargo as cheap in foreign markets as the merchants of such mercantile nations; and with equal art and skill they would be able to sell it cheaper. They would soon, therefore, rival those mercantile nations in this branch of foreign trade, and in due time would jostle them out of it altogether.

According to this liberal and generous system, therefore, the most advantageous method in which a landed nation can raise up artificers, manufacturers, and merchants of its own is to grant the most perfect freedom of trade to the artificers, manufacturers, and merchants of all other nations. It thereby raises the value of the surplus produce of its own land, of which the continual increase gradually establishes a fund, which in due time necessarily raises up all the artificers, manufacturers, and merchants whom it has occasion for.

When a landed nation, on the contrary, oppresses either by high duties or by prohibitions the trade of foreign nations, it necessarily hurts its own interest in two different ways. First, by raising the price of all foreign goods and of all sorts of manufactures, it necessarily sinks the real value of the surplus produce of its own land, with which, or, what comes to the same thing, with the price of which it purchases those foreign goods and manufactures. Secondly, by giving a sort of monopoly of the home market to its own merchants, artificers, and manufacturers, it raises the rate of mercantile and manufacturing profit in proportion to that of agricultural profit, and consequently either draws from agriculture a part of the capital which had before been

employed in it, or hinders from going to it a part of what would otherwise have gone to it. This policy, therefore, discourages agriculture
in two different ways; first, by sinking the real value of its produce,
and thereby lowering the rate of its profit; and, secondly, by raising
the rate of profit in all other employments. Agriculture is rendered
less advantageous, and trade and manufactures more advantageous
than they otherwise would be; and every man is tempted by his own
interest to turn, as much as he can, both his capital and his industry
from the former to the latter employments.

Though, by this oppressive policy, a landed nation should be able
to raise up artificers, manufacturers, and merchants of its own somewhat sooner than it could do by the freedom of trade—a matter, however, which is not a little doubtful—yet it would raise them up, if one
may say so, prematurely, and before it was perfectly ripe for them.
By raising up too hastily one species of industry, it would depress another more valuable species of industry. By raising up too hastily a
species of industry which only replaces the stock which employs it,
together with the ordinary profit, it would depress a species of industry
which, over and above replacing that stock with its profit, affords likewise a net produce, a free rent to the landlord. It would depress productive labour, by encouraging too hastily that labour which is altogether barren and unproductive.

In what manner, according to this system, the sum total of the
annual produce of the land is distributed among the three classes above
mentioned, and in what manner the labour of the unproductive class
does no more than replace the value of its own consumption, without
increasing in any respect the value of that sum total, is represented by
Mr. Quesnai, the very ingenious and profound author of this system,
in some arithmetical formularies. The first of these formularies,
which by way of eminence he peculiarly distinguishes by the name of
the Economical Table, represents the manner in which he supposes
this distribution takes place in a state of the most perfect liberty and
therefore of the highest prosperity—in a state where the annual produce
is such as to afford the greatest possible net produce, and where each
class enjoys its proper share of the whole annual produce. Some subsequent formularies represent the manner in which he supposes this
distribution is made in different states of restraint and regulation; in
which either the class of proprietors or the barren and unproductive
class is more favoured than the class of cultivators, and in which
either the one or the other encroaches more or less upon the share
which ought properly to belong to this productive class. Every such
encroachment, every violation of that natural distribution, which the

most perfect liberty would establish, must, according to this system, necessarily degrade more or less, from one year to another, the value and sum total of the annual produce, and must necessarily occasion a gradual declension in the real wealth and revenue of the society; a declension of which the progress must be quicker or slower, according to the degree of this encroachment, according as that natural distribution which the most perfect liberty would establish is more or less violated. Those subsequent formularies represent the different degrees of declension which, according to this system, correspond to the different degrees in which this natural distribution is violated.

Some speculative physicians seem to have imagined that the health of the human body could be preserved only by a certain precise regimen of diet and exercise, of which every, the smallest, violation necessarily occasioned some degree of disease or disorder proportioned to the degree of the violation. Experience, however, would seem to show that the human body frequently preserves, to all appearance at least, the most perfect state of health under a vast variety of different regimens; even under some which are generally believed to be very far from being perfectly wholesome. But the healthful state of the human body, it would seem, contains in itself some unknown principle of preservation, capable either of preventing or of correcting, in many respects, the bad effects even of a very faulty regimen. Mr. Quesnai, who was himself a physician, and a very speculative physician, seems to have entertained a notion of the same kind concerning the political body, and to have imagined that it would thrive and prosper only under a certain precise regimen, the exact regimen of perfect liberty and perfect justice. He seems not to have considered that, in the political body, the natural effort which every man is continually making to better his own condition is a principle of preservation capable of preventing and correcting, in many respects, the bad effects of a political economy, in some degree, both partial and oppressive. Such a political economy, though it no doubt retards more or less, is not always capable of stopping altogether the natural progress of a nation towards wealth and prosperity, and still less of making it go backwards. If a nation could not prosper without the enjoyment of perfect liberty and perfect justice, there is not in the world a nation which could ever have prospered. In the political body, however, the wisdom of nature has fortunately made ample provision for remedying many of the bad effects of the folly and injustice of man, in the same manner as it has done in the natural body for remedying those of his sloth and intemperance.

The capital error of this system, however, seems to lie in its representing the class of artificers, manufacturers, and merchants as alto-

gether barren and unproductive. The following observations may
serve to show the impropriety of this representation.

First, this class, it is acknowledged, reproduces annually the value
of its own annual consumption, and continues, at least, the existence
of the stock or capital which maintains and employs it. But upon this
account alone the denomination of barren or unproductive should
seem to be very improperly applied to it. We should not call a marriage barren or unproductive though it produced only a son and a
daughter, to replace the father and mother, and though it did not increase the number of the human species, but only continued it as it was
before. Farmers and country labourers, indeed, over and above the
stock which maintains and employs them, reproduce annually a net
produce, a free rent to the landlord. As a marriage which affords
three children is certainly more productive than one which affords
only two; so the labour of farmers and country labourers is certainly
more productive than that of merchants, artificers, and manufacturers.
The superior produce of the one class, however, does not render the
other barren or unproductive.

Secondly, it seems, upon this account, altogether improper to consider artificers, manufacturers, and merchants in the same light as
menial servants. The labour of menial servants does not continue the
existence of the fund which maintains and employs them. Their
maintenance and employment is altogether at the expense of their masters, and the work which they perform is not of a nature to repay that
expense. That work consists in services which perish generally in the
very instant of their performance, and does not fix or realise itself in
any vendible commodity which can replace the value of their wages
and maintenance. The labour, on the contrary, of artificers, manufacturers, and merchants naturally does fix and realise itself in some
such vendible commodity. It is upon this account that, in the chapter
in which I treat of productive and unproductive labour, I have classed
artificers, manufacturers, and merchants among the productive labourers, and menial servants among the barren or unproductive.

Thirdly, it seems upon every supposition improper to say that the
labour of artificers, manufacturers, and merchants does not increase
the real revenue of the society. Though we should suppose, for
example, as it seems to be supposed in this system, that the value of
the daily, monthly, and yearly consumption of this class was exactly
equal to that of its daily, monthly, and yearly production, yet it would
not from thence follow that its labour added nothing to the real revenue,
to the real value of the annual produce of the land and labour of the
society. An artificer, for example, who, in the first six months after

harvest, executes ten pounds' worth of work, though he should in the same time consume ten pounds' worth of corn and other necessaries, yet really adds the value of ten pounds to the annual produce of the land and labour of the society. While he has been consuming a half-yearly revenue of ten pounds' worth of corn and other necessaries, he has produced an equal value of work capable of purchasing, either to himself or to some other person, an equal half-yearly revenue. The value, therefore, of what has been consumed and produced during these six months is equal, not to ten, but to twenty pounds. It is possible, indeed, that no more than ten pounds' worth of this value may ever have existed at any one moment of time. But if the ten pounds' worth of corn and other necessaries, which were consumed by the artificer, had been consumed by a soldier or by a menial servant, the value of that part of the annual produce which existed at the end of the six months would have been ten pounds less than it actually is in consequence of the labour of the artificer. Though the value of what the artificer produces, therefore, should not at any one moment of time be supposed greater than the value he consumes, yet at every moment of time the actually existing value of goods in the market is, in consequence of what he produces, greater than it otherwise would be.

When the patrons of this system assert that the consumption of ar-tificers, manufacturers, and merchants is equal to the value of what they produce, they probably mean no more than that their revenue, or the fund destined for their consumption, is equal to it. But if they had expressed themselves more accurately, and only asserted that the revenue of this class was equal to the value of what they produced, it might readily have occurred to the reader that what would naturally be saved out of this revenue must necessarily increase more or less the real wealth of the society. In order, therefore, to make out some-thing like an argument, it was necessary that they should express them-selves as they have done; and this argument, even supposing things actually were as it seems to presume them to be, turns out to be a very inconclusive one.

Fourthly, farmers and country labourers can no more augment, without parsimony, the real revenue, the annual produce of the land and labour of their society, than artificers, manufacturers, and mer-chants. The annual produce of the land and labour of any society can be augmented only in two ways; either, first, by some improvement in the productive powers of the useful labour actually maintained within it; or, secondly, by some increase in the quantity of that labour.

The improvement in the productive powers of useful labour depend, first, upon the improvement in the ability of the workman; and, sec-

ondly, upon that of the machinery with which he works. But the labour
of artificers and manufacturers, as it is capable of being more sub-
divided, and the labour of each workman reduced to a greater simplicity of operation than that of farmers and country labourers, so it is
likewise capable of both these sorts of improvement in a much higher
degree. In this respect, therefore, the class of cultivators can have no
sort of advantage over that of artificers and manufacturers.

The increase in the quantity of useful labour actually employed
within any society must depend altogether upon the increase of the
capital which employs it; and the increase of that capital again must
be exactly equal to the amount of the savings from the revenue, either
of the particular persons who manage and direct the employment of
that capital, or of some other persons who lend it to them. If merchants, artificers, and manufacturers are, as this system seems to suppose, naturally more inclined to parsimony and saving than proprietors
and cultivators, they are, so far, more likely to augment the quantity
of useful labour employed within their society, and consequently to
increase its real revenue, the annual produce of its land and labour.

Fifthly and lastly, though the revenue of the inhabitants of every
country was supposed to consist altogether, as this system seems to
suppose, in the quantity of subsistence which their industry could procure to them; yet, even upon this supposition, the revenue of a trading and manufacturing country must, other things being equal, always
be much greater than that of one without trade or manufactures. By
means of trade and manufactures, a greater quantity of subsistence can
be annually imported into a particular country than what its own lands,
in the actual state of their cultivation, could afford. The inhabitants
of a town, though they frequently possess no lands of their own, yet
draw to themselves by their industry such a quantity of the rude produce of the lands of other people as supplies them, not only with the
materials of their work, but with the fund of their subsistence. What
a town always is with regard to the country in its neighbourhood, one
independent state or country may frequently be with regard to other
independent states or countries. It is thus that Holland draws a great
part of its subsistence from other countries; live cattle from Holstein
and Jutland, and corn from almost all the different countries of Europe.
A small quantity of manufactured produce purchases a great quantity
of rude produce. A trading and manufacturing country, therefore,
naturally purchases with a small part of its manufactured produce a
great part of the rude produce of other countries; while, on the contrary,
a country without trade and manufactures is generally obliged to purchase, at the expense of a great part of its rude produce, a very small

part of the manufactured produce of other countries. The one exports what can subsist and accommodate but a very few, and imports the subsistence and accommodation of a great number. The other exports the accommodation and subsistence of a great number, and imports that of a very few only. The inhabitants of the one must always enjoy a much greater quantity of subsistence than what their own lands, in the actual state of their cultivation, could afford. The inhabitants of the other must always enjoy a much smaller quantity.

This system, however, with all its imperfections is, perhaps, the nearest approximation to the truth that has yet been published upon the subject of political economy, and is upon that account well worth the consideration of every man who wishes to examine with attention the principles of that very important science. Though in representing the labour which is employed upon land as the only productive labour, the notions which it inculcates are perhaps too narrow and confined; yet in representing the wealth of nations as consisting, not in the un-consumable riches of money, but in the consumable goods annually reproduced by the labour of the society, and in representing perfect liberty as the only effectual expedient for rendering this annual repro-duction the greatest possible, its doctrine seems to be in every respect as just as it is generous and liberal. Its followers are very numerous; and as men are fond of paradoxes, and of appearing to understand what surpasses the comprehension of ordinary people, the paradox which it maintains, concerning the unproductive nature of manufacturing la-bour, has not perhaps contributed a little to increase the number of its admirers. They have for some years past made a pretty consider-able sect, distinguished in the French republic of letters by the name of The Economists. Their works have certainly been of some service to their country; not only by bringing into general discussion many subjects which had never been well examined before, but by influenc-ing in some measure the public administration in favour of agricul-ture. It has been in consequence of their representations, accordingly, that the agriculture of France has been delivered from several of the oppressions which it before laboured under. The term during which such a lease can be granted, as will be valid against every future pur-chaser or proprietor of the land, has been prolonged from nine to twenty-seven years. The ancient provincial restraints upon the trans-portation of corn from one province of the kingdom to another have been entirely taken away, and the liberty of exporting it to all foreign countries has been established as the common law of the kingdom in all ordinary cases. This sect, in their works, which are very numer-ous, and which treat not only of what is properly called Political Economy, or of the nature and causes of the wealth of nations, but of every other branch of the system of civil government, all follow implicitly and without any sensible variation, the doctrine of Mr. Quesnai. There is upon this account little variety in the greater part of their works. The most distinct and best connected account of this doctrine is to be found in a little book written by Mr. Mercier de la Riviere, some time Intendant of Martinico, entitled, *The Natural and Essential Order of Political Societies.* The admiration of this whole sect for their master, who was himself a man of the greatest modesty and simplicity, is not inferior to that of any of the ancient philosophers for the founders of their respective systems. "There have been, since the world began," says a very diligent and respectable author, the Marquis de Mirabeau, "three great inventions which have principally given stability to political societies, independent of many other inventions which have enriched and adorned them. The first is the invention of writing, which alone gives human nature the power of transmitting, without alteration, its laws, its contracts, its annals, and its discoveries. The second is the invention of money, which binds together all the relations between civilised societies. The third is the Economical Table, the result of the other two, which completes them both by perfecting their object; the great discovery of our age, but of which our posterity will reap the benefit."

Marx

—————— on ——————

the Physiocrats

A century after Smith, Karl Marx was to scrutinize the thought of the physiocrats in his *Theories of Surplus Value*. In this survey of economic ideas Marx criticizes many economists in terms of bitter invective. His treatment of the physiocrats is characterized by a poise and moderation rarely found in his writings, and it bears light on some central ideas of Marx's own economic thought.

(On Marx, see pp. 313 ff., below.)

THE ANALYSIS of capital, with the bourgeois horizon, is in its substance the merit of the physiocrats, and that is why they are the true fathers of modern political economy. To begin with, they analyzed the role of the different capital goods in the process of production. One cannot blame them for having considered capital goods such as equipment, raw materials, etc.—like all their successors—in isolation from the social conditions which surround these goods in capitalistic production. In other words, they considered capital goods as elements of a general process of production unrelated to the specific social form which they assume under capitalism. Thereby they turned the capitalistic form of production into an eternal, natural form of production, viewing the bourgeois forms of production as its natural forms. It was their great merit to conceive these forms as physiological forms of social life, arising from natural necessities and independent from volition, politics, etc. They indeed are material laws. The physiocrats made only the mistake of interpreting this material law of a specific historical stage of society as an abstract, general law equally controlling all forms of societies.

Apart from analyzing the tangible elements of which capital consists in the process of production, the physiocrats consider the forms which capital assumes in circulation (fixed capital and circulating capital—although they use different designations) as well as the general relationship between the processes of circulation and of reproduction of capital. With respect to these two matters, Adam Smith has assumed the legacy of the physiocrats. But he must be given credit for having more closely determined the abstract categories and for having securely labeled the differences analyzed by the physiocrats.

It is the basis of capitalistic production that labor power, as a commodity owned by the workers, faces conditions of work, commodities, as it were, which are attached to capital and which exist independently from labor power. Labor power, as a commodity, has value. This value is equal to the labor time required to produce the food necessary for the reproduction of labor power, that is, it is equal to the price

[Translated from Marx's *Theorien über den Mehrwert*, edited by Karl Kautsky, Stuttgart, J. H. W. Dietz Nachf., 1905.]

of the food needed to maintain the existence of the worker as worker. Only on this basis can we postulate the existence of a difference between the value of labor power and the value of its eventual realization. This difference does not exist in the case of any other commodity, because the use value, and, hence, the use of no other commodity, is capable of increasing its exchange value or the exchange values resulting therefrom. The analysis of capitalistic production is the business of modern political economy, and in modern political economy it is basic to consider the value of labor power as a constant, as a given quantity—as it is also in practice in every specific instance. The wage minimum therefore represents quite correctly the axis of the physiocratic doctrine. The physiocrats could arrive at such insight—although they still failed to recognize the nature of value—because the value of labor power manifests itself in the price of the necessary foodstuffs and, hence, in a sum of specific use values. Without being clear about the general nature of value, they therefore were able to consider the value of labor—to the extent to which this was necessary for their investigations—as a given quantity. They also made the mistake of interpreting the wage as a fixed amount, determined exclusively by nature rather than by the historical stage of development—itself a variable subject to change. But all this does not affect the correctness of their conclusions *in abstracto*. The existence of a difference between the value of labor power and the value of its eventual realization does in no way depend upon whether the values are assumed to be large or small.

The physiocrats moved the investigation of the origin of surplus value from the sphere of circulation to the sphere of direct production, thereby laying the foundation for the analysis of capitalistic production.

They are entirely correct when they establish the fundamental proposition that only such labor is productive which creates a surplus value, that is, labor whose product carries a higher value than the sum of values consumed in the production of the product. With the values of primary products and raw materials given, and with the value of labor power being equal to the wage, the surplus value obviously can consist only of the excess of labor, returned by the worker to the capitalist, over the quantity of labor received by the worker in the form of the wage. But, to be sure, this is not the type of surplus value considered by the physiocrats. They still fail to reduce value to its simple substance—the quantity of labor or labor time.

Their presentation necessarily is conditioned by their general view of the nature of value, conceived by them as consisting of matter, of land, nature, and various modifications of matter, rather than as a specific social form of human activity (labor).

Agriculture—primary production—is the branch of production in which the difference between the value of labor power and its realization—that is, the surplus value which the purchaser of labor power acquires—appears in the most conspicuous and irrefutable manner. The total amount of foodstuffs consumed by the worker throughout the years is less than the total amount of foodstuffs produced by him. In industry, on the other hand, one cannot see directly how the worker produces his foodstuffs or an excess of foodstuffs. There the process takes place with the help of the media of purchase and sale, through the various acts of circulation, and its understanding requires a general analysis of value. In agriculture the process manifests itself immediately through the excess of the produced use values over the use values consumed by the worker. This is the reason why it can be understood without a general analysis of value, without a clear perception of the nature of value, even when—as is done by the physiocrats—value is reduced to use value and this to matter. Hence, agricultural labor appears to the physiocrats as the only type of productive labor—as the only type of labor which creates surplus value—and the land rent is the only form of surplus value known to them. An industrial worker, they hold, does not augment matter; he only changes its form. The material—the mass of matter—is given to him by agriculture. To be sure, he adds value to matter, not through his work but through the production cost of his work: through the amount of food which he consumes while at work (and which is equal to his wage obtained from agriculture). Since only agricultural labor is considered productive by the physiocrats, the rent of land is considered the exclusive form of surplus value, characteristic of agricultural but not of industrial labor.

The true profit of capital, of which land rent is only an offshoot, does not exist in physiocratic literature. To the physiocrats, profit simply is a higher type of wage, paid by the landowners and consumed by the capitalists as revenue; entering into cost of production just as the wage of ordinary labor does; and augmenting the value of raw materials because it enters into the cost of the industrialist's (capitalist's) consumption when he produces the product and transforms the raw material into a new product.

Surplus value in the form of money interest—another offshoot of profit—is therefore considered as unnatural usury by the older Mirabeau and some other physiocrats. Turgot, on the other hand, bases the justification of interest on the observation that the owner of money capital could purchase land, and, therefore, land rent, and that for this reason his money capital must create for him as much surplus value as he would obtain were he to transform it into real estate. This analysis does not turn money interest into a newly created value or surplus value. It merely explains why a part of the surplus value acquired by the landowners accrues to the owners of money capital in the form of interest, just as an explanation—based on other reasons— is given why a part of the surplus value accrues to the owners of industrial capital in the form of profit. In the physiocratic view, only agricultural labor is productive. It is the only type of labor which creates a surplus value. Hence, the form of surplus value which distinguishes agricultural from other types of labor, that is, the land rent, becomes the general form of surplus value. Industrial profit and money interest are no more than different names for those parts of the land rent which are passed on from the landowners to other classes. This view is exactly the reverse of that of the later economists following Adam Smith, who correctly consider industrial profit as the form in which surplus value is originally appropriated by capital, that is, as the original, general form of surplus value, with interest and land rent representing only offshoots of industrial profit, distributed by the industrial capitalists among other classes which are co-owners of the surplus value.

Apart from the reason already indicated—that is, because agricultural labor is the type of labor which shows most conspicuously and tangibly the creation of surplus value—and apart from the processes of circulation, we mention the following motives which inspired the physiocrats and help to explain their point of view.

1. In agriculture the land rent appears as a third element, as a form of surplus value of which nothing, or traces only, can be found in industry. It is a surplus value above the surplus value (profit), and, hence, the most obvious and conspicuous form of surplus value, the second power of surplus value, as it were.[1]

2. If one abstracts from foreign trade—as the physiocrats rightly did in order to obtain an abstract view of bourgeois society—then it is clear that the number of workers who are employed in industry and detached from agriculture, the number of "free hands," as Steuart calls them, is determined by the quantity of agricultural products turned out by the agricultural laborers in excess of their own consumption.[2] Agri-

---

[1] As Karl Arnd, the unaffected rural economist, put it: "In agriculture, there is produced a value—land rent—which does not exist in industry and trade: a value which is left over when the entire bill for wages and capital income is met."

[2] "It is obvious that the relative numbers of those persons who can be maintained without agricultural labor, must be measured wholly by the productive powers of the cultivators." Richard Jones, *An Essay on the Distribution of Wealth and on the Sources of Taxation,* London, 1831, pp. 159–160.

cultural labor provides the natural basis for work along related lines in its own sphere and for the emancipation of all other types of work, and, hence, also for the surplus value produced in the latter. Therefore, agricultural labor obviously had to be recognized as the creator of surplus value as long as specific, concrete labor rather than abstract labor and labor time, its measure, were considered as the substance of value.

3. All surplus value, the relative as well as the absolute one,[3] is based on a given productivity of labor. If the productivity of labor were so little developed that one man's labor time would suffice only to maintain his life and to produce and reproduce his own food, there would be no surplus labor and no surplus value. In this case there would be no difference at all between the value of labor power and the value of its eventual realization. Hence, the possibility of surplus labor and of surplus value derives from a given productive power of labor. This productive power enables labor power to reproduce more than its own value, to reproduce in excess of the needs arising from its own existence. This stage of productivity is assumed. As we have noted under (2), it must exist, first of all, with respect to agricultural labor, and it thus appears as a gift of nature, as nature's productive power. In agriculture, there is cooperation on the part of the forces of nature; there the augmentation of human labor power with the help of large-scale application and exploitation of the automatic forces of nature is fundamental. In industry, such large-scale utilization of natural forces comes about only when industry is fully developed. A certain stage of agricultural development, at home or abroad, seems to be the basis of the development of capital, and when this is achieved, absolute and relative surplus value coincide.[4]

[3] In the mercantilist system, the surplus value is only relative: what one gains, the other loses (profit "upon alienation, oscillation or vibration of the balance of wealth between different parties"). Domestically there is no formation of surplus value if the total capital is considered. In this view, surplus value can only arise as a result of international transactions. The surplus which one nation extracts from another is represented by money (balance of trade), because money is the immediate and independent form of exchange value.

In contrast therewith—because the mercantilist system indeed denies the formation of absolute surplus value—the physiocrats desire to explain it: the *produit net*. See J. A. Blanqui, *Histoire de l'économie politique,* Brussels, 1839, p. 139 (English translation, New York, 1880, pp. 353–354).

[4] David Buchanan, the great critic of the physiocrats, pointed this out against Adam Smith, and attempted to prove that the development of modern urban industry was preceded by such an agricultural development.

4. The specific greatness of the physiocrats is based on their derivation of value and surplus value from production rather than from circulation. In contrast to the monetary system of the mercantilists, their
point of departure is the branch of production which can be conceived
as independent of circulation and exchange, and which requires only
an exchange between man and nature rather than between man and
man.

The physiocratic system is indeed the first system which contains
an analysis of capitalistic production, representing, as it does, as eternal,
natural laws of production the conditions under which capital is produced and under which capital serves as productive agent. From another point of view, the physiocratic system appears as a bourgeois
replica of the feudal system with its rule of landed property. The
spheres of industry in which capital for the first time develops independently appear as "unproductive" branches of work, mere appen-
dixes of agriculture. The indispensable condition for the development
of capital is the separation of landed property from labor, with free
labor facing land, the primordial prerequisite of labor, as an independent power controlled by a separate class. In this view the landed
proprietor appears as the true capitalist, that is, the usurper of surplus
labor. Feudalism thus is portrayed and interpreted *sub specie* of
bourgeois production, and agriculture appears as that branch of production in which capitalistic production—the production of surplus
value—can exclusively be found. Feudalism thus acquires bourgeois
characteristics, and in the process the bourgeois society acquires a
feudal appearance. This appearance deceives the noblemen among
the followers of Dr. Quesnay, the older Mirabeau, for example, that
eccentric patriarch. It vanishes among the more broad-minded,
Turgot, for example. Here the physiocratic system represents the new
capitalistic society as it breaks through the framework of feudalism.
The physiocratic system thus mirrors the bourgeois society of the
period, when that society shed the feudal ties. The point of departure
is France, a predominantly agricultural country, rather than England,
an overwhelmingly industrial, commercial, and seafaring country. In
England, circulation calls for major attention: the product obtains
value—becomes a commodity—as the result of general-abstract, social
labor: through its transformation into money. Disregarding the form
of value and concentrating on its size and realization, we may recognize this as the case of "profit upon alienation," that is, relative profit
as characterized by Steuart. But if it is the aim to trace the creation
of surplus value in the sphere of production itself, then one must return

to that branch of labor where surplus value arises irrespective of circulation—to agriculture. This initiative was taken in a predominantly agricultural country. Fragmentary ideas related to those of the physiocrats can be found among the earlier writers, in part in France herself (Boisguillebert). But only the physiocrats turn these ideas into an epoch-making system.

The agricultural laborer, maintaining himself with the help of the wage minimum, the *strict nécessaire,* reproduces a surplus over the *strict nécessaire,* and this surplus is the land rent, the surplus value, which is appropriated by the owner of land, the foremost prerequisite of labor. The physiocrats do not imply that the laborer works longer hours than is necessary for the reproduction of his labor power, and that for this reason the value which he creates is higher than the value of his labor power (or that for this reason the amount of labor which he returns is greater than the amount which he receives in the form of the wage). Instead, it is implied that the sum of the use values which the laborer consumes during the process of production is smaller than the sum of the use values which he creates, and there remains an excess of use values. No such excess would remain if the laborer would work only as long as is necessary to reproduce his own labor power. But this conclusion is not drawn; instead, it is pointed out that the productivity of the land enables the worker, during his working day, which is assumed as given, to produce more than is required by his need for subsistence. Hence, the surplus value appears as a gift of nature.

Nature cooperates by making available organic substances such as seeds of plants and animals, and thereby enables labor to transform unorganic matter into an organic one. It is taken for granted, on the other hand, that the laborer faces the landowner as a capitalist. The landowner pays for the labor power offered as a commodity by the worker, and in return receives not only an equivalent but appropriates the product of the labor power. This exchange assumes the separation of the tangible prerequisites of work from labor power itself. The feudal landowner is the point of departure, but he appears as capitalist, as a mere owner of commodities, who utilizes commodities exchanged by him for labor and in return receives not only an equivalent but a surplus over the equivalent, because he pays only for labor power as a commodity. As an owner of commodities he confronts the free laborer. In other words, this landowner is in substance a capitalist. In this respect the physiocrats hit upon another correct interpretation: the separation of the laborer from land and from landed property is the basic condition of capitalistic production and of the production of capital.

This then brings us to the contradictions of the physiocratic system. It interprets surplus value in terms of the appropriation of the labor of others—appropriation on the basis of an exchange of commodities. But it does not conceive of value as a form of social labor, and not of surplus value as surplus labor. To the physiocrats, value is mere use value, mere matter, and surplus value, to them, is a mere gift of nature, with nature returning to labor in the place of a given quantity of organic matter a larger quantity. Land rent, the true economic expression of landed property, is on the one hand divested of its feudal garb, being reduced to mere surplus value in excess of the wage. On the other hand, however, the source of this surplus value is seen in a feudal manner in nature rather than in society, in the relation to the land rather than in a social relationship. Such value dissolves itself into mere use value and, hence, into matter. Again, the relevant aspect of this matter is its quantity, the excess of the produced use values over the consumed ones, or merely the quantitative relationship of the use values—that is, in the last analysis, only their exchange values which can finally be dissolved into labor time.

All these contradictions are contradictions of capitalistic production emerging from feudal society, with the latter interpreted in bourgeois terms—contradictions of capitalistic production which as yet has not found its own specific form. The analogy of a philosophic system may be helpful, a system originally constructed on the basis of religious consciousness, which then destroys religion while itself moving exclusively in the idealized religious sphere which is dissolved by rationalism.

The conclusions which the physiocrats draw reflect these contradictions. The apparent glorification of landed property turns into its economic negation and into capitalistic production. All taxes are imposed on land rent; in other words, a partial confiscation of landed property takes place—as it was attempted by the legislation of the French Revolution and as it was to be the result of modern political economy developed by Ricardo. The burden of taxation is in its entirety placed on land rent because land rent is the only surplus value. Any tax on other forms of income would eventually fall on landed property, but would do so as the result of a detour, that is, in an economically harmful manner, hampering production. With taxation placed exclusively on landed property, industry becomes exempt from taxation and, thereby, from all government intervention. This is allegedly done in the interest of the landed property, not in that of industry.

From this derives the maxim *laissez faire, laissez aller:* unrestricted, free competition, removal of all government interference, of public monopolies, etc., from industry. In the physiocratic view, industry does not create anything; it merely transforms the values provided by agriculture. It does not add to them any new value but merely returns the equivalent of the received commodities in a different form. Hence, it is obviously desirable from this point of view that the process of transformation occur without disturbances and in the most economical manner. This can be achieved only through free competition under which capitalistic production is left to itself. Thus, bourgeois society becomes emancipated from the absolute monarchy which had established itself on the ruins of feudal society, and this is done only for the sake of the feudal landowners who are transformed into capitalists, inspired merely by the idea of enrichment. The industrial capitalists are capitalists acting only in the interest of landed property, in the same sense in which political economy, when more fully developed, depicts them as acting only in the interest of the working class.

This goes to show how greatly modern interpreters of the physiocrats have misinterpreted them. They present the physiocratic doctrines—the exclusive productivity of agricultural labor, the land rent as exclusive form of surplus value, and the predominant position of the landowner in the system of production—in a piecemeal fashion, without relating them to the proclamation of free competition, the principle of large-scale industry, and that of capitalistic production. One can understand how the feudal appearance of the physiocratic system, similar to the aristocratic garb of the enlightenment, turned the masses of feudal lords into sentimental followers and propagandists of a system which in its substance proclaimed the establishment of the bourgeois system of production on the ruins of feudalism.

The Classical School

Douglas

— on —

Smith

Adam Smith (1723–1790) was the founder of the classical school of economics. This school, composed, in the main, of Smith, Malthus, Ricardo, and Mill, considered labor as the source of all value. It firmly established the advantages of specialization and division of labor in the domestic and international field, and was, on the whole, sceptical of government interference with the free play of individual initiative, which, if left to itself, would harmoniously reconcile the interests of all and result in an optimum state of economic wellbeing.

Adam Smith, born in Kirkcaldy, Scotland, was educated at Glasgow and Oxford. After his return to Scotland he became lecturer at Edinburgh, and eventually professor and vice-rector at Glasgow. In 1764 he resigned from his academic position to provide tutorial guidance to a young nobleman, the Duke of Buccleuch. In this function he traveled extensively on the continent of Europe, and came in contact with the French physiocrats, who, together with the Scottish and English philosophers, were of decisive importance in the formation of his ideas. After his return to England, Smith eventually received an appointment as Commissioner of Customs in Edinburgh. Smith's principal claim to fame, *The Wealth of Nations,* was published in 1776. It won him wide recognition during his lifetime. *The Life of Adam Smith* (1895), by John Rae, stands out among the biographies of great economists.

Paul H. Douglas (1892–   ) is a distinguished American statesman and economist. After a teaching career of nearly twenty years at the University of Chicago, Douglas was elected to the United States Senate in 1948, where his outstanding abilities were soon recognized. As economist, Douglas is best known for his attempts at statistical verification of the marginal productivity theory of distribution, set forth in his *Theory of Wages* (1934).

THE CONTRIBUTIONS of Adam Smith to the theory of value and of distribution were not great, and in commemorating the publication of the *Wealth of Nations* it might seem to be the path of wisdom to pass these topics by in discreet silence and to reserve discussion instead for those subjects, such as the division of labor, where his realistic talents enabled him to appear at a better advantage. Yet the errors of an able thinker are, if properly interpreted, only slightly less illuminating than his substantive contributions, and deserve analysis in the history of economic thought. There is, however, another reason why Smith's doctrines on value and distribution merit examination. This is because Smith's formulation of the problems of exchange value and of the distribution of the national product among the factors of production was such as almost inevitably gave rise to the doctrines of the post-Ricardian socialists and to the labor theory of value and the exploitation theory of Karl Marx.

1. THE REJECTION OF UTILITY AS A DETERMINANT OF VALUE AND THE ACCEPTANCE OF THE LABOR THEORY

In a society with a highly developed division of labor, exchange necessarily becomes ubiquitous, and the ratio at which the goods or services one produces exchange for the goods and services one desires becomes an ingredient element in individual, and indeed in national, prosperity. It is not enough to produce a large physical quantity of goods. If one is to be comfortable it is also necessary, as the farmers in the United States have found, that the exchange ratios of these goods in terms of other products should be sufficiently high to yield a comfortable real income in goods, and hence ultimately in pleasures to the producers. To the theory of production is therefore necessarily joined the theory of value.

What, then, did determine the ratio at which commodities exchanged? Smith had considered the possibility of utility but dismissed

[Paul H. Douglas, "Smith's Theory of Value and Distribution." Reprinted by permission from *Adam Smith, 1776–1926,* The University of Chicago Press, 1928.]

it because of the paradox which Locke, Hutcheson,[1] Law,[2] and Harris had pointed out before him between the relative value of water and diamonds. "Nothing is more useful," wrote Smith,[3] "than water, but it will purchase scarce anything; scarce anything can be had in exchange for it. A diamond, on the contrary, has scarce any value in use; but a very great quantity of other goods may frequently be had in exchange for it." From this he concludes that "value in use," or utility is of an entirely independent nature from "value in exchange" and has no part in the determination of the latter. "The things which have the greatest value in use have frequently little or no value in exchange; and, on the contrary, those which have the greatest value in exchange have frequently little or no value in use." [4] Here the break between the two concepts is complete. Not only is utility not a determinant of exchange value, but—and here Smith goes much farther than Ricardo and later exponents of the labor theory of value—it is not even a necessary prerequisite.

The main reason why Smith and those who followed him abandoned utility as a determinant of value was, of course, because they were comparing the total utilities yielded by varying types of objects rather than their marginal utilities.

The existence of free goods is striking proof of the fact that the utility afforded by a class of commodities need bear no relation to its exchange value. It was not until it was pointed out that we should compare the exchange ratios of individual units rather than of whole classes of commodities that the water-diamond paradox could be solved. When this was done, it was not difficult to see that *a* diamond had a greater value than a gallon of water because in comparison with the intensity of the desires for diamonds and for water, the former was less plentiful than the latter.

Smith's failure to consider the relative scarcity of commodities in connection with their respective utilities is all the more striking in view of the very clear approaches to this point of view which had been made by Locke and Harris. Thus, Locke had written:

What more useful or necessary things are there to the being or well-being of men than air and water? And yet these generally have no price at all, because their quantity is immensely greater than their vent in most places of the earth. But as soon as ever water comes anywhere to be re-

[1] Hutcheson, *A System of Moral Philosophy*, II, 53–54.
[2] Law, *Money and Trade Considered* (1705), Chap. I.
[3] Smith, *Wealth of Nations* (Cannan edition), I, 30.
[4] Smith, *op. cit.*, p. 30.

duced into any proportion to its consumption, it begins presently to have a price and is sometimes sold dearer than wine. Hence it is that the best and most useful things are commonly the cheapest, because, though their consumption be great, yet the bounty of providence has made their production large and suitable to it.[5]

and Harris, applying himself to the very commodities which Smith later considered, had explicitly written that

Water is of great use and yet ordinarily of little or no value because in most places, water flows spontaneously in such great plenty as not to be withheld within the limits of private property; but all may have enough without other expense than that of bringing or conducting it. . . . On the other hand, diamonds being very scarce, have upon that account a great value, though they are but of little use.[6]

By failing to follow up the hints which these writers had developed,[7] Smith helped to divert the writers of the English Classical school into a cul-de-sac from which they did not emerge, in so far as their value theory was concerned, for nearly a century, while he also helped, as we shall see, to give rise to the economic doctrines of nineteenth-century socialism.

When, by observation, by the mathematical assumptions of Dupuit, the demand concepts of Cournot,[7a] and by the experiments of Weber, the principle of diminishing utility was grasped, the further fact emerged that the economic importance of an object was determined by the relative utility yielded by the last of a series of such articles. From these simple phenomena, Gossen,[7b] Jevons,[7c] and Wicksteed[8] built up their elaborate analyses of individual behavior to demonstrate how men would dispose of their time and money in such a way that utilities of the last units of each set of commodities would be equal, while the Austrian school deduced the laws of short-run price.

[5] Locke, *Considerations of the Lowering of Interest and Raising the Value of Money,* p. 41.

[6] Harris, *Essay upon Money and Coins,* p. 5.

[7] For a discussion of the various value theories prior to 1776, see Sewall, *The Theory of Value before Adam Smith,* especially pp. 66–124.

[7a] Cournot, *Recherches sur les principes mathématiques de la Théorie des richesses* (1838). English translation by Bacon, *Mathematical Principles of the Theory of Wealth* (1897).

[7b] Gossen, *Entwickelung der Gesetze des menschlichen Verkehrs* (1854). Gossen to be sure developed this theory independently.

[7c] Jevons, *The Theory of Political Economy,* Chap. III.

[8] Wicksteed, *The Common Sense of Political Economy.*

Smith's moralistic sense was probably a further reason why he failed to follow up the analysis of utility as a possible cause of value. In his thrifty Scotch manner with its opposition to ostentation as almost sinful he concluded that diamonds had "scarce any value in use." But, of course, as the moralists from Ruskin on have pointed out, economic values are not necessarily moral values. It is not necessary that commodities should be "good" for people in order that they may have value. It is only necessary that they be desired and that they exist in less than sufficient quantity to satisfy the demand. A large proportion of what is produced today is indeed "illth" rather than "wealth" in the original sense of the latter word, and yet these articles sell in the market for a money price. We are, indeed, likely to fall into the confusion of Smith if we do not recognize that ethical value and economic value are by no means identical and that the absence of the former by no means signifies the absence of the latter.

Having discarded utility, save in so far as it helped to determine temporary market price, Smith turned to labor as both the measure and the source of value. This in turn necessitated the conception of a unit of labor. What was the common denominator to which all labor could be reduced? Time by itself, Smith pointed out, was not sufficient, since [9] "the different degrees of hardship endured or ingenuity exercised must likewise be taken into account." "There may be more labour," he remarked,[10] "in an hour's application to a trade which it cost ten years labour to learn, than in a month's industry at an ordinary and obvious employment."

2. THE REDUCTION OF TIME, HARDSHIP, AND INGENUITY TO A COMMON MEASURE: THE DISCUSSION OF DIFFERENCES IN WAGES

But to equate time, hardship, and ingenuity to a common unit was, as Smith admitted, "not easy." How, then, was it accomplished? "By the higgling and bargaining of the market," Smith replied,[11] "according to that rough sort of equality which, though not exact, is sufficient for carrying on the basis of common life." There is here the same tendency toward circular reasoning which marks the thinking of both Ricardo and of Marx upon this point. For if it is labor which is to serve as the measure and source of value, then we must explain the

[9] *Wealth of Nations*, p. 33.   [11] Smith, *Wealth of Nations*, I, 33.
[10] *Wealth of Nations*, p. 33.

latter by the quantity of the former. Yet here we find Smith appealing to market values to determine the quantity of labor.[12]

But Smith may perhaps be saved from circuity of reasoning by his celebrated chapter on differences in wages. Differences in monetary remuneration as between occupations are caused, he holds, by differences in (1) the agreeableness of the employments, (2) the relative difficulty in learning them, (3) the degree of regularity of employment, (4) the relative trust imposed on those employed, and (5) the relative possibility of success.

Analyzed more closely, it will be seen that those differences in wages which are caused by differences in the regularity of employment are primarily daily and not yearly differences. Smith pointed out that the wages of the masons were higher than those of journeymen in manufacturing, who had equal skill, in order to compensate the former for the smaller number of days in which they had an opportunity to labor. Over the year—or at best, if we are to use modern parlance, over the course of a business cycle—these differences would be equalized and an equality of earnings for otherwise similar work be established.

In a similar fashion, the necessity for paying skilled labor more than unskilled in order to compensate for the years of apprenticeship when money earnings were lower than those secured by common laborers would not by itself, over the course of a working lifetime, give greater earnings to the skilled than to the less expert. All that Smith tells us is that in later life the former must have higher earnings to balance the lower earnings which they obtained during the earlier years. Equality of money earnings would in the long run be the inevitable result were we not to resort to the relatively modern doctrines of time preference. We may say that the skilled worker is not compensated by receiving later in life the same number of dollars which he had earlier foregone. The higher earlier earnings of the unskilled might in most youthful minds outweigh the greater subsequent earnings of the skilled, and in order to induce some of the boys to forego them, it would probably be necessary to promise them more dollars in the future than they were abandoning in the present. Thus there is probably something in the nature of interest in the wages of the skilled. While this latter point is certainly not Smith's, it is thoroughly con-

---

[12] Ricardo: "The estimation in which different qualities of labor are held comes soon to be adjusted in the market with sufficient precision for all practical purposes." *Principles of Political Economy* (Everyman edition), p. 11. Cf. Marx: "The different proportions in which different sorts of labour are reduced to unskilled labour as their standard are established by a social process which goes on behind the backs of the producers." *Capital* (Kerr edition), I, 52.

sistent with his theory. For here the greater wages received over the
course of a life by the skilled as compared with the unskilled workers
would only be enough to compensate them for the greater psychic loss
which they experienced in giving up their cake in the years of their
youth. For each unit of discomfort experienced, the remuneration of
labor would be the same.

This is the basic principle throughout Smith's discussion. It is
strikingly evidenced in his first reason for such differences, namely,
that wages varied [13] "with the ease or hardship, the cleanliness or dirti-
ness, the honourableness or dishonourableness of the employment."
Blacksmiths, adduced Smith, received more than weavers because their
work was dirtier, while miners received still more because their work
was even more disagreeable. These added money sums had to be paid
to the workers in order to compensate them for the intrinsic unpleas-
antness of their occupations, but supposedly were just enough to provide for this. For equal amounts of sacrifice, however, the remuneration would be equal. Similarly, those whose positions are attended
with public honor will be willing to work for less than will others who
do not receive such social esteem.

The reasoning that wages must be higher in those occupations where
trust is reposed is more ambiguous. Goldsmiths are said to be paid
more than other workmen of equal ingenuity because "of the precious
metals with which they are intrusted." [14] Here, apparently, the reasoning is that those who are subjected to great temptations need added
rewards to prevent them from yielding. A higher wage and a higher
level of living would lessen this pressure of temptation. Since such
workers would then live on a more expensive scale, they would not
need to steal in order to surpass their fellows. Higher wages in such
cases were in the nature of necessary insurance policies against theft
and betrayal. Since men do not believe that virtue is its own reward,
it is necessary to furnish more tangible incentives.

But Smith evidently had more in mind than merely the foregoing:

> We trust our health to the physician . . . our fortune, and sometimes
> our life and reputation, to the lawyer and attorney. Such confidence could
> not safely be reposed in people of a very mean or low condition. Their
> reward must be such therefore as may give them that rank in the society
> which so important a trust requires.[15]

There are two possible explanations of these sentences. The first is
that the responsibility involved in such positions was so irksome that

[13] *Wealth of Nations,* I, 102.   [15] *Ibid.,* p. 107.
[14] *Wealth of Nations,* p. 107.

it was necessary to pay extra sums to attract persons who, without such a compensation, would avoid the responsibility involved. Such an explanation is of course thoroughly consistent with the doctrine that wages are equal for equal amounts of disability experienced.

The other possible explanation is, however, more difficult to reconcile with the general theory. Smith implies that people would not patronize professional men who did not live upon a standard considerably above that of the rest of the community. This may well be true in such a society as our own, where men tend to be valued according to what they spend and waste rather than according to what they are. Under such conditions, lavish personal expenditure may be a necessary competitive advertising expense which is required if one is to secure prestige and consequently public patronage. To maintain this scale of living, higher charges will have to be made. But this is not in harmony with the general tenor of Smith's thought. For in such a case the higher remuneration is being paid not so much to compensate men for added exertions, as to provide the favored professions with those comforts which the snobbish mind of the public persists in regarding as the infallible stamp of worth.

The fifth assigned reason for differences in wages is even less in harmony with the general theory that the differences are but compensatory. In some ocupations, such as the mechanical trades, the entrants would have the surety of making at least a modest living; while in others, such as the law, there would be great and glittering prizes for the few, but very small stipends for most of the remainder. Smith's position here has been frequently interpreted to mean that merely the modal, or most frequent, wage would be lower in those occupations where only a few would rise to the top, but that the very high remuneration of these few would be sufficient to bring the arithmetic average of earnings in these occupations to an equality with that in those occupations where the deviation from the average was but slight. But this was not Smith's meaning. He declares:

> The counsellor at law who at forty begins to make something at his profession, ought to receive the retribution, not only of his own so tedious and expensive education, but of that of more than twenty others who are never likely to make anything by it. How extravagant so ever the fees of counsellors at law may sometimes appear, their real retribution is never equal to this.[16]

Smith believed, therefore, that in those occupations which had great prizes, the average rate of remuneration was lower than in other pur-

[16] *Wealth of Nations,* p. 108.

suits. But if this were so, it may be inquired why men would continue to enter such occupations? Would there not be a tendency for them to turn elsewhere and consequently force the level of payment in the given occupation to rise? Smith saw, however, that this was offset by the almost inveterate tendency of men to overestimate their abilities and their chances for success. Despite the large percentage of failures in these occupations, men would continue to pour into them because each one would believe that he at least would, because of his ability and good fortune, be the one to rise to the top.

Were men perfectly rational and calculating, then, the existence of a few great rewards would not depress the general average below that of other occupations. It does so only because men are not so expert in judging their own qualities and chances as they are in appraising other market situations. Even the Scotchman, whom Bagehot said Smith postulated as inside every man, had a blind spot as regards his own probable advancement.

With the exception of the fifth and, in part, of the fourth reason, however, the differences in wages are not real differences. They either equate out in money terms over the course of a lifetime or are just sufficient in the long run to balance any differences in the relative amounts of sacrifice involved. The force depended upon to effect this nice equilibrium is of course that of competition. If in one occupation the rewards per unit of sacrifice or disutility are greater than in others, then a larger number of men will enter these occupations and a smaller number will enter others until an equilibrium is restored. There is, of course, implied in such reasoning, the assumption that competition is indeed free, and that men are equal in abilities. Smith admitted that competition was not wholly free, but the restrictions which he conceived were legal rather than social and economic in their nature. It remained for Mill and Cairnes to point out the significance of non-competing groups and to demonstrate that equality of remuneration for equal units of sacrifice applied only within, and not between, these non-competing groups.

The assumption that there were no innate differences between men which could enable one man with the same amount of effort to secure a higher wage was natural enough in an age in which Locke's dictum [17] that the mind at birth was a *tabula rasa* upon which experience could write as it would, and in the same year in which Jefferson, on our side of the Atlantic, declared that it was self-evident that "all men are created free and equal." "The difference between the most dissimilar

[17] Locke, *Essay on Human Understanding.*

characters, between a philosopher and a common street porter," wrote Smith,[18] "seems to arise not so much from nature as from habit, custom and education." In a society thus peopled by men of approximately equal talents, freedom of competition was all that was needed to bring wages to an equality. To the modern mind, accustomed by the work of Darwin, Galton, Pearson, and the host of educational psychologists to appreciate the importance of innate differences, this view seems almost incredibly naïve; but it was thoroughly in harmony with the associationist psychology of the day as taught by Smith's bosom friend and fellow-Scotchman, David Hume.

This somewhat lengthy discussion of differences in wages may seem to be a digression from the main theme of the labor theory of value. But it is not in reality. Smith believed he had established the fact that equal units of labor in the sense of disutility were at any one time compensated for by equal amounts of money wages. The market, according to Smith, thus does reduce the various elements composing labor to a common measure.

It should be noted in passing that this doctrine that at any moment of time equal money units represent equal amounts of labor paves the way for a value theory based on the money cost of production, which can also be found lurking in Smith's discussion. Profits and rent need only to be added to wages and then one can say, as Smith did, that

. . . when the price of any commodity is neither more nor less than what is sufficient to pay the rent of the land, the wages of the labour and the profits of the stock employed in raising, preparing, and bringing it to market, according to their natural rates, the commodity is then sold for its natural price.[19]

3. THE LABOR-COST AND LABOR-COMMAND THEORIES OF VALUE [20]

We have hitherto spoken of Smith's labor theory of value as though it were unitary; there are however, in fact, the outlines of two very different theories which are embodied in it, namely, the labor-jelly or labor-cost theory, and the labor-command theory. These two explanations of value are very different in nature, yet they rub elbows with

[18] Smith, *Wealth of Nations*, I, 17.

[19] *Wealth of Nations*, p. 57.

[20] For a competent treatment of this subject, see Whitaker, *History and Criticism of the Labor Theory of Value*, pp. 16–40; see also Wieser, *Natural Value*, pp. xxvii–xxix. See also the suggestive discussion by C. M. Walsh, *The Fundamental Problem of Monetary Science*, pp. 46–53; *The Four Kinds of Value*, pp. 4–10.

each other on almost the same pages. Smith seems, indeed, to give almost equal emphasis to each and to fail to distinguish between them. The labor-jelly theory declares that the value of an object is determined by the quantity of labor units required to produce it, while the labor-command theory declares that the value of an object is determined by the amount of labor which can be purchased with it.

The labor-jelly theory is expressed in the following quotations:

The real price of everything, what everything really costs to the man who wants to acquire it, is the toil and trouble of acquiring it.[21]

At all times and places that is dear which is difficult to come at, or which it costs much labour to acquire; and that cheap which is to be had easily or with very little labour.[22]

That money or those goods . . . contain the value of a certain quantity of labour which we exchange for what is supposed, at the time, to contain the value of an equal quantity.[23]

In that early and rude state of society which precedes both the accumulation of stock and the appropriation of land, the proportion between the quantities of labour necessary for acquiring different objects seems to be the only circumstance which can afford any rule for exchanging them for one another. . . . It is natural that what is usually the produce of two days' or two hours' labour should be worth double of what is usually the produce of one day's or one hour's labour.[24]

On the other hand, the labor-command theory is clearly stated in a number of passages, of which the following are perhaps the most notable:

The value of any commodity therefore, to the person who possesses it, and who means not to use it or consume it himself, but to exchange it for other commodities, is equal to the quantity of labour which it enables him to purchase or command.[25]

Its value [wealth] to those who possess it and want to exchange it for some new productions, is precisely equal to the quantity of labour which it can enable them to purchase or command.[26]

Wealth [Mr. Hobbes says] is power. . . . His fortune is greater or less, precisely in proportion to the extent of this power; or the quantity either of other men's labour or, what is the same thing, of the produce of other men's labour, which it enables him to purchase or command. The exchangeable value of everything must always be precisely equal to the extent of this power which it conveys to its owner.[27]

[21] Smith, *Wealth of Nations*, p. 32.

[22] *Ibid.*, p. 35.

[23] *Ibid.*, p. 32.

[24] *Ibid.*, p. 49.

[25] *Ibid.*, p. 32.

[26] *Ibid.*, p. 33.

[27] *Ibid.*, p. 33.

It is sometimes said, as by Wieser, that the labor-cost theory was only intended for an explanation of value in a primitive society, and that Smith designed the labor-command theory as an explanation of how values were set in more advanced societies. This is only partially true. The labor-cost theory was applied to this primitive stage, but it was also applied at times to more modern communities as well.

What, then, is the difference between these two conceptions? If those who labored to turn out a product received all of that product or all which it brought in exchange, as Smith assumes was the case in primitive times, then the two would be identical. There would be neither a deduction for rent nor for interest; and hence if commodities exchanged according to the amount of labor required to produce them, they would command equal quantities of labor in the form of goods or personal services. Thus, if five hours or "units" of labor were expended on the average to produce a pair of shoes, then this pair of shoes would exchange for a price which would be sufficient to hire other labor for five "units" also. The value of the pair of shoes would then be the same in terms both of labor cost and labor command.

But if rent and profits were deducted from the prices at which all of the articles sold, there would then be a discrepancy between the two measures of value. For if commodities exchanged according to the amount of labor embodied in them, then this would be less than the amount of labor which they could command. Thus, if the share of labor amounted only to two-thirds of the total product, then the workers who expended the five units of labor required for the shoes would receive in return commodities in which only three and one-third labor units were contained. The given pair of shoes would indeed sell in the market for a price which would enable it to purchase seven and one-half units of labor.[28] This would be its value from the standpoint of labor command; but from the standard of labor cost, it would be but five units. There is thus a very real difference between the labor cost of commodities and the command of these commodities over labor. This very real distinction was not perceived by Smith, but was understood by Ricardo, who struggled in some of the most difficult and obscure pages of all economic literature[29] to make the contradiction evident.

[28] I.e., 3.33:5.0 = 5:7.50.

[29] I.e., the latter part of Section I of the first chapter of his *Principles of Political Economy*. It should also be noted that according to the labor-command theory, the amount of commodities offered for a day's labor will always have the same value since they command a constant amount of labor. The wages of the workmen would accordingly not alter in value, although they might increase or decrease as regards their composite physical quantity or the satisfaction afforded.

It was Karl Marx,[30] however—who, as a value theorist, was indeed the last great figure in the classical school—who most clearly pointed out the economic contradictions involved. He tried to restore the labor theory of value by making the value of laboring power (i.e., human effort expended in production) that of the commodities required to support and maintain the laborers and those who were to replace them. In other words, the number of labor "units" expended in producing the food, clothing, and shelter consumed by the workers constituted the value at which their services exchanged for other commodities. Since, however, the laborers expended more units of labor than were embodied in the commodities which they consumed, the balance appropriated by the recipients of rent, interest, and profits was termed by Marx "surplus value." The most distinctive feature of Marxian economics comes directly therefore from Smith's confusion between labor-cost and labor-command.

But it may be objected that while it is true that there is a lack of coincidence between the labor-cost and the labor-command theories as long as we either compare commodities (1) with labor offered for sale, or (2) with each other in terms of absolute units of value, there is nevertheless virtual identity between the two as long as we deal only with the exchange ratios of material commodities for each other. Thus, even though our pair of shoes contained five units of labor and could command seven and one-half such units, nevertheless it would exchange on equal terms for another commodity in which there were five units of labor and which could also command seven and one-half units. The values of these commodities would therefore be equal upon either the labor-cost or labor-command basis.

But while the consistency of Smith's teachings may perhaps be still maintained for the mutual exchange of commodities, the still further inner inconsistencies which were involved in the labor-cost theory were abundantly displayed in the attempts by Ricardo, McCulloch, and Marx to rehabilitate it. In the first place, it soon became apparent that a bushel of wheat produced on good land had an equal exchange value with that raised on poor land, despite the fact that much less labor had been expended upon the former than upon the latter. Ricardo tried to meet this difficulty by comparing only the respective amounts of labor contained in the marginal units of different commodities and of regarding these as setting the exchange ratios between them. Although a city man, he nevertheless could see only the importance of the margin in the case of agriculture and mineral products. Although writing in a period

[30] See Marx, *Capital* (Kerr edition), Vol. I, especially Chaps. I, VI, and VII; also *Value, Price, and Profit*.

when England had just won the Napoleonic Wars because of her newly developed factory system, he persisted in thinking of industry as being conducted under those conditions of constant cost which were so characteristic of handicraft.

But there was an even greater difficulty which grew with the passage of time: the payment of interest, or of profits, as the classicists used the phrase, was a reality. The wages of the workmen were advanced to them by the capitalists for the period intervening between the production of goods and their sale, and for this the capitalists collected interest at a given rate per cent per year. But the period required to produce different commodities varies greatly. Pop corn takes relatively little time to produce, even when the corn is taken into account as well as the popping. But a yard of cloth, if the labor expended upon the machinery as well as upon the textiles themselves be considered, requires labor spread out over a considerable period of time. The amounts of labor expended upon the pop corn and upon the cotton cloth may be equal; but since the wages expended in producing the latter have been advanced over a longer period of time, there has been a greater accumulation of interest upon the cloth than upon the pop corn. Either the rate of wages paid per unit of labor must therefore be less upon the cloth than upon the corn, which in view of Smith's assumptions of free competition is impossible, or the cloth must exchange for pop corn with more units of labor embodied in it. If this is so, however, then commodities plainly do not exchange according to the relative amounts of labor jelly of which they are composed. Ricardo clearly pointed out this difficulty in the fourth and fifth sections of his celebrated first chapter, but, in order to simplify the problem, for the rest of his discussion chose to disregard these troubling factors and to make the heroic assumption that all commodities were produced with capitals of equal duration and with equal rapidity of turnover. And yet the fact that this disturbing issue continued to bother Ricardo is evidenced from his correspondence with McCulloch:

> I sometimes think that if I were to write the chapter on value again which is in my book, I should acknowledge that the relative value of commodities was regulated by two causes instead of by one, namely, by the relative quantity of labour necessary to produce the commodities in question, and by the rate of profit for the time that the capital remained dormant and until the commodities were brought to market.[31]

It was indeed upon this very point that the Marxian theory of value finally collapsed. For if only labor creates exchange value, then it is

[31] *Letters of Ricardo to McCulloch* (edited by J. H. Hollander), p. 71.

only the capital which is advanced in the form of wages which creates a surplus and gives rise to profit. The labor crystals of value supposedly contained in machinery which is used up and in the raw materials fabricated will then merely pass over into the finished product without diminution or increase. But this in turn means that those industries where the proportion of raw materials and machinery is low in comparison with the wages paid must have correspondingly higher profits than those where the situation is reversed. This would mean (1) that equal capitals make different rates of profits according to their "organic composition" and (2) that the less advanced industries make larger profits than those where the process of mechanization has progressed farther. The plain variance of these conclusions from the commonly known facts of economic life led Marx in his third volume to make his famous attempt to reconcile the labor-cost theory with the tendency of profits toward an equality. As is well known, he tried to effect this by declaring that goods sold (1) at the value of the "constant" capital used up in producing them plus (2) the amount advanced in wages or variable capital plus (3) that proportion of the total amount of surplus value secured in society which the sum of the constant and variable capital employed in the given industry formed of the total supply. In this way, although profits were supposed to accrue only from the expenditure of variable capital, they were distributed out over constant as well as over variable capital. Differences in the organic composition of capital thus created no variations in the rates of profit received. A unit of constant capital received as much profit as a unit of variable. But this amounted to the virtual abandonment of the labor-cost theory of value, since accumulations of interest came to affect exchange value as well as the quantity of labor expended. Commodities in actual life did not exchange therefore in proportion to the days of labor embodied within them, but according to the wages advanced to the workers plus an average rate of profit for the time periods during which the wages were advanced.

Marx has been berated by two generations of orthodox economists for his value theory.[32] The most charitable of the critics have called him a fool and the most severe have called him a knave for what they deem to be the transparent contradictions of his theory. Curiously enough, these very critics generally commend Ricardo and Adam Smith very highly. Yet the sober facts are that Marx saw more clearly than

---

[32] As instances of this type of attack, see Böhm-Bawerk, *Karl Marx and the Close of His System;* Joseph, *The Labor Theory of Value in Karl Marx;* Skelton, *Socialism: A Critical Analysis.*

any English economist the differences between the labor-cost and labor-command theories and tried more earnestly than anyone else to solve the contradictions which the adoption of a labor-cost theory inevitably entailed. He failed, of course; but with him Ricardo and Smith failed as well. There are, it seems to me, few more unfair instances in economic thought than the almost complete unanimity with which the English-speaking economists of the chair have heaped condemnation upon the overworked and poverty-stricken Marx, who worked under such great difficulties, and, save for the comments of Jevons and a few others, have heaped praises upon Smith and Ricardo. The failure was the failure not of one man but of a philosophy of value, and the roots of the ultimate contradiction made manifest to the world in the third volume of *Das Kapital* lie imbedded in the first volume of the *Wealth of Nations*.

4. THE DEDUCTIONS FROM THE WHOLE PRODUCE OF LABOR AND THE IMPETUS TO BRITISH SOCIALISM

Smith declared that in the primitive stages of industry, before land is owned privately or capital accumulated, "the whole produce of labour belongs to the labourer." [33] This is a phrase of great importance in the history of socialist thought,[34] and it is most significant to find it in Adam Smith, by whom it was indeed repeated no less than five times.[35]

But this economic Eden does not last long, for

As soon as stock has accumulated in the hands of particular persons some of them will naturally employ it in setting to work industrious people

[33] *Wealth of Nations,* I, 49.

[34] A clear statement of the doctrine is given by Locke in the days when handicraft prevailed, to justify private property: "Every man has a property in his own person; this nobody has any right to but himself. The labour of his body and the work of his hands, we may say, are properly his. Whatsoever then he removes out of the state that nature hath provided and left in, he hath mixed his labour with and joined to it something that is his own and therebye makes it his property. It being by him removed from the common state nature hath placed it in, it hath by this labour something annexed to it, that excludes the common right of other men. For this labour being the unquestionable property of the labourer, no man but he can have a right to what that is once joined to, at least where there is enough, and as good, left in common for others." *Essay on Civil Government,* Chap. V; *On Property,* ss. 27.

[35] See p. 49, already referred to, and also pp. 51, 66, 67, 68. Another similar passage is that of p. 80: "It is but equity, besides, that they who feed, cloath and lodge the whole body of the people, should have such *a share of the produce of their own labour* as to be themselves tolerably well fed, cloathed and lodged" (italics mine).

whom they will supply with materials and subsistence in order to make a profit by the sale of their work, or by what their labour adds to the value of the materials. In exchanging the complete manufacture . . . something must be given for the profits of the undertaker of the work who hazards his stock in this adventure. The value which the workmen add to the materials, therefore, resolves itself in this case into two parts, of which the one pays their wages, the other the profits of their employer upon the whole stock of materials and wages which he advanced.[36]

In other words, the worker adds all value but he does not receive all of it. As Smith says again, "In this state of things the whole produce of labour does not always belong to the labourer. He must in most cases share it with the owner of the stock which employs him." These deductions by the owner of capital are not merely a compensation for the

labour of inspection and direction. They are, however, altogether different, are regulated by quite different principles, and bear no proportion to the quantity, the hardship, or the ingenuity of this supposed labour of inspection and direction. They are regulated altogether by the value of the stock employed, and are greater or smaller in proportion to the extent of this stock.[37]

While Smith did not therefore distinguish the investing capitalist from the entrepreneur—a differentiation which was left for the Frenchman, Say, to make a little over a quarter of a century later—he did distinguish between profits and the wages of management. So also did he distinguish between interest and the compensation for risk as is shown by the passage "the lowest ordinary rate of interest must be something more than what is sufficient to compensate the occasional losses to which lending, even with tolerable prudence, is exposed." [38]

In a similar fashion, Smith seems generally to regard rent as a deduction from values created by labor and one which did not represent any affirmative contribution by land. In a striking passage he writes: "As soon as the land of any country has all become private property, the landlords like to reap where they never sowed and demand a rent even for its natural produce." [39] And in another place he states that "as soon as the land becomes private property, the landlord demands a share of almost all the produce which the laborer can either raise or collect from it." [40]

A natural conclusion from such contentions as these would naturally seem to be that if labor produces all value and if rent and interest are

[36] *Wealth of Nations*, p. 50.
[37] *Ibid.*, p. 51.
[38] *Ibid.*, pp. 97–98.
[39] *Ibid.*, p. 51.
[40] *Ibid.*, p. 67.

but deductions representing no concrete service, it should follow ethically that labor ought to receive all and that wages should be the only share in distribution. But this interpretation seems never to have entered Smith's practical mind. Landlords and men of industrial and commercial property were dominant in the society in which he wrote and he accepted them as part of the order of nature. With his hard-headed Scotch way of accepting the *status quo*, he never thought of inquiring whether it would be possible to create an economic society in which profits and interests would disappear so that thus, as in his suppositious primitive society, the workers should enjoy the full produce of their labor. The doors of Eden had been irrevocably closed to man and there was no possibility of his ever re-entering them.

The declaration that the laborers should receive their full produce was left for the little group of socialist writers, including William Thompson, Thomas Hodgskin, John Gray, and John Francis Bray, who fell between the period of Ricardo and that of Marx and who have been somewhat inappropriately labeled, by Professor Foxwell [41] and Miss Lowenthal,[42] the Ricardian Socialists. They may, however, better be termed the Smithian Socialists, since they derive their inspiration from Smith rather than from Ricardo. This can be demonstrated in a number of ways. In the first place it should be remembered that whereas Adam Smith had taught that labor *caused* value, Ricardo merely held that commodities exchanged in proportion to the relative amounts of labor embodied in them. If there were even ratios of capital to labor in the various lines of industry, which Ricardo assumed for the purpose of his constructive theory, then it would still be possible for capital to make a contribution to the value of commodities and yet, because of this even distribution of capital, for commodities to exchange according to the proportion of labor expended upon them. Labor is thus, in the Ricardian analysis, the measure of value rather than the cause of value.

In the second place, Thomas Hodgskin is apparently the only one of the group who had studied Ricardo at first hand, although Bray makes a few references to him. The others, and possibly Bray as well, knew Ricardo only through the medium of James Mill's and McCulloch's texts. All of the writers, on the other hand, had apparently read Adam Smith, and the phrase "the whole produce of labour" which had

---

[41] Foxwell, Introduction to Menger, *The Right to the Full Produce of Labour*, p. lxxxiii: "It was Ricardo, not Owen, who gave the really effective inspiration to English Socialism." [Foxwell's essay is reprinted below, pp. 269 ff., in abridged form.—Ed.]

[42] In her able monograph, *The Ricardian Socialists*, Miss Lowenthal has pointed out, however, the slight influence of Ricardo upon this group.

been given such wide circulation by Smith, or equivalent expressions are repeated very frequently by them.

Thus Thomas Hodgskin wrote [43] that since the economists have declared that "the labour of a man's body and the work of his hands are to be considered as exclusively his own," they should "henceforth maintain that the whole produce of labour ought to belong to the labourer." This sentiment was frequently repeated with certain differences in phrasing in his *Popular Political Economy*.[44]

William Thompson expressed the same principle when he wrote [45] that "all the products of labour should be secured to the producers of them," and perhaps more frequently than any other of the group used, to justify his position, such phrases as the "whole produce of labour," "entire produce," and characterized the payment of rent and interest by the terms "forced abstraction" and "deduction" or "deprival." [46]

John Gray, by his own statement, owed his initial interest in economics to Adam Smith. After coming up to London as a young man, he writes [47] that he "procured a copy of Dr. Smith's *Wealth of Nations*" and after reading the first volume of it, "I set to work to reduce my theory to a written form." This theory that production should be the cause of demand rather than the effect of it led Gray to a theory of business depressions which was virtually identical with that at present advanced by Foster and Catchings. Depressions were caused by the fact that production increased faster than the supply of gold, which led to a consequent fall in the general price level. As he wrote:

All stocks on hand would therefore require to be sold at a loss. And this is an evil which does not and cannot cure itself, for as commodities must always be produced in apparent super-abundance *before* any fall can take place in their money price, they must uniformly be sold at a loss wherever they are produced in such quantities as to lower themselves in

[43] Hodgskin, *Labour Defended* (Cole edition), p. 83.

[44] Thus, in *Popular Political Economy,* pp. 29, 30, 237, 245, 249, 255. I am indebted to one of my students, Mr. Henry J. Bitterman, for ascertaining these and the subsequently cited page references.

[45] William Thompson, *The Distribution of Wealth* (1850 edition), p. 139.

[46] See the following page references in his *Distribution of Wealth* for the given phrases: (*a*) "Whole produce of labour," pp. 51, 52, 132, 181, 379, 449, 450, 455; (*b*) "Entire produce of labour," pp. 28, 31, 32, 33, 34, 35, 79, 85, 125, 136, 248, 253, 255, 436, 439; (*c*) "Forced abstraction," pp. 4, 33, 46, 50, 51, 52, 53, 54, 91, 126, 172, 252, 308, 321, 439, 442, 445; (*d*) "Deduction" or "deprival," pp. 32, 35, 41, 50, 66, 96, 221, 393; (*e*) "Part of the produce of labour," pp. 28, 30, 92, 133, 135, 169, 446; (*f*) Clear statements of the right to the whole produce of labor can be found on pp. 4, 5, 61, 85, 137, 139.

[47] John Gray, Appendix to *The Social System* (1831), p. 340.

money price; the *higher* price of production preceding the *lower* price of sales.[48]

This to Gray was the force by which [49] "production is constantly checked and retarded by the fear that is ever present in the manufacturer's mind of producing too much. It is the quantity that can be sold at a profit and not the quantity that can be made that is the present limit of production." Gray proposed several measures to meet these difficulties, notably the socialization of production and distribution, and the issuance of paper money to keep pace with the increase in production. He laid especial emphasis upon this second remedy in his later writings,[50] and was thus perhaps the first of those who have sought to stabilize the price level by controlling the issue of money.

But while the control of business depressions was Gray's chief aim, he nevertheless did emphasize the doctrine that labor created all value and should receive it. Thus he called the attention of his readers to what he declared [51] to be the "undisputed doctrine of Political Economy, originally seen and demonstrated by Dr. Adam Smith that labour is the one and only source of wealth." Similar references [52] indicate that Smith's doctrines influenced him greatly on this point. His desire to make the ethical application of the labor theory led him indeed into a proposal which was in reality inconsistent with his program of stabilizing the price level. His belief that a day's labor had the same value-creating powers at one time as another caused him to propose that there should be a fixed daily *money* wage for labor.[53] But as production increased, this would mean lower costs and hence lower prices per unit, which was the very event Gray was trying to avert. In order to stabilize the price level it would be necessary for day wages to rise proportionately with output. Constant piece rates rather than constant day rates were therefore needed to prevent a price fall. To the extent therefore that Gray

[48] *The Social System,* p. 271 (the italics throughout are Gray's).

[49] *Ibid.,* p. 59.

[50] See especially *Lectures on the Nature and Use of Money* (1848), p. 334. One of the most interesting of the parallelisms between Gray and Foster and Catchings is that upon the publication of this book he offered a prize of 100 guineas to anyone who, in the opinion of impartial judges, could successfully disprove his theory! A more comprehensive study of Gray's theories is being made by Mr. Henry J. Bitterman, and will, I hope, shortly be published. [See also Janet Kimball, *The Economic Doctrines of John Gray, 1799–1883,* Washington, D. C., 1948.—Ed.]

[51] Gray, *Lectures on the Nature and Use of Money,* p. 36.

[52] Notably *ibid.,* p. 6.

[53] *Ibid.,* p. 74.

took the labor theory of value into his system, the source of his inspiration is plainly Adam Smith rather than Ricardo.[54]

John Francis Bray, the Socialist printer, quotes Adam Smith as well as Ricardo, James Mill, and McCulloch. The following passage shows the judgment which he passed upon the doctrine that labor created value but that capital received part of it.[55]

The wealth which the capitalist appears to give in exchange for the workman's labour was generated neither by the labour nor the riches of the capitalist, but it was originally obtained by the labour of the workman; and it is still daily taken from him, by a fraudulent system of unequal exchanges. The whole transaction therefore, between the producer and the capitalist, is a palpable deception, a mere farce: it is, in fact, in thousands of instances no other than a barefaced though legalised robbery by means of which the capitalists and proprietors contrive to fasten themselves upon the productive classes, and suck from them their whole subsistence.

In several other passages Bray asserts the right of labor to the entire fruits of industry,[56] although he abstains from using the precise phrase the "whole produce of labour." Taken as a whole, however, there seems to be but little doubt that he was influenced by Adam Smith more than by Ricardo, although this influence may have been in part strained through the writings of Thompson and Gray as well as derived directly from the source.

It is then from the Whiggish pages of the *Wealth of Nations* that the doctrines of the English Socialists, as well as the theoretical exposition of Karl Marx, spring. The history of social thought furnishes many instances where theories elaborated by one writer have been taken over by others to justify social doctrines antagonistic to those to which the promulgator of the theory gave adherence. But had the gift of prevision been granted to those men, few would have been more startled than Adam Smith in seeing himself as the theoretical founder of the doctrines of nineteenth-century socialism.

5. WHAT DETERMINES THE AMOUNTS AND SHARES RECEIVED BY THE OWNERS OF CAPITAL AND LAND AND BY THE LABORERS

Profits and rent are, then, deductions from the annual product for which no corresponding contributions have been made. But what, then,

---

[54] In his "Lecture on Human Happiness" (1825), now chiefly available in Freund's German translation, *Vom menschlichen Glück,* there are several clear references to the "right to the whole produce." See especially pp. 65 and 74.

[55] Bray, *Labour's Wrongs and Labour's Remedies,* pp. 49–50.

[56] See, for instance, the following pages in *Labour's Wrongs:* pp. 57, 60, 87, 100, 101, 153, 181.

makes it possible for their recipients to levy tribute upon industry, and what determines the amount and proportion of their toll?

The capitalist is able to collect profits because it is he who primarily maintains the workers during the period when they are manufacturing commodities prior to their sale.   Here are the main origins of the wages-fund doctrine, as is evidenced by the following passages: [57] "It seldom happens that the person who tills the ground has wherewithal to maintain himself till he reaps the harvest.   His maintenance is generally advanced to him from the stock of a master, the farmer [58] who employs him."   But this is as true of manufacturing as of agriculture, since "In all arts and manufactures the greater part of the workmen stand in need of a master to advance them the materials of their works and their wages and maintenance till it be completed.   He shares in the produce of their labour, or in the value which it adds to the materials upon which it is bestowed, and in this share consists his profit." [59]   The capitalist is then a grub-staker who, by his possession of working capital, is able to induce the workers because of their present necessities to surrender to him a portion of their final product.   It should be noticed, however, that Smith regards the period for which the advances are made as only that which exists at any one stage of production between the purchase of the raw materials and the sale for money of the fabricated article.   This, however, as Taussig has pointed out, is by no means a sufficient analysis, since the incidence of the advances has merely been transferred to another capitalist when the goods at one stage of production are sold to the next.   It is the capitalistic class as a whole, rather than individual capitalists, which makes the advances.

If we ask how it was that the capitalists managed to secure control over capital and why they charge what they do for its use, Smith gives us small comfort.   He indulges in no such suppositious anthropology on the origin of private property and inequality as characterized the musings of the Austrian school on how canoes, fishhooks, and nets came originally to be saved, and a subsequent leisured class to be established.   It was enough for Smith that property did belong to the few.   Once holding such power, it was only natural that they should make a charge for its use, for why would a master employ workmen [60] "unless

[57] *Wealth of Nations,* I, 67.

[58] The word "farmer" is of course used here in the English usage to denote one who is the tenant of a large landowner and who hires laborers in turn to help him on the leased land.

[59] *Wealth of Nations,* p. 67.

[60] *Ibid.,* p. 50; for a similar reference, see p. 67.

he expected from the sale of their work something more than what was sufficient to replace his stock to him, and he could have no interest to employ a great stock rather than a small one, unless his profits were to bear some proportion to the extent of his stock."

But how much "more" does the capitalist expect, and what are the minima, which he will demand as the price of advancing his stock? An attempt to answer these questions would lead us into the very heart of the interest problem; but Adam Smith does not make it.

Smith instead attempts to explain the rate of profits and of interest as varying inversely with the accumulation of capital. When capital is scanty, the owners of it are able to secure a high return; but an increase in its amount "tends to lower its profit." [61] "When the stocks of many rich merchants," Smith writes, "are turned into the same trade, their mutual competition naturally tends to lower its profit; and when there is a like increase of stock in all the different trades carried on in the same society, the same competition must produce the same effect in them all." It might seem that the term "the amount of stock" is quite vague, but by this Smith means the amount relative to the supply of labor. This is clearly evidenced by his explanation that profits are lower in the cities where the amount of "stock" is large in comparison with the number of workers than they are in the country where the ratio of stock of labor is less.

In a thriving town the people who have great stocks to employ, frequently cannot get the number of workmen they want, and therefore bid against one another in order to get as many as they can, which raises the wages of labour and lowers the profits of stock. In the remote parts of the country there is frequently not stock sufficient to employ all the people, who therefore bid against one another in order to get employment which lowers the wages of labour and raises the profits of stock.[62]

Profits and wages thus varied in opposite directions, profits rising as wages fell, and falling as the latter rose. Only in new countries or when new trades or territories were being opened up was it possible to combine high wages and high profits. Here it should be noted that Smith is of course speaking of wages in terms of the amount per worker and of profits in terms of percentage. Unlike Ricardo, he devotes little attention to the relative share of each in the total product.

The minimum below which wages could not permanently fall (save in a decaying society) was the basic amount needed to support a worker, for [63] "a man must always live by his work and his wages must

[61] *Ibid.*, p. 89.   [62] *Ibid.*, p. 91.   [63] *Ibid.*, p. 69.

at least be sufficient to maintain him." Since it is necessary to rear children in order to maintain the population intact without diminution and increase, this minimum tends indeed to be more than this. Cantillon had estimated that the earnings of the wife would serve to maintain her, but that the husband must be given enough to support four children if two were ultimately to be reared. With characteristic caution, however, Smith declines to pass judgment upon the accuracy of Cantillon's estimates,[64] and merely points out that provision must be made for some children unless the population is to decline. This minimum is "the lowest which is consistent with common humanity," although it may well be doubted whether it is the benevolence of the employer which prevents the rate from falling below this point.

But this is only the minimum. Wages may rise above this point if the demand for labor is sufficiently great. This demand for labor consists of the capital set aside by the employing class with which to hire labor, and which in a later section [65] Smith identifies with circulating capital. If the quantity of circulating capital increases, then wages must rise.[66] The greater the relative rise in the amount of capital, the greater must be the advance in wages. This is why in an advancing state of society wages tend to move upward. Where the supply of capital is, on the contrary, decreasing, the wage level will fall.

But—and here is a very clear adumbration of Malthusianism—as the amount of capital swells and wages rise, the population increases, for [67]

Every species of animals naturally multiplies in proportion to the means of its subsistence. . . . The liberal reward of labour, by enabling them to

---

[64] Dr. Louis I. Dublin and A. J. Lotka have recently estimated that *fertile* American families need on the *average* to have 3.1 children if the population is to be held constant. This does not mean, however, that the head of the family will have this number of children dependent upon him *throughout* his working years, for such would be far from the truth. For an analysis of the tangled facts of family composition, see my article, "Is the Family of Five Typical?" *Journal American Statistical Association* (September, 1924), and Chap. III of *Wages and the Family* (1925), and Miss Eleanor Rathbone's *The Disinherited Family*.

[65] *Wealth of Nations*, pp. 265–66: "All useful machines and instruments of trade are originally derived from a circulating capital which furnishes the materials of which they are made and the maintenance of the workmen who make them."

[66] That is, if the supply of labor remained constant or did not increase commensurately.

[67] *Wealth of Nations*, pp. 81–82.

provide better for their children, and consequently to bring up a greater number, naturally tends to widen and extend those limits. It deserves to be remarked, too, that it necessarily does this as nearly as possible in the proportion which the demand for labour requires. If this demand is continually increasing, the reward of labour must necessarily encourage in such a manner the marriage and multiplication of labourers as may enable them to supply that continually increasing demand by a continually increasing population.

If, on the other hand, wages "in the inferior ranks of society" fall below the minimum, then [68] "the scantiness of subsistence can set limits to the further multiplication of the human species, and it can do so in no other way than by destroying a great part of the children which their fruitful marriages produce."

The rate of multiplication of the population thus attunes itself to the rate of increase of stock, for [69]

If the reward should at any time be less than what was requisite for this purpose, the deficiency of hands would soon raise it; and if it should at any time be more, their excessive multiplication would soon lower it to this necessary rate. The market would be so much under-stocked with labour in the one case and so much over-stocked in the other, as would soon force back its price to that proper rate which the circumstances of the society required.

While there is some verbal ambiguity as to the meaning of the term "proper rate," it is nevertheless quite clear that Smith meant by this the ratio between the amount of capital and the number of laborers.

This raises the further question as to whether there was a tendency for this ratio to be approximated and hence establish a wage which would tend to approach uniformity through time. That such was Smith's idea is apparent from a number of passages. It is true that he recognizes a rise in real wages in Great Britain during the eighteenth century which was directly evidenced in the increase in money wages and the fall in the price of necessities. But he does not seem to have regarded this as a permanent tendency. Thus, he states that in a country where the absolute amount of capital is large but where it has not been increasing for some time, which he assumes to be true of China, the population will have already expanded up to the limit permitted by this supply of capital and the rate of wages will in consequence be approximately that low quantum which he had set as the

---

[68] *Ibid.*, p. 81.   [69] *Ibid.*, p. 82.

minimum.[70] This tendency of wages toward the minimum is forecast by implication in the passage,[71] "It is this demand [for men] which regulates and determines the state of propagation in all the different countries of the world, in North America, in Europe, and in China; which renders it rapidly progressive in the first, slow and gradual in the second, and altogether stationary in the last." Though there is here no direct statement, the purport of this sentence seems to be that North America will tend to move into the slow rate of growth of Europe, and the latter into the stationary condition of China.

This tacit forecast of the stationary state which was more fully elaborated three-quarters of a century later by John Stuart Mill is much more directly stated in another passage:

In a country which has acquired that full complement of riches which the nature of its soil and climate, and its situation with respect to other countries allowed it to acquire, which could, therefore, advance no further, and which was not going backwards, both the wage of labour and the profits of stock would probably be very low. In a country fully peopled in proportion to what either its territory could maintain or its stock employ, the competition for employment would necessarily be so great as to reduce the wages of labour to what was barely sufficient to keep up the number of labourers, and, the country being already fully peopled, that number could never be augmented. In a country fully stocked in proportion to all the business it had to transact, as great a quantity of stock would be employed in every particular branch as the nature and extent of the trade would admit. The competition therefore would everywhere be as great and consequently the ordinary profit as low as possible.[72]

Population would therefore ultimately be at a standstill and the rate of profits at that minimum where there would be no inducement for any further savings, since, if such savings were made, the fund available for the payment of labor would rise and wages consequently in-

[70] "Though the wealth of a country should be very great, yet if it has been long stationary, we must not expect to find the wages of labour very high in it. The funds destined for the payment of wages . . . may be of the greatest extent; but if they have continued for several centuries of the same, or very nearly of the same extent, the number of labourers employed every year could easily supply, and even more than supply, the number wanted the following year. . . . If in such a country the wages of labour had ever been more than sufficient to maintain the labourer and to enable him to bring up a family, the competition of the labourers and the interest of the masters would soon reduce them to this lowest rate which is consistent with common humanity" (*ibid.*, p. 73).

[71] *Wealth of Nations*, p. 82.

[72] *Ibid.*, p. 96; for a similar passage, see p. 98.

crease. What this minimum rate was, Smith, like Ricardo and J. S. Mill, did not definitely state beyond the fact that it must be more than a compensation for risk and losses and for management. By his statement,[73] however, that in such a state it would be "impossible for any but the very wealthiest people to live upon the interest of their money," it is plain that he thought of it as quite low. He thought that Holland was "approaching near to this state," [74] and there the rate of interest was 2 per cent.[75] The minimum was then apparently somewhere between 1 and 2 per cent.

Virtually all of the features which characterize the later classical writers were then present in the *Wealth of Nations;* the labor theory of value, Malthusianism, the tendency of profits to a minimum, and the stationary state are all contained in the writings of Adam Smith. The *Wealth of Nations* was indeed a rich quarry in which the later classicists could find the ideas and hints which they molded into more systematic form.

Before passing from the subject of wages, it is well to note (1) Smith's recognition of the disparities in bargaining power between employers and workers, and (2) his sturdy opposition to the mercantilistic doctrine that lower wages were needed in order to force the laborers to work more and thus make England prosperous.

There have been few more pungent summaries of the relative bargaining strength of labor and capital than Smith's quiet comment [76] that while "in the long run the workman may be as necessary to his master as his master is to him; the necessity is not so immediate." Smith also saw that it was easier for the employers to limit competition between each other for workmen than it was for the workers to restrict their competition for positions:

> The masters, being fewer in number, can combine much more easily; and the law, besides, authorizes, or at least does not prohibit their combinations, while it prohibits those of the workmen. . . . We rarely hear, it has been said, of the combinations of masters; though frequently of those of workmen. But whoever imagines, upon this account, that masters rarely combine, is as ignorant of the world as of the subject. Masters are always and everywhere in a sort of tacit, but constant and uniform combination, not to raise the wages of labour above their actual rate.[77]

Smith thus was in a sense a bargain theorist who held that the employer's superiority enabled him to reduce wages below the point at

[73] *Ibid.*, p. 98.
[74] *Ibid.*, p. 98.
[75] *Ibid.*, p. 93.

[76] *Ibid.*, p. 68.
[77] *Ibid.*, p. 68.

which they would otherwise have rested, although they could not fall below that minimum which was needed to maintain the workers.

The English mercantilists had wished to depress the real earnings of the workers in order to force them to work more days in a week, and opposed increasing their remuneration on the ground that it would merely induce them to work for a correspondingly shorter time. This assumed of course that the desires of the workers were relatively fixed and that a higher wage would merely enable them to satisfy those wants, and that the workers would then rest. The way to increase the wealth of the state was therefore thought to lie in decreasing the daily wages of the manual workers.[78] Even Smith's contemporary, Arthur Young, held substantially similar views. Smith, however, could not justify such a public policy which made of the laborers mere instruments for the enrichment of others and which regarded them not as members but as slaves of the state. To his mind, an "improvement in the circumstances of the lower ranks" was of distinct advantage to society, since [79]

> Servants, labourers and workmen of different kinds make up the far greater part of every political society. But what improves the circumstances of the greater part can never be regarded as an inconveniency to the whole. No society can surely be flourishing and happy, of which the far greater part of the members are poor and miserable.

It was here that he added the certainly modest plea that "it was but equity beside that they who feed, cloath, and lodge the whole body of the people, should have such a share of the produce of their own labour as to be themselves tolerably well fed, cloathed, and lodged."

Smith also took decided issue with the doctrine that high wages led to less effort, and asserted on the contrary that they increased "the industry of the common people," for [80] "a plentiful subsistence increases the bodily strength of the labourer and the comfortable hope of bettering his condition . . . animates him to exert that strength to the utmost." In support of this contention he cited the superiority of English workmen to the Scotch artificers, although the wages of the former were appreciably higher. He admitted that high wages might lead some to be idle part of the week, but stoutly asserted that this was "by no means the case with the greater part."

---

[78] For a summary of these doctrines, see E. S. Furniss, *The Position of the Laborer in a System of Nationalism,* and an article by T. E. Gregory in Vol. I of *Economica.*

[79] *Wealth of Nations,* p. 80.

[80] *Ibid.,* p. 83.

In matters of practical policy, therefore, Smith did not sympathize with the efforts of the employing class to reduce wages through superior economic and political power, and he resolutely opposed the reactionary theory of the mercantilists that the great masses of mankind can be driven to work only under the whip-lash of want. The mercantilistic theory has virtually ceased to be applied to white labor, but it has been taken over by the imperialistic countries as a justification of their treatment of tropical labor. What was thought to be true of "trueborn Englishmen" in the seventeenth and eighteenth centuries is now asserted to be true of the black and yellow races.

Turning now to the rent of land, the question naturally presents itself as to how the landlord is able to collect rent and what fixes its amount. In the passages which have been previously quoted the implication is that the landlord secures it because he "demands" it. But we may make the same retort to such an explanation that Hotspur made to Glendower's boast that he "could call the spirits from the vasty deep," namely, "You can call them, but will they come?"

It is not enough to demand rent; it is also necessary to secure it. Analyzed more closely, Smith is, however, seen to have offered no less than three different explanations of rent other than the main one which has been previously quoted. These are, namely, explanations on the ground of (1) monopoly, (2) differential advantages, and (3) the bounty of nature. Thus Smith speaks of rent beginning when *all* of the land of a country "has become private property." And he continues,

> The wood of the forest, the grass of the field and all the natural fruits of the earth, which when land was in common cost the labourer only the trouble of gathering them, come, even to him, to have an additional price fixed upon them. He must then pay for the license to gather them and must give up to the landlord a portion of what his labour either collects or produces.[81]

In another place Smith states [82] directly that "the rent of land therefore . . . is naturally a monopoly price."

In other places Smith approaches the position ultimately worked out by Anderson, West, and Ricardo and makes rent a differential resulting from superior advantages. "The rent of land," he writes,[83] "not only varies with its fertility, whatever be its produce, but with its situation, whatever be its fertility."

[81] *Ibid.*, p. 51.
[82] *Ibid.*, p. 146.
[83] *Ibid.*, p. 148.

A final explanation taken over from Quesnay and the Physiocrats, which Smith offered for rent, was that it was a surplus due to the bounty of nature. In an extraordinary passage [84] he stated that

The labourers and labouring cattle, therefore, employed in agriculture, not only occasion, like the workmen in manufactures, the reproduction of a value equal to their own consumption, or to the capital which employs them together with its owners' profits; but of a much greater value. Over and above the capital of the farmer and all its profits, they regularly occasion the reproduction of the rent of the landlord. This rent may be considered as the produce of those powers of nature, the use of which the landlord lends to the farmer. . . . It is the work of nature which remains after deducting or compensating everything which can be regarded as the work of man. It is seldom less than a fourth and frequently more than a third of the whole produce. No equal quantity of productive labour employed in manufactures can ever occasion so great a reproduction. In them nature does nothing; man does all; and the reproduction must always be in proportion to the strength of the agents that occasion it.

But "in agriculture nature labours along with man, and though her labour costs no expense, its produce has its value, as well as that of the most expensive workmen." Here it is the plenty of nature rather than its niggardliness which enables rent to be paid. It was precisely this position which Malthus, as the defender of the English landlord, urged over forty years later in his discussion with Ricardo [85] when he declared that rent was a payment for added riches rather than a diversion of an existent stock. This position of Smith seems in part inconsistent with his dictum that rent is a subtraction from the whole produce of labor. Yet it might be possible for someone to urge, although Smith did not do so, that although the land might be productive, the landlord was not, and that the bounty of nature should flow to the workers.

As Cannan has pointed out and as we have already stated, Smith interested himself primarily in the question of profits per cent, wages per head, and rent per acre. He did not grapple seriously with the question of the relative share which capital, labor, and land received of the total national product. In one place he asserts [86] that the progress of improvement causes the landlord's share of "the whole produce" to rise, but in another he declares [87] that "in the progress of

---

[84] *Ibid.*, p. 343.

[85] See *Letters of Ricardo to Malthus,* edited by James Bonar, and Malthus, *Principles of Political Economy.*

[86] *Wealth of Nations,* I, 247.

[87] *Ibid.*, p. 317.

improvement, rent, though it increases in proportion to the extent, diminishes in proportion to the produce of the land." He concludes that the interests "of those who live by profit" are opposed to the progress of society, since this will mean a fall in the interest rate.[88] This, however, clearly omits to consider the total amount of capital saved, which might of course be so much greater that even with the reduction in the rate, the total amount of interest and even its share in the total product might be greater than before.

Rent is thought of by Smith in the main as a residual element and not as a cost. It is true that the first edition declared that the price of a commodity must be sufficient to "purchase, command, or exchange for an additional quantity of labour, in order to enable the person who brings it to market to pay this rent," but this was clearly inconsistent with his doctrine that the taxation of rent as such could not be shifted, since "it would fall altogether upon the owner of the ground-rent who acts always as a monopolist and exacts the greatest rent which can be got for the use of his ground." [89] Under the probable influence of Hume the former passage was reworded to make it consistent with his doctrine of incidence.

Profits are said in the first volume to be a necessary cost, but in the second it appears that this only applies to compensation for risk and management, and not to interest:

As a tax upon the rent of land cannot raise rents, because the net produce which remains after replacing the stock of the farmer, together with his reasonable profit can not be greater after the tax than before, so for the same reason, a tax upon the interest of money could not raise the rate of interest, the quantity of stock or money in the country, like the quantity of land, being supposed to remain the same after the tax as before.[90]

This would, of course, be true were the supply of capital to be fixed or to be absolutely inelastic. It is because this is approximately true in the case of land that taxes on economic rent cannot be shifted. Whether capital, however, has such a supply curve may well be doubted, although many, notably the Webbs, have so contended. If not, and if a tax by lowering the rate of interest were to decrease the amounts saved, then other forces would be set into effect which would not make interest such a pure residual.

[88] *Ibid.*, p. 249.   [90] *Ibid.*, II, 332.
[89] *Wealth of Nations*, II, 328.

Bonar, Fay, and Keynes
on
Malthus

Thomas Robert Malthus (1766–1834), a British clergyman, is best known for his population theory, developed in his *Essay on the Principle of Population* (1798). Malthus held that there is a natural tendency of the population to outrun the food supply, and that this natural tendency is checked by "vice," "misery," and "moral restraint." Malthus drew important policy conclusions from his doctrine, pointing out the futility of certain social policies and the danger attaching to generous poor relief. In conjunction with the principle of diminishing returns and the subsistence theory of wages, Malthus' theory opened up a gloomy prospect, and it is largely due to his interpretation that economics came to be characterized as the "dismal science" by Ruskin and Carlyle.

Malthus also is remembered for his *Principles of Political Economy* (1820). In this work he argues against the validity of Say's law, and in a surprisingly modern manner calls attention to the deficiency of effective demand during periods of depression. There is an allusion to this aspect of Malthus' work in the last essay reprinted here.

James Bonar (1852-1941), an outstanding student of the history of economics, devoted a full-length book to Malthus. C. R. Fay (1884–   ) is a well-known scholar in the field of economic history, associated with Cambridge University. On J. M. Keynes see pp. 763 ff. On the occasion of the centenary of Malthus' death the University of Cambridge sponsored a memorial meeting, at which the addresses by Bonar, Fay, and Keynes, which are reprinted here, were delivered.

THE CENTENARY of the death of T. R. Malthus should, in strict chronology, have been celebrated on the 29th December, 1934. As this date fell out of term time, his former College and University postponed its commemoration until the term following. On the afternoon of March 2nd, 1935, members and students of the Faculty of Economics and Politics in the University of Cambridge met in the Hall of King's College to commemorate the occasion. Professor Pigou took the chair, and allocutions to Malthus's memory were delivered by Dr. Bonar, Mr. C. R. Fay and Mr. J. M. Keynes, which are printed below. Later in the day the Master and Fellows of Jesus College gave a dinner in the College Hall at which a number of economists, statisticians and biologists, who had been invited from outside Cambridge, were present. The toast of the evening *In piam memoriam* was given by the Master, coupled with the name of Malthus's biographer, Dr. Bonar, who replied. Mr. Robert Malthus, the last representative in this country of the family of Malthus in the male line, was present. He confirmed the view that the family have always pronounced their name *Maulthus* with the *h* doubtfully sounded.

THE ALLOCUTIONS

I. DR. BONAR

My first duty is to thank King's College and the Faculty of Economics and our Chairman, Professor Pigou, for their welcome to us to-day. By "us" I mean the assembly here, who are guests like myself, but all more or less interested in economics, and therefore in Malthus.

My second duty is to put a question to myself which is likely to be put by the Public outside. I shall try to answer it to my own satisfaction, and I hope to yours, as it affects you and me whether the Public ever thought of it or not: Why do we commemorate this man Malthus at all? Is he deserving of remembrance?

[Reprinted by permission from *Economic Journal,* June 1935.]

I answer: Yes, indeed, if only for the *impulse* he gave to the serious study of a branch of economics which, before him, was hardly a branch at all, but left to be handled in footnotes with apologies.

Ever since the appearance of the first essay of the youthful Malthus (he was thirty-two) in 1798,[1] the subject of Population has been treated by economists as worthy of serious study, a chapter or "Book" to itself and no apologies. Even in that first essay on the principle of Population, Malthus had drawn together the scattered hints of previous writers into a manageable doctrine or rough draft of a doctrine. I do not say it was universally well received, but it excited universal attention. It is true that there was (besides a general murmur of applause) a hurricane of angry criticism. The least fierce of the critics found (and still find) in its opening formulas, the ratios of the increase of population and food, either too much or too little mathematics. Malthus himself observed (and filled up in his second edition of five years afterwards) an omission, not concerned with mathematics.

But in that logically imperfect first edition there was logic enough or eloquence enough to captivate the British Public, and the publisher Johnson wished he had kept up type.

Some may say the impulse given was greater than any contribution of Malthus to doctrine. Very well; let us say that the impulse outlived the criticisms. Here is an example. Utopian Reformers cried out: "He has nothing for us but a Universal Negative; he frowns on Utopias; he frowns on early marriages; when we would go on, he pulls us back— saying, like the obsolete old decalogue, thou shalt not, thou shalt not. What help can such a teacher give to human progress?"

Search his scriptures thoroughly, from the imperfection of the first essay to the maturity of the later edition. You find something better than a Universal Negative; you find a Particular Affirmative; or let me try to sum up his heart's desire for the human race in *three* Particular Affirmatives:

1. A lower death-rate for all.
2. A higher standard of life and livelihood for the Poor.
3. An end of the *waste,* even now going on in this twentieth century, the waste of young human lives.

There might even be a summary in one phrase: he desired economy in human lives. A man who *secured* that would be among the greatest of economists; and a man who spent his life in the *effort* after it has

[1] See *Economic Journal,* 1898, page 200, "The Centenary of Malthus."

surely "acquired merit" enough to deserve even such a Commemoration as to-day's.

It is true that the First Essay has more shadow resting on it than the later essays. Most readers pardoned it in so brilliant a writer as the author of the first. Such gloom as there was could be endured there, while the prosaic work of the later essays needed all the illumination and exhilaration that the subject could bear. As to the vulgar charges of cruelty and atheism, he defends himself in his later editions quite convincingly. Fairer matters of attack were: His exaggerations, slips in reasoning, imperfect statistics; for these he is on his trial still, but no more and no less than all his tribe. It is the reasoner's fate—to endure criticism at every step of the way; and, as all economists are reasoners, they must be prepared to give rebuffs and to take rebuffs as Malthus gave them, and had occasionally (being a mortal man) to take them. Let other writers be happy if in the end they have so small a balance against them as Malthus on his first and chief subject of Population.

There may be a call from the crowd (by no means from the present assembly of chosen spirits) for his tangible achievements which he who runs may read and cannot easily run away from. Here are a few. The impression made by the First Essay whipped up the English census of 1801, and made later censuses certain. Not that Malthus was the originator of the first census; there were many good men pressing for it. But it was of his doing that it could never be held back again as it was fifty years before. Also, he helped Governments to avoid bad mistakes in their Poor Laws—not that he never made mistakes in his own proposals now and then on that field of hard labour.

Again, just before his death in 1834, he joined with Quetelet and Babbage in creating the Statistical Society. Last year in the Annals of the Society he was duly recognised as a "Pious Founder" of it.

Darwin got hints from him in working out the theory of the Survival of the Fittest.

Like Darwin, he has added a new word to the English language, an adjective from his own name.

Paradoxically, Malthus, who was all his life never more rabid in politics than a mild Whig, became a hero of the Philosophical Radicals. John Stuart Mill, once one of them, tells us that Malthus was recognised by them for what he had really done; he had not closed the door to progress, he had for the first time opened it. And his contributions to theory outside the Essay are of high importance if not at the same supreme altitude. He gave rise to the classical theories of Rent and Value, having a fair claim to a large share in the making of both. His support of his arguments by facts, more especially in the Essays, was sufficiently novel to make our dear friend Alfred Marshall (so well known in Cambridge and so powerful an economist) almost persuaded to set him down a leader of Historical Economists. His discussions with his friend Ricardo were carried on in long letters still available to us. If allowed to be nothing more, they must be always a good preliminary training ground for economic students. But there was something more. Many of us feel the gentler pressure of his hand in the argument; and a few of our best men (I have two in my mind) tell us that he would have been a better leader for us than Ricardo. Well, the world is all before us. It is not true of theories as of hard facts that what is done cannot be undone!

Let our friends convert us.

Here is another feather in the cap of Thomas Robert Malthus. So far as I can find out, he was the first in our own country to wear the title Professor of Political Economy.

A friend of mine, more at home in his Shakespeare than in his Economics, wrote of him thus impudently:

"This Malthus of our Dismal Science was the first Professor,—ay he was the first." He was so appointed, in fact, at Haileybury when the East India Company's College for cadets was opened there in 1806. It was not an inspiring place for any professor who could hope now and then to have inspiration from his pupils. But it allowed him leisure to write books and pamphlets and letters to like-minded friends, and leisure enough to pursue his own thoughts. He was not a laughing philosopher like his friend Sydney Smith; but dismal he was not any more than his subject. To be *dismal* is to be afflicted with an extreme form of pessimism, more familiar to Carlyle than to Malthus. If he showed signs of the complaint in 1798 at thirty-two years of age, he recovered from the mild attack. He was personally a normal Englishman more given to merriment than sadness. So his friend Daniel Clarke tells us;—and we all know that about that time of life, thirty-two, a man is just beginning to overcome a certain "oscillation" between melancholy and merriment, such as led Milton to his immortal contrast of them. Malthus was passing out of that stage of our diversified human life and becoming able to see the possibility of a good time coming for his own country and even for Europe and the world after all. He observes both in 1803 (p. 31), and in his farewell edition of the Essay in 1826 (p. 404 of Vol. II) that England stands next to Norway and Switzerland for a good record of infant mortality. We have not had a worse but a better experience since his time. Like Macaulay, we have heard of nothing but decay and seen nothing but progress. Nowhere more evidently than in Public Health.

Certainly at Cambridge Political Economists have been as little dismal as was Malthus. How far from dismal were Marshall and Sidgwick, to say nothing of your still living economists, young and old, and, "as I in this place am specially bound to add," your brother economists at Oxford past and present; and in the regions beyond, including not only Scotland and Ireland, but America; and not only America, but all countries where our study is practised. All have diversities of gifts but, we hope and believe, the same spirit. And it is the spirit that animated our "First Professor."

I should like to think that, when we praise him now, he wakes up and listens. Whether he hears or not, we do right to give him his meed of praise. He had a single-hearted desire to know the truth, with unshaken courage to declare it, were it pleasant or unpleasant. It is often the unpleasant that appears first. The Prophet, himself, unpleasant at first to his hearers,—denouncing, for example, our sins against economy in human lives,—comes to his own pleasanter self again when his work is fully done. He is then shown to us as the Benefactor, worthy to be applauded, as Cambridge is now applauding her trusty and well-beloved son, in a Commemoration to be repeated, I hope, by Cambridge and all of you in 1966, the second centenary of the birth of Thomas Robert Malthus. May you all live to join in it!

II. Mr. Fay

It is of Malthus the social economist that I speak. As Adam Smith was of excellence the economist of policy and Ricardo the path-breaker in monetary thought, so the distinctive contribution of Malthus lay in the field of social economy. He launched the interest and in part the method which travelled through Nassau Senior and Stuart Mill to the social investigations of a later day, where the statistician not less than the theorist is in the line of descent from him. And statisticians can never forget that Malthus' Essay of 1798 was among the influences which provoked the taking of the first census of the people three years later in 1801. By his ratios of increase, arithmetical for Nature and geometrical for Man (for, as our University Calendar reminds us, he was 9th Wrangler of 1788, four places below Gunning of Christ's), he framed a startling disharmony between population with its capacity for cumulative increase and natural resources which are limited and exhaustible. Although the middle link of his doctrine has been broken by the triumphs of technology in transport and agriculture in conjunction with the practice of birth control, yet it remains formidable at either end—in the New World, where resources have been recklessly exploited, and in the old world of Asia, where population teems upon areas so recently reclaimed from flood or desert by the capital and engineering skill of Europe. Malthus, checked by Malthusianism at home, still points a reproachful finger at the plundered land surface of North America and the premature marriage beds of the East.

Now a man may influence his generation by way either of attraction or repulsion; and attraction may show itself in the translation of his teaching to other spheres of knowledge, as well as in the incorporation of it into the policy, practice and literature of the sphere for which it was designed. In every one of these ways the influence of Malthus was potent.

The benign author of the *Essay on Population,* presuming to dispense misery and vice with the certainty of a Benthamite in holy orders, roused to angry protest the rebels of his day. Said William Thompson, the dean of Early English Socialism, "Insult not the suffering, the great majority of mankind, with the glaring falsehood, that by means of limiting population or not eating potatoes their own happiness is in their own hands, whilst the causes are left which render it morally and physically impossible for them to live without potatoes and improvident breeding." [2] And William Cobbett, composing as he rode on horseback through the fertile valleys of his beloved England, reared at the spectre of the Monster Malthus. "How can Malthus and his nasty and silly disciples, how can those who want to abolish the Poor Rates, to prevent the poor from marrying; how can this at once stupid and conceited tribe look the labouring man in the face, while they call on him to take up arms, to risk his life in defence of the land?" [3] And again, "It seemed to me that one way of exposing this mixture of madness and of blasphemy was to take a look, now that the harvest is in, at the produce, the mouths, the condition, and the changes that have taken place, in a spot like this, which God has favoured with every good that he has had to bestow upon man." [4] He was riding that day by the Wiltshire Avon.

But it was otherwise with the scientists whose concern was with Nature more than with Man. The doctrine of Malthus was germinal to the researches of Darwin and Alfred Russel Wallace in the theory of evolution by natural selection; and the testimony of both is unqualified. "In October 1838 (says Darwin), that is fifteen months after I had begun my systematic enquiry, I happened to read for amusement Malthus' *Population,* and being well prepared to appreciate the struggle

[2] W. Thompson, *Distribution of Wealth,* p. 428.

[3] *Poor Man's Friend,* No. 2.

[4] *Rural Rides,* ed. Pitt Cobbett, II, 57.

for existence which everywhere goes on from long-continued observation of animals and plants, it at once struck me that under these circumstances favourable variations would tend to be preserved and unfavourable ones to be destroyed. The result of this would be the formation of a new species. Here then I had at last got hold of a theory by which to work." [5] And Wallace acknowledged a like indebtedness in language just as precise.

Inasmuch, however, as civilised man had left far behind the kind of animals which Darwin chiefly studied, the application of Malthusian teaching to the sphere for which its author designed it was necessarily more oblique. Parliament, indeed, did its best to keep the poor to the strait and natural way, when in 1834, the year of his death, it inscribed on the statute book a new poor law, the first-fruits of Benthamism, as it has been termed—a wreath from England to Malthus as I would rather say. That law with its workhouse test and rule of less eligibility lies outside our province, but the uproar caused only a few days ago by the effort of Government to curtail at points the present scale of unemployment relief measures dramatically the change in social outlook between 1834 and 1935.

An apologist for Malthus might indulge the hope that Parliament wronged him in the Act of 1834. But if it did, it was only because it went less far than he in principle desired, to judge by the evidence which he gave before the House of Commons Emigration Committee of 1827. For after 1815, as large numbers were dismissed from the fighting services, and as Canada, Australia and South Africa dawned on the horizon of settlement, emigration to those quarters of the Empire became the panacea for English ills, of which the chief were the payment of agricultural labour from the poor rates, the influx of Irish immigrants and the distress of the hand-loom weavers. The issue, as envisaged by the Committee, was this. If the English or Scottish poor are emigrated, will the vacuum thus created be filled from Ireland with no better result than to supplant the wheat-fed population of Great Britain by the potato-fed population of Ireland? It was a problem for political economy, and the advice of Malthus was sought. He replied, "I think it is possible that the vacuum might not be filled up because those hovels" (he is referring at this point to Ireland) ". . . might be pulled down and not replaced."

But stopping the holes of habitation, though it might serve for badgers and rabbits, was hardly proper for human beings, even to the mentality of 1827. So they pressed him for another way, and he answered, "No

[5] *Life and Letters of C. Darwin,* I, 83.

other occurs to me except the one I myself proposed a long while ago, that those who were born after a certain time should not be allowed to have any parish assistance." These were the unbidden guests for whom, in the language of the *Essay* (edition 2), there was no vacant cover at Nature's mighty feast—these the unhappy persons who (to employ his earlier metaphor) had drawn a blank in the great lottery of life. But they pressed him further, this venerable witness now over sixty years of age (for they could hardly help remembering that by the laws of England men must not starve to death), and this time they put to him a leading question: "If cheap tracts were written and given to the poor and in some instances taught in the schools, explaining the doctrines you have just laid down with respect to the conditions of the poor, do you imagine they would be able to understand them and that they would apply what they learned to their own case?"

Answer. "I think they are not very difficult to be understood, but they are perhaps rather difficult to apply. I believe some tracts of that kind have been occasionally distributed."

Question. "Have you any knowledge of the effects produced?"

Answer. "I have understood that many of the labouring classes, particularly the artisans, acknowledge the doctrines which have been laid down on the subject of population."

At that the Professor of Haileybury College left it; and perhaps it was as well, for his teaching had sunk into the minds of certain artisans of whom the chief was Francis Place, the tailor of Westminster. And the result was action, furtive at first, that would have horrified its innocent begetter. It had been hinted at in 1818 by James Mill, the father of nine—an inconsistency for which the eldest felt constrained to apologise—and it was expounded later with the courage born of suffering by Francis Place, the father of fifteen. It occupied a corner in the design of the community builders. Through Robert Dale Owen it reached America and returned a generation later to shock Victoria's England in the stirring fight for freedom staged by Charles Bradlaugh and Annie Besant. In 1877 the Neo-Malthusian League was founded. But I am stealing from an American scholar who more than any of us should be here to-day; and I commend to you the writings of Mr. Norman E. Himes; in particular his weighty introduction to Place's *Illustration and Proofs of the Principle of Population* (1822).

Malthus, however, had a friend and admirer who could be trusted to interpret him without imputing the taint of Condorcet, and this was Harriet Martineau, whose first three years of literary fame were the last three years of her master's life. Between 1831 and 1834 she wrote her *Tales Illustrating Political Economy and Taxation,* and in the last of

these advertised the heart of the matter in round conclusions. "The
condition of labourers may be best improved—1. By inventions . . .
and making savings instead of supporting strikes. 2. *By Adjusting the
Proportion of Population to Capital.*" The master and disciple were
alike in that, as they became famous, they were greatly abused. When
she came to the number on Population, she knew there was trouble
ahead. "While writing *Weal and Woe in Garvelock,*" she tells us in
her *Autobiography,* "the perspiration many a time streamed down my
face, though I knew there was not a line in it which might not be read
aloud in any family." [6] But she took comfort for the "tomahawking"
which Messrs. Croker and Lockhart administered in the *Quarterly
Review,* from the example of Mr. Malthus. "I wonder whether it ever
kept you awake a minute?" she asked him. "Never after the first fortnight," was his reply.[7] So beautifully in one number did she portray
the blessedness of domestic life that Malthus called round to thank her
for it. Noble are those who marry when they love, and still nobler are
those "who let it go by for conscience' sake, and do not ask for it
again"—had been the moral of the tale.

How much one would give to have been present at that scene!—he
the married clergyman virtuous and benevolent, she the maiden lady
whose mind, though secular, was as nicely pure, the speaker with his
hollow palate, the listener with her ear trumpet straining to lose no
word, and the two in such spiritual affinity that she did not even need
her trumpet to catch his mild and resonant vowels. To Miss Martineau's keeping we therefore commit this famous ex-Fellow of Jesus.

III. Mr. Keynes

In his preface to *The Revolt of Islam,* Shelley wrote:

Metaphysics, and enquiries into moral and political science, have become
little else than vain attempts to revive exploded superstitions, or sophisms
like those of Mr. Malthus, calculated to lull the oppressors of mankind into
a security of everlasting triumph.

Thus spoke the son-in-law of Godwin, against whose better hopes
for mankind the *Essay on Population* had been directed. Nor did the
other poet, Malthus's fellow-student at Jesus, Coleridge, take a more
favourable view: "Are we now to have a quarto to teach us that
great misery and great vice arise from poverty, and that there must be

---

[6] Harriet Martineau's *Autobiography,* I, 200.
[7] *Ibid.,* 211.

poverty in its worst shape wherever there are more mouths than loaves and more Heads than Brains?"   "The remaining marginal notes," Dr. Bonar writes, "are chiefly of an interjectional character (such as 'Ass!'), many of them not very refined."

Thus to the poet of spiritual revolution and to the poet of spiritual conservatism alike Malthus appeared as a symbol of the sophisms of the economists—the ingenious and hateful tautologists who, out of the bowels of their humanitarianism, can prove, by means of truisms, that all attempts to mitigate poverty and misery are destined to increase it; that impulsive charity is a lesser social virtue than enlightened self-interest; and that all will be for the best possible in a miserable world if the business men are left with the least interference to get on with their beneficent pursuit of the survival of the fittest—meaning those financially most gifted.

This is how two diverse poets, having the highest powers of intel-lectual insight, interpreted what they were being told. Neither is such a charge, directed against the economists of the nineteenth century, wholly false. Nor have we to-day wholly escaped from it. The work begun by Malthus and completed by Ricardo did, in fact, provide an immensely powerful intellectual foundation to justify the *status quo,* to ward off experiments, to damp enthusiasm, and to keep us all in order; and it was a just recompense that they should have thrown up Karl Marx as their misbegotten progeny.

It is not entirely unfair that the memory of Malthus should be thus associated.   As the first edition of the *Essay* was directed against Godwin's *Political Justice,* so in the second appears the often-quoted passage against Paine's *Rights of Man:*

A man who is born into a world already possessed, if he cannot get subsistence from his parents on whom he has a just demand, and if the society do not want his labour, has no claim of *right* to the smallest portion of food, and, in fact, has no business to be where he is. At Nature's mighty feast there is no vacant cover for him. She tells him to be gone. . . .

And when Samuel Whitbread proposed "to empower parishes to build cottages," Malthus wrote a pamphlet to urge that "the difficulty of procuring habitations" must on no account be alleviated.

Yet this association of the name of Malthus overlooks the fact that his life and work as an economist falls into two divided parts, each arising out of the events and influences surrounding him; and that the second part was an unavailing effort to upset the theory which Ricardo and his school were riveting on our necks. In the passage from which I have quoted Shelley continues:

Our works of fiction and poetry have been overshadowed by the same infectious gloom. But mankind appear to me to be emerging from their trance. I am aware, methinks, of a slow, gradual, silent change.

And in a footnote he generously remarks certain changes in the later editions of the *Essay on Population* "as a symptom of the revival of public hope." Let me read to you the passage near the conclusion of the second edition of the *Essay on Population* which Shelley doubtless had in mind:

On the whole, therefore, though our future prospects respecting the mitigation of the evils arising from the principle of population may not be so bright as we could wish, yet they are far from being entirely disheartening, and by no means preclude that gradual and progressive improvement in human society which, before the late wild speculations on the subject, was the object of rational expectation. To the laws of property and marriage, and to the apparently narrow principle of self-love, which prompts each individual to exert himself in bettering his condition, we are indebted for all the noblest exertions of human genius, for everything that distinguishes the civilised from the savage state. A strict inquiry into the principle of population leads us strongly to the conclusion, that we shall never be able to throw down the ladder by which we have risen to this eminence; but it by no means proves that we may not rise higher by the same means. The structure of society, in its great features, will probably always remain unchanged. We have every reason to believe that it will always consist of a class of proprietors, and a class of labourers; but the condition of each, and the proportion which they bear to each other, may be so altered as greatly to improve the harmony and beauty of the whole. It would, indeed, be a melancholy reflection, that, while the views of physical science are daily enlarging, so as scarcely to be bounded by the most distant horizon, the science of moral and political philosophy should be confined within such narrow limits, or at best be so feeble in its influence, as to be unable to counteract the increasing obstacles to human happiness arising from the progress of population. But however formidable these obstacles may have appeared in some parts of this work, it is hoped that the general result of the inquiry is such, as not to make us give up the cause of the improvement of human society in despair. The partial good which seems to be attainable is worthy of all our exertions; is sufficient to direct our efforts and animate our prospects. And although we cannot expect that the virtue and happiness of mankind will keep pace with the brilliant career of physical discovery, yet, if we are not wanting to ourselves, we may confidently indulge the hope that, to no unimportant extent, they will be influenced by its progress, and will partake in its success.

In the closing years of the eighteenth century the misery of the labouring class presented itself to Malthus as chiefly consisting in their low standard of life. In the years after Waterloo and the end of the war it presented itself to him as chiefly a problem of unemployment. To these two problems his work as an economist was successively directed. As the solution of the first, he had offered his principle of population. Nothing, he urged, could raise the low reward of this factor of production except the curtailment of its supply. But whereas in the first edition the stress is on the *difficulty* of curtailing its supply, in the later editions the stress is on the *importance* of curtailing its supply. In the second half of his life he was preoccupied with the post-war unemployment which then first disclosed itself on a formidable scale, and he found the explanation in what he called the insufficiency of effective demand; to cure which he called for a spirit of free expenditure, public works and a policy of expansionism. This time is was Malthus himself who was overwhelmed by the "sophisms of the economists." A hundred years were to pass before there would be anyone to read with even a shadow of sympathy and understanding his powerful and unanswerable attacks on the great Ricardo. So Malthus's name has been immortalised by his *Principle of Population,* and the brilliant intuitions of his more far-reaching *Principle of Effective Demand* have been forgotten.

Let us, however, think of Malthus to-day as the first of the Cambridge economists—as, above all, a great pioneer of the application of a frame of formal thinking to the complex confusion of the world of daily events. Malthus approached the central problems of economic theory by the best of all routes. He began to be interested as a philosopher and moral scientist, one who had been brought up in the Cambridge of Paley, applying the à priori method of the political philosopher. He then immersed himself for several years in the facts of economic history and of the contemporary world, applying the methods of historical induction and filling his mind with a mass of the material of experience. And then finally he returned to à priori thought, but this time to the pure theory of the economist proper, and sought, being one of the very first to seek, to impose the methods of formal thought on the material presented by events, so as to penetrate these events with understanding by a mixture of intuitive selection and formal principle and thus to interpret the problem and propose the remedy. In short, from being a caterpillar of a moral scientist and a chrysalis of an historian, he could at last spread the wings of his thought and survey the world as an economist!

So, let me in conclusion read to you the passage in which Malthus summed up what should be for an economist the relation of experience to theory:

We are continually hearing declamations against theory and theorists, by men who pride themselves upon the distinction of being practical. It must be acknowledged that bad theories are very bad things, and the authors of them useless, and sometimes pernicious members of society. But these advocates of practice do not seem to be aware that they themselves very often come under this description, and that a great part of them may be classed among the most mischievous theorists of their time. When a man faithfully relates any facts which have come within the scope of his own observation, however confined it may have been, he undoubtedly adds to the sum of general knowledge, and confers a benefit on society. But when, from this confined experience, from the management of his own little farm, or the details of the workhouse in his neighbourhood, he draws a general inference, as is very frequently the case, he then at once erects himself into a theorist, and is more dangerous; because experience being the only just foundation for theory, people are often caught merely by the sound of the word, and do not stop to make the distinction between that partial experience which, on such subjects, is no foundation whatever for a just theory, and that general experience on which alone a just theory can be founded.

I claim for Malthus a profound economic intuition and an unusual combination of keeping an open mind to the shifting picture of experience and of constantly applying to its interpretation the principles of formal thought. I believe that a century hence, here in his Alma Mater, we shall commemorate him with undiminished regard.

McCulloch

on

Ricardo

David Ricardo (1772–1823) came to economics as a successful man of affairs who was deeply interested in monetary problems. His *Principles of Political Economy and Taxation* (1817) prove him a master of the analytical technique of abstract reasoning. Adhering to the labor theory of value, Ricardo's work was to acquire great influence on the thought of the socialists as well as of the land reformers. Ricardo is best known for his interpretation of rent as differential return from the "original and indestructible qualities of the soil," which, in conjunction with the subsistence theory of wages, made the landowning class appear as the principal beneficiary of economic development. To the theory of international trade, Ricardo contributed the principle of comparative advantage, which, elaborated by Mill and later writers, served as basis of the free-trade doctrines endorsed by most economists. In the field of taxation, Ricardo emphasized the relevance of the incidence of a tax rather than its yield.

John Ramsay McCulloch (1789–1864) was a contemporary of Ricardo, of whom he was a friend and faithful apostle. Himself an economist of considerable reputation at his time, McCulloch is remembered for his bibliographical and biographical studies as well as for descriptive and statistical investigations. As an original contributor to economic theory, his position is a minor one.

(For another appraisal of Ricardo, by Alfred Marshall, see pp. 173 ff., below.)

MR RICARDO was placed, in early life, under circumstances apparently the least favourable for the formation of those habits of patient and comprehensive investigation, which afterwards raised him to a high rank among political philosophers.

He was the third of a numerous family, and was born on the 19th of April 1772. His father, a native of Holland, and of the Jewish persuasion, settled in this country early in life. He is said to have been a man of good talents and of the strictest integrity; and having become a member of the Stock Exchange, he acquired a respectable fortune, and possessed considerable influence in his circle. David, the subject of the present memoir, was destined for the same line of business as his father; and received, partly in England, and partly at a school in Holland, where he resided two years, such an education as is usually given to young men intended for the mercantile profession. Classical learning formed no part of his early instruction; and it has been questioned, with how much justice we shall not undertake to decide, whether its acquisition would have done him service; and whether it might not probably have made him seek for relaxation in the study of elegant literature, rather than in the severer exercises of the understanding; and prompted him to adopt opinions sanctioned by authority, without inquiring very anxiously into the grounds on which they rested.

Mr Ricardo began to be confidentially employed by his father in the business of the Stock Exchange, when he was only fourteen years of age. Neither then, however, nor at any subsequent period, was he wholly engrossed by the details of his profession. From his earliest years he evinced a taste for abstract reasoning; and manifested that determination to probe every subject of interest to the bottom, and to form his opinion upon it according to the conviction of his mind, which was a distinguishing feature of his character.

Mr Ricardo, senior, had been accustomed to subscribe, without investigation, to the opinions of his ancestors, on all questions connected with religion and politics; and he was desirous that his children should do the same. But this system of passive obedience, and of blind

[Reprinted from *The Works of David Ricardo,* ed. by J. R. McCulloch, London, 1846.]

submission to the dictates of authority, was quite repugnant to the principles of young Ricardo, who, at the same time that he never failed to testify the sincerest affection and respect for his father, found reason to differ from him on many important points, and even to secede from the Hebrew faith.

Not long after this event, and shortly after he had attained the age of majority, Mr Ricardo formed an union, productive of unalloyed domestic happiness, with Miss Wilkinson. Having been separated from his father, he was now thrown on his own resources; and commenced business for himself. At this important epoch of his history, the oldest and most respectable members of the Stock Exchange gave a striking proof of the esteem entertained by them for his talents and character, by voluntarily coming forward to support him in his undertakings. His success exceeded the most sanguine expectations of his friends, and in a few years he realised an ample fortune.

"The talent for obtaining wealth," says one of Mr Ricardo's near relations, from whose account of his life we have borrowed these particulars, "is not held in much estimation; but perhaps in nothing did Mr R. more evince his extraordinary powers, than he did in his business. His complete knowledge of all its intricacies; his surprising quickness at figures and calculation; his capability of getting through, without any apparent exertion, the immense transactions in which he was concerned; his coolness and judgment, combined certainly with (for him) a fortunate tissue of public events, enabled him to leave all his contemporaries at the Stock Exchange far behind, and to raise himself infinitely higher, not only in fortune, but in general character and estimation, than any man had ever done before in that house. Such was the impression which these qualities had made on his competitors, that several of the most discerning among them, long before he had emerged into public notoriety, prognosticated in their admiration, that he would live to fill some of the higher stations in the state." [1]

According as his solicitude about his success in life declined, Mr Ricardo devoted a greater portion of his time to scientific and literary pursuits. When about twenty-five years of age, he began the study of some branches of mathematical science, and made considerable progress in chemistry and mineralogy. He fitted up a laboratory, formed a collection of minerals, and was one of the original members of the Geological Society. But he never entered warmly into the study of these sciences. They were not adapted to the peculiar cast of his

[1] See an Account of the Life of Mr Ricardo in the *Annual Obituary* for 1823, supposed to be written by one of his brothers.

mind; and he abandoned them entirely, as soon as his attention was directed to the more congenial study of Political Economy.

Mr Ricardo is stated to have first become acquainted with the *Wealth of Nations* in 1799, while on a visit at Bath, to which he had accompanied Mrs Ricardo for the benefit of her health. He was highly gratified by its perusal; and it is most probable that the inquiries about which it is conversant, continued henceforth to engage a considerable share of his attention, though it was not till a later period that his spare time was almost exclusively occupied with their study.

Mr Ricardo came, for the first time, before the public as an author in 1809. The rise in the market price of bullion, and the fall of the exchange that had taken place in the course of that year, had excited a good deal of attention. Mr Ricardo applied himself to the consideration of the subject; and the studies in which he had latterly been engaged, combined with the experience he had derived from his moneyed transactions, enabled him not only to perceive the true causes of the phenomena in question, but to trace and exhibit their practical bearing and real effect. He began this investigation without intending to lay the result of his researches before the public. But having shown his manuscript to the late Mr Perry, the proprietor and editor of the *Morning Chronicle,* the latter prevailed upon him, though not without considerable difficulty, to consent to its publication, in the shape of letters, in that journal. The first of these letters appeared on the 6th of September 1809. They made a considerable impression, and elicited various answers. This success, and the increasing interest of the subject, induced Mr Ricardo to commit his opinions upon it to the judgment of the public, in a more enlarged and systematic form, in the tract entitled *"The High Price of Bullion a Proof of the Depreciation of Bank Notes."* This tract led the way in the far-famed bullion controversy. It issued from the press several months previously to the appointment of the Bullion Committee; and is believed to have had no inconsiderable effect in forwarding that important measure. In this tract Mr Ricardo showed that redundancy and deficiency of currency are only *relative* terms; and that so long as the currency of any particular country consists exclusively of gold and silver coins, or of paper immediately convertible into such coins, its value can neither rise above nor fall below the value of the metallic currencies of other countries, by a greater sum than will suffice to defray the expense of importing foreign coin or bullion, if the currency be deficient; or of exporting a portion of the existing supply, if it be redundant. But when a country issues inconvertible paper notes (as was then the case in England), they cannot be exported to other countries in the event of their becoming redundant at home; and whenever, under such circumstances, the exchange with foreign states is depressed below, or the price of bullion rises above, its mint price, more than the cost of sending coin or bullion abroad, it shows conclusively that too much paper has been issued, and that its value is *depreciated from excess*. The principles which pervade the Report of the Bullion Committee, are substantially the same with those established by Mr Ricardo in this pamphlet, but the more comprehensive and popular manner in which they are illustrated in the Report, and the circumstance of their being recommended by a Committee composed of some of the ablest men in the country, gave them a weight and authority which they could not otherwise have obtained. And though the prejudices and ignorance of some, and the interested, and therefore determined, opposition of others, prevented for a while the adoption of the measures proposed by Mr Ricardo and the Committee for restoring the currency to a sound and healthy state, they were afterwards carried into full effect; and afford one of the most memorable examples in our history, of the triumph of principle over selfishness, sophistry, and error.

The *fourth* edition of this tract is the most valuable. An Appendix added to it has some acute observations on some difficult questions in the theory of exchange; and it also contains the first germ of the original idea of making bank notes exchangeable for bars of gold bullion.

Among those who entered the lists in opposition to the principles laid down, and the practical measures suggested in Mr Ricardo's tract, and in the Report of the Bullion Committee, a prominent place is due to Mr Bosanquet. This gentleman had great experience as a merchant; and as he professed that the statements and conclusions embodied in his *"Practical Observations,"* which are completely at variance with those in the Report, were the result of a careful examination of the theoretical opinions of the Committee by the test of fact and experiment, they were well fitted to make, and did make, a very considerable impression. The triumph of Mr Bosanquet was, however, of very short duration. Mr Ricardo did not hesitate to attack this formidable adversary in his stronghold. His tract, entitled, *"Reply to Mr Bosanquet's Practical Observations on the Report of the Bullion Committee,"* was published in 1811, and is one of the best essays that has appeared on any disputed question of Political Economy. In this pamphlet, Mr Ricardo met Mr Bosanquet on his own ground, and overthrew him with his own weapons. He examined all the proofs which Mr Bosanquet had brought forward, of the pretended discrepancy between the facts stated in his own tract, which he said were consistent with experience, and the theory laid down in the Bullion Report; and showed that Mr B. had either mistaken the cases by which he proposed to test the theory, or that the discrepancy was only apparent, and was entirely a consequence of his inability to apply the theory, and not of anything erroneous or deficient in it. The victory of Mr Ricardo was perfect and complete; and the elaborate errors and mis-statements of Mr Bosanquet served only, to use the words of Dr Coppleston, "to illustrate the abilities of the writer who stepped forward to vindicate the truth." [2]

This tract affords a striking example of the ascendency which those who possess a knowledge both of principle and practice, have over those who are familiar only with the latter; and though the interest of the question which led to its publication has now subsided, it will always be read with delight by such as are not insensible of the high gratification which all ingenuous minds must feel in observing the ease with which a superior intellect clears away the irrelevant matter with which a question has been designedly embarrassed, reduces false facts to their just value, and traces and exhibits the constant operation of the same general principle through all the mazy intricacies of practical detail.

The merit of these pamphlets was duly appreciated; and Mr Ricardo's society was, in consequence, courted by men of the first eminence, who were not less pleased with his modesty, and unassuming manners, than with the vigour of his understanding. He formed, about this time, that intimacy with Mr Malthus, and Mr Mill, the historian of British India, which ended only with his death. To the latter he was particularly attached, and readily acknowledged how much he owed to his friendship.

Mr Ricardo next appeared as an author in 1815, during the discussions on the bill, afterwards passed into a law, for raising the limit at which foreign corn might be imported for consumption, to 80s. Mr Malthus, and a "Fellow of University College, Oxford" (afterwards Sir Edward West), had, by a curious coincidence, in tracts published almost consentaneously, elucidated the true theory of rent, which, though discovered by Dr Anderson as early as 1777, appears to have been entirely forgotten. But neither of these gentlemen perceived the bearing of the theory on the question in regard to the restriction of the importation of foreign corn. This was reserved for Mr Ricardo, who, in his *"Essay on the Influence of a Low Price of Corn on the Profits of Stock,"* showed the effect of an increase in the price of raw produce on wages and profits; and founded a strong argument in favour of the

---

[2] First Letter to the Right Hon. Robert Peel, by one of his Constituents, p. 61.

freedom of the corn trade, on the very grounds on which Mr Malthus had endeavoured to show the propriety of subjecting it to fresh restrictions.

In 1816, Mr Ricardo published his *"Proposals for an Economical and Secure Currency, with Observations on the Profits of the Bank of England."* In this pamphlet he examined the circumstances which determine the value of money, when every individual has the power to supply it, and when that power is restricted or placed under a monopoly; and he showed that, in the former case, its value will depend, like that of all other freely supplied articles, on its cost; while in the latter, it will be unaffected by that circumstance, and will depend on the extent to which it may be issued compared with the demand. This is a principle of great importance; for, it shows that intrinsic worth is not necessary to a currency, and that, provided the supply of paper notes, declared to be legal tender, be sufficiently limited, their value may be maintained on a par with the value of gold, or raised to any higher level. If, therefore, it were practicable to devise a plan for preserving the value of paper on a level with that of gold, without making it convertible into coin at the pleasure of the holder, the heavy expense of a metallic currency would be saved. To effect this desirable object, Mr Ricardo proposed that, instead of being made exchangeable for gold coins, bank notes should be made exchangeable for *bars of gold bullion of the standard weight and purity.* This plan, than which nothing can be more simple, was obviously fitted to check the over-issue of paper quite as effectually as it is checked by making it convertible into coin; while, as bars could not be used as currency, it prevented any gold from getting into circulation, and consequently saved the expenses of coinage, and the wear and tear, and loss of coins. Mr Ricardo's proposal was recommended by the Committees of the Houses of Lords and Commons appointed, in 1819, to consider the expediency of the Bank of England resuming cash payments; and was afterwards adopted in the bill for their resumption introduced by Mr (now Sir Robert) Peel. In practice it was found completely to answer the object of checking over-issue. But inasmuch as it required that the place of sovereigns should be filled with one pound notes, the forgery of the latter began to be extensively carried on; and it was wisely judged better to incur the expense of recurring to and keeping up a mixed currency, than to continue a plan which, though productive of a large saving, held out an all but irresistible temptation to crime.

At length, in 1817, Mr Ricardo published his great work on the *"Principles of Political Economy and Taxation."* This was a step which he did not take without much hesitation. He was not, and did not affect to be, insensible of the value of literary and philosophical reputation; but his modesty always led him to undervalue his own powers; and having acquired a very high degree of celebrity as a writer on currency, he was unwilling to risk what he already possessed, by attempting to gain more. Ultimately, however, he was prevailed upon, by the entreaties of his friends, to allow his work to be sent to press. Its appearance forms a memorable æra in the history of political science. Exclusive of many valuable subsidiary inquiries, Mr Ricardo has pointed out, in this work, the source and limiting principle of exchangeable value, and has traced the laws which determine the distribution of wealth among the various ranks and orders of society. The powers of mind displayed in these investigations, the dexterity with which the most abstruse questions are unravelled, the sagacity displayed in tracing the operation of general principles, in disentangling them from such as are of a secondary and accidental nature, and in perceiving and estimating their remote consequences, have never been surpassed; and will for ever secure the name of Ricardo a conspicuous place among those who have done most to unfold the mechanism of society, and to discover the circumstances on which the well-being of its various orders must always mainly depend.

Mr Ricardo maintains, in this work, the fundamental principle, that the exchangeable value of commodities or their relative worth, as compared with each other, depends exclusively on *the quantities of labour* necessarily required to produce them, and bring them to market. Smith had shown that this principle determined the value of commodities in the earlier stages of society, before land had been appropriated and capital accumulated; but he supposed that, after land had become property and rent began to be paid, and after capital had been amassed and workmen began to be hired by capitalists, the value of commodities fluctuated not only according to variations in the labour required to produce and bring them to market, but also according to variations of rents and wages. But Mr Ricardo has shown that this theory is erroneous, and that the value of commodities is determined in all states of society by the same principle, or by the quantity of labour required for their production. He showed that variations of profits or wages, by affecting different commodities to the same, or nearly the same, extent, would either have no influence over their exchangeable value, or if they had any, it would depend upon the degree in which they occasionally affect some products more than others. And Dr Anderson and others having already shown that rent is not an element of cost or value, it follows that the cost or value of all freely produced commodities, the supply of which may be indefinitely increased (abstracting from temporary variations of supply and demand), depends wholly on the quantity of labour required for their production, and not upon the rate at which that labour may be paid; so that, supposing the labour required to produce any number of commodities to remain constant, their cost and value will also remain constant, whether wages fall from 3s. to 1s., or rise from 3s. to 5s. or 7s. a day. This is the fundamental theorem of the science of value, and the clue which unravels the intricate labyrinth of the laws which regulate the distribution of wealth. Its discovery has shed a flood of light on what was previously shrouded in all but impenetrable mystery, and the apparently knotty and hitherto insoluble questions regarding the action of wages and profits on each other and on prices, have since ceased to present any insuperable difficulties. What the researches of Locke and Smith did for the production of wealth, those of Ricardo have done for its value and distribution.

The establishment of general principles being Mr Ricardo's great object, he has paid comparatively little attention to their practical application, and sometimes, indeed, he has in great measure overlooked the circumstances by which they are occasionally countervailed. In illustration of this we may mention, that society being laid under the necessity of constantly resorting to inferior soils to obtain additional supplies of food, Mr Ricardo lays it down that, in the progress of society, raw produce and wages have a constant tendency to rise and profits to fall. And this, no doubt, is in the abstract true. But it must at the same time be observed, that while on the one hand society is obliged constantly to resort to inferior soils, agriculture is on the other hand susceptible of indefinite improvement; and this improvement necessarily in so far countervails the decreasing fertility of the soil; and may, and in fact very frequently does, more than countervail it. Mr Ricardo has also very generally overlooked the influence of increased prices in diminishing consumption and stimulating industry, so that his conclusions, though true according to his assumptions, do not always harmonise with what really takes place. But his is not a practical work; and it did not enter into his plan to exhibit the circumstances that give rise to the discrepancies in question. The *"Principles of Political Economy and Taxation"* is not even a systematic treatise, but is principally an inquiry respecting certain fundamental principles, most of which had previously been undiscovered. And though it be often exceedingly difficult, or, it may be, all but impossible, to estimate the extent to which these principles may in certain cases be modified by other principles and combinations of circumstances, it is obviously of the greatest importance to have ascertained their existence. They are so many land-marks to which to refer and can never be lost sight of even in matters most essentially practical.

That part of Mr Ricardo's work, in which he applies his principles to discover the incidence of taxes on rent, profit, wages, and raw produce, is more practical than the others; and must always be a subject of careful study to those who wish to make themselves well acquainted with this department of political science.

Mr Ricardo had now become an extensive landed proprietor, and had wholly retired from business, with a fortune acquired with the universal respect and esteem of his competitors. But he did not retire from the bustle of active life, to the mere enjoyment of his acres—*Non fuit consilium socordia atque desidia bonum otium conterere*—he had other objects in view; and while his leisure hours, when in the country, were chiefly devoted to inquiries connected with that science, of which he was now confessedly at the head, he determined to extend the sphere of his usefulness, by entering the House of Commons. In 1819 he took his seat as member for Portarlington. His diffidence in his own powers had, however, nearly deprived the public of the services which he rendered in this situation. In a letter to one of his friends, dated the 7th of April 1819, he says: "You will have seen that I have taken my seat in the House of Commons. I fear that I shall be of little use there. I have twice attempted to speak; but I proceeded in the most embarrassed manner; and I have no hope of conquering the alarm with which I am assailed the moment I hear the sound of my own voice." And in a letter to the same gentleman, dated the 22d of June 1819, he says: "I thank you for your endeavours to inspire me with confidence on the occasion of my addressing the House. Their indulgent reception of me has, in some degree, made the task of speaking more easy to me; but there are yet so many formidable obstacles to my success, and some, I fear, of a nature nearly insurmountable, that I apprehend it will be wisdom and sound discretion in me to content myself with giving silent votes." Fortunately he did not adopt this resolution. The difficulties with which he had at first to struggle, and his diffidence in himself, gradually subsided; while the mildness of his manners, the mastery which he possessed over the subjects on which he spoke, and the purity of his intentions, speedily secured him a very extensive influence both in the House and the country, and gave great weight to his opinions.

Mr Ricardo was not one of those who make speeches to suit the ephemeral circumstances and politics of the day: he spoke only from principle, and with a fixed resolution never to diverge in any degree from the path which it pointed out; he neither concealed nor modified an opinion for the purpose of conciliating the favour, or of disarming the prejudices or hostility, of any man or set of men; nor did he ever make a speech or give a vote which he was not well convinced was founded on just principles, and calculated to promote the lasting interests of the public. Trained to habits of profound thinking, independent in his fortune, and inflexible in his principles, Mr Ricardo had little in common with mere party politicians. The public good was the grand object of his parliamentary exertions; and he laboured to promote it, not by engaging in party combinations, but by supporting the rights and liberties of all classes, and by unfolding the true sources of national wealth and general prosperity.

The change that has taken place in the public opinion respecting the financial and commercial policy of the country, since the period when Mr Ricardo obtained a seat in the House of Commons, is as complete as it is gratifying. Not only are the most enlarged principles advocated by all the leading members of both Houses; not only are they now ready to admit that the exclusive system is founded on vicious principles, and that it is sound policy to admit the freest competition in every branch of industry, and to deal with all the world on fair and liberal principles; but they are about to make these doctrines a part of the law of the land, and to give them the sanction of parliamentary authority. Sir Robert Peel has the signal merit of having, despite the most formidable obstacles, carried out and established in their fullest extent the great principles of commercial freedom developed by Smith and his followers. And we believe that that distinguished statesman would readily admit that the writings and speeches of Mr Ricardo have powerfully contributed to pave the way for this most desirable consummation. As he was known to be a master in "the master-science of civil life," his opinion, from the moment he entered the House of Commons, was referred to on all important occasions;[3] and he acquired additional influence and consideration, according as experience served to render the House and the country better acquainted with his talents, and his singleness of purpose.

In 1820, Mr Ricardo contributed an article on the *"Funding System,"* to the Supplement to the "Encyclopædia Britannica." This tract, though somewhat confused in its arrangement, embraces many

---

[3] Mr Ricardo made the first of his prominent appearances on the 24th of May 1819, in the debate on the resolutions proposed by Mr (now Sir Robert) Peel respecting the resumption of cash payments. He did not rise until he was loudly called upon from all sides of the House.

valuable discussions. He was a decided friend to the plan for raising the supplies for a war within the year, by an equivalent increase of taxation; and he also thought (in which opinion few probably will be disposed to concur), that it would be not only expedient but practicable to pay off the public debt by an assessment on capital.

In 1822, Mr Ricardo published, during the parliamentary discussions on the subject of the corn laws, his tract on *"Protection to Agriculture."* This is the best of all his pamphlets, and is, indeed, a *chef-d'œuvre.* The important questions respecting remunerating price, the influence of a low and high value of corn over wages and profits, the influence of taxation over agriculture and manufactures, and many other topics of equal difficulty and interest, are all discussed in the short compass of eighty or ninety pages, with a precision and clearness that leaves nothing to be desired. Had Mr Ricardo never written any thing else, this pamphlet would have placed him in the first rank of political economists.

Though not robust, Mr Ricardo's constitution was apparently good, and his health such as to promise a long life of usefulness. He had, indeed, been subject, for several years, to an affection in one of his ears; but as it had not given him any serious inconvenience, he paid it but little attention. When he retired to his seat in Gloucestershire (Gatcomb Park), subsequently to the close of the session of 1823, he was in excellent health and spirits; and, besides completing a tract, containing a plan for the establishment of a *National Bank,* he engaged, with his usual ardour, in elaborate inquiries regarding some of the more abstruse economical doctrines. But he was not destined to bring these inquiries to a close! Early in September he was suddenly seized with a violent pain in the diseased ear: the symptoms were not, however, considered unfavourable; and the breaking of an imposthume that had been formed within the ear contributed greatly to his relief. But the amendment was only transitory; within two days, inflammation recommenced; and after a period of the greatest agony, pressure on the brain ensued, which produced a stupor that continued until death terminated his sufferings, on the 11th September, in his 52d year.

In private life, Mr Ricardo was most amiable. He was an indulgent father and husband; and an affectionate, and zealous friend. No man was ever more thoroughly free from every species of artifice and pretension; more sincere, plain, and unassuming. He was particularly fond of assembling intelligent men around him, and of conversing in the most unrestrained manner on all topics of interest, but more especially on those connected with his favourite science. On these as on all occasions, he readily gave way to others, and never discovered the least impatience to speak; but when he did speak, the solidity of his judgment, his candour, and his extraordinary talent for resolving a question into its elements, and for setting the most difficult and complicated subjects in the most striking point of view, arrested the attention of every one, and delighted all who heard him. He never entered into an argument, whether in public or private, for the sake of displaying ingenuity, of baffling an opponent, or of gaining a victory. The discovery of truth was his exclusive object. He was ever open to conviction; and if he were satisfied he had either advanced or supported an erroneous opinion, he was the first to acknowledge his error, and to caution others against it.

Few men have possessed in a higher degree than Mr Ricardo, the talent of speaking and conversing with clearness and facility on the abstrusest topics. In this respect, his speeches were greatly superior to his publications. The latter cannot be readily understood and followed without considerable attention; but nothing could exceed the ease and felicity with which he illustrated and explained the most difficult questions of Political Economy, both in private conversation and in his speeches. Without being forcible, his style of speaking was easy, fluent, and agreeable. It was impossible to take him off his guard. To those who were not familiar with his speculations, some of his positions were apt to appear paradoxical; but the paradox was only in appearance. He rarely advanced an opinion on which he had not deeply reflected, and without examining it in every point of view; and the readiness with which he overthrew the most specious objections that the ablest men in the House could make to his doctrines, is the best proof of their correctness, and of the superiority of his understanding. That there were greater orators, and men of more varied and general acquirements in Parliament than Mr Ricardo, we readily allow; but we are bold to say, that in point of deep, clear, and comprehensive intellect, he had no superiors, and very few, if any, equals, either in Parliament or in the country.

He was not less generous than intelligent; he was never slow to come forward to the relief of the poor and the distressed; and while he contributed to almost every charitable institution in the metropolis, he supported, at his own expense, an alms-house for the poor, and two schools for the instruction of the young in the vicinity of his seat in the country.

Besides the publications previously enumerated, Mr Ricardo left one or two manuscripts. Among others, a *"Plan for the Establish-*

ment of a National Bank" was found in a finished state, and was soon
after published.

He also left *"Notes"* on Mr Malthus's Principles of Political Economy; containing a vindication of his own doctrines from the objections
of Mr Malthus, and showing the mistakes into which he conceives Mr
M. had fallen.   But we doubt whether they have sufficient interest to
warrant their publication.[4]

Though not properly belonging to the Whig party, Mr Ricardo
voted almost uniformly with the Opposition. He was impressed with
the conviction, that many advantages would result from giving the people a greater influence over the choice of their representatives in the
House of Commons than they then possessed; and he was so far a
friend to the system of the radical reformers, as to give his cordial support to the plan of voting by ballot; which he considered as the best
means for securing the mass of the electors against improper solicita-
tions, and for enabling them to vote in favour of the candidates whom
they really approved. He did not, however, agree with the radical
reformers in their plan of universal suffrage; he thought the elective
franchise should be given to all who possessed a certain amount of
property; but he was of opinion, that while it would be a very hazardous experiment, no practical good would result from giving the franchise indiscriminately to all. His opinions on these subjects are fully
stated in the *Essay on Parliamentary Reform,* and in the *Speech on
the Ballot.*

Of the value of the services rendered by Mr Ricardo to Political
Economy, there can be, among intelligent men, only one opinion.
His works have made a very great addition to the mass of useful and
universally interesting truths, and afford some of the finest examples
to be met with of discriminating analysis, and of profound and refined discussion.   The brevity with which he has stated some of his
most important propositions; their intimate dependence on each other;
the fewness of his illustrations; and the mathematical cast he has given
to his reasoning, render it sometimes a little difficult for readers, unaccustomed to such investigations, readily to follow him.   But we can
venture to affirm, that those who will give to his works the attention
of which they are so worthy, will find them to be as logical and conclusive as they are profound and important.   It was the opinion of
Quintilian, that the students of eloquence who were highly delighted
with Cicero, had made no inconsiderable progress in their art: and the
same may, without hesitation, be said of the students of Political Econ-

---

[4] [Published in 1928, ed. by J. H. Hollander and T. E. Gregory.—Ed.]

omy who find pleasure in the works of Mr Ricardo: *Ille se profecisse sciat, cui Ricardo valde placebit.*

When the circumstances under which Mr Ricardo spent the greater part of his life are brought under view; and when it is also recollected that he died at the early age of *fifty-one,* it may be truly said that very few have ever achieved so much. His industry was as remarkable as his sagacity and his candour.

"The history of Mr Ricardo," to use the words of Mr Mill, "holds out a bright and inspiring example. Mr Ricardo had every thing to do for himself; and he did every thing. Let not the generous youth, whose aspirations are higher than his circumstances, despair of attaining either the highest intellectual excellence, or the highest influence on the welfare of his species, when he recollects in what circumstances Mr Ricardo opened, and in what he closed, his memorable life. He had his fortune to make; his mind to form; he had even his education to commence and conduct. In a field of the most intense competition, he realized a large fortune, with the universal esteem and affection of those who could best judge of the honour and purity of his acts. Amid this scene of active exertion and practical detail, he cultivated and he acquired habits of intense, and patient, and comprehensive thinking; such as have been rarely equalled, and never excelled."

Marshall

——————————————————— on ———

Ricardo

Alfred Marshall, the founder of the Cambridge school of neo-classical economics, here supplements McCulloch's appraisal of Ricardo. Marshall's essay is specifically devoted to Ricardo's theory of value, the classical statement of the labor theory of value. Marshall examines this theory with especial reference to the criticisms raised against it by Stanley Jevons.

(On Jevons, see pp. 489 ff.; on Marshall, pp. 718 ff.)

§ 1. WHEN RICARDO was addressing a general audience, he drew largely upon his wide and intimate knowledge of the facts of life, using them "for illustration, verification, or the premises of argument." But in his *Principles of Political Economy* "the same questions are treated with a singular exclusion of all reference to the actual world around him." [1] And he wrote to Malthus in May, 1820 (the same year in which Malthus published his *Principles of Political Economy considered with a view to their practical application*), "Our differences may in some respects, I think, be ascribed to your considering my book as more practical than I intended it to be. My object was to elucidate principles, and to do this I imagined strong cases, that I might show the operation of those principles." His book makes no pretence to be systematic. He was with difficulty induced to publish it; and if in writing it he had in view any readers at all, they were chiefly those statesmen and business men with whom he associated. So he purposely omitted many things which were necessary for the logical completeness of his argument, but which they would regard as obvious. And further, as he told Malthus in the following October, he was "but a poor master of language." His exposition is as confused as his thought is profound; he uses words in artificial senses which he does not explain, and to which he does not adhere; and he changes from one hypothesis to another without giving notice.

If then we seek to understand him rightly, we must interpret him generously, more generously than he himself interpreted Adam Smith. When his words are ambiguous, we must give them that interpretation which other passages in his writings indicate that he would have wished us to give them. If we do this with the desire to ascertain what he really meant, his doctrines, though very far from complete, are free from many of the errors that are commonly attributed to them.

He considers, for instance (*Principles,* Ch. I. § 1), that utility is

[1] See an admirable article on "Ricardo's Use of Facts" in the first volume of the Harvard *Quarterly Journal of Economics,* by the late Professor Dunbar.

["Ricardo's Theory of Value." From Alfred Marshall, *Principles of Economics,* eighth ed., London, Macmillan and Company, 1920, Appendix I. By permission of the publishers.]

"absolutely essential" to (normal) value though not its measure; while the value of things "of which there is a very limited quantity . . . varies with the wealth and inclinations of those who are desirous to possess them." And elsewhere (*Ib*. Ch. IV.) he insists on the way in which the market fluctuations of prices are determined by the amount available for sale on the one hand, and "the wants and wishes of mankind" on the other.

Again, in a profound, though very incomplete, discussion of the difference between "Value and Riches" he seems to be feeling his way towards the distinction between marginal and total utility. For by Riches he means total utility, and he seems to be always on the point of stating that value corresponds to the increment of riches which results from that part of the commodity which it is only just worth the while of purchasers to buy; and that when the supply runs short, whether temporarily in consequence of a passing accident, or permanently in consequence of an increase in cost of production, there is a rise in that marginal increment of riches which is measured by value, at the same time that there is a diminution in the aggregate riches, the total utility, derived from the commodity. Throughout the whole discussion he is trying to say, though (being ignorant of the terse language of the differential calculus) he did not get hold of the right words in which to say it neatly, that marginal utility is raised and total utility is lessened by any check to supply.

§ 2. But while not thinking that he had much to say that was of great importance on the subject of utility, he believed that the connection between cost of production and value was imperfectly understood; and that erroneous views on this subject were likely to lead the country astray in practical problems of taxation and finance; and so he addressed himself specially to this subject. But here also he made short cuts.

For, though he was aware that commodities fall into three classes according as they obey the law of diminishing, of constant, or of increasing return; yet he thought it best to ignore this distinction in a theory of value applicable to all kinds of commodities. A commodity chosen at random was just as likely to obey one as the other of the two laws of diminishing and of increasing return; and therefore he thought himself justified in assuming provisionally that they all obeyed the law of constant return. In this perhaps he was justified, but he made a mistake in not stating explicitly what he was doing.

He argued in the first Section of his first Chapter that "in the early stages of society" where there is scarcely any use of capital, and where any one man's labour has nearly the same price as any other man's, it is, broadly speaking, true that "the value of a commodity, or the quantity of a commodity for which it will exchange, depends on the relative quantity of labour which is necessary for its production." That is, if two things are made by twelve and four men's labour for a year, all the men being of the same grade, the normal value of the former will be three times that of the latter. For if ten per cent. has to be added for profits on the capital invested in the one case, ten per cent. will need to be added in the other also. [If w be a year's wages of a worker of this class, the costs of production will be $4w \cdot {}^{11}\!/_{100}$, and $12w \cdot {}^{11}\!/_{100}$: and the ratio of these is $4:12$, or $1:3$.]

But he went on to show that these assumptions cannot be properly made in later stages of civilization, and that the relation of value to cost of production is more complex than that with which he started; and his next step was to introduce in Section II. the consideration that "labour of different qualities is differently rewarded." If the wages of a jeweller are twice as great as those of a working labourer, an hour's work of the one must count for two hours' work of the other. Should there be a change in their relative wages, there will of course be a corresponding change in the relative values of things made by them. But instead of analysing, as economists of this generation do, the causes which make (say) jewellers' wages change from one generation to another relatively to those of ordinary labourers, he contented himself with stating that such variations cannot be great.

Next in Section III. he urged that in reckoning the cost of production of a commodity, account must be taken not only of the labour applied immediately to it, but also of that which is bestowed on the implements, tools and buildings with which such labour is assisted; and here the element of time, which he had carefully kept in the background at starting, was necessarily introduced.

Accordingly in Section IV. he discusses more fully the different influences exerted on the value of "a set of commodities" [he uses this simple method sometimes to evade the difficulties of the distinctions between prime cost and total cost]: and especially he takes account of the different effects of the application of circulating capital which is consumed in a single use, and of fixed capital; and again of the time for which labour must be invested in making machinery to make commodities. If that be long, they will have a greater cost of production and be "more valuable to compensate for the greater length of time, which must elapse before they can be brought to market."

And lastly in Section V. he sums up the influence which different lengths of investment, whether direct or indirect, will have upon relative values; arguing correctly that if wages all rise and fall to-

gether the change will have no permanent effect on the relative values
of different commodities. But he argues if the rate of profits falls it
will lower the relative values of those commodities the production of
which requires capital to be invested a long while before they can be
brought to market. For if in one case the average investment is for
a year and requires ten per cent. to be added to the wages bill for
profits; and in another is for two years and requires twenty per cent. to
be added; then a fall of profits by one-fifth will reduce the addition in
the latter case from 20 to 16, and in the former only from 10 to 8. [If
their direct labour cost is equal the ratio of their values before the
change will be $^{120}\!/_{110}$ or 1.091; and after the change $^{116}\!/_{108}$ or 1.074;
a fall of nearly two per cent.] His argument is avowedly only provisional; in later chapters he takes account of other causes of differences
in profits in different industries, besides the period of investment. But
it seems difficult to imagine how he could more strongly have emphasized the fact that Time or Waiting as well as Labour is an element of
cost of production than by occupying his first chapter with this discussion. Unfortunately however he delighted in short phrases, and he
thought that his readers would always supply for themselves the explanations of which he had given them a hint.

Once indeed, in a note at the end of the sixth Section of his first
Chapter, he says: "Mr Malthus appears to think that it is a part of
my doctrine that the cost and value of a thing should be the same; it is,
if he means by cost, 'cost of production' including profits. In the
above passage, this is what he does not mean, and therefore he has
not clearly understood me." And yet Rodbertus and Karl Marx claim
Ricardo's authority for the statement that the natural value of things
consists solely of the labour spent on them; and even those German
economists who most strenuously combat the conclusions of these
writers, are often found to admit that they have interpreted Ricardo
rightly, and that their conclusions follow logically from his.

This and other facts of a similar kind show that Ricardo's reticence
was an error of judgment. It would have been better if he had occasionally repeated the statement that the values of two commodities
are to be regarded as in the long run proportionate to the amount of
labour required for making them, only on the condition that other
things are equal: *i.e.,* that the labour employed in the two cases is
equally skilled, and therefore equally highly paid; that it is assisted
by proportionate amounts of capital, account being taken of the period
of its investment; and that the rates of profits are equal. He does not
state clearly, and in some cases he perhaps did not fully and clearly
perceive how, in the problem of normal value, the various elements

govern one another *mutually,* and not *successively* in a long chain of causation. And he was more guilty than almost anyone else of the bad habit of endeavouring to express great economic doctrines in short sentences.[2]

§ 3. There are few writers of modern times who have approached as near to the brilliant originality of Ricardo as Jevons has done. But he appears to have judged both Ricardo and Mill harshly, and to have attributed to them doctrines narrower and less scientific than those which they really held. And his desire to emphasize an aspect of value to which they had given insufficient prominence, was probably in some measure accountable for his saying, "Repeated reflection and inquiry have led me to the somewhat novel opinion that *value depends entirely upon utility*" (*Theory,* p. 1). This statement seems to be no less one-sided and fragmentary, and much more misleading, than that into which Ricardo often glided with careless brevity, as to the dependence of value on cost of production; but which he never regarded as more than a part of a larger doctrine, the rest of which he had tried to explain.

Jevons continues: "We have only to trace out carefully the natural laws of variation of utility as depending upon the quantity of commodity in our possession, in order to arrive at a satisfactory theory of exchange, of which the ordinary laws of supply and demand are a necessary consequence. . . . Labour is found often to determine value, but only in an indirect manner by varying the degree of utility of the commodity through an increase or limitation of the supply." As we

---

[2] Prof. Ashley in a suggestive criticism of this Note, as part of an attempted "Rehabilitation of Ricardo" (*Economic Journal,* Vol. I.), insists that it has been commonly believed that Ricardo did in fact habitually think of mere quantities of labour as constituting cost of production, and governing value, subject only to "slight modifications"; and that this interpretation of him is the most consistent with his writings as a whole. It is not disputed that this interpretation has been accepted by many able writers: otherwise there would have been little need for rehabilitating, *i.e.* clothing more fully his somewhat too naked doctrines. But the question whether Ricardo is to be supposed to have meant nothing by the first chapter of his book, merely because he did not constantly repeat the interpretation clauses contained in it, is one which each reader must decide for himself according to his temperament: it does not lend itself to be solved by argument. It is here claimed not that his doctrines contained a complete theory of value: but only that they were in the main true as far as they went. Rodbertus and Marx interpreted Ricardo's doctrine, to mean that interest does not enter into that cost of production which governs (or rather takes part in governing) value: and as regards this Prof. Ashley appears to concede all that is claimed here when (p. 480) he takes it as beyond question that Ricardo "regarded the payment of interest, that is, of something more than the mere replacement of capital, as a matter of course."

shall presently see, the latter of these two statements had been made before in almost the same form, loose and inaccurate as it is, by Ricardo and Mill; but they would not have accepted the former statement. For while they regarded the natural laws of variation of utility as too obvious to require detailed explanation, and while they admitted that cost of production could have no effect upon exchange value if it could have none upon the amount which producers brought forward for sale; their doctrines imply that what is true of supply, is true *mutatis mutandis* of demand, and that the utility of a commodity could have no effect upon its exchange value if it could have none on the amount which purchasers took off the market. Let us then turn to examine the chain of causation in which Jevons' central position is formulated in his Second Edition, and compare it with the position taken up by Ricardo and Mill. He says (p. 179):

> Cost of production determines supply.
> Supply determines final degree of utility.
> Final degree of utility determines value.

Now if this series of causations really existed, there could be no great harm in omitting the intermediate stages and saying that cost of production determines value. For if A is the cause of B, which is the cause of C, which is the cause of D; then A is the cause of D. But in fact there is no such series.

A preliminary objection might be taken to the ambiguity of the terms "cost of production" and "supply"; which Jevons ought to have avoided, by the aid of that technical apparatus of semi-mathematical phrases, which was at his disposal, but not at Ricardo's. A graver objection lies against his third statement. For the price which the various purchasers in a market will pay for a thing, is determined not solely by the final degrees of its utility to them, but by these in conjunction with the amounts of purchasing power severally at their disposal. The exchange value of a thing is the same all over a market; but the final degrees of utility to which it corresponds are not equal at any two parts. Jevons supposed himself to be getting nearer the foundations of exchange value when in his account of the causes which determine it, he substituted the phrase "final degree of utility," for "the price which consumers are only just willing to pay,"—the phrase which in the present treatise is condensed into "marginal demand price." When for instance describing (Second Edition, p. 105) the settlement of exchange between "one trading body possessing only corn, and another possessing only beef," he makes his diagram represent "a person" as gaining a "utility" measured along one line and losing a "utility" measured along another. But that is not what really happens; a trading body is not "a person," it gives up things which represent equal purchasing power to all of its members, but very different utilities. It is true that Jevons was himself aware of this; and that his account can be made consistent with the facts of life by a series of interpretations, which in effect substitute "demand-price" and "supply-price" for "utility" and "disutility": but, when so amended, they lose much of their aggressive force against the older doctrines, and if both are to be held severely to a strictly literal interpretation, then the older method of speaking, though not perfectly accurate, appears to be nearer the truth than that which Jevons and some of his followers have endeavoured to substitute for it.

But the greatest objection of all to his formal statement of his central doctrine is that it does not represent supply price, demand price and amount produced as mutually determining one another (subject to certain other conditions), but as determined one by another in a series. It is as though when three balls *A, B,* and *C* rest against one another in a bowl, instead of saying that the position of the three mutually determines one another under the action of gravity, he had said that *A* determines *B,* and *B* determines *C.* Someone else however with equal justice might say that *C* determines *B* and *B* determines *A.* And in reply to Jevons a catena rather less untrue than his can be made by inverting his order and saying:

Utility determines the amount that has to be supplied,

The amount that has to be supplied determines cost of production,

Cost of production determines value,

because it determines the supply price which is required to make the producers keep to their work.

Let us then turn to Ricardo's doctrine which, though unsystematic and open to many objections, seems to be more philosophic in principle and closer to the actual facts of life. He says, in the letter to Malthus already quoted: "M. Say has not a correct notion of what is meant by value when he contends that a commodity is valuable in proportion to its utility. This would be true if buyers only regulated the value of commodities; then indeed we might expect that all men would be willing to give a price for things in proportion to the estimation in which they held them; but the fact appears to me to be that the buyers have the least in the world to do in regulating price; it is all done by the competition of the sellers, and, however really willing the buyers might be to give more for iron than for gold, they could not, because the supply would be regulated by cost of production. . . . You say demand and supply regulates value [*sic*]; this I think is saying nothing, and for the reason I have given in the beginning of this letter: it is supply which regulates value, and supply is itself controlled by comparative cost of production. Cost of production, in money, means the value of labour as well as of profits." (See pp. 173–6 of Dr Bonar's excellent edition of these letters.) And again in his next letter, "I do not dispute either the influence of demand on the price of corn or on the price of all other things: but supply follows close at its heels and soon takes the power of regulating price in his [*sic*] own hands, and in regulating it he is determined by cost of production."

These letters were not indeed published when Jevons wrote, but there are very similar statements in Ricardo's *Principles*. Mill also, when discussing the value of money (Book III. ch. IX. § 3), speaks of "the law of demand and supply which is acknowledged to be applicable to all commodities, and which in the case of money as of most other things, is controlled but not set aside by the law of cost of production, since cost of production would have no effect on value if it could have none on supply." And again, when summing up his theory of value (Book III. ch. XVI. § 1), he says: "From this it appears that demand and supply govern the fluctuations of prices in all cases, and the permanent values of all things of which the supply is determined by any agency other than that of free competition: but that, under the régime of free competition, things are, on the average, exchanged for each other at such values and sold for such prices as afford equal expectation of advantage to all classes of producers; which can only be when things exchange for one another in the ratio of their cost of production." And, on the next page, speaking of commodities which have a joint cost of production, he says, "since cost of production here fails us we must resort to a law of value anterior to cost of production and more fundamental, the law of demand and supply."

Jevons (p. 215), referring to this last passage, speaks of "the fallacy involved in Mill's idea that he is reverting to *an anterior law of value,* the law of supply and demand, the fact being that in introducing the cost of production principle, he has never quitted the law of supply and demand at all. The cost of production is only one circumstance which governs supply and thus indirectly influences values."

This criticism seems to contain an important truth; though the wording of the last part is open to objection. If it had been made in Mill's time he would probably have accepted it; and would have withdrawn the word "anterior" as not expressing his real meaning. The "cost of production principle" and the "final utility" principle are undoubtedly component parts of the one all-ruling law of supply and demand; each may be compared to one blade of a pair of scissors. When one blade is held still, and the cutting is effected by moving the other, we may say with careless brevity that the cutting is done by the second; but the statement is not one to be made formally, and defended deliberately.[3]

Perhaps Jevons' antagonism to Ricardo and Mill would have been less if he had not himself fallen into the habit of speaking of relations which really exist only between demand price and value as though they held between utility and value; and if he had emphasized as Cournot had done, and as the use of mathematical forms might have been expected to lead him to do, that fundamental symmetry of the general relations in which demand and supply stand to value, which coexists with striking differences in the details of those relations. We must not indeed forget that, at the time at which he wrote, the demand side of the theory of value had been much neglected; and that he did excellent service by calling attention to it and developing it. There are few thinkers whose claims on our gratitude are as high and as various as those of Jevons: but that must not lead us to accept hastily his criticisms on his great predecessors.[4]

It seemed right to select Jevons' attack for reply, because, in England at all events, it has attracted more attention than any other. But somewhat similar attacks on Ricardo's theory of value had been made by many other writers. Among them may specially be mentioned Mr Macleod, whose writings before 1870 anticipated much both of the form and substance of recent criticisms on the classical doctrines of value in relation to cost, by Profs. Walras and Carl Menger, who were

---

[3] See V, iii, 7. [This reference, as well as the one in parentheses in the footnote immediately following, relates to Marshall's *Principles of Economics*.—Ed.]

[4] See an article on Jevons' *Theory* by the present writer in the *Academy* for April 1, 1872. The edition of his *Theory* brought out by his son in 1911, contains an Appendix on his account of interest, with special reference to that article (see also above VI, i, 8). He contends that his father's theory is "true as far as it goes" though he "followed the unfortunate practice of the Ricardian school by abstracting for treatment certain ideas, and assuming that his readers are familiar with their relations and taking his point of view." The son may be accepted as the true interpreter of the father: and the debts of economics to the father are no doubt so great as to be comparable with its transcendent obligations to Ricardo. But Jevons' *Theory* had a combative side, as well as a constructive. In great part it was an attack on what he called in his Preface, "that able but wrong-headed man, David Ricardo" who "shunted the car of Economic science on to a wrong line." His criticisms on Ricardo achieved some apparently unfair dialectical triumphs, by assuming that Ricardo thought of value as governed by cost of production without reference to demand. This misconception of Ricardo was doing great harm in 1872: and it seemed necessary to show that Jevons' Theory of Interest, if interpreted as he interpreted Ricardo, is untenable.

contemporary with Jevons, and Profs. v. Böhm-Bawerk and Wieser, who were later.

The carelessness of Ricardo with regard to the element of Time has been imitated by his critics, and has thus been a source of twofold misunderstanding. For they attempt to disprove doctrines as to the ultimate tendencies, the causes of causes, the *causæ causantes,* of the relations between cost of production and value, by means of arguments based on the causes of temporary changes, and short-period fluctuations of value. Doubtless nearly everything they say when expressing their own opinions is true in the sense in which they mean it; some of it is new and much of it is improved in form. But they do not appear to make any progress towards establishing their claim to have discovered a new doctrine of value which is in sharp contrast to the old; or which calls for any considerable demolition, as distinguished from development and extension, of the old doctrine.

Ricardo's first chapter has been discussed here with sole reference to the causes which govern the relative exchange values of different things; because its chief influence on subsequent thought has been in this direction. But it was originally associated with a controversy as to the extent to which the price of labour affords a good standard for measuring the general purchasing power of money. In this connection its interest is mainly historical: but reference may be made to an illuminating article on it by Prof. Hollander in the *Quarterly Journal of Economics,* 1904.

Mill

on

Bentham

John Stuart Mill (1806–1873), the "saint of rationalism," is remembered for his unusual education (which included training in economics at the age of 13), and for his contributions to philosophy, politics, and economics. During much of his life Mill served as an employee of the India Office in London, and for a short time he was a member of Parliament. His most important works in the field of economics are *Essays on Some Unsettled Questions of Political Economy* (1844), and *Principles of Political Economy* (1848). The authority of the last work, an elaboration of the classical system, was rarely questioned for several decades after its publication.

Mill's work marks a turning point in the history of economic ideas. In his general outlook he gradually shifted from *laisserfaire* to some form of socialistic cooperation.

Mill was attached to the group of "philosophic radicals" whose undisputed head was Jeremy Bentham (1748–1832). Bentham's utilitarian pain-and-pleasure calculus was to influence the outlook of many generations of economists. Bentham's promotion of the social and political changes that went on in nineteenth-century England had results comparable in significance with those achieved by the Webbs during the twentieth century.

A MAN OF great knowledge of the world, and of the highest reputation for practical talent and sagacity among the official men of his time (himself no follower of Bentham, nor of any partial or exclusive school whatever) once said to us, as the result of his observation, that to Bentham more than to any other source might be traced the questioning spirit, the disposition to demand the *why* of everything, which had gained so much ground and was producing such important consequences in these times. The more this assertion is examined, the more true it will be found. Bentham has been in this age and country the great questioner of things established. It is by the influence of the modes of thought with which his writings inoculated a considerable number of thinking men, that the yoke of authority has been broken, and innumerable opinions, formerly received on tradition as incontestable, are put upon their defence, and required to give an account of themselves. Who, before Bentham (whatever controversies might exist on points of detail), dared to speak disrespectfully, in express terms, of the British Constitution, or the English Law? He did so; and his arguments and his example together encouraged others. We do not mean that his writings caused the Reform Bill, or that the Appropriation Clause owns him as its parent: the changes which have been made, and the greater changes which will be made, in our institutions, are not the work of philosophers, but of the interests and instincts of large portions of society recently grown into strength. But Bentham gave voice to those interests and instincts: until he spoke out, those who found our institutions unsuited to them did not dare to say so, did not dare consciously to think so; they had never heard the excellence of those institutions questioned by cultivated men, by men of acknowledged intellect; and it is not in the nature of uninstructed minds to resist the united authority of the instructed. Bentham broke the spell. It was not Bentham by his own writings; it was Bentham through the minds and pens which those writings fed—through the men in more direct contact with the world, into whom his spirit passed. If the superstition about ancestorial wisdom has fallen into decay; if the public are grown familiar with the idea that their laws and institutions are in great part

[Reprinted in abridged form from *Westminster Review*, 1838.]

not the product of intellect and virtue, but of modern corruption grafted upon ancient barbarism; if the hardiest innovation is no longer scouted *because* it is an innovation—establishments no longer considered sacred because they are establishments—it will be found that those who have accustomed the public mind to these ideas have learnt them in Bentham's school, and that the assault on ancient institutions has been, and is, carried on for the most part with his weapons. It matters not although these thinkers, or indeed thinkers of any description, have been but scantily found among the persons prominently and ostensibly at the head of the Reform movement. All movements, except directly revolutionary ones, are headed, not by those who originate them, but by those who know best how to compromise between the old opinions and the new. The father of English innovation, both in doctrines and in institutions, is Bentham: he is the great *subversive,* or, in the language of continental philosophers, the great *critical,* thinker of his age and country.

We consider this, however, to be not his highest title to fame. Were this all, he were only to be ranked among the lowest order of the potentates of mind—the negative, or destructive philosophers; those who can perceive what is false, but not what is true; who awaken the human mind to the inconsistencies and absurdities of time-sanctioned opinions and institutions, but substitute nothing in the place of what they take away. We have no desire to undervalue the services of such persons: mankind have been deeply indebted to them; nor will there ever be a lack of work for them, in a world in which so many false things are believed, in which so many which have been true, are believed long after they have ceased to be true. The qualities, however, which fit men for perceiving anomalies, without perceiving the truths which would rectify them, are not among the rarest of endowments. Courage, verbal acuteness, command over the forms of argumentation, and a popular style, will make, out of the shallowest man, with a sufficient lack of reverence, a considerable negative philosopher. Such men have never been wanting in periods of culture; and the period in which Bentham formed his early impressions was emphatically their reign, in proportion to its barrenness in the more noble products of the human mind. An age of formalism in the Church and corruption in the State, when the most valuable part of the meaning of traditional doctrines had faded from the minds even of those who retained from habit a mechanical belief in them, was the time to raise up all kinds of sceptical philosophy. Accordingly, France had Voltaire, and his school of negative thinkers, and England (or rather Scotland) had the profoundest negative thinker on record, David Hume: a man, the peculiarities of whose mind qualified him to detect failure of proof, and want of logical consistency, at a depth which French sceptics, with their comparatively feeble powers of analysis and abstraction, stopt far short of, and which German subtlety could alone thoroughly appreciate, or hope to rival.

If Bentham had merely continued the work of Hume, he would scarcely have been heard of in philosophy; for he was far inferior to Hume in Hume's qualities, and was in no respect fitted to excel as a metaphysician. We must not look for subtlety, or the power of recondite analysis, among his intellectual characteristics. In the former quality, few great thinkers have ever been so deficient; and to find the latter, in any considerable measure, in a mind acknowledging any kindred with his, we must have recourse to the late Mr. Mill—a man who united the great qualities of the metaphysicians of the eighteenth century, with others of a different complexion, admirably qualifying him to complete and correct their work. Bentham had not these peculiar gifts; but he possessed others, not inferior, which were not possessed by any of his precursors; which have made him a source of light to a generation which has far outgrown their influence, and, as we called him, the chief subversive thinker of an age which has long lost all that they could subvert.

To speak of him first as a merely negative philosopher—as one who refutes illogical arguments, exposes sophistry, detects contradiction and absurdity; even in that capacity there was a wide field left vacant for him by Hume, and which he has occupied to an unprecedented extent; the field of practical abuses. This was Bentham's peculiar province: to this he was called by the whole bent of his disposition: to carry the warfare against absurdity into things practical. His was an essentially practical mind. It was by practical abuses that his mind was first turned to speculation—by the abuses of the profession which was chosen for him, that of the law. He has himself stated what particular abuse first gave that shock to his mind, the recoil of which has made the whole mountain of abuse totter; it was the custom of making the client pay for three attendances in the office of a Master in Chancery, when only one was given. The law, he found, on examination, was full of such things. But were these discoveries of his? No; they were known to every lawyer who practised, to every judge who sat on the bench, and neither before nor for long after did they cause any apparent uneasiness to the consciences of these learned persons, nor hinder them from asserting, whenever occasion offered, in books, in parliament, or on the bench, that the law was the perfection of reason. During so many generations, in each of which thousands of well-educated young men were successively placed in Bentham's position and with Bentham's opportunities, he alone was found with sufficient moral sensibility and self-reliance to say to himself that these things, however profitable they might be, were frauds, and that between them and himself there should be a gulf fixed. To this rare union of self-reliance and moral sensibility we are indebted for all that Bentham has done.   Sent to Oxford by his father at the unusually early age of fifteen—required, on admission, to declare his belief in the Thirty-nine Articles—he felt it necessary to examine them; and the examination suggested scruples, which he sought to get removed, but instead of the satisfaction he expected, was told that it was not for boys like him to set up their judgment against the great men of the Church.   After a struggle, he signed; but the impression that he had done an immoral act, never left him; he considered himself to have committed a falsehood, and throughout life he never relaxed in his indignant denunciations of all laws which command such falsehoods, all institutions which attach rewards to them.

By thus carrying the war of criticism and refutation, the conflict with falsehood and absurdity, into the field of practical evils, Bentham, even if he had done nothing else, would have earned an important place in the history of intellect.   He carried on the warfare without intermission. To this, not only many of his most piquant chapters, but some of the most finished of his entire works, are entirely devoted: the "Defence of Usury"; the "Book of Fallacies"; and the onslaught upon Blackstone, published anonymously under the title of "A Fragment on Government," which, though a first production, and of a writer afterwards so much ridiculed for his style, excited the highest admiration no less for its composition than for its thoughts, and was attributed by turns to Lord Mansfield, to Lord Camden, and (by Dr. Johnson) to Dunning, one of the greatest masters of style among the lawyers of his day.   These writings are altogether original; though of the negative school, they resemble nothing previously produced by negative philosophers; and would have sufficed to create for Bentham, among the subversive thinkers of modern Europe, a place peculiarly his own.   But it is not these writings that constitute the real distinction between him and them. There was a deeper difference.   It was that they were purely negative thinkers, he was positive: they only assailed error, he made it a point of conscience not to do so until he thought he could plant instead the corresponding truth.   Their character was exclusively analytic, his was synthetic.   They took for their starting-point the received opinion on any subject, dug round it with their logical implements, pronounced its foundations defective, and condemned it: he began *de novo,* laid his own foundations deeply and firmly, built up his own structure, and bade mankind compare the two; it was when he had solved the problem him-

self, or thought he had done so, that he declared all other solutions to
be erroneous. Hence, what they produced will not last; it must perish,
much of it has already perished, with the errors which it exploded: what
he did has its own value, by which it must outlast all errors to which
it is opposed. Though we may reject, as we often must, his practical
conclusions, yet his premises, the collections of facts and observations
from which his conclusions were drawn, remain for ever, a part of the
materials of philosophy.

A place, therefore, must be assigned to Bentham among the masters
of wisdom, the great teachers and permanent intellectual ornaments of
the human race. He is among those who have enriched mankind with
imperishable gifts; and although these do not transcend all other gifts,
nor entitle him to those honours "above all Greek, above all Roman
fame," which by a natural reaction against the neglect and contempt of
the world, many of his admirers were once disposed to accumulate upon
him, yet to refuse an admiring recognition of what he was, on account
of what he was not, is a much worse error, and one which, pardonable
in the vulgar, is no longer permitted to any cultivated and instructed
mind.

If we were asked to say, in the fewest possible words, what we conceive to be Bentham's place among these great intellectual benefactors
of humanity; what he was, and what he was not; what kind of service
he did and did not render to truth; we should say—he was not a great
philosopher, but he was a great reformer in philosophy. He brought
into philosophy something which it greatly needed, and for want of
which it was at a stand. It was not his doctrines which did this, it was
his mode of arriving at them. He introduced into morals and politics
those habits of thought and modes of investigation, which are essential
to the idea of science; and the absence of which made those departments
of inquiry, as physics had been before Bacon, a field of interminable
discussion, leading to no result. It was not his opinions, in short, but
his method, that constituted the novelty and the value of what he did;
a value beyond all price, even though we should reject the whole, as we
unquestionably must a large part, of the opinions themselves.

The first question in regard to any man of speculation is, what is his
theory of human life? In the minds of many philosophers, whatever
theory they have of this sort is latent, and it would be a revelation to
themselves to have it pointed out to them in their writings as others
can see it, unconsciously moulding everything to its own likeness. But
Bentham always knew his own premises, and made his reader know
them: it was not his custom to leave the theoretic grounds of his prac-

tical conclusions to conjecture. Few great thinkers have afforded the means of assigning with so much certainty the exact conception which they had formed of man and of man's life.

Man is conceived by Bentham as a being susceptible of pleasures and pains, and governed in all his conduct partly by the different modifications of self-interest, and the passions commonly classed as selfish, partly by sympathies, or occasionally antipathies, towards other beings. And here Bentham's conception of human nature stops. He does not exclude religion; the prospect of divine rewards and punishments he includes under the head of "self-regarding interest," and the devotional feeling under that of sympathy with God. But the whole of the impelling or restraining principles, whether of this or of another world, which he recognises, are either self-love, or love or hatred towards other sentient beings. That there might be no doubt of what he thought on the subject, he has not left us to the general evidence of his writings, but has drawn out a "Table of the Springs of Action," an express enumeration and classification of human motives, with their various names, laudatory, vituperative, and neutral: and this table, to be found in Part I. of his collected works, we recommend to the study of those who would understand his philosophy.

Man is never recognised by him as a being capable of pursuing spiritual perfection as an end; of desiring, for its own sake, the conformity of his own character to his standard of excellence, without hope of good or fear of evil from other source than his own inward consciousness. Even in the more limited form of Conscience, this great fact in human nature escapes him. Nothing is more curious than the absence of recognition in any of his writings of the existence of conscience, as a thing distinct from philanthropy, from affection for God or man, and from self-interest in this world or in the next. There is a studied abstinence from any of the phrases which, in the mouths of others, import the acknowledgment of such a fact.[1] If we find the words "Conscience," "Principle," "Moral Rectitude," "Moral Duty," in his Table of the Springs of Action, it is among the synonymes of the "love of reputation"; with an intimation as to the two former phrases, that they are also sometimes synonymous with the *religious* motive, or the motive of *sympathy*. The feeling of moral approbation or disapprobation prop-

---

[1] In a passage in the last volume of his book on Evidence, and possibly in one or two other places, the "love of justice" is spoken of as a feeling inherent in almost all mankind. It is impossible, without explanations now unattainable, to ascertain what sense is to be put upon casual expressions so inconsistent with the general tenor of his philosophy.

erly so called, either towards ourselves or our fellow-creatures, he seems unaware of the existence of; and neither the word *self-respect,* nor the idea to which that word is appropriated, occurs even once, so far as our recollection serves us, in his whole writings.

Nor is it only the moral part of man's nature, in the strict sense of the term—the desire of perfection, or the feeling of an approving or of an accusing conscience—that he overlooks; he but faintly recognises, as a fact in human nature, the pursuit of any other ideal end for its own sake. The sense of *honour,* and personal dignity—that feeling of personal exaltation and degradation which acts independently of other people's opinion, or even in defiance of it; the love of *beauty,* the passion of the artist; the love of *order,* of congruity, of consistency in all things, and conformity to their end; the love of *power,* not in the limited form of power over other human beings, but abstract power, the power of making our volitions effectual; the love of *action,* the thirst for movement and activity, a principle scarcely of less influence in human life than its opposite, the love of ease:—None of these powerful constituents of human nature are thought worthy of a place among the "Springs of Action"; and though there is possibly no one of them of the existence of which an acknowledgment might not be found in some corner of Bentham's writings, no conclusions are ever founded on the acknowledgment. Man, that most complex being, is a very simple one in his eyes. Even under the head of *sympathy,* his recognition does not extend to the more complex forms of the feeling—the love of *loving,* the need of a sympathising support, or of objects of admiration and reverence. If he thought at all of any of the deeper feelings of human nature, it was but as idiosyncrasies of taste, with which the moralist no more than the legislator had any concern, further than to prohibit such as were mischievous among the actions to which they might chance to lead. To say either that man should, or that he should not, take pleasure in one thing, displeasure in another, appeared to him as much an act of despotism in the moralist as in the political ruler.

It would be most unjust to Bentham to surmise (as narrow-minded and passionate adversaries are apt in such cases to do) that this picture of human nature was copied from himself; that all those constituents of humanity which he rejected from his table of motives, were wanting in his own breast. The unusual strength of his early feelings of virtue, was, as we have seen, the original cause of all his speculations; and a noble sense of morality, and especially of justice, guides and pervades them all. But having been early accustomed to keep before his mind's eye the happiness of mankind (or rather of the whole sentient world), as the only thing desirable in itself, or which rendered anything else desirable, he confounded all disinterested feelings which he found in himself, with the desire of general happiness: just as some religious writers, who loved virtue for its own sake as much perhaps as men could do, habitually confounded their love of virtue with their fear of hell. It would have required greater subtlety than Bentham possessed, to distinguish from each other, feelings which, from long habit, always acted in the same direction; and his want of imagination prevented him from reading the distinction, where it is legible enough, in the hearts of others.

Accordingly, he has not been followed in this grand oversight by any of the able men who, from the extent of their intellectual obligations to him, have been regarded as his disciples. They may have followed him in his doctrine of utility, and in his rejection of a moral sense as the test of right and wrong: but while repudiating it as such, they have, with Hartley, acknowledged it as a fact in human nature; they have endeavoured to account for it, to assign its laws: nor are they justly chargeable either with undervaluing this part of our nature, or with any disposition to throw it into the background of their speculations. If any part of the influence of this cardinal error has extended itself to them, it is circuitously, and through the effect on their minds of other parts of Bentham's doctrines.

Sympathy, the only disinterested motive which Bentham recognised, he felt the inadequacy of, except in certain limited cases, as a security for virtuous action. Personal affection, he well knew, is as liable to operate to the injury of third parties, and requires as much to be kept under government, as any other feeling whatever: and general philanthropy, considered as a motive influencing mankind in general, he estimated at its true value when divorced from the feeling of duty—as the very weakest and most unsteady of all feelings. There remained, as a motive by which mankind are influenced, and by which they may be guided to their good, only personal interest. Accordingly, Bentham's idea of the world is that of a collection of persons pursuing each his separate interest or pleasure, and the prevention of whom from jostling one another more than is unavoidable, may be attempted by hopes and fears derived from three sources—the law, religion, and public opinion. To these three powers, considered as binding human conduct, he gave the name of *sanctions:* the *political* sanction, operating by the rewards and penalties of the law; the *religious* sanction, by those expected from the Ruler of the Universe; and the *popular,* which he characteristically calls also the *moral* sanction, operating through the pains and pleasures arising from the favour or disfavour of our fellow-creatures.

Such is Bentham's theory of the world. And now, in a spirit neither of apology nor of censure, but of calm appreciation, we are to inquire how far this view of human nature and life will carry any one:—how much it will accomplish in morals, and how much in political and social philosophy: what it will do for the individual, and what for society.

It will do nothing for the conduct of the individual, beyond prescribing some of the more obvious dictates of worldly prudence, and outward probity and beneficence. There is no need to expatiate on the deficiencies of a system of ethics which does not pretend to aid individuals in the formation of their own character; which recognises no such wish as that of self-culture, we may even say no such power, as existing in human nature; and if it did recognise, could furnish little assistance to that great duty, because it overlooks the existence of about half of the whole number of mental feelings which human beings are capable of, including all those of which the direct objects are states of their own mind.

Morality consists of two parts. One of these is self-education; the training, by the human being himself, of his affections and will. That department is a blank in Bentham's system. The other and co-equal part, the regulation of his outward actions, must be altogether halting and imperfect without the first: for how can we judge in what manner many an action will affect even the worldly interests of ourselves or others, unless we take in, as part of the question, its influence on the regulation of our, or their, affections and desires? A moralist on Bentham's principles may get as far as this, that he ought not to slay, burn, or steal; but what will be his qualifications for regulating the nicer shades of human behaviour, or for laying down even the greater moralities as to those facts in human life which are liable to influence the depths of the character quite independently of any influence on worldly circumstances—such, for instance, as the sexual relations, or those of family in general, or any other social and sympathetic connexions of an intimate kind? The moralities of these questions depend essentially on considerations which Bentham never so much as took into the account; and when he happened to be in the right, it was always, and necessarily, on wrong or insufficient grounds.

It is fortunate for the world that Bentham's taste lay rather in the direction of jurisprudential than of properly ethical inquiry. Nothing expressly of the latter kind has been published under his name, except the "Deontology"—a book scarcely ever, in our experience, alluded to by any admirer of Bentham without deep regret that it ever saw the light. We did not expect from Bentham correct systematic views of ethics, or a sound treatment of any question the moralities of which require a profound knowledge of the human heart; but we did anticipate that the greater moral questions would have been boldly plunged into, and at least a searching criticism produced of the received opinions; we did not expect that the *petite morale* almost alone would have been treated, and that with the most pedantic minuteness, and on the *quid pro quo* principles which regulate trade. The book has not even the value which would belong to an authentic exhibition of the legitimate consequences of an erroneous line of thought; for the style proves it to have been so entirely rewritten, that it is impossible to tell how much or how little of it is Bentham's. The collected edition, now in progress, will not, it is said, include Bentham's religious writings; these, although we think most of them of exceedingly small value, are at least his, and the world has a right to whatever light they throw upon the constitution of his mind. But the omission of the "Deontology" would be an act of editorial discretion which we should deem entirely justifiable.

If Bentham's theory of life can do so little for the individual, what can it do for society?

It will enable a society which has attained a certain state of spiritual development, and the maintenance of which in that state is otherwise provided for, to prescribe the rules by which it may protect its material interests. It will do nothing (except sometimes as an instrument in the hands of a higher doctrine) for the spiritual interests of society; nor does it suffice of itself even for the material interests. That which alone causes any material interests to exist, which alone enables any body of human beings to exist as a society, is national character; *that* it is, which causes one nation to succeed in what it attempts, another to fail; one nation to understand and aspire to elevated things, another to grovel in mean ones; which makes the greatness of one nation lasting, and dooms another to early and rapid decay. The true teacher of the fitting social arrangements for England, France, or America, is the one who can point out how the English, French, or American character can be improved, and how it has been made what it is. A philosophy of laws and institutions, not founded on a philosophy of national character, is an absurdity. But what could Bentham's opinion be worth on national character? How could he, whose mind contained so few and so poor types of individual character, rise to that higher generalization? All he can do is but to indicate means by which, in any given state of the national mind, the material interests of society can be protected; saving the question, of which others must judge, whether the use of those means would have, on the national character, any injurious influence.

We have arrived, then, at a sort of estimate of what a philosophy like Bentham's can do. It can teach the means of organizing and regulating the merely *business* part of the social arrangements. Whatever can be understood or whatever done without reference to moral influences, his philosophy is equal to; where those influences require to be taken into account, it is at fault. He committed the mistake of supposing that the business part of human affairs was the whole of them; all at least that the legislator and the moralist had to do with. Not that he disregarded moral influences when he perceived them; but his want of imagination, small experience of human feelings, and ignorance of the filiation and connexion of feelings with one another, made this rarely the case.

The business part is accordingly the only province of human affairs which Bentham has cultivated with any success; into which he has introduced any considerable number of comprehensive and luminous practical principles. That is the field of his greatness; and there he is indeed great. He has swept away the accumulated cobwebs of centuries—he has untied knots which the efforts of the ablest thinkers, age after age, had only drawn tighter; and it is no exaggeration to say of him that over a great part of the field he was the first to shed the light of reason.

In the brief view which we have been able to give of Bentham's philosophy, it may surprise the reader that we have said so little about the first principle of it, with which his name is more identified than with anything else; the "principle of utility," or, as he afterwards named it, "the greatest-happiness principle." It is a topic on which much were to be said, if there were room, or if it were in reality necessary for the just estimation of Bentham. On an occasion more suitable for a discussion of the metaphysics of morality, or on which the elucidations necessary to make an opinion on so abstract a subject intelligible could be conveniently given, we should be fully prepared to state what we think on this subject. At present we shall only say, that while, under proper explanations, we entirely agree with Bentham in his principle, we do not hold with him that all right thinking on the details of morals depends on its express assertion. We think utility, or happiness, much too complex and indefinite an end to be sought except through the medium of various secondary ends, concerning which there may be, and often is, agreement among persons who differ in their ultimate standard; and about which there does in fact prevail a much greater unanimity among thinking persons, than might be supposed from their diametrical divergence on the great questions of moral metaphysics. As mankind are much more nearly of one nature, than of one opinion about their own nature, they are more easily brought to agree in their intermediate principles, *vera illa et media axiomata,* as Bacon says, than in their first principles: and the attempt to make the bearings of actions upon the ultimate end more evident than they can be made by referring them to the intermediate ends, and to estimate their value by a direct reference to human happiness, generally terminates in attaching most importance, not to those effects which are really the greatest, but to those which can most easily be pointed to and individually identified. Those who adopt utility as a standard can seldom apply it truly except through the secondary principles; those who reject it, generally do no more than erect those secondary principles into first principles. It is when two or more of the secondary principles conflict, that a direct appeal to some first principle becomes necessary; and then commences the practical importance of the utilitarian controversy; which is in other respects, a question of arrangement and logical subordination rather than of practice; important principally in a purely scientific point of view, for the sake of the systematic unity and coherency of ethical philosophy. It is probable, however, that to the principle of utility we owe all that Bentham did; that it was necessary to him to find a first principle which he could receive as self-evident, and to which he could attach all his other doctrines as logical consequences: that to him systematic unity was an indispensable condition of his confidence in his own intellect. And there is something further to be remarked. Whether happiness be or be not the end to which morality should be referred—that it be referred to an *end* of some sort, and not left in the dominion of vague feeling or inexplicable internal conviction, that it be made a matter of reason and calculation, and not merely of sentiment, is essential to the very idea of moral philosophy; is, in fact, what renders argument or discussion on moral questions possible. That the morality of actions depends on the consequences which they tend to produce, is the doctrine of rational persons of all schools; that the good or evil of those consequences is measured solely by pleasure or pain, is all of the doctrine of the school of utility, which is peculiar to it.

In so far as Bentham's adoption of the principle of utility induced him to fix his attention upon the consequences of actions as the consideration determining their morality, so far he was indisputably in the right path: though to go far in it without wandering, there was needed a greater knowledge of the formation of character, and of the consequences of actions upon the agent's own frame of mind, than Bentham possessed. His want of power to estimate this class of consequences, together with his want of the degree of modest deference which, from those who have not competent experience of their own, is due to the experience of others on that part of the subject, greatly limit the value of his speculations on questions of practical ethics.

He is chargeable also with another error, which it would be improper to pass over, because nothing has tended more to place him in opposition to the common feelings of mankind, and to give to his philosophy that cold, mechanical, and ungenial air which characterizes the popular idea of a Benthamite. This error, or rather one-sidedness, belongs to him not as a utilitarian, but as a moralist by profession, and in common with almost all professed moralists, whether religious or philosophical: it is that of treating the *moral* view of actions and characters, which is unquestionably the first and most important mode of looking at them, as if it were the sole one: whereas it is only one of three, by all of which our sentiments towards the human being may be, ought to be, and without entirely crushing our own nature cannot but be, materially influenced. Every human action has three aspects: its *moral* aspect, or that of its *right* and *wrong;* its *æsthetic* aspect, or that of its *beauty;* its *sympathetic* aspect, or that of its *loveableness.* The first addresses itself to our reason and conscience; the second to our imagination; the third to our human fellow-feeling. According to the first, we approve or disapprove; according to the second, we admire or despise; according to the third, we love, pity, or dislike. The morality of an action depends on its foreseeable consequences; its beauty, and its loveableness, or the reverse, depend on the qualities which it is evidence of. Thus, a lie is *wrong,* because its effect is to mislead, and because it tends to destroy the confidence of man in man; it is also *mean,* because it is cowardly—because it proceeds from not daring to face the consequences of telling the truth—or at best is evidence of want of that *power* to compass our ends by straightforward means, which is conceived as properly belonging to every person not deficient in energy or in understanding. The action of Brutus in sentencing his sons was *right,* because it was executing a law essential to the freedom of his country, against persons of whose guilt there was no doubt: it was *admirable,* because it evinced a rare degree of patriotism, courage, and self-control; but there was nothing *loveable* in it; it affords either no presumption in regard to loveable qualities, or a presumption of their deficiency. If one of the sons had engaged in the conspiracy from affection for the other, his action would have been loveable, though neither moral nor admirable. It is not possible for any sophistry to confound these three modes of viewing an action; but it is very possible to adhere to one of them exclusively, and lose sight of the rest. Sentimentality consists in setting the last two of the three above the first; the error of moralists in general, and of Bentham, is to sink the two latter entirely. This is pre-eminently the case with Bentham: he both wrote and felt as if the moral standard ought not only to be paramount (which it ought), but to be alone; as if it ought to be the sole master of all our actions, and even of all our sentiments; as if either to admire or like, or despise or dislike a person for any action which neither does good nor harm, or which does not do a good or a harm proportioned to the sentiment entertained, were an injustice and a prejudice. He carried this so far, that there were certain phrases which, being expressive of what he considered to be this groundless liking or aversion, he could not bear to hear pronounced in his presence. Among these phrases were those of *good* and *bad taste*. He thought it an insolent piece of dogmatism in one person to praise or condemn another in a matter of taste: as if men's likings and dislikings, on things in themselves indifferent, were not full of the most important inferences as to every point of their character; as if a person's tastes did not show him to be wise or a fool, cultivated or ignorant, gentle or rough, sensitive or callous, generous or sordid, benevolent or selfish, conscientious or depraved.

Connected with the same topic are Bentham's peculiar opinions on poetry. Much more has been said than there is any foundation for, about his contempt for the pleasures of imagination, and for the fine arts. Music was throughout life his favourite amusement; painting, sculpture, and the other arts addressed to the eye, he was so far from holding in any contempt, that he occasionally recognises them as means employable for important social ends; though his ignorance of the deeper springs of human character prevented him (as it prevents most Englishmen) from suspecting how profoundly such things enter into the moral nature of man, and into the education both of the individual and of the race. But towards poetry in the narrower sense, that which employs the language of words, he entertained no favour. Words, he thought, were perverted from their proper office when they were employed in uttering anything but precise logical truth. He says, somewhere in his works, that, "quantity of pleasure being equal, push-pin is as good as poetry": but this is only a paradoxical way of stating what he would equally have said of the things which he most valued and admired. Another aphorism is attributed to him, which is much more characteristic of his view of this subject: "All poetry is misrepresentation." Poetry, he thought, consisted essentially in exaggeration for effect: in proclaiming some one view of a thing very emphatically, and suppressing all the limitations and qualifications. This trait of character seems to us a curious example of what Mr. Carlyle strikingly calls "the completeness of limited men." Here is a philosopher who is happy within his narrow boundary as no man of indefinite range ever was: who flatters himself that he is so completely emancipated from the essential law of poor human intellect, by which it can only see one thing at a time well, that he can even turn round upon the imperfection and lay a solemn interdict upon it. Did Bentham really suppose that it is in poetry only that propositions cannot be exactly true, cannot contain in themselves all the limitations and qualifications with which they require to be taken when applied to practice? We have seen how far his own prose propositions are from realizing this Utopia: and even the attempt to approach it would be incompatible not with poetry merely, but with oratory, and popular writing of every kind. Bentham's charge is true to the fullest extent; all writing which undertakes to make men feel truths as well as see them, does take up one point at a time, does seek to impress that, to drive that home, to make it sink into and colour the whole mind of the reader or hearer. It is justified in doing so, if the portion of truth which it thus enforces be that which is called for by the occasion. All writing addressed to the feelings has a natural tendency to exaggeration; but Bentham should have remembered that in this, as in many things, we must aim at too much, to be assured of doing enough.

From the same principle in Bentham came the intricate and involved style, which makes his later writings books for the student only, not the general reader. It was from his perpetually aiming at impracticable precision. Nearly all his earlier, and many parts of his later writings, are models, as we have already observed, of light, playful, and popular style: a Benthamiana might be made of passages worthy of Addison or Goldsmith. But in his later years and more advanced studies, he fell into a Latin or German structure of sentence, foreign to the genius of the English language. He could not bear, for the sake of clearness and the reader's ease, to say, as ordinary men are content to do, a little more than the truth in one sentence, and correct it in the next. The whole of the qualifying remarks which he intended to make, he insisted upon imbedding as parentheses in the very middle of the sentence itself. And thus the sense being so long suspended, and attention being required to the accessory ideas before the principal idea had been properly seized, it became difficult, without some practice, to make out the train of thought. It is fortunate that so many of the most important parts of his writings are free from this defect. We regard it as a *reductio ad absurdum* of his objection to poetry. In trying to write in a manner against which the same objection should not lie, he could stop nowhere short of utter unreadableness, and after all attained no more accuracy than is compatible with opinions as imperfect and one-

sided as those of any poet or sentimentalist breathing. Judge then in
what state literature and philosophy would be, and what chance they
would have of influencing the multitude, if his objection were allowed,
and all styles of writing banished which would not stand his test.

We must here close this brief and imperfect view of Bentham and
his doctrines; in which many parts of the subject have been entirely untouched, and no part done justice to, but which at least proceeds from
an intimate familiarity with his writings, and is nearly the first attempt
at an impartial estimate of his character as a philosopher, and of the
result of his labours to the world.

After every abatement, and it has been seen whether we have made
our abatements sparingly—there remains to Bentham an indisputable
place among the great intellectual benefactors of mankind. His writings will long form an indispensable part of the education of the highest
order of practical thinkers; and the collected edition of them ought to
be in the hands of every one who would either understand his age, or
take any beneficial part in the great business of it.

Viner

---------- on ----------

Bentham and Mill

Approximately a century after Mill's essay on Bentham was published, the contribution of the two men was newly appraised by Jacob Viner. Viner (1892–   ), educated at McGill and Harvard, is a leading American economist who has brilliantly interpreted several phases of the history of economics. Now teaching at Princeton, he was affiliated for a quarter of a century with the University of Chicago. His principal work, *Studies in the Theory of International Trade* (1937), is dedicated to F. W. Taussig (1859–1940), Viner's teacher at Harvard and the educator of a generation of American economists.

THE ONE-HUNDREDTH anniversary of the publication of J. S. Mill's *Principles of Political Economy* falls in the year 1948, and the American Economic Association in the programming of its meetings takes advantage of anniversaries of births, deaths, and dates of publication to remind its members that our discipline has a past. This is a proper occasion, therefore, for a paper on J. S. Mill. The inclusion of Bentham in the scope of my paper is of my own contriving, but perhaps I can technically legitimatize it by appeal to the fact that British learned circles have been celebrating during 1948 the two-hundredth anniversary of Bentham's birth. There is no intellectual difficulty, however, in associating Bentham with Mill. The intellectual history of Mill is in large part a history, first, of faithful discipleship, then of rebellion from, and finally of substantial return to, the Benthamite set of doctrines.

The general lines of Bentham's thought were wholly of the eighteenth century, as I could demonstrate if there were time. Of English intellectuals who have had great influence, Bentham was perhaps the least original in his stock of general ideas, but clearly the most original in finding means and devices for putting his philosophy to practical use. To the nineteenth century Bentham was important as a carrier of eighteenth-century thought and, still more, as a translator of this thought into a program of social reform. It was the seventeenth century which was the Age of Genius. The philosophers of the eighteenth century were, nonetheless, fertile in ideas. They were, however, almost completely devoid of zeal for the application of these ideas to change of institutions, or even of zeal in generating ideas which would call for change in existing institutions.

We economists like to think of Adam Smith as an exception in this regard, but he was so only to a moderate extent. The one social issue on which Adam Smith was a zealot was the issue of freedom of trade *versus* mercantilism. But Smith had little confidence in the ability of ideas to move worlds. It is often overlooked that it was with reference

[This paper was presented at the meetings of the American Economic Association, December 29, 1948. Reprinted by permission from *American Economic Review,* Vol. 39, No. 2, March 1949.]

to internal and not to international free trade that Adam Smith made his famous statement that "To expect, indeed, that the freedom of trade should ever be entirely restored in Great Britain, is as absurd as to expect that an Oceana or Utopia should ever be established in it," and this although when he wrote, by obsolescence rather than by deliberate repeal, the restrictions on internal freedom of trade had already become largely inoperative. There is no evidence that Smith was more optimistic about the prospects for international than for domestic free trade, or that, beyond writing his book and preparing a few memoranda for the government when called upon, he ever felt moved to do anything, and especially to resort to anything rude or, in the eighteenth-century meaning of the term, to "enthusiasm," to obtain acceptance and execution of his reforming ideas.

The eighteenth century, in Britain if not in France, and before the American and the French Revolutions if not after, was the age of social complacency, political, economic, moral, of satisfaction with the *status quo* at least to the extent of belief that the costs of substantial change would exceed the benefits of removal or moderation of whatever evils were recognized to prevail. British eighteenth-century government was oligarchic, corrupt, inefficient, though it was generally not tyrannical in intent and usually too lax, too inert, too decentralized, and too sceptical to be seriously tyrannical in effect. Until the end of the century there was no major figure who even mildly suggested the need for major political reform. Whether the economic condition of the masses of the people was improving or deteriorating, and whatever its trend, whether it was desperately bad or moderately good as compared to later standards, I frankly have no idea. We may rest assured, however, that it was not idyllic, if only because it never is.

Nevertheless, there was not until the very last moments of the century either a single major political debate which turned on the economic conditions of the poor or a single major writer who had important suggestions as to how to improve them, with the sole exception of Adam Smith's plea for freedom of trade. It was even a common doctrine of the century that the poor should never be relieved of their poverty above the level of a bare subsistence plus perhaps a few crumbs of cake, and it was at least the quasi-official doctrine of the Church of England that the poverty of the poor—and the prosperity of the bishops—were in accordance with the Divine Will.

Bentham and the Benthamites, on the other hand, were never complacent about the condition of the people of England. They were "Radical Reformers," and they worked hard at their reforms: by working out detailed blueprints for them; by propaganda, agitation, intrigue, conspiracy; and, if truth be told, by encouragement to revolutionary movements up to—but not beyond—the point where resort to physical force would be the next step. Bentham, moreover, was a successful social reformer, more successful perhaps than anyone else in history except Karl Marx—I have in mind here only the realization and not the merits of programs of change—if he is given credit for those changes which came after his death as the result largely of the efforts of his disciples.

The list of reforms in England which derive largely from Bentham is a truly impressive one, and I present it here only in part: fundamental law reform in many of its branches; prison reform; adult popular suffrage, including woman suffrage; free trade; reform in colonial government; legalization of trade unions; general education at public expense; free speech and free press; the secret ballot; a civil service appointed and promoted on merit; repeal of the usury laws; general registration of titles to property; reform of local government; a safety code for merchant shipping; sanitary reform and preventive medicine at public expense; systematic collection of statistics; free justice for the poor. Bentham was the first person to propose birth-control as a measure of economic reform, and this *before* Malthus had published his first *Essay on the Principle of Population*.[1] The Ministry of Health which he proposed would be made responsible not only for general sanitation and routine public health work, but also for smoke prevention, local health-museums, and the policing of the medical profession to prevent their formation of monopolies.

Related to the conditions of the time when these reforms were proposed, Bentham's program was comprehensive, radical, and progressive without being visionary. The modern "democratic socialist" would find it wanting, since Bentham did not approve of tampering with the system of private property except through inheritance taxation and insisted on "compensation" where reform measures would involve violation of "reasonable expectations." He apparently never formulated any concrete proposals for social security on an insurance basis, but he approved in principle of government-administered and government-subsidized insurance against every conceivable type of social hazard for which individual prudence could not make adequate provision. It was too early for proposals to stabilize employment through

---

[1] See J. Bentham, "Situation and Relief of the Poor," *Annals of Agriculture,* Vol. XXIX (1797), pp. 422–23 (p. 31, in the separate pamphlet version). See also Norman E. Himes, "Jeremy Bentham and the Genesis of English Neo-Malthusianism," *Economic History* (Suppl. of *The Economic Journal*), Vol. III (1936), pp. 267–76.

monetary or fiscal measures, although Bentham did explore the possibility of increasing real investment and production through the "forced frugality" induced by the issue of paper money.[2] Pronounced individualist though he was, his specific program of reforms in both the content and the processes of legislation, in governmental organization, and in public administration, made him a major source of inspiration for the Fabian socialists as well as for the laissez-faire liberals.

To belief in political democracy Bentham came only slowly, and only as their failure to adopt his proposals eroded his faith in the good intentions of the British aristocratic politicians. The Benthamite case for political democracy was first elaborately expounded by James Mill in his famous essay on Government first published in 1820. It turned out to be an embarrassment for Bentham and his other disciples because by the scholastic formalism of its argument and the extreme lengths to which it carried Bentham's doctrine it was seriously vulnerable to rebuttal and, even worse, to ridicule. Starting out from the proposition that the sole proper purpose of government is to promote the greatest happiness of mankind, James Mill proceeded by purely *a priori* analysis, without any reference to history or to contemporary fact, from the premise that legislators served *only* their "sinister interests"—a stock Benthamite term for the self-interest of rulers or a ruling class—to the conclusion that good government was therefore obtainable only by making it, through popular suffrage and frequent elections, the self-interest of the elected to serve the interests of the electors.

Bentham, writing in the 1780's, had conceded that if at any time legislators "have suffered the nation to be preyed upon by swarms of idle pensioners, or useless place-men, it has rather been from negligence and imbecility, than from any settled plan for oppressing and plundering of the people," but in 1814 he appended a note withdrawing the concession: "So thought Anno 1780 and 1790—Not so Anno 1814.—J. Bentham." [3] By that time he had adopted the doctrine of "Sinister Interests." But James Mill carried the doctrine further than was necessary to meet Bentham's requirements and probably further than Bentham's belief in it. As Tawney has remarked: "To

---

[2] Bentham's treatment of this still remains in large part in manuscript. Extracts from these unpublished manuscripts and comments by Ricardo on them have recently been published by Edmund Silberner, "Un Manuscrit Inédit de David Ricardo sur le Problème Monétaire," *Revue d'Histoire Économique et Sociale,* Vol. XXV (1940), 195–259, and were then also already in page proof in Piero Sraffa's long-forthcoming edition of Ricardo's works.

[3] Bentham, "Principles of Morals and Legislation," *Works* (Edinburgh, 1838–1843), I, 5.

[James Mill] the State is not a band of brothers, but a mutual detective society; the principal advantage of popular government is that there are more detectives, and therefore, presumably, fewer thieves." [4] Bentham always, but James Mill rarely, if ever, conceded that men, even legislators, could not only be influenced by the praise and blame of other men, but could even display some measure of pure benevolence. As Barker has commented: ". . . while all—or nearly all—of the theorems of Mill's article may be found in Bentham, they have undergone a change. The egoism is more egoistic; the negativism is more negative," [5] and it may be added the *a priori* analysis more "high *priori.*" In the seventeenth century Harrington had denied that Hobbes could work the miracle of "making you a king by geometry." Macaulay was now to deny that the Benthamites could depose an aristocracy by geometry.

Macaulay, a young man anxiously seeking fame by his fluent and facile pen, found the opportunity in James Mill's essay on Government. Reviewing in 1829, in the magisterial *Edinburgh Review,* a reprint of this essay of James Mill, Macaulay raked it high and low, primarily on the basis of its use, without benefit of historical induction or of reference to contemporary facts, of the *a priori* or, in the language of the time and earlier, the geometrical method, but also on the more concrete ground that the proposition that legislators *always* and *invariably* act in terms of their selfish interests was preposterous whatever the method by which it was attempted to establish it. [6]

The Benthamites were shaken by the attack, and J. S. Mill most so, as we shall see later. But Macaulay himself, without withdrawing anything of what he had written, soon thereafter made his peace with James Mill and from then on was an exponent of political democracy on the basis of a line of argument which Paxton in his *Civil Polity* had already presented in 1703, and which should have been the original and was to become the standard line of the Benthamites, namely, that only by democratic voting could there be an adequate guarantee that legislators would *always* or predominantly serve the general interest, without denial that they might sometimes do so even in the absence of democracy.

I come now to deal more systematically with the most difficult and

---

[4] R. H. Tawney, preface to *Life and Struggles of William Lovett,* new ed. (New York, 1920), p. xxi.

[5] Sir Ernest Barker, in the preface of his edition of James Mill, *Essay on Government* (Cambridge, England, 1937).

[6] See the preface, pp. ix–xi and pp. 160 ff. of *The Miscellaneous Writings and Speeches of Lord Macaulay,* Popular Edition (London, 1891).

the most controverted aspect of Benthamism, namely, its psychological and ethical justifications for utilitarianism as legislative policy.

Bentham's main concern with ethics was with the ethics which should be followed by moral leaders, not with the ethics of the ordinary man, not with private morals, except as they were data to be operated on by the elite. "The science," he said, "whose foundations we have explored can appeal only to lofty minds with whom the public welfare has become a passion." [7] And by them, Bentham held, its lessons should be pressed on legislators, whether *their* minds were lofty ones or not. As Bentham acknowledged,[8] he sometimes overlooked this, and wrote as if what he had to say was directed at private morals, and critics have made much of this oversight without treating it merely as a lapse from his fundamental purposes. It was Benthamism interpreted as a system of private ethics, didactic as well as descriptive, that has aroused the most violent and the most emotional antagonism. Even as private ethics, however, Benthamism has seemed so vulnerable a target to *odium theologicum* and *odium ethicum* only because the private ethics of the critics permitted them to attack Bentham's words without taking pains to ascertain what the thoughts were which these words were intended to communicate.

Bentham starts from the standard eighteenth-century proposition, common to theologians and to sceptical philosophers alike, that man operates "under the governance of two sovereign masters, pain and pleasure." Happiness is a net sum or aggregate of individually experienced pleasures and pains.[9] Man, he claims, acts only in response to his "interests," by which he usually, and fundamentally, means whatever men are interested in, but, unfortunately, frequently allows to mean what men regard as in their self-interest. Men normally are interested to some extent in the happiness of others than themselves, and in exceptional cases are capable of "universal benevolence," or a dominating concern with the happiness of mankind at large, but generally, if they are left to themselves, there will be serious discrepancy between the actual behavior of individuals and the behavior which would conduce to "the greatest happiness of the greatest number." It is the

---

[7] *Theory of Legislation*, C. M. Atkinson ed. (London, 1914), II, 337.

[8] *Cf.* for example, the preface, first added to the 1823 edition, of his *Introduction to the Principles of Morals and Legislation*, where he says that "an introduction to a penal code" would have been a title better indicating the nature of its contents.

[9] *Cf.* "Gamaliel Smith" [= Jeremy Bentham], *Not Paul, but Jesus* (London, 1823), p. 394: "happiness, to be anything, must be composed of pleasures: and, be the man who he may, of what it is that gives pleasure to him, he alone can be judge."

function of legislation to coerce or bribe individuals to make their behavior coincide with that required by the greatest-happiness principle,
and of education and moral leaders to mould men's desires so that they
spontaneously associate the happiness of others with their own happiness.

Bentham nowhere attempts or asserts the possibility of a positive
demonstration that greatest happiness, whether as hedonism or as
eudaemonism, is the proper moral objective for the common man, the
moral leader, or the legislator, and his only argument in support of
the greatest-happiness principle is the negative one that the rival principles proposed by other ethical systems are either resolvable upon
scrutiny to verbal variants of the utility principle, or are sheer *ipse
dixitism,* or are meaningless patterns of words.

"Pleasure" and "happiness" were to Bentham widely inclusive terms,
involving not only the pleasures of the senses but also those of the
heart and the mind. Pleasures, moreover, which in their "simple" or
primary form, genetically speaking, were pleasures of self could by
"association of ideas" become associated with the pleasures of others.
Man, by living in society, by education, and by acts of parliament,
could be made good. The eighteenth-century utilitarians may have
traded, as a German philosopher has put it, "in the small wares of
usefulness (*Nützlichkeitskrämerei*)." Or it may be that to accept the
pursuit of pleasure as a proper end of man is "swinish doctrine," if
it be proper to assume that man pursues swinish pleasures. But a
utilitarian does not have to be a Philistine. If in Bentham's exposition
of his psychology there was often undue stress on the selfish sentiments,
this fault—which was much more evident in James Mill than in
Bentham—was the result of lack of imagination and of feeling, or of
faulty observation—itself the consequence of these lacks—rather than
any inherent incompatibility of broader views with the logic of his
system. One important manifestation of this—systematic on the part
of James Mill but only occasional and incidental on the part of Bentham—was the assumption that even when one's own pleasure had
through association of ideas become involved in the pleasure of other
persons, the affectionate sentiments toward others still contained an
element of conscious reference back to one's own pleasures. This,
by implication at least, was a proclamation of the universal prevalence
of psychological hedonism.[10]

[10] In notes to his edition of James Mill, *Analysis of the Phenomena of the
Human Mind* (London, 1869), J. S. Mill, without fully admitting that his father
had held this doctrine, points out passages which could be interpreted as implying
it. See II, 217, note; II, 224, note; II, 286 ff., note, etc.

The eighteenth century is often termed the "Age of Reason," and it is correctly so termed if by the phrase is meant that it was the age in which philosophers held that the credibility of all things should be tested by reason. But from the point of view of its prevailing psychological doctrines, it could more properly be called the "Age of the Passions" because of its stress on the emotions and the instincts, the affections and aversions, and its playing down of the role of reason in the behavior of the ordinary man. David Hume was writing in the spirit of his times when he declared that: "Reason is and ought only to be the slave of the passions, and can never pretend to any other office than to serve and obey them." The normal role of reason was that of an obedient servant of the passions, a passive agent for the comparison of their relative intensities and for the justification of the choices made between them. "So convenient a thing," said Bentham in his Autobiography, "it is to be a reasonable creature, since it enables one to find or make a reason for everything one has a mind to do."

For the moral philosopher and the properly conditioned legislator, however, Bentham assigned more important roles to reason, first, that of moulding the passions of individuals so that they would contribute more to the augmentation of general happiness, and second, that of providing a technique for the comparison of passions of individuals with a view to making a socially oriented choice between them where choice had to be or could be made. It was for this social purpose, and not for the routine behavior of routine individuals, that Bentham endeavored to construct what he at different times labelled as a "moral thermometer," a "moral arithmetic," a "felicific calculus."

Much amusement has been derived from Bentham's attempt to develop a technique by which the quantities of pleasure and pain could be measured by the legislator or the benevolent philosopher. Wesley Mitchell's well-known essay on "Bentham's Felicific Calculus," [11] is the fullest and the least unsympathetic account I am acquainted with of Bentham's position on this question. Mitchell points out the excessive degree of hedonism attributed by Bentham to mankind, and comments penetratingly on Bentham's attempt to find a common denominator through money for the pleasures of different persons. Mitchell says that in fact Bentham used the calculus not as an instrument of calculation, but as a basis of ordinal classification. "It pointed out to him what elements should be considered in a given situation, and among these elements *seriatim* he was often able to make comparisons

---

[11] Reprinted in W. C. Mitchell, *The Backward Art of Spending Money* (New York, 1937), pp. 177–202.

in terms of greater and less——." I think this is a somewhat misleading description of Bentham's method. The "classification" was not *seriatim,* was not in terms of higher and lower, but merely of pro and con, of pleasure and pain, and was wholly preliminary to rather than part of the calculus. The "calculus" as he actually used it was merely a mental comparison of the comparative weights of the pros and cons, a technique which neither calls for fancy labels nor is properly conducive either to merriment or to measurement.

Bentham did not invent the concept or the terminology of "moral arithmetic." Play with the idea of measuring the unmeasurable and resort to the language of measurement where it was silly to attempt to apply it goes back to at least the seventeenth century, when the prestige of geometry and later of algebra tended to trap all philosophers with scientific pretensions into casting their analysis into pseudo-mathematical form. Mandeville, as early as 1730, laughed at physicians who studied mathematics because it was fashionable, and cited one who had advised that for certain diseases "the doses of the medicines are to be as the Squares of the Constitutions." [12] Thomas Reid, in his *Essay on Quantity* of 1748, questioned the possibility of reducing to measurement such things as sensations, beauty, pleasure, and the affections and appetites of the mind, even though they "are capable of more and less," and he warned that to apply mathematical language to non-measurable things "is to make a show of mathematical reasoning, without advancing one step in real knowledge." [13]

Bentham never went far afield for the sources of his ideas, and I suspect that Benjamin Franklin was his source, direct or indirect, for this idea of classification by "bipartition" plus "measurement" of the relative weight of the two classes. Franklin a few years earlier, in 1772, had been expounding it in private correspondence with Joseph Priestley and Richard Price—with all three of whom Bentham had personal contacts—in very much the same terms as Bentham was later to use, and under the similar, and already old, label of "moral or prudential algebra." [14]

None of Bentham's immediate disciples showed any interest in this aspect of Bentham's thought, and it was not until Jevons drew attention to it and made it the basis of his subjective theory of economic

[12] Bernard Mandeville, M.D., *A Treatise of the Hypochondriack and Hysterick Diseases,* 2nd ed. (London, 1730), p. 184. Compare the history of "Lullism."

[13] *The Works of Thomas Reid,* Sir William Hamilton, ed., 3rd ed. (Edinburgh, 1852), p. 717.

[14] *The Monthly Repository,* Vol. XII (1817), p. 13, and *Proceedings of the Massachusetts Historical Society,* 2nd ser., Vol. XVII (1903), p. 264.

value that it had any influence, for good or bad. I like to think, more
so probably than Wesley Mitchell would have appreciated, that Bentham's felicific calculus was merely one more manifestation of the
inferiority complex which practitioners of the social "sciences" had in
the eighteenth century, and have reacquired in the twentieth, towards
mathematics, towards the exact sciences, and towards quantification
as one of the higher virtues. Since with the application of "political
arithmetic" to "moral arithmetic" we now all accept without protest
the derivation of measured "propensities" from correlations between
psychologically and otherwise promiscuous statistical aggregates compiled catch-as-catch-can on anything up to global scale, our readiness
to laugh at Bentham's modest and wholly platonic gestures in this direction excites my propensity for amazement.

There remains one question, specially important for economics,
where the influence of Bentham on J. S. Mill is obvious, the question
of laissez-faire, or the economic role of government. Élie Halévy, in
his great but tendentious work on the Benthamites,[15] has made much
of the existence in Bentham's system of a conflict between his juristic
and his economic doctrines. According to Halévy, Bentham in his
juristic theory makes it the primary function of government to create
an *artificial* harmony between the interests of individuals and the
public interest, whereas in his economic theory he reaches laissez-faire
conclusions on the basis of an implied natural or spontaneous harmony
of interests. This has become a stereotype of present-day comments
on Bentham, and although there may be exceptions to the natural
law which proclaims that stereotypes in the field of the history of ideas
provide a light which blinds rather than guides, this is not one of
them.

Bentham did interpret the function of government, under the influence largely of Helvétius, as that of creating, through the application
of rewards and punishments, an approach to harmony between the
interests of individuals and the social interests. He did prescribe
limits for the field for governmental intervention in economic matters,
but these limits were not, as we shall see, very narrow ones, and in
any case were not so narrow as to give scope for a doctrine of natural
harmony of interests, in the sense of a harmony preordained or inherent in the nature of man living in a society unregulated by government. Of explicit formulation by Bentham of a doctrine of natural
harmony I can find not the slightest trace in his writings, and such a

[15] *La Formation du Radicalisme Philosophique*, 3 vols. (Paris, 1901–1904).
There is an inferior edition in English in one volume.

doctrine would be in basic conflict not only with his juristic theories but with his whole cosmological outlook. Faith in natural harmony always stems from either faith in the continuous intervention of a beneficent Author of Nature or faith in the workings of a natural evolutionary process, and the Benthamites rejected the former and had not yet heard of the latter.

It has been common since Adam Smith's day to take for granted *in economics* the role of the state with reference to the protection of legal property rights and the enforcement of contracts, leaving it to juristic inquiry to explore the problems of theory and of practice in this field. Such was also the procedure of Bentham, and in his juristic writings he keeps very much in mind that "passion . . . from the excesses of which, by reason of its strength, constancy, and universality, society has most to apprehend; I mean that which corresponds to the motive of pecuniary interest." [16] Here he deals with the problem of "repression" of harmful economic activity by means of civil and penal law. If Bentham believed that there was a natural harmony of private and public interests in the economic field, it was one, therefore, which would prevail only after the magistrate and the constable had performed their duties. [17]

But Bentham does not advocate anything like "anarchy plus the constable." His most general proposition of a laissez-faire character is as follows:

> With the view of causing an increase to take place in the mass of national wealth, or with a view to increase of the means either of subsistence or enjoyment, without some special reason, the general rule is, that nothing ought to be done or attempted by Government. The motto, or watchword of Government, on these occasions, ought to be—Be Quiet. [18]

This may sound like a sweeping enough support of laissez-faire, if, as is common though rarely desirable practice in such matters, it be read carelessly and out of its context. There are important qualifications, explicit or implied, within this apparently emphatic text. First, the text deals with "encouragement" and not with "repression" of economic activity. As I have already pointed out, Bentham deals with the problem of repression of harmful economic activity as a problem

[16] "Introduction to the Principles of Morals and Legislation," *Works,* Vol. I, pp. 90–91.

[17] Bentham deals briefly with the relations between political economy and law in "A General View of a Complete Code of Laws," *Works,* Vol. III, pp. 203–4.

[18] "Manual of Political Economy," *Works,* Vol. III, p. 33. All subsequent citations of Bentham are from the "Manual."

in law and not in economics. Second, the general rule of doing nothing
positive is applicable only if there is no special reason to the contrary. A rule is not equivalent for him to a principle, nor a "motto"
to a dogma.

Bentham presents three grounds for the general rule against governmental activity of a positive kind in the economic field: (1) in this
field, individuals know their own interest better than government can;
(2) individuals operate more ardently and more skillfully in pursuit
of their own interests than government can or will operate on their
behalf; (3) governmental intervention means coercion, either directly
or indirectly through taxation, and coercion involves "pain" and
therefore is an evil.

Bentham is ready to approve of any departure from the general
rule, however, if a case can be made for such departure on utility
grounds. "Indiscriminate generalizations" are an error, he says, and
"In laying down general rules, [even] fortuitous and transient cases
ought not to be forgotten." And he lives up to his doctrine as, for
instance, when he says that "what ought not to be done with the intention of supporting an unprofitable branch of trade, may yet be proper
for preventing the ruin of the workmen employed in such business," or,
when opposing in general any restrictions on the introduction of labor-
saving machinery, he approves, however, of transitory aid to workmen
injured economically by such introduction.

Bentham does not, moreover, limit his exceptions from the non-
intervention rule to fortuitous and transient cases, but presents an
elaborate analysis of the circumstances under which government should
not ("non-agenda") and those under which it should ("agenda")
intervene. The argument may, to some tastes, be weighted too heavily
on the side of *non-agenda,* but it is free from any dogma except the
utilitarian one with which it is supposed by Halévy to clash.

Whether government should intervene, says Bentham, should depend on the extent of the power, intelligence, and inclination, and
therefore the spontaneous initiative, possessed by the public, and this
will vary as between countries. "In Russia, under Peter the Great,
the list of *sponte acta* being a blank, that of *agenda* was proportionally
abundant." Government has special responsibilities for providing security against food shortages as well as military security. He approves
of government aid in the construction of roads, canals, iron railways,
of public hospitals for the sick, hurt and helpless, of public establishments for the "occasional maintenance and employment of able-bodied
poor," and, as we have seen, of public health activities on a scale still
unknown. He was an ardent advocate of general education at public

expense and he urged the extension of governmental registration services to make fraud more hazardous—and also of the systematic collection of economic statistics, but with a proviso which I suspect saps his concession of most of its virtue for modern statisticians, namely, that "no institution should be set on foot for the furnishing any such articles, without a previous indication of the benefit derivable from such knowledge, and a conviction that it will pay for the expense."

Whatever its merits or defects, this treatment of the economic role of government is not in manner or substance doctrinaire, is not in any detail, as far as I can see, inconsistent with his general "principle of utility," and does not have in it, explicitly or implicitly, any trace of a doctrine of natural harmony of interests. It is to be borne in mind, moreover, that the best Bentham hopes for after all that can be done artificially to harmonize private interests with the public interest will still be far from perfect harmony. This has, indeed, been made the basis from another point of view of attack by moral philosophers of other faiths against utilitarianism: it is taken to task for failing to build a bridge between individual and general happiness. But this would be a valid criticism only if either it had professed to have succeeded in doing so and failed, or if it were a proper demand of *any* moral philosophy that it should provide a *practicable* scheme of perfect harmony of interests. Bentham did not completely bridge the gulf between private interests and the general interest, but neither did he deny the existence of such a gulf, and he did propose two ways, education and government, by which the gulf could be somewhat narrowed—with religion, though grudgingly, accepted as a useful part of education in so far as it educates for virtue. Does anyone know of a third way?

I turn now to John Stuart Mill. His famous *Autobiography*—revealing, but not as much so as he no doubt intended—made generally known the extraordinary intellectual régime to which he had been subjected as a boy by his father, and the precocity which resulted from it. In 1822, at the age of sixteen, he was engaging the redoubtable Robert Torrens in battle in the pages of an important newspaper about the theory of (economic) value. Before he was twenty he had edited Bentham's three-volumed work on the *Rationale of Evidence,* had published at least seven major articles in important periodicals on economic, political, and legal matters, had pointed out with great assurance and even less reverence the literary, political, economic, philosophical, and ethical shortcomings of the august *Edinburgh Review,* and had been arrested for distributing birth-control pamphlets.

In this first stage of his career, drilled to a rigid adherence to the Benthamite canon, J. S. Mill was a zealous exponent of Bentham's, and of his father's moral and political doctrines and of Ricardo's economics. In 1826, however, when still in his twentieth year, he underwent a mental crisis, which continued intermittently for several years and which brought him sieges of mental depression, as well as an intellectual conversion which he was later, in his *Autobiography,* to describe as akin to a religious "conviction of sin," the sin being in effect Benthamism.

It is conceivable that J. S. Mill's main trouble was primarily due to overwork, but his own explanation was that the sudden realization that the Benthamite doctrines left the nobler human feelings too much out of account and did not offer a sufficiently full prospect for human happiness had proved more than he could take. During these and subsequent years, he manifested the characteristic which was to remain prominent in all the rest of his career, his susceptibility to influence from widely diverse ideas or, as he was later to put it in his *Autobiography,* his "great readiness and eagerness to learn from everybody, and to make room in my opinions for every new acquisition by adjusting the old and the new to one another." New winds of doctrine were imping-ing on his mind, which was then as open as a prairie: Wordsworth's nature-poetry, with its reverence for beauty and its revelation—for a Benthamite—that there were other fruitful sources of impressions than those provided by syllogisms; the reading of one of Comte's early works and personal associations with Saint-Simonians, which brought him into contact with the new historical approach to social thought; Macaulay's refutation in the *Edinburgh Review* of his father's *a priori* demonstration of the superiority of democracy to aristocratic govern-ment; the conservative political views and the more-or-less orthodox religious views of his friends John Sterling and Frederick Maurice; the feudalistic and pre-fascistic doctrines being expounded with fiery moral passion by Carlyle; and so forth. From all of them he borrowed some-thing, although never as much as he then supposed, and for the most part not for keeps.

For a time, while his dour and magerful father still lived, the younger Mill did not break openly with the Benthamites, but his per-sonal relations with the school became strained—more so, in fact, than he was ever to be aware of. Bentham, however, died in 1832 and James Mill in 1836, and freed from the restraint of their disapproval and evident disappointment, J. S. Mill began to explore the new ground on which he not too firmly stood by the hazardous procedure of putting his thoughts in print for the public to read.

The break was sharpest in the field of private ethics, where Ben-tham's and James Mill's interest had been least. In his economics,

J. S. Mill remained faithful to the Ricardian doctrines as he understood them—and, to some extent, improved upon them in the process
of interpreting them.   In any case, the Ricardian economics was not
wholly acceptable to Bentham, nor Bentham's economics at all acceptable to Ricardo.   In the fields of politics and of law, J. S. Mill
proclaimed some major departures in his thinking from the views of
Bentham, but he never specified what they were.   I think that, apart
from some wavering as to the virtues of political democracy and some
approaches to the benevolent Toryism of Coleridge, Wordsworth,
Sterling, and Maurice, these were mainly methodological, loss of faith
in the adequacy of the "geometrical" method in politics, rather than
substantive.[19]   With his father's writings he never, it seems to me, dealt
with complete frankness, and he reserved for Bentham blows which
could more justly have been directed against James Mill.   The harsh-
ness and vehemence of the attack on Bentham was no doubt a sub-
conscious manifestation of the urge he was under to free himself from
what he had come to feel was an intellectual straitjacket, but it had
been his father rather than Bentham who had placed it on him.

The attacks on Benthamism began in 1833, while his father was
still living but after Bentham had died, with critical "Remarks on
Bentham's Philosophy" included, under cover of anonymity, as an
appendix to Bulwer-Lytton's *England and the English*.   In 1838, or
two years after his father's death, he published in the *London and
Westminster Review* his famous full-dress article on Bentham, again
anonymous, but with the authorship inevitably known at once to friends
and foes.   In 1840, he published in the same *Review* an article on
Coleridge, which, by its sympathetic treatment of the latter's ethical
and political views, was indirectly a criticism of Benthamism.

Meanwhile, in 1835, in a review in the *London and Westminster* of a
book by Adam Sedgwick which criticized utilitarian ethics as expounded
by Paley, he had defended the principle of utility when properly expounded, but without mentioning any names had remarked that for a
full exposition of it additional materials were needed beyond those
already to be found in the writings of philosophers.

In these articles Mill was clearly endeavoring to salvage, or at least
shrinking from abandoning, a utilitarian system of ethics while reject-

[19] For his attempt to substitute, under Saint-Simonian influence, a philosophy-
of-history approach, see his series of essays on "The Spirit of the Age," originally
published anonymously in the *Examiner* in 1831, and reprinted in 1942 by the
University of Chicago Press, with a characteristically learned and penetrating introduction by F. A. Hayek.

ing such features of Bentham's system as he could no longer tolerate. There was high praise, therefore, for Bentham as well as sharp blame. His main criticism of Bentham related to his treatment of private morals and of psychology, and especially the stress Bentham put on the role played in human behavior by calculation of gain or loss. He objected also that Bentham, by shifting from a technical (or broad) meaning of terms—and especially of the term "interest"—to a popular (or narrow) meaning, often slid into an account of human behavior which pictured it as inherently selfish. He explained this—unkindly—in terms of Bentham's personality. Bentham, said Mill, intellectually recognized the possibility of generous action, of benevolence, but "the incompleteness of his own mind as a representative of universal human nature" led him to regard genuine benevolence as rare and therefore unimportant in real life.

> In many of the most natural and strongest feelings of human nature he had no sympathy; from many of its graver experiences he was altogether cut off; and the faculty by which one mind understands a mind different from itself, and throws itself into the feelings of that other mind, was denied him by his deficiency of Imagination.[20]

There was a basis for Mill's criticisms. That Bentham frequently fell into language which pictured human behavior as if it consisted almost solely of action based on calculations of personal gain and that his imagination was deficient with respect to the possible range of human emotions is beyond dispute. But Mill goes further in his criticism at some points than the texts he cites, or their context, justifies, and in doing so disregards peculiarities of the Benthamite terminology which at other times, when his attitude had changed, he was to invoke against misinterpretations of Bentham at other hands. I can here deal with only one of these misinterpretations. Mill points out that if in Bentham's *Table of the Springs of Action* we find such words as "Conscience," "Principle," "Moral Rectitude," "Moral Duty," which in the mouths of others represent recognition of such a thing as conscience as a thing distinct from philanthropy, affection, or self-interest in this world or the next, it is as synonymous for "love of reputation," and that the word "self-respect" appears not at all either here or in any of Bentham's writings.[21] The critics of Bentham who have since made the same criticism and cited his *Table of the Springs of Action* as evidence are beyond enumeration.

---

[20] "Bentham," reprinted in J. S. Mill, *Dissertations and Discussions*, 3rd ed., L. 1875, I, 353. [Reproduced in abridged form above, pp. 184 ff.—Ed.]
[21] *Ibid.*, I, 359.

There is only too much ground for criticism of Bentham for not using words quite as other men do, provided that deviation on his part from the common use of terms is not taken as reliable evidence of deviation from the common run of thought on the questions with which these words are usually associated. But Mill, who should have known better, makes use here of this kind of argument against the one person of all who by his discussions of the logic of language had made himself least vulnerable to it. Moreover, Bentham in his writings does use "conscience" and "duty" very much as other men do, and if he did not use "self-respect," his stock of synonyms was adequate to fill the void.

The *Table of the Springs of Action,* however, itself provides a more direct, though only a partial, answer to Mill's criticism. The psychology of Hartley and of James Mill from which Bentham started distinguished between "simple" pleasures, and "complex" or "compound" pleasures derived from the "simple" ones genetically by the processes of "association of ideas." Benevolence, generosity, duty, justice, conscience, and so forth would be "compound" pleasures. But Bentham expressly says of the *Table*—which is sufficiently formidable as it stands—that: "The pleasures and pains here brought to view are, every one of them, *simple* and *elementary*." [22] He does cite a few "Compound Pleasures," as illustrative of one broad category of such excluded from the table. One of these, "Love of Justice," has as one of its components "Sympathy for the community at large, in respect of the interest which it has in the maintenance of justice." Mill was later to emphasize love of justice as one of the major virtues. His present refusal to be satisfied with Bentham's recognition of it as one of the "Springs of Action" was perhaps a not too captious suspicion that the words added to it by Bentham made of it a less admirable virtue than if Bentham had written merely "Love of Justice (Period)." But it was common ground among the Benthamites, including J. S. Mill, that the tone and moral significance of "compound pleasures" could be radically different from the tone and original significance of their component elements, the "simple pleasures" from which they had been compounded.

By the time Mill was working on his *Principles of Political Economy,* he had swung back a large part though not all of the way to Bentham's political theory and moral philosophy. What was left of his revolt was confined mostly to a continued insistence on recognition of the complete range of human feelings and a consequent endeavor to avoid exaggerating the role of rationalistic hedonism in human behavior.

[22] *Works,* I, 207.

William Whewell, an anti-utilitarian professor of moral philosophy at Cambridge University where an even narrower type of utilitarianism with hell-fire trimmings—"theological utilitarianism," it was later to be labelled—had until his advent reigned unchallenged for over a century, in 1838, on the appearance of Mill's article on Bentham, had in private correspondence with a friend welcomed Mill's recantation, but complained—with some justice—of its manner:

> It is certainly very encouraging to see on all sides strong tendencies to a reform of the prevalent system of morals. The article [by Mill] in the *London Review* is an indication of this, and appears to me to be in many important points right, and at any rate right in the vigorous rejection of Bentham's doctrines and keen criticism of his character. But I confess I do not look with much respect upon a body of writers, who, after habitually showering the most bitter abuse on those who oppose Bentham's principles, come round to the side of their opponents, without a single word of apology, and with an air of imperturbable complacency, as if they had been right before and after the change. Nor do I see any security, in their present creed, against a change of equal magnitude hereafter.[23]

This was real prescience on Whewell's part. In 1843, in conversation about the surviving disciples of Bentham, Mill made the remark which "though smilingly uttered . . . was not at all a jest" that as for himself: "And I am Peter, who denied his Master."[24] In 1852 Mill was to write a critical review of Whewell's *Lectures on the History of Moral Philosophy in England,* published in the same year. Conceding very little error in the Benthamite doctrine, Mill rejected vehemently Whewell's objections to utilitarian ethics in general and to Bentham in particular, even when they were very similar indeed to his own criticism of Bentham in 1838.

The final stage in Mill's presentation of his ethical views was in 1863, when his essays on Utilitarianism appeared. In form, these still represented an adherence to the doctrine, but so modified by the admission without obvious absorption of foreign elements that they have been the despair of its friends and the delight of its critics ever since. Acts were to be morally appraised solely in terms of their consequences for happiness—a strictly Benthamite proposition. *All* consequences, however, were to be taken into account, including the effects on the character of the agent—an early doctrine of Mill's, which he derived from Coleridge and which he regarded as contrary to Bentham's views,

---

[23] Mrs. Stair Douglas, *Life of William Whewell* (London, 1881), pp. 270–71.
[24] David Masson, "Memories of London in the 'Forties,' " *Blackwood's,* Vol. CLXXXIII (1908), p. 553.

mistakenly, I think. Happiness was conceived broadly enough to cover every type of wish or aspiration man could experience. Mill— unwisely, I think—went a step further than Bentham ever ventured by offering a "proof" that happiness was the proper criterion of virtue: namely, that competent judges accepted it as such, a type of proof which eighteenth-century critics of the "moral sense" school of ethics had exposed to ridicule for its circularity.

Mill now attempted also to incorporate into utilitarianism a novel element for it and one which many moral philosophers hold to be incompatible with it, namely, the recognition of non-homogeneity of pleasures and consequently the existence of qualitative differences of a hierarchical nature, as well as quantitative differences, between pleasures:

> It is quite compatible with the principle of utility to recognize the fact, that some *kinds* of pleasure are more desirable and more valuable than others. It would be absurd that while, in estimating all other things, quality is considered as well as quantity, the estimation of pleasures should be supposed to depend on quantity alone.[25]

The test of quality as between two pleasures was the preference "by those who are competently acquainted with both" of the one above the other despite the fact that the other represented a much greater quantity of pleasure.[26]

I venture to suggest: (1) that the problem as Mill presents it, that is, within the limits of utilitarianism, is a spurious one; (2) that what he proffers as a solution is even more spurious; and (3) that Bentham and his predecessors to some extent and modern economists using utility theory to a larger extent, have provided a technique which, while it does not solve any fundamental moral problem, suffices to show that a dichotomy and possible clash between ratings of values on the basis of quality and their rating on the basis of quantity is not one of the fundamental moral problems.

Pleasures—or desires—are of course not homogeneous with respect to every conceivable quality they may possess—any more than are any other objects of human attention except abstract numbers. Com-

---

[25] J. S. Mill, *Utilitarianism,* 3rd ed. (London, 1867), pp. 11–12.

[26] *Ibid.,* p. 12. In an undated manuscript "On Social Freedom," found in Mill's house at Avignon after his death, and published, among other places, in *Living Age,* 7th ser., Vol. XXXVI (1907), pp. 323–36, there is a stronger statement of the higher-lower thesis with the order of rank made a pure matter of "feeling," not subject to demonstration or to argument—a complete swing back to the eighteenth-century "moral sense" school.

parison is—or should be—always with respect to specified qualities of objects, and if there is possibility of and proper occasion for measurement the measurement is also with reference to these specified qualities.

Mill confuses the issue by attempting at the same time to give predominant importance to the ordering of *classes* of pleasures on a higher-lower scale and to leave room for legitimate preference in particular cases of a pleasure of a lower order over one of a higher. This is the famous and ancient false dilemma of the water-*versus*-diamonds problem in economics, extended to the whole field of values. Whatever may be the case for didactic purposes, for actual behavior—including "moral" behavior—the issues arise in the form of necessary choices between units and not between classes of objects. Bentham's famous dictum "Quantum of pleasure being equal, pushpin [a children's game] is as good as poetry" would meet all the proper requirements of the utilitarian principle if restated somewhat as follows: "Desire being equal at the margin of choice, a marginal unit of pushpin is as good as a marginal unit of poetry." The utilitarian but didactic moralist would still be free to insist that since in fact experienced choosers don't plump for even a first unit of pushpin until they are gorged with poetry, *in that sense* poetry as a class is higher on the scale of values than pushpin as a class.

I come now at long last to Mill's *Principles of Political Economy*. He wrote this two-volume book in less than two years, and when he began it he expected it to take only a few months to write. For at least ten years prior to this, he had not given much attention to economics. It was designed to do for Mill's time what Adam Smith had done for his, and to present what was known of the "Principles of Political Economy" as a science, together with their applications to concrete problems and, in the words of its title page, "some of their Applications to Social Philosophy." By the "science" of political economy Mill meant a body of deductive analysis, resting on psychological premises derived from introspection and observation of one's neighbors, and even with respect to these premises abstracting from all aspects of human behavior except those most intimately and most generally associated with the business of buying and selling. When Malthus, in 1824, objected that the "new school" of Ricardians had "altered the theories of Adam Smith upon pure speculation," Mill had replied: "it would, indeed, have been somewhat surprising if they had altered them on any other ground." [27] Later, as the result of Comtean

---

[27] In a review of the article by Malthus in the *Quarterly Review*, No. LX, criticizing McCulloch's "Political Economy" article in the *Supplement* to the

influence and of his investigations in logical method, Mill was more receptive in principle to the possibilities of historical induction. But it is clear that he never assigned to it the right to an independent role in the "science" of political economy. Writing in 1835 with respect to the historical form of the inductive method, he had said:

> History is not the foundation, but the verification, of the social science; it corroborates, and often suggests, political truths, but cannot prove them. The proof of them is drawn from the laws of human nature; ascertained through the study of ourselves by reflection, and of mankind by actual intercourse with them. . . . The usefulness of history depends upon its being kept in the second place.[28]

This was, of course, standard methodological doctrine, and to a large extent practice, in English social thought since Hobbes. Inquiry was to be pursued by means of deductive reasoning resting on psychological premises obtained empirically, but chiefly through introspection —which, it should always be remembered, was universally regarded in the past, whatever may be the fashion today, as an "empirical" technique of investigation, and sharply distinguished from intuition, or "innate ideas." But in J. S. Mill, as methodological doctrine, it has less significance than for most of his predecessors, since he confines it to the "scientific" part of Political Economy, stresses the importance of "applications" which can proceed by a wider range of logical methods, gives repeatedly at least platonic warnings that any abstraction from reality must be allowed for before the results of such analysis are made the basis for pronouncements on policy, and rejects it for every other established branch of social thought.

Of his earlier rebellion against the psychology of Bentham and of his father, the most important residue for his economics was probably his repeated emphasis on the importance of custom as a rival to the competitive principle, especially in connection with land-tenure and the relations of landlord and tenant. Here he showed the influence of Richard Jones, one of the pioneer advocates of resort to systematic induction in economics. But this presented J. S. Mill with somewhat of a methodological dilemma, which he never succeeded in resolving. "It is unphilosophical," he wrote, "to construct a science out of a few of the agencies by which the phenomena are determined, and leave

fourth edition of the *Encyclopaedia Britannica, Westminster Review,* Vol. III (1825), p. 213.

[28] "Professor Sedgwick's Discourse on the Studies of the University of Cambridge," *Dissertations and Discussions,* Vol. I, pp. 112–13.

the rest to the routine of practice or the sagacity of conjecture." [29]
On the other hand, "only through the principle of competition has
political economy any pretension to the character of a science," [30] a
proposition which F. Y. Edgeworth was later in effect to repeat, when
he wrote that if monopoly should prevail over a large part of the economic order:

> Among those who would suffer by the new regime there would be [in-
> cluded] . . . the abstract economists, who would be deprived of their occu-
> pation, the investigation of the conditions which determine value. There
> would survive only the empirical school, flourishing in a chaos congenial to
> their mentality.[31]

We seem, however, to have found another alternative, that of becoming amateur lawyers.

Mill thus had no technique for dealing systematically with the
analysis of economic process where competition was encroached upon
either by custom or by monopoly, and when he did mention custom—
or monopoly—he left it to the reader to estimate its importance and
to make the necessary corrections in the conclusions he had reached
on the basis of abstractions from these complicating factors.   For himself, he assumed the responsibility only for that "uncertain and slippery
intermediate region," between "ultimate aims" and "the immediately
useful and practicable." [32]   Logicians and physical scientists have the
right, I suppose, to jeer at Mill's failure to extricate himself from this
plight.   For those among us, however, upon whom the redeeming grace
has not as yet been bestowed of that special ideology which takes the
form of faith in the capacity of statistical method to perform logical
miracles, humility is prescribed, since we are all in the same fix.

The *Principles* thus has no single methodological character.   As is
the case with the *Wealth of Nations* of Adam Smith, some portions are
predominantly abstract and *a priori;* in others, there is a substantial
measure of factual data and of inference from history.   Its wide range
of subject matter; the success with which the lucidity of its style and
the nobility of its outlook on life divert attention from its lack of
logical rigor; the patent honesty and open-mindedness with which controversial issues are treated; these and other qualities made it probably

[29] *A System of Logic,* 3rd ed., Vol. II, p. 472.

[30] *Principles of Political Economy,* Bk. II, Chap. IV, "Of Competition and
Custom."

[31] "The Pure Theory of Monopoly" [1897], *Papers Relating to Political Economy* (London, 1925), Vol. I, pp. 138–39.

[32] *Autobiography* (London, 1873), p. 189.

the longest-lived textbook our discipline has ever had or ever will have. It was the text used in the first college course in economics I took, over sixty years after its first publication. Francis Walker's *Political Economy* was also assigned to us, and I think we showed good judgment when we labelled the course, as students will, "Milk and Water." Writing in 1832, Mill had presented a forceful case in defense of ambiguity in language, on the ground that it was for many persons the price which would have to be paid if important ideas which by their richness and variety of content it is difficult to make clear were not to be sacrificed on the altar of logical clarity.[33] The *Principles,* I think, demonstrate that for Mill himself this was good doctrine; it would have been an inferior book, much less rich in content—and much smaller in size—if Mill had thrown out all that was ambiguous and lacking in strict logical consistency.

What most struck his contemporaries in the contents of the *Principles* was the sympathetic manner in which Mill dealt with proposals for radical change along socialist lines in the economic structure of society. The sympathy was in large degree platonic, for in no major concrete instance did Mill actually commit himself to the desirability of a specific drastic change. Mill aspired after the millennium, but he found abundant reason why it was not and should not be wished to be imminent. He looked forward, mostly on ethical and humanitarian grounds, to substantial socialization of the institution of property at some time in the vague future. Meanwhile, however, he warned against any weakening of the institutions of private property, free competition, and the rule of the market. This combination of hard-headed rules and utopian aspirations was just exactly the doctrine that Victorians of goodwill yearned for, and it made a large contribution to the popular success of the book.

Mill's handling of the problem of laissez-faire was a case in point. Except for the difference in tone and feeling, the fuller expression of lofty ideals and impracticable aspirations, it was substantially similar in method of analysis and nature of conclusions to Bentham's treatment. Like Bentham, and like all the other major classical economists except perhaps Senior—who was not a Benthamite—J. S. Mill gave only a very qualified adherence to laissez-faire. It was for him only a rule of expediency, always subordinate to the principle of utility, and never a dogma. The dogmatic exponents of laissez-faire of the time were the Manchester School, and Mill—like Torrens before him and

[33] Review of G. C. Lewis, *Use and Abuse of Political Terms, Tait's Edinburgh Magazine,* Vol. I (1832), p. 164 ff.

Cairnes, Jevons, Sidgwick, Marshall, Edgeworth and others after him
—denied repeatedly, and forcefully almost to the point of blasphemy,
that the Cobdenites had either authority or logic to support them when
they invoked the "Laws of Political Economy" to stop government
from coming to the relief of distress.

It is, fortunately, not part of my assignment to appraise the technical
economics of Mill's *Principles*. What I have tried to do is to show the
intellectual relations between two men important in the history of our
discipline. From these two men several generations of British and
American—and above all Canadian—economists, and to some extent
also "liberal" continental economists, derived in large part the psychological, ethical, political, and methodological presuppositions upon
which they built their economic analysis. With the ebbing of liberalism
in the profession, the importance of knowing what its intellectual
foundations were has become chiefly historical, and to those under
fifty the historical is not obviously important. But for those *over* fifty,
a comment of Tawney's is relevant. "It is a wise philosopher," he
writes, the flatterer really meaning "economist," "who knows the source
of his own premises." [34] I would go even further. It is an unusually
alert economist who knows what his premises are, regardless of their
source. For those over fifty study of Bentham and of Mill can do
something to remedy both of these lacks. Beyond this remark, I make
no attempt to draw any moral from what I have said. But I believe
that in exercising this unaccustomed measure of self-restraint I am
conforming to the "Principle of Utility" if broadly enough interpreted.

[34] Introduction to Raymond W. Firth, *Primitive Economics of the New Zealand
Maori* (London, 1939).

Cairnes
─── on ───
Bastiat

Frédéric Bastiat (1801–1850) was one of the most pronounced exponents of *laisser-faire* ideas in the history of economics. A French publicist and author of numerous popular
essays and allegories, he presented the teachings of the classical
economists in the form of dogmatic truths. Although it is easy
to find fault with Bastiat's exaggerations, parts of his work have
retained their original freshness and suggestiveness. This is true
particularly of Bastiat's celebrated "Petition of the Candlestick
Makers," in which the apparent absurdity of tariffs is demonstrated by means of an imaginary petition of the providers of
artificial light, urging the legislative bodies to prohibit the construction of windows in order to protect the domestic industry of
the candlestick makers against the cut-throat competition of the
sun.

John Elliot Cairnes (1823–1875) taught at Irish and English
universities, following, in the main, the teachings of Mill. He
is remembered for his doctrine of noncompeting groups. His
principal works, *The Character and Logical Method of Political
Economy* (1857) and *Some Leading Principles of Political Economy Newly Expounded* (1874), were designed to defend the
classical position.

THE NAME of Bastiat is, perhaps, the most familiar in this country of all French economists; a result to which several circumstances have contributed besides the merit of his writings. At a critical period of our reforming career he threw himself with extraordinary ardour into our contests, and lent effective assistance to the side that has triumphed. He is known on more than one occasion to have made himself the generous defender of English policy and character against the unreasoning prejudices of his countrymen. He was, moreover, the friend of Cobden—in itself, in the judgment of most, a sufficient voucher for economic acquirement; and he has been fortunate enough to find excellent translators for his principal works. This last circumstance cannot, indeed, be fairly separated from the merits of the writings themselves; and it must be owned that these were in some respects of a high and rare order. As examples of dialectical skill in reducing an opponent to absurdity, of simple and felicitous illustration, of delicate and polished raillery, attaining occasionally the pitch of a refined irony, the "Sophismes Économiques" might almost claim a place beside the "Provincial Letters." The petition of the candle-makers and other manufacturers of light to the Legislative Body, praying the exclusion by legislative enactment of the light of the sun, is alone almost enough to make a reputation in this line; and Swift himself has hardly shown greater art in the logical conduct of an absurd proposition than that with which the reader, in this modest proposal, is led, step by step, from the avowed premisses of Protection, through a series of the most natural and irrefragable deductions, straight to the preposterous conclusion advocated by the petitioners.

What we pray for is, that it may please you to pass a law ordering the shutting up of all windows, skylights, dormer-windows, outside and inside shutters, curtains, blinds, bull's-eyes—in a word, of all openings, holes, chinks, clefts, and fissures, by or through which the light of the sun has been allowed to enter houses, to the prejudice of the meritorious manufactures with which we flatter ourselves we have accommodated our country—a country which, in gratitude, ought not to abandon us now to a strife so unequal. . . .

[Reprinted in abridged form from *Fortnightly Review,* October 1870.]

And, first, if you shut up as much as possible all access to natural light, and create a demand for artificial light, which of our French manufactures will not be encouraged by it?

If more tallow is consumed, then there must be more oxen and sheep; and, consequently, we shall behold the increase of artificial meadows, meat, wool, hides, and, above all, manure, which is the basis and foundation of all agricultural wealth.

If more oil is consumed, then we shall have an extended cultivation of the poppy, of the olive, and of colewort. These rich and exhausting plants will come at the right time to enable us to avail ourselves of the increased fertility which the rearing of additional cattle will impart to our lands.

Our heaths will be covered with resinous trees. Numerous swarms of bees will, on the mountains, gather perfumed treasures, now wasting their fragrance on the desert air, like the flowers from which they are derived. No branch of agriculture but will then exhibit a cheering development. . . .

If you urge that the light of the sun is a gratuitous gift of nature, and that to reject such gifts is to reject wealth itself under pretence of encouraging the means of acquiring it, we would caution you against giving a death-blow to your own policy. Remember that hitherto you have always repelled foreign products, *because* they approximate more nearly than home products to the character of gratuitous gifts. To comply with the exactions of other monopolists, you have only *half a motive;* and to repulse us simply because we stand on a stronger vantage-ground than others, would be to adopt the equation $+ \times + = -$; in other words, it would be to heap *absurdity* upon *absurdity*. . . .

.   .   .   .

Make your choice, but be logical; for as long as you exclude, as you do, coal, iron, corn, foreign fabrics, *in proportion* as their price approximates to *zero,* what inconsistency would it be to admit the light of the sun, the price of which is already at *zero* during the entire day!

But it was not on the "Sophismes Économiques" that Bastiat would have been content to take the verdict of posterity as to his pretensions as an economist. Indeed, whatever might be the controversial and literary merits of these admirable tracts, they added nothing to already familiar economic truths. The theory of Free Trade had been fully thought out by a succession of able writers before Bastiat took it in hand, and all that he here could do was what, in fact, he did—furnish new and apt illustrations of a familiar doctrine, or, by well-selected instances, reduce opponents to glaring absurdity. But in 1848 the advent of the democratic republic brought other questions to the front, and stirred controversies more fitted to try the metal of a philosophic thinker. Socialism had raised its grim visage, and was propounding those solutions of the social problem, the mere recollection of which has since so often sufficed to frighten France from her propriety.   Louis Blanc, Considérant, Leroux, Proudhon, were thundering against the existing industrial order; and for those who cared to maintain that order the need of the hour was a philosophy adapted to the popular apprehension, which should be capable of furnishing a plausible reply to their attacks.   At this time Bastiat was at the height of his reputation in Paris.   He had frankly and sincerely accepted the Revolution, though sensible of the unpreparedness of the country for the new *régime,* and alive to the inevitable dangers incident to this state of things.   His views, however, did not extend beyond political changes, and while recognizing the generous aims of the Socialists, he shrank with horror from their subversive proposals.   He accordingly came forward eagerly to defend the menaced social structure.   In a series of clever brochures—"Propriété et la Loi," "Propriété et Spoliation," "Justice et Fraternité," "Capital et Rente," "Maudit Argent"—he propounded his reply to the "despotic organizers"—"ces pétrisseurs de l'argile humaine."   As he wrote, his ideas took firmer hold of his mind, and gradually shaped themselves into a system.   The needed philosophy was, he thought, to be found in a recast of Political Economy, and the "new exposition" he undertook to furnish in his "Harmonies Éco- nomiques."   Unfortunately, Bastiat did not live to complete this work; but enough was accomplished to render perfectly clear the essential character of the conception and the general scope of his design.   The English reader has now an opportunity of studying it in Mr. Stirling's excellent Translation.

  Political Economy, as treated by the predecessors of Bastiat—by Adam Smith and his successors in this country, by Say and his suc- cessors in France—aimed at unfolding the natural principles—natural in the sense of having their foundation in the nature of man and of his environments—which govern the facts of material well-being.   Those economists did not, indeed, hold themselves precluded from pointing out, when occasion offered, the moral and social bearing of their doc- trines; but, in general, they recognized the distinction between such practical lessons as they believed deducible from their expositions and the doctrines of the science which they taught.   In effect, Political Economy, in their hands, was a positive science, in the modern sense of that expression; its methods were combined induction and deduc- tion; its conclusions embodied hypothetical truths of precisely the same character as those of any of the deductive physical sciences; and its purpose was to explain phenomena.   As thus constituted, however, Political Economy did not meet the need which it was the object of

Bastiat to satisfy. What he aimed at supplying was, not a positive science, not a body of doctrines which should simply *explain* the facts of wealth, but one which, while explaining, should also *justify* those facts,—should justify them, that is to say, as manifested in the results of those fundamental institutions of modern society, private property, freedom of industry, of contract, and of exchange. As his biographer, M. de Fontenay, puts it, his aim was

To combine together and fuse into one the two distinct aspects of Fact and of Right; to recur to the formula of the Physiocrats—"La science des faits au point de vue du droit naturel"; to prove that *that which is,* in its actual *ensemble,* and still more in its progressive tendency, is conformable to *that which ought to be,* according to the aspirations of the universal conscience.

In Bastiat's own words, he sought

To demonstrate the Harmony of those laws of Providence which govern human society [by showing] that all principles, all motives, all springs of action, all interests, co-operate towards a grand final result, . . . the indefinite approximation of all classes towards a level which is always rising; in other words, the *equalization* of individuals in the general *amelioration.*[1]

"The conclusion of the Economists," he says in another place, "is for liberty. But, in order that this conclusion should take hold of men's minds and hearts, it must be solidly based on this fundamental principle:—Interests, left to themselves, tend to harmonious combinations, and to the progressive preponderance of the general good." [2]

Such was the scheme of renovated economic science propounded by Bastiat; and the question which I desire here to consider is, how far this conception of the inquiry represents a legitimate philosophical speculation, and, more particularly, how far the actual treatment of economic questions from this point of view by Bastiat has resulted in what all will allow to be among the primary and main ends of economical investigation—the elucidation of the facts of wealth.

And here the first remark that occurs is, that, as set forth in the above extracts, the problem of Political Economy is not properly the problem of a science at all. Not only is it not *the* problem of a science, it is not even a scientific problem; for I apprehend it is of the essence of all scientific investigation that the conclusion be left free to shape itself according to the results of the inquiry. Science has no foregone conclusions; but to prove a foregone conclusion is *the* problem of

[1] Stirling's "Translation," p. 105.
[2] Ibid., p. 7.

Political Economy, as propounded by Bastiat. What Bastiat proposes to do is, not to ascertain what the consequences of a given set of social arrangements are—that would have been a scientific investigation—but *to prove that they are of a certain kind;* to prove that "left to themselves, human interests are harmonious." By the very form in which he states his case, he constitutes himself the advocate of a system, instead of the expositor of a science.

But his conception of the problem involves a still graver error: as we have seen, it was of the essence of his scheme to "fuse together the two distinct aspects of Fact and Right." The "harmony" of human interests which he undertook to establish was not a mere coincidence of certain manifestations of material well-being with certain others, but extended to the moral consequences involved—an extension of view which, according to his biographer, constituted the great merit of his speculation. In effect, Bastiat, however widely separated from his opponents on the question of practical policy, was thoroughly at one with them on the most fundamental article of his philosophic creed: he and they alike accepted the doctrine of "natural rights." They differed, indeed, in their interpretation of the code of nature, but they were quite agreed as to its existence, and as to the obligation of bringing their doctrines to the test of its maxims. A new order of ideas thus found entrance among the premises of economic science; and the appeal, which had formerly been to facts,—to facts exclusively, mental or physical,—as the ground and evidence of doctrine, was henceforth extended to "rights," *"les plus simples éléments de la justice,"* *"bonne équité,"* and phrases of similar import.[3] It was thus that Fact and Right were fused. The principle of value, as understood by Bastiat, was not simply the law to which the facts of value conform, but such a presentation of that law as should reconcile the facts with what the expositor held to be the dictates of natural justice. The problem involved in the payment of interest on capital was not simply the determination of the physical and mental conditions which render possible the permanent payment of interest, and which govern its amount and fluctuations, but such a mode of presenting the practice as should

---

[3] His Essay on Free Trade opens with this announcement:—"Exchange is a natural right, like Property. Every citizen who has created or acquired a product, *ought* to have the option either of applying it immediately to his own use, or of ceding it to whosoever, on the surface of the globe, consents to give him in exchange the object of his desires. To deprive him of this faculty, while he makes no use of it contrary to public order or good morals, and solely to satisfy the convenience of another citizen, is to legalize spoliation, is to do violence to the law of justice."

amount to its moral vindication,—to show that it is "natural, just, legitimate, as useful to him who pays as to him who receives it." [4] And so of the other problems of the science. Political Economy, in short, became in Bastiat's hands one more example of that style of reasoning on political and social affairs which flourished so luxuriantly in France during the latter half of the last century, and is not yet quite extinct, of which the "Social Contract" may be taken as the type, and the "Declaration of the Rights of Man" as the best known practical outcome—a species of hybrid philosophy, consisting, to borrow the language of Mr. Mill, "of attempts to treat an art like a science, and to have a deductive art." "I speak," says Mr. Mill, "of those who deduce political conclusions, not from laws of nature, not from sequences of phenomena, real or imaginary, but from unbending practical maxims. Such are all who found their theory of politics on what is called abstract right." [5]

Now is such a mode of speculation philosophically legitimate? It seems to me not, and for this reason—that, from the very form in which the problem is stated, the argument is involved from its outset in a *petitio principii*. The question, What is? and the question, What ought to be? are distinct questions. It may be that the answers to them coincide; that *that which is,* is also *that which ought to be;* but, then, this is a thing to be proved, not to be taken for granted; and it can only be proved by working out each problem independently of the other. Instead of this, Bastiat formally identifies them—"fuses" them into one. But fusion of the questions implies fusion of the answers;— that is to say, it is assumed that the same form of words which tells us what is, will tell us also what ought to be. Such a scheme of speculation, it is obvious, could only be worked out in one way—namely, through the instrumentality of terms capable of lending themselves at need to either point of view—capable either of simply expressing a matter of fact, or of connoting with the fact expressed a moral judgment. And such, in truth, is Bastiat's method of proceeding. Availing himself of the double meaning of such "passionate" terms as "principle," "value," "worth," "service," and the like, he has produced a theory which affects to cover both solutions—at once to explain and to justify the facts to which it applies. The economic vocabulary unfortunately lends itself only too readily to this sort of theorizing, and few writers have entirely escaped illusion from this cause. Bastiat's distinction is that he has contrived so to propound the problem of Political Economy that it can only be answered by an *équivoque*.

---

[4] "Œuvres Complètes," vol. V, p. 26.
[5] "System of Logic," vol. II, p. 466. Third ed.

It may be added, that even though the questions of Fact and Right, of Science and Morality, were conceived and argued as distinct, there would still be strong, and, I venture to think, decisive reasons against combining them in the same scheme of speculation. To mention one reason only: such a mode of investigation would present the constant temptation to sacrifice one solution to the other, the scientific to the moral, or the moral to the scientific. The student would be constantly solicited to overlook or ignore, or, on the other hand, to strain or over-rate, data, according as they might seem to involve conclusions in one branch of the speculation in conflict with, or corroborative of, conclusions deemed to be of more importance in the other. Investigation, thus pursued, would no longer be disinterested; science would lose its singleness of purpose. This objection would lie against the combined treatment of the two problems even if they were conceived and discussed as distinct. But the objection to Bastiat's method goes far deeper than this: that method not merely combines science and morality, it confounds them.

Passing from the question of the logical legitimacy of Bastiat's conception of Economic Science, let us consider now the results which have accrued from this mode of conceiving and dealing with the problems of wealth. What, in a word, have been the scientific fruits of Bastiat's method? What new light have his speculations shed on the facts which form the subject-matter of his inquiry?

The doctrine on which Bastiat founded his pretensions as an original thinker in Political Economy was his Theory of Value. According to him this theory comprised potentially the whole of Economic Science; and, in point of fact, all that is peculiar to his views flows directly from this source: his conception of value is the *idée mère* of his entire scheme.

Bastiat's doctrine resolved itself into the statement that exchange-value under all circumstances is due to human effort as its sole and exclusive cause—to human effort as distinguished from natural gift and endowment, material or mental. What was given to man by nature was not only, he conceived, gratuitous in its origin, but must, in all cases, and (so long as exchange is free) under all circumstances, be incapable of acquiring value. Stated thus nakedly, however, the doctrine is not easily reconcilable with some very obvious facts. For example, the value of a pearl picked up accidentally on the sea-shore; the high remuneration obtained by persons endowed with natural gifts of an exceptional kind—painters, singers, and *artistes* generally; above all, the value of land possessing natural fertility or peculiar advantages of situation;—value in these and other similar instances does not seem to lend itself very easily to the doctrine that all value consists in and represents human effort. To give the theory plausibility, it needed to be clothed in other words. A term, in short, was wanting, which, while designating "effort," should be capable also of suggesting other considerations fitted to meet cases of the above kind. More than this, it was necessary (bearing in mind the moral side of the problem as conceived by Bastiat) that the term, while satisfying the conditions indicated, should also be capable of conveying a moral judgment on the facts to which it was applicable. Such a term Bastiat found in the word "service"; and it is in the uses to which he turns this word—as at once universal solvent of economic difficulties, and what Bentham would call a "sacramental" term in the warfare with Socialism—that the peculiar character of his speculation reveals itself.

In propriety of speech the term "service" should, I apprehend, be limited to personal exertions made in another's behalf. It is in this sense that it is commonly used in economic writings, and, so understood, it is a convenient economic term. But it is obviously possible, without doing any great violence to language, to give it a wider signification. Thus, for example, if a friend were to warn me that I was about to drink poison, he might be said to render me a service, though the effort involved in the announcement would be quite inappreciable. Similarly, a musician might be said to render a service to an audience whom he gratified by the performance of a piece of music, however slight the effort incident to the performance might happen to be. And so, again, might the owner of an island just risen from the sea, on which no human being had ever set foot, be said to render a "service" to the person to whom he should consent to transfer his property so circumstanced. Service, in short, may be understood to mean, not exclusively personal effort in another's behalf, but any act whereby another is served, *i.e.* benefited, wholly irrespective of whether the act consist in onerous exertion, in the passive surrender of property to another's use, or in a mere utterance of words from which some useful or pleasant consequence may flow. "Service" thus fulfilled the first of the conditions required; and it is accordingly substituted by Bastiat for "human effort" in the exposition of his theory. "Value" is said to depend upon "service," and to vary with the magnitude of the "service"; and all exchange is described as an "exchange of services." In a word, what Bastiat did was this: having been at infinite pains to exclude gratuitous gifts of nature from the possible elements of value, and pointedly identified the phenomenon with "human effort" as its exclusive source, he designates human effort by the term "service," and then employs this term to admit as sources of value those very gratuitous natural gifts the exclusion of which in this capacity constituted the essence of his doctrine. I acknowledge it seems scarcely credible that a writer of Bastiat's distinguished reputation should put forward an elaborate speculation, purporting to be "a new exposition of economic science," in which principles established or accepted by a succession of eminent predecessors are challenged, and which should after all resolve itself into so gross a fallacy as this; but a few quotations will show whether I have overstated the case.

To make an effort in order to satisfy another's want is to render him a service. If a service is stipulated in return, there is an exchange of services. . . . If the exchange is free, the two services exchanged are worth each other. . . . Less effort implies less service, and less service implies less value.[6]

So far he is propounding (doubtless in vague and somewhat equivocal terms, and without the due limitations) the doctrine of cost of production, and to this he for some time adheres; but, further on, we find this passage:

I take a walk along the sea-beach, and I find by chance a magnificent diamond. I am thus put in possession of a great value. Why? Am I about to confer a great benefit on the human race? Have I devoted myself to a long and laborious work? Neither the one nor the other. Why then does this diamond possess so much value? Undoubtedly because the person to whom I transfer it considers that I have rendered him a great *service* —all the greater that many rich people desire it, and that I alone can render it.

Here, it will be observed, he wholly abandons the idea of "effort" as the fundamental consideration. It is no longer "effort in satisfying another's want" that creates and measures the "service," but the capacity of the *natural object* in this respect in connection with the limitation set by *nature* to objects possessing this capacity. Further on, having to deal with the case of the high remuneration obtained by eminent *artistes,* he has these remarks:

Among the amusements which the people of Paris relish most is the pleasure of hearing the music of Rossini sung by Malibran or the admirable poetry of Racine interpreted by Rachel. There are in the world only two women who can furnish these noble and delicate kinds of entertainments, and unless we subject them to the torture, which would probably not succeed, we have no other way of procuring their services but by addressing

[6] Stirling's "Translation," pp. 44, 45.

ourselves to their good-will. Thus the services which we expect from Malibran and Rachel are possessed of great value.[7]

The reason assigned, it will be observed, being the same as in the case of the diamond—the power of satisfying a widely felt desire, coupled with the limitation of the number of persons possessing the natural endowments which give the power.

These, however, are rather "fancy" cases: the real hitch lies in the application of the theory to value in the case of land. I beg the reader's attention to Bastiat's mode of dealing with this point:

Land [he says] has value, because it can no longer be acquired without giving in exchange the equivalent of this labour [the labour expended upon it]. But what I contend for is that this land, on which its natural productive powers had not originally conferred any value, has still no value in this respect. This natural power which was gratuitous then is gratuitous now, and will be always gratuitous. We may say that the land has *value,* but when we go to the root of the matter we find that what possesses value is the human labour which has improved the land, and the capital which has been expended on it.[8]

But then comes the question, which he puts into the mouth of an objector, how is this doctrine reconcilable with the fact of the value attaching to natural fertility?

Everyone [says the objector] who purchases a land estate examines its quality, and pays for it accordingly. If of two properties which lie alongside each other, the one consists of rich alluvium, and the other of barren sand, the first is surely of more value than the second, although both may have absorbed the same capital, and, to say truth, the purchaser gives himself no trouble on that score.[9]

The objection is fairly stated; and now mark the answer:

The answer to the objection now under consideration is to be found in the theory of value explained in the fifth chapter of this work. I there said that value does not essentially imply labour; still less is it necessarily proportionate to labour. I have shown that the foundation of value is not so much the *pains taken* by the person who transfers it as the *pains saved* to the person who receives it; and it is for that reason that I have made it to reside in something which embraces these two elements—in *service.* I have said that a person may render a great service with very little effort, or that with a great effort one may render a very trifling service. The sole result is that labour does not obtain necessarily a remuneration which is in

[7] Ibid., p. 121.   [9] Ibid., p. 255.
[8] Ibid., pp. 249, 250.

proportion to its intensity, in the case either of man in an isolated condition, or of man in the social state.[10]

In other words, the difficulty is surmounted through the equivocal meaning of "service," which, with curious *naïveté,* we are informed in this passage was selected by the philosopher expressly because its meaning was equivocal.

Now what is the significance and what the worth of a theory, of which the efficacy, as a means of elucidating phenomena, lies entirely in the shifting uses of an ambiguous term? After the concessions made in these passages, it is evident that there is no longer any question of fact between Bastiat and the economists whose views he controverts. In entire disregard of what he had contended for as a fundamental principle, he here admits that value depends upon other conditions than human effort—upon such condition as the degree of satisfaction which the valuable object or act is capable of conferring; upon such condition, again, as the degree of limitation set to the supply of natural objects or of acts depending upon natural endowment; lastly, upon such condition as the natural superiority of some agents furnished by nature over others—for this is what the explanation in the passage last quoted obviously comes to. After these concessions, I say, there is no longer between Bastiat and those whom he so vehemently controverts anything that can be called a question of fact; and yet the issue is very far from being verbal merely. The real difference is not as to the facts, nor yet as to the names by which the facts are to be called, but as to the method of dealing with them—a difference again which resolves itself into the different aims with which Bastiat and those whom he opposes have gone into the inquiry. Thus Ricardo, seeking to ascertain the laws to which exchange-value in its various manifestations conforms, analyses the various conditions under which the phenomenon is found to present itself, classifies them according to their essential distinctions, marking these distinctions by distinct names, and is thus enabled to show in what way and under what circumstances each class contributes to the ultimate result—the phenomenon of value. Bastiat, aiming, not at the interpretation of facts, but at the defence of a system, proceeds by a wholly different course—repudiates analysis, classification, distinctive nomenclature; nay, avowedly selects as the central term of his doctrine a word which designates combinations of facts of the most diverse character. The difference of aim leads to difference of method, and issues in a different

10 Ibid., p. 256.

result; for whereas Ricardo's doctrine *does* succeed in explaining a vast variety of the most important and most complicated facts of exchange-value, Bastiat's, I have no hesitation in asserting, fails to solve even the simplest case. Let us test it by an example:—I desire to know if the recent gold discoveries will lower the value of gold. How am I helped to this by being told that value represents "service," and is in proportion to "service"? "Service" may import half-a-dozen things—effort exerted, effort saved, satisfaction conferred by the possession of natural objects, limitation of supply, and various combinations of these—and its import in the case in hand I have no means of determining. Gold, it is true, is now obtained by less "effort" than formerly. With Ricardo's doctrine before me I know what interpretation to place upon that circumstance. Enlightened by Bastiat's, I am precluded from drawing any inference whatever; for though the effort of production has been diminished, it may not be on effort that "service" in this case depends: "On peut rendre un grand service avec un très-leger effort, comme avec un grand effort on peut ne rendre qu'un très-médiocre service." Take a simpler case still. A machine is invented which cheapens the production of cloth:—will this lower the value of cloth? It would be quite consistent with Bastiat's theory that it should not do so, because it would be open to him to say, as he does say in the case of the diamond and of Madame Malibran's singing, that though the effort of production was diminished, the satisfaction which the commodity was capable of conferring remained unaffected. To tell me then that value represents "service" and varies with "service" is to tell me nothing, unless I am told further the elements of "service" which are operative in the given case. This is what Ricardo's theory in effect does: this is what Bastiat's theory fails to do; and in this difference lies the entire difference between the two doctrines. It is much as if a chemist were to propound as a solution of the problem of the composition of bodies, that matter is composed of elementary atoms, omitting to classify the various forms of matter according to their elementary constitution, or to say in what proportion in each class the elements combine. Such a generalization is no generalization in the scientific sense of the term: it is a mere confounding of a crowd of unanalysed phenomena under an ambiguous word.

So utterly, so glaringly inadequate is Bastiat's Theory of Value as a means of explaining phenomena, that its enunciation by a reasoner of Bastiat's remarkable acuteness would be altogether inexplicable had economic explanation been his principal object. But this, as we have seen, if an object with Bastiat at all, was quite secondary in his scheme. His paramount aim was, in truth, not economic, but moral; he sought,

not simply to explain, but also, and mainly, to justify the social facts
which he undertook to expound. And this brings me to the second and
more important *rôle* played by the term "service" in his theory. For
service not merely designates a fact, but connotes a moral judgment.
No one will deny that a man's services are properly his own—that he
has a right to be remunerated for his services by him who requires to
have them rendered to him; if, therefore, property is resolvable into
the right to certain values, and values in all cases represent, and vary
with, services, we have the moral sentiment at once enlisted in the support of property. To maintain property—property, let us say, in the
ground-rent of houses in the centre of London—is to maintain the
right of a man to the product of "services"—of "services" rendered to
society by himself or by those from whom he has derived. To maintain
freedom of contract is to maintain the right of one who has rendered
"services" to exchange those "services" on such terms as he pleases
against the "services" of others who are equally free. Thus all industrial and commercial operations under a *régime* of freedom were resolved by Bastiat into instances of the reciprocity of services—*"services
pour services";* than which, he asks, what can be more just? *"Services
pour services"*—the phrase has the unmistakable ring of an axiom of
"natural justice." Like the "droit du travail," "a fair day's wages for a
fair day's work," and other kindred expressions, it, so to speak, sounds
in equity. Whatever can be brought under the formula of *"services
pour services"* has already received its moral ratification. We see, then,
what Bastiat really accomplished. By dint of such explanations as I
have given examples of, he succeeded in bringing the principal phenomena of value within the comprehension of a single term; this term
being one which, from its etymological associations, connoted a moral
judgment on the facts to which it was applied. Armed with the shib-
boleth of *services pour services,* Bastiat felt himself strong to encounter
Communists on their own ground, and was able to return in kind the
bolts launched at him from the arsenal of the Rights of Man.

So much for the "new exposition of Political Economy," by which
Bastiat proposed to defend social order menaced by socialistic attacks.
The degree of faith which he placed in his specific is certainly surprising; for, however he may have failed to convince others, it is beyond
question that he succeeded in fully convincing himself. He entirely
believed that the Theory of Value set forth above contained the key to
the social problem—furnished the sufficient foundation for a policy of
the most rigid *laissez-faire.* Considered with reference to the practical
purpose for which it was designed—as a corrective to the intoxicating
appeals of socialistic writers—the antidote must, I think, be pronounced

to be extraordinarily weak, a veritable pill to cure an earthquake. Nor would it seem that Bastiat's writings have produced any sensible impression upon the general course of economic thought in France. He has left no school, and even those who yield a general assent to his system for the most part qualify their adhesion by reservations on essential points.

List
on
Say

The work of Friedrich List (1789–1846) marks an early revolt against the tenets of classical economics. List had a varied career, which led him from Germany to the United States. In his *National System of Political Economy,* first published in German in 1841, he develops a theory of productive forces, in contrast with the classical doctrine of exchange value. In List's work, individualism and cosmopolitanism give way to nationalism and protectionism. Emphasis on the concrete historical situation and on government intervention makes List a forerunner of the historical school.

It is not surprising that List had little use for Jean Baptiste Say (1767–1832), the principal apostle of Adam Smith on the continent of Europe. His appraisal of Say fails to mention Say's discussion of the role of the entrepreneur ("master-agent" or "adventurer") as well as Say's celebrated law of markets: "It is production which opens a demand for products. . . . A product is no sooner created, than it, from that instant, affords a market for other products to the full extent of its own value" (*A Treatise on Political Economy,* first French ed. 1803, English transl. 1821, Bk. I. Chap. 15).

JEAN BAPTISTE SAY on the whole has merely endeavoured to systematise, to elucidate, and to popularise, the materials which Adam Smith had gathered together after an irregular fashion. In that he has perfectly succeeded, inasmuch as he possessed in a high degree the gift of systematisation and elucidation. Nothing new or original is to be found in his writings, save only that he asserted the productiveness of mental labours, which Adam Smith denied. Only, this view, which is quite correct according to the theory of the productive powers, stands opposed to the theory of exchangeable values, and hence Smith is clearly more consistent than Say. Mental labourers produce directly no exchangeable values; nay, more, they diminish by their consumption the total amount of material productions and savings, and hence the total of material wealth. Moreover, the ground on which Say from his point of view includes mental labourers among the productive class, viz. because they are paid with exchangeable values, is an utterly baseless one, inasmuch as those values have been already produced before they reach the hands of the mental labourers; their possessor alone is changed, but by that change their amount is not increased. We can only term mental labourers productive if we regard the productive powers of the nation, and not the mere possession of exchangeable values, as national wealth. Say found himself opposed to Smith in this respect, exactly as Smith had found himself opposed to the physiocrats.

In order to include manufacturers among the productive class, Smith had been obliged to enlarge the idea of what constitutes wealth; and Say on his part had no other alternative than either to adopt the absurd view that mental labourers are not productive, as it was handed down to him by Adam Smith, or else to enlarge the idea of wealth as Adam Smith had done in opposition to the physiocrats, namely, to make it comprise productive power; and to argue, national wealth does not consist in the possession of exchangeable values, but in the possession of power to produce, just as the wealth of a fisherman does

[Reprinted by permission from Friedrich List, *The National System of Political Economy,* transl. by S. S. Lloyd, London, Longmans, Green and Company, 1916.]

not consist in the possession of fish, but in the ability and the means of continually catching fish to satisfy his wants.

It is noteworthy, and, so far as we are aware, not generally known, that Jean Baptiste Say had a brother whose plain clear common sense led him clearly to perceive the fundamental error of the theory of values, and that J. B. Say himself expressed to his doubting brother doubts as to the soundness of his own doctrine.

Louis Say wrote from Nantes, that a technical language had become prevalent in political economy which had led to much false reasoning, and that his brother Jean himself was not free from it.[1] According to Louis Say, the wealth of nations does not consist in material goods and their value in exchange, but in the ability continuously to produce such goods. The exchange theory of Smith and J. B. Say regards wealth from the narrow point of view of an individual merchant, and this system, which would reform the (so-called) mercantile system, is itself nothing else than a restricted mercantile system.[2] To these doubts and objections J. B. Say replied to his brother that "his (J. B. Say's) method (method?) (viz. the theory of exchangeable values) was certainly not the best, but that the difficulty was, to find a better." [3]

What! difficult to find a better? Had not brother Louis, then, found one? No, the real difficulty was that people had not the requisite acuteness to grasp and to follow out the idea which the brother had (certainly only in general terms) expressed; or rather, perhaps, because it was very distasteful to have to overturn the already established school, and to have to teach the precise opposite of the doctrine by which one had acquired celebrity. The only original thing in J. B. Say's writings is the form of his system, viz. that he defined political economy as the science which shows how *material wealth is produced, distributed, and consumed.* It was by this classification and by his exposition of it that J. B. Say made his success and also his school, and no wonder: for here everything lay ready to his hand; he knew how to explain so clearly

[1] Louis Say, *Etudes sur la Richesse des Nations,* Preface, p. iv.

[2] The following are the actual words of Louis Say (p. 10): "La richesse ne consiste pas dans les choses qui satisfont nos besoins ou nos goûts, mais dans le pouvoir d'en jouir annuellement." And further (pp. 14 to 15): "Le faux système mercantil, fondé sur la richesse en métaux précieux, a été remplacé par un autre fondé sur la richesse en valeurs vénales ou échangeables, qui consiste à n'évaluer ce qui compose la richesse d'une nation que comme le fait un marchand." And (note, p. 14): "L'école moderne qui refute le système mercantil a elle-même créé un système qui lui-même doit être appelé le système mercantil."

[3] *Etudes sur la Richesse des Nations,* p. 36 (quoting J. B. Say's words): "Que cette méthode était loin d'être bonne, mais que la difficulté était d'en trouver une meilleure."

and intelligibly the special process of production, and the individual powers engaged in it; he could set forth so lucidly (within the limits of his own narrow circle) the principle of the division of labour, and so clearly expound the trade of individuals. Every working potter, every huckster could understand him, and do so the more readily, the less J. B. Say told him that was new or unknown. For that in the work of the potter, hands and skill (labour) must be combined with clay (natural material) in order by means of the potter's wheel, the oven, and fuel (capital), to produce pots (valuable products or values in exchange), had been well known long before in every respectable potter's workshop, only they had not known how to describe these things in scientific language, and by means of it to generalise upon them. Also there were probably very few hucksters who did not know before J. B. Say's time, that by exchange both parties could gain values in exchange, and that if anyone exported 1,000 thalers' worth of goods, and got for them 1,500 thalers' worth of other goods from abroad, he would gain 500 thalers.

It was also well known before, that work leads to wealth, and idleness to beggary; that private self-interest is the most powerful stimulus to active industry; and that he who desires to obtain young chickens, must not first eat the eggs. Certainly people had not known before that all this was political economy; but they were delighted to be initiated with so little trouble into the deepest mysteries of the science, and thus to get rid of the hateful duties which make our favourite luxuries so dear, and to get perpetual peace, universal brotherhood, and the millennium into the bargain. It is also no cause for surprise that so many learned men and State officials ranked themselves among the admirers of Smith and Say; for the principle of "laissez faire et laissez aller" demands no sagacity from any save those who first introduced and expounded it; authors who succeeded them had nothing to do but to reiterate, embellish, and elucidate their argument; and who might not feel the wish and have the ability to be a great statesman, if all one had to do was to fold one's hands in one's bosom? It is a strange peculiarity of these systems, that one need only adopt their first propositions, and let oneself be led credulously and confidingly by the hand by the author, through a few chapters, and one is lost. We must say to M. Jean Baptiste Say at the outset that *political* economy is not, in our opinion, that science which teaches only how values in exchange are produced by individuals, distributed among them, and consumed by them; we say to him that a statesman will know and must know, over and above that, how the productive powers of a whole *nation* can be awakened, increased, and protected, and how on the other hand they are weakened, laid to sleep, or utterly destroyed; and how by means of those national productive powers the national resources can be utilised in the wisest and best manner so as to produce national existence, national independence, national prosperity, national strength, national culture, and a national future.

This system (of Say) has rushed from one extreme view—that the State can and ought to regulate everything—into the opposite extreme —that the State can and ought to do nothing: that the individual is everything, and the State nothing at all. The opinion of M. Say as to the omnipotence of individuals and the impotence of the State verges on the ridiculous. Where he cannot forbear from expressing a word of praise on the efficacy of Colbert's measures for the industrial education of France, he exclaims, "One could hardly have given *private persons* credit for such a high degree of wisdom."

If we turn our attention from the system to its author, we see in him a man who, without a comprehensive knowledge of history, without deep insight into State policy or State administration, without political or philosophical views, with merely one idea adopted from others in his head, rummages through history, politics, statistics, commercial and industrial relations, in order to discover isolated proofs and facts which may serve to support his idea. If anyone will read his remarks on the Navigation Laws, the Methuen Treaty, the system of Colbert, the Eden Treaty, &c. he will find this judgment confirmed. It did not suit him to follow out connectedly the commercial and industrial history of nations. That nations have become rich and mighty under protective tariffs he admits, only in his opinion they became so in spite of that system and not in consequence of it; and he requires that we should believe that conclusion on his word alone. He maintains that the Dutch were induced to trade directly with the East Indies, because Philip II forbade them to enter the harbour of Portugal; as though the protective system would justify that prohibition, as though the Dutch would not have found their way to the East Indies without it. With statistics and politics M. Say is as dissatisfied as with history; with the former because no doubt they produce the inconvenient facts which he says "have so often proved contradictory of his system"—with the latter because he understood nothing at all of it. He cannot desist from his warnings against the pitfalls into which statistical facts may mislead us, or from reminding us that politics have nothing to do with political economy, which sounds about as wise as if anyone were to maintain that pewter must not be taken into account in the consideration of a pewter platter.

First a merchant, then a manufacturer, then an unsuccessful politician, Say laid hold of political economy just as a man grasps at some new undertaking when the old one cannot go on any longer. We have his own confession on record, that he stood in doubt at first whether he should advocate the (so-called) mercantile system, or the system of free trade. Hatred of the Continental system (of Napoleon) which had ruined his manufactory, and against the author of it who had turned him out of the magistracy, determined him to espouse the cause of absolute freedom of trade.

The term "freedom" in whatever connection it is used has for fifty years past exercised a magical influence in France. Hence it happened that Say, under the Empire as well as under the Restoration, belonged to the Opposition, and that he incessantly advocated economy. Thus his writings became popular for quite other reasons than what they contained. Otherwise would it not be incomprehensible that their popularity should have continued after the fall of Napoleon, at a period when the adoption of Say's system would inevitably have ruined the French manufacturers? His firm adherence to the cosmopolitical principle under such circumstances proves how little political insight the man had. How little he knew the world, is shown by his firm belief in the cosmopolitical tendencies of Canning and Huskisson. One thing only was lacking to his fame, that neither Louis XVIII nor Charles X made him minister of commerce and of finance. In that case history would have coupled his name with that of Colbert, the one as the creator of the national industry, the other as its destroyer.

Never has any author with such small materials exercised such a wide scientific terrorism as J. B. Say; the slightest doubt as to the infallibility of his doctrine was branded as obscurantism; and even men like Chaptal feared the anathemas of this politico-economical Pope. Chaptal's work on the industry of France, from the beginning to the end, is nothing else than an exposition of the effects of the French protective system; he states that expressly; he says distinctly that under the existing circumstances of the world, prosperity for France can only be hoped for under the system of protection. At the same time Chaptal endeavours by an article in praise of free trade, directly in opposition to the whole tendency of his book, to solicit pardon for his heresy from the school of Say. Say imitated the Papacy even so far as to its "Index." He certainly did not prohibit heretical writings individually by name, but he was stricter still; he prohibits all, the non-heretical as well as the heretical; he warns the young students of political economy not to read too many books, as they might thus too easily be misled into errors; they ought to read only a few, but those good books, which means in other words, "You ought only to read me and Adam Smith, no others."

But that none too great sympathy should accrue to the immortal father of the school from the adoration of his disciples, his successor and interpreter on earth took good care, for, according to Say, Adam Smith's books are full of confusion, imperfection, and contradictions; and he clearly gives us to understand that one can only learn from himself "how one ought to read Adam Smith."

Notwithstanding, when Say was at the zenith of his fame, certain young heretics arose who attacked the basis of his system so effectually and so boldly, that he preferred privately to reply to them, and meekly to avoid any public discussion. Among these, Tanneguy du Châtel (more than once a minister of State) was the most vigorous and the most ingenious.

"Selon vous, mon cher critique," said Say to Du Châtel in a private letter, "il ne reste plus dans mon économie politique que des actions sans motifs, des faits sans explication, une chaîne de rapports dont les extrémités manquent et dont les anneaux les plus importants sont brisés. Je partage donc l'infortune d'Adam Smith, dont un de nos critiques a dit qu'il avait fait rétrograder l'économie politique." [4]   In a postscript to this letter he remarks very naïvely, "Dans le second article que vous annoncez, il est bien inutile de revenir sur cette polémique, *par laquelle nous pouvions bien ennuyer le public.*"

At the present day the school of Smith and Say has been exploded in France, and the rigid and spiritless influence of the Theory of Exchangeable Values has been succeeded by a revolution and an anarchy, which neither M. Rossi nor M. Blanqui are able to exorcise. The Saint-Simonians and the Fourrierists, with remarkable talent at their head, instead of reforming the old doctrines, have cast them entirely aside, and have framed for themselves a Utopian system. Quite recently the most ingenious persons among them have been seeking to discover the connection of their doctrines with those of the previous schools, and to make their ideas compatible with existing circumstances. Important results may be expected from their labours, especially from those of the talented Michel Chevalier. The amount of truth, and of what is practically applicable in our day, which their doctrines contain, consists chiefly in their expounding the *principle of the confederation and the harmony of the productive powers.* Their annihilation of individual freedom and independence is their weak side; with them the individual is entirely absorbed in the community, in direct contradiction to the Theory of Exchangeable Values, according to which the individual ought to be everything and the State nothing.

[4] Say, *Cours complet d'Economie politique pratique,* VII, p. 378.

It may be that the spirit of the world is tending to the realisation of the state of things which these sects dream of or prognosticate; in any case, however, I believe that many centuries must elapse before that can be possible. It is given to no mortal to estimate the progress of future centuries in discoveries and in the condition of society. Even the mind of a Plato could not have foretold that after the lapse of thousands of years the instruments which do the work of society would be constructed of iron, steel, and brass, nor could that of a Cicero have foreseen that the printing press would render it possible to extend the representative system over whole kingdoms, perhaps over whole quarters of the globe, and over the entire human race. If meanwhile it is given to only a few great minds to foresee a few instances of the progress of future thousands of years, yet to every age is assigned its own special task. But the task of the age in which we live appears not to be to break up mankind into Fourrierist "phalanstères," in order to give each individual as nearly as possible an equal share of mental and bodily enjoyments, but to perfect the productive powers, the mental culture, the political condition, and the power of whole nationalities, and by equalising them in these respects as far as is possible, to prepare them beforehand for universal union. For even if we admit that under the existing circumstances of the world the immediate object which its apostles had in view could be attained by each "phalanstère," what would be its effect on the power and independence of the nation? And would not the nation which was broken up into "phalanstères," run the risk of being conquered by some less advanced nation which continued to live in the old way, and of thus having its premature institutions destroyed together with its entire nationality? At present the Theory of Exchangeable Values has so completely lost its influence, that it is almost exclusively occupied with inquiries into the nature of Rent, and that Ricardo in his "Principles of Political Economy" could write, "The chief object of political economy is to determine the laws by which the produce of the soil ought to be shared between the landowner, the farmer, and the labourer."

While some persons are firmly convinced that this science is complete, and that nothing essential can further be added to it, those, on the other hand, who read these writings with philosophical or practical insight, maintain, that as yet there is no political economy at all, that that science has yet to be constructed; that until it is so, what goes by its name is merely an astrology, but that it is both possible and desirable out of it to produce an astronomy.

Finally, we must remark, in order not to be misunderstood, that our criticism of the writings alike of J. B. Say and of his predecessors and successors refers only to their national and international bearing; and that we recognise their value as expositions of subordinate doctrines. It is evident that an author may form very valuable views and inductions on individual branches of a science, while all the while the basis of his system may be entirely erroneous.

Socialists and Reformers

Halévy
— on —
Sismondi

Simonde de Sismondi (1773–1842), a Swiss historian and student of literary history, is the author of an early critque of classical economics, *Nouveaux principes d'économie politique* (1819). In this work, Sismondi notes the lack of economic stability under competition, and he is concerned with economic depressions resulting from underconsumption. Sismondi's work marks the beginning of a discussion which was resumed by a variety of later schools of thought.

Élie Halévy (1870–1937), the author of the essay on Sismondi which is reproduced here, was a French historian with early training in philosophy. Halévy made a name for himself as a profound student of the wellsprings of the social and intellectual movements in nineteenth-century Britain. His emphasis on the influence of the Methodist revival on British life and thought parallels Tawney's interpretation of the role of Puritanism in the early development of capitalism. Halévy's best-known works are his *History of the English People in the Nineteenth Century* (English translation 1924–1947), and *The Growth of Philosophic Radicalism* (English translation 1928), a brilliant account of Benthamism and British utilitarianism in general.

J EAN CHARLES LEONARD SIMONDE—this was originally the name of the man who later on called himself Sismondi—was born in Geneva on May 9, 1773. Geneva—the ancient holy city of Calvin, mellowed by the influence of Rousseau and Voltaire, the home of liberal protestantism. Geneva—the meeting place of the Latin and of the Teutonic genius, the seat of benign cosmopolitanism, the future capital of the League of Nations. Charles Simonde's family came from the French Dauphiné, having taken refuge in Geneva during the times of the religious wars. His father Gidion was a Calvinist minister. Charles was barely fifteen years old when economic ruin overcame his family, compelling him to earn his own living and preventing him from completing the formal education, solid but austere, which was characteristic of eighteenth-century Geneva. The family's ruin was connected with the world events of the day. The Geneva banker Necker had been called by Louis XVI to come to the aid of the finances of France; he had opened up a huge credit which was subscribed by a large number of his enthusiastic countrymen. Gidion was one of them, and he lost his entire fortune.

Charles Simonde was sent to Lyons to become a banker. Meanwhile the French Revolution broke out in Paris and its impact was soon to be felt in Geneva. With their finances becoming more and more strained, and in flight from the Revolution, the whole family Simonde eventually went to England. Charles learned to speak English like a native, and he came to love England like a second homeland. He came to reflect on, and to accept without reservation, the principles of political and economic liberalism. In 1803 he published a treatise, *De la richesse commerciale, ou principes d'économie politique appliqués à la législation du commerce* (Commercial Wealth, or Principles of Political Economy Applied to Commercial Legislation), a work lacking in originality, being in the nature of a popularization of the ideas of Adam Smith. Nevertheless, it attracted considerable attention. J. B. Say's treatise had not yet been published, and Simonde's work met the special needs of the French-speaking countries. We may add that

[Translated from Élie Halévy's Introduction to *Morceaux Choisies de Sismondi,* Paris, Alcan, 1933. By permission.]

Geneva, by that time, had become, against its wishes, a French city, and that Simonde, using the disguise of economics, attacked in his work the despotic administration of the French regime. It is interesting to note the final sentences of this book, in which Simonde expresses with great vigor the same ideas which were to be so badly shaken in his later work: "The legislators of Europe are afraid that there are not buyers of the products turned out by the several nations; they fail to be aware of the fact that production is woefully inadequate to satisfy the requirements of the buyers. . . . They take precautions against abundance, but abundance pursues them. They are unable to recognize the consoling truth that, whatever the misfortune of a few producers, the national wealth will never be idle in the hands of its owners but will always be employed by them to maintain productive labor, to diffuse welfare among the workers, and to undo, through the opening of a new line of production, the fall of those who have been defeated by adverse circumstances."

The treatise on Commercial Wealth was not the first publication of the young Simonde. Two years earlier he had come out with a *Tableau de l'agriculture toscane.* Why this interest in the agriculture of Tuscany? After the trip to London, a new foreign influence had come to affect the man from Geneva, this time that of Italy. In 1792 the family Simonde, which had been led back to Geneva by nostalgia, was compelled again to seek refuge abroad, this time in flight from the regime of Terror. Having crossed the Alps, they purchased an estate in Tuscany. Simonde took a great liking to this new country, becoming enamored of its simple customs and of the happy balance of its economy. He wanted to depict the happiness of the tenant in Tuscany, and did so in a poetic manner. Working out a political philosophy, he infused British liberalism with the republicanism of Geneva and with his admiration for the relics of the ancient spirit of autonomy, characteristic of the free municipalities of the Middle Ages, a spirit which seemed to subsist in Italy. His whole family became half Italian; he himself divided his time between the neighborhood of Geneva and that of Pescia, and undertook to write a *Histoire des Républiques italiennes au Moyen Age,* whose first volume was published in 1804 and which was to make him famous. In his own eyes and in the eyes of the whole western public, he had become an Italian patriot and at the same time a citizen of Geneva. In the course of his historical studies he made what to him seemed an important discovery. One of the "seven first families of Florence," the family de Sismondi, had fled from the ravages of the fifteenth-century civil war, and had taken refuge in the Dauphiné. Now, it was from the Dauphiné that a century later the family Simonde

(which at that time called itself Symond) had departed for Geneva.
No doubt, it must have been the same family. Charles Simonde became Simonde de Sismondi, S. de Sismondi, de Sismondi. There was
laughter in Geneva when the good citizen returned from the country
beyond the mountains, masquerading in a fancy title. But this naive
humbug succeeded in the end; it needed only time. How many people
today would doubt that Sismondi acquired his name by birth?

After his return from Tuscany to Geneva, Charles Simonde—whom
from now on we shall call Sismondi, as all the world does—cultivated
the friendship of Madame de Staël; together with Benjamin Constant
he became a member of the group at Coppet. Was he now to discover
Germany, after having discovered England and Italy? It seems that
the new discovery left hardly any effect on his mind. He continued
the publication of the sixteen volumes of his monumental *Histoire des
Républiques italiennes,* and also plunged into investigations of comparative literature.

As paradoxical as it may appear at first glance—Sismondi was still
to discover France. He did not care much for the France of bygone
times, the France of St. Bartholomew and of the revocation of the
Edict of Nantes; the Jacobin and the Imperial France, with her centralized despotism which was to deprive Geneva of its liberty. "I have
never seen Paris," he wrote in 1809, "but I despise it, and, besides, I
am afraid of it: I would not want the bit of pleasure which I might find
there to diminish my aversion against the city and its inhabitants and
the nation whose capital it is." Nevertheless, he was soon to travel
to Paris, for reasons connected with his books and their publication.
At once the *salons* of the Faubourg Saint-Germain vied with each other
in the conquest of the grave man from Geneva who loved so much the
company of the ladies. "After five months of an existence so animated
by a continuous festival of the spirit," he writes right after his return to
Geneva, "I think only of the society which I have left, I live on
memories, and I can understand better than before the lively regrets
of those who are exiled from Paris." But was it only a "bit of pleasure"
which had mellowed his will to resist? In truth, his reconciliation with
the French civilization, which began so abruptly and whose consequences were to be so lasting, is based on more profound reasons. We
must turn to them for a moment if we wish to understand the nature
of the "conversion" which took place in Sismondi's mind during that
period.

He had come to Paris at a time when the disasters of Napoleon's
Grand Army were beginning; when the western liberals were recognizing—moving, like history itself, from one extreme to the other—that

they must cease to hate France as a centre of warlike arrogance but love it as the last refuge of liberty. As the speed of the disaster quickened, Sismondi's attachment to France grew. "I continue to feel a strong aversion against Napoleon—but I feel no affection or esteem for any of his opponents." "I understand the hatred inspired by a ruler of mad ambition, but it is not equivalent to the contempt which I feel for imbecile sovereigns; I don't know whether my indignation or my chagrin is stronger when I see so many kings and so many governments reestablished only by virtue of their stupidity and their profound incapacity." In spite of all this, his sympathy for England persisted. With the intention of making British public opinion favorably inclined to his native country, he presented Geneva to the British public as "an English city on the Continent, . . . the champion both of civil and of religious liberty, of the British liberty, so wise and strong, so progressive and conservative as well." He also declared that in his estimation "no nation stands higher than the British." England is to him "without equal." France comes only afterwards. But he could not fail to be shaken in his cult of British civilization when during the Hundred Days he vigorously sided with Napoleon. To understand this attitude, one must take into account the profound revolution which took place during these days among so many liberal minds—when Jean Baptiste Say, the apostle of the ideas of Adam Smith and the most obstinate opponent of Napoleon among French scholars, devoted an entire little book to a denunciation of the vices of British society, pointing out the contrast between extreme wealth and extreme poverty, the decline of education among the lower class and the decline of civilization among the middle class. In spite of all, however, Jean Baptiste Say remained loyal to the doctrine of Adam Smith, attributing many of the faults of British society to the betrayal, by the ruling classes, of the great traditions of the nation by turning to warlike policies and to agrarian protectionism. He recommended reduction of military expenditures, abandonment of colonial expansion, and lowering or elimination of the duties on imported grain—then prosperity, combined with liberty, would rule again. Two years later Sismondi was to go much farther than Say in his criticism of British society—by insisting on the inadequacy of the remedies proposed by the classical economists and on the theoretical weakness of this school.

The *Encyclopaedia Britannica* was a publication famous in England. It had become a sort of permanent institution which was constantly brought up to date in the form of revised editions. At the moment, the publishers decided to bring out a supplement of six volumes rather than incur the expenses of an entirely reset work. They commissioned

the author of the *Richesse commerciale,* who always had been very
popular in England, to write the article on "Political Economy," and
Sismondi began to work on it. This was his first return to economics
after an interlude of fifteen years, during which he had busied himself
with entirely different matters. When comparing his ideas of fifteen
years and more ago with the facts, he noted a profound disaccord between the two. He did a good job writing the commissioned article in
the spirit expected by those who had ordered it. But at the same time
he went to work on a full-length treatise which was differently inspired.
Completed at the end of 1818, it was published early in 1819. The
title of this work was *Nouveaux principes* (*Nouveau principes d'économie politique, ou de la richesse dans ses rapports avec la population,*
that is, New Principles of Political Economy, or, on Wealth and Its
Relations to Population), in contrast with the subtitle of his work of
1803 (Principles of Political Economy Applied to Commercial Legislation) and with the title of Ricardo's work of 1817 (Principles of Political Economy and Taxation). Behind the façade of England's political
liberalism he now discovered an economic organization whose true
name was serfdom rather than liberty, and he went on in this vein to
pronounce a judgment on British civilization such as he would not have
dreamed of pronouncing before. "In one nation alone there is always
a contrast between its apparent wealth and the abject misery of one
tenth of its population, which is reduced to a life maintained by public
charity. But this nation, which in certain respects is so deserving of
being imitated, whose very defects are so dazzling—this nation has
seduced through its example all statesmen of the Continent. If the
reflections presented here should fail to be useful to Britain herself, I
at least hope to have done a service for humanity and for my countrymen by pointing out the dangers of her course and by making clear,
in the light of the British example, that unlimited competition as basic
principle of economic organization implies the justification of a struggle
of all against society and the sacrifice of the interests of humanity to
the simultaneous action of all those who are inspired by greed."

Let us now attempt to define the "new principles" which form the
basis of Sismondi's economics. To show them in full perspective, we
may contrast them with "orthodox economics"—an expression coined
by Sismondi—which he intended to demolish. The foundation of
orthodox economics was a theory, implicit in the great work of Adam
Smith, stated by Sismondi in 1803 in the final passages of his *Commercial Wealth,* and given its classical form by Jean Baptiste Say and
James Mill: the so-called law of markets. In terms of this theory, the
gluts of markets and the lack of saleability of goods are matters which

can be taken lightly: they are temporary and particular disorders, bound to disappear swiftly once order is again restored. This is so because goods are exchanged for goods; all goods for all goods. Any one good which is brought to the market constitutes in itself the demand for another good. If there is general overproduction every once in a while, this would never be a general overproduction of the same good. It rather means that in a certain part of the world certain products find no buyers, while in another part of the world other products likewise find no buyers, because tariff duties constitute artificial obstacles to their exchange. This obstacle should be removed, and all things be permitted to obey the natural law of exchange. Free trade brings abundance and equality.

Ricardo incorporated this law into his doctrine in 1819, at the same time basing the latter on a law which Adam Smith had not known: the Malthusian principle of population. In the terms of this "principle," if it is divested of its pseudo-mathematical garb, mankind increases incessantly and exercises constant pressure on the means of subsistence, their habitat being a world whose extension and fertility are limited. According to Ricardo's doctrine—whose details we cannot discuss here —there results from this the division of society into three classes, which struggle against each other and whose struggles, in certain respects, become aggravated as mankind progresses and increases: landowners, capitalists, and laborers. Is Sismondi going to retain this pessimistic aspect of Ricardian economics, to set it up against the optimism of the law of markets? Others will do it, but not he, failing, as he did, to note that Ricardo's thought could be turned against Ricardo himself. A strange illusion, but one which was common among many of his contemporaries and for whose reasons one must look to Sismondi.

Sismondi confesses at once that he is repelled by the abstract simplicity of the speculations of the modern school of economists, so much so that he is hardly able to read Ricardo. "Our mind puts up resistance to the admission of the abstractions which they require from us; but this resistance itself is a hint that we move away from truth when we aim, in the social sciences, at the isolation of a principle, seeing nothing besides it." Adam Smith had proceeded quite differently, being a historian who appealed to experience all the time. That is why Sismondi never ceased to consider himself a disciple of Adam Smith, in spite of unavoidable differences, whereas he assumed the position of an irreconcilable opponent of the later economists who desired to transform economics into a science of principles. He made it a point to insist on the complex character of the object of social science. Because of its complexity, it is not the same everywhere and at all times, and it can be varied according to the discretion of the investigator within the limits of empirical possibilities. Sismondi further hoped to avoid what he considered the second defect of the Ricardian doctrine, that is, its fatalism. In the hands of the orthodox economists, economics has become "speculative to such an extent that it appears to detach itself from all practice." Ricardo's system tends to prove that "nothing makes any difference and nothing can do harm to anything else." Fatalism, perhaps, goes with simplicity. In the light of orthodox economics, the class division of society is based on certain simple data; naturally, it must itself also be simple, and the emergence of the three separate classes of landowners, capitalists, and laborers appears as necessary in the sense characteristic of the simple laws of nature. Sismondi took a completely different view. He did not deny the possibility of scientific economics, but the class distinctions, which are the product of an ever-changing and infinitely complex history, are to be its point of departure, not its point of destination. On the basis of a given class division of economic society one can establish the laws under which the society composing such classes operates; and one can further establish the effects which the operation of these laws has on the welfare of the individual members of society. If the effects are bad, one must search, guided by experience, for ways and means to modify relations which are not unchangeable at all. This is the art of politics, which is firmly based on science, but on a science less abstract and therefore less passive than the science of the economists in vogue at Sismondi's time.

According to Sismondi, we are members of a society whose characteristic mark of distinction compared with all earlier forms of society is its division into two classes. One class is composed of proprietors who receive income without work, and the other is composed of laborers who do not own any property. The former, capitalist, class includes the landowners as well as the owners of industrial capital. The second class is the proletariat. To the economist, such a status of society poses a two-fold problem: a theoretical one and a practical one. The theoretical problem is to know how the laws of exchange function in this society, laws which form the basis of the science founded by Adam Smith. The practical problem is to know whether the operation of these laws, if they are left to themselves in a society of the described type, is favorable to the interests of mankind, and to formulate proposals for desirable and feasible reforms of the institutions of this society in order to correct the ill effects of *laisser faire*.

Is the division of society into two classes of such nature that the progress of free competition is bound to allay all the time, and thereby

to correct, the ill effects? This was the thesis maintained by the orthodox school. Let us assume, for example, that a manufacturer has made
an innovation which enables him to turn out his products at lower
cost. According to the orthodox school, he will derive from the reduction of cost no more than a temporary advantage. Very soon knowledge of his innovation will spread; other producers will imitate him;
and for all of them, without distinction, cost of production and selling
price will fall. But, according to Sismondi, things take quite a different
course. From the point of view of the manufacturers the introduction
of the new process requires the sacrifice of a large amount of fixed
capital as well as of habits of work acquired by them and by their
workers—a sacrifice to which they will resign themselves only if there
is no other way out. On the other hand, it will be much easier for the
innovator to expand the application of the new process, to increase his
plant, to reduce the price of his merchandise, and, by offering a quantity capable of satisfying the increased demand, to ruin his competitors.
In summary, competition, instead of tending in the end to reestablish
equality between him and his competitors, makes him the master of
the market. Through large-scale production, division of labor, and
the use of machinery, competition leads to the concentration of wealth
among a smaller and smaller number of individuals, and to the concentration of production in larger and larger plants.

Does such a society, which is based on inequality of wealth, enjoy
stability in lieu of justice? Not at all, according to Sismondi. This
is the second point of his demonstration, and perhaps the most important. With the number of small producers diminishing, the middle class
shrinks. Concentration leads to the existence of a restricted number
of very wealthy individuals side by side with a large number of very
poor persons. With a given quantity of labor input the workers, in
the large factories, produce a constantly growing volume of output.
Who is to buy it? The workers? As a result of the new distribution
of social wealth, they become poorer and poorer; their purchasing
power diminishes. The employers? Besides being very small in number, they can consume products which are in the nature of necessities
only within limits. Only luxury goods can be bought and consumed
without limits. But the characteristic feature of large-scale industry
is not the production of luxuries but of articles of ordinary quality and
general usefulness. In brief, the effect of large-scale industry is the
increase of the capacity to produce, and, at the same time, the reduction of the capacity to consume. The only relief available to the manufacturers in search of markets is the export of goods to regions not
yet invaded by large-scale industry. When one market has been

saturated, or when large-scale industry has been established there, it ceases to be an export market. A new crisis of overproduction makes itself felt until such time as a new foreign market has been discovered. And so forth, until the whole world finds itself invaded by the products of large-scale industry and the utter absurdity of the system becomes evident. Contrary to the pretensions of the "law of markets," the congestion of markets is a characteristic feature of the present economic era, the normal effect of the regime of large-scale industry.

This then is, according to Sismondi, the fundamental defect of ortho-dox economics. It does not take the point of view of society as a com-plex whole but that of the proprietor who enriches himself by selling the products of his land or of his factory. Although it has definitively refuted the error of mercantilism, it constitutes a new type of mer-cantilism, taking into account only the interests of the merchant and believing thereby to have safeguarded the interests of the entire com-munity—which would only be the case if the latter were to consist exclusively of merchants. This is not true political economy, that is, the art of guiding the affairs of the community in the general interest, but rather the art of individual enrichment, "chrematistics," according to the term coined by Sismondi. This accounts for the contradictions of orthodox economics. Naturally, the proprietor is interested only in the increase in the "net product" of human labor, whereas mankind is interested in the "gross product." Naturally, the proprietor is in-terested in what in economics is known as the "value in exchange" of the goods which he throws on the market—the price at which they will be exchanged for other goods—whereas to society their utility, their "value in use," is the important matter. The doctrinaires of the "law of markets" recognize only independent producers who engage in mutual exchange transactions, exchanging, after their wants are satisfied in part, the excess of their produce with the view of obtaining complete want satisfaction by satisfying the wants of others. But they fail to understand the true character of modern industrial society, whose inter-preters they pride themselves to be: It is only in order to sell that the masters of production themselves work and make others work for wages. Though the originators of the law of markets are not aware of this, this law is the true expression of the old world, the obsolete world of "landed wealth" in which production was carried on for a restricted market known in advance. The modern world is the world of "commercial wealth," of blind and frantic production for a market which runs away, as it were, from the merchant. Production closes its own outlets by placing a steadily increasing number of poor workers in the service of the masters of production and exposing them to regular unemployment.

Which remedies can relieve these evils? Is it the remedy which later on will be called "socialistic"? Sismondi was acquainted with the founders of socialism. He saw Robert Owen in Paris in 1818, that is, exactly at the time when economic problems occupied him again. Can one not surmise either that he desired to meet Owen, having been struck by the ideas set forth in the latter's numerous pamphlets, in which Owen insists on the reality of industrial overproduction, on the urgent need for legal restrictions on the working day, and on the inevitable replacement of a society which produces for exchange by one which produces for use? Or can one perhaps go as far as to surmise that the knowledge of these writings brought about the conversion of Sismondi and turned him to his attempt at founding economics on "new principles"? The doctrine of Robert Owen had gained much prestige in these years; a whole group of disciples, inspired by Owen's ideas, extolled the replacement of existing society, based on exchange, by a "cooperative" society. And in France Fourier began to find followers. However, Sismondi's interest in the propaganda of Owen's and Fourier's disciples reflected only his attachment to their critique of existing institutions. He never went along with the remedies which they extolled, being too prudent a historian, too firmly convinced of the complexity of human affairs. "Who is the man," he writes, "strong enough to conjure up the vision of an organization not yet existing, strong enough to size up the future, when we already find it so difficult to size up the present?" With respect to the followers of Saint-Simon, whose propaganda was soon to become so noisy, it is unnecessary to point out that they never had the sympathy of Sismondi. These opponents of competition have one point in common with the theorists of unbridled competition: both do not admit the existence of a problem of overproduction. Sismondi always distrusted and despised the frantic optimism of either school of thought.

He does not aim at a comprehensive regulation of conditions of work. Although neither Fourier nor Saint-Simon nor their followers are egalitarians in the strict sense of this word, he ponders, in his critiques, especially over Owenism, which is an egalitarianism. He does not believe in the possibility of an absolute equalization of wealth without violence, which would make the new regime odious and precarious. He is satisfied with a moderate inequality of conditions, similar to one which he observes in certain regions not yet invaded by industrialism. Does he dream of a return to the past, of a return which could be called a "reaction" in the philosophical sense of this term? One sometimes might think so. Thus, when discussing the possibility of government intervention to alleviate the ills from which modern society suffers, he runs into the familiar objection of the orthodox economists who insist that any legal intervention in the realm of production is bad because it tends to retard production. But he replies: What does this matter if the disease from which modern society suffers is an excess of productivity? However, his thought can be interpreted as less thoroughly reactionary. He declares explicitly that he is not opposed to the progress of mechanization, under the condition only that it should entail a reduction of the workload of the people, of all the people, and that it should not lead to the opulence of a few while the masses toil and suffer. He insists that the rich should not abuse their increasing power—vested in them through the ownership of machinery—to raise their profits by impairing the living conditions of their employees. Such restraint, he points out, would protect the rich themselves against their imprudent rapacity: with the workers less pinched, and with their purchasing power strengthened, society will be less exposed to the periodic congestions of the market, which are a permanent source of insecurity for all, the rich and the poor. He insists that the increase in production should surely not be arrested but that it should be regulated by law; that this increase should follow the progress of consumption instead of moving ahead of it with giant strides—as, he believes, it happens, to the general misfortune, in his own monstrous society.

Concerning landed property, the legislator should favor the development of small holdings—not so much by means of new legislation but rather by abrogating the ancient laws which hamper such a development. The legislator is advised to take similar measures also with respect to personal property. In a world in which a small number of wealthy people are in command of armies of the poor, the legislator should bestow on workers the freedom to form associations, enabling them, through the union of weak individuals, to put up some resistance to oppression by employers. Furthermore, the legislator—and this time by means of positive laws—should secure the limitation of the working day, the prohibition of child labor, a weekly day of rest; and he should aim at a reorganization of the industrial order—inspired, as Sismondi recognized almost with regret, by the ancient guild system —which would give the worker "a guaranteed right against the employer," with the latter obliged by law to protect the workers against the hazards attending their occupational life, especially against unemployment. When Sismondi suggests these remedies, he proceeds haltingly and in an extremely cautious manner. "I confess," he writes, "that, after having indicated what to my mind is justice, I don't feel strong enough to indicate the means to bring about justice." But if he goes so far as to consider the task as "beyond human power," we must take into account that here he meets a difficulty which arises from the depth of his philosophy. His irresolution is irresolution based on reason.

When he confesses that he must separate himself from friends whose political opinions he shares, we must take into account that in the bottom of his heart he always remains loyal to their liberalism. These liberals are no anarchists, no enemies of all laws. They want laws in order to protect the individual against the excessive power of the sovereign, be it a man or a mass. It is in this spirit that Sismondi, having seen unbridled competition giving birth to serfdom, wants liberty to be restrained, but always with prudence and in an experimental manner, as it were, because in the last analysis liberty is only to be restrained in order to preserve it. When Sismondi insists that the worker should have "guaranteed rights" against his employer, does he not borrow the word "guarantee" from the language of constitutional law? And does he not reveal what is at the bottom of his thought when he characterizes as "extra-constitutional" the power of the capitalist over the proletariat?

The first edition of the *New Principles of Political Economy* appeared in 1819 and a second edition was published in 1827. At the head of the second edition Sismondi could place a triumphant preface. After a few years of calm, a new crisis of overproduction had broken out in England, and France, having begun to industrialize, was likewise to have her first crisis. In this manner Sismondi's predictions fulfilled themselves. Did this mean that the years of glory would now come to him? This, perhaps, was his hope. He was convinced of his economic and political doctrines, and, in passing his fifties, had attained the full measure of maturity. But, in reality, the years which followed were to him years of decline.

He did not again meet with the success achieved with his *History of the Italian Republics of the Middle Ages*. Publishing a *History of the French* in more than forty dreary volumes, he had to see one volume after the other fall flat in an atmosphere of general indifference. He took much interest in the causes cherished by liberals: the abolition of the slave trade and of slavery, the freedom of Italy. But the heterodox opinions which he had pronounced in his *New Principles* had turned him into an eccentric thinker who was slighted by all.

When a workers' revolt was bloodily subdued in Lyons in 1834, Sismondi, in Geneva, "infuriates the whole world" by declaring "the massacres of innocuous persons by the moderates and by the friends of order to be the most atrocious thing which has happened during these 45 years of revolution." The bourgeosie of Geneva now counted him among the Jacobins. The Swiss radicals, on the other hand, were then insisting on the transformation of Switzerland into a single and undivided democracy. This sufficed to throw Sismondi, the enemy of all centralization and unrepentant federalist, back into the camp of the aristocrats. Sick, partner to a marriage—a love match—which had turned out well but by no means delightful, he ended his days as a lonely and hypochondriac old man. His neighbors tell a story how he, inspired by hatred of overproduction, selected for work on his farm the slowest and oldest day laborer, and for the repair of his house the worker least in demand. Who understood him in France? Villermé, in a monograph on the status of the laboring classes, did not mention his name, to the chagrin of Sismondi. Villeneuve Bargemont, in his *Economie politique chrétienne,* paid tribute to him, but with this tribute Sismondi would readily dispense, having his own interpretation of the return to the Middle Ages. To him, the Middle Ages denoted weakness of the central power, federalism, local autonomy. To Villeneuve, as to many others, they denoted order, hierarchy, and "sacerdotalism" —which Sismondi detested. In order to explain, once for all, his entire social philosophy, Sismondi had the happy idea to assemble, and to publish under the title *Etudes sur les sciences sociales,* an old treatise on political constitutions which forty years earlier he had been unable to publish, as well as a complete series of selections from his large and small works and articles on economics. It seems that the work attracted very little attention. "I leave this world," he wrote shortly before his death—he died on June 25, 1842—"without having made the slightest impression, and nothing will be done."

"Without having made the slightest impression." How he exaggerates, if he really expresses here his innermost thoughts! Will he not rather say that he has exercised an influence different from the one he desired to exercise, that his influence was exerted in the wrong direction? Because there developed in France what may be called a Sismondism of the left, which exploited his critical analysis of capitalism with the view of using it in support of socialism—although Sismondi was opposed to socialism as well as to capitalism, seeing in either only the left and the right side of the same type of centralized and oppressive society. When Proudhon declares that property "is theft," that it is, in other words, identical with his opposite and constitutes a contradictory notion, that it is not only "unjust" but "impossible"—he continuously derives his inspiration from Sismondi, although he does not say so explicitly, and, perhaps, is not always aware of it. When Louis Blanc states that "competition is for the people a system of extermination and for the middle class an incessant cause of impoverishment and ruin," this is nothing but dramatized Sismondism. Sismondi could not have read Proudhon's *Mémoire sur la propriété* or Blanc's *Organisation du travail* without being alarmed to see his denunciations of industrialism bring about the triumph either of a levelling anarchism or—worse still—of an egalitarian terrorism.

Sismondi has died, and there arrives in Paris, from Cologne, a young philosopher of the Hegelian left, a young revolutionary, Karl Marx, who intends to join the group of French socialists. He has assigned to himself the task of applying to the economic and social reality the grand philosophy—rooting it somehow in the earth—which interprets the development of the universe as a dialectical game of contradictions which are constantly resolved and which constantly arise again. Sismondism provides him with the key to the problem which occupies him. The existing society courts its own disaster; it leads directly to communism—which is at the same time its negation and its necessary consequence—because of the disequilibrated, contradictory character of its structure. It can be maintained, and not as a paradox, that the critical parts of Sismondism serve as the basis of the Communist Manifesto, published only a little later than five years after Sismondi's death. Why not admit that Sismondi foresaw with much alarm this revolutionary interpretation of his doctrine, and that he was disturbed to see that "nothing was to be done" to prevent society from drifting into what unhappily was in store for it if left to itself—that is, in the opinion of Sismondi, into a catastrophe.

Almost a century has passed since the publication of the *New Principles,* almost a century since the death of Sismondi.[1] An economic depression without precedent in history plagues mankind. It fits into the scheme outlined by Sismondi, being a world crisis of agricultural and industrial overproduction, a congestion of all markets. The friends of peace who consider the war responsible for so many ills are not altogether wrong; but the relationship between the war and the economic suffering which followed in its wake is less direct than they believe. War, taken by itself, destroys capital and retards production; it must lead, and it does lead, directly to underproduction, to shortages. The war has created new national units, has intensified national feelings, multiplied and heightened tariff barriers; but has it not led to the congestion of all markets only because of the fetters imposed on exchange? This would prove the point of the ancient theory of markets, the thesis of J. B. Say and Ricardo. But should one not rather say that, if all countries surround themselves with increased tariff barriers, they

---

[1] [Written in 1933.—Ed.]

do so because each suffers from an abundance of products of all sorts
and does not wish to see an internal disease aggravated by the invasion
of foreign products?   Only in an indirect sense is the war the cause of
all the evils from which we suffer.   The art of war has been industrial-
ized like the arts of peace.   Perhaps the last great war has had an effect
which is new in the military history of mankind.   Perhaps it has brought
about the over-industrialization of the belligerent nations and speeded
up the coming of the depression—which, if the advance of industrial
technology had remained normal, might have broken out only half a
century or a century later.   Shall the over-industrialized nations turn
the wheels of history back, according to Sismondi's plan, or shall they
move forward to a new regime which the western Marxists apparently
find difficult to organize?   Whatever the outcome of our suffering will
be, this, it seems to me, is the problem, and it was Sismondi, not Jean
Baptiste Say, who formulated it a century ago for the first time.

Foxwell

on

Ricardian Socialists

The Ricardian socialists were forerunners of Marx. Like Marx, they developed theories of surplus value and exploitation on the basis of Ricardo's thought and of the labor theory of value. The principal members of this group were Charles Hall (c. 1740–c. 1820), William Thompson (1785–1833), Thomas Hodgskin (1783–1869), John Francis Bray (1809–1897), and John Gray (1799–1883). Bray was born in the city of Washington and died near Detroit, having spent twenty years of his life in England. The others were Englishmen. All had varied careers. Hall, a physician, died in debtor's prison. Thompson was a man of wealth and leisure, Hodgskin a navy officer who turned to journalism, Bray a humble man of many trades, and Gray the founder of a successful printing business.

Herbert Somerton Foxwell (1849–1936) was a British economist affiliated with the Universities of Cambridge and London for a period of over fifty years. His special interests were in book collecting and in the fields of economic history, socialism, and money, an unusual combination indicative of Foxwell's detachment from the more austere type of economic theorizing as carried on by his contemporary in Cambridge, Alfred Marshall. Foxwell is chiefly remembered for his essay on the Ricardian socialists, which is reproduced here in part.

W E MAY REGARD socialism as a protest against the extravagances of the individualistic movement of the Renaissance and the Reformation, against the disintegration of the settled order and inner harmony of medieval life. This protest was constantly noticeable at periods of change, as, for instance, after the Civil War; and it became general and acute during the ferment of thought caused by the American and French Revolutions, and during the terrible sufferings of the masses, nowhere more severe than in England, which resulted from the industrial revolution and the Great War. As a reaction against the anarchy of individualism, socialism naturally developed in proportion to the exaggerations of the fashionable philosophy; and when this found its *reductio ad absurdum* in the extreme *laisser-faire* of the "New School" of economists, about the early 1840's, the tide of socialist influence reached its first high-water mark. If this is a true view of the nature of the socialist movement, it is not surprising that it should have originated in England; and even those to whom socialism is the gospel of the future have no ground for national self-glorification on this account. It is only natural that the reaction against the power of modern capital, and the mischiefs incident to license and absence of control, should begin in the country where that power first made itself felt, where its license was most unbounded, and where it attained the most striking proportions. English genius perhaps does not so commonly show itself in work of pure originality as in the successful adaptation to useful purpose of ideas derived from other races. But this is not so true in the region of politics, and especially of social politics. It is notorious that all the great *remedial* measures which have proved the most effective checks to the abuses of capitalistic competition are of English origin. Trade unions, co-operation, and factory legislation are all products of English soil. That the *revolutionary* reaction against capitalism is equally English in its inspiration is not so generally known.

It was a handful of English writers, brought up in the classic country of capitalistic production, and reflecting upon the terrible wreckage of

[From H. S. Foxwell's Introduction to Anton Menger's *Right to the Whole Produce of Labour*, London, Macmillan and Company, 1899. By permission. Copyright of heirs and assigns of H. S. Foxwell.]

the early pre-regulation period, who laid down the broad lines of thought upon which the socialistic criticism of capitalism has ever since proceeded. Original, independent, trenchant, and radical as they were, this little school of writers stand apart, clearly distinguishable from the various groups of contemporary social reformers, as well as from that English socialism whose form was determined by foreign influences. Not content, as the common English habit is, to attempt to palliate the miseries of the time by specific and detailed legislation, they challenged the very principles upon which the system of society rested: and while others were absorbed in the advocacy of social utopias, they devoted themselves to asserting the inherent defects and injustice of the existing system, and demanded that these defects should be dealt with by radical and preventive, rather than by regulative and remedial methods.

Of this English School, the chief names are undoubtedly those of Godwin, Hall, Thompson, Gray, Hodgskin, and Bray. It will seem to many that Robert Owen should be added to this list. But though it is impossible to exaggerate the importance of the Owenite movement as a propagandist and remedial agency, and as a means of giving asylum and resonance to socialist ideas, Robert Owen himself was not remarkable as a militant and destructive thinker. Thomas Spence and Tom Paine, and even William Cobbett in some respects, might have a stronger title to be regarded as leaders of the revolutionary movement. Much more, I think, may be said for the claims of William Ogilvie. But in spite of the undoubted ability and influence of Ogilvie's work, we may here follow Dr. Menger in placing Godwin at the head of the English Socialist School. "Godwin," he says, "may be regarded as the first scientific socialist of modern times, in whom are to be found in germ all the ideas of modern socialism and anarchism." Traces of these ideas, no doubt, exist here and there in many of his predecessors, not merely in Ogilvie, Spence, and Paine, but in other minor writings; and socialist yeast even lurks, where perhaps it might least be suspected, in that wonderfully catholic work, the *Wealth of Nations*. Still Godwin fairly deserves the position assigned to him by Dr. Menger. By its philosophic completeness, its rigorous and fearless, if somewhat puerile logic, and its admirably lucid exposition, the *Political Justice* may fairly entitle its author to be regarded as the Adam Smith of socialistic speculation.

WILLIAM GODWIN

Godwin's *Political Justice* is so well known that I need say little of
it here. It was an attempt, Godwin tells us, to systematize political
views and principles after the new light thrown upon them by the discussions in France and America. From French speculation, he says,
he derived a bent toward simplicity in political constructions; and possibly this, too, was the source of that confirmed optimism, that faith
in the unlimited possibilities of social improvement, and the irresistible
sway of intellectual conviction, which is the most striking character of
the work. These premises were required to give even a superficial
plausibility to his social philosophy. It was a combination of the
purest communism with the most anarchic individualism. "The subject
of Property," he says, "is the keystone that completes the fabric of social justice"; and in his last book, where he treats of property, we
have an epitome of the whole. Individuals have no rights, neither
has society: hence he cannot admit the claim of labor to the product
of industry, except on its negative sides. In the established system of
property he saw the root of all social evil, and attacked it with un-
sparing vigor. For it he would substitute a system of equal property,
where distribution is determined by want, or "the capacity of the
subject." In the Arcadia he imagined, this system would require "no
restrictions or superintendence whatever." "It grows out of a simple,
clear, and unanswerable theory of the human mind, that we first stand
in need of a certain animal subsistence and shelter, and after that, our
only true felicity consists in the expansion of our intellectual powers,
the knowledge of truth, and the practice of virtue." Here we soar
quite out of sight of the work-a-day world. Godwin only appeals to
that very rare class of mind which is mainly swayed by intellectual
considerations: his book, for ordinary men, was destitute of motive
force. He was too dispassionate in temper, too extravagantly optimistic in his belief in the ultimate empire of reason, too innocently
blind to the impulses that animate the average man—in short, too hopelessly impracticable and unworldly ever to lead, or even to stimulate,
a revolutionary movement. His political insight may be measured by
his adoption of that most chimerical of all utopias, an anarchical communism. Here is Godwin, who regards want as the only equitable
title to property, objecting to any control over the individual disposition of property, even in bequest. Contrast this with the position of
that statesman socialist, Saint-Simon; who, with views on the equities
of property not very different from those of an average British jury-

man, was a strenuous advocate of heavy death duties. However, Godwin was perhaps saved by his extravagances. The *Political Justice* appeared in 1793, at the height of the Reaction and the Terror, and no book even of that perturbed period was more profoundly subversive and revolutionary in its teaching. But the Government, who rigorously prosecuted many lesser men, felt that they could afford to ignore Godwin. A man who dwelt in regions of thought so far removed from the world of everyday life was quite harmless for all immediate practical purposes, and Governments do not trouble themselves about the future. Godwin's influence on the socialistic movement was, in fact, almost wholly indirect; and I am inclined to think that it might have been almost inappreciable, but for the elaborate development of his views by William Thompson, and the existence of a great propagandist agency for Thompson's ideas in the Owenite co-operative societies.

CHARLES HALL

In Charles Hall we come to a writer of a very different, and to my mind, far more stimulating quality. The *Political Justice* may be said to have had an academic origin. It was an attempt to systematize political views and principles after a period of ferment and criticism, which had disturbed the symmetry and acceptance of the traditional systems. Hall's inspiration was derived from direct contact with human misery in the exercise of his calling as a physician. His book is not the result of a philosophic desire to bring political science up to date, or to draft a more perfect scheme of society. It springs directly from a burning sense of injustice and wrong, and a first-hand acquaintance with widespread, undeserved suffering and destitution. The more grave social abuses generally leave their mark on the public health, so that medical men can hardly fail to observe them; and Hall is one of the most notable examples of a long series of physicians who made a noble use of their opportunities, and play an honorable part in the history of English industrial reform. Forced by his daily duties, he tells us, to observe the deplorable condition of the masses at that time, he was led to reflect upon the causes which had brought it about. He finds the cause in what he calls civilization; and hence the title of his remarkable work, *The Effects of Civilisation on the People in European States*. By civilization, Hall practically means just what Godwin means by "the established system of property," viz. a certain legalized inequality, with the consequences incident to it. His central idea is that wealth is power over the labor of the poor; leading under the then-existing conditions to inequality and oppression. This at least, as he very forcibly and impressively argues, is the usual effect of civilization, though not a necessary one. It really results, he maintains, from the arbitrary and forcible assumption of land which has prevailed in most societies. Accordingly his remedy is a more equal distribution of land.

Regarded in bare abstract, Hall's argument may not appear specially noteworthy, or to entitle him to distinction from the crowd of land-nationalizers whom we always have with us. Nothing but a study of the book itself will give an adequate idea of the restrained intensity of its purpose, the rigorous march of its argument, and the grandeur of its general conception. But the dominant effect perhaps which it leaves on the mind is a sense of the existence of a great impersonal power, arising out of faulty social institutions, necessarily operating to degrade the masses; a power of whose nature victims and instruments are alike unconscious. This impression is the more vivid on account of the scientific spirit and transparent sincerity of the work. Hall everywhere keeps his indignation in check, and never suffers it to provoke him to personal or class attacks. His criticism is inexorable and relentless, but not passionate or intemperate. Nor is the discussion disfigured by theoretical jargon, trumped up to give a pseudo-scientific basis to conclusions really derived from a hasty and partial induction. In these and many other respects, Hall's *Effects of Civilisation* is honorably distinguished from Marx's *Kapital*. It is not so well adapted to appeal to a popular audience as the more famous work, nor I think was written with this intention; but it has just the kind of originality and force which turn the current of cultivated opinion in new directions. It was undoubtedly influential amongst the Owenite socialists, who constantly recommend it to the societies; and it must be held to entitle its author to a permanent place in the history of one of the most important movements of modern thought.

I am inclined to doubt whether Hall was acquainted with Godwin's writings. Neither in his principal work, nor in the *Observations on Malthus* which he appended to it, is there any reference to Godwin. It is true that Godwin, like Hall, pleaded the remoteness of the pressure which Malthus apprehended; but their general arguments are essentially different. Godwin immediately leaves the material question of more or less food, and passes to the visions of intellectual progress, of "triumph of mind over matter," on which he really relies. Hall, who is too serious to indulge in mere speculation, meets Malthus on his own ground, and keeps close to the real issues. The question of remoteness seems to him vital for practical purposes. It is an enormous gain if we can "lay the reprieve at one hundred years." But this physical limit may be extended by political action. "Nature's remedy, colonization," should be adopted; and "marriage may be regulated by law." If all fails, and over-population ensues, its evils will be less in a state of equality than at present. In any case, the denial of the right to existence is unjust and iniquitous. It is not nature's laws, as Malthus asserts, that doom the laborer to starve; that cruel doom is brought on him by the rich. He produces six or eight times what he requires in order to live, but this is taken from him by those who produce nothing. In fine, Hall says that Malthus's system "will operate as an encouragement to those who were too much before inclined to oppress to push their tyranny still further,—but I am very far from thinking this was the design of the author" (p. 349). This is a far more practical reply to the objection on the ground of over-population than Godwin's. I have referred to it at some length, because the tract seems to be unknown; and it appears to me to confirm the view that Hall was an essentially independent thinker, and that he was unaware of previous work published by Godwin on somewhat similar lines.

If, indeed, we are to find a precursor for Hall, we must look to Tom Paine, and especially to Paine's *Agrarian Justice*. This notable essay, which resembles Hall's work in its incisiveness and fearless logic, presents civilization under just the aspect in which it appeared to Hall. "Poverty," says Paine, "is a thing created by that which is called civilized life. It exists not in the natural state." "Civilization therefore . . . has operated two ways, to make one part of society more affluent, and the other part more wretched, than could have been the lot of either in a natural state." "The condition of millions in every country of Europe is far worse than if they had been born before civilization began, or had been born among the Indians of North America on the present day." "The contrast of affluence and wretchedness continually meeting and offending the eye, is like dead and living bodies chained together." He attributes these mischiefs to "the landed monopoly." The diagnosis and the agrarian remedy remind us of Hall. But Paine lacks Hall's intensity and economic insight. He is pre-eminently a politician; "the founder of political ideas among the people of England," as Holyoake styles him; but he cannot claim to have seriously raised the social question, as we now understand it. The merit, or demerit, the fame in any case, which attaches to this achievement, must I think belong to Hall. Godwin and Ogilvie stated the formal issues with some precision, Ogilvie with some practical conception of what was at stake. But both writers had a certain academic air. Dr.

Bain says of the *Political Justice,* "It was a splendid ideal or political romance, and may fitly be compared with the *Republic* of Plato. It set people thinking, made them dissatisfied with the present state of things." [1] Without pretending to put the *Political Justice* on the same level as the *Republic* of Plato, we must admit that it was rather the dream of a philosophical optimist than the bitter cry of protest against injustice and suffering. It was much better calculated to set scholars thinking, than to turn the widespread dissatisfaction of serious men into revolutionary channels. But Hall was the man to preach a social crusade. His book does not seem to have been noticed by the authorities, owing to its very small and private circulation, or it would no doubt have been suppressed. It is difficult to say what might not have been its effects had it been more widely read. As it was, Hall's influence, though limited and indirect, was very considerable. His work was carefully studied by the leaders of the Owenite societies, and had much to do with the rise and shaping of that critical socialism which was the life-blood of the movement in the second quarter of the nineteenth century.

WILLIAM THOMPSON

I pass now to the better-known William Thompson, who, perhaps, deserves by the completeness of his exposition, the wide influence of his writings, and the devotion of his life and fortune to the movement, to be regarded as chief of the English Socialist School. Socialistic propagandism has been mainly carried on by men of Celtic or Semitic blood, and Thompson appears to have been an Irishman, a native of County Cork, where he died at Clonnkeen in 1833, aged about fifty. In 1827, he tells us that for about twelve years he had been "living on what is called rent, the produce of the labor of others"; as an Irish landlord, in fact. For twenty years he was a vegetarian and teetotaller. His life was spent in advocating and aiding the formation of Owenite co-operative societies; and he left the great bulk of his property by will in 1830 to be applied to the same purposes. This will, however, was successfully contested by relatives on the ground that "immoral" objects were included in its benefits; and very little of his property seems actually to have been used as he had directed.

He was a pupil and an enthusiastic admirer of Bentham, "who has done more," he says, "for moral science than Bacon did for physical science"; and he describes himself as merely working out the applica-

[1] *Life of James Mill,* p. 435.

tions of his master's principles. In Owen's system of equality he
hoped to realize Bentham's conception of a maximum of happiness.
There is indeed a tendency to formal enumerations and elaborate
classifications in Thompson's work which was probably derived from
Bentham; but not much else, I think, except the perpetual insistence
upon a rigorous, systematic and impartial calculation of utility, upon
which all its argument proceeds. There was another obvious influence
which was at least equally potent in forming his views. From first to
last his work is saturated with the spirit of Godwin, though the teachings of Bentham no doubt gave him a practical turn and a regard for
facts and detail conspicuously wanting in the author of *Political Justice.*
Like Godwin, Thompson shows a strong preference for purely voluntary methods, and hopes for great results from the development of the
intellectual side of human nature. But he distinctly advocates communistic organization as against individual economy. He is filled with
almost the Owenite detestation of competition as the root of all social
evil; though he goes so far with Godwin as to admit that a genuine
system of *laisser faire* would be infinitely preferable to the system of
"restraint by force and fraud," or of "forced inequality of wealth,"—
his way of describing the then-existing social institutions. His own
account of his position, in the *Preliminary Observations,* is that he
steered a middle course between the purely intellectual speculation
of Godwin and the merely mechanical philosophy of Malthus. Following on Bentham's lines, his object was to apply to social science the
ascertained truths of political economy, making these and all other
branches of knowledge subservient to that just distribution of wealth
which tends most to human happiness.

"The ascertained truths of political economy" were, of course, the
doctrines of the new or Ricardian School. I am more and more
impressed, as I study the literature of socialism, with the far-reaching,
disastrous consequences of the unfortunate color given to economic
teaching by Ricardo, and the little band of able, but somewhat hard
and narrow writers who called themselves by his name. It was
Ricardo's crude generalizations which gave modern socialism its
fancied scientific basis, and provoked, if they did not justify, its revolutionary form. There are times when we are disposed to underrate
the value of that drill in method which is a principal part of academic
training. At such times we should think of Ricardo. Ricardo, and
still more those who popularized him, may stand as an example for all
time of the extreme danger which may arise from the unscientific use
of hypothesis in social speculations, from the failure to appreciate the
limited application to actual affairs of a highly artificial and arbitrary

analysis. His ingenious, though perhaps over-elaborated reasonings became positively mischievous and misleading when they were unhesitatingly applied to determine grave practical issues without the smallest sense of the thoroughly abstract and unreal character of the assumptions on which they were founded. Thus, as Jevons has observed, Ricardo gave the whole course of English economics a wrong twist. It became unhistorical and unrealistic; it lost its scientific independence, and became the tool of a political party. At one time indeed it went very near to losing its rightful authority in legislation and affairs; nor did it regain its old position until by the greater precision of the theorists on the one side, and the broader treatment of real questions by the historical school on the other side, this elementary blunder in method was rectified. Meanwhile, by a singular irony of fate, it happened that Ricardo, by this imperfect presentation of economic doctrine, did more than any intentionally socialist writer to sap the foundations of that form of society which he was trying to explain, and which he believed to be the typical and natural, if not, indeed, the ideal social state. William Thompson was only one of a series of socialist writers, culminating in Marx and Lassalle, who take the Ricardian position as the very basis of their argument. His first section has the familiar Ricardian ring. "Wealth is produced by labor; no other ingredient but labor makes any object of desire an object of wealth. Labor is the sole universal measure, as well as the characteristic distinction of wealth." Give the word "labor" its popular meaning, and it is merely an affair of logic to deduce a large part of modern socialism from this position. Whatever qualifications Ricardo may have made upon it in his own mind, ninety-nine readers out of a hundred took him literally, and the main impression left by his book was that while wealth was almost exclusively due to labor, it was mainly absorbed by rent and other payments to the unproductive classes. This was the text which Thompson and the English socialists proceeded to elaborate.

The whole school, and especially Thompson and Gray, were greatly impressed by the distinction between the productive and unproductive classes. Patrick Colquhoun, in his *Treatise on the Wealth, Power, and Resources of the British Empire,* which first appeared in 1814, published a celebrated Table, which he describes as "An Attempt to exhibit a General View of Society; and to shew how the New Property [or National Income] . . . is *distributed* among the different Classes of the Community." This Map of Civil Society, as Colquhoun calls it, was the statistical foundation of the socialist movement. We meet with constant references to it, not only in the text-books of the school, but in its periodical literature. There is no doubt that the statistical detail given by Colquhoun, at a time when the nation was groaning under a crushing weight of taxation, gave quite a new vividness and realism to the formal distinction between productive and unproductive labor, and very much fostered the disposition to divide society into productive and unproductive classes. This again, under the conditions of popular agitation, inevitably tended to that narrow view of productivity which is characteristic of revolutionary socialism in all its forms. Like Hall and Gray, Thompson's view of rational consumption is somewhat narrow; it seems to be limited to the "ordinary wants and comforts of society—food, clothing, and dwellings"; what goes beyond these is due to luxury and caprice: and it was one of his chief objections to the "system of inequality" that it diverted production from the supply of the more necessary objects to "a species of industry—the least conducive to the public good." But outside all distinction between kinds of producers was the great distinction between producers and non-producers. It is upon this latter distinction, not always clearly separated from the distinction between kinds of producers, that Thompson's main argument turns.

He starts from the three *natural* laws of distribution. Labor is to be free: to enjoy the whole of its products: to exchange these products voluntarily. In all three respects Thompson finds the existing system of distribution vicious. Labor is not free, either as to its direction or continuance; there are heavy deductions from its product, in the shape of rent, profits, and taxes; exchanges are impeded by various forms of monopoly and protection. On all three heads Thompson argues at great length; though he is not as trenchant as Gray, and he is everywhere careful to deprecate the employment of force. Godwin himself is not more profoundly attached to the voluntary principle; it is the characteristic mark of his system. "Do we ask," he says, "whether any abstraction of the products of labor is just? The sufficient and only answer ought to be, 'Is it voluntary?'" But it is evident that no system of *laisser faire,* however perfectly realized, will ever give us equality. This brings us to a difficulty which Thompson recognizes at the outset of his inquiry, but in my opinion utterly fails to overcome. "Here," he says, "is the cruel dilemma in which mankind have been placed. Here is the important problem of moral science to be solved, *'how to reconcile equality with security;* how to reconcile *just distribution with continued production.'"* He sees clearly enough how hard it is to retain an effective stimulus to production, and to conform to the communist ideal of distribution; but it cannot be said that his solution is very convincing. It is of the nature of a compromise. At first indeed he contends that there is no real conflict between the principles. "It is only by an undeviating adherence to (real) equal security that any approach can be made to equality." Candor obliges him to abandon this position in favor of a curious evasion. "Labor should enjoy the use of the whole products of its exertions: the shares of the products of labor should be equal to all contributing, according to their capacities of mind or body, to the common stock." [2] I need not point out how completely the passage from the laborer as individual to labor in the abstract surrenders the whole contention of equity. There is less objection to the second form of his compromise, though it is obviously unpractical. "Though labor has the *right* to the whole product of its exertions, it may *voluntarily agree before production* to equality of remuneration." In any case, the supposed necessary incentive to production has vanished. The fact is that there is a radical contradiction between the equities of production and the equities of consumption. "To each according to his work," "to each according to his needs," are hopelessly inconsistent maxims, though each is plausible enough in itself. Our present happy-go-lucky system of competitive exchange makes a confessedly imperfect compromise between the two principles, but we have yet to be shown the socialistic system which would make a better one.

There is an unfortunate omission in Thompson's treatise, which deprives us of what would have been a good opportunity for judging of his practical statesmanship. He had prepared, he says, a chapter of 100 pages, devoted to the criticism of the then-existing institutions of society. For the present he withholds it, in order to prevent unnecessary irritation. It might have been expected that William Pare, his literary trustee, would have discovered and published this chapter in his second edition of the book; but we are still left with only the table of headings. We have to judge Thompson therefore as a practical reformer, by his projects for voluntary schemes. These show the inevitable drift to communism which must be the end of all speculations based on considerations of equity. "Would you like," he writes to the distressed Spitalfields weavers, "to enjoy yourselves the whole products of your labor? You have nothing more to do than simply to *alter the direction of your labor*. Instead of working for you know not whom, *work for each other*." He had said in 1824 that if any departure is made from the principle of securing the whole product to labor it should be in the direction of equality. At that time he thought that such a departure "ought scarcely ever, if ever, to occur." But after 1830 he devoted himself, body, mind, and estate, to the advocacy of communis-

---

[2] *Labor Rewarded*, p. 37.

tic societies of the Owenite type: and the "principle of security" seems to have been practically abandoned in favor of the principle of equality. The sacrifice of equity involved in this result is perhaps not so great as even Thompson himself imagined. A careful analysis of the real contribution of individuals to the work of production, under modern conditions, if conducted in the spirit of Comte's philosophy, might considerably modify our *prima facie* impressions as to the inequity of equal remuneration. Still something would undoubtedly remain. But we need not further discuss the equity of arrangements so hopelessly impracticable. Thompson's fame will not rest upon his advocacy of Owenite co-operation, devoted and public-spirited as that was; but upon the fact that he was the first writer to elevate the question of the just distribution of wealth to the supreme position it has since held in English political economy. Up to his time, political economy had been rather commercial than industrial; indeed he finds it necessary to explain the very meaning of the term *industrial,* which he says was from the French, and no doubt adopted from Saint-Simon. When we get to John Stuart Mill we find production definitely subordinated to distribution, the great and distinguishing theme of his work. I cannot doubt that this change was largely due to Thompson, whose influence on Mill is conspicuous, in more directions than one.

JOHN GRAY

John Gray, the next writer who claims notice, though he cannot pretend to anything like the authority and following of Thompson, was the author of a *Lecture on Human Happiness,* which is perhaps the most striking and effective socialist manifesto of the time. Like Fourier, his first experience of life was gained in trade. Educated at Repton, he left school early to serve first as clerk, and then as traveller in a great London wholesale house. The great city cast its spell over him, and raised doubts in his mind as to the social harmonies. London and its myriads, he tells us, were to him for many years an intricate problem that he could hardly venture to hope ever to be able to solve. At an early age, and long before he had even heard of Owen, he became convinced that "something was wrong . . . the commercial proceedings of mankind were at variance with the whole system of nature." After some reflection he arrived at the conclusion that production, instead of being the *effect* of demand, ought to be its *cause.* Full of his discovery, he turned to Adam Smith, read the first volume of the *Wealth of Nations,* and then "compiled a violent, puerile, unintelligible, and unmendable volume," which he called *The National Com-*

mercial System. He was dissuaded from publishing this book. Afterwards, advised by his brother, he read Owen's writings; and finding in them some support to his own views, he then (in 1825) published a fragment of the discarded work in the shape of the famous *Lecture,* which was a favorite text-book with English socialists for the next twenty years. Part of the edition was lost, and the circulation in England was therefore restricted; but the lecture was reprinted in Philadelphia, where a thousand copies were rapidly sold, and it no doubt aided the growth of the American socialist group which rallied around Frances Wright, R. Dale Owen, and the *Free Enquirer.* We know, at all events, that it gave rise to one of the earliest of American socialist utterances, an *Address to the Members of Trade Societies,* written by a journeyman bootmaker; a tract which so impressed Robert Owen that he brought a copy over with him from America, and caused it to be reprinted in London in 1827. Meanwhile Gray, though differing considerably from Owen on many vital points, offered his services at Orbiston, and came to Scotland to assist; but disapproving of the plans, and not being able to make his remonstrances effective, he resolved to have nothing to do with the scheme, and wrote an article in criticism of it called *A Word of Advice to the Orbistonians.* He seems afterwards to have settled in Scotland, and embarked on various newspaper ventures, presumably with some success; for we find him later in life offering substantial prizes, and circulating his books gratuitously in large numbers.

Gray was very careful to assert his own originality, especially as against Owen. "Neither in whole nor in part," he says, "have I gathered these opinions from any man." But his independence of Owen is obvious enough. He was too revolutionary in his early work, and too individualistic throughout for Robert Owen. He owed more to Colquhoun, whose *Map of Civil Society* is the central topic and object-lesson of the *Lecture on Happiness.* It may have been reflection on the facts exhibited in the *Map* which roused in Gray the biting irony of this vigorous tract. Nothing could be more unlike the temper and method of Robert Owen. Besides, there is a certain continuity and individuality about all Gray's work; it has a character of its own. From first to last his great theme was the avoidance of dislocations in industry by the better adjustment of production and demand. As he advanced in years his tone became more commercial, and we miss any trace of the revolutionary socialism which animates his first tract. Indeed, in 1848, he goes so far as to apologize for having used the term "Social System" in the title of his 1831 book, and to explain that the word *Social* did not then carry with it the communistic associations it had since acquired. He had come to identify the cause of commercial mischief with a bullion-based currency, and devoted the greater part of his life to the advocacy of a scheme of paper currency, almost as wild and impracticable as Owen's Labor Exchange.

Looked at as a whole, Gray's career was a curious one, and not such as would justify us in classing him as a socialist. And yet the *Lecture on Human Happiness* is certainly one of the most remarkable of socialist writings. How it could have been written by Gray, I have always found hard to understand. It is a solitary flash of lightning from an otherwise peaceful sky. The ostensible object of the lecture is to advocate Owen's schemes, though Gray did not really believe in the communistic principle.[3] He may possibly have regarded Owenism as a counsel of perfection; at any rate he promises in a future lecture to propound a scheme of his own, "quite different."

The book is so rare now,[4] that it may be convenient if, in summarizing the argument, I quote a few typical passages. After some general remarks intended to meet any prejudices against Owen on account of the novelty of his proposals, Gray inquires into the nature of existing commercial arrangements, and gives a critical analysis of Colquhoun's tables, laying great stress, and much in the same way as Thompson, on the distinction between the productive and unproductive classes. Following Colquhoun, he estimates the whole income of the country as £430,000,000, of which he considers that the productive classes produced £426,000,000: "being very nearly *fifty-four pounds a year* for each man, woman, and child in the productive classes: of which they received about *eleven pounds,* being but a small trifle more than one-fifth part of the produce of their own labor!!!" "Every unproductive member of society is a direct tax upon the productive classes." "Numbers, even of the productive classes, are compelled by the present system to become useless members of society." "The persons who compose the Independent classes are Dependent upon two things: first upon the *industry* of their fellow-creatures; second, upon *injustice* which enables them to command it." He denies that there can be any just title to land. "The foundation of all property is labor, and there is no other just foundation for it." "The interest of money is another mode of obtaining labor without giving any equivalent for it." "What does the productive laborer obtain for that portion of the produce of

---

[3] Cf. *The Social System,* 1831, p. 106: "I look upon all systems of equality as unjust in principle, and quite impracticable."

[4] [A reprint of the *Lecture* was published by the London School of Economics in 1931.—Ed.]

his industry which is annually taken from him by incomes obtained by the lenders of money? He obtains nothing. Then, we ask, is a man the natural proprietor of the produce of his own labor? If he is not, what foundation is there for property at all? . . . If he is, . . . there is no justice in requiring interest for the use of money." Passing from the question of right, Gray next contends (like Godwin) that there is no real happiness in any rank under the competitive system of society, not even among the pensioned rich; and remarks especially upon the distressed state of Ireland. The great cause of poverty he finds in the existence of an unnatural limit to production, in the shape of the principle of competition. "The division of the interests of men, in their mode of employing capital, and in the distribution of the produce of their labor, is the tremendous engine of mischief which is the curse of the human race, and the cause of almost every evil by which we are surrounded." "In consequence of the ability of the few to produce all that competition will allow the many to consume, competition will be still further increased." "The grand feature of Mr. Owen's plan . . . is that it abolishes the circumstance which now limits production, and gives to the producers the wealth that they create."

Finally, he sums up in a passage which deserves to be quoted at length.

Upon the whole, then, we have endeavored to exhibit society as it now is. We have endeavored to show by whom wealth is created, and by whom it is consumed. We have endeavored to show that it is from human labor that every description of wealth proceeds; that the productive classes do now support, not only themselves, but every unproductive member of society! that *they only* are productive members of society who apply *their own hands* either to the cultivation of the earth itself, or to the preparing or appropriating the produce of the earth to the uses of life; that every individual not so employed, is a direct tax upon those who are so employed; that (to say nothing of the numerous and expensive class of persons who have not even the pretension to utility in any way whatever) all merchants, manufacturers, wholesale and retail tradesmen, together with their clerks, assistants, and shopmen, are either directors and superintendents of production, or mere distributors of wealth, who are paid by the labor of those who create it; and that such persons are useful only in a *sufficient number,* so as to direct and superintend labor, and to distribute its produce.

We have endeavored to show that the real income of the country, which consists in the quantity of wealth annually created by the labor of the people, is taken from its producers chiefly by the rent of land, by the rent of houses, by the interest of money, and by the profit obtained by persons who buy their labor from them at one price, and sell it at another; that these immense taxes of rent, interest, and profits on labor must ever continue while the system of individual competition stands; that in the new communities *all* would be productive members of society; excepting only the persons *absolutely required* in unproductive occupations, who would also devote their time and talents to the general good, and that *no one* would be taxed either with rent, interest, or profit on his labor.

This is a definite programme clearly and logically expressed, and it will easily be understood how it would appeal to the Owenite societies. Some of its extravagances, such as classing as unproductive services "absolutely required" by society, the economists had already taught them to swallow; and the great abuses of property then common made others sound more plausible than they do to the more critical readers of today. It cannot be said positively whether Gray wrote before Thompson, and in independence of him. I think he did. He makes no reference to him so far as I know. In any case, I think Gray must be regarded as the pioneer of modern, militant, aggressive socialism; and his little tract must be preferred, in point of originality, terseness, and effect, to the elaborate and methodical treatise of Thompson, more notable in many other respects. Gray's convictions were less solid and matured than Thompson's, and they seem, as so often happens, to have been considerably modified by his success in life, or else by larger experience. But so far as this early writing is concerned, Gray left little for Marx to add, except in the way of incitement to the use of force. To this Gray was firmly opposed; he deprecates every form of violence, and he even says that it has been no pleasant task to him to criticize thus faithfully "the established customs of the country."

THOMAS HODGSKIN

The next writer of this little group, and one of the most original, is Thomas Hodgskin. His first socialistic utterance appeared in 1825, the same year as Gray's famous lecture; but Gray's lecture, as we have seen, was really written much earlier. All Hodgskin's writing shows him to have been a man of liberal education and some philosophic training. He quotes throughout from the best authorities on economics and social philosophy; especially from Locke, Adam Smith, and Millar. To Adam Smith he constantly refers; and he never tires of contrasting Smith's "natural system" with the "political economy" of the contemporary school. Before 1820 he travelled in North Germany, and published an account of his impressions in two volumes; and he states that he knew from personal observation the condition of the legally emancipated serfs in Austria and Prussia. John Lalor tells us [5] that Hodgskin was well known as an able and accomplished journalist; he appears to have been on the staff of, or at least a frequent contributor to, the *Morning Chronicle*. At one time he was Honorary Secretary to the London Mechanics' Institution, where in 1826 he delivered four lectures, published in 1827 under the title of *Popular Political Economy*. James Mill, writing to Brougham, speaks of him as "our friend Hodgskin." Both Brougham and Mill would probably know of Hodgskin through Black and the *Chronicle,* then their great organ in the press; and also, no doubt, through his connection with the Mechanics' Institution.[6]

But, apart from personal acquaintance, there was something in Hodgskin's writing well calculated to attract the attention of those who had any real insight into the signs of the times. No member of the English socialist group seems to have been more widely read on both sides of the Atlantic, and the significance of his position was instantly recognized. He was controverted, amongst others, by Samuel Read in 1829, Thomas Cooper in 1830, and Brougham in 1831. He is quoted by Marx in the first draft for his larger work, which he published in 1859; and Cooper speaks of his doctrines as having influenced the New York School of socialists and the *Free Inquirer*.

For our present purposes the two most important works of Hodgskin are his *Labour Defended,* published in 1825, and his *Right of Property,* which appeared in 1831. In his *Popular Political Economy,* from the circumstances in which it was prepared, Hodgskin no doubt felt bound to subordinate his peculiar opinions, and at any rate they are not developed with the same freedom and originality as in the other works named. The occasion of the first of these writings, justly described by Marx as a "vorzügliche Schrift," will appear from its full title:—*Labour Defended against the Claims of Capital; or the Unproductiveness of*

---

[5] Cf. *Money and Morals,* 1852, Pref. p. xxiv.

[6] Since the above was written, the appearance of Mr. Wallas's admirable *Life of Francis Place* has thrown further light on the personality of Hodgskin, and on his friendship with Place and James Mill (cf. especially, pp. 267–269). Like so many turbulent thinkers, Hodgskin seems to have been the victim of injustice. A young naval lieutenant, he was in 1813 placed on half-pay for writing a pamphlet against pressing. From this year onwards he was in intimate correspondence with Place, and once acted as travelling companion to Place's eldest son. In 1820, Hodgskin read Ricardo's *Principles,* and from this time the correspondence often related to that "Ricardian Socialism" which Hodgskin, more than any other individual, may claim to have originated. In one of the letters, according to Mr. Wallas, Hodgskin sketches a book "curiously like Marx's *Capital,*" but Place dissuaded him from writing it.

Capital proved with reference to the Present Combinations amongst Journeymen. By a Labourer. In 1824, the Combination Laws, at the instance of Joseph Hume's Committee, had been repealed. But there followed a great development of trade union activity, and with it such an outburst of strikes as to cause general alarm. This led in 1825 to the appointment of another Committee, with a view to the re-enactment of the old anti-combination laws. By the tactical skill of Francis Place, however, this result was averted, and the new Act of 1825, while imposing certain restrictions, left the right of agreement and discussion in wages questions substantially unimpaired. Hodgskin's tract was intended as a theoretical contribution to the settlement of this question.

In all the debates [he says], much stress is laid on the necessity of protecting capital. What capital performs is therefore a question of considerable importance, which the author was on this account induced to examine. As the result of this examination, it is his opinion that all the benefits attributed to capital arise from co-existing and skilled labor. He feels himself, on this account, called on to deny that capital has any just claim to the large share of the national produce now bestowed on it. This large share, he has endeavored to show, is the cause of the poverty of the laborer; and he ventures to assert that the condition of the laborer can never be permanently improved till he can refute the theory, and is determined to oppose the practice, of giving nearly everything to capital.

The thesis perhaps is rather clumsily stated, but the development of the argument is very able. There is an analysis of capital which would interest Dr. Irving Fisher and Mr. Cannan. Hodgskin insists that most of what is called capital is not so much a hoard or stock, as an income or flow estimated at a particular point of time, all of which is the product of labor. "As far as food, drink, and clothing are concerned, it is quite plain that no species of laborer depends on any previously prepared stock, for, in fact, no such stock exists; but every species of laborer does constantly, and at all times, depend for his supplies on the co-existing labor of some other laborers." "All the effects usually attributed to accumulation of circulating capital are derived from the *accumulation and storing up of skilled labor.*" Fixed capital, no doubt, is stored; but "fixed capital does not derive its utility from previous, but present labor; and does not bring its owner a profit because it has been stored up, but because it is a means of obtaining a command over labor." The inventor deserves his reward, and so does the skilled artisan who uses the invention. "But betwixt him who makes instruments and him who uses them, in steps the capitalist, who neither makes nor uses them, and appropriates to himself the produce of both . . . he is the middleman of all the laborers." But while the middlemen of Ireland are stigmatized as oppressors, the middlemen of England are honored as benefactors. "At least such are the doctrines of political economy." I quote these passages, not to endorse them, but to explain Hodgskin's position, and to enable the reader to judge how far he anticipates Marx.

In one respect he was in advance both of Marx and the economists. He carefully distinguishes between the capitalist and the *entrepreneur*. "Masters, it is evident, are *laborers* as well as their journeymen. In this character their interest is precisely the same as that of their men. But they are also either capitalists or the agents of the capitalist, and in this respect their interest is decidedly opposed to the interest of their workmen." "The contest now appears to be between masters and journeymen, or between one species of labor and another, but it will soon be displayed in its proper characters; and will stand confessed a war of honest industry against . . . idle profligacy." Among other points made in the argument, which is too compressed and continuous to be fairly represented by quotations, I may note that he refers to Ricardo, "not as caring much to illustrate the subtleties of that ingenious and profound writer, but because his theory confirms . . . that the exactions of the capitalist cause the poverty of the laborer," and he proceeds to claim his authority for the Iron Law. He recognizes that under division of labor "there is no longer anything which we can call the natural reward of individual labor." But this difficulty might be left to the "higgling of the market," if labor were perfectly free. But if he is in favor of competition as the principle by which to determine the division of labor's share between the various ranks of laborers, he is for combination against capital in order to make labor's share as large as possible. By combining, the journeymen "may reduce or destroy altogether the profit of the idle capitalist . . . but they will augment the wages and rewards of industry, and will give the genius and skill their due share of the national produce."

Thus Hodgskin, while retaining an individualistic form of society, aimed, by means of combination, at depriving capital of any share in the produce. Thompson considered this position an impossible one. In an answer to Hodgskin published in 1827, called *Labor Rewarded*, Thompson urges that "individual competition is incompatible with equal remuneration, as it is also with securing to labor the entire products of its exertions." "The author of *Labour Defended* stands alone, as far as I know, amongst the advocates of individual competition, in even *wishing* that labor should possess the whole of the products of its exertions. All other advocates of individual competition look on the notion as visionary, under the Competitive System." We know Thompson's solution of the difficulty. Laborers must become capitalists, and unite in communities to regulate their own labor. To ascertain for each the exact product of his own labor is impracticable. If this could be done, then justice would give each individual a property in that product. But moral considerations would force him to share that product with others. The human race could not otherwise be preserved. This voluntary distribution is best carried out under the equitable arrangements of co-operative communities, with their regulated exchanges. "It is on the regulation of exchanges," he concludes, "that the industrious classes must depend for realizing the general proposition that 'the whole produce of labor should belong to the laborer.'" We shall see later how this theme was developed by Bray.

While Hodgskin in his *Labour Defended* adopted a position of his own, sufficiently distinct from those of Gray and Thompson, his most characteristic and original doctrine is contained in *The Natural and Artificial Rights of Property Contrasted*. This work, published in 1832, and "practically written," he tells us, in 1829, is in form of a series of letters addressed to Brougham, who in February 1828 had moved for a Commission on the State of the Law. It opposes to Brougham's demand for detailed reform a drastic, radical indictment of the whole foundation of the existing property law. The vein of anarchism which is a salient feature of English socialism, and which may even be traced, thanks to Physiocratic influence, in Adam Smith himself, is nowhere more conspicuous than in Hodgskin, and especially in this his last work. It would appear that Hodgskin was mainly inspired in his attack by the teaching of the *Wealth of Nations,* for whose author he had a profound respect. Both here and in his *Popular Political Economy* he quotes Adam Smith copiously, and he is greatly impressed by Smith's well-known distinction, in Book III., between "human institutions" and "the natural order of things." "That great man," he says, "carefully distinguished the natural distribution of wealth from the distribution which is derived from our artificial right of property. His successors, on the contrary, make no such distinction, and in their writings the consequences of this right are stated to be the laws of nature." [7] The distinction appeared to Hodgskin of the very first importance. "The contest now going on in society, the preternatural throes and heavings which frightfully convulse it from

[7] *Popular Political Economy,* p. xxii.

one end to the other, arise exclusively and altogether from the right of property, and can be neither understood nor relieved, but by attending to the great distinction . . . between the natural and the legal right of property." As he somewhat bluntly puts it, "the law of nature is that industry shall be rewarded by wealth, and idleness be punished by destitution; the law of the land is to give wealth to idleness, and fleece industry till it be destitute." "To the violation of the natural right of property, effected by the law, we owe most of our social miseries." Among these are the exploitation of labor and industrial crises. Speaking of the "comparative pauperism and destitution" of the laboring classes, he says, "it cannot be doubted . . . that the immediate and proximate cause of their poverty and destitution, seeing how much they labor, and how many people their labor nourishes in opulence, is the law which appropriates their produce, in the shape of revenue, rent, tithes, and profit." "To our legal right of property we are indebted for those gleams of false wealth and real panic, which within the last fifty years have so frequently shook to its centre the whole trading world." He was not surprised at the respect professed for the law by the Irish gentry and similar classes. "The law is the creature of their passions, and they rightly endeavor, according to their own views, to substitute it for the violence which is the offspring of the passions of other people." The law, in short, "is a great scheme of rules, intended to preserve the power of government, secure the wealth of the landowner, the priest, and the capitalist, but never to secure his produce to the laborer. The law-maker is never a laborer, and has no natural right to any wealth." However, Hodgskin really did not wish to destroy, but to reform, the law of property. "Amend the laws as to property; for all the crimes which afflict society grow from them." Nor was he prepared with a scheme of reform. "Individual man does not make society, and cannot organize it. . . . I trust to that great power, call it Nature, or call it God, which has brought society forth out of the wilderness, to provide for its future welfare. When you ask me for plans and schemes, my reply is, trust in that power, do justice, and fear not."

The practical outcome of Hodgskin's inquiry seems tame, and, as often happens with anarchist essays, hardly in keeping with the pretensions of the critical part of the work. But at any rate it avoids the blundering absurdities into which more ambitious writers have fallen. Hodgskin was a man of affairs, and his general tone, for a socialist, was unusually practical. Much of his writing, especially in *Labour Defended,* was in advance of his time, and even now has a modern ring about it. This applies particularly to his trades union policy, and to his excellent economic analysis, and broad view of social philosophy. Indeed his orthodox contemporaries might have learnt much from him which was not actually incorporated in English economics till fifty years later. One distinction in any case Hodgskin can claim to have achieved. Not only did he inspire men like Marx, the founders of the modern socialist movement, but he was the first (and perhaps the last) to attract the attention of the orthodox school, and had the honor to be singled out for special attack by the great Chancellor Brougham.

JOHN FRANCIS BRAY

John Francis Bray, the last of the six writers I have selected for special notice, seems to have been a journeyman printer, of whom little is known, except that he was the author of the remarkable book, *Labour's Wrongs and Labour's Remedy,* published at Leeds in 1839. At this time political agitation ran high, and great things were hoped from constitutional changes and Whig reforms. Bray's purpose was to recall men's attention to fundamentals, to those radical social reforms without which, in his opinion, mere political remedies would be ineffective. "There is wanted," he says, "not a mere governmental or particular remedy, but a general remedy—one which will apply to all social wrongs and evils, great and small." "The producers have merely to determine whether it be not possible to change *that social whole which keeps them poor,* as well as that governmental part which oppresses them because they are poor." "Every social and governmental wrong owes its rise to the existing social system—*to the institution of property as it at present exists.*" Tracing the mischief to its root, he finds it in "the principle of unequal exchanges," and the inequality of condition which results from this. This was old Vanderlint's doctrine, and Bray might have adopted his motto, "The destruction of the poor is their poverty." Robert Dale Owen, too, had arrived at a similar result in 1828. "The present system of commercial exchange deprives Britain's laborers, in some way or other, of $\frac{38}{40}$ths of the produce of their industry." [8] Under the present social system, "which gives to irresponsible individuals the power of grinding masses of labor between masses of capital," "the whole of the working class are dependent upon the capitalist or employer for the means of labor, and therefore for the means of life." Wealth acquired by trading is derived, by unequal exchanges, from the exertions of others. "All profit must come from labor . . . the gain of an idle class must necessarily be the loss

[8] *Co-operative Magazine,* March 1828, pp. 62, 102, 52, 61, 67, 49, 50.

of an industrious class." "Capitalists and proprietors do no more than give the working man, for his labor of one week, a part of the wealth which they obtained from him the week before." "Thus, view the matter as we will, there is to be seen no towering pile of wealth which has not been heaped together by rapacity." These passages, and I might quote many others to the same effect, will enable the reader to judge how far there was any originality in Marx's famous theory of profit. Like Gray and Thompson, Bray goes to Colquhoun's statistics to estimate the extent of this robbery of labor. "Of six millions of adult men, five assist in producing and distributing wealth; four belong to the working class. These last receive scarcely £200,000,000 of the £500,000,000 annually created, which averages £11 per head for the men, women, and children comprised in this class, and for this they toil on the average 11 hours a day." As he elsewhere puts it, the system of unequal exchanges "robs every working man of two-thirds of his just earnings, to keep up the supremacy and the wealth of those who are not working men." The Whig remedies, free trade, machinery, and emigration, are worthless. The trade union movement, though sound in principle (for Bray saw through the wage-fund theory), has failed, and must have failed; for neither political nor trades unions go to the root of the matter. They do not touch the system of unequal exchanges. American experience shows the futility of merely political reform. "Society is upon the same principle in all countries . . . they, like ourselves, are divided into rich and poor, into capitalists and pro-ducers, and the last are there as they are here, at the mercy of the first."

A really equitable system, according to Bray, must be one of universal labor and equal exchanges. He takes as his first principle the plausible but vague axiom on which Mr. Spencer afterwards based his *Social Statics.* "Every man has a right to do what he likes, *provided the so-doing interferes not with the equal rights of his fellow-men.*" He holds that this principle excludes property in land, and implies a right to the whole produce of labor. "Equal labor of all kinds should be equally remunerated . . . inequality in the value of labor to society is no argument for inequality of reward." For this communistic prin-ciple he tries to obtain the authority of Ricardo, whose highly spec-ulative analysis Bray and the socialists generally took too seriously. Ricardo, he says, tells us that "it is not to any one commodity, or set of commodities, but to some given *quantity of labor,* that we must refer for an unvarying standard of real value. Here is a recognition of the principle that real value is dependent upon labor; and the only inference we can draw from it is that all men who perform an equal quantity of labor ought to receive an equal remuneration."

These principles clearly land us in communism; and Bray's ideal system is one of community of possessions. But he recognizes the extreme difficulty of establishing such a system; and therefore, as a transitional measure, he proposes a kind of National Joint-Stock Scheme. Let the whole 5,000,000 of adult producers be formed into a number of joint-stock companies, containing from 100 to 1000 men each. Each company is to be confined to one trade. They are to have in use, by hire or purchase, the land and fixed capital of the country; and to be set in motion by a circulating bank-note capital equivalent to £100 for each associated member. Their affairs are to be conducted by general and local boards of trade; the members being paid weekly wages for their labor, and receiving equal wages for equal amounts of labor. All would have a common interest, working for a common end, and deriving a common benefit from all that is produced.

For assistance in establishing "this joint-stock modification of society," Bray looked to the Friendly Societies, with their 1,500,000 members, and the Trade Unions. Together they might bring into relation 2,000,000 producers. The finance of the scheme is original. Bray is as weak on the theory of money as socialists usually are. He thinks it quite practicable to issue paper against the whole mass of national property. Accordingly he proposes that the working class should obtain possession of the land and capital by the issue of notes on their joint credit to the amount of 2000 millions sterling. "The past, the present, and the future transactions of capital all depend on labor for their fulfillment. Such being the case, why should not labor itself make a purchase? Why should not the bond of *labor,* to pay at a future time what itself only can produce, be as valuable as the bond of *capital,* to pay what this very same labor is to produce? . . . Is the security offered by a people of less worth than that offered by an individual?" In any case there must be no resort to violence. "Reason, and not force, conviction, and not compulsion, purchase, and not a plunder, a systematic application of combined forces, and not an undisciplined and chaotic movement, are the proper instruments to be employed." For popular revolutions to be effectual, conviction must always precede force; for force may establish, but it cannot always preserve.

Bray's scheme, it must be admitted, is more practical than the pure communism of Owen and Thompson, which he regarded as a counsel of perfection. It admits of individual property in products together with common property in productive powers, and thus combines the stimulus of private property with the equities of common interest. His companies, too, are far more practical units for industrial organization than the self-sufficing communities of his predecessors. Indeed, if we can imagine a system of federated productive co-operation, national in its scope, and somewhat communistic in its distribution of wages, we shall have gone far towards realizing what Bray seems to have intended. It might be said, indeed, that as he has foreshadowed in his financial proposals the principle of modern labor banks, so his general conception is not without analogies in the aims of the wholesale co-operative societies of our day.

Within its limits, which though narrow are not narrower than those of the *laissez faire* school of economists whom he was opposing, Bray's essay must be considered a closely reasoned and philosophical piece of work. It was long a classic in the propagandist literature of the English socialists. No one can read the work without perceiving that it had clearly anticipated many of the ideas which are supposed to be most characteristic of Karl Marx. That Marx was greatly impressed by the book is beyond question. In his *Misère de la Philosophie,* 1847, when his object is to discredit Proudhon, he quotes Bray to the extent of nine pages, and describes his essay as a remarkable performance, little known in France, but containing the key to all the works of Proudhon, past, present, and future. In 1859, when he had begun to develop his own theory, the notice of Bray is limited to the mention of his name in a footnote. Even his name does not occur in *Das Kapital,* 1867, though the list of works quoted in that book extends to sixteen pages, and it is here that Marx develops the theory of profit which Bray had so vigorously put forward in 1839. It was fortunate for Marx that in Germany also Bray was then "little known."

It must be evident from this brief survey of the writings of six principal English socialists, that the body of doctrine they advanced was of such a character as to deserve the serious attention of all who were concerned with social philosophy. It was closely reasoned, original in conception, striking at the very root of the principles on which existing society was based, and expounded in such vigorous fashion as to exert widespread influence over the mass of the people, at that time distressed and disaffected. Why did the English economists for the most part ignore ideas of such a revolutionary and far-reaching nature? We can imagine how they would have interested Adam Smith; and Malthus and Sismondi, each in his way critical of the orthodox school, might at least have been expected to see their importance. Malthus and Sismondi, however, though critical, were not radical in their criticism; both writers accepting the general social philosophy of the dominant school. Neither succeeded in founding a school of his own, or in appreciably modifying the direction impressed upon current thought by the Ricardian group. After James Mill and Brougham, no leading economist seems to have thought the English revolutionary socialism worth notice, and the very names of its chief writers were unknown to most of them until quite recent times. John Stuart Mill gives no sign that he was aware of the existence of his contemporaries, Marx, Engels, and Lassalle, much less of the men from whom they drew their inspiration. Socialism for him meant the romantic utopias of Fourier and Owen, or the academic industrialism of Saint-Simon and Comte.

After the appearance of Mill's *Principles,* English economists, for a whole generation, were men of one book; and it must be admitted that the influence of this book did not tend to correct the distaste for historical study and the somewhat narrow range of investigation which were already becoming traditional in the English school. Hence, half a century elapsed before the ideas of the originators of modern social-ism were appreciated, or even recognized, by the official representatives of social philosophy in the country of their birth. This must always be a matter of profound regret. Perhaps it is idle to speculate on what might have resulted had their pregnant teaching been subjected at the time to searching criticism by the best English economists of the day. But we can hardly doubt that a thorough discussion would have cleared the air of a good deal of confused and revolutionary socialism, and it would certainly have very much broadened and developed the current exposition of economic science.

Meanwhile the ideas were not dead. It was the Owenite institutions, and their political literature, that served to propagate the doctrines of the Ricardian socialists. The name Socialist was of Owenite origin, and does not seem to have been commonly applied to the Owenites till May 1835. But the ideas which we associate with the term today came not so much from Owen as from Thompson and his school. I cannot find that this school were in any way indebted to Owen for inspiration. But the Ricardian socialism was the yeast of the Owenite movement, and the foundation of all the more able contributions to Owenite literature; while it had no small share in stimulating the polit-ical offshoot of Owenism which rallied around the Charter.

It was Ricardo, not Owen, who gave the really effective inspiration to English socialism. That inspiration was indirect and negative, but it is unmistakable. Thompson and the rest took for granted the ac-curacy of Ricardo's unfortunate and strained deductions, and quote him as an unquestioned authority. Finding that certain of their con-clusions were abhorrent to their sense of right, and assuming that he had taken the existing conditions of society as his premises, they naturally directed all the force of their attack against these conditions. This was the real intellectual origin of revolutionary socialism, and it is for this reason I have called it Ricardian.

The revived socialism in England [during the 1880's] was a purely exotic growth. It seemed to have altogether lost touch with the parent school of Thompson and his contemporaries; and, except for such slight countenance as it derived from the teaching of John Stuart Mill, was entirely inspired from foreign sources, and especially by the writings of Marx and Lassalle, and the crusade of Henry George. Of late years, the authority of Marx and George has greatly waned in this country. The current forms of socialism are once more of native origin, and like most really English movements, have gradually purged themselves of the revolutionary temper. The Fabian Society, in particular, though genuinely socialistic in its ulterior aims, appears from its latest manifesto to have adopted a policy of gradual and detailed reform, so practical and opportunist that it can hardly be called socialistic in the sense here given to that term.

Cole
on
Owen

Another strand of socialist thought derives from the work of Robert Owen (1771–1858). Owen is generally classified among the "utopian" socialists, who developed elaborate schemes of a new order of social life. He was an active reformer and pioneer in the cooperative movement. The cooperative colonies which he founded included a settlement in the United States (New Harmony, Indiana).

Owen, born in Wales, was a man of many accomplishments. His reformist zeal did not prevent him from becoming a successful manufacturer. His most important works, *A New View of Society and Other Writings,* are available in an edition by G. D. H. Cole (1927).

G. D. H. Cole (1889–   ) is the author of the standard biography of Owen. Cole has been associated with Oxford University as student and teacher, since 1945 as professor of social and political theory. Professor Cole and his wife, Margaret Cole, have for many years been associated with the British labor movement and the Fabian Society. He has published a large number of books in the field of social and economic history, biography, and theory. Together with Mrs. Cole, he has also made a name for himself as a writer of detective stories.

ROBERT OWEN, shop-boy and manufacturer, factory reformer and educationist, Socialist and Co-operative pioneer, Trade Union leader and secularist, founder of ideal communities and practical man of business, was something of a puzzle to his own generation, and is no less a puzzle to posterity. Surely no man ever founded so many movements, and yet had so simple and unvarying a body of ideas. Surely no man was ever at once so practical and so visionary, so lovable and so impossible to work with, so laughed at and yet so influential. And there are few men who are so much talked about, and whose works are so little read.

There is a reason for this. Owen wrote voluminously, and often ill. He lived to be eighty-seven, and he was writing steadily up to the last weeks of his life. But of his later works, which make up the great bulk of his writings, by far the larger part is valueless. Owen said what he had to say in his earlier books; his later works are merely more and more elaborate and prosy repetitions of his better writings. There is but one exception: his Life of himself, of which he completed only a first volume, is delightfully fresh and attractive—the best and most readable of all his books, though it was published in his eighty-sixth year. It can best be read as a companion volume to his expository writings; for it gives Owen's own version of the circumstances which attended their issue.

With this one exception, all Owen's later works can be disregarded, except by the specialist. Indeed, one volume, even one slender volume, is enough to contain all the best of Owen's writings with the exception of his unfinished Autobiography. And all that need be included in such a volume was issued within a space of eight years. The opening essay of the *New View of Society* appeared in 1813, and the *Report to the County of Lanark* in 1821. In these eight years Robert Owen made his essential contribution to human knowledge. And, incidentally out of his work during these years arose in Great Britain the two great movements of Socialism and Co-operation.

[From G. D. H. Cole, *Persons and Periods*. Copyright 1938 by Macmillan and Company. Used with permission.]

In order to understand Owen's doctrines aright, it is necessary to know something both of the man himself and of the circumstances in which his ideas were developed. Owen was born in 1771, and the years of his manhood coincided with the most critical years of the great social change which we call the "Industrial Revolution." And his doctrines were above all designed as answers to the vast social and economic problems which the Industrial Revolution had raised up.

Let us begin with the man himself. Robert Owen was born in Newtown, Montgomeryshire, in Central Wales, on the Upper Severn. His father was a saddler and ironmonger, and also the local postmaster. Owen was a weakly boy, much given to introspection, but intelligent beyond his fellows. He was only seven years old when he became a sort of pupil-teacher in the local school. At nine, he left school and began work as shop-boy in a neighbour's shop. At ten, after a brief visit to London, he was apprenticed to a draper in good business at Stamford in Lincolnshire. There he remained three years, and then became assistant at a draper's in London. A year later he migrated to Manchester, and for four years was assistant there in a good drapery house. Then, at eighteen, his chance came, and the boy set up in business for himself.

Manchester, which was to be the scene of Owen's first considerable successes, was then at the height of a great and rapid industrial transformation. The great inventions of Hargreaves, Arkwright, and Crompton were in process of revolutionising the methods of cotton manufacture, and new factories for preparing, roving and spinning the cotton were springing up right and left. It was a time when great fortunes were to be made by the fortunate and the adventurous; and young Owen seized his chance. He began business for himself, with a borrowed hundred pounds, in partnership with a mechanic who knew how to make certain of the new machines. Before long his partner left him, in search of a better-equipped colleague, and Owen was left on his own. No longer able to make machines, he set out to use those which remained in his hands. He succeeded; but within a few months a better chance came his way. The position of manager to one of the largest and best-equipped spinning mills in Lancashire fell vacant, and Owen, still under twenty, was appointed, at a salary of three hundred a year— a handsome remuneration in those days. At twenty he found himself in full charge of a factory in which five hundred workers were employed.

Again Owen made good. The products of his factory became well known for excellence in the trade, not only in Manchester but as far away as Glasgow. His employer, a Mr. Drinkwater, offered him a partnership; but difficulties arose, and instead Owen entered into part-

nership with two younger men who were starting a new company for
the manufacture of yarn. He remained for some years in sole control
of the new mill, and then on behalf of his company acquired from
David Dale, whose daughter he soon afterwards married, the famous
New Lanark Mills, the largest and best equipped spinning mills in
Scotland.

This bald summary does far less than justice to the romance of
Owen's early career. Every episode in it was an adventure, through
which he climbed steadily to a further success. At twenty-eight, when
he became managing partner in the New Lanark establishment, Owen
was already a wealthy manufacturer according to the standards of the
times, and bade fair to be before long very wealthy indeed.

Owen was by now well known as a successful business man; but,
beyond a small circle of friends, that was his only claim to distinction.
He had, indeed, as a leading member of the Manchester Literary and
Philosophic Society, given utterance to some peculiar opinions on the
subject of religion and the formation of character; but these did not
appear to possess any special significance in relation to his business.
Only when he was established at New Lanark did it appear that he
was aiming at something very much bigger than mere money-making or
business success.

Owen remained at New Lanark for more than a quarter of a century.
He made of it not only a most successful commercial establishment,
but a show place which visitors came from all over the world to see.
Through all the successive partnerships in which he was associated—
and he quarrelled with each group of partners in turn because they
would not give him full freedom to follow out his ideas—he aimed at
making New Lanark, not merely an efficient factory, but a well-governed human community based on his ideals. The manufacturer of
those days—especially when his factory stood in an isolated place—
had a tremendous hold over his employees. The houses in which they
lived, the shops at which they bought their provisions, the entire village
as well as the factory belonged to the employer, who gathered together
his force of labourers from far and near, and could rule over them as
a benevolent or malevolent despot. Owen had a high idea of the duties
which this vast power entailed. In his view, the employer had no right
merely to treat his employees as a means to profit. It was his duty to
ensure to them all the means of good living—to pay good wages, to
avoid unreasonably long hours of work, to provide good houses and
good food and clothing at reasonable prices, to make the factory village
a sanitary and a pleasant place, and, above all, to ensure to the children,
whether employed in the factory or not, the best education that sym-

pathy and knowledge could place at their command. In his later partnerships, when he was in a position to make his own terms, Owen
strictly limited the reward of capital to a fixed amount, and insisted
that all surplus profits should be applied to the provision of communal
services on the employees' behalf.

At New Lanark, Owen paid better wages, worked shorter hours, and
gave infinitely better conditions than most of his competitors. He
abolished all "pauper apprentice" labour immediately on assuming
control, and refused to employ children at less than ten years of age
when others were freely working them intolerably long hours at less than
six years old. And yet he had no difficulty in making the factory pay,
despite the large sums he was constantly spending on all manner of
improvements and amenities. In short, he gave an astonishingly convincing demonstration of what later generations have called the "economy of high wages," at a time when appalling under-payment and overwork were almost everywhere regarded as the indispensable conditions
of commercial success.

Owen's earlier writings, such as the *New View of Society* and the
Address to the Inhabitants of New Lanark, reflect this phase of his
career. And they make it clear that there was already a quite definite
theory behind his activities. He did what he did because he believed
that in no other way could the foundations of a reasonable social order
be truly laid. His main purpose, he insisted throughout, was educational. There was no way of making good citizens except by educating
men and women so as to make them such. And there was no way of
so educating them save by providing an environment in which their
better natures would be encouraged to grow, and body and mind together be well cared for and trained in right habits and ways of living.

"Man's character is made for, and not by, him," Owen was never
weary of proclaiming; and his whole system at New Lanark was based
on this belief. What appalled him about the new "manufacturing system" was not only its inhumanity, but also that it seemed to him to
result in a perversion of the characters of those who were subjected to
its rule. What chance had the child, forced into the factory at a tender
age and there remorselessly compelled to labour under rigid discipline
for the profits of others, of becoming a good citizen? What sort of civic
virtues was the rule of unlimited competition and "devil take the hind-
most" likely to breed up in both master and man? The child should
not labour at all until it had been thoroughly grounded by education
in right social principles. When it did go to work, the labour must be
suited to its years, and animated by a social, instead of a competitive,
motive. And education, while it must begin with the child, must not

stop with the child; it must continue throughout life. Above all, a man's occupation has so strong an influence on his character that, if the factory is wrongly organised so as to appeal to the wrong motives in men, the whole of society will be poisoned by it.

It is important to understand exactly what Owen meant by his view of human character. He did not mean, as some people have supposed, that man's individuality has no real existence, or that the individual is merely the result of the circumstances in which he has been placed. On the contrary, he insisted strongly on the importance of individuality and on the large differences between one man and another, and made these differences in individuality an essential foundation of the system of education which he established at New Lanark. He held, however, that each individual would react in a different way according to the environment in which he was placed, and that, in particular, men's social and ethical ideas—what, in effect, he meant by their "character" —were taken by them from the environment and the social and economic institutions under which they lived. Accordingly, he held that the evils which existed in the world of his own day, the competition between man and man which he regarded as the root of social antagonisms, and the competition between country and country which prevented concerted effort to develop the resources of the whole world in the common interests of its inhabitants, were the result of evil social institutions, including wrong traditional doctrines, and could be eradicated by a change in these institutions. including a change in men's beliefs. In particular he thought that the doctrine of individual responsibility, preached by the Churches, was a powerful influence in perpetuating social evils, because it led men to impute social misfortunes to individual sinfulness rather than to faulty social arrangements. This was the basis of his famous denunciation of all existing religions and of his attempt to create a new rational religion based on the denial of man's individual responsibility and the recognition that men's characters are formed for them and not by them. On this foundation too, he built up his system of education at New Lanark, and on the same principle the Owenites founded at a later period the numerous educational experiments which they carried on throughout the country in their Halls of Science.

Owen, then, set out to find a new basis for society in place of the existing competitive system, with the idea of establishing a set of social institutions on the basis of which men and nations would be brought to live in harmony one with another, and taught from infancy the moral doctrine of social co-operation. This was for him the significance of the Villages of Co-operation which, largely on the model of his own experiment at New Lanark, he proposed everywhere to establish. For he held that, if the basic unit of society came to be a small co-operative group working not for individual profit but for common service, this would effect a fundamental change in men's character and remove all danger of class rivalries within communities, or of war and competition between one community and another.

Although Owen ranks as the pioneer of the Co-operative Movement, he had little interest in consumers' co-operation as such. Indeed, at the outset the consumers' co-operative stores which grew up under the influence of his ideas, such as the famous Toad Lane Store of the Rochdale Pioneers of 1844, did not regard the retailing of goods on a non-profit-making basis as an end in itself, but only as a preparatory step towards the building-up among the members of a system of co-operative production and self-employment which would get rid of competition and the need for a separate employing class. The declared object, for example, of the Rochdale Pioneers, when they founded their store, was not shopkeeping on a mutual basis, but the building-up of a collective fund which could be subsequently used for co-operative production and ultimately for the establishment of an Owenite Co-operative Community.

These ideas of Owen's bear certain marked resemblances to the theory on which the Communists of the Soviet Union have been working of late in their plans of industrialisation, and above all in their intensive efforts to bring about the socialisation of agriculture. For the Russian experiment is not only, or even at bottom mainly, an attempt to raise the material standard of living of the Russian people, but far more an attempt to change the basis of men's thought by bringing them under the influence of a different social and economic environment. The Russians want, as Owen wanted, gradually to abolish the difference between town and country and the difference between industrial and agricultural conditions. They want to industrialise and collectivise agriculture because they believe that only by causing the peasants, as well as the industrial workers, to live in an environment of collective institutions based on co-operative rather than competitive principles can they hope to bring into existence a mental condition consistent with the successful functioning of a Communist community. In other words, they, like Owen, believe that man's "character," in the Owenite sense, is made for him and not by him, as the product of his social and economic environment. This doctrine, commonly regarded as distinctively Marxian, is in effect Owenite, and it is impossible to doubt that Marx, though he regarded Owen as a "Utopian" Socialist, owed far more to him in the formulation of the Materialist Conception of History than has generally been admitted. Owen, in this as in other respects, deserves much more credit than he has ever received as the true progenitor of modern Socialist ideas.

It can, no doubt, be urged that this root idea of Owenism concerning the influence of environment upon character was not original, and that Owen himself may have derived it largely from Godwin, who in turn was influenced by such eighteenth-century rationalists as d'Holbach and Helvetius. This is doubtless true, but the fact remains that Owen was the first person definitely to link up this doctrine of social determinism with economic conditions, and particularly with the new industrial system which was coming into existence in his day, and that he anticipated Marx in urging that the problems of the new industrialism demanded a co-operative rather than a competitive solution and accordingly a radical change from competition to co-operation as the basis of social institutions.

Owen lived on until 1858, and in his last years when his powers were failing became involved in spiritualist experiments. He had in fact finished his constructive work long before these later mental meanderings set in. His real importance to history is that, as an employer, he was the first man to demonstrate clearly the advantages of good wages and conditions and a pleasant hygienic factory environment; that, as an educationist, he was in many respects a pioneer of new methods which are only now beginning to find substantial recognition, especially in his insistence on the inadequacy of mere book teaching and the necessity of an appeal to the eye and ear of the child and on the immense formative importance of the earliest years of life; and, finally, that, as a Socialist and Co-operative thinker, he was the first person to formulate in the light of the new industrialism a doctrine plainly relating the possibilities of social and economic improvement to the material and mental environment in which men had to live, and to urge the necessity of a complete transformation of the social system based on the essentially co-operative character of modern large-scale processes of production.

We may think that, in the *New View of Society,* Owen pushed his view of the effect of environment on character too far. But it can hardly be disputed that, in the circumstances of his own time, his insistence on it was wholly salutary. Owen's contemporaries were for the most part acting on very different principles—treating the acquisition of wealth as the highest good, and justifying the most ruthless exploitation of labour by an appeal to that standard. By insisting that the acquisition of wealth on such terms might mean the destruction of men, Owen put forward a different ideal, and became the pioneer of new views both of education and of factory management.

By common consent, the schools at New Lanark were pronounced the outstanding success of that astonishing factory. Both in ideas of education and in their practical working out Owen was far ahead of his time. He saw at once the inadequacy of Lancaster's monitorial system, and insisted that the first aim of education must be not to cram the memory but to equip the mind. He realised the limitations of books, especially in their appeal to the younger children, and the place of dancing, of physical exercises, of appeals to eye and ear in any sensible system of education. He trained his own teachers in his own methods, and raised up a host of disciples in his faith. And, above all, he realised that a tired mind cannot learn, and that long hours of toil are incompatible with the making of good citizens.

In all his work at New Lanark, Owen was doubtless very much the benevolent autocrat, whose word all men in his village were bound to obey. And, as he came to wish to apply his doctrines over a sphere wider than his own factory, he began to visualise a world made in the image of New Lanark. He had done wonders. Why should not others do as much? His employees were orderly, prosperous and happy. Why should other employers complain of the turbulence, laziness, drunkenness of their workers? Why should there be so much misery in the world? Need there be any misery at all, if the world would but follow his example?

So Owen became gradually the leader of a crusade. For more than twelve years after his coming to New Lanark he worked away quietly, testing his theories and gradually proving their soundness. Then he set to work to convert others. His *New View of Society* was his first effort at propaganda of his views. For it seemed to him that if he could but convince the world of his doctrine concerning the formation of character, everything else would follow as a matter of course. If the world knew that "man's character is formed for, and not by, him," it would cease to blame the poor for being what they were, and would set out to provide an environment in which they would speedily become, as the workers at New Lanark were becoming under his guidance, industrious, prosperous, good and happy. It would cease to blame the poor for their condition, and would take the obvious steps necessary to improve it.

Side by side with this wider crusade, Owen set on foot another. He began to work hard for a Factory Act which would prohibit the labour of young children, regulate hours of work, and set up a State system of factory inspection. Owen was the great pioneer of the movement for factory reform. Principally to his initiative the first Factory Act—

that of 1819—was due, though he repudiated it as falling far short of what he held to be both just and expedient.

Owen was engaged in this double crusade when the ending of the Napoleonic wars ushered in a period of intense unemployment and economic crisis. "On the day the peace was signed," he wrote, "the great customer of the producers died." Everywhere trade stagnated, thousands were flung out of work, wages came tumbling down. Soon there were throughout the country mutterings of discontent from the starving operatives; and before long the mutterings swelled to a mighty clamour. The workers were driven in masses to the Poor Law for support; and the parishes, appalled at the heavy rates, barely kept them from sheer mass starvation. The workers cried out for the Reform of Parliament as a means to the redress of their grievances; the Government, fearing revolution, retaliated with the "Peterloo" massacre, the Six Acts of 1819, and a general campaign of repression.

To Owen, meanwhile, it seemed as if the world had gone mad. He had no belief in political reform as a means to the remedying of economic grievances; but the repression of the workers seemed to him utterly beside the point. The thing to do was to remove the causes of distress, instead of tinkering with its effects. As early as 1816 he developed, with this end in view, the first outline of his famous "Plan," the germ of Socialism and of Co-operation, but in its first inception essentially a practical scheme for relieving the economic distress of the years immediately after the war.

The gist of Owen's plan can be very shortly stated. He proposed that, instead of paying out doles, the Government should employ the poor in "Villages of Co-operation" modelled on his own establishment at New Lanark and, like it, essentially centres of social life and rational education as well as of productive activity. These "Villages," Owen suggested, should be in the main self-supporting. They should be agricultural as well as industrial, and should raise the produce needed for their own consumption, exchanging their surplus products of different kinds one with another. As they would be based on rational principles of education, they would not compete but co-operate one with another, and their aim would be as much to train good citizens as to relieve the necessities of the poor. If this were done, Owen argued, the need for poor rates would speedily disappear, and, by the same token, the foundations of a new and better social order for the whole community would speedily be laid.

This is the "Plan" which, with minor variations, is expounded in many of Owen's writings, but most fully and maturely in the *Report to the County of Lanark*. As Owen expounded it, the conception of it

broadened out in his mind. He began by preaching it as a cure for
unemployment; but soon he was putting it forward as a complete and
immediately practicable social Utopia, destined speedily to sweep away
capitalism and the competitive system, and to inaugurate for all the
world a new era of peace and brotherhood based on a rational idea of
the formation and development of human character under the influence
of environment. "Any character from the best to the worst, from the
most ignorant to the most enlightened, may be given to any community,
even to the world at large, by applying certain means, which are to a
great extent at the command, and under the control, or easily made so,
of those who possess the government of nations." So Owen had written
in his *New View of Society;* and in his "Plan" he was proposing the
actual means by which the great change might be brought about.

There was, at the outset, nothing "Radical" or democratic in Owen's
conception. He appealed for its execution to the Tory Government and
the Unreformed Parliament. He enlisted for a time the respectful
interest of Lord Sidmouth, the Tory Home Secretary and noted perse-
cutor of Radicals. His projects were blessed by the Archbishop of
Canterbury, and supported by the Duke of Kent. David Ricardo and
other noted economists sat on a committee pledged to further his "Plan."
As the famous and successful manufacturer of New Lanark, he received
a respectful hearing in high quarters. But it was one thing to listen,
and another to act; and, as the cries of distress and anger among the
poor grew louder, the Government and the Parliament turned more
and more from considering ways of relieving distress to taking measures
for the suppression of disturbance and riot. Owen found himself less
and less respectfully received; he made up his mind to appeal from the
Government to the general public.

This wider appeal is embodied in the Addresses and Manifestoes
which Owen poured out one after another during the troublous years
after 1815. In one of them occurs Owen's famous denunciation of all
established religions as inveterate foes to the progress of mankind.
There was nothing particularly novel in this declaration, save its out-
spokenness. All the religions, Owen held, treated man as a responsible
agent—responsible for his own misdoings, whereas his faults of character and his sins were really the products of his environment, and
could be washed away by a better moral and physical education. Owen
had been preaching this doctrine for years, though he had never before
declared so plainly his hostility to the Churches. But it was largely
as a stick wherewith to beat his growingly unpopular social doctrines
that the remark was seized upon, and quoted against him in every accent
of horrified surprise. Owen suddenly ceased to be respectable; and,

though some of his highly placed friends stood by him for a time, yet from the date of this declaration his main appeal was made in effect to the working class.

Indeed, it became clear within a few years that a section of the workers was almost alone in taking Owen seriously. For a time he had still a following among the middle and professional classes, and produced for their consumption successive elaborations of his "Plan," culminating in the famous *Report to the County of Lanark*. But gradually, in despair of seeing any practical outcome of his labours in Great Britain, he conceived the idea of trying out his schemes in the more congenial, because less contaminated, air of the New World. In 1824 Owen left for the United States, and there, the following year, he founded the Co-operative Community of New Harmony.

The story of that failure has been often told. How the settlers, a motley band of enthusiasts and adventurers of every sort, fell out among themselves, how the parent community broke into several lesser communities, how finally the communal basis of settlement was given up, and New Harmony relapsed into a successful pioneer town based on individual tenure, and how Owen, having sunk his whole fortune in the venture, emerged poor but not discouraged from its collapse, cannot here be described. It is enough to say that in 1829 Owen returned to Great Britain to find that the face of the world had greatly changed in his absence.

For now Owenism had attracted a new body of disciples, and these were chiefly found among the most intelligent leaders of the working class. The Combination Acts had been repealed in 1824, and a rapid growth of Trade Unionism had immediately followed. The great political uprising which culminated in the Reform Act of 1832 was nearing its height; but the workers were organising for industrial protection as well as for political agitation. There had begun too among the workers a growth of little Co-operative Societies and stores for mutual trading, explicitly based on Owen's teaching, and regarding themselves as forerunners of purely working-class "Villages of Co-operation" to be founded when the surplus funds accumulated through mutual trade grew large enough for so ambitious a venture.

After a momentary hesitation, Owen, who had by this time severed his connection with New Lanark and ceased to be an employer of labour, put himself at the head of the movement. All over the country his disciples set to work to bring the Trade Unions and other working-class bodies over to their way of thinking. John Doherty, the great Trade Union leader of the North and secretary of the Spinners, was a convinced Owenite. One after another, the Unions were converted:

there was a rapid growth of Co-operative Stores, and many Unions set on foot Producers' Co-operative Societies of their own.

The Operative Builders' Union, the most powerful of the new Trade Unions which had sprung up during the excitements of the preceding years, went over completely to Owenism after Owen himself had addressed its national conference, ambitiously styled the "Builders' Parliament." Plans were made for basing on the Union a Grand National Guild of Builders, which was to dispense altogether with employers and new-fangled "building contractors," and to take the entire industry into its own hands. Moreover, in order to provide a market for the rapidly growing number of Producers' Co-operative Societies, or "Union Shops," Owen founded in 1832 his National Equitable Labour Exchange, of which branches were speedily opened in Birmingham, Liverpool, and Glasgow, as well as London. In these Exchanges, Owen's principle of "labour value," as expounded in his *Report to the County of Lanark,* was to be put into practice, and goods were to be exchanged for goods between the various groups of producers by means of "labour notes" standing for definite amounts of "labour time" embodied in each commodity.

Till the end of 1832 the preoccupation of the main body of the workers with the Reform struggle had delayed the growth of the movement. But thereafter disillusionment with the fruits of the political agitation, which had enfranchised the middle classes and left the workers voteless, had brought fresh recruits thronging into the Trade Unions and Owenite Societies. Political means having failed, the workers were minded to try Trade Unionism and Co-operation as the roads to social emancipation. By 1833 Owen found himself at the head of a huge working-class movement eagerly demanding a lead.

It was at this stage that most of the numerous Trade Unions which had come into being were organised under Owen's leadership into a Grand National Consolidated Trades Union with an Owenite programme. A little later, in the North, the Owenites, through the National Regeneration Society, placed themselves at the head of a movement for factory reform and the eight-hour day, which they set out to secure not by legislation but by industrial action. The Grand National Consolidated Trades Union at the height of its influence in 1834 is said to have had over half a million members, and another half million are said to have been enrolled in Unions, such as the Builders' Union, which were working in association with it.

The Grand National Consolidated Trades Union, known to its contemporaries as *the Trades Union,* speedily came to be feared as a vast and potentially revolutionary uprising of the working class. For a while Owen dreamed great dreams. In 1816 it had seemed to him that, if only his "Plan" were adopted, the whole face of the world could be at once changed. The failure of New Harmony had not taught him to moderate his hopes; he had become steadily more Utopian and millennial as he grew older. Now, he proclaimed to the workers that by their might and rationality there should come speedily a great change by which all misery and poverty would at once be swept away.

How rapidly this great movement crumbled students of the history of the Trade Union movement are well aware. The Owenites had projected a General Strike, to be followed by the sudden and complete institution of the new Co-operative system which Owen had preached. But in fact the "Trades Union," as it was commonly called, soon found itself involved in a large number of sectional disputes, mostly lock-outs declared by employers who refused to employ anyone who admitted membership of the "Trades Union." Moreover, the trial and transportation for the administration of unlawful oaths of the Dorchester labourers who had formed a branch of the "Trades Union" indicated the readiness of the Government to go to all lengths in repressing the new movement. Under these blows the "Trades Union" rapidly crumbled away, and in the summer of 1834 Owen, realising its failure, decreed its dissolution. Thereafter Owen played little direct part in the fortunes of the organised working-class movement. For the rest of his life he devoted the whole of his energies to a social propaganda which became more and more ethical and rationalistic rather than directly political and industrial.

Within a year of its formation, the great Trades Union was shattered into a thousand fragments, and Owen had ceased to be the leader of the British working class. Within two years more, a new political agitation—the Chartist Movement—was arising, and the great Trade Union struggle of 1834 was no more than a memory.

Owenism, however, did not die. From one stream of Owenite influence sprang the modern Co-operative Movement; another went on to give birth to the Secularist agitation. Owen himself, turning more and more from reformer to prophet, became the apostle of a "Rational Religion" which was the forerunner of the modern Ethical movement. For more than twenty years longer he poured out books, pamphlets and magazines in an endless stream, and a body of faithful disciples continued to spread his gospel. But he was already an old man when the great Trades Union collapsed; and his later work was no more than a repetition of his earlier writings. The new Co-operative Colony, Queenwood, or Harmony Hall, which he founded in Hampshire in

1839, only repeated the failure of New Harmony in the 'twenties. Owen's real work was over in 1834.

I began by calling Robert Owen something of a puzzle. Leslie Stephen called him "one of those bores who are the salt of the earth." He was essentially a man of one idea, which he preached tirelessly, in and out of season, through the whole of his public life. In pursuit of this idea, practical business man though he had been, he lost all sense of the difference between conception and accomplishment. The millennium seemed to him always just round the next corner; he was endlessly and fatuously hopeful and sure of success. He aimed constantly at the impossible, and was never in the least deterred by failure from aiming at it again. Consequently he became, despite his early and outstanding successes, an exceedingly bad leader of men. He was, moreover, more than a little autocratic in his ways—a habit bred in him by his position of unquestioned command at New Lanark, and confirmed by his unswerving and absolute assurance of being on all occasions perfectly right.

This sounds an unlovable picture; and yet, by the general testimony of those who knew him, Owen was a most lovable man. He was utterly without taint of self-seeking, a real and feeling lover of his fellow men, an unfailing favourite with children. His own children loved him very dearly, and were ardent disciples of his doctrine. Perhaps the easiest answer to the riddle of his personality is that he was a little mad.

If there are grave faults to be found with Owen's practical qualities of leadership, and many failures to his record, few men of the nineteenth century have more solid achievements to their credit. It was a very great thing to have demonstrated, as he did in the worst days of the Industrial Revolution, that low wages, long hours, and bad conditions of labour were not the indispensable foundations of Britain's greatness. It was a fine thing to have realised the need for a liberalising education as the basis of a rational citizenship at a time when the Lancasterian monitorial system was regarded as the last word in progressive education for the poor. And it was a fine thing to have spoken, even for the time in vain, a word of hope and promise to the unfortunate victims of the Industrial Revolution, and to have set them building up their Trade Unions and their Co-operative Societies with a new vision of self-government and freedom before their eyes. Long before Carlyle or Ruskin, Owen looked upon the new world which the "Manchester School" was making, and called it "evil"; and his calling it so was the more remarkable because he was himself one of the most successful learners in that school. But Owen was greatest because he not only re-

volted against the horrors of the Industrial Revolution, but also sought
a constructive way of escape. His Co-operative Colonies and his great
Trades Union alike failed; but he laid the foundations on which a later
generation was better able to build. Few men have exerted a wider
or more beneficent influence; and none has been more whole-hearted in
the service of his faith.

Veblen

——— on ———

Marx

Karl Marx (1818–1883) was born at Trier, in the German Rhineland, and educated at the Universities of Bonn and Berlin, where he studied law, history, and philosophy. Unable to secure a university appointment, he turned to journalism. His radical views compelled him to leave Germany, and he moved first to Paris, later to Brussels, and eventually to London, where he spent over thirty years of his life. Of Marx's principal work, *Capital*, the first volume was published in 1867; the second and third volumes were published after his death by his friend and associate Friedrich Engels (1820–1895) in 1885 and 1894.

Marx's economic views are formed on the basis of the classical labor theory of value, from which he derives theories of surplus value and exploitation. Marx's dialectic materialism considers history primarily as a reflex of the prevailing structure of production. Change is generated by the class struggle, which, according to Marx, will end when the millennium, the classless society, begins.

Marx's theories are appraised here by Thorstein Veblen (1857–1929), himself a brilliant and bitter critic of business civilization but neither a socialist nor a Marxist.

(On Veblen, see pp. 378 ff., below.)

THE SYSTEM of doctrines worked out by Marx is characterized by a certain boldness of conception and a great logical consistency. Taken in detail, the constituent elements of the system are neither novel nor iconoclastic, nor does Marx at any point claim to have discovered previously hidden facts or to have invented recondite formulations of facts already known; but the system as a whole has an air of originality and initiative such as is rarely met with among the sciences that deal with any phase of human culture. How much of this distinctive character the Marxian system owes to the personal traits of its creator is not easy to say, but what marks it off from all other systems of economic theory is not a matter of personal idiosyncrasy. It differs characteristically from all systems of theory that had preceded it, both in its premises and in its aims. The (hostile) critics of Marx have not sufficiently appreciated the radical character of his departure in both of these respects, and have, therefore, commonly lost themselves in a tangled scrutiny of supposedly abstruse details; whereas those writers who have been in sympathy with his teachings have too commonly been disciples bent on exegesis and on confirming their fellow-disciples in the faith.

Except as a whole and except in the light of its postulates and aims, the Marxian system is not only not tenable, but it is not even intelligible. A discussion of a given isolated feature of the system (such as the theory of value) from the point of view of classical economics (such as that offered by Böhm-Bawerk) is as futile as a discussion of solids in terms of two dimensions.

Neither as regards his postulates and preconceptions nor as regards the aim of his inquiry is Marx's position an altogether single-minded one. In neither respect does his position come of a single line of antecedents. He is of no single school of philosophy, nor are his ideals those of any single group of speculators living before his time. For this reason he takes his place as an originator of a school of thought as well as the leader of a movement looking to a practical end.

[The substance of lectures before students in Harvard University in April 1906. Originally published in *Quarterly Journal of Economics*, August 1906, and reprinted in Veblen's *The Place of Science in Modern Civilization*, New York, The Viking Press, 1919. By permission.]

As to the motives which drive him and the aspirations which guide him, in destructive criticism and in creative speculation alike, he is primarily a theoretician busied with the analysis of economic phenomena and their organization into a consistent and faithful system of scientific knowledge; but he is, at the same time, consistently and tenaciously alert to the bearing which each step in the progress of his theoretical work has upon the propaganda. His work has, therefore, an air of bias, such as belongs to an advocate's argument; but it is not, therefore, to be assumed, nor indeed to be credited, that his propagandist aims have in any substantial way deflected his inquiry or his speculations from the faithful pursuit of scientific truth. His socialistic bias may color his polemics, but his logical grasp is too neat and firm to admit of any bias, other than that of his metaphysical preconceptions, affecting his theoretical work.

There is no system of economic theory more logical than that of Marx. No member of the system, no single article of doctrine, is fairly to be understood, criticised, or defended except as an articulate member of the whole and in the light of the preconceptions and postulates which afford the point of departure and the controlling norm of the whole. As regards these preconceptions and postulates, Marx draws on two distinct lines of antecedents,—the Materialistic Hegelianism and the English system of Natural Rights. By his earlier training he is an adept in the Hegelian method of speculation and inoculated with the metaphysics of development underlying the Hegelian system. By his later training he is an expert in the system of Natural Rights and Natural Liberty, ingrained in his ideals of life and held inviolate throughout. He does not take a critical attitude toward the underlying principles of Natural Rights. Even his Hegelian preconceptions of development never carry him the length of questioning the fundamental principles of that system. He is only more ruthlessly consistent in working out their content than his natural-rights antagonists in the liberal-classical school. His polemics run against the specific tenets of the liberal school, but they run wholly on the ground afforded by the premises of that school. The ideals of his propaganda are natural-rights ideals, but his theory of the working out of these ideals in the course of history rests on the Hegelian metaphysics of development, and his method of speculation and construction of theory is given by the Hegelian dialectic.

What first and most vividly centred interest on Marx and his speculations was his relation to the revolutionary socialistic movement; and it is those features of his doctrines which bear immediately on the propaganda that still continue to hold the attention of the greater number of his critics. Chief among these doctrines, in the apprehension of his critics, is the theory of value, with its corollaries: (a) the doctrines of the exploitation of labor by capital; and (b) the laborer's claim to the whole product of his labor. Avowedly, Marx traces his doctrine of labor value to Ricardo, and through him to the classical economists.[1] The laborer's claim to the whole product of labor, which is pretty constantly implied, though not frequently avowed by Marx, he has in all probability taken from English writers of the early nineteenth century,[2] more particularly from William Thompson. These doctrines are, on their face, nothing but a development of the conceptions of natural rights which then pervaded English speculation and afforded the metaphysical ground of the liberal movement. The more formidable critics of the Marxian socialism have made much of these doctrinal elements that further the propaganda, and have, by laying the stress on these, diverted attention from other elements that are of more vital consequence to the system as a body of theory. Their exclusive interest in this side of "scientific socialism" has even led them to deny the Marxian system all substantial originality, and make it a (doubtfully legitimate) offshoot of English Liberalism and natural rights.[3] But this is one-sided criticism. It may hold as against certain tenets of the so-called "scientific socialism," but it is not altogether to the point as regards the Marxian system of theory. Even the Marxian theory of value, surplus value, and exploitation, is not simply the doctrine of William Thompson, transcribed and sophisticated in a forbidding terminology, however great the superficial resemblance and however large Marx's unacknowledged debt to Thompson may be on these heads. For many details and for much of his animus Marx may be indebted to the Utilitarians; but, after all, his system of theory, taken as a whole, lies within the frontiers of neo-Hegelianism, and even the details are worked out in accord with the preconceptions of that school of thought and have taken on the complexion that would properly belong to them on that ground. It is, therefore, not by an itemized scrutiny of the details of doctrine and by tracing their pedigree in detail that a fair conception of Marx and his contribution to eco-

[1] Cf. Critique of Political Economy, Chap. I, "Notes on the History of the Theory of Commodities," pp. 56–73 (English translation, New York, 1904).

[2] See Menger, Right to the Whole Produce of Labor, Sections III–V and VIII–IX, and Foxwell's admirable Introduction to Menger. [Reprinted in abridged form above, pp. 269 ff.—Ed.]

[3] See Menger and Foxwell, as above, and Schaeffle, Quintessence of Socialism and The Impossibility of Social Democracy.

nomics may be reached, but rather by following him from his own point of departure out into the ramifications of his theory, and so overlooking the whole in the perspective which the lapse of time now affords us, but which he could not himself attain, since he was too near to his own work to see why he went about it as he did.

The comprehensive system of Marxism is comprised within the scheme of the Materialistic Conception of History.[4] This materialistic conception is essentially Hegelian,[5] although it belongs with the Hegelian Left, and its immediate affiliation is with Feuerbach, not with the direct line of Hegelian orthodoxy. The chief point of interest here, in identifying the materialistic conception with Hegelianism, is that this identification throws it immediately and uncompromisingly into contrast with Darwinism and the post-Darwinian conceptions of evolution. Even if a plausible English pedigree should be worked out for this Materialistic Conception, or "Scientific Socialism," as has been attempted, it remains none the less true that the conception with which Marx went to his work was a transmuted framework of Hegelian dialectic.[6]

Roughly, Hegelian materialism differs from Hegelian orthodoxy by inverting the main logical sequence, not by discarding the logic or resorting to new tests of truth or finality. One might say, though perhaps with excessive crudity, that, where Hegel pronounces his dictum, *Das Denken ist das Sein,* the materialists, particularly Marx and Engels, would say *Das Sein macht das Denken.* But in both cases some sort of a creative primacy is assigned to one or the other member of the complex, and in neither case is the relation between the two members a causal relation. In the materialistic conception man's spiritual life—what man thinks—is a reflex of what he is in the material respect, very much in the same fashion as the orthodox Hegelian would make the material world a reflex of the spirit. In both the dominant norm of speculation and formulation of theory is the conception of movement, development, evolution, progress; and in both the movement is conceived necessarily to take place by the method of conflict or struggle. The movement is of the nature of progress,—gradual advance towards a goal, toward the realization in explicit

    [4] See Engels, *The Development of Socialism from Utopia to Science,* especially Section II and the opening paragraphs of Section III; also the preface of *Zur Kritik der politischen Oekonomie.*

    [5] See Engels, as above, and also his *Feuerbach: The Roots of Socialist Philosophy* (translation, Chicago, Kerr & Co., 1903).

    [6] See, *e.g.,* Seligman, *The Economic Interpretation of History,* Part I.

form of all that is implicit in the substantial activity involved in the movement. The movement is, further, self-conditioned and self-acting: it is an unfolding by inner necessity. The struggle which constitutes the method of movement or evolution is, in the Hegelian system proper, the struggle of the spirit for self-realization by the process of the well-known three-phase dialectic. In the materialistic conception of history this dialectical movement becomes the class struggle of the Marxian system.

The class struggle is conceived to be "material," but the term "material" is in this connection used in a metaphorical sense. It does not mean mechanical or physical, or even physiological, but economic. It is material in the sense that it is a struggle between classes for the material means of life. "The materialistic conception of history proceeds on the principle that production and, next to production, the exchange of its products is the groundwork of every social order." [7] The social order takes its form through the class struggle, and the character of the class struggle at any given phase of the unfolding development of society is determined by "the prevailing mode of economic production and exchange." The dialectic of the movement of social progress, therefore, moves on the spiritual plane of human desire and passion, not on the (literally) material plane of mechanical and physiological stress, on which the developmental process of brute creation unfolds itself. It is a sublimated materialism, sublimated by the dominating presence of the conscious human spirit; but it is conditioned by the material facts of the production of the means of life. [8] The ultimately active forces involved in the process of unfolding social life are (apparently) the material agencies engaged in the mechanics of production; but the dialectic of the process—the class struggle—runs its course only among and in terms of the secondary (epigenetic) forces of human consciousness engaged in the valuation of the material products of industry. A consistently materialistic conception, consistently adhering to a materialistic interpretation of the process of development as well as of the facts involved in the process, could scarcely avoid making its putative dialectic struggle a mere unconscious and irrelevant conflict of the brute material forces. This would have amounted to an interpretation in terms of opaque cause and effect, without recourse to the concept of a conscious class strug-

---

[7] Engels, *Development of Socialism,* beginning of Section III.

[8] *Cf.,* on this point, Max Adler, "Kausalität und Teleologie im Streite um die Wissenschaft" (included in *Marx—Studien,* edited by Adler and Hilferding, Vol. I), particularly Section XI; *cf.* also Ludwig Stein, *Die soziale Frage im Lichte der Philosophie,* whom Adler criticises and claims to have refuted.

gle, and it might have led to a concept of evolution similar to the unteleological Darwinian concept of natural selection. It could scarcely have led to the Marxian notion of a conscious class struggle as the one necessary method of social progress, though it might conceivably, by the aid of empirical generalization, have led to a scheme of social process in which a class struggle would be included as an incidental though perhaps highly efficient factor.[9] It would have led, as Darwinism has, to a concept of a process of cumulative change in social structure and function; but this process, being essentially a cumulative sequence of causation, opaque and unteleological, could not, without an infusion of pious fancy by the speculator, be asserted to involve progress as distinct from retrogression or to tend to a "realization" or "self-realization" of the human spirit or of anything else. Neither could it conceivably be asserted to lead up to a final term, a goal to which all lines of the process should converge and beyond which the process would not go, such as the assumed goal of the Marxian process of class struggle which is conceived to cease in the classless economic structure of the socialistic final term. In Darwinianism there is no such final or perfect term, and no definitive equilibrium.

The disparity between Marxism and Darwinism, as well as the disparity within the Marxian system between the range of material facts that are conceived to be the fundamental forces of the process, on the one hand, and the range of spiritual facts within which the dialectic movement proceeds,—this disparity is shown in the character assigned the class struggle by Marx and Engels. The struggle is asserted to be a conscious one, and proceeds on a recognition by the competing classes of their mutually incompatible interests with regard to the material means of life. The class struggle proceeds on motives of interest, and a recognition of class interest can, of course, be reached only by reflection on the facts of the case. There is, therefore, not even a direct causal connection between the material forces in the case and the choice of a given interested line of conduct. The attitude of the interested party does not result from the material forces so immediately as to place it within the relation of direct cause and effect, nor even with such a degree of intimacy as to admit of its being classed as a tropismatic, or even instinctive, response to the impact of the material force in question. The sequence of reflection, and the consequent choice of sides to a quarrel, run entirely alongside of the range of material facts concerned.

[9] Cf. Adler as above.

A further characteristic of the doctrine of class struggle requires mention. While the concept is not Darwinian, it is also not legitimately Hegelian, whether of the Right or the Left. It is of a utilitarian origin and of English pedigree, and it belongs to Marx by virtue of his having borrowed its elements from the system of self-interest. It is in fact a piece of hedonism, and is related to Bentham rather than to Hegel. It proceeds on the grounds of the hedonistic calculus, which is equally foreign to the Hegelian notion of an unfolding process and to the post-Darwinian notions of cumulative causation. As regards the tenability of the doctrine, apart from the question of its derivation and its compatibility with the neo-Hegelian postulates, it is to be added that it is quite out of harmony with the later results of psychological inquiry,—just as is true of the use made of the hedonistic calculus by the classical (Austrian) economics.

Within the domain covered by the materialistic conception, that is to say within the domain of unfolding human culture, which is the field of Marxian speculation at large, Marx has more particularly devoted his efforts to an analysis and theoretical formulation of the present situation,—the current phase of the process, the capitalistic system. And, since the prevailing mode of the production of goods determines the institutional, intellectual, and spiritual life of the epoch, by determining the form and method of the current class struggle, the discussion necessarily begins with the theory of "capitalistic production," or production as carried on under the capitalistic system.[10] Under the capitalistic system, that is to say under the system of modern business traffic, production is a production of commodities, merchantable goods, with a view to the price to be obtained for them in the market. The great fact on which all industry under this system hinges is the price of marketable goods. Therefore it is at this point that Marx strikes into the system of capitalistic production, and therefore the theory of value becomes the dominant feature of his eco-

[10] It may be noted, by way of caution to readers familiar with the terms only as employed by the classical (English and Austrian) economists, that in Marxian usage "capitalistic production" means production of goods for the market by hired labor under the direction of employers who own (or control) the means of production and are engaged in industry for the sake of a profit. "Capital" is wealth (primarily funds) so employed. In these and other related points of terminological usage Marx is, of course, much more closely in touch with colloquial usage than those economists of the classical line who make capital signify "the products of past industry used as aids to further production." With Marx "Capitalism" implies certain relations of ownership, no less than the "productive use" which is alone insisted on by so many later economists in defining the term.

nomics and the point of departure for the whole analysis, in all its voluminous ramifications.[11]

It is scarcely worth while to question what serves as the beginning of wisdom in the current criticisms of Marx; namely, that he offers no adequate proof of his labor-value theory.[12] It is even safe to go farther, and say that he offers no proof of it. The feint which occupies the opening paragraphs of the *Kapital* and the corresponding passages of *Zur Kritik,* etc., is not to be taken seriously as an attempt to prove his position on this head by the ordinary recourse to argument. It is rather a self-satisfied superior's playful mystification of those readers (critics) whose limited powers do not enable them to see that his proposition is self-evident. Taken on the Hegelian (neo-Hegelian) ground, and seen in the light of the general materialistic conception, the proposition that value = labor-cost is self-evident, not to say tautological. Seen in any other light, it has no particular force.

In the Hegelian scheme of things the only substantial reality is the unfolding life of the spirit. In the neo-Hegelian scheme, as embodied in the materialistic conception, this reality is translated into terms of the unfolding (material) life of man in society.[13] In so far as the goods are products of industry, they are the output of this unfolding life of man, a material residue embodying a given fraction of this forceful life process. In this life process lies all substantial reality, and all finally valid relations of quantivalence between the products of this life process must run in its terms. The life process, which, when it

[11] In the sense that the theory of value affords the point of departure and the fundamental concepts out of which the further theory of the workings of capitalism is constructed,—in this sense, and in this sense only, is the theory of value the central doctrine and the critical tenet of Marxism. It does not follow that the Marxist doctrine of an irresistible drift towards a socialistic consummation hangs on the defensibility of the labor-value theory, nor even that the general structure of the Marxist economics would collapse if translated into other terms than those of this doctrine of labor value. *Cf.* Böhm-Bawerk, *Karl Marx and the Close of His System;* and, on the other hand, Franz Oppenheimer, *Das Grundgesetz der Marx'schen Gesellschaftslehre,* and Rudolf Goldscheid, *Verelendungs- oder Meliorationstheorie.*

[12] *Cf., e.g.,* Böhm-Bawerk, as above; Georg Adler, *Grundlagen der Karl Marx'schen Kritik.*

[13] In much the same way, and with an analogous effect on their theoretical work, in the preconceptions of the classical (including the Austrian) economists, the balance of pleasure and pain is taken to be the ultimate reality in terms of which all economic theory must be stated and to terms of which all phenomena should finally be reduced in any definitive analysis of economic life. It is not the present purpose to inquire whether the one of these uncritical assumptions is in any degree more meritorious or more serviceable than the other.

takes the specific form of an expenditure of labor power, goes to produce goods, is a process of material forces, the spiritual or mental
features of the life process and of labor being only its insubstantial
reflex. It is consequently only in the material changes wrought by
this expenditure of labor power that the metaphysical substance of
life—labor power—can be embodied; but in these changes of material
fact it cannot but be embodied, since these are the end to which it is
directed.

This balance between goods in respect of their magnitude as output of human labor holds good indefeasibly, in point of the metaphysical reality of the life process, whatever superficial (phenomenal)
variations from this norm may occur in men's dealings with the goods
under the stress of the strategy of self-interest. Such is the value of
the goods in reality; they are equivalents of one another in the proportion in which they partake of this substantial quality, although their
true ratio of equivalence may never come to an adequate expression in
the transactions involved in the distribution of the goods. This real or
true value of the goods is a fact of production, and holds true under
all systems and methods of production, whereas the exchange value
(the "phenomenal form" of the real value) is a fact of distribution,
and expresses the real value more or less adequately according as the
scheme of distribution in force at the given time conforms more or
less closely to the equities given by production. If the output of industry were distributed to the productive agents strictly in proportion
to their shares in production, the exchange value of the goods would
be presumed to conform to their real value. But, under the current,
capitalistic system, distribution is not in any sensible degree based on
the equities of production, and the exchange value of goods under this
system can therefore express their real value only with a very rough,
and in the main fortuitous, approximation. Under a socialistic régime,
where the laborer would get the full product of his labor, or where
the whole system of ownership, and consequently the system of distribution, would lapse, values would reach a true expression, if any.

Under the capitalistic system the determination of exchange value
is a matter of competitive profit-making, and exchange values therefore depart erratically and incontinently from the proportions that
would legitimately be given them by the real values whose only expression they are. Marx's critics commonly identify the concept of
"value" with that of "exchange value," [14] and show that the theory

[14] Böhm-Bawerk, *Capital and Interest*, Book VI, Chap. III; also *Karl Marx and
the Close of His System*, particularly Chap. IV; Adler, *Grundlagen*, Chaps. II
and III.

of "value" does not square with the run of the facts of price under the existing system of distribution, piously hoping thereby to have refuted the Marxian doctrine; whereas, of course, they have for the most part not touched it.   The misapprehension of the critics may be due to a (possibly intentional) oracular obscurity on the part of Marx.   Whether by his fault or their own, their refutations have hitherto been quite inconclusive.   Marx's severest stricture on the iniquities of the capitalistic system is that contained by implication in his development of the manner in which actual exchange value of goods systematically diverges from their real (labor-cost) value. Herein, indeed, lies not only the inherent iniquity of the existing system, but also its fateful infirmity, according to Marx.

The theory of value, then, is *contained in* the main postulates of the Marxian system rather than derived from them.   Marx identifies this doctrine, in its elements, with the labor-value theory of Ricardo,[15] but the relationship between the two is that of a superficial coincidence in their main propositions rather than a substantial identity of theoretic contents.   In Ricardo's theory the source and measure of value is sought in the effort and sacrifice undergone by the producer, consistently, on the whole, with the Benthamite-utilitarian position to which Ricardo somewhat loosely and uncritically adhered.   The decisive fact about labor, that quality by virtue of which it is assumed to be the final term in the theory of production, is its irksomeness.   Such is of course not the case in the labor-value theory of Marx, to whom the question of the irksomeness of labor is quite irrelevant, so far as regards the relation between labor and production.   The substantial diversity or incompatibility of the two theories shows itself directly when each is employed by its creator in the further analysis of economic phenomena.   Since with Ricardo the crucial point is the degree of irksomeness of labor, which serves as a measure both of the labor expended and the value produced, and since in Ricardo's utilitarian philosophy there is no more vital fact underlying this irksomeness, therefore no surplus-value theory follows from the main position.   The productiveness of labor is not cumulative, in its own working; and the Ricardian economics goes on to seek the cumulative productiveness of industry in the functioning of the products of labor when employed in further production and in the irksomeness of the capitalist's absti-

---

[15] *Cf. Kapital,* Vol. I, Chap. XV, p. 486 (4th ed.).   See also notes 9 and 16 to Chap. I of the same volume, where Marx discusses the labor-value doctrines of Adam Smith and an earlier (anonymous) English writer and compares them with his own.   Similar comparisons with the early—classical—value theories recur from time to time in the later portions of *Kapital.*

nence. From which duly follows the general position of classical economics on the theory of production.

With Marx, on the other hand, the labor power expended in production being itself a product and having a substantial value corresponding to its own labor cost, the value of the labor power expended and the value of the product created by its expenditure need not be the same. They are not the same, by supposition, as they would be in any hedonistic interpretation of the facts. Hence a discrepancy arises between the value of the labor power expended in production and the value of the product created, and this discrepancy is covered by the concept of surplus value. Under the capitalistic system, wages being the value (price) of the labor power consumed in industry, it follows that the surplus product of their labor cannot go to the laborers, but becomes the profits of capital and the source of its accumulation and increase. From the fact that wages are measured by the value of labor power rather than by the (greater) value of the product of labor, it follows also that the laborers are unable to buy the whole product of their labor, and so that the capitalists are unable to sell the whole product of industry continuously at its full value, whence arise difficulties of the gravest nature in the capitalistic system, in the way of overproduction and the like.

But the gravest outcome of this systematic discrepancy between the value of labor power and the value of its product is the accumulation of capital out of unpaid labor and the effect of this accumulation on the laboring population. The law of accumulation, with its corollary, the doctrine of the industrial reserve army, is the final term and the objective point of Marx's theory of capitalist production, just as the theory of labor value is his point of departure.[16] While the theory of value and surplus value are Marx's explanation of the possibility of existence of the capitalistic system, the law of the accumulation of capital is his exposition of the causes which must lead to the collapse of that system and of the manner in which the collapse will come. And since Marx is, always and everywhere, a socialist agitator as well as a theoretical economist, it may be said without hesitation that the law of accumulation is the climax of his great work, from whatever

---

[16] Oppenheimer (*Das Grundgesetz der Marx'schen Gesellschaftslehre*) is right in making the theory of accumulation the central element in the doctrines of Marxist socialism, but it does not follow, as Oppenheimer contends, that this doctrine is the keystone of Marx's economic theories. It follows logically from the theory of surplus value, as indicated above, and rests on that theory in such a way that it would fail (in the form in which it is held by Marx) with the failure of the doctrine of surplus value.

point of view it is looked at, whether as an economic theorem or as a tenet of socialistic doctrine.

The law of capitalistic accumulation may be paraphrased as follows: [17] Wages being the (approximately exact) value of the labor power bought in the wage contract; the price of the product being the (similarly approximate) value of the goods produced; and since the value of the product exceeds that of the labor power by a given amount (surplus value), which by force of the wage contract passes into the possession of the capitalist and is by him in part laid by as savings and added to the capital already in hand, it follows (a) that, other things equal, the larger the surplus value, the more rapid the increase of capital; and, also (b), that the greater the increase of capital relatively to the labor force employed, the more productive the labor employed and the larger the surplus product available for accumulation. The process of accumulation, therefore, is evidently a cumulative one; and, also evidently, the increase added to capital is an unearned increment drawn from the unpaid surplus product of labor.

But with an appreciable increase of the aggregate capital a change takes place in its technological composition, whereby the "constant" capital (equipment and raw materials) increases disproportionately as compared with the "variable" capital (wages fund). "Labor-saving devices" are used to a greater extent than before, and labor is saved. A larger proportion of the expenses of production goes for the purchase of equipment and raw materials, and a smaller proportion— though perhaps an absolutely increased amount—goes for the purchase of labor power. Less labor is needed relatively to the aggregate capital employed as well as relatively to the quantity of goods produced. Hence some portion of the increasing labor supply will not be wanted, and an "industrial reserve army," a "surplus labor population," an army of unemployed, comes into existence. This reserve grows relatively larger as the accumulation of capital proceeds and as technological improvements consequently gain ground; so that there result two divergent cumulative changes in the situation,—antagonistic, but due to the same set of forces and, therefore, inseparable: capital increases, and the number of unemployed laborers (relatively) increases also.

This divergence between the amount of capital and output, on the one hand, and the amount received by laborers as wages, on the other hand, has an incidental consequence of some importance. The purchasing power of the laborers, represented by their wages, being the

[17] See *Kapital,* Vol. I, Chap. XXIII.

largest part of the demand for consumable goods, and being at the same time, in the nature of the case, progressively less adequate for the purchase of the product, represented by the price of the goods produced, it follows that the market is progressively more subject to glut from overproduction, and hence to commercial crises and depression. It has been argued, as if it were a direct inference from Marx's position, that this maladjustment between production and markets, due to the laborer not getting the full product of his labor, leads directly to the breakdown of the capitalistic system, and so by its own force will bring on the socialistic consummation. Such is not Marx's position, however, although crises and depression play an important part in the course of development that is to lead up to socialism. In Marx's theory, socialism is to come by way of a conscious class movement on the part of the propertyless laborers, who will act advisedly on their own interest and force the revolutionary movement for their own gain. But crises and depression will have a large share in bringing the laborers to a frame of mind suitable for such a move.

Given a growing aggregate capital, as indicated above, and a concomitant reserve of unemployed laborers growing at a still higher rate, as is involved in Marx's position, this body of unemployed labor can be, and will be, used by the capitalists to depress wages, in order to increase profits. Logically, it follows that, the farther and faster capital accumulates, the larger will be the reserve of unemployed, both absolutely and relatively to the work to be done, and the more severe will be the pressure acting to reduce wages and lower the standard of living, and the deeper will be the degradation and misery of the working class and the more precipitately will their condition decline to a still lower depth. Every period of depression, with its increased body of unemployed labor seeking work, will act to hasten and accentuate the depression of wages, until there is no warrant even for holding that wages will, on an average, be kept up to the subsistence minimum.[18] Marx, indeed, is explicit to the effect that such will be the case,—that wages will decline below the subsistence minimum; and he cites English conditions of child labor, misery, and degeneration to substantiate his views.[19] When this has gone far enough, when capitalist production comes near enough to occupying the whole field of industry and has depressed the condition of its

[18] The "subsistence minimum" is here taken in the sense used by Marx and the classical economists, as meaning what is necessary to keep up the supply of labor at its current rate of efficiency.

[19] See *Kapital,* Vol. I, Chap. XXIII, Sections 4 and 5.

laborers sufficiently to make them an effective majority of the community with nothing to lose, then, having taken advice together, they will move, by legal or extra-legal means, by absorbing the state or by subverting it, to establish the social revolution.

Socialism is to come through class antagonism due to the absence of all property interests from the laboring class, coupled with a generally prevalent misery so 'profound as to involve some degree of physical degeneration. This misery is to be brought about by the heightened productivity of labor due to an increased accumulation of capital and large improvements in the industrial arts; which in turn is caused by the fact that under a system of private enterprise with hired labor the laborer does not get the whole product of his labor; which, again, is only saying in other words that private ownership of capital goods enables the capitalist to appropriate and accumulate the surplus product of labor. As to what the régime is to be which the social revolution will bring in, Marx has nothing particular to say beyond the general thesis that there will be no private ownership, at least not of the means of production.

Such are the outlines of the Marxian system of socialism. In all that has been said so far no recourse is had to the second and third volumes of *Kapital*. Nor is it necessary to resort to these two volumes for the general theory of socialism. They add nothing essential, although many of the details of the processes concerned in the working out of the capitalist scheme are treated with greater fulness, and the analysis is carried out with great consistency and with admirable results. For economic theory at large these further two volumes are important enough, but an inquiry into their contents in that connection is not called for here.

Nothing much need be said as to the tenability of this theory. In its essentials, or at least in its characteristic elements, it has for the most part been given up by latter-day socialist writers. The number of those who hold to it without essential deviation is growing gradually smaller. Such is necessarily the case, and for more than one reason. The facts are not bearing it out on certain critical points, such as the doctrine of increasing misery; and the Hegelian philosophical postulates, without which the Marxism of Marx is groundless, are for the most part forgotten by the dogmatists of to-day. Darwinism has largely supplanted Hegelianism in their habits of thought.

The particular point at which the theory is most fragile, considered simply as a theory of social growth, is its implied doctrine of population,—implied in the doctrine of a growing reserve of unemployed workmen. The doctrine of the reserve of unemployed labor involves as a postulate that population will increase anyway, without reference to current or prospective means of life. The empirical facts give at least a very persuasive apparent support to the view expressed by Marx, that misery is, or has hitherto been, no hindrance to the propagation of the race; but they afford no conclusive evidence in support of a thesis to the effect that the number of laborers must increase independently of an increase of the means of life. No one since Darwin would have the hardihood to say that the increase of the human species is not conditioned by the means of living.

But all that does not really touch Marx's position. To Marx, the neo-Hegelian, history, including the economic development, is the life-history of the human species; and the main fact in this life-history, particularly in the economic aspect of it, is the growing volume of human life. This, in a manner of speaking, is the base-line of the whole analysis of the process of economic life, including the phase of capitalist production with the rest. The growth of population is the first principle, the most substantial, most material factor in this process of economic life, so long as it is a process of growth, of unfolding, of exfoliation, and not a phase of decrepitude and decay. Had Marx found that his analysis led him to a view adverse to this position, he would logically have held that the capitalist system is the mortal agony of the race and the manner of its taking off. Such a conclusion is precluded by his Hegelian point of departure, according to which the goal of the life-history of the race in a large way controls the course of that life-history in all its phases, including the phase of capitalism. This goal or end, which controls the process of human development, is the complete realization of life in all its fulness, and the realization is to be reached by a process analogous to the three-phase dialectic, of thesis, antithesis, and synthesis, into which scheme the capitalist system, with its overflowing measure of misery and degradation, fits as the last and most dreadful phase of antithesis. Marx, as a Hegelian,—that is to say, a romantic philosopher,—is necessarily an optimist, and the evil (antithetical element) in life is to him a logically necessary evil, as the antithesis is a necessary phase of the dialectic; and it is a means to the consummation, as the antithesis is a means to the synthesis.

Hobson
on
George

Henry George (1839–1897), an American born in Philadelphia, was the founder of a movement for economic reform which at times had a wide popular appeal. Observing the drastic increase in land values which occurred in the United States during the nineteenth century, George became inclined to attribute the ills of society to this "unearned increment." He proposed the levy of a "single tax" which was to absorb all rent and from which the cost of government could be defrayed. Henry George's *Progress and Poverty* (1879), in which these ideas are developed, has been one of the most widely read tracts in the history of economic literature.

John A. Hobson (1858–1940), educated at Oxford, was an economic thinker of much originality, attracted by the ideas of John Ruskin and Thorstein Veblen. A prolific journalist and author of many volumes, Hobson had developed, in an early work, *The Physiology of Industry* (1889), an unorthodox theory of oversaving. Of the orthodox economic theory he was highly critical, insisting on the need for valuation in human rather than in monetary terms, and assailing as apologetic the character of traditional economic science. Hobson did not secure an academic appointment, but his influence and stature have grown with the years. His most important works include *Work and Wealth* (1914), and *Wealth and Life* (1929). The story of his life is told in his autobiography, *Confessions of an Economic Heretic* (1938).

THE SOCIAL philosophy of the West-End club contains a doctrine of "agitation" which easily explains the influence of such a man as Henry George. "Agitation" thus interpreted implies neither a genuine grievance in the agitated, nor an honest purpose in the agitator; for the one is substituted an irrational discontent, for the other a mere lust for popularity and power. The agitator thus conceived is an uninstructed "spouter," who plays upon a natural fund of envy and cupidity latent in the masses, stimulating an attack upon the established order of things. By such foolish and dishonest means, somehow or other, dangerous social forces are generated, threatening the material and moral prosperity of society. Quite unsupported by history or psychology, this doctrine is completely satisfactory to those who hold it. Yet it is evidently of such a nature as not to merit serious refutation. Deriving something from nothing, assigning an effect without anything that can be called a cause, it stands upon the same level of irrationality with that "rationalism" to which the religions of the world are nothing but recurrent bubbles of illusion created by a persistent human capacity for error.

Plain contradiction is the only appropriate refutation. It must, therefore, suffice to say that an agitation can only succeed if there is something to agitate, some real, deep-grounded passion or conviction to which an appeal can be made, the product of the pressure of some genuine need or aspiration. Henry George was indeed distinctively a great "agitator," but in order to understand the nature of his power, it is best to turn first to the matter agitated, and afterwards to the mode of his agitation. The specifically economic character of George's "mission" is its peculiar note. But we must recognise at the outset that the substance of George's land theory and policy was nothing new; he is not to be looked upon as a fanatic, who conjured out of his imagination, or his private experience, some brand-new doctrine which he sought to impose upon the popular mind. Those who would thus conceive him are forgetful or ignorant of the tenor of the peculiarly English science of Political Economy, which, from John Locke to J. S. Mill, may be regarded as continually engaged in undermining

[Reprinted by permission from *Fortnightly Review,* December 1897.]

the ideas of justice and social utility attaching to private property in
land. The anomalous position of the landowner received early emphasis in English theories of "Distribution." In *The Wealth of Nations*,
Adam Smith never tires of pointing the contrast between labourers
and capitalists, who receive their remuneration for services personally
rendered, and landowners who do nothing for the rent they take. He
also plainly indicates the power of the landowner to enhance his taxation of the rising national wealth. "Every improvement in the circumstances of the society tends, either directly or indirectly, to raise
the real rent of land, to increase the real wealth of the landlord, his
power of purchasing the labour, or the produce of the labour, of other
people." It is significant that from the heterogeneous armoury of
Ricardo, not only the social democrat, but the land nationaliser, draws
his most effective weapons. The more rigorous formulation of the
law of rent obliged Ricardo to take a step in advance of Adam Smith,
by assigning to landowners the economic power to take not merely an
absolutely larger rent, but a constantly growing proportion of the national wealth at the expense of the industrial classes. "The economical
progress of a society constituted of landlords, capitalists, and labourers
tends to the progressive enrichment of the landlord class; while the cost
of the labourers' subsistence tends on the whole to increase and profits
to fall." It only remained for J. S. Mill to impart a fuller meaning to
this theory by illustrating the power of the landowner to take in en-
hanced rent the results definitely due to the skill and energy of other
persons, and to develop a curative policy of taxation of "unearned
increment."

These allusions to the most prominent teachers of political economy
will suffice to show that the trend of economic theory in this country
has been to lay stress upon the opposition of interests between landowners and other industrial classes, and to impute to the former an
increasing power to extort from the latter a growing proportion of the
wealth produced by them.

It is true that most political economists, sometimes induced by a
proper regard for the limits of science, sometimes by timidity, have
abstained from the plain advocacy of a remedy, and have contented
themselves with pointing out the theoretic powers of landowners to
reap where they have not sown. But the margin between theory and
practice is here peculiarly thin, and not only Mill, but other teachers
of political economy, both in England and on the Continent, have
stepped from the indicative mood of economic science into the impera-

tive mood of politics in advocating social defence against the antisocial powers of the landowner.

George did not even originate the policy of the "Single-tax" on land
most distinctively associated with his name. The small step from the
physiocratic doctrine that all taxation was, in fact, borne by rent, to
the position that all taxation ought to be so borne, was taken by more
than one would-be reformer of this century.

The real importance of Henry George is derived from the fact that
he was able to drive an abstract notion, that of economic rent, into the
minds of a large number of "practical" men, and to generate therefrom
a social movement. It must be understood that the minds into which
George dropped his seed were, for the most part, "virgin soil"; the
teaching of economists to whom allusion has been made had never
reached the ear of most of them, or had passed unheeded. The pop-
ulariser of a new idea requires for his task a certain capacity of dramatic
exaggeration. This is needed to teach, it is still more needed if the
direct object of the teacher is to incite to action.

In this work personality and opportunity alike favoured Henry
George. Keenly intelligent, genial and sympathetic, his nature contained that flavour of obstinacy which borders on fascination, and which
is rightly recognised as essential to the missionary. A passionate attachment to the cause of the poor, derived from the experiences of a
varied life, was the true source of his power with tongue and pen. The
habit of speaking and of writing in America is less restrained than ours,
the academic influences are weaker, even in the intellectual world more
dramatic modes of expression are practised. Henry George had all
the popular gifts of the American orator and journalist, with something
more. Sincerity rang out of every utterance. Sparing in book knowledge, he had hammered out his thoughts upon the forge of personal
experience, and showed them hot from the hammer, rude and unfinished
in form. For this very reason *Progress and Poverty,* a stumbling block
to responsible politicians, to the economic professor foolishness, struck
the common mind of the thinking people with convincing and dramatic
force. The influence of this first book of serious economic import
which ever reached the outer circle of the English reading public, is not
to be slighted. It is a matter of deep significance that such a book
should have reached a circulation of far upwards of a hundred thousand copies. Upon the pressure of the early popularity of his book,
Henry George threw the weight of his present personality, and his
great gifts as orator and debater secured his influence, and widely advertised his doctrines at a time particularly favourable to their reception. His dialectic may not have satisfied the trained critic in economic

issues, but the persuasive and effective illustrations which it carried
were well calculated to impress the average man. Nor is this designed
as a depreciatory criticism. The refusal to qualify, the dramatic exaggeration, even the *argumentum ad hominem* are justifiable and indeed
necessary instruments in such work of education. A single illustration
brings home the nature of this power. When Henry George was present
at a meeting of the Lords' Committee upon Sweating, a number of
miserable workers from Cradley Heath were there for examination.
George turned to a friend and said, "Why have you brought these
people here? To find out why they are poor? Why, here is the cause,"
pointing to the noble lords who constituted the committee, "and here
is the effect," pointing to the witnesses.

But while a powerful, perhaps a fanatical, passion motived his career
as agitator, it never dominated his speech or writing. He was essentially argumentative in method; though passionate rhetorical appeals
are not infrequent, such passages were appendages to, and not substitutes for, reasoning. Henry George clearly understood that his
business was to teach men to think who were not in the habit of thinking on such matters, and few writers upon economic subjects are so
lucid, simple, and consecutive in their presentation of an argument.
For this very reason, those who find his "economics" faulty and reject
his conclusions, are able to lay their finger upon the precise points of
error, which the critics of more involved and more metaphysical exponents of revolutionary doctrine, as, for example, Marx, are notori-
ously incapable of doing. Bright, pointed, and vigorous, he never
failed to make his meaning understood, and he must rank extremely
high as a teacher who first brought home to a large section of the public
the need and the interest of economic study.

A certain dramatic opportuneness attending the advent of *Progress
and Poverty* gave to Henry George the public ear. A voice from the
Far West of America, a land of boundless promise, where, if anywhere,
it might seem that freedom and material progress were secure possessions of honest labour, announced grinding poverty, the squalor of
congested city life, unemployment, and utter helplessness. Though
huge tracts of uncultivated land awaited the spade and plough, the
willing and able hands which could work the soil were shut out of all
access to the raw materials of wealth. California and the rich West
had fallen into the hands of private owners, wealthy syndicates, or
domineering railway companies, taken from the people, sold for an
old song, or assigned as a gift to persons who had no intention of
occupying or working the land, but who held it for profit. Hence in
the newest portion of the bright New World, amidst a sparse population

of civilised white men, perhaps better educated and more energetic than any other people in the world, endowed with political freedom and institutions of self-government, the same social maladies arose which the sanguine temperament of America had hitherto regarded as natural results of congestion, misgovernment, or incapacity in the effete old world. The picture which George presented, even if highly coloured, was substantially correct, though his analysis of causes was defective, and it dealt a severe shock to that doctrine of progress by the normal development of industrialism upon the existing basis of property which prophets of free trade had preached for two generations in this country. When *Progress and Poverty* appeared, the vast majority of those who seriously concerned themselves with "the condition of the people" in this country believed that the expansion of education and intelligence among the working classes, the growth of thrift and of other organised habits of self-help, improved administration of the Poor Law and of charitable energy, assisted by the higher wages which, it was held, must follow the rapid development of modern methods of production, were gradually reducing the sum of poverty and misery, and that the unfettered action of these forces sufficed for the gradual and safe solution of the darkest social problems.

Although the thinking members of the working classes had never thoroughly accepted this *laisser-faire* theory of the doctrinaire radical and the political free trader, they had unconsciously absorbed some of its complacency and its disbelief in the need of governmental action.

Henry George shook this complacency, and, what is more, he gave definiteness to the feeling of discontent by assigning an easily intelligible economic cause. It is not without significance that *Progress and Poverty* appeared in the year 1879, which marks the turn in the tide of agricultural prosperity in this country. The following years of gradually deepening depression brought rural land questions more and more to the front and that divorcement of the people from the soil, which formed the kernel of the social problem according to George, assumed increasing prominence. The phenomenally rapid growth of large industrial towns, with their close concentration of working population, the direct and obvious result of our free trade policy, had been quickly ripening the land question in the towns, and the rising standard of sanitation and of other civic needs was driving home to municipal reformers a sense of conflict between the public interest of the town and the private interests of the owners of town land.

The pressure of these forces had awakened a good deal of incoherent sentiment directed against landlordism. George welded this loose sentiment into a coherent positive conviction. So far as his appeal was directed to personal and obvious interests, England was even a more favourable field than the United States. For in America, notwithstanding the encroachment of large landownership and the growth of mortgages and tenancy, a very large proportion of citizens had a direct stake in the land. England, on the other hand, is vested in a smaller number of owners than any other country of equal population, and nowhere else have the vast majority of actual cultivators so slight a property or interest in the land they cultivate. Thus a peculiarly effective presentment of the iniquity of landlordism, dramatically concentrated in a small class, was possible in England. Moreover, George's ability enabled him to fully utilise that advantage which land grievances possess over most other economic issues, their susceptibility to powerful concrete local illustration. Many of our towns belong to a few noblemen or wealthy persons who are familiar personages, and whose actual economic power is visibly and constantly exercised. The nature of economic rent and the power of the landowner can thus be made clear to the meanest intelligence.

To some it has seemed strange that the highly exaggerated power which George assigned to landowners should have gained acceptance among any class of Englishmen.

By what is termed the "Crusoe method" of illustration, it was not difficult for George to show that a single landowner or a small body of landowners might, by a ruthless use of their economic might as controllers of the raw material of wealth and the conditions of physical subsistence, keep down in utter servitude the rest of the population, taking in rent the results of all improvements in the arts of industry, and leaving to the producers only so much of the produce as would keep them alive and in working efficiency.

Some have found it hard to understand that many in this country should accept a theory which posits the landowner as the "residual claimant" in the scheme of distribution, and assigns him the power to take every increase of wealth beyond the minimum requisite to sustain labour and capital. The most casual reflection upon the recent course of English industrial history would seem to make it evident that other classes have partaken, and more fully than the landowners, in the immense growth of industrial wealth during this century. If England were enclosed by a ring fence of prohibitive tariffs, if all the land were engaged in producing food and other raw materials of wealth, if the full powers to draw economic rents were rigidly enforced, George's contention would have some tolerably close relation to the truth. But the merest tyro in economic thinking must perceive that the power of competing landowners to tax the manufacturing and commercial classes falls far short of their power over the agricultural and mining classes, and that even in the latter case the constant expansion of the area of production of food and raw materials for our market clips the wings of English landlordism.

Those who regard the nationalisation of the land of England as a cure for all the ills that states are heir to, ignore the leading feature of our modern commercial policy, its internationalism. Grant their major premiss, that common ownership and control of land will secure equality of economic opportunities for all citizens and cut away the natural supports of all industrial monopolies, can such a consummation be attained for us by nationalising the land of England? Is not the land of America, China, Egypt, Russia, and all other countries, which by trade intercourse supply us with food and materials of manufacture, as integral a part of England for economic purposes as the land of Kent or Devon? No ultimate solution of the land question or any other social problem is even theoretically possible upon a strictly national basis. Neither the theory which posits "land" as the residual claimant in distribution, nor the policy which assumes that political limits are coterminous with economic limits, can gain any wide and permanent acceptance among thoughtful people.

The adoption of George's theoretic position, so far as it has gained ground, must be imputed to a certain tendency among lovers of abstract reasoning to swallow premisses which will yield a compact and portable body of judgments conformable to certain preconceived opinions. Even such notable thinkers as Ricardo and J. S. Mill, we saw, stopped only a little short of George's conclusions when they closed their eyes to the facts of industrial life and abandoned themselves to an abstract analysis of rent.

Indeed, this fallacy of a residual claimant is not by any means confined to land nationalisers. The whole structure of economic science is honeycombed by the fallacy of a theory of distribution which assumes that of the three factors of production, land, labour, and capital, two of them may be considered to be fixed charges upon the product, while the third is in the position to take all the surplus that remains after the others are paid off. The Marxian Socialists practically place capital in this position. Other "orthodox" economists—General Walker, for example—give the place to labour. Henry George and his followers merely play the third remaining variation of the fallacy.

But George's true influence is not rightly measured by the small following of theorists who impute to landlords this supreme power of monopoly. Large numbers who would not press this extreme contention are disciples of Henry George because they regard unqualified private ownership of land to be the most obviously unjust and burdensome feature in our present social economy. The spirit of humanitarian and religious appeal which suffuses *Progress and Poverty* wrought powerfully upon a large section of what I may call typical English moralists. In my lectures upon Political Economy about the country, I have found in almost every centre a certain little knot of men of ‚the lower-middle or upper-working class, men of grit and character, largely self-educated, keen citizens, mostly nonconformists in religion, to whom Land Nationalisation, taxation of unearned increment, or other radical reforms of land tenure, are doctrines resting upon a plain moral sanction. These free-trading Radical dissenters regard common ownership of and equal access to the land as a "natural right," essential to individual freedom. It is this attitude of mind which serves to explain why, when both theoretic students of society and the man in the street regard Land Nationalisation as a first and a large step in the direction of Socialism, organized Socialists regard the followers of Henry George with undisguised hostility and contempt.

In fact, Land Nationalisation stands upon two widely different and philosophically inconsistent bases. To those who take their stand upon the "natural rights" of the individual it is the coping-stone of a free-trade policy. Equal access to the resources of nature seems essential, if liberty to labour and to accumulate property is to be equally secured to all. To such thinkers "The earth is the Lord's and the fulness thereof," constitutes at once sound morality and useful policy: that an absentee landowner should take away the value which God or man's labour has imparted to land appears a plain violation of honesty and a direct discouragement to industry. "To every one the right to work on land and to enjoy the full fruits of his labour,"—this sums up the Individualist basis of Land Nationalisation. Such men sternly repudiate the notion of extending public ownership and control to capital, and of "nationalising" all the instruments of production. Land and labour they hold are the only original requisites of wealth-production: let each man own himself and have an equal use of nature with every other man, and all will be well. George himself stood out boldly in his repudiation of Socialism and entered a strong and ingenious defence of profit and interest. How comes it, then, that Georgism is so closely associated in the public mind with Socialism? It is not due to mere laxity of thought. For while George has many followers who stand by his ideal of full free trade, there are many more to whom *Progress and Poverty* has been a stepping-stone to a more or less formal Socialism. This is explained by the other basis of Land Nationalisation, the recognition not of the rights of the individual, but of the definitely social origin and character of land-values, the apprehension of the truth that they spring from and embody, not merely the energy of this or that tenant or labourer, but the common activities of an organised society, and the constantly growing material needs of an increasing population. This idea of rent as a definitely social product emerges with tolerable frequency in George's writings, but it does not form the main strand of his argument; his appeal is more usually to individual than to social rights. He, therefore, never fully confronted the question which takes this shape: "Are not all values, those which reside in forms of capital as well as in land, due to the operation of social forces, arising from the needs and activities of organised society, and not resoluble into the results of the action of the several units which form the society?"

The answer to such a question depends upon the conception we form of the relation of individuals to one another in society—i.e., of the organic character imputed to society. George never clearly faced this question. Among his followers many have accustomed themselves to draw their arguments, now from the Individualist now from the Socialist armoury, and to stand aloof from the wider issue. Others accept Land Nationalisation either as avowed Individualists or as Socialists. The rift is curiously visible in the policy of the two English societies which attack the land question as a whole. The Land Nationalisation Society, though rejecting the "no compensation" policy of George, visibly clings to the idea of individual rights, claiming for every citizen the option to occupy a definite piece of land with full effective proprietorship. The Land Restoration League, on the other hand, fastens its eyes definitely upon the social origin of rent and land-values, and seeks to secure this public property by process of taxation.

The influence of George is not, however, to be measured by the number or zeal of the advocates of a wholesale policy of nationalisation of the land. It is rather to be traced in the energy which, during the last fifteen years, has freely flowed into many channels of land reform.

Heroic remedies are little to the taste of Englishmen: a more discriminative logic rules their policy. The spirit of reform awakened by Henry George manifested itself, not in one, but in many movements directed to the redress of specific grievances and the attainment of specific aspirations in connection with the land. For practical purposes, therefore, there is not one land question, but many. Town and country, agriculture, mines, manufacture, transport, residential and industrial use, each discloses its own set of problems claiming study and solution. A vast reticulation of separate organisations has arisen to enforce existing laws and to secure further legislation curtailing the powers of landowners; societies for the preservation of existing public rights over footpaths and commons; for the protection of tenant rights and the attainment of freedom of cultivation and security of property in improvements; for the registration of titles to land and mortgages; for the abolition of tithes, the enfranchisement of leasehold land, abolition of entail, and the removal of all other barriers which separate land from other forms of property, and prevent its free transfer. Many of these movements are not in just line with the tenor of George's policy, but all of them have been vitalised by the spirit of his agitation. No one can fail to perceive in every legislative and administrative body in the country, from the House of Commons to the Board of Guardians and the Parish Council, an increased desire to confront, in a more liberal public spirit, the particular problems of land policy which lie within their purview. In various ways and at various paces these numerous land-issues are ripening in England. Size and the pressure of social needs are bringing a few of them rapidly to the front of the political platform. Though England will never attack the land question *en bloc,* certain large sections have visibly advanced during the last few years. The demand for effective national control of the railroads, our modern highways, is the most definite advance towards a policy of nationalisation, and probably commands a wider and more heterogeneous support than any other movement of radical reform. In the field of municipal politics, the taxation of ground rents and values has already won the complete formal adherence of one great political party, while the justice of taxation of "unearned increment" from public improvements may be considered to have gained an even wider theoretic recognition. Practical difficulties, however, in enforcing public claims by the instrument of taxation are generating a powerful support for a policy of municipal ownership, which receives material assistance from the successful experience of several of our most progressive municipalities. Corresponding to this growing tendency to recognise the utility of municipal ownership and control of town lands, is the tendency to seek some solution for the more urgent rural grievances, by placing more power to acquire the ownership or practical control of agricultural land in the hands of locally elected bodies.

While a clearer apprehension of the complexity of the land question has thus led practical reformers to resolve unity into multiplicity, it is not difficult to discern a cohesive and co-operative character underlying these several movements of land reform. Most of them are definitely, and in part consciously, aiming to secure that fuller public property in the resources of nature, that fuller social control over the uses of land for human industry and human enjoyment which found in Henry George their most powerful advocate.

No doubt it is easy to impute excessive influence to the mouthpiece of a rising popular sentiment. George, like other prophets, co-operated with the "spirit of the age." But after this just allowance has been made, Henry George may be considered to have exercised a more directly powerful formative and educative influence over English radicalism of the last fifteen years than any other man.

Tawney

——— on ———

the Webbs

Sidney (1859–1947) and Beatrice Webb (1858–1943) were outstanding representatives of modern British socialism. Their writings, largely fact-finding, and personal influence made them prime movers behind the social changes which have occurred in Britain during our time. Their work is the outcome of a unique marriage partnership, lasting over fifty years and leading from early membership in the Fabian Society to the founding of the London School of Economics and to widespread activities on behalf of the labor movement. Both participated in the work of numerous official bodies and served as inspiration, directly and indirectly, of important parts of the program of the British Labour Party.

The writings of the Webbs include some 25 volumes. The best-known are *The History of Trade Unionism* (1894), *Industrial Democracy* (1897), *English Local Government* (1906–1929), and *The Decay of Capitalist Civilization* (1923).

R. H. Tawney (see above, p. 16) here pays a personal tribute to the Webbs.

THE TOPIC on which I have been asked to speak requires no apology, but I approach it with some diffidence. There are many in my audience who knew the Webbs too well to require an account of them; nor am I sure that the indefatigable lecturers, who are the subject of my remarks, would have enjoyed being turned into the text for a lecture. They submitted patiently to publicity, as to everything else, when the cause required it, and no one knew better, if limelight was the order of the day, what buttons to press; but they were not lovers of honorific ritual. Their air, when the thing was over, was, "There, that's done; now for something serious." I suspect that they would have regarded an address devoted to themselves as among the emotional substitutes for work which they were accustomed to dismiss, in their more frivolous moments, under the name of "religious exercises."

So my sensations are much what they were when, as a youth who had not yet got over his education, I paid my first visit to 41 Grosvenor Road, and was so unfortunate as to depart with the headgear of another guest. I felt, as a more than ordinarily massive bowler settled heavily on my shoulders, a momentary surprise; but I had not yet learned from my hosts that investigation, measurement and verification are among the first duties of man, and I assumed, with the casual optimism of youth, that, though the incubus seemed unfamiliar, it would come all right somehow. It was not till next morning that a scorching letter from Mrs. Webb informed me that I had eloped with the property of one whom I hope it is not disrespectful to describe as taking, in all senses of the expression, an out-size in hats, the then about to be Right Honourable John Burns, over whom at the moment she was casting her flies, and was anxious to retain in a humour to swallow them. The episode confirmed her conviction of the incorrigible incompetence, unreliability, moral laxity and mental imbecility of most products, however insignificant, of the older universities, and took some years to live down. I feel now somewhat the same embarrassment as I experienced then, an embarrassment at once softened and reinforced by later memories, as though Beatrice, her skirts turned back and crouching over the

[R. H. Tawney, *The Webbs and Their Work*, published by the Fabian Society and reprinted by permission.]

fire, were ejaculating into one ear, "Beware of dilettantism," and Sidney, full-length on the sofa, were murmuring into the other, "Above all, no intimacies."

The latter injunction I proposed to follow. In the library of hell a special stack is reserved for those biographies—a vast and dreary host—of great men and women, which throw light on every aspect of their victims' personalities, from their taste in dress to their second cousins' Christian names, except the characteristics in which their greatness consisted. I should be sorry to add another item to it. The Webbs, when off duty, were known to their friends as two sociable people, with a psychological curiosity not too elevated to enjoy gossip, an engaging capacity for laughing at themselves, and an appetite on the part of one partner for physical exercise, defended by her with arguments, hygienic and ethical, of terrifying cogency, against which the other occasionally rebelled, but always, in my experience, rebelled in vain. They are also, however, historical figures, and figures whose stature increases as their world recedes. They faced great issues, and grappled with them in a great way. They changed thought and action. They founded new institutions and launched ideas which re-made old ones. They conquered for knowledge and made habitable for men departments of social life which, before them, were a trackless jungle. They forced upon national attention the importance of movements which today are a power, but which, till the Webbs' searchlight was turned on them, still awaited recognition; revealed their significance to a public sceptical and often hostile; and charted some segments of their course to their goal. They researched, wrote, agitated, administered and—since only the last stages of legislation take place in Parliament—were not the less legislators because, save for ten years when both of them were over sixty, County Hall and the British Museum saw more of them than the House of Commons.

The study of social institutions with a view to transforming them, which was their special sphere of work, does not lend itself to treatment in terms of the spectacular exploits of extraordinary individuals. But there is authority for the statement that the serpent on the rock is as miraculous, in his own way, as the eagle in the air; and what the Webbs' unflagging war on ignorance, apathy, and prejudice may lack in drama it gains in the impressiveness of positive accomplishment. If a man looks back on the successive chapters of British social history from 1880 to 1930—if he reflects on such movements as Trade Unionism, Co-operation and the rise of the Labour Party; or considers, in another sphere, industrial policy, financial policy, public education and public health, unemployment, the Poor Law, the development of municipal enterprise and Local Government in general; or ponders the advance in civilisation which the changed public attitude to all these subjects represents—he is unlikely, I think, to conclude that the patient labourers ploughed the sands. He will find few problems which they failed to illumine, few abuses against which their blows were not the heaviest struck, and few reforms in which they did not play a decisive, if often a deliberately self-effacing, part. Whatever our individual interests and creeds—whether we are active workers in social movements, or merely students of them, or ordinary citizens concerned for decency, good sense and fair play in the management of our common concerns—we are all their pupils. The authors of such achievements have no need of the small change of reminiscences to perpetuate their memory. The noblest of all titles, they used to say, is that of servant. The legacy, scientific and practical, of their half-century of devoted labour is the monument by which we may most fittingly recall them.

If the work of the Webbs is too massive for biographical gossip, an attempt to provide them with intellectual ancestors is equally superfluous. Historians of political thought are apt to be obsessed with origins and pedigrees, as though ideas were transmitted in the same manner as property, and different attitudes to society and theories about it succeeded each other by direct descent. To most of us, who take our views at second-hand, that procedure may apply. Where creative minds are concerned, it is absurdly off the mark. Original people are not links in a chain; more often they are breaks in one. Presented with the metaphorical torch which each generation is supposed to hand on to the next, they insist on making certain that it is what it is alleged to be. If it turns out on investigation, as not infrequently it does, to be, not an authentic illuminant, but a smelly taper, they incontinently blow it out, and proceed to replace it with lamps of their own. The Webbs were voracious readers, endowed with memories of embarrassing efficiency, which armed them with precedents for every innovation, and rarely left them at a loss for apt quotations from authors who would have trembled with apprehension at the alarming causes they were cited to support. But they possessed—a quality which all readers should have, and most of us have not—a high degree of resisting power. They took from their predecessors hints which served their purpose, and let the rest slide off them. The clue to their outlook on the world of their day is to be found less in what they absorbed of its prevalent assumptions and fashionable philosophies than in what they ignored or dropped into the dustbin.

Their position is not to be understood, therefore, by analysing it into elements derived from different sources. It was too much their own. It is interesting that Beatrice should have been brought up in an atmos-

phere compounded of London Society, country houses, and the Big
Business which kept both the merry-go-rounds spinning; that she should
have mixed from childhood with the scientists and men of letters whom
her father, a civilised capitalist, invited to his house; and that the most
intimate of her parents' friends, at whose feet for a time she sat, should
have been that forgotten celebrity, Herbert Spencer. It is more significant that at twenty-five she had outgrown him; that, when the sage,
whose long suit was not humour, urged her, with kindly obtuseness, to
begin her life-work with a study of "the absorbent organs in the leaves,
roots and seeds of plants," she already knew that the subject on which
her heart was set was the strange ways of man in commerce with his
kind; that, with grandfathers floated to fortune from farm and weaver's
cottage when cotton became king, and then, *via* radical politics into the
reformed House of Commons, she saw the Industrial Revolution and
its political sequel, not as a story in books, but as a chapter of her family
history; and that the influence which finally clinched her decision to
devote her life to research into the social system came, not from books
or teachers, but from sympathies aroused and lessons learned on the
occasion of a month's visit to some Lancashire cousins, who, when her
own branch of the family had been wafted upwards, had remained
operatives at Bacup. It is interesting that Sidney should have been
nurtured on the purest milk of Victorian radicalism; that he should
have attended lectures on Natural Science by Huxley—an occasion on
which, since the course was confined to workers in industry, he put
down his trade as that of a wood-carver, on the ground that he would
carve if he could—that the only contemporary economist whom he
respected should have been Mill, with whose deductions from Ricardo's
theory of rent he later himself did much execution; and that he should
have thought that, if a theory of value was necessary to salvation, the
article supplied by Jevons was, on the whole, a less unhandy instrument
than that of Marx. It is more significant that, at an age when most
well-to-do young people have not left the University, he had seen the
inside of a broker's office in the City and of three Government Departments; that his first paper to the Fabian Society, at the age of twenty-
six, had the characteristically curt and trenchant title, *The Way Out;* and
that, when offered Liberal constituencies to stop his mouth, he decided
that there was more both to be done and to be learned on the L.C.C.
than in Parliament.

The truth is that neither of our friends was of the kind which is disposed to take opinions from a master. Each of them independently had
gone young through the business of settling accounts with current cant,
whether to right or left, which is the necessary preliminary to serious

work. Apart from the influence of science, in whose disciplined attack on its problems they saw an example for sociologists, both of them owed more to experience than to the doctrines of the schools. One partner, according to his own account, had been converted to Socialism by a lecturer at Birkbeck College, an otherwise unknown Mr. Smith. As, however, what convinced him of the virtues of nationalisation, and set him agog to propound plans for applying it, was the fatuity of the arguments advanced by Mr. Smith against it, his debt to his teacher was more negative than positive, and he is not an example of the docile disciple. The abandonment by the other of a creed which she described as "agnosticism tempered by individualist economics" was slower and more painful. It had begun, to her own surprise, in the course of her collaboration with Booth in his *Life and Labour in London*. It had taken place, in all but name, before she had completed her book on Co-operation.

Both possessed the fire at the centre without which great things are not done; but, having made up their minds on first principles, they took their work too seriously to be emotional about it, and there is a sense in which the fact that they were Socialists is less important than the kind of Socialists they were. They looked at facts through plain glass; held that light, not heat, was the world's main need; saw no reason why the devil should have a monopoly of the business virtues; and thought that capitalism was most likely to be brought to terms, not by blowing trumpets round its walls, but by mobilising against it, not only the qualities which it despised, but also the organising ability and concentrated effort which were its special boast. They regarded the Co-operative Commonwealth neither as a distant Utopia, nor as the inevitable climax of an irresistible evolution, but as an edifice to be built piecemeal by hard, practical labour, an edifice which—since its building was a long-term job—should be begun here and now, and to the erection of which system, method, application, technical skill, a reasonable consideration for the prejudices and susceptibilities of ordinary men and women, and, above all, knowledge, were not less indispensable than enthusiasm and eloquence. Their first contributions to that programme were made when they were under thirty. They were continuing to make them when they were both over eighty.

Their business, as they saw it when they joined forces in 1892, was pioneering on two fronts. The first essential was to know exactly and in detail what required to be done; the second to mobilise the energy to do it, which meant, till the distant day when a Government of their own persuasion should be in power, the education of public opinion and the instruction of politicians in matters about which both at the time were ill-informed and the latter, when not actively hostile, were commonly indifferent. They approached that task from slightly different angles. Mrs. Webb's introduction to economic questions had been that of an investigator, not of a propagandist. She joined the Fabian Society in 1893, but a long interval elapsed before she played an active part in it. For a decade following her marriage, she remained primarily a student, though a student who found in the service of social causes the inspiration to her work. Her husband, after ten years in the Colonial Office, to which a generation later he returned as Minister, had been elected to the London County Council in 1892. As chairman of its Technical Education Committee, into whose orbit he contrived to sweep, much to the advantage of the service, almost the whole of London's higher education, he was a busy administrator, though an administrator with a profound conviction of the dependence of social progress on systematic research and the application of its results. But they saw theory and practice as complementary aspects—the staff-work and operations—of a single campaign. Each laboured unceasingly and simultaneously at both, and both threw their whole selves into each. The London School of Economics, the chief venture of their early years, was designed by them, not as a cloistered college, but as a mundane institution around which should eddy the full tide and roar of London life. The supercilious description of it given me in a more secluded University—"one of those places like Selfridge's, isn't it?"—though its hint of financial prosperity is unfortunately unfounded, conveys a suggestion of workman-like realism which the founders of the School, so far from resenting, would have welcomed as a compliment. If, therefore, I touch separately on their literary work and their practical activities, the reason is not that they themselves distinguished between them. It is merely considerations of practical convenience.

The first publications of both the authors appeared in the same year, when, in 1887, one produced the first edition of *Facts for Socialists,* and the other an article on *The Dock Life of East London.* The last, a joint-work, *The Truth About Soviet Russia,* was published in 1942. In the intervening half-century, they were together responsible, usually as partners, for some forty-five volumes, apart from a long list of pamphlets—Webb produced not less than forty-seven for the Fabian Society alone—articles, essays and introductions to books composed by other writers. Their more important works may be classified, perhaps, into five main groups. They include four books on working-class organisation and policy; ten volumes on English Local Government; four substantial works and various shorter pieces on the reform of the Poor Laws; four books—two of them by Sidney alone and two of them by both together—specifically devoted to Socialism; and a group of miscellaneous writings, of which the most striking are *My Apprenticeship*—the least egotistical of autobiographies, which characteristically turned into a social history—the elaborate study of *Soviet Communism,* and the two shorter books on the same subject which followed it.

Continuous labour by two busy people on so ambitious a scale demanded system and method. Both of them believed in planning, and the industry which they planned first was their own. They were assisted by secretaries, their one extravagance—there was a period, I believe, when they found work for six at once—but they did not spare themselves. The materials required for their historical works were widely dispersed. The authors, who had started their honeymoon with a visit to Dublin to examine the records of Irish trade societies, spent part of each summer, when the Council was in recess, on voyages of exploration. For the books on Trade Unionism, they not only used the wealth of sources available in London, but ransacked the archives of all important unions in the provinces and of the great majority of smaller ones. The sources for their study of Local Government were even more voluminous. In the process of discovering and making extracts from parish, county, manorial and borough records, they visited, singly or together, some hundreds of villages and towns, from Cornwall to Northumberland, and from Neath to Norwich.

They did not rely only on documents, but made a point of seeing in action the organisations concerned, by obtaining permission to attend in person the meetings of Trade Unions, Trades Councils, Co-operative Societies and Local Government bodies. Nor did they confine themselves to the information to be obtained by watching institutions at work. An interviewer at once charming and inexorable, with a unique gift for making the dumb speak, and the loquacious talk to the point, Mrs. Webb had discovered, when she worked for Booth, the lessons to be learned from conversations with a purpose. In the course of her inquiries into dock labour and the clothing trade, she had put through their paces a long list of employers, workers, factory and sanitary inspectors, school board officers, and social agencies of different kinds; had taken lessons in tailoring; and finally, to see how a sweated industry looked from the inside, had obtained employment in a succession of workshops as a "plain trouser hand." They did not forget the value of oral evidence, or the methods of eliciting it, when the time came for their more massive works. The "method of the interview," as they called it, added not a little to the realism of the Webbs' interpretations. To watch a witness undergoing their skilful third degree was sometimes amusing.

To appraise in their totality the contributions of authors so wide in their range and so exhaustive in detail is a task, not for individuals, but for a corps of specialists. Even the layman, however, can hardly fail to be impressed by certain features of their work, which are found in the same degree in no other sociologists. Like those of most writers who have been active over a long period, the books of the Webbs reflect different phases in their authors' lives and thought. Some, like *The History of Trade Unionism* and *English Local Government,* the latter of which appeared at intervals over a period of nearly thirty years, were the result of prolonged investigations in fields which had previously been little explored. Others were written quickly and deal with topics of the moment. The common characteristic which sets its stamp on all of them, so that a reader familiar with their writings can tell at a glance whether an anonymous pamphlet is from their mint or not, is a matter less of style than of substance. It is the impression conveyed of large reserves of ordered knowledge. Whatever the subject, it is handled with respect. Whether the result is a *brochure* like *English Teachers and Their Professional Organisations* or a volume of 800-odd pages, like *The Parish and the County,* there is the same patient care in assembling materials and the same self-restraint in refusing to suggest conclusions till the evidence has been sifted. Even their slighter books are marked by a wealth of information and a maturity of thought which set them apart from other occasional pieces. The opinions advanced in them may be summarily expressed, but they have not been reached in haste. If the object of their authors is to persuade, as well as to inform, it is persuasion by an appeal, not to ignorance, but to knowledge.

That quality of their work does not stand alone. It is accompanied by two others, which are even more impressive. The first is an extraordinary gift for illuminating generalisation. The Webbs, for all their wealth of data, were never at the mercy of them. They were at the opposite extreme from the legendary bookworm, and valued facts, not for themselves, but for the meaning to be extracted from them. If discovery is the revelation of significant, but previously unrealised, relations between phenomena, then in their own field they were discoverers, and discoverers whose finds yielded fruit, as well as light. The second characteristic is equally remarkable. It is their power to carry conviction to their readers, and to do so not by pathos, or eloquence, or other literary artifices, but by the weight of massed evidence and a measured force of argument which strikes home to the mind with a kind of inevitability, as though what spoke were the voice, not of two fallible mortals, but of society herself, instructing her children how to learn to live together.

The researches of Miss Potter—as she then was—into sweating and Co-operation, are early cases in point. As a result of her work on the former, the picturesque myth of an endless chain of sub-contractors, with a parasitic Jewish middleman as the villain of the piece, went the way of other legends. Henceforward, it was evident, the problem was, not merely the removal of exceptional scandals, but the maintenance by voluntary combinations and legislative enactments of proper standards of employment over the whole field of industry. The ability to see facts as they are, and to cause others to do the same, was equally conspicuous in her study of the Co-operative Movement. Co-operation—to a generation conscious of tightening social strains a word of reassurance—had been widely interpreted to mean the multiplication of societies of producers dividing profits among all participants in the business. She showed that, except here and there, the British version of Co-operation meant nothing of the kind. Economic democracy as practised by Co-operators implied neither self-governing workshops nor profit-sharing with employees. It involved—a statement today a platitude, but then a revelation—the supply of goods, and whenever possible, their production, for the service of consumers by agents appointed by them; the payment of a fixed rate of interest on capital; and the eliminations of profit by the return to the purchaser of surpluses arising between prices and costs.

The same qualities of insight in penetrating realities and of persuasiveness in expounding them were displayed on a broader canvas in their books on Trade Unionism and on Local Government. To appreciate the significance of the former, they must be seen against the murky background of the age in which they appeared. On the publication of the second of them, in 1897, a reviewer, not more imbecile than most, could write in a journal not otherwise inane that it was regrettable that writers so gifted should have wasted their talents on the investigation of institutions so unimportant as Trade Unions. The observation is memorable, not because it was exceptional, but because it was typical. The right of professional association was secure on the Statute book; but a generation had elapsed without the morals from it being drawn. Public ignorance of the object and methods of Trade Unions; a prejudice slow to die among professional economists; misrepresentation in the press; persecution by employers outside the staple industries; and a hostility on the part of Courts which they hardly troubled to conceal— these forces combined to produce in the England of the eighteen-nineties an attitude to Organised Labour somewhat resembling that still common down to 1935 in the United States. And deeper depths than that no mortal eye can plumb.

To suggest that this mountainous load of un-informed or interested opposition could have been rolled back by two books, or indeed, by any dynamic less powerful than the will to freedom of those who suffered from it, would be, no doubt, absurd.   But what authors could do the Webbs did, and did superbly.   They had few earlier works to help them—they had to compile their own census of trade unionists, which figures later published by the Board of Trade confirmed—but the influence of the *History of Trade Unionism* and of *Industrial Democracy* was due as much to the spirit in which they were written as to the addition which they made to knowledge.   Studiously unemotional in tone, commanding respect by their scholarship, and arguing their case with unanswerable logic, they lowered feverish temperatures and turned on sensationalism a cooling stream of facts.   The former showed combinations of wage-earners bargaining collectively as to the terms of their employment to be a concomitant of modern industry as normal, inevitable and permanent as power-driven machinery or an urban civilisation.   The latter carried the war into the enemy's camp.   Trade Unionism had been denounced, and was to be denounced again, as an obstacle to economic progress.   Trade Unionism, the Webbs retorted, so far from being the enemy of industrial efficiency, was actually its ally.   By prescribing minimum standards of employment, which no employer, however hard pressed or unscrupulous, could evade, it diverted competition from exploiting human beings into channels more compatible with social well-being; stimulated management to discover methods of reducing costs by the progressive improvement of machinery and organisation; and promoted the most effective utilisation of the nation's resources by compelling trades which were parasitic, in the sense of using up the energies of the workers in them under conditions incompatible with health and vigour, either to mend their ways or to go out of existence.   Few historical or economic works can expect a life of as much as ten years.   The Webbs' books on Trade Unionism contain some statements and interpretations which may need, in the light of later work, much of which they inspired, to be qualified or recast.   They remain, however, after the lapse of half a century, not only alive, but incomparably the best English books on the subject. That successive generations of readers should have learned to see the world of Organised Labour through the eyes of authors with the Webbs' profound knowledge of it and faith in its future has been an inestimable service, not only to them, but to the Labour Movement as a whole.

The bearing on contemporary issues of the great study of Local Government from the Revolution to the Reform Bill seems, at first sight, more remote.   In reality, if less obvious, it is hardly less direct.   The

two preceding decades had seen the modernisation of county administration and an impressive expansion of municipal enterprise. The
growth of the house-keeping state, as distinct from the police state,
could already faintly be discerned. The Webbs' interest had always
been concentrated on what they called the "spontaneous under-growth
of social tissue," rather than on the more dramatic aspects of political
action. It was natural that, once the books on Trade Unionism were
out of the way, they should regard the study of Local Government as
their next most urgent task. The practical morals for the present which
their researches yielded are best stated in the two concluding chapters
of *Statutory Authorities for Special Purposes*—the cheerless title of a
great book—with which the students of their ten volumes would be wise
to begin. The story, as they tell it, is one, not only of the elaboration
of machinery, but of the emergence of new principles. The central
theme in their account of the transition from the old order to the new
is the transference of authority from little oligarchies of traders and
property-owners to representative bodies employing salaried officials to
organise the services necessary to health and civilisation for all residents
in their areas. It is, in short, the rise of the citizen-consumer as the
controlling power in local government. The conclusion agrees so admirably with the Webbs' own philosophy that the reader is half-tempted
to believe that their success in producing at the right moment a lively
rabbit from the hat must be due to the fact that they first put it there;
but, if they did any conjuring, I, at least, have failed to detect the sleight
of hand. It is simpler to believe that history was kind enough to confirm their theories, because from the start they based their theories on
history.

It belonged to the studies which the Webbs made their own, as well
as to their personal convictions, that knowledge and its application
should go hand in hand. Their literary work was not the harvest of a
life of leisure. It was planned, and should be read, as a product, not
only of scholarship, but of the civic temper crusading for great ends.
Immediate objectives and tactics naturally changed with changing circumstances; and to recount their activities would require a volume, not
a lecture. It is sufficient to say that, from the time of their marriage,
and, indeed, before it, down to the twenties of the present century, they
were never without some campaign on their hands.

They were not of the generals who rarely see the line, and they took
their full share of hard fighting, as well as of staff work. In the nineties,
when the London County Council is struggling on to its feet, one partner
not only provides it, in *The London Programme,* with a policy of large-
scale municipal socialism, and himself does more than any other indi-

vidual to carry it out, but attempts, not without some success, to inoculate the Liberal Party with a virus of Fabianism suitably diluted for infants; writes the Minority Report which remains the part best worth reading of the twelve portentous volumes of the Labour Commission; and struggles to convert the disorderly welter of London colleges into a Peoples' University. The other, in addition to her work for the same causes, and to the continuous research which was the basis of their practical activities, does what one person can to turn Conservative Factory Legislation into something not wholly futile. Both, as the principal authorities among economists on Trade Unionism, labour hard to counter the attack on it of which the Taff Vale judgment fired, if not the opening, the loudest, gun, and in the intervals are floating their child, the London School of Economics, over the shoals which beset its youth.

The early years of the next century were equally strenuous. They saw Webb's tract on *The Education Muddle and the Way Out,* which supplied the ideas for the Education Act of 1902; and the withdrawal next year by the Government of its preposterous first draft of a bill for London proposing to entrust the service to twenty-eight Borough Councils, before a storm of opposition in the Conservative press—a storm which might have astonished ministers less could they have heard the question which Sidney once put to me: "Did you know that for a week I was editor of *The Daily Mail?*" They saw also, what was not less important, the launching of the programme for a national minimum of subsistence and civilisation, which contained the germs of a multitude of subsequent policies, some partially carried out, others still awaiting application. Then came the epic labours of Mrs. Webb on the Poor Law Commission of 1905–1909, when she fought the Local Government Board and its allies to a standstill; the two famous reports on the Break-up of the Poor Law and the Prevention of Destitution; and the three years' campaign by herself and her husband to extort action on them from a government whose members disliked their proposals in proportion as they understood them. They had made up their minds at an early stage of the first world war that it could be turned into a watershed, not only in international, but in social, history; and the fourth chapter, which opened in 1915, is not the least crowded. Webb's co-operation with Arthur Henderson on the executive of the Labour Party; his joint-authorship with him of the new constitution of the Party adopted at the Conference of 1918; the two pamphlets from his pen, *Labour and Peace* and *Labour and the New Social Order,* the latter a classic which might with advantage be reprinted today; and the magnificent services which he rendered, in the following year, both to the miners and also—if only it had had the wits to realise the fact—to the general public, by his masterly advocacy of nationalisation on the Commission presided over by Lord Sankey, are high landmarks in the development of Socialist policy.   Together with the work of Mrs. Webb on the Reconstruction Committee, and on the Committee on Women in Industry, for which she wrote a report that is still not out of date, they stand out from the sterility of those feverish years like oases in a desert.

With the country what it was—and, it may be, still is—to see reforms carried out at the time when they are proposed and in the form in which they are advanced is rarely given to their sponsors, however skilful and pertinacious; but some of the measures launched and championed by the Webbs, if not all that they were meant to be when they left their hands, staggered at last into port.   A legal minimum wage in trades once notorious for sweating; the extension of the services of health, education and pensions on a scale which, inadequate though it is, would thirty years ago have seemed hardly credible; the abolition of the Guardians and the break-up of the Poor Law long after the authorship of the proposal was forgotten; the admission, in principle, of the responsibility of the State for the victims of unemployment; the prevention of mass unemployment itself, long declared to be beyond the wit of man, now blessed by most economists and endorsed in a White Paper; the tardy acquisition by the nation of the most important of minerals, and the prospective nationalisation of a group of key industries—all these and much else had been not only preached by them when there were few to listen, but turned into workable schemes.   Before their retirement, they could have pointed, had they been interested in doing so, to that most convincing of compliments which is paid when former opponents claim the credit for measures once denounced by them, and friends dismiss reforms for which formerly they laboured as antiquated trivialities too commonplace to deserve mention.

In reality, there is nothing which would have interested the Webbs less.   Two-thirds of their working lives were passed in a world where not only was capitalism firmly seated in the saddle, with its prestige undimmed and its *moral* unimpaired, but outside small circles, the bare possibility of a practicable alternative to it was regarded as, at best, an interesting speculation.   Like the scientist who commands nature by first obeying her, they accepted that situation, with all the limitations and disillusionments it involved, in order to end it.   They played to the score; did first things first; if successful at one point, did not pause to congratulate themselves, but hurried on to the next; if blocked in their course by an obstacle, did not waste time in lamentations, but found some other path which turned it.   They never, however, lost sight of their destination, or forgot, amid all their preoccupations with the dusty business of the day, what that destination was. Studiously moderate in speech; regular in their habits, and frugal in their expenditure; a model of domestic felicity; Beatrice with a touch of ascetic austerity, as of the lay-sister of some order; Sidney with the air of scientific detachment—as though if suitably fee'd, he not only could, but would, argue any case—which is said to have caused one ingenuous mine-owner to be overheard in 1919 saying sadly to another, "I told you we made a mistake in not hiring that man Webb," these demure representatives of the bourgeois virtues belonged, in reality, to the dangerous handful of human beings, perhaps half-a-dozen in a generation, who live for an idea. They organised their lives as the servants of a cause for which no labour could be too great, and no task too small.

Between the appearance of *Fabian Essays* in 1889 and the 'twenties of the present century, the Webbs' version of Socialism became, it may fairly be said, the characteristic British version. As such, it was naturally honoured with hard knocks, from more than one quarter. An accusation whose validity they would not have admitted is that, perhaps, most often brought against them. It is the charge of a bureaucratic indifference to individual freedom. They would have replied to it that liberty means, not the right of particular individuals or groups to use as they may think fit such powers as past history or present social arrangements may happen to have conferred on them, but "the utmost possible development of faculty" in every human being, and that liberty in that sense, has law as its mother. In an urban and industrial civilisation, the alternative to planning by a democratic state for the general good is not, they observed, the freedom of every individual to arrange his own affairs as best suits himself. It is the acquiescence, under economic duress, of the mass of mankind in an environment and style of life created by the self-interest of powerful minorities. In such conditions, the extension of collective action, so far from impairing freedom, is the necessary condition of it.

Nor, again, was their Socialism the unbending skeleton of bloodless formulæ, neatly classified and labelled with exasperating finality, which set successive generations of young lions sniffing nervously and sometimes growling angrily, as at an unnutritious dinner of dehydrated truth. The four-fold way of the years before 1914—regulation, communal services, the taxation to extinction of unearned incomes, and a wide variety of different forms of public ownership—continued to summarise not too inadequately the main heads of their programme; but its authors, long after they had acquired the status of an oracle, returning with collective wisdom—"We think"—unambiguous answers to perplexed inquirers, remained personally humble-minded. They did not cease to

learn, and later statements of their position revealed concessions both
to criticism and to the teaching of events. Under the influence of the
gild socialists, they came to give a larger place to the participation in
the conduct of nationalised industries of the representatives of the
workers than at one time they would have admitted. They were quick
to grasp the significance both of the war-time experiments in State-
organisation and of the capitalist ramp which insisted on their abolition.
More surprising, they underwent a re-birth when they were over sev-
enty. Not being simpletons, they did not suppose that the achievements
of the Russian Revolution could be replanted, as they stood, in a different soil and climate; nor were they wholly at ease in the atmosphere
created by what they described as "the disease of conformity." But the
deliberate adjustment of economic means to social ends; the reliance on
science; the glad tidings, in short, of "planned production for community consumption" with which, for ten years after their visit, it was
the exhilarating practice of Mrs. Webb to welcome the coming, and
speed the parting, guest, not only appealed to their intellects, but profoundly stirred their emotions. Whether their chapters on the Soviet
economic system are a reliable picture of Russia I have not the
knowledge to say. As an account of one type—though not, of course,
the only possible type—of planned economy, they are in a class by
themselves.

It is of the nature of political thought that much of its best work is
topical. It achieves immortality, if at all, not by eschewing the limitations of time and place, but by making them its platform. It is both
inevitable and satisfactory that some of the problems with which the
Webbs dealt should be now, partly thanks to them, less urgent than they
were, and that on others, which occupy today the fore-front of the stage,
they should have thrown out pregnant hints, while leaving it to later
hands to elaborate and apply them. As is not uncommon in the case of
great people, their premises were more important than the particular
conclusions which they themselves derived from them. The essence of
their work can be simply stated. It was to reveal the methods by which
a political democracy can become, if it pleases, a Socialist democracy.

The fathers of Socialist thought, both British and Continental, had
belonged to the pre-democratic era. Their conception of the political
strategy required to accomplish the transition to Socialism had taken—
inevitably taken—its character from that fact. The Webbs realised,
not, indeed, alone, but with an unrivalled comprehension of the full
consequences of the change, that Liberalism had created a political tool
which Liberals themselves, inhibited both by interests and by doctrines,
were incapable of using, but which Socialists could employ for the crea-

tion of a Socialist State based on the deliberate choice of the great majority of their fellow-countrymen.

The things necessary to salvation they believed to be two. The first was primarily a matter of the intellect. The conception of a social order planned, with general consent, for the common good, has a long history behind it; but earlier prophets of the destination had rarely mapped the road. The Webbs were strong where their predecessors had been weak. Prescription without diagnosis appeared to them charlatanism, and diagnosis was a task to which virtuous intentions were less important than hard work and a sound technique. Hence their long list of books on particular topics, and their refusal to formulate a philosophy of Socialism except by way of comment on the specific subject on hand. Hence also their view of the path which Socialists must tread. Their gradualism was not, as was absurdly suggested, the statement of a preference, as though loitering were their favourite foible, but a recognition of the facts of a world where life is lived in time. They were the last persons to wait on events, when it was in their power to accelerate them, and for the authors of real changes, whether small or great, whether a clause in a Factory Act or a Five-year Plan, they had a profound respect. But they were not of the intellectuals who see in the Labour Movement a substitute for the cinema, and who relapse into paroxysms of grief, scorn and indignation at its lamentable indifference to their appetite for melodrama. Believers themselves in persuasion by an appeal to reason, and holding that "morality," as Webb used to say, "is in the nature of things," they were impatient of criticisms without affirmations, refused to preach ideals until they had found a way to realise them, and thought that invention and construction, not eloquence in denunciation, were the root of the matter. Romantic or self-advertising revolutionaries, all rhetoric and blank cartridges, usually bored, and sometimes irritated, them.

The truth that social processes, in order to be controlled, must be known thoroughly and in detail was the Webbs' first legacy to the Movement to which they gave their lives. The second, if less obvious, was not less important. It was the temper and attitude of mind which they brought to the service of it. Trenchancy and good sense, audacity and prudence, the nerve to take risks for great ends and a reasonable adaptability in the choice of means, are not necessarily antithetic. Sad experience suggests, however, that they are not easily run in harness, and that the proud possessors of one set of qualities are too often disposed to proceed instantly to stultify it by a resolute refusal to combine it with the other. The Webbs thought that both types of character and mentality are equally indispensable, and themselves united them to an unusual degree.

Like most of us, they would have welcomed the discovery of a short cut to the Co-operative Commonwealth; but they knew too much of Socialist history, contemporary affairs, and the nature of their fellow-countrymen to suppose that that recurrent illusion has any basis in realities. While not of the kind to shrink from drastic action, when circumstances called for it, they were impatient of the pretence that mere emotional demonstrations are either action or drastic. Having made up their mind that Socialism could be made to come in England by the procedure of democratic government—of course, suitably accelerated—and could not be made to come by any other, they were at pains to exemplify in themselves and to encourage in others the mentality and habits which democracy requires. They were consistently unsectarian, insisted that the points on which British Socialists are agreed are both more numerous and more important than those on which they differ, and were tolerant, not only of opponents, but—a more difficult accomplishment—of embarrassing friends, possibly with the reflection that a *modicum* of imbecility is a necessary ingredient in any party which aspires to be representative. Themselves formidable in debate, they were not of the controversialists to whom any argument is good which brings down its bird. They cared too intensely for the cause to be interested in winning dialectical victories. They took as much pains to make Socialism acceptable to the weaker brethren among their fellow-countrymen as have some of its more voluble exponents to render it repulsive to them.

The Webbs' belief in democracy, however, was a creed not less exacting, but more exacting, than most more truculent evangels. They did not under-estimate the severity of the struggle which lay before the Labour Movement, and cherished no illusions as to the resourcefulness of its opponents. They knew from experience that the plutocracy consists of agreeable, astute, forcible, self-confident, and, when hard pressed, unscrupulous people; that, if seriously threatened, it will use every piece on the board, political and economic, in the honest belief that it is saving civilisation; and that, in the meantime, one of the trades—by no means the least profitable—of which it is master is lion-taming by kindness. Not the crudities of forcible repression, but flattery, blandishments and caresses, which would ensure, if the animal succumbed to them, that there would be nothing to repress, seemed to them the gravest danger. It was against these arts of seduction that Mrs. Webb, when a minister's wife, made a characteristic protest, and that her husband, in an article written shortly after he left office, uttered his warning of the perils of "the aristocratic embrace." Independence of spirit, and a contempt for the discreet, gentlemanly bribes employed to undermine it, were, in short, as essential a part of their testament as the belief in knowledge. They have not done the job for us, but they have given us the tools, both intellectual and moral, with which to do it. It is for us to use them.

Historical and
—————————————— *Institutional* ——
Approaches

Schmoller

——————— *on* ———————

Roscher

Wilhelm Roscher (1817–1894) taught at the Universities of Göttingen and Leipzig. With Karl Knies and Bruno Hildebrand he is remembered as a founder of the "older historical school" of German economists. Roscher's point of view was closer to British liberalism than was true of later generations of German economists, and his attitude in questions of methodology was characterized by moderation. Of one of his works, an English translation was published in 1878 under the title *Principles of Political Economy*.

Gustav von Schmoller (1838–1917) taught at the Universities of Halle, Strasbourg, and Berlin, and became the undisputed head of the "younger historical school" of economics in Germany. Critical of the value of abstract generalization in economics, Schmoller wrote and promoted a great variety of historical studies replete with descriptions of concrete details. A bitter opponent of the Austrian school, he participated in the *Methodenstreit* which raged during the last decades of the nineteenth century. He supported an active role of the government in economic affairs and was among the founders of the *Verein für Sozialpolitik,* the organization of the "socialists of the chair." An English translation of one of Schmoller's works, his interpretation of mercantilism, was published in 1896 under the title *The Mercantile System.*

ALL HISTORICAL development obtains life and color from the opposing forces which make themselves felt in every human action, forces which sometimes are in conflict with one another and which at other times are fused into a single blend. In a similar manner the progress of science is promoted by such contrasting forces as empiricism and rationalism. These always face each other, take each other's place, and correct each other—although the sensible empiricist will never fail to admit that all experience is only the result of his thinking, and the rationalist, as a rule, does not deny that the stuff of his thoughts is made available to him by the world of the senses. As an eminent thinker recently has said, the conflict of the schools means in the last analysis that the rationalist attributes a higher value to the associations of ideas produced by our own volition, in contrast with the empiricist, who attaches higher value to those associations which impress themselves by force of circumstances irrespective of our volition. However much truth there may be in this, however much every great scholar and thinker may be empiricist as well as rationalist, it is from the different combination of these elements that the different schools of thought spring, schools which are in conflict with each other and which follow one upon the other.

The method characteristic of the economic literature of the seventeenth and eighteenth centuries, which preceded that of the physiocrats, was predominantly empirical. Those purely theoretical statements which can be found in that literature were hasty generalizations, based on crudely conceived empirical facts. Its practical doctrines, however, often had a truth content much more substantial than that of its rationalist successors because they were rooted in real experience and because there was still a direct link between life and doctrine. Throughout the entire older literature of mercantilism and cameralism the reader finds a naive enjoyment of facts, of statistical data, and of commercial, technological, and agricultural detail. This stock of knowl-

[Translated in slightly abridged form from Gustav Schmoller, *Zur Litteraturgeschichte der Staats- und Socialwissenschaften,* Leipzig, Duncker und Humblot, 1888. By permission.]

edge was gathered into broad compilations and encyclopaedias. An
economic encyclopaedia, that of the German cameralist J. G. Krünitz,
went into 149 volumes to absorb all that knowledge (started in 1773).

Compared with this, the rationalism of the physiocrats meant libera-
tion, even though it started out as, and was blended with, playful
phantasy. On their shoulders there could rise fast and splendidly the
English-Scotch school of thought, culminating in Adam Smith. Smith
was a brilliant observer of the life of the human soul and of the
simple economic processes of his period. Being attached to the views
of his time concerning natural science and natural law, he drew simple
conclusions from the general and uniform nature of man which the
eighteenth century believed to have established. He knew how to
start out with a few dominating causal relationships of great conspicuousness and thus to clear up causes and effects over wide regions.
His rationalism broke the path for the practical aims of the century
and for the long number of his theoretical successors. While he still
combined empiricism and rationalism in a superior manner, the empirical element evaporated more and more in Ricardo's work. Among
the later economists the rationalistic element is greatly exaggerated.
The increase in acumen and in wealth of speculative thought could
not protect the late-comers from losing more and more the ground
of reality under their feet. More and more did they turn into completely drab, abstract arm-chair scholars, interested in divisions and
definitions; into socialist visionaries; into calculating mathematicians;
into doctrinaire, all-embracing theorists of natural law and of Robinson-
Crusoe stories. In this manner, intellectual rot was the outcome of a
rationalism entirely divorced from experience.

Only one remedy offered itself in this situation: the return to empirical reality. Such a return has set in in many ways. Statistics, with
its quantitative analysis of population, trade, and industry, had for
long represented a counterweight to abstract theory. Old German
cameralism, with its elaborate knowledge of technology and administrative law, had never been completely eliminated by Adam Smith's
elegant theory of the fashion. Some of its later exponents, informed,
intelligent, and moderate, represented a marriage of cameralism and
British economic liberalism. Officials, practitioners, and statesmen
such as Galiani, Necker, Büsch, and others had stated many matters
more truthfully than Turgot and Ricardo since they represented a
happier combination of experience and rationalism. Friedrich List,
with the ingenious insight and the passion of a great statesman, had
destroyed the theoretical basis of the old system, just as his countrymen, Hegel and Schelling, pushed aside the old, individualistic, natural

law and replaced it with a more profound and nobler concept of the state. But all these countercurrents were partly more practical, partly likewise rationalistic-speculative.

It was on the foundation of German philology and German historical science that there developed the truly scientific and scholarly movement which again, and for good, filled the veins of the consumptive body of economics with blood and life. Rationalistic anemia was to be cured with the help of a strong dose of empirical-historical knowledge of the world; the proven methods of strictly scholarly, specialized work were to be applied to a field of human knowledge which until then had been the playground of bookish ideas and political tendencies, the stage for amateurs and journalists.

Many men have participated in this, inside as well as outside of Germany. List, Hildebrand, Knies, and a number of less important teammates joined the principal spokesman of the new movement almost simultaneously in his own country. But the true founder of the historical school of German economics is Wilhelm Roscher. List, in his thoughts, was much more ingenious, bold, and pioneering. But he was not a man of science proper, not of the academic brand. Hildebrand was a politician, full of ideas, replete with classical-historical education. He imparted much stimulation to practice and to science, but he frittered away his powers. Knies showed the historical path to economics, but he himself worked along other lines. Wilhelm Roscher began as philologist and historian. He devoted his whole life, simple and quiet as it was, and full of attachment to his science and teaching, to the task of founding a historical basis for abstract economics, to the task of transforming the theories of the cameralists and the natural-law theories of the British into historical theories. And this aim he has achieved.

He worked on it in three ways. First, he prepared a number of historical investigations, writing monographs on the life, work, and age of Thucydides, on the development of socialism and communism, on the various forms of government, on colonies, colonial policy, and emigration, on agricultural policy and statistics, and on various other subjects. These contributions are collected in part in Roscher's *Economics Viewed from the Historical Standpoint,* published in 1861 and reprinted in a third edition in 1878. Second, he has produced a scholarly history of economic literature and thought. A monograph on the history of British economic thought in the sixteenth and seventeenth centuries, published in 1854, was followed by numerous long articles, preparatory works for Roscher's *History of Economic Thought in Germany* of 1874. Third, he published in 1854–1856 a *System of Economics,* a hand- and textbook for businessmen and students. The single volumes of which this work is composed have been published time and again in new editions. It is, no doubt, the most widely used text in present-day Germany, and has also been translated into several foreign languages. Whereas the other products of Roscher's pen appealed to the narrow circle of scholars and specialists, his *System* had the widest effects. Often he is judged solely on the basis of the *System.* This is not quite the right thing to do: his true scientific importance rests at least as much, if not more so, on the writings which we have mentioned before.

The subject matters of these principal publications of Roscher's give an approximate indication of the direction of his thought. He is not an economic historian proper, in the sense that he would investigate critically and descriptively certain periods of German or foreign economic development. His primary concern is not the critical analysis of historical sources. Nor is he exclusively interested—as was Savigny —in furnishing proof that human institutions are not the product of rational deliberations but that they unnoticeably grow out of the national character of a people. He is, in the first line, a student of cultural history, the disciple of a group of men who, in Goettingen and elsewhere, formed so wholesome a counterweight to the smooth rationalism of the eighteenth century. This group fused philology and technology, politics and legal history, into a universal cultural history— uncritical sometimes, but valuable nevertheless. The collecting industry of these men succeeded in producing a basic foundation for cultural and economic history rather than a scientific integration. It often happened later on that their works were deprecated and overlooked by the exponents of critical methods. In part they had not been altogether successful in bringing their economic and historical training into a substantive relationship. But regardless of this they represented the wholesome beginnings of comparative historical methods, gathering material, as they did, for a universal cultural history. In the hands of Roscher the various threads were combined and woven into a new pattern true to life.

Roscher is the most universally trained cultural historian among the economists. His strength derives from an extremely rare breadth of education and reading, from a realistic sense for all the detail of economic life. He is interested in the first line in the great questions of the historical development of peoples and nations, questions posed already by Aristotle and Macchiavelli. He attempts to make the questions of public life more profound by laying bare the economic processes. He searches for natural laws which control the general process of economic development. The study of antiquity, the perusal of recent historical writing, the investigation of statistical data—all this serves him only as empirical material for the formulation of general principles relating to the march of political and economic history. In certain respects his views coincide with those of Buckle, whose only aim is the uncovering of historical laws. One could almost say that Roscher has in mind a general theory of history, laws of general historical development. Perhaps this is an aim too high for the present generation. But it is an aim for which great minds always reach out —for which those may reach out who combine subtlety of mind and observation with universal education.

II

Roscher views with favor and almost with admiration the liberal basis and the more significant doctrines of the older, so-called classical school of economics. It was always his true nature to take cognizance of entirely different minds, to see their good qualities rather than their imperfections.

His textbooks, replete of scientific truth as they are, are also designed to point out to the future government officials the aims of practical policies which appear justified to him. In view of the present status of our knowledge, this cannot always be done by ascertaining causal relationships but rather by professing certain ideals whose validity is considered as *prima facie* given—unless counter-evidence should be presented. Roscher decided such issues as a far-sighted, cautious historian. His judgment in practical questions is illuminated by the study of the ancient writers, the lessons of history, and the ideas of the administrative practice of Hanover and Britain. The school of historical thinking indeed provides the very best method to arrive at the proper understanding of social, economic, and political processes.

Roscher is principally interested in questions which neither the cameralists nor the British economists had posed. The latter had in the main raised only this question: What are the causes of the simplest economic phenomena which repeat themselves everywhere, and what must the rational modern individual and the wisely organized government do in order to see to it that these developments take place as normally as possible? What the older economists had taught in this respect was presented by Roscher in a very similar fashion. But he, in addition, desired to fit into a larger historical context what was found to exist at a given time. He did not only want to describe the present distribution of income but wished to explain how it developed.

He did not only want to enumerate the factors which today determine wages but desired to explain the present-day wage relation as a link in social development. He did not want to examine whether the Malthusian theory of overpopulation was correct at the present time but desired to interweave the present population problems into the general history of population movements.

One may complain that Roscher in his textbooks does not exclusively present the philosophy of economic history, that he often compiles theoretical and practical knowledge of the nonhistorical variety, blending it with historical digressions—but such criticism would completely neglect the aim pursued with these texts. Roscher very definitely intends to adopt and present the existing doctrines to the extent to which they are justified. But even when he does no more than this—and he does so in a very conservative spirit—he nevertheless rises to a higher scientific level because he develops his argument on the basis of a broader knowledge of man and the world, and because he rejects the old rationalistic scheme as it had prevailed among the older cameralists. This scheme may be illustrated with the help of an example such as this: there are six causes supporting organization in closed guilds, and seven causes supporting free business enterprise; therefore we shall decide in favor of the latter. It is one of Roscher's greatest merits that he went as far as possible in the elimination of such an unhistorical and unscientific procedure. Sometimes a person may hesitate in the face of practical decisions; he may not be fully aware of the relevant causal relationships, and may not be under the sway of great leading ideas. In such a situation one frequently may have to decide in the described haphazard manner—there are still people who count their buttons whether to take a trip, whether to vote for the conservative party, etc. But such counting is a sad makeshift. It is the function of science to eliminate it.

Obviously, the opportunities for fitting phenomena into a chain of historical causation are not equally favorable everywhere. The empirical history of prices and statistics has eliminated many older errors; but the basic fact of price movements repeats itself everywhere, and for this reason does not stand much in need of historical investigation. A similar situation obtains with respect to many elemental psychological and natural facts which constitute and influence economic life. Historical information fails in many of these matters, and for this reason other approaches must predominate or suffice. Nobody went farther in recognizing this than Roscher—a careful, reverent, and conservative man who maintained direct contacts with a large number of outstanding, nonhistorical economists.

This factor also explains the different character of the several volumes of his *System*. The first volume, the "Foundations of Economics" (first published in 1854), centers around the distribution of goods and the formation of prices. It contains very little that is new. In many chapters of this book historical erudition is displayed, not in order to modify the doctrines but rather to illustrate them with the help of notes on cultural history. In this volume, Roscher's special studies bear more fruit in connection with minor rather than with principal questions. Here it matters least if characteristics are wanting which rarely are combined with historical aptitude. Here the system remains entirely the old one, with the population doctrine placed awkwardly in an appendix.

If I should classify all four volumes of the *System*, I would place next to this the volume on "Public Finance" (published in 1886). It contains a number of excellent historical discussions, and is marked by the detached wisdom which only an experienced thinker brings to the realm of practical policies—but in the light of other, newer achievements in this field this book does not represent such striking progress as the two volumes on applied economics. The volume on "Agricultural Economics" (first published in 1859) and that on the "Economics of Industry and Commerce" (first published in 1881) stand much above the other volumes, and the reason for this is not far to seek. Here economic institutions are described. Here is the most suitable field for the cultural historian, for comparative history, for the identification of necessary historical sequences. Here the special investigations of the author could be utilized to the fullest extent. Here Roscher has created something new and epoch-making. Here the preparatory works of all the older economists offer only sporadic beginnings and sketches of the complete picture which Roscher unfolds. Here also the organization is new, following the lines of history. Everywhere the background is provided by the cultural life of the newer peoples of Western Europe from the beginning of the Middle Ages to the present time; their cultural life is compared with that of the peoples of antiquity, the primitive peoples, with America, the colonies, the communities of Asia. The discussion of agricultural policy is preceded by a general discussion of the state (as contrasted with families, corporations, and municipalities); that of industrial and commercial policy is preceded by a general discussion of the city. This is followed by a series of chapters which describe the typical forms of historical development of primary production, commerce, and industry. It is concluded by a theoretical and practical discussion of the great economic and social issues of the present time. The organi-

zation of agriculture, of commerce, and of industry stands in its fore-
ground. The spheres are examined in which government intervention and individual action come into contact with one another, spheres
in which the historical formations of custom and law are in conflict
with new interests and new attempts at organization, spheres in which
the national outlook, the stage of civilization, and the geographic conditions, in different combinations, influence the general and homogeneous elements of production, transportation, and credit.

In these spheres any point of view other than the historical is misplaced—yet before Roscher it was almost entirely lacking. A glance
at recent English and French historical works, valuable as they are,
indicates how much Roscher has accomplished. How funny is the
unhistorical free-trade doctrinalism in Levasseur's work on the history
of the French laboring classes, or in Rogers' history of British agriculture; how tortuously do these gentlemen work their way between their
attachment to modern economic ideals and the necessity to grant the
older economic institutions some measure of justification. Compared
with these works, how simple and natural are Roscher's attempts to
understand the older times first psychologically and morally, then economically and socially; to explain their institutions in the light of
given conditions, to classify their origin, their flowering, and their
eventual decay.

Having devoted years of my life to the history of the guilds, the
medieval organization of the city, and of commerce, and having worked
on documents and in archives, I am surprised how Roscher was able
—even when preparatory works were lacking and when he himself did
not make any special investigation—to collect a large amount of
factual material, to order and classify it properly, to use it with the
right tact and with ingenuity when drawing general conclusions, and
to determine the development on the whole correctly. To be sure, in
many of these fields more rigorous investigations have started only
now, and they surely will show certain phenomena in a somewhat
different light. But in order to promote work along the right lines,
nothing was more necessary than to break the first paths through the
virgin forest of our science. Roscher did this with energy and good
luck. He has taught us which further questions we should ask, which
further investigations we should make. This was not so difficult in
those fields in which a rich literature was produced during the past
few decades—as in the history of guilds—but it was a great scientific
achievement in those fields where this was not the case, for example,
in the discussion of the staples, the markets, and fairs.

III

As everybody knows, neither the English nor the French have been able to bring together a history of economic doctrines. At least the books by Twiss, Blanqui, Villeneuve de Bargement, not to mention others, do not deserve this name. They are colorful collections of casual notes, mixed with remarks on the older and newer practice of economic policy. In Germany, too, and for a long time, one had copied in the main Adam Smith's remarks on mercantilism and the physiocrats. As late as 1840, J. B. Say had said, with the applause of those economists who thought in terms of natural science: "What can we gain by collecting the absurd opinions and rejected theories which deserve oblivion? It would be useless as well as boring to disinter them. Errors must be forgotten, not studied. The history of economic doctrine serves only idle curiosity."

To be sure, such triteness met opposition also in France, but more still in Germany. And it was Roscher who, first in 1854 in his discussion of the writings of Sir Walter Raleigh, Bacon, Mun, Hobbes, Harrington, Child, Petty, North, Locke, and Davenant, eliminated the phrases on mercantilism which had been traditional since Adam Smith. It was Roscher who prepared the ground for a scholarly history of economic doctrine by actually studying the old writings and unassumingly narrating their contents. With Dühring's critical *History of Economics and of Socialism* (1871 and 1875) and with Roscher's *History of Economics in Germany* (1874), German scholars accomplished an achievement not enjoyed by any other country nor by a number of related sciences.

Roscher had been called upon to undertake this work by the historical commission of the Munich Academy of Sciences, which had commissioned, in accordance with a uniform plan, the writing of histories of the various sciences in Germany by the appropriate authors. This explains the fact that Roscher's work was devoted to Germany only—a fact which one could deplore if the author had not at least in an introductory fashion taken up the important English and French literatures and their influence on the German. It is also possible that Roscher's individuality was less suited for an exposition of the older foreign theories than for the detailed and devoted presentation of the entire economic literature of Germany.

Roscher's work is, in the first line, a bibliographically exhaustive work of learning. In a long series of monographic investigations he himself had during more than a decade created the preparatory studies for his book. Many of these should be used, in addition to the summaries contained in the principal work, by any student of the period, the persons treated, and their writings. In the principal study Roscher records the works of more than one thousand authors, their contents, and the attitudes taken to the more important problems of economics. He has read everything which he mentions. In the first line, he wishes to present a report and an exposition, not a critique. His moderate judgment always is properly balanced. Hardly anybody is censured; but his praise, the fine shade of his approval and characterization, always indicates exactly the impression which a writer has left with him.

Taking up all authors one by one, Roscher investigates their position relative to the various doctrines of present-day economic theory. This naturally entails some monotony. It is a method which makes the book useful as a work of reference rather than as a work which is to be read. This procedure pushes the subjective opinions of Roscher into the background and adds to the objectivity of the work; but it also pushes into the background the principal points and leading ideas. To those who consider a number of traditional economic theories, divisions, and points of view as antiquated scholasticism, many of the remarks will not have as much significance as to Roscher himself. They will perhaps attach little value, for example, to the statement that Leibniz, in his sentence *"regionis potentia consistit in terra, rebus, hominibus"* (the power of a region consists of its land, the things on it, and the men), proved a precursor of those who later on developed the doctrine of the three factors of production, land, capital, and labor. But this way of writing is so intimately connected with Roscher's attitude to the traditional doctrines, and with his method of objectively reporting, that to him any other treatment surely would appear as inexact and subjective.

The entire development is divided by Roscher into three periods, a theological-humanistic one which lasts until 1648, a cameralistic period which goes on approximately until 1750–1780, and a scientific period which extends to the present time and absorbs more than one-half of the work. Theoretical and applied economics as well as public finance are treated, but also administrative law and the general concept of the state. Everywhere economic history forms the background.

IV

In England, the self-satisfied trainbearers of so-called classical economics insisted until recently that our science, although very young, has attained the highest status of perfection, and that it already has reached its deductive stage—like mathematics, astronomy, and other branches of natural science. As if it were not obvious that only the very simplest phenomena open themselves up easily and swiftly to complete knowledge; as if it were not to be taken for granted that the opening up of the most complicated field of human observation, the social one, must necessarily suffer from much delay.

Such vain and exaggerated self-confidence was the result of the discovery of a sort of general causal clue to some of the most elemental economic phenomena. It surely was a great step ahead to explain market phenomena on the basis of the desire for gain and of the mechanics of production cost. But this was only a part of the economic data. Its exploration had been facilitated with the help of psychological considerations—all human, social, and historical life having been more accessible to us since thousands of years than the external nature. But after the simplest matters were thus explained, there remained the important task of arriving at an understanding of the more complex phenomena. And this requires first their scientific description. For long there has been undue neglect of the fact that every science requires a descriptive part as a basis for anything further. People who feel contempt for historical methods should have watched the example of the natural sciences: in botany, mineralogy, zoology, and anatomy, the most distinguished scholars have devoted decades of selfless labor to such preparatory work. With a clear understanding of the situation they limited themselves temporarily to fact-finding, before turning to the explanation of facts.

Statistics has taken over the task of stating economic facts in quantitative terms. The observation and description of qualitative relationships, their modifications, and their development, are more difficult matters. There one has to consider not only individual, but also collective entities, their motives, activities, and methods of organization. This requires a rare art of distilling the most important, the typical, the general, and of tracing a picture on the basis of inexhaustible, thousand-fold detail. The more difficult this task, the more easily is the picture distorted—by subjective influences and political passions, by the difficulty of considering from the same point of view what one has seen and what one has read in books—and the more grateful we should be for good descriptions. Marx and Engels are masters of description but the pictures which they draw are not inspired by the search for truth but by social passion. In contrast with them, Roscher is a master of calm, objective description.

From his work dates an important advance in the art of objective economic description—the successful formation of a construction from the combination of the most distant building stones. His monographs —on large and small industry, on the economic importance of the machine industry, on gluts and surpluses, on the location of cities and industries—are primarily descriptions of present-day situations. It is their aim to resolve the problems of the day, as well as to point out causes and to recommend remedies—but all this is presented in the simple form of a well-arranged description. The subject of these studies is not formed by a single industry or by a single country, but by the composite average of our present-day European countries, their techniques, and their economic organization. Roscher could rightly apply to himself the proud and modest word of the historian Ranke: he wanted only to show how things really are. Is it not a tremendous matter to know how things really are?

But in his most remarkable monographs Roscher is not concerned with an average complex of the economic facts of a certain period. He wants, in a manner similar to that applied in the best parts of his *System,* to single out a group of integrated phenomena and institutions of a number of different peoples and to pursue it through the centuries; for example, luxury, colonization, agricultural systems, the Jews, socialism and communism, the forms of government. He wants to demonstrate that the development of the peoples of antiquity was similar to that occurring in more recent times. In these investigations the material is fitted into a historical scheme, which then is filled in by means of detailed descriptions. The typical and general which is abstracted from the development of each period serves then as illumination and explanation of the detail. In this manner, the description of the field systems turns into a process of historical development and is brought into relationship with such diverse matters as Thünen's doctrines of gross returns, cost of production, net returns, and location; with the history of the family, of municipal organization, and of serfdom. The interrelations between these social institutions and the technological development of the field systems is made clear, and an attempt is made to demonstrate how the distinctive features of the agricultural organization of various periods are always based on certain conditions: when these disappear, the institution loses its justification.

Everywhere the same aim, the same method: a number of collective entities, their characteristics, are compared and placed side by side. They are ordered in a historical series. The attempt is made to identify the causes of institutions which prevailed under parallel circumstances. This should lead to laws of historical development and produce benchmarks for the appraisal of economic policies and of old and modern institutions. Statements are formulated, as general as is possible, "natural laws," as Roscher likes to call them, which are designed to facilitate judgment on the basis of causal relationships and to show the way to the solution of practical problems better than this or that abstract ideal can do.

When Roscher contrasts his historical-physiological method with the older method of idealism, when he promises to produce an anatomy and physiology of economics, when he wants to place comparison next to observation in order to make observation less one-sided, richer in points of view, and more profound, when he considers as the highest achievement the survey of the history of mankind as a sequence of developmental stages, when he wants to accustom the student, first of all, to see always the whole of the economy and of national life in order to judge the detail more correctly and practically—then it is clear that he does not have in mind all parts of his *System,* all intellectual operations which he himself engages in, but first of all the explanation of economic institutions of different times and countries, in which he is primarily interested.

It is exactly because of his basic views that Roscher has been attacked from the right and from the left. Some objected that the detail must be much more rigorously investigated before comparisons can be made. Others considered his method of comparing the most diverse times and countries as a regression to Bodinus. They argued that differences should be explained on the basis of simple, ever-recurring elements rather than with the help of broad comparisons. Naturally, if one moves the centre of gravity of Roscher's scientific work from the middle ground which he holds to the left or to the right, one can find fault with specific points. But it is an unjustified reproach if an able observer and narrator, who has brought new honor to the descriptive method, is told: we now want to produce descriptions which are more exact than yours; you must not begin to make comparisons until all preparations are completed. It surely is necessary today to dig more deeply at many places than was done by Roscher—than could be done by him in the light of the methods and means of his time. But the rudiments of a comparative view are a necessary accompaniment of observation and description of detail; they show us the way and enable us to pose the right questions.

Clearly, not all problems are tractable with the help of Roscher's method; clearly, in the initial stages comparisons of the type made by him are liable to be based on relatively inadequate material; admittedly, the first attempt often will yield no more than a scheme, a series of stages, without complete explanation of the causal development; the notions of youth, flowering, and decay, the analogy with individual human life, slip in. But Roscher is well aware of these imperfections. He emphasizes that every analogy of this type is only a means to an end—to a many-sided and more profound explanation. He warns against the analogy which compares the entire history with the periods of an individual life—we do not know whether we are in the first or in the last tenth of the history of mankind. He points out explicitly that in all comparisons differences must be brought into focus just as much as similarities.

Roscher shares the universal-historical view with the older school of cultural historians. He has taken over from the older generation of economists the great respect for Adam Smith, Ricardo, and Malthus. He is a fine, detached scholar who does not want to destroy but to rebuild slowly. It was as much his aim to remain a theoretical economist as to make the statements of the old school historically more profound. He holds middle ground between two scientific epochs, winding up the older period and ushering in the new one. More than all other scholars he has helped to elevate economics to the level of scientific, systematic, specialized work, of historical investigations of cause and effect. His innermost being is characterized by pure idealism, by the belief in the great moral powers in history. He recognizes no other progress than the moral improvement of man. He measures every economic and technological advance by its effects on the intellectual and moral life.

We are fortunate indeed that such a mind is the master of our science, that the necessary return to empirical methods in our science is ennobled in this manner by a rationalism so exalted and high-minded.

Mitchell
—— on ——
Veblen

Institutional economics in the United States will always be connected with the names of Veblen, Commons, and Mitchell. Thorstein Veblen (1857–1929), the offspring of Norwegian immigrants, had a varied teaching career, made difficult by his unorthodox views and erratic personality. Applying his highly developed critical acumen both to the teachings of orthodox economics and to social institutions—defined as widely prevalent habits of thought and action—he wrote eleven influential books and numerous smaller essays. His best-known works are *The Theory of the Leisure Class* (1899), *The Theory of Business Enterprise* (1904), *The Instinct of Workmanship* (1914), *The Engineers and the Price System* (1921), and *Absentee Ownership* (1923). Veblen's essays have been collected in three volumes. A selection from his writings was edited by Max Lerner in 1948 (*The Portable Veblen*), and a biography, *Thorstein Veblen and His America,* was published by Joseph Dorfman in 1934.

Wesley Clair Mitchell (see below, pp. 413 ff.) was a student and friend of Veblen, whom he admired and loyally supported together with such conservative economists as J. Laurence Laughlin (1850–1933), the founder of the economics department at the University of Chicago, and Herbert J. Davenport (1861–1931), a distinguished price economist.

To EXPLAIN the characteristic animus for which Hume stands, on grounds that might appeal to Hume, we should have to inquire into the peculiar circumstances—ultimately material circumstances—that have gone to shape the habitual view of things within the British community." [1] Thus Thorstein Veblen formulates the problem of accounting for the preconceptions of another "placid unbeliever."

To explain the characteristic animus for which Veblen stands, on grounds that might appeal to Veblen, we need a similar inquiry into the peculiar circumstances that have gone to shape the habitual view of things within the American community of his own day. That need is readily met—Veblen has made the inquiry for us. By logical implication, his explanation of the preconceptions of modern science is an explanation of his own characteristic animus. Though there is scarcely a word about himself in all his writings, we can piece together from various books and essays his account of those elements in his thinking which he deems it feasible and interesting to explain.

But this explanation will not satisfy our "idle curiosity" about Thorstein Veblen. There are other elements in the make-up of a thinker besides the habitual view of things that prevails in the community from which he springs. For example, note what further Veblen says about Hume:

Hume was not gifted with a facile acceptance of the group inheritance that made the habit of mind of his generation. Indeed, he was gifted with an alert, though somewhat histrionic, skepticism touching everything that was well received. . . .

There is in Hume . . . an insistence on the prosy, not to say the seamy, side of human affairs. . . . He insists, in season and out of season, on an exhibition of the efficient causes engaged in any sequence of phenomena; and he is skeptical—irreverently skeptical—as to the need or the use of any formulation of knowledge that outruns the reach of his own matter-of-fact, step-by-step argument from cause to effect.

[1] "The Preconceptions of Economic Science," 1899. Reprinted in *The Place of Science in Modern Civilisation and Other Essays,* p. 96, New York, 1919.

In short, he is too modern to be wholly intelligible to those of his contemporaries who are most neatly abreast of their time. He out-Britishes
the British; and, in his footsore quest for a perfectly tame explanation of
things, he finds little comfort, and indeed scant courtesy, at the hands of
his own generation. He is not in sufficiently naïve accord with the range
of preconceptions then in vogue.

These comments have a double interest. If one knows Veblen, what
jumps to mind is that his characterization of Hume might pass as a
characterization of himself. Veblen, too, is unable to accept his group
inheritance; he is skeptical, he has a histrionic bent, he insists on the
seamy side of life, he practices an irreverent neglect of all theories not
cast in the matter-of-fact mold. Hence, like Hume, he has not been
wholly intelligible to his contemporaries, and he has received scant
courtesy at their hands.

A second impression is that Veblen seems to contradict himself.
Hume was and was not the child of his time. He was more British
than the British, yet he did not accept the habit of mind of his generation. Of course, the contradiction is one in seeming only. Human
culture is a crazy quilt of durable patches from the spiritual garments
man has worn at successive ages in the past, pieced out by a few
patches sewed on recently. Hence, the quilt has many patterns; which
one a thinker will prefer depends upon his taste. Hume's contemporaries who treated him with scant courtesy were likewise legitimate
children of their time. They liked the older patterns in the crazy
quilt—the relics of their ancestors' clothing. Yet a man in advance
of the age, repudiated by his generation, may appear in historical
perspective to have been the most authentic spokesman for what that
generation was adding to culture. He may be typical, for all that he is
unique.

This solution of the seeming contradiction throws the problem of the
thinker's personality into higher relief. To explain Hume's work, we
need not only an inquiry into the peculiar circumstances that shaped
the habitual view of things within the British community, but also an
inquiry into the circumstances that shaped David Hume into the individual he became, and set him in opposition to his age.

These two inquiries run on different lines and encounter different
hazards. One is a venture in cultural history, the other is a venture
in psychological biography. It is hard enough to demonstrate an
explanation of cultural developments. It is impossible to demonstrate
an explanation of personal idiosyncrasies. Veblen, who dealt so confidently with mass habits of thought, left the individual out, or took

him for granted.   The part of prudence is to follow his example.
But Veblen's personality is too intriguing a problem for my prudence.
I shall sketch the circumstances of his early years and add a few conjectures, wrested from his own writings, concerning the way in which
these circumstances contributed to his characteristics.   All of which
will do but little to dispel the mystery.

I

The son of Norwegian immigrants, Veblen was born on a Wisconsin
farm, July 30, 1857.   When he was eight years old, his parents moved
to a larger farm in Minnesota.   There he grew up in a frontier settlement with eight brothers and sisters who continued to speak Norwegian at home while they learned English in school.   The Veblens
prospered as efficient farmers may, and gave their children better educational opportunities than most native American farmers have thought
worth while.   An intellectual drive seems to characterize the family.
An elder brother of Thorstein's became a professor of physics and
one of his nephews is a distinguished mathematician.

At seventeen Veblen entered the academy of Carleton College; at
twenty he entered the college, and at twenty-three he graduated with
the class of 1880.   Carleton was then a small Congregational school
that gave a youth predisposed to skepticism abundant provocation to
amuse himself with the infirmities of traditional wisdom.   By all accounts, the undergraduate impressed his college circle much as the
adult was to impress the reading public.   But however gravely folk
might reprobate his views, everyone acknowledged his extraordinary
capacity for assimilating knowledge and putting it to strange uses.

John Bates Clark, later to win fame as one of the foremost economic
theoreticians of his generation, was teaching in Carleton in the late
seventies.   Thus Veblen was introduced early to the subject about
which he finally organized his interests.   But for the time being he was
engrossed by classical philology, natural history, and philosophy.   When
he went to Johns Hopkins University in 1881, philosophy was his
major subject and economics his minor.   Not finding what he wanted,
Veblen transferred to Yale, where he took a Doctor's degree in philosophy in 1884, with a dissertation entitled "Ethical Grounds of a
Doctrine of Retribution."   In that same year he published a paper on
"Kant's Critique of Judgment" [2] in the *Journal of Speculative Philosophy*.

[2] Reprinted in *Essays in Our Changing Order,* New York, 1934.

All this looked like the fair beginning of an academic career. But in those days there were not many openings for young philosophers whose preconceptions resembled Hume's. Veblen was never one who could "sell himself," as advertisers have taught us to say. So he returned to Minnesota, presently married a classmate of literary gifts, and entered on a desultory course of life with wide reading, some writing, and a bit of nondescript office work. This period of incubation lasted some six or seven years. Doubtless the difficulty of obtaining an academic appointment reinforced Veblen's critical attitude toward American "seminaries of the higher learning." Hope deferred is a bitter diet. But the lack of regular occupation and of intellectual companions other than his wife gave Veblen long hours to follow his own thoughts wherever they led. He became more detached than ever from conventional viewpoints and more firmly rooted in his own habit of mind.

A new phase of Veblen's life began in 1891, when he entered Cornell as a graduate student of the social sciences. While there he published a paper called "Some Neglected Points in the Theory of Socialism." [3] It was "offered in the spirit of the disciple" to Herbert Spencer—in the spirit of the disciple who demonstrated that his master misconceived the grounds of popular dissatisfaction with economic "freedom." Professor J. Laurence Laughlin, then at Cornell, appreciated the quality of this essay. When asked to take charge of the department of economics at the newly founded University of Chicago, Laughlin invited Veblen to go with him. Thus Veblen became one of that extraordinary faculty which President Harper gathered about him—perhaps the most stimulating group of scholars in the country, certainly the group with the most varied traditions.

Teaching courses on agricultural economics, socialism, and the history of economic theory, plus managing the *Journal of Political Economy,* was a heavy load for one of Veblen's physique and temperament. But he seems to have worked best under pressure. In 1898 he published his first critique of economic theory, "Why Is Economics Not an Evolutionary Science?" [4] and in 1899 brought out his first book, *The Theory of the Leisure Class.* From that year he was a man

---

[3] *The Annals of the American Academy of Political and Social Science,* November, 1891; reprinted in *The Place of Science in Modern Civilisation,* New York, 1919.

[4] *The Quarterly Journal of Economics;* reprinted in *The Place of Science in Modern Civilisation,* New York, 1919.

of mark, known as widely to the intelligentsia as to his professional brethren.[5]

II

The essence of Veblen's critical work and the type of his constructive efforts, as we have known them since, are revealed in the article of 1898 (which was elaborated in "The Preconceptions of Economic Science," 1899–1900) and the book of 1899. It is time to see what account we can make his writings yield of their author's viewpoint.

In that effort my bald sketch of his early life gives a hint. It suggests that as an observer of social behaviour in the American field, Veblen had the initial advantage of coming from a different culture. In his essay on "The Intellectual Pre-eminence of Jews in Modern Europe," [6] Veblen explains how such an experience fits a youth for scientific inquiry.

The first requisite for constructive work in modern science, and indeed for any work of inquiry that shall bring enduring results, is a skeptical frame of mind. . . .

The young Jew who is at all gifted with a taste for knowledge will unavoidably go afield into that domain of learning where the gentile interests dominate and the gentile orientation gives the outcome. There is nowhere else to go on this quest. . . .

Now it happens that the home-bred Jewish scheme of things, human and divine . . . all bears the datemark, "B.C." . . . it runs on a logic of personal and spiritual traits, qualities and relations, a class of imponderables which are no longer of the substance of those things that are inquired into by men to whom the ever increasingly mechanistic orientation of the modern times becomes habitual.

When the gifted young Jew, still flexible in respect of his mental habits, is set loose among the iron pots of this mechanistic orientation, the clay vessel of Jewish archaism suffers that fortune which is due and coming to clay vessels among the iron pots. . . . He is divested of those archaic conventional preconceptions which will not comport with the intellectual environment in which he finds himself. But he is not thereby invested with the gentile's peculiar heritage of conventional preconceptions which have stood over, by inertia of habit, out of the gentile past, which go, on the one hand, to make the safe and sane gentile conservative and complacent, and

---

[5] Dr. Joseph Dorfman has given a full account of Veblen's life and an admirable analysis of his work in *Thorstein Veblen and His America*, New York, 1934.

[6] *Political Science Quarterly*, Vol. XXXIV, March, 1919; reprinted in *Essays in Our Changing Order*, pp. 226–230, New York, 1934.

which conduce also, on the other hand, to blur the safe and sane gentile's intellectual vision, and to leave him intellectually sessile. . . .

By consequence [the young Jew] is in a peculiar degree exposed to the unmediated facts of the current situation; and in a peculiar degree, therefore, he takes his orientation from the run of the facts as he finds them, rather than from the traditional interpretation of analogous facts in the past. In short, he is a skeptic by force of circumstances over which he has no control. Which comes to saying that he is in line to become a guide and leader of men in that intellectual enterprise out of which comes the increase and diffusion of knowledge among men, provided always that he is by native gift endowed with that net modicum of intelligence which takes effect in the play of the idle curiosity.

Now, a Norwegian family of farmer folk is like an orthodox Jewish family at least in one respect: it also has a culture that differs widely from the culture of modern America. The Norwegian brand is not date-marked "B.C.," but it savors of the sagas. There is less of business in the Norwegian than in the Jewish heritage, and the former is by so much the more remote in spirit from today. A boy brought up in such a family, largely sufficient unto itself, acquires an outlook upon life unlike that of the son of thoroughly acclimated parents. As he ventures into the world, he finds much strange which those to the manner born take for granted. If endowed with curiosity, he wonders both about the notions that his parents cherish and about the notions that his mates accept. That was Thorstein Veblen's case. And he was insatiably curious about everything he encountered—minerals, plants, and animals, the tongues men speak, the arts they practice, the faiths they venerate, and the proofs they find convincing. He had no collection of established truths to check his questioning; for the truths taken for granted at home and the truths taken for granted in school raised doubts about one another. Thus he, like the Jewish boy of his analysis, became "a skeptic by force of circumstances over which he had no control." On some such lines, the creature of these circumstances might explain his own preparation for scientific inquiry.

But scientific inquiry does not exhaust itself in asking questions; it seeks also to find answers. Veblen's constructive bent is not less marked than his skepticism, though of course it is more specialized. An inquisitive youth may come to doubt all things on principle; but when he begins to contrive explanations, he must limit himself within a range that he can study intensively. What fixed Veblen's choice of problems?

All I can say in answer is that, given his temperament, Veblen's final choice seems a natural outcome of his circumstances. A son of immigrant farmers must wonder about differences among people. That theme is both obvious and subtle; it is beset by prejudices, difficult to treat objectively, fascinating, and slippery. Veblen found its dangers, open and concealed, alluring; for in the realm of thought he was bold as a Viking, and as fond of wiles. Yet differences among people are manifold; no one can explore and explain them all. Veblen might have held fast to his early philological interest, fed by his bilingual upbringing. He might have stuck to his first "major," philosophy. Perhaps he would have done so, had he secured a position in that department of learning. He might have pushed deeper into biology, which in the days of Darwinian speculation seemed neatly fitted to his talents. In the end he found for himself a field more attractive than any one of these. He could fuse his leading interests by studying human cultures. That large venture gave scope to his double heritage from home and school, to his linguistic equipment and facility, to his inveterate skepticism, to his liking for organized systems of thought, to his interest in biology. Also it gave free play to another set of impulses that were as much a part of him as curiosity.

Veblen loved to play with the feelings of people not less than he loved to play with ideas. Now, there are few objects of scientific scrutiny more exciting to our feelings than cultural differences. These differences touch our dear selves. Recall how fond we are of making invidious comparisons between people of our own kind and others. We feel magnanimous if we let the comparisons turn to our disadvantage; we feel resentful if others point out inferiorities in us. However objectively our traits are analyzed, we react emotionally. The delicate nature of this subject must repel men who dislike complex and ambiguous situations; it attracted Veblen. He usually wrote with one eye on the scientific merits of his analysis, and his other eye fixed on the squirming reader. To him, this reader is the creature of cultural circumstances that have produced standard habits of feeling as well as norms of thinking. Veblen practices vivisection upon his contemporaries; he uses no anaesthetic; he has his notions about what emotional reactions each type will exhibit. Instead of seeking to facilitate the reception of his analysis by minimizing the reader's emotions, he artfully stimulates them for his own delectation.

Of course, most critics of modern culture have strong feelings of their own, which they strive to impart to their readers. Moral indignation is the commonest note, and the one to which we respond most readily. We get a certain satisfaction from being preached at; even when we think the preacher bears down rather hard upon our amiable weaknesses, we respect his zeal. Also we are used to the open satirist who seeks to laugh us out of our follies. Veblen repudiates preaching. As an evolutionist, his office is to understand, not to praise, or blame, or lead us into righteousness. From his point of view, any notions he may entertain concerning what is right and wrong are vestiges of the cultural environment to which he has been exposed. They have no authority, and it would be a futile impertinence to try to impose them upon others. There is much of the satirist in him; but it is satire of an unfamiliar and a disconcerting kind. Professedly, he seeks merely to describe and to explain our cultural traits in plain terms. But he likes to put his explanations in a form that will make the commonplaces of our daily lives startling and ridiculous to us. It is this histrionic foible which gives his writing its peculiar flavor.

Veblen is an inveterate phrasemaker, and he designs his phrases to get under our skins. "Conspicuous waste" fits our habits of consumption like a whiplash. Our philanthropies are "essays in pragmatic romance." Modern industry is so "inordinately productive" that prosperity requires "a conscientious withdrawal of efficiency" by the businessmen in control—their chief service to production is to practice "capitalistic sabotage." The common stock of trusts formed by combining companies that had competed with one another represents "defunct good-will." As individuals, we find our places either in the "kept classes" or among the "underlying population"—and either ranking makes us wince. His wit spares nothing and no one. If the pulpit is "the accredited vent for the exudation of effete matter from the cultural organism," the scientist is a "finikin skeptic," an "animated slide-rule," "machine made."

To explain this quirk in Veblen's humor would require the assurance of an amateur psychoanalyst. One who lacks that qualification must take the trait for granted, and merely register its consequences. I think Veblen's fondness for quizzing folk helped to determine his choice of problems and to shape the course of his analysis. I am sure it has been largely responsible for the reactions of readers, both professional and lay, to his work. One must be highly sophisticated to enjoy his books.

Within the field of human culture, an investigator must make a more definite choice of themes. Anthropology, history, sociology, economics, political science, social psychology, all deal with culture. A worker in that field must know something of all these disciplines, and Veblen knew much. In the end he organized his inquiries about economics. Perhaps his early contact with an original, though widely different, thinker in that line had some influence upon his choice.

But there is an explanation in terms of logic that carries more conviction than psychological conjectures.

Darwin tells what stimulation he received from reflecting upon Malthus's theory of population when he was groping after his own theory of natural selection. An installment upon this debt of biology to economics was paid by the stimulation that Darwin's doctrines gave to Veblen's theory of cultures. Cultures are complexes of "prevalent habits of thought with respect to particular relations and particular functions of the individual and of the community." [7] The significant question about these habits is the question that Darwin asked about animal species: How did they develop into the forms that we observe?

The biological view of man's evolution suggests that habits of thought are formed by the activities in which individuals engage. The activities that occupy most hours are likely to exercise most influence in making the mind. The task of getting a living has busied incomparably more men and women for more time than any other task. Hence, economic factors have had and still have a major share in shaping mass habits of thought; that is, in making human culture what it has been under varying circumstances in the past, and what it is today. Other types of activity get whatever time and attention the peremptory job of finding food and shelter leaves free. Where the economic activities themselves are efficient, this margin for indulging such human propensities as emulation, propitiation, predation, and idle curiosity becomes appreciable. A good many individuals can spend most of their time in other tasks than making a living, and so can build up a considerable body of habits not drilled in by the exigencies of humdrum work. Yet there is perforce a certain congruence among all the mental habits formed in any single brain, and even among the habits prevalent in any community at a given time. So the emancipation even of our religious, aesthetic, and scientific notions from economic determination is but partial.

Only one other factor can conceivably rival the influence of getting a living in shaping culture. That is the strictly biological factor of breeding. Veblen thinks, however, that the evidence is all against supposing that *homo sapiens* has undergone any substantial change in anatomy or physiology for thousands of years. Our brains are about as efficient organs as were the brains of neolithic men. Selective breeding under stress of changing circumstances doubtless tends to lower the reproduction rate of individuals whose propensities run toward violence in exceptional degree. Perhaps other generalizations

---

[7] *The Theory of the Leisure Class,* p. 190, New York, 1899.

of that type may be made. But the effects of the breeding factor are slight and dubious in comparison with the effects of cumulative changes in habits of thinking under the discipline of cumulative changes in modes of getting a living. That the lives we live today are so vastly different from the lives lived by our ancestors who left their sketches on the walls of caves and lost their stone implements in the kitchen middens is due in but minor measure to bodily modifications. The theory of evolution begun by biologists must be continued by students of culture, and primarily by economists.

III

Needless to say, economists found this a novel conception of their office when Veblen began writing. The "science of wealth," as they commonly defined their subject, dealt with production, exchange, and distribution, as these processes run in modern times. About the way in which the modern scheme of institutions has evolved, the professed theorists knew little and cared little, for they did not see that such knowledge would help to solve what they took to be their central problem—how prices are determined now, particularly the prices that effect the distribution of income.

Veblen does not claim that genetic studies will answer the questions that economists have posed in the form they have chosen. His fundamental criticism is that economists have asked the wrong questions. Their conception of science and its problems is antiquated, pre-Darwinian.

The sciences which are in any peculiar sense modern take as an (unavowed) postulate the fact of consecutive change. Their inquiry always centers upon some manner of process. This notion of process about which the researches of modern science cluster, is a notion of a sequence, or complex, of consecutive change in which the nexus of the sequence, that by virtue of which the change inquired into is consecutive, is the relation of cause and effect.[8]

Neither the theory of value and distribution as worked out by Ricardo nor the refined form of this theory presented by Veblen's teacher, J. B. Clark, deals with consecutive change in any sustained fashion. The more classical political economy was purified, the more

[8] "The Evolution of the Scientific Point of View." Read before the Kosmos Club, at the University of California, May 4, 1908; first published in *University of California Chronicle*, Vol. X, no. 4; reprinted in *The Place of Science in Modern Civilisation*, p. 32, New York, 1919.

strictly was it limited to what happens in an imaginary "static state." Hence, orthodox economics belongs to the "taxonomic" stage of inquiry represented, say, by the pre-Darwinian botany of Asa Gray. Therefore, it possesses but meager scientific interest. If political economy is to modernize itself, it must become "an evolutionary science," and it can become an evolutionary science only by addressing itself to the problem: How do economic institutions evolve?

In so far as modern science inquires into the phenomena of life, whether inanimate, brute, or human, it is occupied about questions of genesis and cumulative change, and it converges upon a theoretical formulation in the shape of a life-history drawn in causal terms. In so far as it is a science in the current sense of the term, any science, such as economics, which has to do with human conduct, becomes a genetic inquiry into the human scheme of life; and where, as in economics, the subject of inquiry is the conduct of man in his dealings with the material means of life, the science is necessarily an inquiry into the life-history of material civilization, on a more or less extended or restricted plan. . . . Like all human culture this material civilization is a scheme of institutions—institutional fabric and institutional growth.[9]

Associated with this fundamental charge, that economists have mistaken their chief problem, is a second criticism, that they have worked with an antiquated conception of human nature.

In all the received formulations of economic theory . . . the human material with which the inquiry is concerned is conceived in hedonistic terms; that is to say, in terms of a passive and substantially inert and immutably given human nature. The psychological and anthropological preconceptions of the economists have been those which were accepted by the psychological and social sciences some generations ago. The hedonistic conception of man is that of a lightning calculator of pleasures and pains, who oscillates like a homogeneous globule of desire of happiness under the impulse of stimuli that shift him about the area, but leave him intact.[10]

Veblen molded his own notions of human nature on Darwin, William James, and anthropological records. To the biologist and the open-eyed observer, man is essentially active. He is not placed "under the governance of two sovereign masters, pain and pleasure," as Jeremy Bentham held; on the contrary, he is forever doing something on his own initiative. Instead of studying pleasures and pains, or satisfactions

9 "The Limitations of Marginal Utility," 1909. Reprinted in *The Place of Science in Modern Civilisation*, pp. 240–241, New York, 1919.

10 "Why Is Economics Not an Evolutionary Science?" 1898. Reprinted in *The Place of Science in Modern Civilisation*, p. 73, New York, 1919.

and sacrifices, on the supposition that these "real forces" determine what men do, economists should study the processes of human behavior at first hand. For this purpose, the important psychological categories are not the felicific calculus and the association of ideas, but propensities and habits. The human individual is born with a vaguely known equipment of tropisms and instincts. Instincts differ from tropisms in that they involve an element of intelligence; in other words, they are susceptible of modification by experience. What modifications instincts will undergo, into what habits they will develop, depends upon the nature of the experience encountered, and that depends in turn upon the environment, especially the human environment, in which the individual grows up. The human environment is of critical importance because through tradition, training, and education "the young acquire what the old have learned."

Cumulatively, therefore, habit creates usages, customs, conventions, preconceptions, composite principles of conduct that run back only indirectly to the native predispositions of the race, but that may affect the working out of any given line of endeavor in much the same way as if these habitual elements were of the nature of a native bias. Along with this body of derivative standards and canons of conduct, and handed on by the same discipline of habituation, goes a cumulative body of knowledge, made up in part of matter-of-fact acquaintance with phenomena and in greater part of conventional wisdom embodying certain acquired predilections and preconceptions current in the community.[11]

This emphasis upon the cumulative character of cultural changes takes us back to Veblen's conception of what constitutes the problems of science and to his fundamental criticism of economics. The distinctively modern sciences, we have found him contending, deal with consecutive change. He might have added, though I do not recall his doing so, that the consecutive changes studied by different sciences appear to be cumulative in varying degree. Even physics and chemistry, when applied to the history of the cosmos, are concerned with a situation that develops from millennium to millennium. Biology has its branches that deal with processes conceived to repeat themselves over and over without marked alteration in the total situation to be accounted for; but the problems in which cumulative change is prominent bulk larger in biological than in physicochemical theory. Cumulation rises to its highest pitch, however, in the social sciences, because the behavior of men changes in the course of experience far more rapidly than does the behavior of stars and infra-human species. For

[11] *The Instinct of Workmanship*, p. 39, New York, 1914.

that reason, the major explanation of human behavior at any point in the life-history of our race must be sought in the preceding installments of the story. As Veblen put it: "Each new situation is a variation of what has gone before it and embodies as causal factors all that has been effected by what went before." [12] To take economic institutions as they stand at a given moment for granted, and merely to inquire into their working, cuts out of economics that behavior trait which differentiates human activities most clearly from all other subjects of scientific inquiry.

Yet Veblen might have admitted that the quasi-mechanical economics, which takes existing institutions for granted and inquires how they work, has a certain value. This type of inquiry may be regarded as elaborating the logic implicit in the institutions of which it takes cognizance, usually without recognizing their transient character in the life-history of mankind. For example, pecuniary institutions are a prominent feature of current life in the Western world. Most of us make money incomes and buy what we want at money prices. To some extent all of us are drilled by experience into the habit of thinking in dollars; all of us acquire some skill in "the exact science of making change"; all of us accept in part "the private and acquisitive point of view." Now, a theory such as Veblen's warm admirer, Herbert J. Davenport, developed on the express assumption that all men are animated by the desire for gain throws light on our economic behavior just to the extent that men are perfect products of the countinghouse. The logician who excogitates this mechanical system is prone to exaggerate its adequacy as an account of contemporary behavior. But Veblen would be the last to deny the importance of pecuniary institutions in modern culture. He does not, in fact, hold that work such as Davenport has done is wrong, or wholly futile. Yet he inclines to take what is valuable in it for granted, much as Davenport takes for granted the existing scheme of institutions. For Veblen is impatient of the well known and eager to develop aspects of the modern situation about which more orthodox types of economic theory have little to say. Men whose conception of what is "scientific" has been molded by mechanics, criticize his precipitate neglect of their problems, much as Veblen, who builds upon Darwinian biology, criticizes them for their precipitate neglect of evolutionary problems.

One more characteristic of Veblen's procedure must be noted. Representatives of the "exact" sciences stress the importance of measure-

[12] "The Limitations of Marginal Utility," 1909. Reprinted in *The Place of Science in Modern Civilisation*, p. 242, New York, 1919.

ment. There are those, indeed, who go so far as to claim that the outstanding characteristic of scientific thought is its quantitative precision. Now, Darwinian biology was not an exact science; it made but slight use of measurements in any form; it confined itself mainly to "qualitative analysis," supplemented by a recognition that certain factors have played major and other factors minor roles in the development of species. In comparison with Darwin's method, Mendel's experiments in heredity seem precise, and we all know what an impetus the rediscovery of Mendel's work gave to biological research.[13]

Veblen was a good Darwinian in this respect also. His native bent was toward speculation of a philosophical sort. No one had keener insight or nicer subtlety in dealing with ideas, and like all efficient inquirers, he used the tools of which he was master. Further, the statistical invasion of the biological and social sciences was but just starting in Veblen's youth. Galton was not then recognized as a figure of the first magnitude; Pearson's and Edgeworth's work on quantitative methods lay in the future. It was easy for one who had little liking for mathematical procedures to overlook the promise of statistics. Finally and most important, problems of cumulative change in "life-history" are exceedingly difficult to treat by any method of measurement. Each change is by hypothesis a unique event, begotten by an indefinite number of causes. To disentangle the tangled skein is impossible. Without the aid of an elaborate technique it is hard to do more with such problems than what Darwin and Veblen have done— that is, to study the evidence and select for particular attention what seem to be the salient factors. That might go without saying concerning all parts of man's history before social statistics were collected on a liberal scale and preserved for analysis. It is only when he comes to

[13] That Veblen grasped the significance of Mendel's work and of the experiments to which it led is shown by his paper on "The Mutation Theory and the Blond Race," reprinted in *The Place of Science in Modern Civilisation*, pp. 457–476, New York, 1919. See also his references to "the Mendelian rules of hybridization" in *The Instinct of Workmanship*, pp. 21–25, New York, 1914, and in *Imperial Germany and the Industrial Revolution*, pp. 277–278, New York, 1915. But this appreciation, supplemented by his admiration for the experiments of Jacques Loeb, did not induce him to attempt close quantitative work of his own. Two early articles on the price of wheat and "A Schedule of Prices for the Staple Foodstuffs" drawn up for the Food Administration in 1918 are the only papers I recall in which Veblen made detailed statistical inquiries. The articles appeared in *Journal of Political Economy*, Vol. I, pp. 68–103, 156–161, December, 1892, and 365–379, June, 1893; the memorandum for the Food Administration was unearthed by Dr. Dorfman and may be found, minus the statistics, in *Essays in Our Changing Order*, pp. 347–354, New York, 1934.

recent changes that an investigator has tolerably accurate data. These materials Veblen did not reject; but he made no great effort to exploit them. In this respect, at least, his practice resembled that of most orthodox economists.

While not addicted to the quantitative method, Veblen was a keen observer. Having climbed to Darwin's mountain peak, his eyes ranged over a vast stretch of human experience. About many matters quite invisible to economists immersed in the nineteenth century he thought intensively. The Neolithic age in Europe, the feudal system in Japan, the lives of the Australian blackfellows, and a thousand things equally remote in time or space from present-day America seemed strictly pertinent to his problem. Even what he saw of his immediate surroundings differed from what was patent to his contemporaries.

"All perception," said William James, "is apperception." Every scientific inquirer sees what his mind is prepared to see, and preparation of the mind is a compound of previous experiences and the thoughts to which they have given rise. Recall how Darwin's vision was clarified when, after long fumbling with a mass of observations, he hit upon the idea of natural selection.

What Veblen saw when he looked at man's activities differed from what other economists saw because his mind was equipped with later psychological notions. How widely Veblen's conception of human nature departed from that which he imputed to his predecessors has been remarked. It remains to show how his ideas upon "original nature" and "culture" controlled the larger issues of his theorizing, just as notions concerning man's substantial rationality controlled the larger issues of earlier speculation.

There are two ways of studying behavior. One may observe men "objectively," as an experimental psychologist observes animals, and try to form generalizations concerning their activities without pretending to know what goes on inside their heads. Or one may take his stand inside human consciousness and think how that organ works. If the latter method is chosen, the results arrived at depend upon the thinker's notions about consciousness. Logically, these notions form one premise—usually tacit—in a syllogism. The procedure at this stage is "deductive," though it may have been preceded by an "inductive" derivation of the psychological premise, and it may be followed by an "inductive" testing of the conclusions.

Veblen adhered to the standard practice of the classical masters—he chose to reason out human behavior. But he sought to explain actual behavior, not what men will "normally" do; his conclusions are supposed to conform to "facts" and to be open to testing by observation in a directer fashion than are most expositions of "economic laws." Also Veblen gave closer attention than his predecessors to the character of his psychological premise and made it explicit. Profiting by two generations of active research in biology and anthropology as well as in psychology, he could reach what is certainly a later, and presumably a juster, conception of human nature. In so far as his economic theories rest upon psychological premises, they may be rated a more "scientific" account of human behavior than theories which rest upon what latter-day writers call the "intellectualist fallacy of the nineteenth century." Yet in so far as any theories of behavior are conclusions deduced from some conception of human nature, they must be subject to change as knowledge of human nature grows.

Veblen's dealings with psychology, however, are not confined to borrowing ideas from other sciences for use as premises in economics. Anyone who gives an enlightening account of any phase of human behavior is himself contributing toward our understanding of ourselves. By working with psychological conceptions, he develops them and makes their value and limitations clearer. Thus Jevons contributed to the breakdown of hedonism by applying Bentham's felicific calculus in good faith to explain how exchange value is determined. His literal exposition helped economists to realize the artificiality of ideas which seem plausible so long as they remain vague. The more clearly a social scientist sees that he is dealing with human behavior, and the more explicit he is about the conceptions of human nature with which he works, the larger the service which he can render to our self-knowledge. Veblen's service in this direction is that he has applied the instinct-habit psychology of Darwin and William James to explain a wide range of human activities. The nascent science of social psychology owes him a heavy debt of gratitude for this accomplishment—a debt which will be all the heavier if his work helps future investigators to do something better than he accomplished.

One of the ways to press forward along Veblen's path is to turn back and test for conformity to "fact" our plausible reasonings about how men behave—that is, to see how our theories about what men do agree with what we can observe. Of course, what we can observe is not wholly objective. As recalled above, it depends upon what we are mentally prepared to see, and also upon our techniques. Yet when we can apply them, factual tests of ideas are one of our most effective ways of promoting knowledge. The men who laid the foundations of economics recognized this point, and in their writings upon method admitted the desirability of "inductive verification." But in practice they spent little effort upon this desideratum—it seemed too hopeless a task as matters stood. The notion that inquiries should be framed from the start in such a way as to permit of testing the hypothetical conclusions was not common property in their time. Unless such plans are laid in advance, and laid with skill, it is more than likely that the results attained by reasoning will be in such form that no inquirer can either confirm or refute them by an appeal to facts. Observing this run of affairs, the classical methodologists spoke disparagingly of induction in general and of statistical induction in particular: it seemed to them a tool limited to a narrow range of uses in economics.

Veblen's case is not so very different, except that he deals with actual as distinguished from "normal" behavior. He does not plan in advance for testing his conclusions. Of course, he is bound to be skeptical about them—that attitude is not merely logical in him, but also congenial to his temperament. There is always an aura of playfulness about his attitude toward his own work in marked contrast to the deadly seriousness of most economists. Yet, when the opportunity offers, he will cite evidence to support a contention. Usually it is evidence of a sweeping sort which those who do not agree with his viewpoint can interpret in a different sense. Sometimes the evidence is an illustrative case, and the question remains open how representative the case may be. Rarely does he undertake a factual survey. Many of his propositions are not of the type that can be tested objectively with the means now at our disposal. His work as a whole is like Darwin's—a speculative system uniting a vast range of observations in a highly organized whole, extraordinarily stimulating both to the layman and to the investigator, but waiting for its ultimate validation upon more intensive and tamer inquiries.

IV

All this about the man, his problems, his viewpoint, and his methods of work. What constructive results did he reach?

Veblen's studies in the life-history of mankind range over the whole interval between "the origin of the blond type" and the future prospects of business enterprise. Into this range he has dipped at will, preferring always the little-known features of the story. He has never written a systematic treatise upon economics; instead, he has produced numerous essays and ten monographs. An adequate summary of the ideas he has contributed to the social sciences would fill another volume as large as *Absentee Ownership*. All that is feasible here is to select topics illustrative of his conclusions. The whole body of writing is so much of one piece that almost any of his disquisitions would serve as an introduction to the whole. Doubtless it is best to take discussions of matters with which everyone is familiar.

Looking over the modern world, Veblen marked a difference between industrial and pecuniary employments; that is, between the work of making goods and the work of making money; in still other terms, between the machine process and business enterprise. No fact of daily life is more commonplace than this difference; neither men on the street nor economic theorists see in it anything exciting or novel. What comments it seems to call for have been made long since. Adam Smith pointed out in the *Wealth of Nations* that division of labor requires exchange of products and that exchange is greatly facilitated by money. But money is merely an intermediary; we must not exaggerate its importance, as the mercantilists did. Bentham's psychology reinforced this view. Pleasures and pains are the only things that really matter to men; commodities and services are important as instruments of pleasures and pains; money stands at a further remove—it is a means of getting commodities and services. The prevalent common sense on the subject was summed up by John Stuart Mill in a famous passage:

> There cannot, in short, be intrinsically a more insignificant thing in the economy of society, than money; except in the character of a contrivance for sparing time and labor. It is a machine for doing quickly and commodiously, what would be done, though less quickly and commodiously, without it; and like many other kinds of machinery, it only exerts a distinct and independent influence of its own when it gets out of order.[14]

Acting on this conviction, economists have paid a great deal of attention to the monetary mechanism—the best ways of designing it and of keeping it in order. But they treat this problem as a specialty that has little to do with general economic theory. In discussing value and distribution they take money as a tool for investigating more important matters. Thus Alfred Marshall declares that money

> is the center around which economic science clusters . . . not because money or material wealth is regarded as the main aim of human effort, nor even as affording the main subject-matter for the study of the economist, but because in this world of ours it is the one convenient means of measuring human motive on a large scale.[15]

The "real forces" that control behavior, on Marshall's showing, are satisfactions and sacrifices. It is these real forces, and the balancing

[14] *Principles of Political Economy,* Ashley's ed., p. 488, London and New York, 1909.

[15] *Principles of Economics,* 6th ed., p. 22, London and New York, 1910.

of one set of them against the other set, that require analysis. Money is an indispensable tool for measuring the force of opposing motives; but it remains merely a tool so far as the fundamental principles of economics are concerned.

This view of the place of money in economic theory is perfectly consistent with the conception of human nature entertained by Marshall. Despite his substitution of less colorful terms for "pleasure" and "pain," he thought after Bentham's fashion. Men practice a sort of double-entry bookkeeping, satisfactions on the credit and sacrifices on the debit side of the account; they discount for futurity and for uncertainty; they are ready reckoners. To tell what they will do, one needs to know the motive force of the satisfactions and sacrifices promised by alternative lines of action. That force can best be expressed in terms of money; but the use of money does not alter the substantial character of economic behavior.[16]

Shift from Marshall's psychological notions to Veblen's, and the whole picture changes. Money becomes a most significant thing in the economy of society, because it shapes the habits of thought into which our native propensities grow. Instead of being "a machine for doing quickly and commodiously what would be done, though less quickly and commodiously, without it," the use of money "exerts a distinct and independent influence of its own" upon our wants as consumers, upon our skill as planners, upon our methods as producers, and upon our ideals as citizens. And since the discipline that the use of money imposes upon our minds affects some classes far more than it does others, this institution produces social stresses—stresses that may disrupt the present polity.

To begin where Veblen began: In a society where money-making is the commonly accepted test of success in life, our native propensity toward emulation takes on a pecuniary twist. We wish to seem well-to-do, and to attain that agreeable rating we cultivate an air of careless affluence as much as our means permit. We like goods that look expensive, we keep up with the changing styles however uncomfortable they may be, we subject ourselves to inane and fatiguing social frivolities, we teach our children accomplishments that are elegant because they are costly. Our sense of beauty is stamped with the dollar sign. We stand in awe of the very rich, and approach as close to their reputed manner of life as we can. Though born with an instinct of workman-

---

[16] In fairness it should be noted that Marshall's discussions of economic behavior are far more realistic than this schematic framework seems to promise.

ship that makes futility disagreeable, we get satisfaction from conspicuous waste.   Though active creatures, we practice conspicuous
leisure, or make our wives and menials do it for us.   The higher
modern technology raises our standards of living above the "minimum
of subsistence," the wider the scope of our invidious consumption.
Money cannot be intrinsically insignificant in the economy of a society
whose inner cravings bear so deep an impress of pecuniary standards.
All this and much more was set forth in Veblen's first volume, *The
Theory of the Leisure Class.*

Secondly, money-making drills into us a certain type of rationality—
the type that reaches its flower in modern accounting.   The monetary
unit provides us with a common denominator in terms of which the
best drilled among us can express all values, not excepting the value
of human lives.   However vagrant our fancies, we are all forced by the
environment of prices to be somewhat systematic in planning.   We
learn to reckon costs and income, to make change, to compare the
advantages of different types of expenditure.   It is the habit of mind
begotten by the use of money that makes the pleasure-pain calculus
plausible as an account of our own functioning.   Thus the use of
money lays the psychological basis for that philosophy of human behavior which Bentham and Mill, Marshall and Clark, represent—a
philosophy which, ignorant of its origins, treats money as a thing of
slight moment except in facilitating trade and research.   As pointed out
above, economic theory written from the private and acquisitive viewpoint becomes a system of pecuniary logic that exaggerates the importance of one institutional factor in behavior to the neglect of others.

Thirdly, money-making both promotes and obstructs the fundamental task of getting a living.   Veblen pictures two sets of economic
activities running side by side through the life of a modern community.
One set is concerned with producing raw materials, working them up
into serviceable goods, transporting and distributing the things men
desire to use.   The other set is the endless series of concatenated bar-
gains by which men determine how much each individual can take to
himself of what others have made.   The material welfare of the community as a whole depends solely upon the quantity and quality of the
goods brought to consumers by the first set of activities.   Money-
making conduces to material well-being just in so far as it enlarges
the quantity or improves the quality of the serviceable goods obtained
from a given expenditure of energy.   From a common-sense viewpoint, therefore, money-making is a means to getting goods.   But in
practice we reverse the relation.   We make goods in order to make

money. Veblen never wearies of expounding that central paradox and of developing its consequences.

He grants the commonplaces about the economic advantages of this scheme of organization. Adam Smith was right: industrial efficiency requires division of labor, division of labor requires exchange, and exchange requires money. No other scheme of organization that men have tried out in practice yields so large a per capita flow of goods to consumers as the current scheme of making goods for profit. Business accounting is a marvelous device for controlling complicated undertakings. Industry requires capital and credit, and, as matters now stand, who can supply capital and credit but the capitalist and the banker? The businessman is the central figure in modern economic life, the prime mover, what you will. There is no call to quarrel with encomiums of this sort which anyone is moved to pronounce upon the present order. But it is interesting to reflect upon certain features of the situation that are less obvious to business-trained eyes.

One is that the recurrent crises and depressions which ever and again reduce the flow of goods to consumers are due to business, not to industry. There is no technological reason why every few years we should have idle factories and unemployed men walking the streets, while thousands lack the goods employers and men would like to supply. The trouble is that business enterprises are run for profit, not to meet human needs. When times are good, prices rise, profits are high, businessmen borrow freely and enlarge their output. But such prosperity works its own undoing. The substantial security behind the loans is prospective net earnings capitalized at the current rate of interest. When the rate of interest rises, as it does during prosperity, the capitalized value of a given net income declines, and the loans become less safe. More than that, net earnings in many cases prove less than had been expected in the optimistic days of the nascent boom. Prices cannot be pushed up indefinitely; the costs of doing business rise and encroach upon profits; bank reserves fall and it becomes difficult to get additional credit. When fading profits are added to high interest, creditors become nervous. In such a strained situation, the embarrassment of a few conspicuous concerns will bring down the unstable structure which had seemed so imposing. A demand for liquidation starts and spreads rapidly, for the enterprises pressed for payment put pressure upon their debtors to pay up. So prosperity ends in a crisis, followed by depression. In short, business enterprises cannot prosper without committing business errors that bring on a crisis, and from these errors the whole community suffers.

More serious in the long run than these acute fits of indigestion is
a chronic malady of the present order. Businessmen seek to fix their
selling prices at the maximum net-revenue point. There is always
danger that an oversupply of products will reduce prices more than the
increased turnover will compensate for. This danger is peculiarly great
because of the "inordinate" productivity of the modern machine process.
Give the engineers their heads and the markets might be swamped by a
flood of goods. Businessmen are constantly on their guard against this
peril. It is their office to adjust supply to demand; that is, to prevent
an unprofitable rate of output; that is, to keep industrial efficiency "sub-
normal"; that is, to practice "capitalistic sabotage."

Indeed, by their very training, businessmen are incompetent to serve
as captains of industry. Technology is becoming more and more an
affair of applied science. We have elaborate schools for engineers in
which mathematics, physics, chemistry, and electrical theory are the
basic subjects of instruction. The graduates from these schools are the
men who know how to make goods. If permitted to organize production on a continental scale, they might, with their present knowledge,
double or triple the current output of industry. That they will not be
suffered to do, so long as they are subject to the higher authority of
businessmen, who do not understand technology and who distrust the
vaulting plans of their own engineers. And this distrust is well founded,
so long as business enterprise is organized in many units. To set engineering science free from business shackles would smash the independent enterprises of today, and lay out the process of making goods
on much broader lines. In the early days of the industrial revolution,
the businessman was an industrial leader; in these later days the development of technology has turned him into an industrial incubus.

Yet the situation of business enterprise which seems so firmly
entrenched is becoming precarious, because the habits of thinking
engendered in men by modern life are undermining the habits of thinking on which business traffic rests. If businessmen do not speak the
same language as engineers, or enter into their thoughts, neither do
engineers speak the language or share the ideas of businessmen. The
one group talks in terms of physical science, the other talks in terms of
natural rights, particularly the right of ownership. It is increasingly
difficult for the engineer to see why he should not be allowed to develop his plans for increasing output to the limit. He asks why the
pecuniary interests of a handful of families should stand in the way of
a doubled per capita income for the community as a whole. Demonstrations that absentee owners have a perfect right to draw dividends
from industry without contributing personal service leave him cold.
What is more threatening than this doubting mood of the technologists

is a growing disaffection among the masses of factory hands. Though not schooled in physical science, these people fall into a somewhat similar habit of thought. Their daily work with materials and machines teaches them to seek an explanation of all things in terms of cause and effect. They tend to become skeptical, matter of fact, materialistic, unmoral, unpatriotic, undevout, blind to the metaphysical niceties of natural rights. And nothing effective can be done to check the spread of these subversive habits of thought so long as the workers must be kept at their machines. So it appears that the time is coming when the present order of society, dominated by business enterprise in the interests of absentee ownership, will no longer seem right and good to the mass of mankind.

Veblen has no definite specifications for the new structure of institutions that will grow up in place of the present one, beyond an expectation that technically qualified engineers will have a larger share in managing industry. His evolutionary theory forbids him to anticipate a cataclysm, or to forecast a millennium. What will happen in the inscrutable future is what has been happening since the origin of man. As ways of working shift, they will engender new habits of thinking, which will crystallize into new institutions, which will form the cultural setting for further cumulative changes in ways of working, world without end.

V

If Veblen has descried aright the trend of cultural change, his economic theories will commend themselves to a wider circle in the next generation than in his own. For on his showing, science, like all other cultural excrescences, is a by-product of the kind of work folk do. Circumstances made a certain Thorstein Veblen one of the early recruits in the growing army of men who will look at all social conventions with skeptical, matter-of-fact eyes. Just before his time the German historical school had perceived the relativity of orthodox economics; but they had not produced a scientific substitute for the doctrine they belittled or discarded. Karl Marx had been more constructive. In Veblen's view, Marx had made a brave beginning in cultural analysis, though handicapped by a superficial psychology derived from Bentham and by a romantic metaphysics derived from Hegel. Bentham's influence led Marx to develop a commonplace theory of class interests that overlooked the way in which certain habits of thought are drilled into businessmen by their pecuniary occupations and quite different habits of thought are drilled into wage earners by the machine process in which they are caught. Hegel's influence made the Marxian theory of social evolution essentially an intellectual sequence that tends to a

goal, "the classless economic structure of the socialistic final term,"
whereas the Darwinian scheme of thought envisages a "blindly cumulative causation, in which there is no trend, no final term, no consummation." Hence, Marx strayed from the narrow trail of scientific
analysis appropriate to a mechanistic age and attained an optimistic
vision of the future that fulfilled his wish for a socialist revolution.[17]
The Darwinian viewpoint, which supplies the needed working program,
will spread among social scientists, not because it is less metaphysical
than its predecessors or nearer the truth (whatever that may mean), but
because it harmonizes better with the thoughts begotten by daily work
in the twentieth century. That the majority of economists still cling
to their traditional analysis is to Veblen merely the latest illustration of
the cultural lag in social theory—a lag readily accounted for by the
institutional approach.

Yet Veblen remains an inveterate doubter even of his own work.
The Darwinian viewpoint is due to be superseded in men's minds; the
instinct-habit psychology will yield to some other conception of human
nature. The body of factual knowledge will continue its cumulative
growth, and idle curiosity will find new ways of organizing the data.
His own view of the world is date-marked "A.D. 1880–1930," as definitely as Jewish culture is date-marked "B.C."

A heretic needs a high heart, though sustained by faith that he is
everlastingly right and sure of his reward hereafter. The heretic who
views his own ideas as but tomorrow's fashion in thought needs still
firmer courage. Such courage Veblen had. All his uneasy life he faced
outer hostility and inner doubt with a quizzical smile. Uncertain what
the future has in store, he did the day's work as best he might, getting
a philosopher's pleasures from playing with ideas and exercising "his
swift wit and his slow irony" upon his fellows. However matters went
with him, and often they went ill, he made no intellectual compromises.
In his retreat among the lovely coast hills of California, he died on
August 3, 1929, a "placid unbeliever" to the end.

[17] See Veblen's two papers on "The Socialist Economics of Karl Marx and His
Followers," originally published in *Quarterly Journal of Economics,* August, 1906,
and February, 1907; reprinted in *The Place of Science in Modern Civilisation,*
pp. 409–456, New York, 1919. The phrases quoted are from pp. 417, 436.

After dilating upon the "disparity between Marxism and Darwinism," Veblen
points out that "the socialists of today" have shifted from "the Marxism of Marx"
to "the materialism of Darwin," though "of course" without admitting that "any
substantial change or departure from the original position has taken place." See
pp. 417, 432, 433.

Perlman
on
Commons

John R. Commons (1862–1944), educated at Oberlin and Johns Hopkins, had a varied teaching career until he was called to the University of Wisconsin in 1904. Commons defined an institution as collective action in control of individual action. He developed considerable interest in legal institutions, and his "investigational" approach to institutional economics, similar to the fact-finding of the Webbs, brought fruitful cooperation with state and federal authorities, making Commons the sponsor of a number of now flourishing fields of applied economics. Under Commons and his associates, the department of economics at the University of Wisconsin attained high rank.

Commons' principal works are *Legal Foundations of Capitalism* (1924), and *Institutional Economics* (1934). He also published an autobiography, *Myself* (1934).

Selig Perlman (1888–   ) was educated in Poland, Italy, and at the University of Wisconsin, with which he has been associated as a student and teacher for a period of over forty years. Perlman was befriended by Commons and became one of his favorite disciples. He is the author of *A Theory of the Labor Movement* (1928) and of other works in the field of labor history which continue the institutionalist tradition.

INSTITUTIONALISM is subject to a Nemesis that is implacable, inescapable and renders judgment with relative celerity. Since it concentrates on the trends in the ultra-visible total socio-economic pattern, institutionalism is as exposed to the ravages of time as were the early farmer almanacs with their predictions of the weather. For, to merit the name at all, any economic institutionalism must claim to have found, presumably through intuition-pointed research, which specific areas in the changing kaleidoscopic picture of economic behavior and relations are the "critical" ones, namely controlling the total process of change. Hence, to use the same analogy of the almanac, a number of seasons of drought or of excessive rain, where good growing weather has been predicted, will suffice to disqualify the institutionalist's claim to be a scientist.

Where, indeed, is Marxism as a science, after the "proletariats" of the technically most advanced countries have refused to emulate the Bolshevists, while instead of the predicted classlessness after the revolution, there is in the Soviet Union a brand-new social hierarchy? What of the Webbs' discerned trend in trade unionism away from the earlier "vested interests" doctrine and of "demand and supply" bargaining to an acceptance of the "common rule" principle in a planned society soon due to leave private capitalism behind, outlined by Sidney Webb in the first official program of the Labour Party, when the six years of Labour Party rule have been studied with instances of persistent particularism by individual trade unions and when the rank and file has shown a clear lack of interest in the program of nationalization of industry so dear to the Party intellectuals? Further, what of the proclaimed dichotomy between the "engineer" and the "businessman" with a future rule by a "Soviet of technicians" clearly adumbrated, when the biggest CIO unions, in steel and automobiles, born in revolt against the AFL's "vested interest" craftism, are hopefully joining in an "industrial government" with "vested interests" managements, which are showing their capitalist self-confidence through this very willingness to play with

[Certain passages of this essay were originally published in the *American Economic Review*, Vol. 35, No. 4, September 1945, and are reprinted by permission.]

union recognition? Yet, each of these groups of institutional thinkers— the Marxian, Webbian, and Veblenian—has shaped the thinking of one or more generations of intellectuals in at least one large country, and compared with their self-confidence as analysts of trends and as drafts- men of blueprints of the society to come, the John R. Commons con- tribution appears indeed self-limiting and even pitifully pedestrian. On the other hand, the "march of history" must be literally a foot soldier's exercise to have extended validation, as we now find it did, to the Commons approach and not to the others.

A major cause of the vitality of Commons' institutionalism lies in the unique quality of his objectivity. To be sure, none of the above- enumerated institutionalists has succumbed to the self-deception of those social thinkers who, in order to render their "objectivity" above suspicion, have loudly divorced themselves from "value" or ethical judgments, thereby frequently leaving the door open to vesting sheer "whimsies" with intellectual trappings. Commons, however, even went further than his brother institutionalists: he not only wrote, spoke, and taught as though his ethical commitment to the advancement in status and opportunity of the so-called common man were so self-understood that no further comment was needed, but showed clearly that this very concern of his precluded a lightminded espousal of unrealistic theories and programs which would only put upon the common man the burden of functions he was not fit to discharge. As regards what "did make or did not make sense" in such diagnoses and prescriptions, Commons was, in addition, completely free of the most insidious species of snobbery, that of condescendingly lending one's "superior brain" to the cause of the lowly. Commons genuinely believed that the "common men," especially their leaders, busy at their perpetual task of attracting mem- bers to the organizations and of holding them, are as capable of making valid and meaningful intellectual discoveries as himself and his col- leagues in the social scientists' guild. In a word, Commons practiced the most difficult sort of democracy—intellectual democracy. For this, his reward was steadily at hand; he was never in danger of substituting an "abstract mass in the grip of an abstract force" [1] for the concrete human beings, and his generalizations had a "close-to-life" quality and a power to carry conviction that come only from "living with one's subject" with no barriers between.

Commons' intellectual democracy showed strikingly even when he was interviewing people. His was no "technique of modesty" or a

---

[1] S. Perlman, *A Theory of the Labor Movement* (New York: The Macmillan Company, 1928, 1949), pp. 280–283.

simulated ignorance to appeal to the other's ego and thus evoke information. It was a genuine groping, questions without any definite goal—a mere stabbing in this direction and in that. What kept the conversation from degenerating into a boring experience to the person interviewed was Commons' deep earnestness and his unmistakable assumption that the latter's problems were not just his own private worries but of general concern and deeply instructive to any serious-minded interrogator. And then, sometimes after hours had elapsed, a question or a series of questions would come forth which not only touched the nerve of the whole situation but, as if by sleight-of-hand, made the earlier groping appear as an orderly quest with little waste motion. The result was a fuller grasp of the problem and a suggested solution possessing both freshness and promise. To the bystander it was an absorbing spectacle of intuition and reason pulling in common harness.

In his search for generalizations bearing on the life cycle of economic institutions—"collective action in control of individual action," as Commons defined an institution—he was untiring in the use of what he delighted to call the "dig it up" method. Commons had no liking for either the winged phrase or for what one might call the winged theory as devices for circumventing the necessity for "digging," since he knew from experience that human motives have a way of appearing in innumerable combinations. He, therefore, doubted such master juxtapositions as bourgeoisie and proletariat, technician and businessman, and felt that they appeared convincing only from a seat in the British Museum or from an academic armchair. To him the social terrain was far too broken to conform to any sweeping description, but demanded the labor of tireless and meticulous topographers who had the experimenter's imagination and were unafraid to "wade in." He began with the institutions of labor, to which he had received an early introduction as a member of the Typographical Union.

Commons accorded a supreme attentiveness to the institutions contrived by workingmen without the aid of mentors from those of high social station and education—institutions such as trade unions, cooperative buying clubs, cooperative workshops, and the like. He rejoiced in tracing the steps of the unlettered statesmen—the phrase is the Webbs'—whereby these movements laid stable foundations underneath these organizations by the method of trial and error. And as a student of such movements, he knew how incompatible such creativeness from below was with external domination by employers, messianic intellectuals, or government.

To Commons the workingmen were not building blocks out of which a jealous deity called "History" was to shape the architecture of the

new society, but beings with legitimate ambitions for a higher standard
of living and for more dignity in their lives. Both objectives, he agreed
with labor, were primarily realizable through the attainment of citizenship status in the places of employment, paralleling the worker's status
in the democratic state. As self-determining beings, the workers and
their movements were to set their *own* objectives, their *own* values, and
were entitled to claim from the intellectuals expert aid in the road they
should take to attain the goals set by leaders risen in their midst. If
labor's goals were mutually contradictory, the intellectual should so
inform them. If labor's objectives were not for the benefit of society
and ultimately not for its own, he should tell that too. And above all,
the intellectual should be an expert social topographer and trained fore-
caster of group behavior.

Commons applied this same pattern of fruitful interplay between the
undogmatic intellectual and struggling movements to past history. He
thus came to formulate a gripping theory of the interrelation between
group customs and the common law, of the rise of new social classes,
and of their struggle for recognition. In his *Legal Foundations of
Capitalism,* he showed how in the struggle around the "rent bargain"
the barons had reduced the King of England from an over-all owner to
a recipient of a land tax fixed by collective bargaining between their
representatives and his. In a similar way, the merchants of England
began through their participation in the piepowder courts at the fairs
to impose the customs of their group upon the presiding judge, who was
only too glad thus to fill the void of his ignorance. Out of this un-
impressive beginning, through a process of osmosis over several centuries between judges increasingly appreciative of the growing importance of the merchants to the Commonwealth of England and a
continuous custom-making by that merchant class to suit changing
conditions, came the law merchant, and finally the latter's incorporation
in the common law. What produced this significant result was the
unremitting pushing by the merchant class; the willingness of undogmatic intellectuals, the judges, to absorb pressures from below and thus
prevent frustration; and ultimately a judicial sifting of these merchant
customs, the rejection of some and the acceptance of those that looked
acceptable from the standpoint of the moving pattern of the law. The
intellectual mechanism employed was the expansion of the meaning of
property from the mere "physical" to embrace the "incorporeal" and
the "intangible."

Commons delighted in seeing the judges of America, during the last
years of his life, do with the customs of the labor movement—the fair
wage, the normal working day, the union shop, and seniority—what

their English predecessors had done with the customs of the merchants. Earlier he had been greatly impressed by the statesmanship of Australia's Court of Conciliation and Arbitration, although not by her system of compulsory arbitration of labor disputes. But the shift away from dogmatism by our official "intellectuals" came only after the labor movement had gathered momentum both in industry and government under the salutary climate of the New Deal—altogether in conformity with Commons' conception of how social change takes place.

In this American scene, in which perhaps, among the major countries of the West, private property and freedom of enterprise have shown their strongest entrenchment, Commons was known as an advanced liberal, if not a radical. It is noteworthy, though, that conservatives frequently understood him better than did the conventional radicals: while yielding to his charm, they proclaimed that he was "fifty years ahead of his time." The left-wing liberals applauded him as a toiler in their own vineyard, but were definitely puzzled and disappointed at his refusal to join them in indicting capitalism as a system. Nor were matters helped much when he, on his part, indulged in puncturing, however gently, their fondest dreams by blandly declaring that his labor history studies have shown that "labor cannot manage" and that operative management by government, except in certain areas such as municipal and power-generating utilities, would not be sufficiently above management by labor. For Commons was convinced that, in order that the standard of living of the many might keep going up, society needed the profit-stimulated drive of privately appointed management, a drive which must be supervised, to be sure, by society's attention to the rules of the game, including not a few of his own devising, while accompanied by social policies encouraging the barter of the union rules hampering efficiency for management's concessions on wages and status.

Commons' dictum that "labor cannot manage" was derived from his vast studies which resulted in the ten-volume *Documentary History of American Industrial Society,* and on which he concentrated during 1904–1910. He saw the repeated failures of the idea of the self-governing or cooperative workshop, from the forties of the past century to the eighties. These attempts, running into the hundreds, to escape the wage system into self-employment by small groups of mutually congenial people, invariably ended in the dissipation of the invested capital and of the idealistic hopes of the participants (in rare cases, these shops survived, but then only as the property of some of the "smarter" co-operators). In addition, these "co-ops," in their keenness to get orders, usually hampered their foster parent, the labor union, by foisting upon the private employer a severer market competition, which in his eyes was both destructive and unfair and which he was certain to use as an argument in his wage bargaining.

In the *Documentary History* and the two-volume *History of Labor in the United States* which followed in 1918, both published as joint products of Commons and his students, Commons has unobtrusively brought forth an almost casual answer to both the Marxian and the Fabian theories of the labor movement. In it, there were the first tying-up of labor movement behavior with business fluctuations; the first genetic treatment of America's unique psychological classlessness, despite the growing contrasts shown in her income and property statistics; the factual foundation of a theory of the origins of "economic classes" (*"bargaining* classes" as Commons called them); and, finally, the *rationale* of American labor's striving for a fulsome and dignified class collaboration under "union recognition," but still under capitalism. All this achieved an epitome in a theory of "industrial stages" in the *American Shoemakers, 1648–1895,* the preface to Volume III of the *Documentary History.* Commons built his "stages" upon the testimony given in the early labor conspiracy trials by strikers, "scabs," master workmen, and "gentlemen of the trade." Little did these witnesses realize that they were providing material for a future economist who would emulate the reconstruction work of the paleontologist!

In several of the earlier stages—the "itinerant," the "custom order," and the "retail shop"—there was a virtual harmony between consumer, master workman, and journeyman. During the ensuing "wholesale-order stage," when goods could find a widened market through being transported by turnpike and by river, aspiring masters from different places, in order to expand their scale of operation, resort to the inducement of lower price in a competition which had already become impersonal and ruthless. The journeymen meet their employer's new "cost consciousness" with a wage consciousness and thus there arise the first stable unions, which practice a sort of a "class struggle" through cutting off the employer's access to cheaper labor, namely the suppression of the legitimate craftsman's "competitive menaces."

But it is in the stage that followed, in which the ultimate authority lies with the merchant-capitalist, a person not necessarily risen from the trade, that the class conflict becomes truly bitter, in consequence of still greater pressure on price in a market which has grown still larger and with the competition between the sellers more fierce than before— all of it causing a more relentless pressure upon wages and, as a reaction, a more frantic protective labor effort. In the next stage, in which machinery comes in, the immediate employer, now a small manufacturer, is under the thumb of the merchant-jobber, who is in control of the outlet to the consumer and by playing off one manufacturer against the other, forces them to depress wages still further, an act which the latter finds within his capacity, as the machine had exposed the craftsman to the competitive menace of "green hands." This is accordingly the stage of the most exasperated "class struggles." Presently, however, the manufacturer eliminates the jobber by reaching out directly to the consumer, and with this greater case won, is in a position either to become a "welfare employer" minus a union or to go the full length in "industrial democracy" by signing a time agreement with the union.

Once we accept the view that a broadly conceived aim to control competitive menaces is the key to the conduct of organized labor in America, the real causes of the American industrial class struggles stand revealed. In place of looking for these causes, with the Marxians, in the domain of technique and production, we look for them on the market, where all developments which affect labor as a bargainer and competitor, of which technical change is one, are bound sooner or later to register themselves. It then becomes possible to account for the long stretch of industrial class struggle in America prior to the factory system, while industry was still on the handicraft basis. Also we are able to render to ourselves a clearer account of the changes, with time, in the intensity of the struggle and, above all, of the turn to a "joint industrial government" by management and the union, which, were we to follow the Marxian theory, would appear hopelessly irregular if not subversive of "history's purpose." [2]

[2] In Commons' own words: "The foregoing sketch of industrial evolution in America brings into prominence the part played by the ever-widening area of competition, and the effort of protective organizations to ward off the peculiar competitive menace of each stage of development. From this standpoint the sketch may be compared with the investigations of Marx, Schmoller, and Bücher. Karl Marx was the first to challenge the world with a keen analysis of economic evolution, but his standpoint is that of the mode of production and not the extension of the market. His two assumptions of a given 'use value' and a given 'average social labor' serve to obliterate, the one the part played by the price-bargain, the other the part played by the wage-bargain. With these assumptions out of the way he is able to concern himself with the production of 'surplus value' by his theory of the working day and the cost of living. But these are secondary factors, results, not causes. The primary factors are on the side of the market where competition is carried on at different levels. Instead of 'exploitation,' growing out of the nature of production, our industrial evolution shows certain evils of competition imposed by an 'unfair' menace. Instead, therefore, of an idealistic remedy sought for in common ownership, the practical remedy always

Commons is thus the father of a labor struggle theory which is not a class struggle theory in the Marxian sense. It is not a struggle by the rising group to liquidate the old class or to raze the social structure which the latter controlled, but essaying instead to add to the old edifice new and spacious wings to serve as the dwelling places of the customs of the rising class. Such a "class struggle" might appear to some as pathetically limited in its objective, but there was nothing pathetic about its driving qualities. And those who pioneered in the struggle of recognition were to him in the front ranks of the history makers. As an intellectual democrat Commons held in the highest esteem Samuel Gompers, who had to develop his theory of the American labor movement as he went about keeping the American Federation of Labor from disintegrating on his hands.

But great as Commons was as a social investigator inspired by the ideal of the equivalence of all men, he was no less great as a statesman. In fact, with him scholarship and practical statesmanship were forever inseparable. As a statesman he knew that the democratic objective in industrial relations could not be attained through a bureaucracy, however well intentioned or trained, but depended on self-action by all the groups concerned, the government aiding but not dominating. Nor would he enthrone the underdog group. For much as he identified himself with the so-called "common man," he was far from disdainful of employers' and manufacturers' associations and other organizations among the better-situated groups. Though he fought them before legislative committees when they impeded industrial safety, workmen's compensation, shorter hours for women and the like, he strove to harness the power of these same organizations alongside the trade unions on behalf of an efficient administration of the laws enacted.

And within the groups on the conservative side of the alignment, he sought to enlist and to energize on behalf of those measures the individuals of high purpose and high standards. He thus came to grapple as early as forty years ago with the so-called "road to serfdom," the alleged discovery of our own day, and in the device of the "advisory committee" of the leaders of the groups concerned he provided for an effective preventive of the bureaucratization of the governmental process.

As teacher and inspirer of graduate and undergraduate students, Professor Commons ranks with America's greatest. In Commons'

actually sought out has been the elimination of the competitive menace through a protective organization or protective legislation." John R. Commons, *Labor and Administration* (New York: The Macmillan Company, 1913), p. 259.

presence the student while aware of contact with greatness yet never felt dwarfed, for Commons made him feel that he was genuinely dependent on his contribution whether to check a theoretical point or to invent a workable device. Professor Commons never tired of acclaiming such contributions, as when a member of his seminar suggested the "employer election device" in the workmen's compensation law of 1911, for long the keystone of that law's constitutionality. In fact, his generosity in allotting credit to his students and co-workers was a source of endless embarrassment to the latter. The same generosity and solicitude extended to the students' other concerns and wants.

There are hundreds of Commons' students, including some most prominent in the academic life and in the public services of this country, who largely owe their careers to the untiring and tender encouragement by Professor and Mrs. Commons. At the Commons' weekly "Friday Nights" at their home near Mendota Beach, students, frequently numbering as many as sixty, had the opportunity of meeting some of the most prominent economists and public men of the world and to present before the group their own observation in the "field." To the Commons' "Friday Nights" many a public man today looks back as the informal and friendly "Parliament" that heard his "maiden speech."

Wesley Clair Mitchell (1874–1948), educated at the Universities of Chicago, Halle, and Vienna, had a distinguished teaching career, with over thirty years of service at Columbia University. Mitchell's method of statistical fact-finding made him the leading exponent of the quantitative approach to institutional economics. He was one of the founders of the National Bureau of Economic Research, and did pioneering work in the study of business cycles. His principal books include three volumes devoted to this subject: *Business Cycles* (1913), *Business Cycles: The Problem and Its Setting* (1927), and *Measuring Business Cycles* (1946, with A. F. Burns). A collection of his essays, treating in part of the history of economics, was published under the title *The Backward Art of Spending Money* (1937).

Arthur F. Burns (1904–   ) was educated at Columbia University, where he has been teaching since 1941. Burns, a student and associate of Wesley Clair Mitchell, has been affiliated with the National Bureau of Economic Research since 1930, succeeding Mitchell as director of research in 1945. Burns's work, *Production Trends in the United States since 1870* (1934), has been characterized by Mitchell as "the most important contribution to our knowledge of increase in production which has been made since Mill."

W ESLEY MITCHELL is best known for his studies of business cycles and his leadership of the National Bureau of Economic Research. Fired by a bold conception of economic science and the part it might play in building a better world, he specialized in order to test his novel approach to economic problems. But Mitchell never ceased being a general economist, and throughout his life took the whole of economic experience as his intellectual province.

I

Mitchell once related that his family claimed to be descended from an Experience Mitchell, said to have come over on the *Mayflower*. He added dryly that he could not vouch for the justice of the claim. However that may be, it is known that Mitchell's forebears hailed from New England. His father, John Wesley Mitchell, was born on a farm in Avon, Maine, December 30, 1837. In time he became a physician, saw service in the Civil War as an army surgeon, leaving with the rank of brevet colonel. He married Lucy Medora McClellan, the daughter of a Middle Western farmer, whose ancestors can be traced to Massachusetts. Wesley Clair was their second child, born on August 5, 1874, in Rushville, Illinois. Soon the number of children grew to seven.

Young Clair matured rapidly. The family's means were scant, and his father repeatedly ill. Clair had the opportunity to learn at first hand about economic struggle, and its moral concomitants in sturdy folk. In a letter to Lucy Sprague, shortly before their marriage, he wrote of his parents:

Such strength of character as they possess I've never found elsewhere. But they could not help resting a part of family responsibilities on me, as the eldest son, far too early. I had to think about money matters, to learn the hard side of life, when most children are free from care. No doubt this fact strengthened my bent for reading and the world of imagination which reading helps to enlarge.[1]

[1] Letter to Lucy Sprague, October 18, 1911.

[Adapted by the author from Twenty-Ninth Annual Report of the National Bureau of Economic Research, New York, 1949.]

414

Clair found another refuge in spinning logical exercises and relating them to facts. Often he engaged in theological discussions with his grand aunt, who "was the best of Baptists, and knew exactly how the Lord had planned the world." Mitchell liked to tell of his "impish delight in dressing up logical difficulties" for her. Unable to dispose of them, she "always slipped back into the logical scheme, and blinked the facts in which" he "came to take a proprietary interest." [2]

Despite the straitened circumstances of his family, Clair managed to go off to Chicago, where he studied under the remarkable faculty assembled by President Harper at the new university. In the summers he worked on the family farm, and in the winters he knew how to live on next to nothing. To a boy of his "experience and temperament college was a shining opportunity, not a dull duty." [3] Years later he drew a lively sketch of his college days:

I began studying philosophy and economics about the same time. The similarity of the two disciplines struck me at once. I found no difficulty in grasping the differences between the great philosophical systems as they were presented by our text-books and our teachers. Economic theory was easier still. Indeed, I thought the successive systems of economics were rather crude affairs compared with the subtleties of the metaphysicians. Having run the gamut from Plato to T. H. Green (as undergraduates do) I felt the gamut from Quesnay to Marshall was a minor theme. The technical part of the theory was easy. Give me premises and I could spin speculations by the yard. Also I knew that my "deductions" were futile. . . .

Meanwhile I was finding something really interesting in philosophy and in economics. John Dewey was giving courses under all sorts of titles and every one of them dealt with the same problem—how we think. . . . And, if one wanted to try his own hand at constructive theorizing, Dewey's notion pointed the way. It is a misconception to suppose that consumers guide their course by ratiocination—they don't think except under stress. There is no way of deducing from certain principles what they will do, just because their behavior is not itself rational. One has to find out what they do. That is a matter of observation, which the economic theorists had taken all too lightly. Economic theory became a fascinating subject—the orthodox types particularly—when one began to take the mental operations of the theorists as the problem. . . .

Of course Veblen fitted perfectly into this set of notions. What drew me to him was his artistic side. . . . There was a man who really could

[2] Letter to John Maurice Clark, August 9, 1928. See Clark, *Preface to Social Economics*, p. 410. Originally printed in *Methods in Social Science*, edited by Stuart Rice.

[3] See note 1.

play with ideas! If one wanted to indulge in the game of spinning theories who could match his skill and humor? But if anything were needed to convince me that the standard procedure of orthodox economics could meet no scientific tests, it was that Veblen got nothing more certain by his dazzling performances with another set of premises. . . .

William Hill set me a course paper on "Wool Growing and the Tariff." I read a lot of the tariff speeches and got a new sidelight on the uses to which economic theory is adapted, and the ease with which it is brushed aside on occasion. Also I wanted to find out what really had happened to wool growers as a result of protection. The obvious thing to do was to collect and analyze the statistical data. . . . That was my first "investigation." . . .[4]

By the time he graduated from college, Mitchell knew he should devote himself to economic research. Laughlin and Dewey busied themselves on his account, and helped him find the material path to the doctorate, which he attained in 1899 *summa cum laude*. Mitchell embraced a university career eagerly. He began teaching at the University of Chicago in the autumn of 1900. In January 1903 he followed Adolph Miller, one of his former teachers, to the University of California. Mitchell liked teaching and always attended conscientiously to his classes, but he was the investigator first and teacher second. He valued the career of a university professor primarily because it enabled him to engage in creative investigation. From a year spent with the Census Office, he had learned that he could not be happy except as his own master. For a while he was an editorial writer for the *Chicago Tribune,* but newspaper work involved too many compromises with his sense of craftsmanship. He had a sample of executive work at Red Cross Headquarters in San Francisco after the earthquake, and as the superintendent of field work for the Immigration Commission while it was being organized. But he did not deem any of these tasks as significant as those he had found for himself.

II

The eighteen-nineties were an exciting period for a young man entering the study of economics. Agrarian discontent was widespread, and labor disputes ominous. Tariffs, trusts, railroads, and the income tax were much discussed, but the fate of the nation's monetary system dominated every other issue. The price of silver was declining, and the proponents of "easy money" campaigned actively for its "free and

[4] See Clark, *op. cit.,* pp. 411–2. Mitchell warned Clark that he might be rationalizing, and consented to the publication of the letter with considerable reluctance.

unlimited" coinage. Their cause was measurably advanced by an Act of 1890 requiring sharply increased purchases of silver by the Treasury. Fear for the safety of the gold standard and the established economic order spread. The Senate's passage of a free-coinage measure in 1892 intensified the anxiety of reputable circles. Foreign capitalists sought safety by dumping securities on the New York market, and withdrawing their balances in gold. Domestic hoarders added to the drain on bank reserves and on the Treasury's gold stocks. In May 1893 an old-fashioned panic broke loose, banks suspended or limited payments, and a severe depression of economic activity developed. Grave uncertainty about the nation's money continued until Bryan's decisive defeat at the polls in 1896 practically closed the issue for a generation.

These stirring events imparted a monetary slant to Wesley Mitchell's economic thinking, which deepened with the years. In the realistic atmosphere of Chicago's economics department, the subject of money was steadily and vigorously threshed out. To Professor J. Laurence Laughlin it was a plain duty to enlist the interest of students in the unsolved problem of the monetary standard. An apostle of "sound money," he fought heresy with unfailing energy. But he was as honest as he was orthodox, and did more to stimulate students to think for themselves than his more original colleagues. Laughlin warmly encouraged able youth. In March 1896 the *Journal of Political Economy,* of which he was editor, featured an article on "The Quantity Theory of the Value of Money" by Wesley Mitchell, then a senior at college.

This essay played a role in the polemical literature of its day, and makes interesting reading still, despite its youthful crudities. Some of the traits that made Mitchell a strong constructive force in economics—a concern with basic issues, analytical skill, lucidity, and predilection for statistical testing—are already in evidence. Most revealing of all is his emphasis on the complexity of the forces at work and the need for empirical testing. Let me quote a passage:

Deductive reasoning . . . is proverbially likely to lead the inquirer astray, unless its results are checked and corrected by inductive investigation. Such a theoretical examination as the above might well be complemented by applying the test of fact to the theory. If it were found to offer a satisfactory explanation of the price phenomena of actual life, a strong presumption would be created against the criticisms suggested. If, on the other hand, the theory failed to account for observed facts, the case against it would be more complete.[5]

[5] *Journal of Political Economy,* March 1896, pp. 157–8.

And having given his first public sermon on methodology, Mitchell proceeded to practice what he had preached. This college youth took it as a matter of course that a "workman who wanted to become a scientific worker" had a responsibility to check his speculative reasoning.[6]

During the next several years Mitchell contributed regularly to the *Journal of Political Economy*. Several of his articles dealt with the greenback issues of the Civil War—the subject of his doctoral dissertation. He got interested in the economic consequences of the greenbacks and, not being content with a qualitative analysis, "had to invent ways of measuring their effects." [7] The result was the substantial volume, *History of the Greenbacks,* which has served as a standard authority on the Civil War inflation since its publication in 1903.

In this work Mitchell analyzed the fiscal embarrassments of the federal government that led to the greenbacks, but he put the main emphasis on their broad consequences—the confusion in the monetary circulation, the premium on gold, the rise of commodity prices at wholesale and retail, and the intricate and painful readjustments of the earnings of the people. He did not explicitly raise any important questions about the theory of value and distribution, but his quantitative and historical approach forced to the surface various features of economic organization which had not received much attention in the theoretical literature. The usual explanations of the value of money stressed the quantity in circulation; yet Mitchell noticed that the premium on gold shifted regularly with the fortunes of the Northern armies. This fact among others led him to attribute the variations in the premium to the "varying estimates which the community was all the time making" of the government's ability to redeem its notes.[8] His studies indicated that during the Civil War the recipients of profits gained at the expense of the rest of the community, especially of persons who lent capital at interest. But why did the high rate of profit not lift the rate of interest? Here Mitchell found a place for uncertainty—that is, the inability to foresee changes in the price level. Again, Mitchell observed that the revolution in prices left some commodities behind, that wages lagged behind prices, and that the lag was not the same in all industries. These facts led him to examine the obstacles to "readjustment in the scale of money payments" [9]—contracts, convention, and the push and pull of the bargaining process. At a time when most economic theorists were busy reformulating the essentials of

[6] See Clark, *op. cit.*, p. 413.
[7] See note 1.

[8] *History of the Greenbacks,* p. 199.
[9] *Ibid.,* p. 139.

Ricardo's theory of competitive price or Cournot's theory of monopoly price, Mitchell was beginning to hammer out a new problem in price theory—the relations that bound prices together in a system of responses through time.

This problem came to his attention in the course of work with factual records. Mitchell's prodigious industry was revealed for the first time in his *History,* as was his superb skill in organizing a great mass of factual material and extracting from it significant generalizations. He made extensive new calculations, set out the statistical records in full, explained their derivation, and noted their shortcomings. An experimental mind was obviously at work, carefully checking one piece of evidence against another, yet stopping short of pedantry. So gracefully did Mitchell move back and forth between theoretical reasoning and factual documentation that the need for whatever statistical detail he presented was hardly ever left in doubt. These traits became more prominent still in Mitchell's later work.

The extensive experience with statistical records gained in writing the *History of the Greenbacks* led Mitchell to more discriminating views on the quantity theory of the value of money than he had expressed in his early essay. He now observed that statistical attempts to deal with the quantity theory "must always be inconclusive so long as there are no accurate data regarding the volume of exchanges to be performed by the use of money and the rapidity of circulation." Since even the quantity of money during the Civil War was shrouded in obscurity, "a rigorous comparison between the quantity and the gold value of the currency or between quantity and prices" was "out of the question." Mitchell nevertheless remained critical of the quantity theory, and advanced the hypothesis that "the quantity of the greenbacks influenced their specie value rather by affecting the credit of the government than by altering the volume of the circulating medium." [10] In an article published shortly after the *History of the Greenbacks,* Mitchell took a more constructive approach to the quantity theory, pointing out that the participants in the continuing debate failed to define basic concepts precisely or to measure the importance of variations in the money supply relatively to other factors. Repeating the self-criticism already made in the *History,* he noted also that his youthful essay on the subject was by no means blameless.[11] Forthrightness was one of Mitchell's outstanding traits, and is no less re-

[10] *Ibid.,* pp. 207–8.
[11] "The Real Issues in the Quantity Theory Controversy," *Journal of Political Economy,* June 1904, p. 405; and *History of the Greenbacks,* p. 208.

sponsible than his scientific craftsmanship for the moral authority he later exercised over his colleagues and, for that matter, over the entire profession of economics.

III

The California decade was decisive for Mitchell's personal and scientific life. Here he discovered Lucy Sprague, the gifted Dean of Women who in 1912 became his wife. Here he glimpsed the vision of an expanding money economy, and expressed its fundamental rhythm in his unforgettable *Business Cycles*. Here also he learned to get on with the two conflicting sides of his nature, each becoming more insistent: one driving him furiously to hypotheses of ever wider scope, the other holding him down to the facts needed to support or refute the generalizations.

Mitchell was a lonely man in these years of intellectual struggle, despite tennis and billiards, dining out and dancing parties. The last few years at California he withdrew more and more into himself, and worked hard even by his own standards. To Lucy Sprague he wrote before their marriage:

Outwardly I live in the accredited academic fashion, and doubtless I have insensibly acquired through long association pedantic modes of expression. But spiritually I acknowledge no kinship with these passive folk. My world is the world of thought; but the world of thought has a realm of action and I live there. It is a place where one has to depend upon himself—his own initiative, his own sustaining faith. My danger in this realm is not from lack of vigor, but from lack of caution.[12]

While working on the monetary upheaval of the Civil War, Mitchell gave much of his leisure to the history of economic institutions and ideas. These studies led him into ethnology and psychology, which soon consumed an increasing part of his energies. At California he had the opportunity to teach whatever subjects he liked and to experiment as he would. Mitchell flourished in this atmosphere of freedom. Promptly he settled on a course in primitive culture, exploring the "origin and early development of fundamental economic customs and institutions." This course in Economic Origins he supplemented with several on current organization—Principles of Economics, Money, Banking, and Problems of Labor. The experiment brought out in sharp relief the peculiar sway of pecuniary forces in modern society. Soon Mitchell was at work on a course in the Theory and History of Banking, trying to forge links between man's remote past and the current

[12] See note 1.

scheme of pecuniary institutions. At the same time he busied himself with technicalities of international finance, which he felt he needed to round out his knowledge of money. In the academic year 1905–06 he gave for the first time a course on the relation between the money economy and business fluctuations. Thus, his offering that year included Economic Origins, the Theory and History of Banking, and Economic Crises and Depressions in the fall semester; and Money, International Exchanges, and Problems of Labor in the spring. Two years later he began reaping the harvest of this extraordinary preparation for constructive work in economic theory. The courses on Economic Origins, Labor, and International Exchanges had served their purpose, and he supplanted them with the History of Economic Thought and Economic Psychology.

Mitchell has described succinctly this period of storm and stress:

When I came to California I still had the proofs of the *History of the Greenbacks* to read and the plan of a continuation from the close of the war to the resumption of specie payments to execute. While I was working on the latter, the ferment of philosophy and ethnology was gradually widening my notions of what economics ought to be. I held to my old tasks long enough to complete the statistical apparatus for the second volume on the greenbacks and to publish it as *Gold, Prices, and Wages under the Greenback Standard.* But I wanted to be at something larger in its scope and more penetrating in its interest than this detailed work with a passing episode in monetary history. My rather vague notions gradually crystallized into the idea that the important matter to understand about money is the money economy—that is, the cultural significance of the highly organized group of pecuniary institutions, how they have developed since the middle ages, how they have gained a quasi-independence, and how they have reacted upon the activity and the minds of their makers.[13]

Gold, Prices, and Wages was published in 1908. It satisfied Mitchell even less than the *History.* To a mind bent on large generalizations but willing to accept only what is rooted in experience, it was natural to think of *Gold, Prices, and Wages* as the "statistical apparatus of a book still to be written," just as it was natural to regard the *History* as a mere fragment.[14] The *History* was a monograph of a "fragmentary character" because it stopped short of the downward revolution in prices that followed the Civil War; also because it failed to compare the Civil War inflation with similar episodes across the centuries in this country and abroad. *Gold, Prices, and Wages* was the "statistical apparatus of a book still to be written" because it remedied

[13] *Ibid.*   [14] See the prefaces to both volumes.

only in part the first of these deficiencies of the *History*. But Mitchell's contemporaries shared neither his imperial conceptions nor his misgivings. The formidable companion piece of the *History* was quickly recognized as a great work of scholarship, and remains an authoritative source on the period from 1862 to 1878.

The statistical materials for the greenback period gave Mitchell a lively impression of the magnitude and diversity of economic fluctuations. During 1862–78 the country experienced two price revolutions, a major boom, a crisis, a great depression, and sundry minor fluctuations. These movements stood out in time series, clamoring for attention. At the close of the book Mitchell noted that his tables "suggest more problems than they solve." Let me quote from his concluding section on the "economic significance of the price-revolutions of the greenback period":

Perhaps the clearest conception of the price-revolutions is gained by regarding them as changes made by the business community in its effort to adapt itself to the monetary conditions created by an inconvertible paper currency. . . . An economic theorist, accustomed to imagine immediate and accurately gauged changes of prices occurring in a frictionless hypothetical market under the stimulus of some "disturbing factor," might perhaps regard this lagging of one class of prices behind another as an important deviation from the "natural" course of events. But a student of prices in less highly organized business communities, or an economic historian familiar with earlier price-revolutions, would be much more impressed by the rapidity and system with which prices of different classes of goods were changed, than by the lack of completeness in the adjustment.[15]

The "economic theorist" and "economic historian" of this quotation are, of course, none other than Wesley Mitchell himself. He had arrived at the conception of an interdependent system of prices, as had Walras and Marshall before him; and now, pondering the results of his statistical inquiries, he was feeling his way to the theory that this interdependent system, shot through as it was with lagged responses, generated business cycles instead of equilibrium.

IV

Monetary theory before 1914 was concerned mainly, if not exclusively, with the causes of variations in the value of money. This problem attracted Mitchell at the start of his scientific career, but

[15] *Gold, Prices, and Wages under the Greenback Standard*, pp. 281–3.

before a dozen years elapsed he broke through to a new conception. From the quantity theory of money he passed first to the analysis of a particular monetary inflation, next to the evolution of the price system and its impact on human behavior, later to the "recurring readjustments of prices" [16] which led him into business cycles.

Mitchell's interest during his early years at California centered on the evolution of the price system, its current institutions and their interactions. Ethnological studies had shown him that money was far more than the mere "contrivance for sparing time and labor" the classical economists had supposed it to be. The fact most suggestive of its part in economic development was that society has gradually evolved an economic organization based on the making and spending of money incomes. Between men's activities as producers of goods and their activities as consumers, a vast network of financial machinery and prices has intervened. "Monetary and banking systems, practices regarding mercantile credits, the pecuniary organization of business enterprises, the financial policies of governments, the interadjustments of the system of prices, the machinery of security markets, all are features of the money economy which man has made only to fall under their power." [17] The interrelations of prices, not industrial capacity or men's desire for useful commodities, determine what is now produced, how much is produced, and the shares of the final product accruing to participants in the productive process. Since money is the key to the understanding of economic life, it must be the root of economic science. Mitchell turned to this grand theme, and started writing a "Theory of the Money Economy."

The manuscript of *Gold, Prices, and Wages* was completed toward the end of June 1907. Several weeks earlier Mitchell had begun drafting the first chapter of the "Theory of the Money Economy." He stayed with this manuscript until March 1908, when he shifted to work he had agreed to do for the Immigration Commission. From the end of April through the summer he was fully occupied with this activity. The following academic year he lectured at Harvard on money and business cycles. Although his academic duties left little time for the "Theory of the Money Economy," he managed to go through a considerable amount of historical literature and to look into statistical records, especially such as bore on the crisis of 1907. Meanwhile he

[16] See Clark, *op. cit.,* p. 414.

[17] Mitchell, "The Rationality of Economic Activity," *Journal of Political Economy,* March 1910, p. 209.

had become uneasy about his manuscript, and began modifying plans in a fateful direction. In his own words:

I was working away from any solid foundation—having a good time, but sliding gayly over abysses I had not explored. One of the most formidable was the recurring readjustments of prices, which economists treated apart from their general theories of value, under the caption "Crises." I had to look into the problem.[18]

When Mitchell returned to California in the autumn of 1909, he brought with him a firm resolve to work out promptly "the subject of 'Business Cycles' as a *Vorarbeit* of the 'Money Economy.' " [19]

He lost no time getting started and worked at a feverish pace, seeking to embrace every significant aspect of economic activity in the countries in which the money economy had reached its fullest expression—the United States, Great Britain, Germany, and France. Not finding the statistics he needed on commodity prices, wages, stock prices, bond prices, bond yields, or the money supply, he made extensive calculations, pioneering boldly in each field. The work prospered. In April 1911 Mitchell wrote exultantly: "The various difficulties of explanation seem to dissolve of themselves as I approach." There were occasional setbacks: "Now that I've come to the point of discussing crises themselves I am temporarily at a loss. Everything happens all at once, and to arrange an orderly exposition is more difficult than I had supposed." But the setback was momentary; within a fortnight the chapter on "Crises" was drafted. Mitchell was pleased as he stopped to look back: "My own impression is that the chapters are rather good—particularly the crucial one on the breeding of crises." [20] Months of recasting and revision followed. Finally, on October 15, 1912, he sent the last of the manuscript off to the printer. Except for the proofs, *Business Cycles,* a 600 page quarto, was completed. In the amazingly short time of three years, Mitchell had worked out and written one of the masterpieces in the world's economic literature. And this burst of creative activity carried with it other outstanding achievements, among them the articles on "The Rationality of Economic Activity" and "The Backward Art of Spending Money."

Business Cycles is a beautifully organized and closely reasoned treatise. More than that, it is a landmark in the development of economics. No other work between Marshall's *Principles* and Keynes' *General Theory* has had as big an influence on the economic thought

[18] Clark, *op. cit.,* p. 414.
[19] See note 1.
[20] From letters to a friend, between April 3 and May 2, 1911.

of the Western World. The simplest way to make clear the novelty and scientific force of Mitchell's work is to compare his approach to business cycles with that of earlier investigators.

The traditional method of accounting for business cycles was to start from simple assumptions, based on common sense, concerning the state of business in equilibrium or in "late" prosperity or depression; then call attention to some new factor arising from within or outside the business situation; finally, show how the adaptations of the business community to the new factor generated a cyclical movement. Since imaginative thinkers had no difficulty in assigning a critical role to one factor after another, plausible theories of business cycles multiplied abundantly. Occasionally a theorist would use statistical data, but as a rule their function, when called upon at all, was merely to support or illustrate a particular stage of an argument. Mitchell broke with this tradition. Instead of starting theoretical analysis with assumptions concerning the state of business in late depression, such as might be suggested by common sense, he started with assumptions derived from systematic observations of experience. Again, instead of passing from these assumptions, reinforced by others about the arts and human motives, to supposedly tight inferences concerning the condition of business in the next stage of the cycle and stopping there, Mitchell checked his reasoning by consulting systematic observations of experience. This plan of working had two revolutionary consequences. First, business cycle theory became, or at least approached, a tested explanation of experience instead of an exercise in logic. Second, in the process of observing economic life in its many ramifications, the theory of business cycles broadened into a theory of how our economic organization works.

Mitchell began with a review of current theories of business cycles, then paused to outline his method of investigation:

One seeking to understand the recurrent ebb and flow of economic activity characteristic of the present day finds these numerous explanations both suggestive and perplexing. All are plausible, but which is valid? None necessarily excludes all the others, but which is the most important? . . .

There is slight hope of getting answers to these questions by a logical process of proving and criticizing the theories. For whatever merits of ingenuity and consistency they may possess, these theories have slight value except as they give keener insight into the phenomena of business cycles. It is by study of the facts which they purport to interpret that the theories must be tested.

But the perspective of the investigation would be distorted if we set out to test each theory in turn. . . . For the point of interest is not the validity of any writer's views, but clear comprehension of the facts. To observe, analyze, and systematize the phenomena of prosperity, crisis, and depression is the chief task.[21]

Before passing to this task, Mitchell developed his theoretical orientation in a chapter on the organization of the money economy, so that the statistical facts could be seen as "details of a larger system." The "system" rests on the proposition that the ebb and flow of activity depends on the prospects of profits, except in times of crisis when a quest for solvency supplants profits as the main driving force of business enterprise. Mitchell used current theories of business cycles as suggestions concerning the processes that were worth examining, and his sketch of the money economy as the analytical framework into which the statistical chapters of Part II were fitted. Every one of these chapters "bears upon the crucial problem of business profits, either by dealing with factors which determine profits, like prices and the volume of trade; or by dealing with necessary conditions for the successful quest of profits, like the currency, banking, and investment; or by offering direct gauges of business success and failure, like the statistics of profits themselves and of bankruptcies." And just as Mitchell's theoretical sketch of the "controlling factors" in a money economy provided a framework for the statistical analysis in Part II, so also it provided a framework for the theoretical analysis of "The Rhythm of Business Activity" in Part III.[22]

Mitchell's theory is cast in a mould of evolutionary concepts. Business cycles are not merely fluctuations in aggregate activity, but fluctuations that are widely diffused through the economy. They are therefore a product of culture, and arise only when economic activities have become largely organized on the basis of making and spending money incomes. Again, business cycles are not minor or accidental disruptions of equilibrium, but fluctuations systematically generated by economic organization itself. As prosperity cumulates, costs in many lines of activity encroach upon selling prices, money markets become strained, and numerous investment projects are set aside until costs of financing seem more favorable; these accumulating stresses within the system of business enterprise lead to a recession of activity, which spreads over the economy and for a time gathers force; but the realignment of costs and prices, reduction of inventories, improvement of bank

[21] *Business Cycles*, pp. 19–20. Part III of this volume was reprinted in 1941 by the original publisher, the University of California Press, under the title *Business Cycles and Their Causes*.
[22] *Business Cycles*, pp. 20, 91, 92.

reserves, and other developments of depression gradually pave the way for a renewed expansion of activity. In this theoretical scheme "the recurring readjustments of prices," which first attracted Mitchell's curiosity, play a crucial role, but so too do a host of interrelated industrial and financial changes. Each phase of the business cycle evolves into its successor, while economic organization itself gradually undergoes cumulative changes. Hence, Mitchell believed, "it is probable that the economists of each generation will see reason to recast the theory of business cycles which they learned in their youth." [23]

"The case for the present theory," Mitchell concluded, "and also the case against it, is to be found . . . in an independent effort to use it in interpreting the ceaseless ebb and flow of economic activity." In the years that have elapsed since the publication of Mitchell's classic, knowledge of business fluctuations has been appreciably extended. Yet I know of no theoretical work that, taken as a whole, has met as well as Mitchell's old book "the practical test of accounting for actual business experience." [24] No one else has succeeded in tracing with comparable skill or knowledge the interlacing and readjustment of economic activities in the course of a business cycle, or developed as fully or as faithfully the typical process by which one stage of the business cycle gradually evolves into the next. I venture the prophecy that if Mitchell's homely work of 1913 were translated into the picturesque vocabulary of "propensities," "multipliers," "acceleration coefficients" and the like, it would create a sensation in the theoretical world, especially if the translator were mindful enough to shift passages here and there from the indicative to the conditional mood. However that may be, it is worth noting and remembering that much of the special vocabulary of today's theorizing centers around economic fluctuations, and that this was already Mitchell's central theoretical problem before World War I.

V

Mitchell put the finishing touches on the manuscript of *Business Cycles* in London during October 1912. Upon his return in December he took up residence in New York, wishing to observe the nerve center of the money economy at close range. He joined the Columbia faculty in 1913, and soon achieved outstanding success as a teacher. Between the completion of *Business Cycles* and the inception of his researches at the National Bureau, Mitchell largely devoted his time to empirical studies of prices and critical and historical studies of economic theory.

[23] *Ibid.*, p. 583.   [24] *Ibid.*, p. 570.

During this period he wrote a masterly paper on Wieser's *Social Economics,* then unknown to English-speaking readers, and the famous essays "The Role of Money in Economic Theory" and "Bentham's Felicific Calculus." [25]   The latter was originally intended as a chapter of a book on Types of Economic Theory which Mitchell began writing in 1916. Upon entering government service early in 1918, as Chief of the Price Section of the War Industries Board, he had to lay this manuscript aside. He returned to it briefly after the war and looked forward to completing it when he finished his new work on business cycles. But he never reached this stage, and the manuscript on types of theory remains an unpublished fragment. Some notion of its intellectual flavor may be gained from the essays [26] collected in 1937 by Professor Joseph Dorfman under the title *The Backward Art of Spending Money;* though this volume gives hardly an inkling of the historical range of Mitchell's uncompleted manuscript, or of his brilliant analysis of the social conditions out of which classical political economy and its offshoots developed.

In 1914 Royal Meeker invited Mitchell to write an introduction to a bulletin by the Bureau of Labor Statistics on index numbers of wholesale prices. Mitchell responded with "The Making and Using of Index Numbers" [27]—a monograph in which he extended his earlier experiments in measurement, and discussed at length the practical problems involved in constructing and using index numbers. This study has had an enormous influence on statistical understanding and practice, both in this country and elsewhere. As late as 1938 the Bureau of Labor Statistics reissued the monograph to meet the "continuing demand, particularly in colleges and universities." [28]   After completing the work on indexes of wholesale prices, Mitchell turned to a companion piece on stock prices, which was published in the *Journal of Political Economy* for July 1916.

Another of Mitchell's achievements just before the National Bureau got under way was the preparation of the *History of Prices during the War* under the auspices of the War Industries Board. Mitchell edited

[25] All three are reprinted in *The Backward Art of Spending Money.*

[26] Besides the one on Bentham, the paper on "Postulates and Preconceptions of Ricardian Economics," published in 1929, was adapted from his manuscript, which was the foundation also of some of his lectures at Columbia on Types of Economic Theory. A mimeographed edition of the lectures, taken down stenographically by a student on his own responsibility, has circulated fairly widely, and has recently been reissued by Augustus M. Kelley, Inc. (New York).

[27] *Index Numbers of Wholesale Prices in the United States and Foreign Countries,* Bulletin of the U. S. Bureau of Labor Statistics, No. 173, July 1915.

[28] Bulletin No. 656 of the Bureau of Labor Statistics, p. iii.

the publication and wrote two of its fifty-seven bulletins—*International Price Comparisons* and the *Summary*. One scientific novelty of the *Summary* is a production index constructed so as to be precisely comparable with a price index. As far as I know, no one had ever carried out this obvious but significant step before. Indeed, Mitchell was the first investigator to attack systematically the technical problems of weighting and industry grouping in the construction of a production index.

VI

At heart Wesley Mitchell was a reformer. Ever since taking up residence in New York he had participated in social causes—settlement work, woman suffrage, better schooling, adult education. These activities were dear to Mitchell, yet he had no great faith in the improvisations of reformers. The reliable path to social reform, he felt, was through scientific investigation of social processes.

The course of events during 1914–20 tested and favored Mitchell's approach to economics. The threatening rise in prices was turning men's minds to the problem of business cycles. The war experience with economic mobilization emphasized the need for accurate quantitative information on national income, inventories, prices, the labor supply, and other basic factors in the economy. An increasing number of men now shared a sense of urgency about empirical research, if not faith in an empirical science of economics. In this atmosphere of social thinking Wesley Mitchell joined Malcolm Rorty, N. I. Stone, and Edwin F. Gay in organizing the National Bureau of Economic Research "to encourage, in the broadest and most liberal manner, investigation, research and discovery, and the application of knowledge to the well-being of mankind; and in particular to conduct, or assist in the making of, exact and impartial investigations in the field of economic, social and industrial science." [29]

Mitchell was forty-five when he assumed, early in 1920, direction of the National Bureau. He brought rich personal gifts to the venture: character, a judicial temperament, self-assurance mellowed by wisdom, exacting scientific standards, a kind and understanding nature. More than that, he was a tireless scientific explorer, committed to social improvement through science and reason. He regarded the Bureau as an experiment which, if successful, might lead to similar work by others, the joint effort becoming in time a powerful instrumentality of progress. The Bureau meant also personal fulfillment. Here empirical investi-

[29] National Bureau, *Charter and By-Laws.*

gations might be undertaken, broader and more fundamental than any yet attempted by economists. Here complementary technical skills could be pooled, and the process of developing new knowledge made more efficient. Here an investigator could subject his methods and results to the steady and searching scrutiny of skilled colleagues. Here hypotheses could be checked by statistical data, statistical data stimulate new hypotheses, and hypotheses new data. Here tested findings could cumulate, reinforce one another, and open up new problems, as was routine in the established sciences. Most important of all, here was an experiment in democratic action, men of many shades of political opinion joining in the undramatic enterprise of reviewing the factual findings of a technical staff. If a group so constituted as the National Bureau's Board of Directors could work harmoniously and accept staff investigations of a controversial question such as the proportion of the national income paid out in wages or accruing as profits, might not reason triumph over passion in an ever widening circle of men? Stirred by this vision, Mitchell put his great energies to the Bureau's task at once. His faith never wavered.

The subject selected by the Board of Directors for its first study was the size of the national income and its distribution. Nothing could have been more congenial to Mitchell. If modern economic life is organized on the basis of making and spending money incomes, economic analysis should start from that fact. From its original focus of national income, the National Bureau's research program moved outward, not according to a rigid plan, but on a principle enunciated by Mitchell at the beginning. Let me quote from his First Annual Report to the Board: [30]

I should like to submit a general suggestion, regarding the principle upon which future topics should be chosen. I think we should plan to complete our studies of the National Income, and work outward from that central field. It may be desirable to take up a few incidental inquiries . . . which we can manage without serious derangement of our main program; but it would be poor policy to scatter our energy over a considerable number of unrelated topics, however fascinating.

If you approve of the general policy I am suggesting, it would probably mean that after the current report is finished, we should take up for careful study the shares of wages, rent, interest and profits, and the subject of savings versus current consumption. . . . It is quite possible that still other investigations supplementing our first report may seem to be desirable by the time that report is finished.

May I also suggest one topic on which we shall come as soon as we move

[30] Presented February 7, 1921, not published.

outward from our central field? Our preliminary figures indicate that the
National Income can scarcely be large enough to secure what we consider
a decent standard of living for all American families. If the final figures
are not much larger than we anticipate, they will lend new emphasis to the
call for a greater output of staple commodities. But while all the producing interests may admit the desirability of having more and better food,
clothing, and housing for our people, they also point out the difficulty of
finding profitable markets for the current output. Here lies, indeed, the
great economic problem of the future. . . .

Mitchell's suggestion of a basis for choosing new topics guided the
National Bureau's development over the years. First, the subject of
business cycles was added to the program, then the labor market, commodity prices, industrial productivity, financial operations, fiscal problems, and recently, international economic relations. From time to
time the Bureau has undertaken *ad hoc* investigations, but its broad
history has been one of concentration on relatively few subjects, not
piecemeal research. The program has developed from within the investigations themselves, one study growing out of another, reinforcing
the studies in progress, making its direct contribution, and in turn raising fresh problems. Thus the deliberateness and consistency which
guided Mitchell's life since boyhood became imbedded in the Bureau's
work and shaped its development. By creating an atmosphere in which
scientific work could flourish and in which capable investigators could
work cooperatively, Mitchell laid the foundation for a research program
that in time became cumulative and self-reinforcing, and which established the Bureau as one of the leading agencies in the world for scientific research in economics.

VII

Mitchell remained a working scientist while he served as Director of
Research of the National Bureau. Although he gave up this office in
1945, he continued as an active member of the research staff until his
death. Mitchell did not permit administrative work at the Bureau or
professorial duties at Columbia to consume all his energy, as they easily
might have. He was co-author of the first National Bureau publication,
Income in the United States, Vol. I (1921). In 1927 his *Business
Cycles: The Problem and Its Setting* was published. He was co-author
of several other Bureau volumes: *Business Cycles and Unemployment*
(1923), *Business Annals* (1926), *Recent Economic Changes* (1929),
Measuring Business Cycles (1946), and *Economic Research and the
Development of Economic Science and Public Policy* (1946). He con-

tributed to the Bureau's *Bulletin* and *Occasional Papers,* wrote enlightening introductions to many Bureau monographs, and a long series
of *Annual Reports* which stimulated economic thinking and research at
large. But the publications that bear Mitchell's name cannot by themselves convey his part in the Bureau's work on business cycles, or his
role in inspiring and bringing to fruition its other investigations.

In economic literature there are many concepts of business cycles,
not just one. Some familiarity with Mitchell's particular concept is
essential if the epic proportions of the investigation he launched in 1922
are to be understood. To Mitchell a business cycle meant more than
a fluctuation in a single aggregate such as national income or employment. It meant also that the fluctuation is recurrent, and that certain
repetitive features run through the recurrences. And especially it
meant that the fluctuation is diffused through economic activity—appearing, as a rule, in prices as well as industrial activities, in markets
for securities as well as for commodities and labor, in processes of
saving and investment, in finance as well as in industry and commerce.
Systematic fluctuations of this character are distinct from the irregular
disturbances and seasonal rhythms to which business is commonly exposed. Not only that, they emerge at a late stage in the evolution of
the money economy, when processes of production and consumption
have become broadly organized on the basis of making and spending
money incomes. Fluctuations of this type—that is, business cycles—
can hardly occur until the different parts of an economy have been
linked together by complex agencies of transport and credit. To understand how business cycles have emerged is to understand how our
"business economy" has developed. And if business cycles are "not
one phenomenon, but a congeries of interrelated phenomena," [31] any
distinction between the problem of how business cycles run their course
and of how our economic organization works cannot be other than
artificial. In an outline of an Introductory Course in Economics that
Mitchell once drew up, he put a section at the end entitled "Economic
Process in Motion." [32] Its content was expressed in the following note:
"Business prosperity, crisis, depression, and revival, discussed so as to
bring in and review all that has gone before." In other words, business
cycles encompassed the entire field of economics, and a theory of business cycles was to be a theory of capitalism itself.

[31] *Business Cycles: The Problem and Its Setting,* pp. 63, 454.

[32] The outline is undated. From Mitchell's correspondence I judge that it was
probably drafted May 23, 1909, in preparation for Introduction to Economics,
which he was scheduled to teach in the fall. Note that he was then not yet working on his *Business Cycles.*

This sweeping notion was already contained in Mitchell's 1913 volume, but he now tried to work out its implications more fully. The statistical basis of the old book was restricted to a brief period, 1890–1911. It leaned heavily upon annual data, which often obscure essential features of business fluctuations. Its statistical techniques seemed primitive in the light of devices that time-series analysts were beginning to develop. Most serious of all, there were gaps in the evidence—especially on construction, inventories, retail trade, personal incom~ and business profits. In view of the rapid accumulation of new r~ and the improving knowledge about business fluctuations, Mi~ eager to make a fresh attack upon the entire problem. At ~ ning he expected that a single volume would suffice for a "sy~ treatise." But as his irrepressible instinct of workmanship as~ its authority, the investigation deepened and lengthened. In reporting to the Board early in 1924 Mitchell observed: "I am eager to get the work done as rapidly as possible, but I am still more eager to do it as well as I can—and that takes time." [33] The first instalment, *Business Cycles: The Problem and Its Setting,* did not appear until 1927.

In the preface Mitchell explained that he was conducting the inquiry on the "general plan" of the 1913 volume. He added:

My earlier impressions that business cycles consist of exceedingly complex interactions among a considerable number of economic processes, that to gain insight into these interactions one must combine historical studies with quantitative and qualitative analysis, that the phenomena are peculiar to a certain form of economic organization, and that understanding of this scheme of institutions is prerequisite to an understanding of cyclical fluctuations—these impressions have been confirmed. . . .

The confirmation came through extensive new research. Mitchell was now investigating business cycles on a scale that made his formidable 1913 volume look like an introductory sketch. While *The Problem and Its Setting* is a book of substantial size, its scope corresponds merely to the first three chapters of the 1913 volume—that is, to ninety of its six hundred pages. In the new volume Mitchell recorded what he had discovered in his extensive intellectual travels: what hypotheses concerning business cycles the theorists have developed, what statisticians have found out about various types of fluctuations, and how reporters have described each year's business since 1790 in the United States and Great Britain and for shorter periods in another fifteen countries. But Mitchell went beyond an encyclopedic report. His interpretation of the

[33] Annual Report of the Director of Research, Feb. 4, 1924 (unpublished).

procedures and findings of time-series specialists illuminated a new literature for both novice and expert. His description of modern economic organization, while designed from the viewpoint of a student of business cycles, is virtually a survey of the field of economics, and I believe one of the most instructive ever written. His analysis of the duration of business cycles is still the one authoritative treatment of that complex subject. His handling of the factor of time in the equation of exchange is a theoretical contribution of lasting value. Mitchell's scholarly feat was acclaimed by professional and lay readers alike. The first printing was soon exhausted, and the book has been reprinted a dozen times. It was translated into Russian and German. No volume published by the National Bureau has approximated its sales.

Only at the end of *The Problem and Its Setting* was Mitchell prepared to define business cycles, and the definition he framed was a working definition—that is, a definition to guide research. How have wage rates behaved during recent and distant depressions? Does consumer spending characteristically lead or lag behind investment at recoveries? What are the relations in time between consumer spending and national income? between consumer spending and employment? How do inventories behave from stage to stage of the business cycle? Does the volume of the circulating medium rise and fall in harmony with industrial activity? Is the volume of investment materially affected in the short run by the rate of change in sales? How are the cyclical turning points in the profits of individual concerns distributed around the turning points of aggregate profits? Questions of this character go to the very heart of the operation of our economic system. Since reliable answers did not exist, Mitchell felt that economists and men of affairs lacked a solid foundation for dealing with business cycles. "Overtaken by a series of strange experiences our predecessors leaped to a broad conception" of economic cycles, "gave it a name, and began to invent explanations, as if they knew what their words meant." [34] This method of working yielded quick results, but they could not be depended upon. To theorize responsibly it was essential to know definitely the actual behavior for which the theory was supposed to account. Instead of undertaking a fresh explanation of business cycles, Mitchell therefore first set about determining as precisely as he could what the business cycles of actual life have been like. In so doing he no more ignored the theories of other writers than his own; but he took existing explanations as guides to research, rather than as objects of research.

[34] *Business Cycles: The Problem and Its Setting*, p. 2.

An economist who works with only a few time series can get along without a special technique of analysis. Mitchell's plan, however, compelled work with a wide range of observations. To gain a just view of business cycles and their causes, the number of time series could hardly be smaller than the number of processes that reputable theorists have alleged to be strategic. That the number should, in fact, be much larger was plain at an early stage, partly because it seemed wise to examine the records of at least several countries, partly because the frequent imperfections of statistical data made extensive crosschecks necessary, partly because new theoretical problems were suggested in the course of work with the data. But if hundreds of time series are to be compared—some covering little more than a decade and others over a century, some representing one country and others a second or third—a systematic technique becomes necessary. In the closing chapter of *The Problem and Its Setting* Mitchell sketched a novel method of analyzing the cyclical behavior of time series. This method he amended after some experimentation. Other investigators soon joined in the task of developing the technique, and improved its power to establish what characteristics of business cycles are stable and what characteristics are variable. Preliminary versions of the technique appeared from time to time as the work progressed. But a full and definitive account was postponed until 1946 when *Measuring Business Cycles,* on which I collaborated with Mitchell, was published.

Even before *The Problem and Its Setting* was completed, Mitchell began experimenting with the results yielded by his new apparatus. The interpretation of results thus went hand in hand with compiling time series, developing a technique of measurement, and applying the technique to the data—each operation reacting on the others. In his first use of the results, Mitchell followed a plan similar to that of Part III in his 1913 volume. But as he attempted to carry out an analytical trip around the business cycle, he found gaps in his knowledge—some of which could be filled by a more thorough mastery of the statistical materials. Hence he embarked on an intensive analysis of the cyclical behavior of leading economic processes—production of commodities, construction work, transportation and communication, commodity prices, wholesale and retail trade, inventories in different hands, foreign commerce, personal incomes, business profits and losses, security markets, savings and investment, interest rates, banking and the currency. In the 1913 volume Mitchell had written:

The present theory of business cycles deals almost wholly with the pecuniary phases of economic activity. The processes described are concerned with changes in prices, investments of funds, margins of profit, market capitalization of business enterprises, credits, the maintenance of solvency, and the like—all relating to the making of money, rather than to the making of goods or to the satisfaction of wants. Only two nonpecuniary factors command much attention—changes in the physical volume of trade and in the efficiency of labor—and even these two are treated with reference to their bearing upon present and prospective profits.[35]

In his new investigation, Mitchell put greater emphasis on the physical side of economic activity. He began his examination of the cyclical behavior of individual processes with production instead of prices, and explored the organization and technology of different industries, seeking to distinguish situations in which output could respond readily to business motives in the short run from others in which output was not subject to close business control. The physical processes of employing labor and other resources, and of ordering, producing, holding, and using commodities were still interpreted in their pecuniary bearings. But Mitchell was steadily broadening his analysis of the workings of our economic organization, and he did not shrink from going as far below the "money surface" as seemed necessary to comprehend the impulses originating changes in output, and the agencies—technical, legal, psychological, or financial—through which adaptations to new circumstances were continually being made.

By 1932 Mitchell had drafted a sizable manuscript on the cyclical behavior of leading economic activities, taken singly and in combination. He expected to follow this volume with another devoted to theoretical analysis. But he was not satisfied with the manuscript, and after rewriting it more than once continued to feel that he had not mastered adequately the vital processes of which his time series were only the symbols. Around 1938 he reached the conclusion that the authoritative investigation of the operations of our economic system for which he was, in fact, striving required expert knowledge of business and industrial practices beyond what he possessed or could easily acquire. The upshot was an enlargement of the staff. Several collaborators took on the task of extending and refining Mitchell's analysis of the cyclical behavior of leading processes, while he shifted his focus from specific activities to the changes in the internal organization of the economy that occur during a typical business cycle.

Thus the simple conception of the original plan [36]—that is, a "systematic treatise" by Mitchell, supplemented by "two or three special

[35] *Business Cycles*, pp. 596–7.

[36] See *A Bold Experiment: The Story of the National Bureau of Economic Research* (Second Annual Report of the Director of Research, February 6, 1922), pp. 9, 10.

studies of topics that have never been adequately investigated"—was progressively modified as the investigation of business cycles unfolded. In the hands of an alert investigator, empirical research has the refreshing quality of springing ever new surprises. In working on the systematic treatise, Mitchell discovered not "two or three," but numerous topics that had never been adequately investigated, and that nevertheless seemed indispensable to a scientific understanding of business cycles in the actual world. He had the habit of examining new evidence all the time, and this kept reminding him of what he did not know. As his task grew, he invited other investigators to join in the enterprise, who in their turn opened up new problems. Work on "special studies" therefore expanded, the "systematic treatise" burst through the limits of a single volume, and various byproducts of that treatise developed into independent studies. For example, Kuznets' study of seasonal fluctuations grew directly out of Mitchell's investigation of business cycles; so did Macaulay's work on interest rates and security markets, Thorp's on business annals, Wolman's on trade unionism, Clark's on "strategic factors," Hultgren's on transportation, Evans' on incorporations, Abramovitz' on inventories, much of Mills' on prices, and so on. A general idea of how the program developed in the course of a quarter century's research may be derived from the Bureau's numerous publications that take business cycles as their main theme.

Through all changes of plan and conception, a systematic treatise that would deal comprehensively with business cycles and their causes remained Mitchell's goal. Its living shape is the National Bureau's series, Studies in Business Cycles. The final instalment of the series was to be a theoretical account of what business cycles are, how they typically run their course, and of their tendencies toward variation. Mitchell devoted his last years to this effort, trying to fit together the pieces on which his colleagues were at work. He planned a "progress report" in two volumes that would sum up what he had been able to learn about business cycles. The subtitle of the first volume was to be "The Many in the One," and of the second "The One in the Many." As a scientist and philosopher Mitchell had searched long and patiently for "the many in the one, the one in the many." His first volume was nearly completed when he died on October 29, 1948, at the age of seventy-four. It is only a fragment of the work he had planned, yet no other study in existence elucidates so fully or so authoritatively how economic activities fare, both severally and collectively, during a typical business cycle of our modern economy. This work was recently published by the National Bureau under the title *What Happens during Business Cycles.*

VIII

During the long years of specialization in business cycles, which made Mitchell the foremost world authority on the subject, he remained a general economist concerned with the whole social process—at once economist and statistician, theorist and historian, philosopher and social scientist. Although he never returned to his manuscript on "The Theory of the Money Economy," its intellectual impulse remained with him. In one paper after another, he developed his basic theme that if economic theory was to play a useful role in social reform, it had to grasp "the relations between the pecuniary institutions which civilized man is perfecting, the human nature which he inherits from savage ancestors, and the new forces which science lends him." [37] Time and again, also, he developed his implemental theme that objective, quantitative studies are essential to a scientific understanding of economic life in its current institutional setting.

One of Mitchell's last essays, "The Role of Money in Economic History," sums up his reflections on "how monetary forms have infiltrated one human relation after another, and their effects upon men's practices and habits of thought." I shall quote what Mitchell has to say concerning the influence of the money economy on "man's efforts to know himself":

By giving economic activity an immediate objective aim, and by providing a common denominator in terms of which all costs and all gains can be adequately expressed for business purposes, the use of money provided a technically rational scheme for guiding economic effort. It thereby paved the way for economic theory; for technically rational conduct can be reasoned out, and in that sense explained. But money economy does this job of rationalizing conduct only in a superficial sense, and unwary observers of human behavior fell into the trap it had set. Thoroughly disciplined citizens of the money economy readily assumed that all economic behavior is rational, and when they tried to penetrate beneath the money surface of things they found no absurdity in supposing that men do psychic bookkeeping in pains and pleasures as they do pecuniary bookkeeping in outgo and income. . . . Following the money-making pattern, economic theory became, not an account of actual behavior such as historians attempt to provide, but an analysis of what it is to the interest of men to do under a variety of imagined conditions. . . .[38]

Mitchell found much of the traditional body of economic theory faulty, not because it was mechanical, but because, lacking institutional

[37] *Business Cycles,* p. 599.
[38] *Journal of Economic History,* Supplement IV, December 1944, pp. 61, 64–5.

perspective, it was naively mechanical. He well knew that "the use
of money and the pecuniary way of thinking it begets is a most important factor in the modern situation." Hence "to isolate this factor,
to show what economic life would be if it dominated human nature, is
to clarify our understanding of economic processes." But he regretted
that the theorists who worked on this plan "have not emphasized the
monographic character of their work." [39] He put his criticism as
follows:

A man who realizes that he is studying an institution keeps his work in
historical perspective, even when he confines himself to analyzing the form
that the institution has assumed at a particular stage of its evolution. By
so doing he opens vistas enticing to future exploration, instead of suggesting
a closed system of knowledge. He does not delude himself into believing
that anyone's personal experience is an adequate basis for theorizing about
how men behave; rather is he eager to profit by any light shed upon his
problem by any branch of learning—history, statistics, ethnology, psychology.[40]

Veblen's and Commons' work, Mitchell felt, was also of a monographic
character, and of course the "institutionalists" were not the only economists concerned with institutions. Let me quote another telling passage:

Veblen's analysis of the cultural incidence of the machine process and of
business traffic takes for granted knowledge of how prices are fixed and
of the bearing of prices upon the distribution of income. Every scheme
of institutions has an implicit logic of its own, and it is no less important
to know what that logic is than to know how the institutions came into
being and what they are becoming. When . . . Davenport defined economics as the science that treats phenomena from the standpoint of price,
and insisted that it must be written "from the private and acquisitive point
of view," he was elaborating the logic of pecuniary institutions. . . .
Though Davenport explicitly ruled cultural evolution out of economics, he
was contributing toward the understanding of one set of institutions.[41]

Thus orthodox price theory was "institutional" but "monographic,"
since it was not concerned with the evolution of economic organization.
It was "monographic" also because it failed to differentiate sufficiently
between the "work of the captains" of modern business, where its
reasonings applied tolerably well, and "the work of the rank and file"
and "activities of consumption," where its reasonings applied badly.[42]

[39] *The Backward Art of Spending Money,* p. 158.
[40] *Ibid.,* p. 256.
[41] *Ibid.,* pp. 338–9.
[42] "The Rationality of Economic Activity," *Journal of Political Economy,*
March 1910, p. 201.

Hence, it was critically important to determine what men actually do, and not take on faith attempts to think out what it is in the interest of men to do.

Games and puzzles of all sorts, not least those contrived by the more subtle of the economic theorists, fascinated Mitchell; but he found the solution of puzzles turned up by actual events not less delightful and much more rewarding. He looked forward to an economics that would be immersed in "the objective validity of the account it gives of economic processes." He put his "ultimate trust in observation" and expected this approach ultimately to prevail. As economists concerned themselves increasingly with actual human behavior, rather than equilibrating adjustments under assumed conditions, the efforts of economic historians and theorists would be fused and the scope of economic theory expanded. Hypothetical schedules of utility and disutility would give way to realistic accounts of processes by which the valuations of men are moulded. But the striving of economists to fashion a science of human behavior would not render equilibrium price theory useless. "On the contrary, not only will it make clear the limitations of the older work, but it will also show how the old inquiries may be carried further, and how they may be fitted into a comprehensive study of economic behavior." The theory of value and distribution, in its traditional sense, would therefore remain a concern of economists, although it would recede from its central position.[43]

Mitchell's faith in social science sprang from his faith in mankind. He expected that as economics took on the shape of a cumulating quantitative science, it would become an increasingly potent factor in social change.

Such topics as the economic serviceability of advertising, the reactions of an unstable price level upon production, the effect of various systems of public regulation upon the services rendered by public utilities will be treated with incisive vigor as we become able to make the indispensable measurements. And investigations of this type will broaden out into a constructive criticism of that dominant complex of institutions known as the money economy—a constructive criticism which may guide the efforts of our children to make that marvelously flexible form of organization better fitted to their needs.[44]

Repeatedly Mitchell pointed to the shortcomings of our economic organization. "The frequent recurrence of economic crises and depressions," he noted, "is evidence that the automatic functioning of our

---

[43] *The Backward Art of Spending Money,* pp. 36, 371, 376.
[44] *Ibid.,* p. 30.

business system is defective." [45] Business planning had found no effective means of checking depressions, or preventing developments that tend to increase the business cycle hazard, or providing economic security for wage earners, or restraining the formation of monster combinations, or conserving the nation's heritage of natural resources, or providing for the satisfactory training of underprivileged youth for responsibilities of industry and citizenship. To Mitchell the existence of these grave problems demonstrated a need for greater knowledge of human behavior. The following is a characteristic utterance:

When for any reason it is not profitable to make goods we are forced to sacrifice our will as human beings to our will as money makers. . . . What we have to do is to find out just how the rules of our own making thwart our wishes and to change them in detail or change them drastically as the case may require. Not that this task is easy. On the contrary, the work of analysis is difficult intellectually and the work of devising remedies and putting them into effect is harder still. But one has slender confidence in the vitality of the race and in the power of scientific method if he thinks a task of this technical sort is beyond man's power.[46]

Mitchell realized poignantly that of itself science was neither good nor evil, and that in recent years many of its findings have been put to antisocial uses. But he felt that in a free society this danger is likely to be reduced as knowledge of man's own nature is improved.

Mitchell recognized also that government must play a key role in applying the results of social investigations. He favored national planning on a broad and continuing basis—by which he meant mobilization of a democratic society's intelligence "to deal seriously with social problems before they have produced national emergencies." He followed eagerly the bold experiments in social organization being made in different parts of the world, and our own modest efforts at economic planning under the aegis of the Council of Economic Advisers. That society would evolve a form of organization that will satisfy men's emotional and material needs better than our money economy was his constant hope. Mitchell admired rebels in politics as in economic theory, feeling that deliberate experimentation is essential to the learning process. Yet he thought it necessary to recall "the historical fact . . . that, in the countries that have given wide scope to private initiative . . . , the masses of mankind attained a higher degree of material comfort and a larger measure of liberty than at any earlier time of which

[45] *Ibid.,* p. 91.
[46] "The Crisis of 1920 and the Problem of Controlling Business Cycles," *American Economic Review,* Supplement, March 1922, pp. 31–2.

we have knowledge, or under any other form of organization that mankind has tried out in practice." [47]   The one element in our society that he deemed worth preserving at all costs was democracy itself.

These, in brief, are the leading thoughts that run through Mitchell's scattered papers.   Their moral sincerity, simplicity, humor, and literary grace won for them a large audience beyond the ranks of professional economists.   They played their part, besides his more technical contributions, in shunting the car of economics onto the tracks of empirical science.   Under the stimulus of Mitchell's leadership quantitative research on national income, prices, investment, money markets, and business cycles developed rapidly in the United States and abroad.   The reconstruction of economics now under way may be traced in large part to his influence—to his bold views on the scope and method of economics, to his pioneering studies of the money economy, and to his vigor in stimulating research by others.

[47] *The Backward Art of Spending Money,* pp. 94, 100.

The Rise of Marginalism

Schneider

——————————————————————— *on* ———

Thünen

Johann Heinrich von Thünen (1783–1850) was a learned agriculturist, whose *Isolated State* (1826–1863) anticipated many innovations of modern economics. Thünen seems to have had a clear notion of marginal values, applied chiefly in the realm of production and distribution. He is the forerunner of the modern, mathematical approach to economics, and has laid the foundations for the theory of location. Next to List, Thünen's was the principal contribution to economic thought made in Germany during the early part of the nineteenth century.

Erich Schneider (1900–   ) is the leading exponent of modern economic theory in Germany. Having been associated during the 1930's with the University of Aarhus in Denmark, he now teaches at the University of Kiel. Schneider's contributions include studies of the theory of production and of monopoly as well as a three-volume introduction to economic theory.

Schneider

on

Thünen

J OHANN HEINRICH VON THÜNEN was born June 24, 1783, on his father's estate Kanarienhausen in the Grand Duchy of Oldenburg, the descendant of an old feudal family. His father, Edo Christian von Thünen, who is described as a man of remarkable knowledge, especially in mathematics and mechanics, Thünen lost when he was two years old. In 1789 his mother married a merchant named von Buttel, and with the children of her first marriage moved to Hooksiel, a little town on the Jahde. Johann Heinrich von Thünen received his first instruction in the town-school of this place. We are told that he was a quiet, studious pupil, who was especially gifted in arithmetic. When he had completed his thirteenth year, von Thünen was sent to Jever to attend the secondary school. Here he occupied himself with special zeal and success with mathematics. He was always busy with some mathematical problem, and in the papers which he left from that time we find solutions of problems which give testimony of extraordinary talent.

His natural leaning towards agriculture, and the expectation of having to take over his father's estate some time in the future, induced him to devote himself to practical farming. In 1799 he went as a student to the estate of Gerrietshausen near Hooksiel, where he became thoroughly acquainted with the purely practical labors of a farm. After completing his apprenticeship, he went to the Agricultural College at Gross-Flottbeck near Hamburg, which was administered by Lukas Andreas Staudinger, who subsequently remained his lifelong, paternal friend. Here in Gross-Flottbeck, in 1803, when he was but twenty years old, he conceived the idea of the Isolated State. In a treatise, *Description of the Agriculture in the Village of Gross-Flottbeck,* he wrote:

Assume that a large city is located in the center of a country with a diameter of forty miles; that the country can sell its products exclusively in this city; and that the agricultural development of this region has ad-

[Reprinted by permission from *Econometrica,* January 1934. Translated by Anne von Bibra Sutton. Quotations translated by the Editor.]

446

vanced to its highest stage. Then one could conclude that the economic systems around this city would divide themselves into four groups.[1]

Schumacher here notes that it was clear even to this mere lad that there was no ideal of agriculture which would be applicable to all circumstances, but that the distance of a farm from its market, the prices of products, the richness of the soil, and so forth, were of decisive influence in the choice of a system of agriculture, in order to get the highest possible net revenue. "Even as a wanderer in the dark forest listens to the mysterious rushing of water as yet invisible, the youth here listens gropingly at the very source of immortal laws. As yet the water gushes forth troubled and over rough stones. It was to be through the labors and cares of the man, the diligence and night watches of the scientist, that he was finally to succeed in damming its shores so that it might flow on as a clear stream." [2]

During this same year von Thünen attended the lectures of Thaer in Celle, whose work had the greatest influence on him. In Celle he was also busy with his mathematical studies. In 1803 he went to the University of Göttingen. But he abandoned his courses after two semesters. During his college year he had made the acquaintance of Helene Berlin, the sister of one of his fellow-students, and became engaged to her in the autumn of 1804. Following the advice of his father-in-law, he sold his paternal estate in the Jever country, was married in the year 1806, and leased the estate of Rubkow near Anclam. A life of care and worry began. A mediocre soil produced only small harvests; in addition to this it was a time of war, there were quarterings of soldiers, and cattle-pests, and altogether he was spared none of the bitter experiences of life. June 24, 1808, was finally the day of release. He left Rubkow and went with his family to the house of his brother-in-law, and from here he quietly looked around for a new farm. In 1810, after von Thünen had confined himself to a closer choice of thirteen farms, he bought the estate of Tellow in Mecklenburg, and the soil of this farm became to him an inexhaustible source of deep scientific truths. Here, in calm and quiet work, he finally had the opportunity to win from his own estate the necessary foundations for his research studies, the data which other farm accounts had only given him spasmodically up until now.

[1] H. Schumacher-Zarchlin, *Johann Heinrich von Thünen. Ein Forscherleben*, Rostock, 1868, pp. 15–16.

[2] *Ibid.* All passages from the letters of von Thünen are quoted from this source.

After ten years of the most intensive labor he attained his first goal. On New Year's Eve of the year 1820 he wrote to his brother:

The present day marks a significant and pleasant turning point in my life. Today I have completed a very laborious ten-year work. Fifteen years ago, when for the first time I came across the laws pertaining to the exhaustion of the soil, my enthusiasm became aroused by these ideas. They impressed me as important enough to devote my life to their elaboration. I had a wonderful time, giving free play to my imagination, building conclusions on conclusions, and advancing continuously toward new discoveries. But I was sorry to notice soon that the final results of everything which I produced in this manner could never agree with reality, and *that I would have to derive the basis for my speculations from observation* [3] if I wanted to produce something really useful and practical. After having recognized this clearly, I imposed upon myself a severe rule—to bring to a stop the progress of ideas, and devote all my time and energy to the exploration of reality. This was the decisive factor in the ensuing period of my life. I began to keep records of my observations at Tellow, as extensively as it was within my powers, to serve the purposes of my calculation. Accounting had to be done in terms of labor, grain, and money, and with the same standards of comprehensiveness and exactness throughout. All this I had to do myself. Otherwise the whole work would have been without unity and internal consistence.

Nature provides the reply to my enquiry on every farm. Still, everybody, including the scientifically trained agriculturist, must learn it through long and costly experience, because everybody shuns away from keeping proper records and is thus unable to cumulate his experience.

To be sure, I did not realize in the beginning how large an amount of toil and work I imposed upon myself with this record-keeping. I had to devote to it almost the entire leisure time of the winter season, and had to forego social and domestic amenities as well as, in part, even the study of other sciences. When nature herself put in my way obstacles in the form of ailments and eye troubles, I felt induced on several occasions to abandon the uncompleted task. But an inner compulsion, and the firm intention not to relinquish the chosen goal of my life, gave me the courage to persist.

I have now before me an *account for ten years*. The goal which I have pursued so long is reached. I still need the leisure time of several years to bring order into my collection of data and make them useful for others. But any work devoted thereto shows a tangible result. It is rewarding as well as pleasant. I now shall reap the fruits of my earlier efforts, and a happy future opens itself up for subsequent work.

[3] Italics here and in the following quotations are supplied by the author of this article.

During a number of years I have put in writing my thoughts relating to the "influence of soil productivity and of grain prices on agricultural systems." But, to attain unity, and to base the work on the ten-year experience, a revision is required. I have all but lost the desire to publish this work. Most farmers will fail to understand it; the others, whose doctrines are refuted therein, will attack it.

If one observes the activities of the literary world, one cannot fail to see that the pursuit of truth is misinterpreted whenever a petty personal bias of the critic collides with it. If one sees how the greatest men attack each other, placing personal considerations above science, one surely loses all desire to enter this realm. I would feel insulted by unjust censure. Exaggerated praise would harm me, in part because I still am not insusceptible enough, and, principally, because it would throw upon me many new social connections and visits which would be incompatible with my financial condition and domestic situation. On the other hand, however, the development of my views has become the purpose of my life. I can resign myself to the irresistible passage of time only because I may leave behind, once my life reaches its end, some useful accomplishment.

It is my present plan to proceed only slowly with the work on the manuscript, combining with it the study of all related disciplines. It is the relationship between these disciplines and my subject which makes them interesting to me—and this relationship reaches very far: "In the tops of the trees all sciences come together," as Madame de Staël says. In this manner I hope to combine professional work with further education, spending my leisure-time in the most pleasant manner.

It was only after six years that the first part of the book was ready for printing under the title *The Isolated State in Relation to Agriculture and Political Economy, or Researches on the Influence which the Price of Wheat, the Richness of the Soil, and the Market, Have on Agriculture.*[4] However, Thünen could not make up his mind to publish the book because he was afraid of being attacked and misunderstood. On December 29, 1821, von Thünen wrote to his brother:

The *ideal* state has now fallen into oblivion. With my many side-line occupations I have no hope that I shall complete the work. In this field of science, very few persons are able to understand new views. Those who do understand them are specialists who have been trained in the same field, and whose opinions are biased. The new views are interpreted in the light of their systems of thought, being rejected or approved depending upon whether or not they are compatible with these systems. This should not deter the publication. *Truth as well as error always has been compelled to combat the prevailing opinion.* But, with the sacrifice implied

---

[4] Originally Thünen intended to give his book the title *The Ideal State*. At the instigation of his brother, the expression *ideal* was supplanted by *isolated* in 1823.

by this anticipated reaction to the publication, there is no need to hurry with it. Did you read Malthus' book on population growth? If you read it, you will not be sorry, even though you may have to cut a few classes.

His friends, however, succeeded in persuading him to put aside these apprehensions and to give his permission for printing. Perthes in Hamburg undertook the edition. One could not expect that a book which was so completely different from the usual way of thinking should find wide understanding and acceptance. As Staudinger wrote to Thünen: "Your work is too strong and potent for this generation, which can stand only soft food."

Indeed, the reception which the book had in Germany was not encouraging for Thünen in spite of all the brilliant reviews and the manifold honors which he received. The textbooks on agriculture and political economy quoted his views, many different publications tried to secure him as collaborator, the University of Rostock bestowed upon him the Degree of Doctor of Philosophy *honoris causa:*

I almost have the impression that the public feels no desire to gain insight into the matters in which I always had the liveliest interest. Among all the reviews of my book, laudatory as they may be, there is not a single one which *penetrated into the substance* of my work, to give me the aid of just censure and stimulate further work. To my friend and brother, who knows me well enough, I may be permitted to say this without being considered arrogant.

Only after the appearance in 1842 of the second edition, which had been provided with supplements and improved in certain points, did the world begin to discover the gold which was hidden in this book. Recognition came from all sides, and Tellow became a place of pilgrimage for the most distinguished men of all countries. In 1845, Roscher declared: "I do not hesitate a moment to characterize this work as one of the most significant contributions made in Germany to the exact science of the state."

Even during the printing of the first edition of *The Isolated State* in April of 1826, Thünen continued his researches on the relation of the rate of interest to the wage, which were to occupy him for the following years. On April 12, 1826, he wrote to his brother:

While suffering from an ailment which was physically painful but left my mind completely free, I succeeded in gaining insight into the nature of the rate of interest which is still satisfactory to me. The light, so long desired, came during a sleepless night from February 3rd to 4th. As yet I am still unable to trace the connection between the discovered theorems and reality. But I surely will find it once I have leisure and peace of mind.

On March 8, 1829, he again wrote to his brother:

During the fall I again was intensely occupied with the investigation of
the rate of interest. On the last day of the year I succeeded in bringing the
matter close to the decisive point. Since then I have allowed it to rest, occupying myself only with the accounts and other incidental business. But
unless I devote myself to a serious, fully absorbing investigation, I feel as
if my mind were split, as if I were in conflict with myself, and I feel the
urgent desire soon to resume my research.

These researches seem to have come to a preliminary conclusion
with the finding of the well-known formula of the natural wage, as we
see from a letter addressed to his brother on November 7, 1830:

I was driven back with such force to my earlier investigations into the
relationship between interest rates and wages, which I had carried on for
years, that during four weeks I was not capable of another thought—
although my health suffered badly. Finally, the desired light went on, and
the effort was highly rewarded.

He then presented to his brother some of his main results and continued:

The results of the investigation, expressed here in words, are derived
in formulae of pure mathematics. You can imagine my delight when
looking at these formulae.

However, as long as the relation between Capital and the Product of
Labor was not known, no practical use could be made of the found
formula. Eighteen years more of hard labor were necessary to bring
the problem also to a successful solution.

Right after New Year's Day I had decided to abandon everything else
and devote myself entirely to the investigation of the *relationship between
wages and interest rates*. I have always been driven to this investigation
by a truly mysterious power, and I enjoy the progress I make. Meanwhile
I received Fischer's malevolent, disparaging review of the *Isolated State*.
What little inclination I have to work for publication, has been turned into
aversion by this review, against which the contents of a book cannot provide protection. Nevertheless, the zeal for my work has remained unchanged. [Letter to his brother, March 20.]

The happiness which I would derive from the continuation of my book
has unfortunately still been denied to me. This is not only the fault of my
state of health. *It is my peculiar nature that I can only construct on the
basis of a mathematically secure foundation.* For the natural wage, the
expression $\sqrt{ap}$ has been found. This may be absolutely correct. But

to apply it numerically, *the principle relating* q *with* p (*capital and product*) *must be found and expressed.* The search for this principle has occupied me during a period of twenty years. But since reality does not produce any suitable data, the search has been in vain. Last spring, when I worked on the continuation of the *Isolated State,* I again and again was confronted by this difficulty, and my work broke down. Since then the problem has been on my mind every day during the whole summer, and I have come much closer to the solution. But I am still not entirely satisfied. Knowledge that the wage is $\sqrt{ap}$ has led to very important results. But to continue in true happiness, I must know the relationship between q and p. I feel the inactivity especially painful because during the past summer I received so much evidence that my earlier efforts were not in vain. [Letter to his brother, November 26, 1845.]

In 1848 finally he could write full of joy to his son Heinrich:

The problem of finding an equation of capital and labor product has tormented me for twenty years, has deprived me of rest, and prevented the continuation of my work. Now it has suddenly been cleared up. During the three days from January 17 to 19 I have found a scale which satisfies all my present requirements, although I do not know whether it will satisfy my future requirements. It may be doubtful whether the gain is as great as the effort spent. Perhaps the matter is of interest to nobody else but me. How often have I told this to myself—it did not help; the problem did not let me rest and prevented me from continuing my work. Now at least I have gotten rid of a tormentor, and the melancholic memory of the three days is fused with exhilaration. Hidden in the recesses of the human mind there are secrets of which we become conscious only on rare and special occasions.

Still Thünen could not make up his mind to publish the researches which he had made after the appearance of the first edition of *The Isolated State,* that is, after 1826. It was only due to the urging of the Revisionsrat Schumacher and his son that he finally declared himself willing to publish the researches on the Natural Wage and its relation to the Rate of Interest and to Rent of Land.

I must confess that I have been disloyal to myself, as it were, yielding to the Schumachers (father and son) and turning over for publication the first section of Part 2 of the *Isolated State.* [Letter to his daughter, January 18, 1850.]

He did not live to see the effects which these researches to which he had devoted twenty years of his life had on the specialists in his field. On September 22, 1850, a stroke of apoplexy put an end to his full and rich life. His friends and relatives escorted him to his last

rest. In fulfillment of a wish which he had once uttered, his tomb-
stone carries as inscription that result of his laborious researches which
seemed most important to him, namely the relation of the Wage to the
Rate of Interest and the Rent of Land:

$$\text{The Natural Wage} = \sqrt{ap}.$$

A thorough perusal of Thünen's rich scientific legacy was made by
his friend and pupil, H. Schumacher. The most valuable manuscripts,
among them especially the important researches on the relation between Capital and the Product of Labor and the numerical bases for
the investigations in *The Isolated State,* were published by Schumacher
in the year 1863 as the second part of the second volume of *The
Isolated State.* A third volume published by Schumacher in 1863
contains the "Grundsätze zur Bestimmung der Bodenrente, der vorteil-
haftesten Umtriebszeit und des Werts der Holzbestände von verschied-
enem Alter für Kieferwaldungen." [5]

II

For a long time most of the scientific world looked upon Thünen's
work as a *noli me tangere,* which was admired with reverent awe by
most and understood by few. Thünen, with Gossen and Cournot,
shared the fate of all great men who leave the travelled paths of traditional thought and work, and thus, hurrying far in advance of their
own time, become the pathfinders for a later scientific generation.
Even today we must sadly admit that Thünen's unique accomplishments still stand on a lonely pinnacle far from the great broad highway
which leads through the realm of our science. Only few dared, and
still dare today, to make the difficult ascent to this summit; the greater
number of those who started out to conquer it stopped halfway, and
therefore still try to find his importance in secondary things and in
other directions from where it really lies. It is certainly not wrong,
as Ehrenberg did, to see in him a representative of detailed research
in the field of economics, or to claim him as an empiricist, or to praise
him as a great social politician. But that is not going to the core of his
labors, it does not characterize his true scientific bearing. What he
really was has been strikingly expressed by Marshall who, as he himself gratefully recognizes, was lastingly influenced by him. "Von

[5] "Principles Pertaining to the Determination of Ground Rent, of the Most
Profitable Length of Growth, and of the Value of the Standing Timber at Different Ages, for Pine Forests."

Thünen was a bona fide mathematician, but of less power: his blunder as to the natural wage is not of the same order as Cournot's little slips. But, to make up, *he was a careful experimenter and student of facts, and with the mind at least as fully developed on the inductive as on the deductive side.* Above all he was an ardent philanthropist. . . . I loved Thünen above all my other masters." [6]

These qualities and abilities which Marshall praises in Thünen, are the very ones which mark an economist as an econometrist. Thünen was one of us, one of the great pioneers on the way to a goal which is beginning to become universal. He did not descend from the height of his ideas down to reality, but he ascended from reality to ideas. He shows us with classic examples "how theory grows out of the observation of business practice." [7] Only he who sees in Thünen the great econometrist sees him correctly, and has the proper approach to his work. Thünen may have made many mistakes in individual results, as for instance in the deduction of the famous formula for the Natural Wage, which he himself considered to be the crown of his achievements, to which instance critics, by the way, confined themselves almost exclusively, and herewith believed they had found again a case by which could be demonstrated in a concrete and convincing manner the absolute inefficacy of mathematical reasoning for the solution of economic problems, instead of seeking the mistake in the assumptions and in the reasoning as a whole. However, this changes nothing of the fundamental importance of his mission for the development of econometrics; and does not in the least minimize its enduring value.

Of course he alone really understands the true content of the message which Thünen's work carries who treads the thorny path that leads him to the very end. Whoever does not dread this labor will be richly rewarded. He will recognize Thünen as the master of theoretical methods of work, and find that ideas which today we use as a matter of course in our daily work, have been formed and executed by him with rare clearness. Let us only sketch shortly the most essential points and verify them with the corresponding quotations from the *Isolated State.*

1. Thünen saw with remarkable definiteness that the economic mechanism is a great system of functional relations.

[6] *Memorials of Alfred Marshall,* edited by A. C. Pigou, London, 1925, p. 360. Italics are supplied by the author of the present article.

[7] Schumpeter in *Econometrica,* Vol. 1, p. 9.

In most sciences the investigation takes its starting point from a few established propositions which are considered as given. In the present context, however, we are concerned with quantities which continuously act upon each other, and none of which may be assumed as given.

That is why our investigation becomes so difficult and complicated. It is questionable whether as many equations can be found as are necessary for the determination of the unknown magnitudes. [*Der isolierte Staat*, Pt. II, Section 1, p. 532.] [8]

2. Thünen convincingly proves that only the method of successive approximations is suitable for the disentanglement of the variegated tangle of economic interrelations.

I urge the reader not to be discouraged by assumptions which deviate from reality, and not to consider them as arbitrary and useless. These assumptions are necessary in order to show in isolation the effect of a certain power, of which we obtain only an obscure picture in the real world because there it always appears in conflict with other, simultaneously effective powers.

This type of approach has helped me to clear up so many matters, and seems to me capable of so extensive an application, that I consider it as the most important contribution of this work. [Preface to the second ed. of Pt. I of *The Isolated State*.]

3. The idea of the static equilibrium state and the importance of the construction of this term for economic theory, is clearly understood by Thünen, and he develops it in a way which deserves our fullest admiration.

In the isolated state the condition of rest is the basis of the argument. [p. 419] We always have in view the eventual success, the attained goal. Once this is reached, the state of rest ensues—and here we find the rule of laws, whereas in the period of transition many things appear in inextricable confusion. However, for the following reasons the state of rest cannot exist in reality. [Thünen then sets forth these reasons, and continues:] But, in spite of this changeableness, specific matters under consideration here contain the germ of a certain development. Just as we know that a tree will eventually spring from the acorn put into the ground, so we can predict and contemplate in our mind the eventual success. This justifies the use of the state of rest as basis for our considerations.

Knowledge obtained with the help of this method can render substantial aid in clearing up the confusing phenomena which occur during the period of development and transition. [p. 432]

[8] All quotations, unless marked otherwise, refer to Waentig's edition of *The Isolated State* in the *Sammlung sozialwissenschaftlicher Meister,* Jena, Fischer, Vol. XIII.

4. But especially—and in this we may see his greatest achievement from the point of view of the pure theorist—is Thünen the ingenious creator of the instrument of marginal analysis, which he employed with such admirable skill and which led him to results that even today belong to the fundamentals of modern economic theory. The application of marginal analysis for the determination of the amount of wages and the amount of the rate of interest under conditions of competition then leads him to the fundamental problem of Imputation theory.

The output of labor is the common product of labor and capital.

How can we measure the contribution of each of the two factors to the common product?
We measure the efficiency of capital in terms of the increment to the product of labor which accrues as the result of an increase in capital. Here labor is a constant, and capital a variable quantity.
If we retain this procedure, but consider capital as constant and labor increasing, then the efficiency of labor must also be interpreted in terms of the increase in the total product due to an additional laborer. [p. 584]

5. It is evident that a scientist like Thünen, who stresses the quantitative character of economic theory with such emphasis, positively takes his stand on the side of the "mathematical method" and lays stress upon the use of mathematical methods for the investigation of the complex phenomena of agriculture and economics.

The employment of mathematics must be permitted when the truth cannot be found without it.
If there had been in other branches of knowledge as much aversion to mathematical calculation as in agriculture and economics, we would still be in complete ignorance about the laws guiding the movements of the celestial bodies. Navigation, which because of the development of astronomy links all parts of the world, would be limited to coastwise movements. [p. 569]

Up to this point, that which Thünen has given us has today become general knowledge, and if this had been the sum total of his achievements, it would now be only of interest from the point of view of the history of our science. But even if the historian may see in Thünen merely the great theorist of a past time, his work means more to the present student of pure theory than just a climax in the history of economic theory. Only a few of us realize that problems which now stand in the very center of our present investigations had been already recognized by von Thünen in their full significance with incomparable clearness; and that, moreover, there are contained in his books many valuable hints and data as to their efficient treatment. One needs but read carefully the introduction of the first part of the second volume of *The Isolated State* to be convinced of this; and one will be surprised to find problems posed in it, which belong to our own day and which even now await a satisfactory solution:

How does the quantity of money affect interest rates and commodity prices? [p. 402]

What influence is exercised by significant improvements in agriculture and by the invention of new machinery for manufacturing, when these are introduced first, and what is their final effect? [p. 402]

How must the type of cultivation change with the increasing distance from the city, if the net yield of the soil is to be maximized? [p. 404]

What law controls rent, if, instead of one large city, there are located in the isolated state a number of small cities, of equal size and equally distant from each other; and what relationship is there between the degree of diligence of labor and the grain prices? [p. 423]

Assuming given conditions, how can one identify the size of farms which will maximize the yield of the soil? [p. 428]

Does different distance from the market affect the optimum size of farms? [p. 428]

What influence does an increase in the richness of the soil have on the optimum size of farms? [p. 428]

This is only a very small part of the great wealth of suggestions and fruitful thought which have been given to us here. For the econometrist, Thünen's work is moreover a source of most valuable, as yet entirely unused, and almost entirely unnoticed, material for econometric researches. I only refer to the statistical investigations on the Relation between Capital and the Product of Labor in the second part of the second volume of *The Isolated State*. In this respect it has an incalculable value.

"There will be a time when one will eagerly bring to the light of day the pure precious metal from its rich mines," Staudinger wrote to Thünen in 1826. Today, about a hundred years after the first appearance of the book, we have finally progressed far enough to understand and appreciate the great wealth of this work of genius. Now is the time to bring to light the treasures which lie hidden in this immortal book, and to complete that which its creator had to leave unfinished.

Fisher
on
Cournot

Augustin Cournot (1801–1877) was a French mathematician, philosopher, and student of probability theory. Cournot published in 1838 his celebrated *Researches into the Mathematical Principles of the Theory of Wealth* (English translation, 1897), the first treatise to contain a systematic application of mathematical economics to classical economics. To Cournot is due the interpretation of demand and supply as functions or schedules. His solution of the oligopoly problem is still widely quoted. It was not until the 1870's, however, that Cournot's pioneering work received some measure of recognition.

Irving Fisher (1867–1947), educated at Yale, Berlin, and Paris, was associated with Yale University from 1890 to 1935, beginning his teaching career as a tutor in mathematics. Fisher was one of the first exponents of mathematical economics in the United States, and the editor of the English translation of Cournot's work. His principal writings, devoted to the theory of capital and interest, include *The Nature of Capital and Income* (1906), *The Rate of Interest* (1907), and *The Theory of Interest* (1930). His *Mathematical Investigations into the Theory of Value and Price* (1892) anticipates Pareto's use of the indifference curve.

> *"Cournot's genius must give a new mental activity to every one who passes through his hands."*—MARSHALL

THE APPEARANCE in English [1] of Cournot's *Principes Mathématiques* offers a suitable occasion for a review of that remarkable work and of the later developments of economic method which it foreshadowed. In the six decades since the original work was published, a decided change has taken place in the modes of conceiving and treating economic problems. For good or for ill the mathematical method has finally taken root, and is flourishing with a vigor of which both its friends and enemies little dreamed. Sixty years ago the mathematical treatise of Cournot was passed over in silence, if not contempt. To-day the equally mathematical work of Pareto is received with almost universal praise. In Cournot's time "mathematical economists" could be counted on one's fingers, or even thumbs. To-day they muster some thirty active enthusiasts and a much larger number of followers and sympathizers. In 1838 there seems to have been no institution of learning besides the Academy at Grenoble, of which Cournot was rector, where "mathematical economics" were employed or approved. In 1898 there are at least a dozen such institutions, and in England alone half that number, Oxford and Cambridge among them. It is in France, the prophet's own country, where he is still without honor. When Cournot wrote, no journal existed in which such investigations as his could find a welcome. To-day the *Economic Journal,* the *Journal of the Royal Statistical Society,* the *Giornale degli Economisti,* and the *Nationaloekonomisk Tidsskrift* receive such material with more or less regularity; while, within the last eight years alone, twenty other journals have occasionally published economic articles containing mathematics. Opponents of the new method no longer venture to ignore or ridicule it, but, in academic circles at least, seek to acquaint themselves with its history and present aims as matters of necessary

---

[1] *Researches into the Mathematical Principles of the Theory of Wealth.* By Augustin Cournot, 1838, translated by Nathaniel T. Bacon. In the "Economic Classics" series. Macmillan, 1897.

[Reprinted in slightly abridged form from *Quarterly Journal of Economics,* January 1898.]

and professional information. In recognition of such wide-spread interest the latest Dictionary of Political Economy devotes some forty articles to the history, writings, methods, and terminology of the "mathematical school."

It may fairly be claimed that Cournot was the principal founder of this school.[2] For this reason, if for no other, his book is an "economic classic," and as such deserves careful study. But its interest is not simply historical. The bulk of its reasoning and conclusions has never yet been superseded. Those who now read it for the first time will find it as new and fresh as any modern investigation.

In his preface Cournot defends his method of treating economic science. Few better statements exist of the aims and merits of "deductive" and "mathematical" economics. While welcoming all study of facts, Cournot insists on a framework of *theory* in which those facts fit. A very few facts (such as that demand increases with a decrease of price) suffice to determine the main outlines of that theory, though its exact form depends on the specific circumstances of each particular case. He answers the alleged objection to a mathematical treatment that economic problems lack the data for numerical solution:

> Those skilled in mathematical analysis know that its object is not simply to calculate numbers, but that it is also employed to find the relations between magnitudes which cannot be expressed in numbers and between *functions* whose law is not capable of algebraic expression. . . . Thus . . . theoretical mechanics furnishes to practical mechanics general theorems of most useful application, although in almost all cases recourse to experience is necessary for the numerical results which practice requires.[3]

Entering upon the book itself, we find that it naturally falls under three heads. The introductory chapters, treating of value, "absolute and relative," and of the foreign exchanges, are quite apart from the rest of the book. Chapters IV–X inclusive discuss the determination of prices under different conditions as to monopoly and competition, taxes and bounties. This portion of the work is the most distinctive and the most widely celebrated. The remaining two chapters give an ambitious but erroneous theory of "Social Income."

Chapter I is devoted to defining wealth, which term Cournot uses in the sense of value in exchange. He carefully distinguishes this idea from *utility,* with which he conceives the economist has no direct concern. Here, of course, he differs materially from modern mathematical economists, beginning with Jevons and Walras. To prevent all mis-

---

[2] Cf. Walras, *Théorie Mathématique de la Richesse Sociale,* 1883, p. 9.
[3] Page 3.

understanding, Cournot points out that, under his definition of wealth, the destruction of spices by the East India Company, though opposed to the general good, was a "real creation of *wealth* in the commercial sense of the word." What relations exist between wealth thus conceived and the welfare of the human race Cournot regards as too difficult a problem to admit of present solution. Yet he does not disparage efforts towards that end.

Chapter II deals with "Changes in Value, Absolute and Relative,"— a subject of engaging interest in these latter days of conflicting monetary standards. The reader will be filled with surprise and admiration at Cournot's anticipations of modern thought on this difficult topic. The *values* of a system of commodities are compared to the positions of a system of particles. The value of each commodity is expressed relatively to other commodities, just as the position of each particle is expressed by reference to the other particles. When a change occurs in the relative values or positions, the question arises, Which term of the comparison has suffered an *absolute* change? Clinging to physical analogy, Cournot cites the remarkable passage in Newton's *Principia* in which an "absolute space" is supposed as a background for mechanical motion, distinct from the "relative space" made up of the system of moving points. He does not despair of distinguishing statistically absolute and relative changes, and observes that in case all commodities except one, such as gold or silver, preserve the same relative values, the probability is greater that the one commodity has changed than that all the others have changed. Although the whole discussion lacks one of its modern elements,—the idea of utility,—it must nevertheless be regarded as more profound and worthy of serious consideration than most contemporaneous treatments of the same theme.

Of the third chapter, on foreign exchange, Jevons says, rather dubiously, that it is "highly ingenious, if not particularly useful." [4] Its utility, however, seems commensurate with the utility of the subject of which it treats. It is a correct first approximation, based on the hypothesis of a regularly recurring annual indebtedness between nations or "centres of exchange." So far as it fails to explain the complex facts of the exchange market, the failure is due to this arbitrary hypothesis, which neglects "dynamic" causes. When a completer theory is developed (so far as I am aware, none such exists as yet), it will establish laws governing the *oscillations* of exchanges and the part played by foresight and speculation in such transitions.

---

[4] *Theory of Political Economy,* 3rd edition, p. xxix.

Supposing only two centres of exchange, (1) and (2), and supposing (1) to be annually indebted to (2) the sum of $m_{1,2}$ francs, and (2) to (1) $m_{2,1}$ francs, if $c_{1,2}$ is the rate of exchange at (1) on (2), "or the amount of silver given at the place (2) in exchange for a weight of silver expressed by 1 and payable at the place (1)," then $c_{1,2} = m_{2,1}/m_{1,2}$. If three centres are taken instead of two, the formula becomes more complicated; but it is still possible to derive the six rates of exchange in terms of the six sums of indebtedness between the three centres, and so on for any number of centres. The limits set by the "specie points" are discussed, and the case of exchange between gold and silver countries without a par of exchange is briefly touched upon.

With Chapter IV, the main portion of the work, the theory of prices, begins. Cournot assumes that the demand for an article, in the sense of the quantity of it annually consumed, varies with (i.e., is a "function" of) its price. The relation between price and demand is delineated by the now familiar "demand curve," which Cournot was the first to introduce. The character of this relation—i.e., the form of the demand curve—depends on "the kind of utility of the article, on the nature of the services it can render or the enjoyments it can procure, on the habits and customs of the people, on the average wealth, and on the scale on which wealth is distributed." [5] As is well known, Walras and later writers have gone a step deeper into the analysis, and have shown how to deduce the *general* demand curve used by Cournot from a system of *individual* demand curves, and have in turn deduced the individual curves from systems of relations between the "utility of the article" and its quantity, and from the "nature and habits of the people" and the "scale on which wealth is distributed." In doing this, they have not superseded Cournot, but have simply laid bare the foundations on which he built.

Given the law of demand, Cournot first supposes a complete monopoly of the article in question, and shows what price will yield the maximum profit. He points out (§ 30) that *fixed charges,* or costs which do not vary with the output, have no influence on price,—a theorem whose truth and importance are often overlooked to-day, except, perhaps, in America, where it has been made conspicuous both in railway experience and theory.[6] Only the *running expenses* figure in the determination of rates. Cournot shows that an increase of what

[5] Page 47.

[6] See Hadley, *Railway Transportation,* p. 265.

would now be called marginal cost always causes an increase in the price under a monopoly, but that the rise of price is sometimes more and sometimes less than the amount of the increase of cost. The criterion for distinguishing the two cases is deduced and discussed.

In passing from the study of perfect monopoly to that of perfect competition, Cournot considers also the intermediate case of a few, say two, competitors. The operation of self-interest in this case will, Cournot contends, cause an equilibrium price to emerge, which will be lower than if the two rivals had combined, but higher than if a third competitor should enter the field.

Cournot's treatment of this difficult problem is brilliant and suggestive, but not free from serious objections. The fault to be found with the reasoning is in his premise that each individual will act on the assumption that his rival's output is constant, and will strive only to so regulate his own output as to secure the largest profits. He is regarded as oblivious of the consequences of his action on the tactics of his rival, and as assuming that the price which will be charged by that rival will be neither more nor less than that necessary to take off the fixed output imputed to him plus the output decided upon by himself. Under these conditions, Cournot's conclusions will hold true. But the conditions are not those which actually apply to competition between two producers. A more natural hypothesis, and one often tacitly adopted, is that each assumes his rival's *price* will remain fixed, while his own price is adjusted. Under this hypothesis each would undersell the other as long as any profit remained,[7] so that the final result would be identical with the result of unlimited competition. But, as a matter of fact, no business man assumes either that his rival's output or price will remain constant any more than a chess player assumes that his opponent will not interfere with his effort to capture a knight. On the contrary, his whole thought is to forecast what move the rival will make in response to one of his own. He may lower his price to steal his rival's business temporarily or with the hope of driving him out of business entirely. He may take great care to preserve the *modus vivendi,* so as not to break the market and provoke a rate war. He may raise his price, if ruinously low, in hopes that his rival, who is in the same difficulty, may welcome the change, and follow suit. The whole study is a "dynamic" one, and far more complex than Cournot makes it out to be. The completest treatment of this intricate and

[7] Cf. Bertrand, *Journal des Savants,* 1883, p. 503; Marshall, *Principles,* I, 2nd edition, p. 457; Pareto, *Cours d'Économie Politique,* 1, p. 67; Edgeworth, *Giornale degli Economisti,* June, 1897, p. 24.

neglected problem is contained in Professor Edgeworth's brilliant articles in the *Giornale degli Economisti*.[8]

Passing on to the case of "unlimited competition" (Chapter VIII), Cournot shows that the price is, in this case, equal to the "marginal cost of production." Cournot himself does not use this term nor any other verbal description of the magnitude involved. He confines himself to mathematical symbolism. $\phi(x)$ being the total cost, to a particular producer, of producing x units, $\phi'(x)$ will be equal to the price. Since $\phi'(x)$ is the rate of increase of cost per unit of increased product,—i.e., "marginal cost,"—Cournot must be counted among the anticipators of Jevons, Menger, and Walras. These anticipators now appear to be Bernouilli, Anderson, Ricardo, Von Thünen, Rae, Cournot, Dupuit, and Gossen.

If we plot the relation between the product of each individual and his resulting marginal cost, we have a system of individual supply curves. These may be combined into a single general supply curve, which Cournot uses. He shows, what is now familiar to every student, that the intersection of this general supply curve with the general demand curve determines price. It is significant of the slow growth of economic science that these graphic pictures of supply and demand, now in almost universal use in text-book and class-room, were ignored or forgotten by Cournot's contemporaries, and were only restored in 1870, when independently obtained by Fleeming Jenkin. With his name, rather than with Cournot's, they are generally associated to-day.

In the same chapter Cournot enunciates two other principles which have become classic, though, like that just mentioned, they are seldom duly credited to him. One is in regard to the law of diminishing returns (p. 91), and the other is that a tax on an article subject to "unlimited competition" will raise the price by an amount less than the tax itself (p. 93).

Cournot next considers the "mutual relations of producers" or the connections between complementary materials, such as copper and zinc, which enter jointly into the production of a composite, such as brass. Cournot was apparently the first to investigate such "joint demand." His study here, unlike the rest of his work, is confined to a special case; namely, that where the component articles enter in perfectly definite proportions into the joint article. He shows, among other things, that the control by a single monopolist of both copper and zinc will result in a lower price of brass than the control of copper by one monopoly and zinc by the other. That is, in the case of complementary

[8] 1897, June, October, and November.

commodities, it is better for the consumer to be at the mercy of one monopolist than two. An important application, Professor Edgeworth points out, is to railway rates, where, as is well known, lower fares follow the consolidation of connecting lines. But, although Cournot's conclusions are in the main consonant with facts, his analysis of motives in the minds of the two monopolists is subject to much the same objection as above expressed in the case of two competitors.[9] Turning to the more trustworthy case of unlimited competition, Cournot develops several interesting results, among them that a tax levied on one of the two component articles will raise the price of that article and of the composite article, but will *lower* the price of the other component.

In introducing the subject of import duties or bounties, "without pretending, which would be absurd, to contradict the opinion which has been very generally formed, of the advantages for the community procured by improvements in the means of communication or by the extension of markets," [10] Cournot suggests that the extreme position of free traders is untenable. In following out this contention, Cournot commits a mathematical blunder which invalidates his main thesis; namely, that a tariff on imports may, under certain peculiar circumstances, lower prices of the goods imported. Formulæ (6) on page 122 are erroneous [11] for reasons explained in the appended notes (No. 50). The correct formulæ may be transcribed from those given by putting zero for ϵ. With this change it will be seen that Cournot's arguments on pages 123 and 124 are quite destroyed.

This singular error supplies one of many examples of a serious fault in our talented author,—gross carelessness. In spite of extraordinary acuteness and precision of mind, Cournot was neglectful of his duties as verifier and proofreader. The translator, Mr. Bacon, has convicted him of some thirty-five inaccuracies. Though most of these are obvious misprints, some are clearly due to hasty and heedless mathematical transformations. Fortunately, only two of them affect the economic conclusions drawn. The first has just been mentioned, and the second will soon appear. It was not ignorance or unfamiliarity with mathematics which caused these slips. The evidence, internal and external, is decisive against this view. Rather was it his very facility in employing the mathematical apparatus which led Cournot to omit the essential labor of reviewing his reasoning and of checking his

[9] See Edgeworth, *Giornale degli Economisti,* 1897, June and October.
[10] Page 121.
[11] Cf. Edgeworth, in Palgrave's Dictionary, article "Cournot," and Berry and Sanger, quoted by Edgeworth, *Economic Journal,* 1894, p. 627. [The "appended notes" are not reprinted here.—Ed.]

results by common sense. The impossibility of formulæ (6), page 122, appears from the simplest inspection; for it is *a priori* evident that δ (the effect of the tax) ought to vanish when *u* (the tax) vanishes, which it does not do.[12]

Most readers of Cournot have trusted his mathematics, but been puzzled by his conclusions. Professor Bastable tries to explain the matter by the influence of some prejudice on his judgment.[13] But such an explanation does not seem to be required. Cournot's "curious views" are in large measure due to the mathematical error above mentioned. Moreover, his whole book stamps him as the most dispassionate of truth-seekers. He expressly disclaims any feeling in favor of protection:

> If we have tried to overthrow the doctrine of Smith's school as to barriers, it was only from theoretical considerations, and not in the least to make ourselves the advocates of prohibitory and restrictive laws.[14]

Again, in his preface, he says:

> I am far from having thought of writing in support of any system, and from joining the banners of any party; I believe that there is an immense step in passing from theory to governmental applications; I believe that theory loses none of its value in thus remaining preserved from contact with impassioned polemics; and I believe, if this essay is of any practical value, it will be chiefly in making clear how far we are from being able to solve, with full knowledge of the case, a multitude of questions which are boldly decided every day.

The two concluding chapters on "Social Income" are the most unsatisfactory in the book. They form one of those innumerable and futile attempts to define the income of a community and analyze its variations. Cournot here loses his accustomed perspicuity. He first describes social income as the sum of individual incomes, the latter term being regarded as self-explanatory. He then redefines it as the sum of commodities "for consumption." He thinks he bridges over the gap between these two descriptions of income on the theory that the price of any commodity "for consumption" consists of parts ascribable to the different agents of production. This being the case,

---

[12] Cf. Arthur Berry, quoted by Edgeworth, *Economic Journal*, 1894, p. 627.

[13] "The treatment of the topic [the benefits of a tariff] in so defective a manner by an able and critical investigator suggests the belief that some disturbing cause must have influenced his judgment, and his evident desire to discover a scientific foundation for protectionism furnishes us with a very probable explanation of his curious views." *International Trade*, 2nd edition, p. 179.

[14] Page 171.

if D be the entire consumption of a "commodity for consumption," and p the price, "the product pD will express the sum to the extent of which this commodity co-operates in making up the social income." If p_0D_0 be the value of this product at one time, and p_1D_1 that at another, the difference between them, $p_0D_0 - p_1D_1$, expresses the diminution of social income (assuming for illustration that p_1D_1 is the lesser of the two products). This diminution occurs in the incomes of the various persons contributing to the *production* of the commodity in question; and Cournot argues that the incomes of all other persons may be considered unchanged, for perturbations in the prices of other commodities are apt to occur as much in one direction as in the other (pp. 129–132).

According to this reckoning, a dearth of a necessity of life may cause an *increase* of social income if the price rises faster than the quantity consumed falls! To overcome this difficulty, Cournot distinguishes between the "nominal" reduction of income just described $(p_0D_0 - p_1D_1)$ and a *real* reduction of income. He attempts to describe this real reduction of income without describing any "real income." The real reduction is found by taking into account the sacrifices that *consumers* of the commodity suffer in paying higher prices. Although it was already shown that the incomes of consumers, as a whole, may be considered as unchanged, still those who continue to buy after the price has risen have to pay the rise $p_1 - p_0$ on their purchase D_1, thus expending $(p_1 - p_0)D_1$ more income for precisely the same return. Hence they "are really in just the same situation as to fortune as if the commodity had not risen and their incomes had been diminished by $(p_1 - p_0)D_1$." Adding this virtual loss of income for consumers to the loss already shown for producers,—namely, $p_0D_0 - p_1D_1$,—Cournot obtains $p_0(D_0 - D_1)$ as the *total* real loss. He confesses, however, that, even with this amendment, he has not taken account of the loss to consumers who have ceased to buy the commodity because of the increased price, or of part of the loss (in the shape of reduced purchases) to those who do buy, but buy less. He pleads in extenuation of this omission: "But this kind of damage cannot be estimated numerically. . . . Here comes in one of those relations of size which numbers can indicate, indeed, but cannot measure." Had Cournot reached the conception of "consumers' rent," he would have seen that numbers can measure as well as indicate the damage in question.[15]

[15] Cf. Edgeworth, *Economic Journal*, 1894, p. 628. If the price rises from OT to OT' (see Fig. 6, in Cournot), the loss to consumers, as estimated by Cournot,

In the final chapter Cournot applies his ideas of income to international trade, and attempts to show in particular that a protective tariff may, under special circumstances, increase the national income. Inasmuch as the idea of income is so arbitrary and faulty, little or no importance attaches to such speculations.[16]

Such, in brief, are some of the main outlines of Cournot's economic doctrines. It is not possible, however, to reproduce the striking and ingenious observations with which his pages bristle, or to reflect the strong, clear style in which those observations are expressed. To feel Cournot's power and stimulus, the reader must actually "pass through his hands." He will scarcely fail to come away with a "new mental activity."

And yet it is not surprising that the book seemed a failure when first published. It was too far in advance of the times. Its methods were too strange, its reasonings too intricate, for the crude and confident notions of political economy then current. It was quite inevitable that it should be neglected and forgotten until such kindred spirits as Jevons and Walras pointed out its virtues. Cournot accepted the situation philosophically, and tried to make his theories more palatable by divesting them of the mathematical form. He published his *Principes de la Théorie des Richesses* in 1863, and in 1876, the year before his death, his *Revue sommaire des Doctrines Économiques*. Both contain new matter. The second is said to retain the more successfully the strength and virtues of the *Principes Mathématiques*. I have seen only the first. Of this Jevons [17] said, with justice, that it "does not compare favorably in interest and importance with" the *Principes Mathématiques*.

In the seventies the main work began to show signs of coming to life. Walras quoted and praised it in his *Éléments d'Économie Politique*,[18] published in 1874, and in later works.[19] In 1875 an Italian

is the rectangle *TS'*, whereas the loss of consumers' rent is the trapezoid *STT'S'*. That is, the loss due to consumers giving up consumption, which loss was neglected by Cournot, is the triangle of which *SS'* is hypotenuse. Evidently, this triangle may be very large. Cournot's erroneous views on social income are treated at length by Pareto, *Giornale degli Economisti*, 1891, Vol. IV, pp. 1–14.

[16] In one of them Cournot falls again into mathematical error. The inequality near the end of p. 158—namely, $E < E - (D_b - D'_b)$—is incorrect. It implies that $D_b < D'_b$, which contradicts what was said on p. 155, line 9. The author seems to have forgotten that D'_b does not here mean quantity consumed, but quantity produced (see p. 151, § 88, line 9).

[17] *Theory*, 3rd edition, p. xxx.

[18] *E.g.*, preface and p. 423.

[19] *E.g.*, *Théorie Mathématique de la Richesse Sociale*, 1883, p. 9.

translation appeared in the excellent series of Boccardo, *Biblioteca dell' Economista.* In 1879 Jevons, in the preface to the second edition of his *Theory of Political Economy,* described the contents of the book, a copy of which he had found as early as 1872. With these sponsors the work was brought into prominence, and studied with care.

Cournot's influence and eminence have not been confined to economics. He was something of a man of affairs, as is evident from the positions which he occupied. His literary work was many-sided. In addition to editing and translating, he published several works of note, both on Mathematics, pure and applied, and on Philosophy.

Yet it is as economist rather than philosopher or mathematician that Cournot is to-day most remembered. He is fulfilling Jevons's prophecy that he would "occupy a remarkable position in the history of the subject." [20] Although some score of writers had preceded him in attempting to apply mathematical processes to political economy, he was the first to win substantial results. He alone of the early writers exerts to-day a powerful influence on economic thought. It is with him, therefore, that any survey of modern mathematical economics should begin.

[20] *Theory,* 3rd edition, p. xxviii.

Walras

on

Gossen

Hermann Heinrich Gossen (1810–1858), another forerunner of modern economics, did not enjoy even the small measure of recognition which came to Cournot during the latter's life. Gossen's book, *Entwicklung der Gesetze des menschlichen Verkehrs* (1854), which contains a clear formulation of the marginal principle as applied to utility, was disregarded for a period of 25 years and resuscitated only after Gossen's death.

Léon Walras (1834–1910), considered by many the greatest economic thinker of all times, reports here on the discovery of the work of his predecessor. Walras' article reviews a number of ideas developed by himself, and thus serves as an introduction to his own work.

(On Walras, see pp. 580 ff., below.)

READERS OF the *Journal des Économistes* who are interested in mathematical economics—I have no illusions concerning their number —will perhaps recall a memoir, *Principe d'une théorie mathématique de l'échange,* which I read before the Academy of Moral and Political Sciences in August, 1873, and which was printed in the *Journal* of August, 1874. In this memoir I developed the mathematical theory of barter with two goods in the following manner. Taking as first point of departure the demand of each owner of one good for the other good, I expressed the demand in the form of a curve which falls as a function of the price, and demonstrated that *the supply of one good is equal to the demand for the other multiplied by the price of the latter in terms of the first.* On the basis of partial or total demand curves I was thus able to derive supply curves. The intersection of the demand and supply curves yielded the equilibrium price at which the quantity demanded is equal to the quantity supplied.

Taking then as point of departure the utility of each good to each exchanger, I expressed utility in the form of curves which fall as a function of the quantity consumed, and demonstrated the condition of maximum satisfaction. When a person, at a certain price, exchanges a certain quantity of a good which he has in his possession for a certain quantity of another good which he does not have in his possession, *the condition of maximum satisfaction of his desire requires that the ratio of the intensities of the desires which are satisfied last, or of the rarities, be equal to the price.* I was then able to derive, from the utility curves in conjunction with the quantities possessed, demand curves, the quantity demanded being one which procures the greatest possible satisfaction at any given price. In this manner I established the relationship which links the utility and the quantity of goods with their price on the market, demonstrating successively (1) how equilibrium prices depend on demand curves, and (2) how the demand curves themselves depend on the utility and quantity of goods.[1]

[1] Mr. Joseph Bertrand, who has devoted an important article to my *Théorie mathématique de la richesse sociale* in the *Journal des Savants* of September,

[Translated in slightly abridged form from *Journal des Économistes,* 1885. By permission.]

There are here, as one can see, two distinct problems, which both are equally essential to the solution of the question of barter with two goods. The first leads to the equilibrium price, the second relates to the elements of this price. The latter is the base of the former, and the theory thus developed, which I call "theorem of maximum satisfaction," is the cornerstone of mathematical economics. It would be wrong to judge its importance in the light of its immediate practical usefulness—there being none. This would indeed be a manifestation of a very mediocre scientific intellect. As statics teaches us, a body, which is supported by a horizontal plane at several points, is in equilibrium if the vertical line, which passes through its centre of gravity, lies in the interior of the polygon formed by all points of contact. This theorem, which is so fruitful of consequences along theoretical and

1883, has raised two objections to two fundamental points. These objections are more of an economic than of a mathematical character. To me, their refutation seems quite easy. Mr. Bertrand insists that the problem of exchange is not determinate: when the quantity demanded exceeds the quantity supplied, or when the quantity supplied exceeds the quantity demanded, only some buyers or some sellers will be satisfied; to satisfy the other buyers or sellers, there must then take place an increase in price or a price fall. In reply to this argument I may point out that, when the quantity demanded exceeds the quantity supplied on the theoretical market, or when the quantity supplied exceeds the quantity demanded, nobody will be satisfied; instead, the exchange remains suspended until an increase or decrease in price has brought about equality of the quantities demanded and supplied. The theoretical equilibrium price is essentially a unitary price, resulting, at a given time, from a general exchange. Under these conditions, the problem of exchange is perfectly determinate. With respect to the condition of maximum satisfaction, which makes the demand and supply curves depend on the utility and quantity of goods, Mr. Bertrand raises the following objection. Considerations of the utility of goods, he points out, may help in the explanation of the consumer demand for goods and services, but not so in the case of the demand of industrial or commercial producers who do not desire the goods for the satisfaction of their own wants. In reply to this I may point out that, although I abstracted from the problems of production and capitalization in my first memoir and in the second which followed, I have written the third and the fourth expressedly in order to introduce these matters. There I treat of the entrepreneur, who is in charge of them, and I consider the loss and profit of an enterprise which are the controlling factors in the entrepreneurs' demand for services and their supply of products. Much more fearful of the criticism of mathematicians than of that of economists, as I was, I confess that my theory, after its examination by the illustrious secretary of the Academy of Sciences, seems to me well-founded and to deserve the small effort which I assume in order to divide equitably the scientific property between Gossen, Jevons, and myself. I may add that at the time of publication of this article, Mr. W. Launhardt, director of the College of Engineering at Hanover, is coming out with a book, *Mathematische Begründung der Volkswirtschaftslehre,* which is based on the two conditions of maximum utility and equilibrium price.

practical lines, does not help us to keep ourselves upright. This is the meaning of Lépine's answer, when he has let himself fall down and is told by Philaminte and Bélise: [2] "You awkward fellow! Ought people to fall after they have learned the equilibrium of things? Do you not see the causes of your fall, you ignoramus, and that it proceeded from your deviation from the fixed point which we call the centre of gravity?" To this Lépine replies, with a marked degree of irony: "I became aware of it, Madam, when I was on the ground."

But if this facetious young man would go farther and would wish to insinuate that knowledge of the properties of the centre of gravity and of the mathematical conditions of the equilibrium of bodies is of no use, he would be the one who would make us laugh. It is in the nature of science to seek and find the how and the why of facts which the ordinary individual accomplishes, or to which he submits, without giving himself an account of them. We hope that it now will be understood that the knowledge of the mathematical conditions of market equilibrium can be fundamental knowledge in pure economics, although everyone of us, when he exchanges a good for another, obtains the maximum satisfaction of his desires without investigating whether the ratio of the intensities of his desires which are satisfied last is equal to the price, and without even suspecting that they must be equal.

This being so, it is not surprising that, after having read my memoir, Mr. W. Stanley Jevons, then professor of political economy at Owens College, Manchester, claimed at once his own priority with respect to this theory. He had given, in 1871, in his *Theory of Political Economy,* the mathematical expression of utility and of the condition of maximum satisfaction. Any reader of the *Journal des Économistes* for June, 1874, can find our correspondence, he claiming this priority and I satisfying his claim. It is only natural that Mr. Jevons and I, put on our guard by this singular coincidence, have carefully investigated various attempts which preceded our own, and have compiled jointly the "bibliography of works relating to the application of mathematics to economics" which was published in the *Journal des Économistes* of December, 1878. It is the aim of my present article to do the same justice to Gossen which I have done to Jevons. In a sense, it is the last act of an incident whose successive phases I am going to describe. I hope that the editor of the review will lend me his hospitality—and my few readers their attention. When they have read what I have to say, they will recognize, I believe, that among the many examples of coincidences in the history of science, there are few as

[2] Molière, *Les femmes savantes,* iii, 2. (Tr. by Henri van Laun.)

curious as the rencounter of Gossen, Mr. Jevons, and myself at the origin of mathematical economics. For my part, I will go farther and state that, among the equally numerous examples of scientific injustice, there is none more grave than the ingratitude shown to Gossen. This man, in my opinion one of the most remarkable economists who have ever lived, made his way completely unnoticed. My aim here is not to say everything that should be said about his work and career, but only to make known what I know of him, to put those on their way who later on will do justice to this great, misprized man in a manner worthy of him.

On September 15, 1878, just after I had sent to Mr. Joseph Garnier the corrected proof of the bibliography which I have mentioned here, Mr. Jevons wrote to me: "The question becomes more complicated because of the discovery of a work, published in Brunswick in 1854, which contains some of the principal points of our theory in a clearly elucidated form. It is by Hermann Heinrich Gossen, and its title reads about like this: *Entwickelung der Gesetze des menschlichen Verkehrs.* This work seems to be entirely unknown even in Germany; and since I don't read German, I was absolutely ignorant of its existence. My successor at Owens College, Professor Adamson, has found it mentioned in a history of economics, but not in that by Roscher, who seems to ignore it. . . . Adamson is going to prepare for me an analysis of the book with the help of a copy which he has been able to obtain." A year later, that is, in the summer of 1879, Mr. Jevons published the second edition of his *Theory of Political Economy,* and, in a new preface, gave a detailed account of the discovery of Gossen's work and its contents. Mr. Robert Adamson had found it mentioned, a few years before, as a work containing a theory of pleasure and pain, in *Theorie und Geschichte der National-Oekonomik* by Kautz, a book published in 1858.[3] He had advertised for a copy, but with no success; only in August, 1878, when he accidentally discovered it in the catalog of a German bookseller, had he succeeded in purchasing a copy. He apparently did not know that there was one in the British Museum, acquired in 1865. Be this as it may, the following is Mr. Jevons' account of the book, based on information from Adamson:

"Gossen evidently held the highest possible opinion of the importance of his own theory, for he commences by claiming honors in economic science equal to those of Copernicus in astronomy. He

---

[3] Gossen is mentioned favorably in *Die Arbeiterfrage. Ihre Bedeutung für Gegenwart und Zukunft,* by Friedrich Albert Lange. Dritte umgearbeitete und vermehrte Auflage. Winterthur, 1875, p. 124.

then at once insists that mathematical treatment, being the only sound one, must be applied throughout; but, out of consideration for the reader, the higher analysis will be explicitly introduced only when it is requisite to determine maxima and minima. The treatise then opens with the consideration of Economics as the theory of pleasure and pain, that is as the theory of the procedure by which the individual and the aggregate of individuals constituting society, may realize the maximum of pleasure with the minimum of painful effort. The natural law of pleasure is then clearly stated, somewhat as follows: *Increase of the same kind of consumption yields pleasure continuously diminishing up to the point of satiety.* This law he illustrates geometrically, and then proceeds to investigate the conditions under which the total pleasure from one or more objects may be raised to a maximum.

"The term *Werth* is next introduced, which may, Professor Adamson thinks, be rendered with strict accuracy, as *utility,* and Gossen points out that the quantity of utility, material or immaterial, is measured by the quantity of pleasure which it affords. He classifies useful objects as, (1) those which possess pleasure-giving powers in themselves; (2) those which only possess such powers when in combination with other objects; (3) those which only serve as means toward the production of pleasure-giving objects. He is careful to point out that there is no such thing as absolute utility, utility being purely a relation between a thing and a person. He next proceeds to give the derivative laws of utility somewhat in the following manner: That separate portions of the same pleasure-giving object have very different degrees of utility, and that in general for each person only a limited number of such portions has utility; any addition beyond this limit is useless, but the point of uselessness is only reached after the utility has gone through all the stages or degrees of intensity. Hence he draws the practical conclusion that each person should so distribute his resources as to render the final increments of each pleasure-giving commodity of equal utility for him.

"In the next place Gossen deals with labor, starting from the proposition that the utility of any product must be estimated after deduction of the pains of labor required to produce it. He describes the variation of the pain of labor much as I have done, exhibiting it graphically, and inferring that we must carry on labor to the point at which the utility of the product equals the pain of production. In treating the theory of exchange he shows how barter gives rise to an immense increase of utility, and he infers that exchange will proceed up to the point at which the utilities of the portions next to be given

and received are equal. A complicated geometrical representation of
the theory of exchange is given. The theory of rent is investigated
in a most general manner, and the work concludes with somewhat
vague social speculations, which, in Professor Adamson's opinion, are
of inferior merit compared with the earlier portions of the treatise." [4]

This résumé probably does not tell much to those who are not acquainted with the problem. But to those who have read my first
memoir and Mr. Jevons' work, the preceding paragraphs will immediately indicate that Gossen has given mathematical expression to
utility and has established a mathematical condition of maximum
satisfaction before this was done by myself and by Mr. Jevons. Indeed,
Mr. Jevons, when yielding to Gossen, does so with no more hesitation
and ado than shown by myself when I yielded to him. He censures
Gossen for using straight lines in his diagrams instead of undetermined
curves, and he states that Gossen has not reached the equations of
exchange. But, taken all in all, he recognizes that his own theory,
although it loses nothing of its importance, is by no means as completely novel as he had believed, and he restricts himself to protesting
that, at the time of his writing, he did not know of Gossen nor of his
work—an existence then so little known to the whole world that it
was more difficult to uncover it than to uncover the theory of pleasure
and pain.

"Almost nothing," he says in conclusion, "is known to me concerning Gossen; it is uncertain whether he is living or not. On the
title-page he describes himself as Königlich preussischer Regierungs-
Assessor ausser Dienst, which may be translated 'Royal Prussian Government Assessor, retired'; but the tone of his remarks here and
there seems to indicate that he was a disappointed if not an injured
man. The reception of his one work can have lent no relief to these
feelings; rather it must have much deepened them. The book seems
to have contained his one cherished theory; for I can find under the
name of Gossen no trace of any other publication or scientific memoir
whatever. The history of these forgotten works is, indeed, a strange
and discouraging one; but the day must come when the eyes of those
who cannot see will be opened. Then will due honor be given to all
who like Cournot and Gossen have labored in a thankless field of
human knowledge, and have met with the neglect or ridicule they
might well have expected. Not indeed that such men do really work for

    [4] W. Stanley Jevons, *The Theory of Political Economy,* second ed., London,
Macmillan and Company, 1879, pp. xxxvi–xxxviii.

the sake of honor; they bring forth a theory as the tree brings forth its fruit." [5]

Most certainly, the true scientist pursues truth only because of the pleasure of this pursuit, just as the genuine amateur of whist plays this noble game only because of the pleasure conveyed thereby. There is no need to emphasize that the search and discovery of theories such as those relating mathematics to various sciences exert an attraction incomparably greater than that exerted by any sort of game. But, just as it is legitimate to take a chance with small amounts of money while playing whist, so it is permitted, in the pursuit of scientific truth, to derive additional satisfaction from the thought that one is going to attach his name to an important result. The very greatest men of science have not felt disdain for this feeling of satisfaction. Remember that those who were ingenious enough to invent the infinitesimal calculus were not free enough from self-love to share in propriety the honor of this invention. Nor was Gossen above this sentiment, and Mr. Jevons confesses in all sincerity that he has felt it. I myself have no pretension at all of being above human weaknesses and ordinarily play whist for chips. So I will confess that on receiving Mr. Jevons' letter of September 15, 1878, that is, a year before I was to read the preface to the second edition of his *Theory of Political Economy,* I was much disturbed and a bit worried about what would remain as my own after all the successively evolving priority claims had been satisfied.

The first thing to do was to search for a copy of Gossen's work, and I had much trouble obtaining one. Vieweg and Son, the publishers in Brunswick, informed me that Gossen had lived in Cologne around 1850, and that they had returned to him at that time, and on his request, all remaining copies of his work, "which was only an article of commission." While inquiring about the book with the publishers, I also addressed myself to various public libraries. Finally Mr. Halm, librarian in Munich, sent it to Mr. Charles Secrétan, his son-in-law and my colleague and friend. Together with him I read it with much attention during the first weeks of 1879, and made a complete translation.

The title of Gossen's work is: *Entwickelung der Gesetze des menschlichen Verkehrs und der daraus fliessenden Regeln für menschliches Handeln, von* Hermann Heinrich Gossen, *königlich preussischem Regierungs-Assessor ausser Dienst. Braunschweig, Druck und Verlag von Friedrich Vieweg und Sohn,* 1854. This I would try to translate

[5] *Ibid.,* pp. xli–xlii.

a bit freely as *Exposition of the Laws of Exchange and of the Principles of Industry Derived Therefrom,* by Hermann Heinrich Gossen, formerly Assessor of the Royal Prussian Government. Brunswick, Frederick Vieweg and Son, Publishers, 1854. It forms a volume of 277 pages of text, preceded by a preface of four pages, and is not divided into parts or chapters. A simple dash line, without heading, separates the various subjects treated successively by the author. Altogether this absence of divisions does no harm to the organization of the book, which in a natural manner falls into two parts of approximately equal length. The first part, devoted to pure theory, comprises the "laws of enjoyment and of work," with discussion and arithmetical tables, the "laws of exchange," and the "theory of rent." The other part, devoted to applied theory, comprises "rules of conduct pertaining to desires and pleasures," and the refutation of certain social errors concerning "education," "money," "credit," and "property." For each of his subjects the author provides a plan of organization. He is a strict utilitarian and liberal, that is, he is strongly opposed to government intervention, especially under conditions when individual initiative and free competition suffice as guiding principles of the economic order. The style is quite German, that is, somewhat diffuse and redundant. But the development of the ideas is always perfectly logical and clear.

With respect to the first part of the work, Jevons' résumé and critique, based on Professor Adamson's report, impress me as exact and just. But I, for my part, wish to add a few remarks, because my position vis-à-vis Gossen differs from that of Mr. Jevons. "From this statement," Mr. Jevons says, "it is quite apparent that Gossen has completely anticipated me as regards the general principles and method of the theory of Economics. So far as I can gather, his treatment of the fundamental theory is even more general and thorough than what I was able to scheme out." [6] Well, more happily than Mr. Jevons, I believe to have pushed matters forward to a degree not attained by Gossen, and thus I believe I can protect the priority of a good part of my discoveries. This is a point which I shall take the liberty of discussing in all frankness.

Gossen and Mr. Jevons have found, before me, the mathematical expression of utility, and have formulated the condition of maximum utility in the exchange, by an individual, of one good for another. This is indisputable. Mr. Jevons seems inclined to recognize a certain superiority of Gossen with respect to the first point, and to claim the second for himself. He is right. Gossen has formulated only the

[6] *Ibid.,* p. xxxviii.

condition of the absolute maximum, whereas Jevons was the first to formulate the condition of the relative maximum coexisting with equality of the quantities supplied and demanded.[7] But at this point of the discussion of exchange both have stopped. Neither Gossen nor Mr. Jevons has as much as touched the question of the determination of the equilibrium price of each of the two goods in terms of the other on the basis of an infinitely large number of exchangers. This is precisely one of the two questions resolved by me in the memoir, *Principe d'une théorie mathématique de l'échange,* of August, 1873, leading to the establishment of the equilibrium price as a result of an increase in price when the quantity demanded exceeds the quantity supplied, and as a result of a fall in price in the opposite case of an excess of the quantity supplied. In this way there exists, side by side, the greatest possible satisfaction of desires, or maximum satisfaction, and unity of the exchange ratio for all exchangers, or unity of the market price. The theory of exchange, even in the very restricted case of barter with two goods, is complete only with these two particulars. Exchange under the mechanism of free competition is an operation which enables all exchangers to obtain the greatest satisfaction of their desires compatible with the condition that they turn over the goods which they sell, and receive the goods which they buy, in common and identical proportion. In combining the second condition with the first, I have completed the foundation of the mathematical theory of exchange. In following up this twofold condition for the case of exchange of any number of goods for each other, facilitated by the use of a unit of account—as I have done in my second memoir, *Équations de l'échange,* of December, 1875—I have completed the mathematical theory of exchange itself. Besides the law of price determination, I have formulated the law of price variation, and am convinced that in doing so I not only have formulated the law of supply and demand but have rigorously proved it.

So much about the problems of exchange and of price determination of goods. I should like to state with the same sincerity my conviction that neither Gossen nor Mr. Jevons has analyzed as completely as I the problems of production and of price determination of productive services. These matters are taken up in Gossen's investigations of the "laws of labor" and of the "theory of rent," and in Jevons' "theory of labor," "theory of rent," and "theory of capital." In this respect, the difference between myself and my two predecessors can

---

[7] See Léon Walras, *Études d'économie sociale,* Lausanne, F. Rouge, 1936, pp. 207 ff.

be reduced to the following points, which I wish to call to the attention of the readers.

Gossen and Mr. Jevons always assume an individual or a group of individuals who turn out products, sometimes with labor alone, sometimes with labor and land combined, sometimes with labor and capital combined. They then investigate, usually with great ingenuity, the mathematical conditions of production, determined by the aim of maximization of pleasure and minimization of pain. Well, I for my part do not believe that these studies, ingenious and accomplished as they are, represent a definitive and fruitful advantage, because I consider the assumptions on which they are based as special, exceptional, and deviating from the general case. Their assumptions mirror the organization of production on Robinson Crusoe's island; also, perhaps, production in isolation or under primitive conditions. This is not how production is carried on—I shall not say under our own socio-economic conditions, but under the abstract and ideal socio-economic conditions on which pure economics is based. Under these conditions an economic agent does not always have labor, land, and capital, and he never has all the types of labor, land, and capital which are required if he himself is to turn out the various products which he desires. So, what does he do? He sells his labor, or the services of his personal faculties, for wages; he sells the services of his land for rent; he sells the services of his capital for interest; and with the wages, rent, and interest thus obtained he purchases products. This is the point of view which I have taken in my third memoir, *Équations de la production,* of January and February, 1876, with the aim of defining the mechanism of production under free competition, just as I had defined, in my first memoir, the mechanism of exchange under free competition. The entrepreneur is portrayed by me as a person absolutely distinct from the worker, the landowner, and the capitalist, charged with the function of transforming the productive services of labor, land, and capital into products. At one market, known as market of productive services, the entrepreneur bids for the labor, land, and capital services offered by the worker, the landowner, and the capitalist. For all types of labor, land, and capital services there is, thus, at the market of productive services a demand, a supply, and an equilibrium price: wage, rent, and interest. At a second market, known as product market, the same entrepreneur supplies the products demanded by the worker, the landowner, and the capitalist. For all types of products there is thus, at the product market, a supply, a demand, and an equilibrium price. Just as the equilibrium of exchange is brought about by equality of the quantities supplied and demanded—of productive services or of products—the equilibrium of production is brought about by equality of the selling prices of the products and of the prices of the productive services employed in their production. Here we have, it seems to me, the mechanism surmised by the economists, by means of which services are exchanged for services. The case examined by Gossen and Mr. Jevons—that of an individual producing goods for his own use—is a special case fully included in the general case: the individual then becomes an entrepreneur and should not, in theory, devote himself to the activities of transformation unless he extracts from his labor, his land, and his capital a quantity of products at least equal to that which would have been obtained by passing through the two markets.

In a fourth memoir, *Équations de la capitalisation et du crédit,* of July, 1876, I have discussed the difference between natural and artificial capital. Personal faculties and land are natural capital, available always in kind. Artificial capital consists of products which result from saving—a function of the rate of interest—and which are most often made available in the form of money. Taking thus up the problems of capitalization and of credit after those of exchange and production, I have developed the theory of the determination of the rate of interest following upon the theories of the determination of the prices of products and services. In all these investigations I have carefully maintained the condition of a uniform price—at the market for products, at that for services, and at that for money capital—side by side with the condition of maximum satisfaction. This has enabled me to get to the bottom of the fact of exchange value. In the case of barter with two goods, it follows at once that each exchanger proportions the intensities of his last satisfied desires, or rarities, with the values, because this is the condition of maximum satisfaction. It further follows that the ratio of the values is the same for all exchangers because this is the condition of the uniformity of the price. Therefore, the ratio of the intensities of the last satisfied desires also is the same for all exchangers, and *the values are proportional* to the rarities. I have proved that this proportionality of the values and rarities obtains also in the case of the exchange of several goods for one another with intervention of a unit of account, in the case of production, of capitalization, and of credit. Finally, I have derived from this the principles guiding the variation of values. I might criticize Gossen for having left aside this whole series of investigations—if this were not quite the wrong word to use in such a case. I do not owe him criticisms but great thanks, and these I wish to extend to Gossen and Mr. Jevons. Although they have snatched from me the priority concerning the point of departure of all pure economics, they have most tactfully left me almost entirely in the possession of all further conclusions.

I do not share the opinion of Professor Adamson concerning the applied section which constitutes the second part of Gossen's work. No epithet seems to me less fitting than the word "vague" in connection with the "principles of industry" which Gossen bases on his "laws of exchange." His theories of money, credit, and property are perfectly lucid and precise. Even if these theories should be faulty, the abundance of detail with which they are developed would still attach to them a high value. But they are not faulty. To mention only his theory of property, of which I have presented a critical examination in my memoir, *Théorie mathématique du prix des terres et de leur rachat par l'État,* of November, 1880: this is one of the most beautiful theories which I have ever come across in economics.

The general theory of price determination under free competition, which in my opinion forms the proper subject matter of pure economics, comprises, as we have seen, a theory of rent. Ricardo's theory was developed on the assumption of products obtained with the help of a single variety of land; it expressed the value of the rent in terms of units of the product; and it could explain the surplus element in rent in a progressive society only with the help of an assumed increase in product prices. It is a crude and childish theory, such as could be developed without the aid of mathematics. Rent, the price of the services of land, is determined, as I have said above, at the market for productive services as the result of the supply by the landowners and of the demand either by the entrepreneurs who wish to utilize the respective services in production or by the consumers who wish to devote them directly to their own use. The values of all capital services, labor services, and land services are always proportional to the intensities of the desires satisfied last, or rarities, by the services of capital, labor, and land which are directly consumed. The intensities of the desires satisfied last, or rarities, by the services of land which are directly consumed increase gradually in a society in proportion to the increase in population. The size of parks and gardens diminishes; buildings increase in height; dwelling units, halls, and stairs become smaller. It follows that the value of land services also increases gradually in a progressive society. That is how it must be and that is how it is. Here as in many other cases it suffices to substitute the notion of rarity, which is an absolute element, for the notion of value, which is a relative element, in order to remove all incertitude.[8]

The existence of a surplus element in rent in a progressive society is well established by experience and well explained by reason. Consequently, if the land is abandoned to individuals instead of being reserved for the state, a parasitical class is enabled to profit from an appreciation which should furnish the means to pay for the ever-growing public services. I recall a discussion which I had with Mr. Laboulaye one evening as we returned together from a meeting of the Economic Society at Douix. He insisted that all value derived from labor, but after we had taken a few steps I was able to point out to him a number of vacant lots into which no labor whatever had been sunk and which nevertheless had an enormous value. "This value," he said to me, "is derived from the social labor of the environment." "Well," I asked, "if the value is derived from society, why does society not profit from it?" Let the past be buried, but let the future be safeguarded. Perhaps the state could bring the loss to an end by land nationalization. And if the state, instead of profiting immediately from

---

[8] This is not the place to carry further the current discussion of the important question of land nationalization. However, I am unable to resist the temptation to refute in two words an argument which claims to destroy the entire basis of our theory. I have in mind the prodigious argument which insists that the landowners, far from profiting from a social surplus element in rent, fail to recover by a wide margin from the value of land the value of capital sunk into it since the beginning of society. In a study of *"Le cadastre et l'impôt foncier,"* published in the *Bibliothèque universelle et Revue suisse* of November and December, 1873, I have made the following observations. How little of economics one may know, one must admit that capital rationally employed in agriculture yields its return and its amortization in the form of the price of the agricultural products. Consequently, one can always figure out the value of land before improvements by subtracting from the total value of the landed property the value of the fixed and circulating capital listed in the inventory. The economists of the school of Carey, I said, observe distinctly how capital is sunk into the land in the form of seed, cultivation, improvement, drainage, irrigation, etc. But they fail to notice how it departs in the form of grain, vegetables, and fruits of all kinds. These gentlemen are guilty of an oversight: they are present when the farmer irrigates, works, seeds, fertilizes, plants, and builds; they are absent or absentminded when he mows, harvests, and collects. And these same economists—who delight in the phantasmagoria of an enormous mass of capital, invisible and imperceptible, buried in the land—accuse us of living in a world of abstractions and of confusing the fancies of our imagination with the facts of reality, because we have demonstrated a hundred times the existence of a surplus element in rent in a progressive society and have explained it by relating it to the laws of exchange value.

the surplus element in rent, devoted first the surplus rent to the payment for the land, it might not only save the future but set right the past.

Here an objection poses itself which Gossen did not notice. If the surplus element in rent in a progressive society is an economic fact demonstrated by experience and reason, the equilibrium price of land must reflect it. If now the state pays the landowners the equilibrium price, it can easily find in the increasing rental receipts a normal return on its outlay but not enough to amortize the capital used for the acquisition of land. Obviously, in order to avoid this difficulty, a new element must be introduced into the solution of the problem. I have adduced this element in my memoir, *Théorie mathématique du prix des terres et de leur rachat par l'État,* in the following manner. Together with several economists of authority I believe that mankind at the present time passes through an important economic evolution, turning from the agricultural regime under which it has lived for several thousand years to the industrial and commercial regime. The principal characteristic of the latter relates to the fact that under it agriculture is compelled to employ a large amount of capital in order to maintain a much more numerous population. In my opinion this evolution will add to the surplus element in rent, with no increase in the scarcity or in the value of agricultural products—but up to now this has only been noticed by a few alert and advanced minds and thus cannot as yet have been discounted by the landowners.[9] If the state were to nationalize the land before the evolution under study has taken place, and if it then would do all within its power to pro-

[9] The new surplus element in rent, which results from the economic evolution here described, will arise only after the present crisis, which is characterized by the equalization of rents in the whole world, has abated. This crisis has broken out in consequence of the developments in the field of transportation and of improved communication among the markets. Far from weakening it, it confirms our theory of land services and their surplus value in a progressive society. This theory can indeed in its entirety be traced back to the determination of the price for land services in accordance with the law of supply and demand. When communication is established between two regions of the same country, or between two different countries, unequally rich and peopled, land services will be exported in the form of agricultural products from the point where their scarcity is less to the point where it is more pronounced. There is thus an increase in supply with attending price fall at this last point, and a decline in supply with attending increase in price at the first point. This is what takes place at the present time between England and France, on the one hand, and the less highly developed countries of Europe, America, and Australia on the other. Complicated, perhaps, by an inadequate money supply, it has brought about what is known as agricultural crisis.

mote this evolution—and nationalization would act in this sense—I believe that the new surplus element in the rent would provide ample means for the amortization of the purchase price. I do not believe, it is true, that the democratic and parliamentary state which we enjoy is in the position to undertake such an operation; but the value of an economic and social theory does not necessarily depend on its chance of immediate practical application. Assume that in the second or third century of our era some stoic philosopher gave the exact and precise formula for a social organization without slavery, with ways and means to emancipate the slaves. Shortsighted people, who would have had reasons for being satisfied with the existing state of affairs, would easily have succeeded in demonstrating to him that his plan contradicted the entire social order of Rome and in assuring him that in any event it would never be adopted. But all this would not have prevented truth and the future from being on his side. The situation is similar with respect to Gossen's theory of land nationalization with amortization of the purchase price from rental receipts. Gossen claimed the glory of Copernicus, which is due to him because of his concept of the mathematical equilibrium of the economic world. In my opinion he combines the glory of Copernicus with that of Newton because of his solution of the social question. I have nothing else to say to express my opinion of his merits.

I was much disturbed by the thought that a book such as his could pass unnoticed in a country such as Germany, where scientific work is claimed to be organized so efficiently that no ideas can get lost. I know that mankind, just as nature, finds delight in creation for the sake of subsequent destruction. Often I have said to myself that there are Copernicuses and Newtons who perish in their germinal stage or in their flower. But to see with my own eyes, and to hold in my hands, a great book, which had cost its author years of meditation and study and which almost had fallen into eternal oblivion—for this I was not prepared. I decided to obtain information concerning Gossen's life and to hold up his name for all the world to see. To obtain information of a man who once had been a Prussian official did not seem extremely difficult. But, nevertheless, three years had to pass since the moment when I heard of Gossen for the first time, before I was in the position to prepare this note.

Lausanne being a place where many foreigners reside, and among them some of distinction, I did not have much trouble to find someone in the position to make enquiries with the Prussian administration. In February, 1879, when I had prepared with the help of Mr. Charles Secrétan the French translation of Gossen's book, I had located useful channels for the expression of my desire to obtain detailed information concerning the administrative and scientific career of the author. I pointed out that some relative of Gossen's, if there existed one, could easily furnish this information. At the end of only one year I received a note letting me know that Gossen had died, at age 47, in Cologne on February 13, 1859, and that he had left a sister, mother of Dr. Hermann Kortum, Professor of Mathematics at the University of Bonn. In the possession of this name, I addressed myself to Professor Kortum on February 21, 1880. He promised at once to fulfill my wishes; but not until July 29, 1881, when he had completed the necessary investigations among the papers of his uncle, did he send me the information summarized in the following.[10]

Hermann Heinrich Gossen was born in Düren on September 7, 1810. The city of Düren, located between Aix-la-Chapelle and Cologne, was at that time part of the Ruhr district. His father, of German nationality, was a tax collector in the service of the French government. After the fall of the French empire he was transferred, in the same position, to the Prussian government. In 1824 he gave up his job and went to Cologne, later to Muffendorf, near Bonn, and devoted himself to an agricultural enterprise. There Gossen obtained his early education, with his mathematical inclination soon becoming apparent. In the fall of 1829, after having graduated, he entered the University of Bonn with the view of preparing himself, in accordance with the wishes of his father, for a career in public administration.

In February, 1834, he underwent the first state examination. One of the reports written for this purpose had as subject "the comparative value of direct and indirect taxes from the point of view of the public credit." Gossen treated this question thoroughly, not historically but with the help of the theoretical method, which was to remain his characteristic. He then was appointed "referendary" at Cologne. Not only lacking the inclination for administrative duties but feeling aversion to such a career, he attempted, though in vain, to obtain from his father the permission and the means to spend two more years at the university in order to prepare himself for some other profession. He did not go through his second state examination until 1841, and in July, 1844, was appointed "assessor" at Magdeburg, later at Erfurt. In 1847, after the death of his father, he quit the government service and went to Berlin. A liberal in politics, and already at that time occupied with social

---

[10] I reserve his complete report for publication in conjunction with a translation of Gossen's work.

questions, he stood behind the revolution of 1848 with interest and sympathy but without taking any active part in it.

He then became acquainted with a Belgian who intended to found a general insurance company to undertake successively all types of insurance. Gossen associated himself with this project and took charge of hail and livestock insurance in Cologne in 1849. At that time he prepared with much care and effort the plan for a "General German Savings Bank" designed to do life-insurance business. But after the hail and livestock insurance failed to show good results, he withdrew from it in 1850 in order not to lose too large a portion of the amount which he had invested in it.

These various enterprises had supplied confirmation and precision to his economic ideas. He felt moved to present them in systematic form, and from 1850 to 1854 devoted himself entirely to this pursuit, living in Cologne in seclusion except for the company of his two sisters. He attached great importance to his work and placed high hopes on its publication. But the mathematical form—which was its original feature—prevented it from making any sort of impression, and even from being read by more than a few persons.

The lack of success, combined with poor health, darkened the last few years of Gossen's life. His health, which had been vigorous before, was ruined by a severe attack of typhoid fever in 1853. Soon there became apparent the first symptoms of tuberculosis of the lungs. The rapid aggravation of this disease prevented Gossen from establishing himself in a new position and confined him to seclusion. As he was a musician and violinist, he found some diversion in music and took up the serious study of its mathematical theory. Attended by his sisters with affectionate care, he died on February 13, 1858, a man of idealistic and optimistic tendencies, lacking in practical sense and with little concern about his personal interests, very kindhearted and amiable, full of frankness, sincerity, and probity, naive in demeanor and childlike, as it were, of a nature which opened him all hearts.

Such was Gossen's life—the life of a man easily recognized as the German type of character of olden days, made up of genius and naiveté; a man who died at the age of 47 years, surely without doubting the value of his ideas but probably convinced that they would never bring honor to his name. In this article I try to render honor to him as scrupulously as possible without despoiling myself. The foregoing remarks as well as the translation of Professor Kortum's biographical note were put on paper by me during the first days of August, 1881, exactly as they are printed here, with the only exception of three footnotes which I have added later. Subsequently I put the manuscript aside, fearful, as I was, of attributing excessive and premature importance to theories in whose success I am personally interested. But at the present time I do not believe I should hold it back any longer. Jevons died in 1882, and at once the significance of his work was appreciated. A group of admirers, comprising all outstanding English statesmen and scientists, have joined in an appeal for a foundation in honor of his memory. In this appeal, which is signed, among others, by Messrs. Foxwell and Adamson, successors of Jevons at the University College of London and at Owens College in Manchester, respectively, it is said: "Great logician, which he was, he was a still greater economist. . . . It is no exaggeration to state that his *Theory of Political Economy* was the most original economic work of the time and that, through this book as well as through his admirable statistical investigations, he has marked a distinct period in the development of economic thought, establishing its scientific character beyond all dispute." Nothing could be more just. But is this not an occasion suitable for recalling that Gossen has founded pure economics in the mathematical form which is to be its definitive form—before Jevons and as much as Jevons, according to Jevons' own words?

It seems to me that the time has come to see to it that—in the case of Gossen as in other cases—an injustice which started through negligence be not perpetuated intentionally. That is why I have decided to call his name and his works to the attention of the economists, with much emphasis, and to urge French science and critique to honor itself by treating with the respect which he deserves an original and profound thinker who is not adequately appreciated in his own country.

Keynes
————————— on ———
Jevons

W. Stanley Jevons (1835–1882) was educated at University College in London. As a young man he interrupted his studies and went to Australia, working as an assayer for the mint. Upon his return—*via* the United States—to England he resumed his academic work and turned to economic investigations. He taught at Manchester, and, toward the end of his life, at University College in London.

Jevons' writings are in the fields of logic, statistics, and economics. He is best known for his *Theory of Political Economy* (1871), which introduced the principle of marginal utility to the English-speaking economists. Jevons was a bitter critic of Mill, and his work marks the end of the supreme rule of classical economics as interpreted by Mill. It stands out as an early example of mathematical reasoning applied to economics.

John Maynard Keynes (see below, pp. 763 ff.) was not only a great economist but also a master of biographical writing. His essay on Jevons shows him at his best.

(See also Marshall's essay on Ricardo's theory of value, above, pp. 173 ff., for a discussion of Jevons' views on value.)

I

STANLEY JEVONS [1] was born in the year after Malthus's death. But he was only seven years senior to Marshall and ten years senior to Edgeworth. Professor Foxwell lectured in his stead at University College *before* Jevons took up his professorship there. He examined my father in the Moral Sciences Tripos of 1875, his name being known to me from my early years as, in my father's mind, the pattern of what an economist and logician should be. Thus, though we celebrate to-day (a little late) the centenary of his birth, though it is sixty years ago that Professor Foxwell lectured in his stead and more than fifty years since his death; nevertheless, Jevons belongs to the group of economists whose school of thought dominated the subject for the half-century after the death of Mill in 1873, who are the immediate teachers and predecessors of ourselves here assembled to pay our duty to his memory.

His family belonged to the class of educated nonconformists, who, without academic connections, made up, in the first half of the nineteenth century, the intelligentsia of Liverpool, Manchester, Leeds and Birmingham, and became the backbone of Bentham's foundation (in 1826) at University College, London, and of Owens College, Manchester (founded in 1846). The family, and many of their connections, were Unitarians; and in substance Stanley Jevons remained of that faith to the end of his life. His father was an iron merchant, a friend of Stephenson, much interested in the engineering innovations of the age, said to have constructed (in 1815) the first iron boat that sailed on sea-water, a supporter of the construction of the Thames Tunnel to his own financial loss, author of a small book on law and of an economic pamphlet. His mother, whose ninth child he was, herself a poetess, was the eldest of the gifted family of William Roscoe, the solicitor and banker of Liverpool, collector and dilettante, but also

---

[1] I have, of course, drawn freely on the main source for Jevons's life—his *Letters and Journal* edited by his wife. I am also much indebted for information to his son, H. S. Jevons, who is a member of our Council to-day.

[Reprinted by permission of the Royal Statistical Society from *Journal of the Royal Statistical Society*, 1936.]

a learned historian, author of the *Life of Lorenzo de Medici* and the *Life and Pontificate of Leo X* amongst much else (including the children's classic *The Butterfly's Ball and the Grasshopper's Feast* [2]). Stanley Jevons himself married a daughter of J. E. Taylor, the founder of the *Manchester Guardian,* and was a connection by marriage of R. H. Hutton of the *Spectator*.

His father and his grandfather Roscoe, though both unusually gifted and of unquestioned probity, were both of them bankrupted, the former in the financial crisis of 1848 and the latter through a run on his bank in 1816; so that he had good hereditary cause not to overlook the phenomenon of business fluctuations. Stanley Jevons took much interest in his own investments and financial position, which he managed, if certain hints in his correspondence are to be trusted, with close regard to his theories concerning the Trade Cycle and the gradual exhaustion of our reserves of coal. His own capital was small, but his wife had some means of her own, and Jevons, I am told, augmented their income by good investment of their savings. He was an example of a man who at every critical stage of his affairs sacrificed his income relentlessly in order to secure his major purposes in life, but was far, nevertheless, from despising money, and suffered severe pangs each time that a sacrifice was called for. In many, perhaps in most, respects he was a good Victorian, averse both intellectually and morally to the outlook of the extreme Left, appreciative alike of a Conservative Party "desirous at all costs"—I quote his own words—"to secure the continued and exclusive prosperity of this country as a main bulwark of the general good," and, on the other hand, of a Liberal Party "less cautious, more trustful in abstract principles and the unfettered tendencies of nature." [3]

The circle in which Stanley Jevons grew up was interested in social and economic problems. His grandfather, William Roscoe, was an ardent social reformer, active over the abolition of the slave trade. His father wrote a pamphlet entitled *The Prosperity of the Landlords not Dependent on the Corn Laws*. It is recorded that his mother read with him Archbishop Whateley's *Easy Lessons on Money Matters*. His headmaster, Dr. Hodgson, at the Mechanics' Institute High School in

---

[2] "With Step so majestic the *Snail* did advance,
And promis'd the Gazers a Minuet to dance.
But they all laugh'd so loud that he pulled in his Head,
And went in his own little Chamber to bed."

Written to amuse his own children, it was published in 1807, sold 40,000 copies in the first year and was popular for at least three-quarters of a century after that.

[3] *The Coal Question,* p. xviii.

Liverpool, where he first went to school, was afterwards Professor of Political Economy at Edinburgh. Nevertheless, Jevons was educated, not in the moral sciences, but in mathematics and in biology, chemistry and metallurgy.[4] In 1852, seven years before the publication of Darwin's *Origin of Species,* when he was seventeen years old he wrote in his journal:

I have had several rather learned discussions with Harry about moral philosophy, from which it appears that I am decidedly a "dependent moralist," not believing that we have any "moral sense" altogether separate and of a different kind from our animal feelings. I have also had a talk about the origin of species, or the manner in which the innumerable races of animals have been produced. I, as far as I can understand at present, firmly believe that all animals have been transformed out of one primitive form by the continued influence, for thousands and perhaps millions of years, of climate, geography, etc. Lyell makes great fun of Lamarck's, that is, of this theory, but appears to me not to give any good reason against it.[5]

When he was eighteen the financial difficulties of his family led to his accepting an appointment as an assayer at the Sydney Mint, lately opened as a result of the Australian gold discoveries. In this post he remained for nearly five years. To his ambitions it was a great disappointment to leave University College half-way through his studies, and his main object in leaving Australia was to return there to complete his course for the M.A. degree. But his long period of solitary thought and slow gestation in Australia, at an age when the powers of pure originality are at their highest, had been abundantly fruitful. For soon after his return, the outlines of his principal contributions to knowledge were firmly fixed in his mind. The last third of Jevons's life after he was thirty was mainly devoted to the elucidation and amplification of what in essence he had already discovered.

The results of his solitary thinking in Australia and afterwards, which were produced in a series of studies covering a little more than the decade following his return to England at the end of 1859, fall into two distinct groups, both foreshadowed by his communications to the Cambridge meeting of the British Association in 1862—the first concerned with his inductive studies of fluctuations, and the second with his de-

---

[4] The influence of his scientific training on his approach to economics, statistics and logic was recognized by his election (in 1872) as a Fellow of the Royal Society—the first economist so elected, I think, since Sir William Petty, and followed only by Giffen and Palgrave.

[5] *Letters and Journal,* p. 23.

ductive contributions to pure theory. But before considering these in detail, it will be convenient to mention *The Coal Question,* his first book and the first occasion of his coming prominently before the public.

II

The Coal Question; an Inquiry concerning the Progress of the Nation and the Probable Exhaustion of our Coal Mines is by no means one of Jevons's best works. It is most brilliantly and engagingly written, with nothing omitted which could add to its attractiveness and the effect of its impact. But its prophecies have not been fulfilled, the arguments on which they were based are unsound, and re-read to-day it appears over-strained and exaggerated.

It was Jevons's thesis in this book that the maintenance of Great Britain's prosperity and industrial leadership required a continuous growth of her heavy industries on a scale which would mean a demand for coal increasing in a geometrical progression. Jevons advanced this principle as an extension of Malthus's law of population, and he designated it the *Natural Law of Social Growth.* In the form in which he enunciated the principle—namely, "that living beings of the same nature and in the same circumstances multiply in the same geometrical ratio"—it is, as he said, "self-evident when the meanings of the words are understood." [6] Yet in spite of his warning that "even if we do not change in inward character, yet our exterior circumstances are usually changing," Jevons's extension of the truism can easily mislead. For he continues:

Now what is true of the mere number of the people is true of other elements of their condition. If our parents made a definite social advance, then, unless we are unworthy of our parents, or in different circumstances, we should make a similar advance. If our parents doubled their income, or doubled the use of iron, or the agricultural produce of the country, then so ought we, unless we are either changed in character or circumstances. [7]

From this it is a short step to put *coal* into the position occupied in Malthus's theory by *corn:*

Our subsistence no longer depends upon our produce of corn. The momentous repeal of the Corn Laws throws us from corn upon coal. It marks, at any rate, the epoch when coal was finally recognized as the staple product of the country; it marks the ascendancy of the manufacturing interest, which is only another name for the development of the use of coal. [8]

[6] *The Coal Question,* p. 149.   [8] *Op. cit.,* p. 150.
[7] *Op. cit.,* p. 149.

It is easy to see what alarming deductions from this could be made convincing to a generation which accepted without question a crude version of Malthus. For, as Jevons pointed out, "the quantity of coal consumed is really a quantity of two dimensions, the number of the people, and the average quantity used by each. In round numbers, the population has about doubled since the beginning of the century, but the consumption of coal has increased eightfold and more. Again, the quantity consumed by each individual is a composite quantity, increased either by multiplying the scale of former applications of coal, or finding wholly new applications. We cannot, indeed, always be doubling the length of our railways, the magnitude of our ships, and bridges, and factories. But the new applications of coal are of an unlimited character." [9]

By this time the reader has been carried away from the carefully qualified truisms with which he began, and Jevons concludes in splendid and exciting terms:

We are growing rich and numerous upon a source of wealth of which the fertility does not yet apparently decrease with our demands upon it. Hence the uniform and extraordinary rate of growth which this country presents. We are like settlers spreading in a new country of which the boundaries are yet unknown and unfelt.

But then I must point out the painful fact that such a rate of growth will before long render our consumption of coal comparable with the total supply. In the increasing depth and difficulty of coal mining we shall meet that vague, but inevitable boundary that will stop our progress. We shall begin as it were to see the further shore of our Black Indies. The wave of population will break upon that shore, and roll back upon itself. And as settlers, unable to choose in the fair inland new and virgin soil of unexceeded fertility, will fall back upon that which is next best, and will advance their tillage up the mountain side, so we, unable to discover new coal-fields as shallow as before, must deepen our mines with pain and cost.

There is, too, this most serious difference to be noted. A farm, however far pushed, will under proper cultivation continue to yield for ever a constant crop. But in a mine there is no reproduction and the produce once pushed to the utmost will soon begin to fail and sink to zero.

So far, then, as our wealth and progress depend upon the superior command of coal, we must not only stop—we must go back.[10]

Jevons, it must be confessed, meant the book to be *épatant*. For it is not, I think, unfair to attribute the striking manner in which it is written to his extreme anxiety that his ideas should not be overlooked.

[9] *Op. cit.,* pp. 150, 151, slightly abridged.
[10] *Op. cit.,* p. 154.

His highly original communications to the British Association (in 1862) had fallen flat. His diagrams for business forecasting (also in 1862), the precursor, sixty years too soon, of so many half-baked loaves, had been published at his own expense and, barely mentioned in *The Times* and the *Economist,* lost him money. His pamphlet on Gold [11] (in 1863), though it attracted attention a little later on,[12] had sold 74 copies.[13] Yet he had a passionate sense of vocation and of having something valuable to give the world. On April 25, 1863, he wrote in his Journal:

Now, I suppose I am low because my essay on "Gold" is out, and as yet no one has said a word in its favour except my sister, who of course does it as a sister. What if all I do or can do were to be received so? In the first place, one might be led to doubt whether all one's convictions concerning oneself were not mere delusions. Secondly, one might at last learn that even the best productions may never be caught by the breath of popular approval and praise. It would take infinite time and space to write all I have thought about my position lately. As I have even thought myself in many ways a fool, I am in no way surprised to find that many notions which I have had are ridiculous. At last I fairly allow that the one great way of getting on in this world is to get friends, and impress them with a notion of your cleverness. Send them about to advertise your cleverness, get their testimonials like so many levers to force yourself where you wish to go. How well did Shakespeare see through all these things when he wrote his sixty-sixth sonnet.

It is quite obvious to me that it is useless to go on printing works which cost great labour, much money, and are scarcely noticed by any soul. I must begin life again, and by another way, ingratiating myself where and when I can: only after long years of slow progress can one's notions be brought out with any chance of being even examined by those capable of judging of them.

Faulty as I am in so many ways, I yet feel that my inmost motives are hardly selfish. I believe they grow by degrees less so. Sometimes I even feel that I should not care for reputation, wealth, comfort, or even life

---

[11] *A Serious Fall in the Value of Gold ascertained, and its Social effects set forth, with two Diagrams.*

[12] Fawcett quoted it in an address to the British Association, and Cairnes wrote to *The Times* about it. Jevons records that the *Economist* (*semper idem*) "has been induced to notice the subject in a cautious manner, and, though attributing to me some exaggeration of the matter, comes over to my conclusion substantially" (*Letters and Journal,* p. 191).

[13] "I have just received the bill for my pamphlet on Gold, the total cost of printing, advertising, etc., is £43, and the offset by sales only £10; only seventy-four copies seem to have been sold as yet, which is a singularly small number" (Letter of July 24, 1863, *Letters and Journal,* p. 188).

itself, if I could feel that all my efforts were not without their use. Could I do it all anonymously I perhaps might consent to it. And yet the condemnation of friends and all you meet is hard to be borne, and their praise or admiration must be sweet. . . . I must go upon a different tack.[14]

This time, therefore, he was determined that the public should listen to him. All the arts of showmanship are exercised to recall Political Economy from Saturn. It took Mr. Alexander Macmillan but a few days to perceive that he had been sent a best-seller.[15] Within a year success was complete. He wrote in his Journal:

Sunday Evening, 3rd December, 1865.—The work of the thinker and inventor may indeed prove for ever futile and mistaken; but even if it be in the true and successful path, it is not, and perhaps can hardly be, recognized at once. At least it is not. One of my chief reasons for the little love of society, is that in most company my hopes and feelings seem snuffed out.

14th December, 1865.—Yesterday I had a letter from Sir John Herschel, approving in the most complete manner of my *Coal Question,* which I lately had sent to him. Long periods of labour and depression have to be repaid in brief moments of such satisfaction as that letter gave me— perhaps I may say amply repaid. If the book, which was to me a work of intense interest and feeling, is read by few and understood by fewer, it has at least the endorsement of one scientific man whom I should perhaps of all in the world select as the most competent judge of the subject as a whole.[16]

The shrewd publisher sent a copy to Mr. Gladstone, who replied, "I think it is a masterly review of a vast, indeed a boundless subject," [17] and invited the author to call upon him. "My visit to Gladstone, however, was the striking event, which I shall not easily forget—as an author to meet a great minister in the height of his power." [18] Mill drew attention to the book in Parliament in a speech "in which he urged, for the sake of posterity, the present duty of making greater

---

[14] *Letters and Journal,* p. 181.

[15] *The Coal Question* was published (as were nearly all his subsequent books) by Macmillan, whose treatment of the young and unknown author should serve as a model of promptness to all succeeding generations of publishers. Jevons's entry in his note-book is as follows: "First attention given to the subject in 1861 or 1862. Inquiry commenced in January 1864. Chiefly carried out at Museum Library, June and July 1864. Writing completed before Christmas. Transmitted to Mr. Macmillan about 28th December. Accepted 6th January, 1865. Published during the week 24th and 30th April, 1865" (*Letters and Journal,* p. 203).

[16] *Loc. cit.,* p. 215.

[17] *Loc. cit.,* p. 219.

[18] *Loc. cit.,* p. 226.

efforts for the reduction of the National Debt." [19]   Indeed, the book
came opportunely as political ammunition in the controversy over the
Sinking Fund. Jevons had written:

A multiplying population, with a constant void for it to fill; a growing
revenue, with lessened taxation; accumulating capital, with rising profits
and interest. *This is a union of happy conditions which hardly any country
has before enjoyed, and which no country can long expect to enjoy.*[20]

Thus it was easy to invoke the proposition that we were living on our
natural capital, as a reason why the times were suitable for the rapid
reduction of the dead-weight debt. Yet a little reflection might have
shown that, if our demand for coal was going to increase indefinitely
in a geometrical ratio, our future national income would be so much
greater than our present income that the dead-weight debt would become of little account. Indeed, there is not much in Jevons's scare
which can survive cool criticism. His conclusions were influenced, I
suspect, by a psychological trait, unusually strong in him, which many
other people share, a certain hoarding instinct, a readiness to be alarmed
and excited by the idea of the exhaustion of resources. Mr. H. S.
Jevons has communicated to me an amusing illustration of this. Jevons
held similar ideas as to the approaching scarcity of paper as a result
of the vastness of the demand in relation to the supplies of suitable
material (and here again he omitted to make adequate allowance for the
progress of technical methods). Moreover, he acted on his fears and
laid in such large stores not only of writing-paper, but also of thin brown
packing paper, that even to-day, more than fifty years after his death,
his children have not used up the stock he left behind him of the latter;
though his purchases seem to have been more in the nature of a speculation than for his personal use, since his own notes were mostly written
on the backs of old envelopes and odd scraps of paper, of which the
proper place was the waste-paper basket.[21]

III

We must now turn back to Jevons's long series of inductive studies
of commercial fluctuations and of prices which began with his paper
"On the Study of Periodic Commercial Fluctuations, with Five Diagrams" read before the British Association in 1862.[22] This brief paper

[19] *Loc. cit.,* p. 222.
[20] *The Coal Question,* p. 179.
[21] Prof. Gregory has lately recorded the similar propensity of Edwin Cannan.
[22] Reprinted in *Investigations in Currency and Finance.*

of less than a dozen pages marks the beginning of a new stage in economic science. Others before Jevons had noticed seasonal changes and the alternations of good and bad business. He was not the first to plot economic statistics in diagrams; some of his diagrams bear, indeed, a close resemblance to Playfair's, with whose work he seems to have been acquainted.[23] But Jevons compiled and arranged economic statistics for a new purpose and pondered them in a new way. The significance of his method may be expressed by saying that he approached the complex economic facts of the real world, both literally and metaphorically, as a meteorologist. Most of his previous papers were in fact concerned with meteorology,[24] and he begins his association with economics by the declaration:

> It seems necessary, then, that all commercial fluctuations should be investigated according to the same scientific methods with which we are familiar in other complicated sciences, such especially as meteorology and terrestrial magnetism.[25]

As we shall see subsequently, Jevons was equally at home in the simplified abstractions of pure theory. But this did not blind him to the fact that the material to be handled is shifting and complicated, and will only yield up its answer if it is arranged, compared and analysed for the discovery of uniformities and tendencies. Jevons was the first theoretical economist to survey his material with the prying eyes and fertile, controlled imagination of the natural scientist. He would spend hours arranging his charts, plotting them, sifting them, tinting them neatly with delicate pale colours like the slides of the anatomist, and all the time poring over them and brooding over them to discover their secret. It is remarkable, looking back, how few followers and imitators he had in the black arts of inductive economics in the fifty years after 1862. But to-day he can certainly claim an unnumbered progeny, though the

[23] The *Charts of Trade,* mentioned by Jevons in the passage quoted in the footnote to p. 526 below, was doubtless Playfair's *Commercial and Political Atlas,* published in 1786.

[24] He had published in Waugh's *Australian Almanac* for 1859, "Some Data concerning the Climate of Australia and New Zealand," a paper over fifty pages in length, which is best described by his closing words: "My object has been to present in an available form such accurate numerical data as are attainable, and secondly, to group together general information as to the winds, rains, rivers, floods, the geographical features of the country, and the meteorological circumstances of this part of the globe, so as to show what remarkable problems have to be solved, and what interesting connections of cause and effect may ultimately be traced and proved" (*Letters and Journal,* p. 112).

[25] *Op. cit.,* p. 4.

scientific flair which can safely read the shifting sands of economic statistics is no commoner than it was.

In the first instance Jevons was primarily interested in the discovery and elimination of *seasonal* fluctuations. Indeed, the title of his early paper before the British Association is misleading if it suggests that it was concerned with the trade cycle. He points out that, although there had always been an unwritten knowledge of seasonal fluctuations in the minds of business men, he was only aware of two scientific studies of such matters—Gilbart on the bank-note circulation, and Babbage on the Clearing House statistics, published in the *Statistical Journal* for 1854 and 1856 respectively; and he then proceeds to study the seasonal movements of the rate of discount, of bankruptcies, of the price of Consols and of the price of wheat. He is not yet concerned with the larger swings, and his meteorological interests have not yet led him to sunspots. Nevertheless, his study of the monthly prices of many articles since 1844 put an idea into his head. "I was so much struck with the enormous and almost general rise of prices about the year 1853, that I was led to suspect an alteration of the standard of value." [26] As a result, in the next year (1863) his pamphlet on *A Serious Fall in the Value of Gold* leads him, not to cyclical, but to secular movements.

The state of the subject, when this unknown young man spent his savings on printing his notions about it, was extraordinarily backward. The Californian and Australian gold discoveries had led Chevalier (in 1859) to predict a large fall in the value of gold. But the meaning to be attached to the latter phrase and the method of measurement appropriate to the problem were involved in deep obscurity. Newmarch (in 1857) and McCulloch (in 1858) doubted the existence of any depreciation in the purchasing power of gold, and subsequently in the pages of the *Statistical Journal* (1859, 1860 and 1861) Newmarch had suspended judgment. Jevons had to solve the problem of price index-numbers practically from the beginning; [27] and it is scarcely an exaggeration to say that he made as much progress in this brief pamphlet as has been made by all succeeding authors put together. He examines the logical and dialectical problem, the question of weighting, the choice between an arithmetic and a geometric mean, whether articles which have moved abnormally should be excluded, and, generally speaking, what classes of commodities can best be taken as representative. He then compiles a series of index numbers based on the

[26] *Investigations,* p. 16.

[27] As was habitual with Jevons, he took great interest in discovering and recording the work of his precursors.

average monthly prices of thirty-nine commodities for each of the years 1845 to 1862; and supplements and checks the results by considering a further seventy-nine minor articles. His final conclusion he expressed as follows:

> While I must assert the fact of a depreciation of gold with the utmost confidence, I assign the numerical amount of it with equal diffidence. The lowest estimate of the fall that I arrive at is 9 per cent., and I shall be satisfied if my readers accept this. At the same time, in my own opinion the fall is nearer 15 per cent. It may even be more than this. Many years, however, must pass before numerical estimates can be properly stated to possess more than a slight degree of probability.[28]

Finally, Jevons examined the social consequences of the change in the value of money, classifying incomes according as they suffer from depreciation, estimating its effect on the Budget and the National Debt, enquiring "Whether a remedy is needful or possible," "Ought gold as a standard of value to be abandoned?" "Have the gold discoveries added to the wealth of the world?" and concluding:

> I cannot but agree with Macculloch, that, putting out of sight individual cases of hardship, if such exist, a fall in the value of gold must have, and, as I should say, has already, a most powerfully beneficial effect. It loosens the country, as nothing else could, from its old bonds of debt and habit. It throws increased rewards before all who are making and acquiring wealth. It excites the active and skilful classes of the community to new exertions, and is, to some extent, like a discharge from his debts is to the bankrupt long struggling against his burdens. All this is effected without a breach of national good faith, which nothing could compensate.[29]

For unceasing fertility and originality of mind applied, with a sure touch and unfailing control of the material, to a mass of statistics, involving immense labours for an unaided individual ploughing his way through with no precedents and labour-saving devices to relieve his task, this pamphlet stands unrivalled in the history of our subject. The numerous diagrams and charts which accompany are also of high interest in the history of statistical description.

Just as Jevons's study of seasonal fluctuations had led to his detection of the secular movement of prices, so his task of analysing the latter brought to the surface the character of the cyclical movements over the same period. The analysis and elimination of the latter played, indeed, an important part in his controversial objective. For the doubt which existed as to the secular depreciation of gold was due to the movement

---

[28] *Op. cit.*, p. 17.
[29] *Investigations in Currency and Finance*, p. 96.

being overlaid by the price changes of the trade cycle; those who denied the long-period change in the value of the standard, ascribing the observed movements to the familiar alternation of good and bad trade. It was, therefore, necessary for Jevons to endeavour to eliminate the effect of the latter, which led him, incidentally, to date and to measure the trade cycle with a new precision. This was to lead him at a later date to famous conclusions. For the time being his observations on the underlying causes of the trade cycle, though merely *obiter dicta,* strike deeper, in my judgment, than those which he popularized later. He summed them up as follows:

That great commercial fluctuations, completing their course in some ten years, diversify the progress of trade, is familiar to all who attend to mercantile matters. The remote cause of these commercial tides has not been so well ascertained. It seems to lie in the *varying proportion which the capital devoted to permanent and remote investment bears to that which is but temporarily invested soon to reproduce itself.*[30]

Were a certain definite proportion of the capital of the country set apart every year for such long-dated investments, the returns of capital which they would make would be as regular as the absorption of capital. But this is not the case. It is the peculiarity of these great and permanent works to be multiplied at particular periods.[31]

Jevons supported this conclusion by a graph showing annually over a period of thirty-seven years the quantity of bricks made in the United Kingdom, the loads of timber imported and the price of iron—a remarkable example (in what is merely a parenthesis) of the range of Jevons's inductive curiosity and of his intense industry at this period of his life.[32]

Speaking in this place, it is suitable to mention that at this point Jevons felt himself ripe to apply for membership of our body. In his Journal of June 4, 1864, he wrote:

[30] Jevons's own italics.

[31] *Op. cit.,* p. 28.

[32] This parenthesis had been originally a part of the *Statistical Atlas* which he had been working at in 1861. In a letter to his brother (April 7, 1861) he wrote: "The chief interest of the work will be in the light thrown upon the commercial storms of 1793, 1815, 1826, 1839, 1847, 1857, etc., the causes of which will be rendered more or less apparent. I find that the number of Acts of Parliament, the number of patents, and the number of bricks manufactured, are the best indications of an approaching panic, which arises generally from a large investment of labour in works not immediately profitable, as machinery, canals, railways, etc. It is truly curious how well the curve of *bricks produced* shows this, bricks and mortar being the most enduring form of product. Most of the statistics, of course, are generally known, but have never been so fully combined or exhibited *graphically*. The statistics of patents, and some concerning literature,

I am on the point of getting myself proposed and perhaps elected a Fellow of the Statistical Society, as the use of the title F.S.S., the use of the library, and possible acquaintance with other statisticians, will be of high advantage to me.[33]

His next contribution, *On the Variation of Prices and the Value of the Currency since 1782,* in which he further developed his theory of index numbers and carried through the immense labour of continuing his series backwards into the eighteenth century, was read before the Statistical Society in May 1865; and in the following year he read before the Society his extensive study *On the Frequent Autumnal Pressure in the Money Market, and the Action of the Bank of England.* These papers were the beginning of a close association, which in 1877 culminated in his becoming one of the secretaries of the Society and a member of the Council. By this time he was resident in London, and frequently attended our meetings. In 1880 he was appointed a Vice-President on resigning his secretaryship.

The four years from 1862 to 1866 had been a period of intense activity of mind.[34] Jevons was living on the money he had saved in Australia. He had no post, and had a sense of loneliness and failure. Even in the early part of 1866, when his name had been established, his Journal shows that he suffered from anxiety and depression. So is it always. In May 1866 he was appointed Professor of Logic and Mental and Moral Philosophy and Cobden Professor of Political Economy in Owens College, Manchester. "I shall now have about £300 a year from the college," he wrote in his Journal, "and nearly £108 from my own money. What can I not do with it?" But he now had much to do besides think and write; and in 1867 he married. Nearly ten years were to pass before he again attempted a major statistical enquiry.[35]

will be quite new. The mode of exhibiting numbers by curves and lines has, of course, been practised more or less any time on this side the Deluge. At the end of last century, indeed, I find that a book of *Charts of Trade* was published, exactly resembling mine in principle; but in statistics the method, never much used, has fallen almost entirely into disuse. It ought, I consider, to be almost as much used as *maps* are used in geography" (*Letters and Journal,* pp. 157, 158).

[33] *Letters and Journal,* p. 199.

[34] In addition to what I have recorded, his *Pure Logic, or the Logic of Quality apart from Quantity, with Remarks on System and on the Relation of Logic and Mathematics* was published in 1863.

[35] His paper *On the Condition of the Gold Coinage of the United Kingdom, with reference to the question of International Currency,* read before the Statistical Society in 1868, is of secondary importance, though ingenious and laborious.

It is often forgotten how comparatively late in his career Jevons developed the theory of solar variation as the explanation of the period of the Trade Cycle, which is immortally associated with his name. It was published in two papers read before the British Association in 1875 and 1878. The first of these papers is brief and goes little further than to suggest a matter for enquiry. In 1801 Sir William Herschel had "endeavoured to discover a connection between the price of corn and the power of the sun's rays as marked by the decennial variation of the sun's spots." [36] In 1861 R. C. Carrington, "in his standard work upon the sun, gave a diagram comparing the price of corn with the sunspot curve during portions of the last and present centuries." [37] The results of both these enquiries were negative. But Arthur Schuster, Jevons's colleague at Owens College, revived the matter by pointing out "that the years of good vintage in Western Europe have occurred at intervals somewhat approximating to eleven years, the average length of the principal sunspot cycle." [38] Thorold Rogers' *History of Agriculture and Prices in England,* which began to appear in 1866, provided Jevons with material for analysing wheat prices over a long period. The commercial crises in his own lifetime had occurred at intervals of ten or eleven years: 1825, 1836–39, 1847, 1857, 1866. Might there not be a connection between these things? "I am aware," Jevons concluded, "that speculations of this kind may seem somewhat far-fetched and finely-wrought; but financial collapses have recurred with such approach to regularity in the last fifty years, that either this or some other explanation is needed." [39] Nevertheless, he soon repented of publishing what was no better than a bright idea. "Subsequent enquiry convinced me that my figures would not support the conclusion I derived from them, and I withdrew the paper from publication." [40]

The virus, however, had entered into his system. No one who has once deeply engaged himself in coincidence-fitting of this character will easily disembarrass himself of the enquiry. In 1878 Jevons returned to it in his second paper before the British Association, and in an article contributed to *Nature* in which the argument was recapitulated. Three new discoveries were his excuse. In the first place, he had succeeded in carrying back the history of commercial crises at ten- or

[36] *Investigations,* p. 206.

[37] *Op. cit.,* p. 195.

[38] *Op. cit.,* p. 195.

[39] *Op. cit.,* p. 204.

[40] *Op. cit.,* p. 207. The paper was reprinted posthumously in the *Investigations in Currency and Finance.*

eleven-year intervals almost to the beginning of the eighteenth century. In the second place, he was now advised by his astronomical friends that the solar period was not 11.1 years, as he had previously supposed, but 10.45 years, which fitted much better his series of commercial crises. In the third place, he now abandoned European harvests, the price statistics for which yielded negative results, as the intermediary through which sunspots affected business, in favour of Indian harvests, which, he argued, transmitted prosperity to Europe through the greater margin of purchasing power available to the Indian peasant to buy imported goods.[41]

Jevons's argument is by no means so clear as is usual with him. He produced considerable evidence for the view that commercial crises had occurred at intervals of about 10½ years. The astronomers told him that the solar period was about 10½ years. This "beautiful coincidence," as he called it, produced in him an unduly strong conviction of causal nexus. "I beg leave to affirm," he wrote in his article for *Nature,* "that I never was more in earnest, and that after some further careful enquiry, I am perfectly convinced that these decennial crises do depend upon meteorological variations of like period." [42]   But he devoted far too little attention to the exact dating of deficient harvests in relation to the dating of commercial crises, which was a necessary first step to tracing the intermediate links. In his paper of 1875, when he believed his evidence to depend on European harvests, he discovered the link in the spirit of optimism produced by good crops:

Mr. John Mills in his very excellent papers upon Credit Cycles in the *Transactions of the Manchester Statistical Society* (1867–68) has shown that these periodic collapses are really mental in their nature, depending upon variations of despondency, hopefulness, excitement, disappointment and panic.[43] . . . Assuming that variations of commercial credit and enterprise are essentially mental in their nature, must there not be external events to excite hopefulness at one time or disappointment and despondency at another? It may be that the commercial classes of the English nation, as at present constituted, form a body suited by mental and other conditions to go through a complete oscillation in a period nearly corresponding to that of the sunspots. In such conditions a comparatively slight variation of

[41] Mr. J. C. Ollerenshaw had explained in a communication to the Manchester Statistical Society in 1869 "that the secret of good trade in Lancashire is the low price of rice and other grain in India" (*op. cit.,* p. 236).

[42] *Op. cit.,* p. 235.

[43] Already in 1869 (in his Inaugural Address to the Manchester Statistical Society) Jevons had adopted Mills's theory of the trade cycle.

the prices of food, repeated in a similar manner, at corresponding points of the oscillation, would suffice to produce violent effects.[44]

But in 1878 he described this theory as a "rather fanciful hypothesis," [45] and made everything to depend on the decennial fluctuations in foreign trade consequent on cyclical crop changes in India and elsewhere. Unfortunately this involved a difficulty in dating which he passes over with surprising levity:

> One difficulty which presents itself is that the commercial crises in England occur simultaneously with the high prices in Delhi, or even in anticipation of the latter; now the effect cannot precede its cause, and in commercial matters we should expect an interval of a year or two to elapse before bad seasons in India made their effects felt here. The fact, however, is that the famines in Bengal appear to follow similar events in Madras.[46]

Thus the details of the inductive argument are decidedly flimsy. If, however, it could be established that, generally speaking and on the average of different crops and countries, years when the world draws for current consumption on the stocks carried forward from one harvest to another alternate, in accordance with the solar period, with years when bountiful harvests serve to increase the stocks carried forward, Jevons could have linked his thesis, on the broadest possible grounds, with his forgotten theory of 1863 that the trade cycle depended on fluctuations of investment. For alternating investment and disinvestment in the aggregate stocks of the produce of the soil held in excess of current consumption might be capable of consequences closely analogous to those he had previously ascribed to fluctuations in the rate of new investment in durable goods.

Whether or not Jevons was wrong or rash in the hypotheses he framed on the basis of his inductive studies, it was a revolutionary change, for one who was a logician and a deductive economist, to approach the subject in this way. By using these methods Jevons carried economics a long stride from the *à priori* moral sciences towards the natural sciences built on a firm foundation of experience. But the material of economics is shifting as well as complex. Jevons was pursuing a singularly difficult art, and he has had almost as few successors as predecessors, who have attained to his own level of skill.

The sun-spot papers cannot be ranked on at all the same plane of genius or of achievement as *A Serious Fall in the Value of Gold*. Since

[44] *Op. cit.*, pp. 203–4.   [46] *Op. cit.*, pp. 239–40.
[45] *Op. cit.*, p. 226.

his time, unfortunately for his conclusions, the astronomers have reverted to 11.125 as the average of the solar period,[47] whilst the trade cycles have recurred at intervals of 7 or 8, rather than of 10 or 11 years. In 1909 the problem was reconsidered in an ingenious manner by his son Prof. H. S. Jevons,[48] who argued that the harvest statistics could be interpreted in terms of a 3½-year cycle, which was combined in twos or threes to produce either 7- or 10½-year periods. This was followed up after the War by Sir William Beveridge's much more elaborate studies of harvest statistics, which led him to the conclusion of a complex 15.2-years period which he further analysed into sub-periods.[49] It is now generally agreed that, even if a harvest period can be found associated with the solar period or with more complex meteorological phenomena, this cannot afford a complete explanation of the trade cycle. The theory was prejudiced by being stated in too precise and categorical a form. Nevertheless, Jevons's notion, that meteorological phenomena play a part in harvest fluctuations and that harvest fluctuations play a part (though more important formerly than to-day) in the trade cycle, is not to be lightly dismissed.

IV

Meanwhile Jevons was contributing with equal originality to the study of deductive economics based on simplified and abstract assumptions. His thoughts can be traced back to his period of solitary thought in Australia in 1858–9 when he was 22 or 23 years old.[50] By 1860, when he was working at University College, a definite theory was taking shape in his mind. On June 1, 1860, he wrote to his brother Herbert:

During the last session I have worked a good deal at political economy; in the last few months I have fortunately struck out what I have no doubt

---

[47] Whilst this is now believed to be the *average* interval, it is not a uniform one; and over the limited period which Jevons had particularly examined the average interval actually was, as he believed, about 10.45 years.

[48] *The Sun's Heat and Trade Activity,* supplemented by his paper on "The Causes of Fluctuations of Industrial Activity and the Price-level," *Statistical Journal* (1933), Vol. XCVI, pp. 545–605.

[49] Published in articles in the *Economic Journal* in 1920 and 1921 and in the *Statistical Journal* in 1922. In the discussion at the Statistical Society serious objections were raised by Mr. Yule and others to the further analysis of the (apparent) 15.2-years period.

[50] In December 1862 he wrote in his Journal: "I thought what I did very clever then (i.e., in Sydney), but it seems foolishness to me now and my first efforts at a theory of economy look strange beside the theory which has gradually opened before me."

is *the true Theory of Economy,* so thorough-going and consistent, that I cannot now read other books on the subject without indignation. While the theory is entirely mathematical in principle, I show, at the same time, how the data of calculation are so complicated as to be for the present hopeless. Nevertheless, I obtain from the mathematical principles all the chief laws at which political economists have previously arrived, only arranged in a series of definitions, axioms, and theories almost as rigorous and connected as if they were so many geometrical problems. One of the most important axioms is, that as the quantity of any commodity, for instance, plain food, which a man has to consume, increases, so the utility or benefit derived from the last portion used decreases in degree. The decrease of enjoyment between the beginning and end of a meal may be taken as an example. And I assume that on an average, the *ratio of utility* is some continuous mathematical function of the quantity of commodity. This law of utility has, in fact, always been assumed by political economists under the more complex form and name of the Law of Supply and Demand. But once fairly stated in its simple form, it opens up the whole of the subject. Most of the conclusions are, of course, the old ones stated in a consistent form; but my definition of capital and law of the interest of capital are, as far as I have seen, quite new. I have no idea of letting these things lie by till somebody else has the advantage of them, and shall therefore try to publish them next spring.[51]

More than two years passed by, however, before the outline of his theory was made public. Jevons sent a short paper entitled *Notice of a General Mathematical Theory of Political Economy* to Section F of the British Association to be read in his absence before the 1862 Meeting held at Cambridge, where Marshall was an undergraduate in his first year. He had no diffidence about its worth and high, though doubtful, hopes about its effect. He wrote to his brother in September 1862:

Although I know pretty well the paper is perhaps worth all the others that will be read there put together, I cannot pretend to say how it will be received—whether it will be read at all, or whether it won't be considered nonsense. . . . I am very curious, indeed, to know what effect my theory will have both upon my friends and the world in general. I shall watch it like an artilleryman watches the flight of a shell or shot, to see whether its effects equal his intentions.[52]

The paper attracted no attention whatever and was not printed, the Secretary of the British Association writing to him that "a further explanation and publication of the above-mentioned theory is deferred until a more suitable period for establishing a matter of such difficulty."

[51] *Letters and Journal,* p. 151.   [52] *Loc. cit.,* p. 169.

Four years later it was published in the *Statistical Journal* (June 1866), where it occupies about five pages.[53] Though to a modern reader Jevons's 27 paragraphs are perfectly lucid, they are little more than an abstract or syllabus of a complete theory. But the substance of all his subsequent ideas is there. A hedonistic calculus allows us to balance the utility of consumption against the disutility of labour. The price of a commodity is determined not by its aggregate utility but by balancing the marginal utility of its consumption, or, as he here expresses it, "the *coefficient of utility* (which) is the ratio between the last increment or infinitely small supply of the object, and the increment of pleasure which it occasions," against the marginal disutility of its production, "labour (being) exerted both in intensity and duration until a further increment will be more painful than the increment of produce thereby obtained is pleasurable." [54] The amount of capital is estimated by the amount of utility of which the enjoyment is deferred. . . . As labour must be supposed to be aided with some capital, the rate of interest is always determined by the *ratio which a new increment of produce bears to the increment of capital by which it was produced.*" [55] In a concluding sentence the extent of his departure from the classical school is indicated: "The interest of capital has no relation to the absolute returns to labour, but only to the increased return which the last increment of capital allows." [56]

Another five years passed by before this abstract, which had attracted no more attention than at its first reading, was fully clothed, *The Theory of Political Economy* being published in October 1871. Prof. H. S. Jevons records [57] that "according to one of my father's MS. notes,[58] the publication might have been delayed considerably later than 1871 had it not been for the appearance in 1868 and 1870 of articles by Pro-

[53] Reprinted (as an appendix) in the fourth edition of Jevons's *Theory of Political Economy,* edited by H. S. Jevons in 1911.

[54] *Statistical Journal* (1866), Vol. XXIX, pp. 283, 284.

[55] *Loc. cit.,* p. 286.

[56] *Loc. cit.,* p. 287.

[57] In editing the fourth edition of *The Theory,* p. lvii.

[58] This note (as nearly as I can decipher it—written, as usual, on the back of an old envelope) runs as follows:

"In regard to this & certain other essays of Professor Fleeming Jenkin, it seems desirable that I should make the following explanation, to prevent misapprehension. My theory was originally read at the Brit. Assoc. in 1862, & printed in the Stat. Journal in 1867 (*sic*). In March 1868 Prof Jenkin wrote an article for the Br. Quarterly Review (*sic*) in which he restated (?) . . . the law of supply & demand in math language. He courteously sent a copy to me and requested my opinion thereon; in replying I sent a copy of the paper mentioned above, & a

fessor Fleeming Jenkin." The book follows very closely both the order and substance of the abstract of nearly ten years before. But it carries out what was only the promise of the latter to "reduce the main problem of this science to a mathematical form," by introducing diagrams and expressing the argument in mathematical form with a frequent use of the notation of the differential calculus.

Jevons's *Theory of Political Economy* and the place it occupies in the history of the subject are so well known that I need not spend time in describing its contents. It was not as uniquely original in 1871 as it would have been in 1862. For, leaving on one side the precursors Cournot, Gossen, Dupuit, Von Thünen and the rest, there were several economists, notably Walras and Marshall, who by 1871, were scribbling equations with x's and y's, big Deltas and little d's. Nevertheless, Jevons's *Theory* is the first treatise to present in a finished form the theory of value based on subjective valuations, the marginal principle and the now familiar technique of the algebra and diagrams of the subject. The first modern book on economics, it has proved singularly ✻ attractive to all bright minds newly attacking the subject;—simple, lucid, unfaltering, chiselled in stone where Marshall knits in wool. Let me open it almost at random and quote you a passage to remind you of its quality:

> The fact is, that *labour once spent has no influence on the future value of any article:* it is gone and lost for ever. In commerce bygones are for ever bygones; and we are always starting clear at each moment, judging the values of things with a view to future utility. Industry is essentially prospective, not retrospective; and seldom does the result of any undertaking exactly coincide with the first intentions of its promoters.
>
> But though labour is never the cause of value, it is in a large proportion of cases the determining circumstance, and in the following way: *Value depends solely on the final degree of utility. How can we vary this degree of utility?—By having more or less of the commodity to consume. And how shall we get more or less of it?—By spending more or less labour in obtaining a supply.* According to this view, then, there are two steps between labour and value. Labour affects supply, and supply affects the degree of utility, which governs value, or the ratio of exchange. In order

correspondence ensued concerning the correctness of the theory, in the course of which curves were used in illustration by both parties.

"In 1870 appeared Prof. Jenkins 'Graphic Illustration (*sic*)' in which no reference is made to my previous (?).

"Partly in consequence of this I was led to write & publish the Theory in 1871.

"In 1872 Prof. Fleeming Jenkin published in the Proceedings of the Roy Soc Edin (?)."

that there may be no possible mistake about this all-important series of relations, I will re-state it in a tabular form, as follows:

> *Cost of production determines supply;*
> *Supply determines final degree of utility;*
> *Final degree of utility determines value.*[59]

In recent times Jevons has received special praise for his Theory of Capital, inasmuch as he anticipated the Austrian School by emphasizing as two distinct dimensions the quantity of capital and the period for which it has to be employed in order to yield up its product. Nevertheless, his treatment as a whole is somewhat vitiated (as Prof. Robbins has pointed out) by echoes of "wage-fund" ideas. Capital, according to Jevons, "consists merely in the aggregate of those commodities which are required for sustaining labourers of any kind or class engaged in work." [60] He prefers to say, "not that a factory, or dock, or railway, or ship *is capital,* but that *it represents so much capital sunk in the enterprise.*" "Accordingly, I would not say that a railway *is fixed capital,* but that *capital is fixed in the railway.* The capital is not the railway, but the food of those who made the railway." [61] On the other hand, there are admirable passages where he conceives of capital as being measured on the supply side by the amount of the present utility foregone and on the demand side by the discounted value of the future utilities expected from it.

It is somewhat surprising that even the book did not win any immediate success.[62] The only reviews of importance were those by Cairnes, representing the older generation, and by Alfred Marshall, representing the younger, in what was the latter's first appearance in print. Cairnes declared that ignorance of mathematics made most of the book unintelligible to him, but this did not prevent him from concluding that it was all wrong. Marshall's review was tepid and grudging. "We may read far into the present book," he wrote, "without finding any important proposition which is new in substance." [63] "The main value of the book does not lie in its more prominent theories, but in its original treatment of a number of minor points, its suggestive remarks and careful analogies." [64] And he characteristically concludes: "The book before us would be improved if the mathematics

---

[59] *Theory of Political Economy*, p. 164.
[60] *Theory of Political Economy* (4th ed.), p. 223.
[61] *Op. cit.,* p. 243.
[62] Seven years passed before it had sold 1,000 copies.
[63] *Memorials of Alfred Marshall*, p. 94.
[64] *Loc. cit.,* p. 95.

were omitted, but the diagrams retained." [65]   Jevons, writing to a correspondent, commented as follows: "There was indeed a review in the *Academy* of 1st April, 1872, but though more fair than that of the *Saturday Review,* it contained no criticism worthy of your notice." [66] So late as 1874 Jevons wrote:

While I am not aware that my views have been accepted by any well-known English economist, there are a certain number of younger mathematicians and economists who have entered into the subject, and treated it in a very different manner.   Among these I may mention Mr. George Darwin, the son of the eminent naturalist; he is a very good mathematician and an acute economist. [67]

The relations between Jevons and Marshall are of some interest. Nearly twenty years later, and eight years after Jevons's death, the references to Jevons in the *Principles* are still somewhat grudging. [68] Marshall was extraordinarily reluctant to admit that he owed anything to Jevons.   There is no evidence that Jevons was aware of the authorship of the *Academy* review.   He never visited Cambridge before 1874, when he first examined in the Moral Sciences Tripos.   "The only time I saw him," Mrs. Marshall writes to me, "was in 1874 when he was one of my examiners and gave rise to Dr. Kennedy's lines:

> "Were they at sixes and at sevens?
> Oh Pearson Gardiner Foxwell Jevons." [69]

He was, of course, close friends with Professor Foxwell, with whom he frequently corresponded, and whom he again visited at Cambridge towards the end of 1880.   In a letter of Jevons's to Professor Foxwell written in 1875 and again in 1879 there are echoes of talk in which

[65] *Loc. cit.,* p. 99.

[66] *Letters and Journal,* p. 309.

[67] *Loc. cit.,* p. 311 (in the same letter as that from which the immediately preceding quotation is taken).

[68] *Vide* my *Essays in Biography,* pp. 186–188.

[69] When *The Economics of Industry,* by Alfred and Mary Marshall, was published in 1879, the authors sent Jevons a copy, which is now in the possession of his son.   At the beginning and at the end Jevons has pasted in letters from Marshall.   In the first of these, printed in *Memorials of Alfred Marshall,* p. 371, Marshall speaks of "the results of abstract quantitative reasoning in Economics of which I recognize in you the chief author."   The second responds to Jevons's acknowledgment of the book and begins: "My dear Jevons, My wife and I have often wondered what you would think of our book; we were more anxious for your good opinion of it than for anyone else's. . . ."   When Marshall applied for an appointment at Bristol (1877), Jevons furnished him with a testimonial (*vide* my *Essays in Biography,* p. 195).

Professor Foxwell seems to have been advancing Marshall's claims. In 1875 Jevons writes:

I have been very much interested in your letter concerning my paper. It has told me much, which I had no previous means of knowing, concerning the ideas current in philosophical subjects in Cambridge. I was not aware that Marshall had so long entertained notions of a quantitative theory of political economy, and think it a pity that he has so long delayed publishing something on the subject.

It is, of course, open to you or him or others to object to the special way in which I have applied mathematics, and I should like to see other attempts in different directions, but what I contend is that my notion of utility is the correct one, and the only sound way of laying the foundation for a mathematical theory.[70]

And in 1879:

As regards the analogy of the laws of wages and rents, of course I do not know what Marshall gave in his lectures in 1869, as I neither attended them nor have seen notes, unless, indeed, the answers of some of the candidates. But I do not remember that they said anything on the matter. . . .

As regards Marshall's originality, I never called it in question in the slightest degree, having neither the wish nor the grounds. On the other hand, you seem to forget that the essential points of my theory were fully indicated as far back as 1862, at the Cambridge Meeting of the British Association. I have no reason to suppose that Marshall saw any printed report of my first brief paper; but of course, on the other hand, in my book of 1871 (*Theory of Political Economy*) I could not possibly have borrowed anything from Marshall. But these questions are really of little or no importance now that we have found such earlier books as those of Gossen, Cournot, Dupuit, etc. We are all shelved on the matter of priority, except, of course, as regards details and general method of exposition, etc.[71]

Jevons omits to point out that an abstract of his whole theory had been printed in the *Statistical Journal* in 1866—not a very obscure source. Indeed, it was preposterous to suggest that Jevons could have derived anything from Marshall. But for more than another decade after Jevons wrote the above, "what Marshall gave in his lectures in 1869" was to be an inhibition and a taboo on the publications of others. In later years Marshall was, perhaps, a little uneasy whether a certain fundamental lack of sympathy had led him to do injustice to Jevons. The following undated [72] fragment was found amongst his papers:

[70] *Letters and Journal*, p. 331.   [72] Apparently written in 1897.
[71] *Loc. cit.*, p. 408.

I looked with great excitement for Jevons's *Theory:* but he gave me no help in my difficulties and I was vexed. I have since learnt to estimate him better. His many-sidedness, his power of combining statistical with analytical investigations, his ever fresh honest sparkling individuality and suggestiveness impressed me gradually; and I reverence him now as among the very greatest of economists. But even now I think that the central argument of his *Theory* stands on a lower plane than the work of Cournot and von Thünen. They handled their mathematics gracefully: he seemed like David in Saul's armour. They held a mirror up to the manifold interactions of nature's forces: and, though none could do that better than Jevons when writing on money or statistics or on practical issues, he was so encumbered by his mathematics in his central argument, that he tried to draw nature's actions out into a long queue. This was partly because the one weakness of his otherwise loyal and generous character showed itself here: he was impressed by the mischief which the almost pontifical authority of Mill exercised on young students; and he seemed perversely to twist his own doctrines so as to make them appear more inconsistent with Mill's and Ricardo's than they really were. But the genius which enabled Ricardo —it was not so with Mill—to tread his way safely through the most slippery paths of mathematical reasoning, though he had no aid from mathematical training, had made him one of my heroes; and my youthful loyalty to him boiled over when I read Jevons' *Theory.* The editor of the *Academy* having heard that I had been working on the same lines, asked me to review the book: and, though a quarter of a century has passed, I have a vivid memory of the angry phrases which would force themselves into my draft, only to be cut out and then reappear in another form a little later on, and then to be cut out again. . . . On many aspects of economics I have learnt more from Jevons than from any one else. But the obligations which I had to acknowledge in the Preface to my *Principles* were to Cournot and von Thünen and not to Jevons.[73]

This passage brings to the surface a deeper cause of the lack of sympathy between these two founders of modern economics than a sense of rivalry arising out of the similarity of their approach—namely, out of their *dissimilarity* in standing, each with the deep emotion which the subject commands, on opposite sides in the still unresolved debate whether Ricardo was a true or a false prophet. In 1875 Jevons wrote to Professor Foxwell:

[73] *Memorials of Alfred Marshall,* p. 99. To this may be added Marshall's tribute to Jevons printed by Professor Foxwell in his introduction (p. xliii) to the *Investigations in Currency and Finance,* to the effect that the great body of Jevons's work "will probably be found to have more constructive force than any save that of Ricardo, that has been done during the last hundred years," and that "the pure honesty of Mr. Jevons's mind, combined with his special intellectual fitness for the work, have made them models for all time."

"I am beginning to think very strongly that the true line of economic science descends from Smith through Malthus to Senior, while another branch through Ricardo to Mill has put as much error into the science as they have truth." [74] And the preface to the second edition of his *Theory of Political Economy* (1879) concludes as follows:

When at length a true system of Economics comes to be established, it will be seen that that able but wrong-headed man, David Ricardo, shunted the car of Economic science on to a wrong line, a line, however, on which it was further urged towards confusion by his equally able and wrong-headed admirer John Stuart Mill. There were Economists, such as Malthus and Senior, who had a far better comprehension of the true doctrines (though not free from the Ricardian errors), but they were driven out of the field by the unity and influence of the Ricardo-Mill school. It will be a work of labour to pick up the fragments of a shattered science and to start anew, but it is a work from which they must not shrink who wish to see any advance of Economic Science.[75]

The violence of Jevons's aversion to Mill, pursued almost to the point of morbidity, is well known. All Jevons's nonconformist heredity rose up against the orthodoxy which the prestige of Mill in the 'sixties and 'seventies imposed on the subject and particularly on its educational side. He wrote to a correspondent in 1874:

I fear it is impossible to criticize Mr. Mill's writings without incurring the danger of rousing animosity, but I hope and believe you are right in saying that I have said nothing from petulance or passion. Whatever I have said or shall say of Mr. Mill is due to a very long consideration of his works, and to a growing conviction that, however valuable they are in exciting thought and leading to the study of social subjects, they must not be imposed upon us as a new creed.[76]

Of the younger men with whom he was intimate, he fully converted Professor Foxwell to his point of view, and it was a bond of sympathy. But he could not forgive Edgeworth, with whom he used to walk on Hampstead Heath, by which they both lived in the last years of his life, for being "still deep in the fallacies of Mill." The aversion had some of its roots, I think, in a personal experience. In 1860, shortly after his return from Australia, he was working at University College for the B.A. degree. At this time his own theories were seething in his head.[77]

[74] *Letters and Journal,* p. 344.
[75] *Theory of Political Economy* (2nd ed.), p. lvii.
[76] *Letters and Journal,* p. 329.
[77] Cf. the letter to his brother written at this time from which I have quoted above, p. 531.

In his heart he believed himself to be in embryo the only economist in the world with a conception of the truth. This was a dangerous state of mind for an examinee, and after the College Examinations in June, 1860, he has to confess:

In political economy I had a sad reverse, such indeed as I never had before, for in spite of having studied the subject independently and originally, and having read some dozens of the best works in it, almost neglecting other classes for the purpose, I was placed third or fourth when I felt confident of the first prize. This I can only attribute to a difference of opinion, which is perfectly allowable, having prejudiced the professor against my answers. However, I shall fully avenge myself when I bring out my *Theory of Economy,* and re-establish the science on a sensible basis.[78]

It is interesting to record that the first prize was awarded to H. H. Cozens-Hardy, afterwards Master of the Rolls, who was, however, three years Jevons's junior, and that in the examination for the Ricardo Scholarship in Political Economy, a few months later in the same year, Jevons defeated Cozens-Hardy and was awarded the scholarship.[79] Moreover in the June examination in Philosophy of Mind and Logic Jevons was bracketed first (with Theodore Waterhouse). So he had not, in fact, much to complain of. Nevertheless the effect on his mind was curious. The students whom he had to teach when he became Professor at Owens College were accustomed to sit for the London examinations. As he thought it would be unfair to expose his own pupils to the rebuff he himself had suffered, his conscience did not allow him to teach them his own characteristic doctrine. His courses at Manchester were mainly confined to an exposition of Mill.[80] I had long

[78] *Letters and Journal,* p. 154.
[79] This and other information relating to the teaching of Economics at University College has been very kindly supplied to me by Miss C. E. Collet (who was examined by Jevons in 1880 in the philosophical subjects for the London B.A.). She tells me that the sessional examination was confined to the work done during the year under the Professor (Jacob Waley, who was more of a lawyer than an economist), and gave little scope for showing superiority outside this course, whereas the scholarship examination was wider and brought in an external examiner (R. H. Hutton in 1860, Bagehot having been the external examiner in the previous year). The actual papers set are to be found in the U.C.L. Calendars for 1860–1 and 1861–2.
[80] In explaining his methods of teaching at Owens College (*Letters and Journal,* p. 284) he writes: "I have generally followed somewhat the order of subjects in Mill's Pol. Econ. in perfect independence, however, of his views and methods when desirable. In the subject of currency I have always abandoned his book altogether." But this fell far short, I believe, of his venturing to teach the mar-

ago heard this from my father, and how this repression of his own theories had brought his feeling against Mill to boiling point. A book of careful lecture notes taken down by a member of his class, which I lately came across, confirms that this was so.[81]

V

In my memoir of Alfred Marshall I called attention to the many-sidedness which seems to be a necessary equipment for an economist.[82] Jevons was certainly a notable example of this. To his scientific and experimental training which led him to his inductive studies and his logical and analytical bent which led him to his deductive studies there was added an unusually strong historical, and even antiquarian, bias. From his earliest days Jevons had a native inclination to carry his inductive studies backwards in point of time, and to discover the historical

ginal principle and other characteristic doctrines of his own *Theory;* whilst on currency his own outlook did not differ significantly from Mill's. Cf. also *Letters and Journal,* p. 409, where many years later (1879) he defended his recommendation of Mill's *Political Economy* for the Bankers' Institute examinations on the ground that "it is one thing to put forward views for rational judgment of competent readers, it is another thing to force these views on young men by means of examinations." Miss Collet tells me that, since Political Economy was a subject only for the London M.A. degree and not for the London B.A., those of Jevons's pupils at Owens College who sat for the London examinations in Political Economy were very few indeed as compared with those who sat in Logic for the B.A. examination, and she argues that Jevons's irritation against Mill was concerned more with his Logic than with his Political Economy. But there can, I think, be little doubt as to the strength of Jevons's hostility to Mill's *Political Economy,* at least equally with his Logic.

[81] Some qualification to the above is suggested by the following note appended by Jevons in his list of his mathematico-economic books: "From about the year 1863 I regularly employed intersecting curves to illustrate the determination of the market price in my lectures at Owens College." The lecture notes referred to above do, indeed, include a sketch of a demand curve, but the accompanying text contains no reference to the marginal principle.

[82] There are many passages which show Jevons's own awareness of the complex qualities required by an economist. *Vide Letters and Journal,* p. 101 (also pp. 116–18): "*Economy,* scientifically speaking, is a very contracted science; it is in fact a sort of vague mathematics which calculates the causes and effects of man's industry, and shows how it may best be applied. There are a multitude of allied branches of knowledge connected with man's condition; the relation of these to political economy is analogous to the connection of mechanics, astronomy, optics, sound, heat, and every other branch more or less of physical science, with pure mathematics. . . . There are plenty of people engaged with physical science, and practical science and arts may be left to look after themselves, but thoroughly to understand the principles of society appears to me now the most cogent business."

origins of any theory in which he was interested. This is first apparent in the quantity of historical material with which he adorned the *Coal Question,* material much of which it would have occurred to few other authors to bring in. He carried back his series of index numbers into the eighteenth century. When he came to study solar variations, he traced back the history of the trade cycle to the beginning of the eighteenth century and examined harvest statistics over many centuries. Thus in the field of economic history he made himself a pioneer in the history of prices and of trade fluctuations.

In the history of economic thought and theory he was even more deeply interested. In every branch of the subject that he touched he sought out the unknown or forgotten precursors of his favourite theories. His most brilliant contribution in this field was his discovery of the work and significance of Cantillon; whilst his most substantial contribution was his pioneer work in economic bibliography summed up in his hand-list of "Mathematico-Economic Books, Memoirs, and other published Writings," printed as an appendix to the second edition of his *Theory of Political Economy* and in his handlist of writings on monetary problems appended to the *Investigations in Currency and Finance.*

Beyond this, Jevons was a born collector, the first of the distinguished tribe of economic bibliomaniacs who have contrived to set a fashion amongst librarians which has entitled the booksellers to run the obscurest fragments of economic literature up to fancy figures. Jevons invented the collecting of obscure economic books and pamphlets; though it was, of course, Lord Macaulay who first drew attention to their importance as historical sources. Professor Foxwell [83] first caught the affliction from him; though Jevons never paid high prices or proceeded to the extremer stages where condition and collector's "points" are paramount,—his was primarily a far-flung working library for which any usable copy would do. Nevertheless, there are entries scattered through his letters tantalizing to the modern collector. On April 8, 1879, he writes to his wife from The Three Swans, Salisbury:

> I have done a great stroke in book-buying, having bought a remarkable collection of nearly five hundred economical and political pamphlets at

[83] "Why," said Jevons to Foxwell one day, "don't you walk sometimes down Great Portland Street" (then a centre of the secondhand booksellers, especially where it joins the Euston Road, as it is to-day of secondhand cars), "there are few days I don't find something there." And that, Prof. Foxwell tells me, was the beginning. In 1881 he wrote to Prof. Foxwell: "I hear of you at the booksellers' occasionally, and fancy you must be getting a good collection of economic books," a remark which has remained *à propos* any day in the fifty-five years since then.

about a halfpenny each. Some of them are evidently valuable and rare. One of them contains copperplate diagrams of prices for some centuries. One or two are by Robert Owen. I also got a carefully-written list of them all, as good as a catalogue.[84]

In 1881 he writes from Paris:

A large part of my time has been taken up in book-hunting on the banks of the Seine. I have secured almost a trunkfull of books on economics, of much scientific and historic value, but often at ridiculously low prices.[85]

His wife records:

On a leisure afternoon he thoroughly enjoyed making a round of several old bookshops, and his kindly, courteous manners—as courteous always to his inferiors in position as to those of his own station—were fully appreciated by the owners. At two at least of the shops which he most frequented he was regarded as a friend, and the booksellers took a pleasure in looking out at the sales they attended for the books they thought might suit him, reserving them from their other customers until he had seen them.[86]

By the end of his life he had accumulated several thousand volumes, lining the walls and passages of the house and packed in heaps in the attics, an embarrassment to his wife and family both then and in their subsequent removals. These latter led to the gradual dispersal of the books. In 1907 the Library of Owens College, Manchester, was given the first choice to take what they wanted and some 2,400 volumes are incorporated in that library with a special label. After that the Library of University College, London, was given the opportunity to take some hundreds. Out of the residue his son, Prof. H. S. Jevons maintained a working collection, mainly of the more modern books, which he added to the notable economics library which he had built up at the University of Allahabad, when he gave up his Professorship there. Jevons also had a collection of old bank-notes which he described as "such a collection as probably hardly anyone else has." [87]

VI

We have now traversed Jevons's outstanding contributions to Economics and Statistics. But we are far from having surveyed the whole of his work. During his lifetime the reputation of Jevons as a logician stood nearly as high as his reputation as an economist. The English

[84] *Letters and Journal*, p. 397.   [86] *Letters and Journal*, p. 428.
[85] *Letters and Journal*, p. 436.   [87] *Op. cit.*, p. 421.

school of Logic of the post-Mill period has not held its own in the judgment of modern opinion, and the interest of Jevons's work has declined along with that of his contemporaries. But during the second phase of his work from about 1866 to 1876 logic occupied a large part of his time and thought, and also (so long as he was at Owens College) of his teaching duties. More than half of the books published during his lifetime related to logic. One of them, *The Principles of Science, A Treatise on Logic and Scientific Method,* is his largest work, and was widely used for many years. Nevertheless, the part Jevons played in the development of logic is in no way comparable to his position in the history of Economics and Statistics. It is, however, no part of my present task to review his contributions to knowledge in that field.

In the last decade of his life he discovered in himself a remarkable aptitude for writing in a simple, clear and interesting style the elementary outlines of his favourite subjects. Apart from numerous editions printed in America and in six or seven foreign languages, there have sold up to the present time 130,000 copies of his *Elementary Lessons in Logic* (published in 1870), 148,000 copies of his *Primer of Logic* (1876), and 98,000 copies of his *Primer of Political Economy* (1878). Another elementary book, though on a somewhat larger scale, his *Money and the Mechanism of Exchange* (1875), has sold about 20,000 copies in this country, apart from large sales in America, where there was at one time a cheap pirated edition. For a period of half a century practically all elementary students both of Logic and of Political Economy in Great Britain and also in India and the Dominions were brought up on Jevons. His little books involve few perplexities, are never dull, and give the effect of lucidity and certainty of outlook without undue dogmatism,—indeed ideal for the purpose. Simple and definite examination questions can be set upon them;—no blame to them in the eyes of Jevons, who was, rightly, a great believer in the system of examinations which was one of the great contributions of his generation to education and administration. The conclusion of his article on "Cram," published in *Mind* (1877), is worth quoting:

I should not venture to defend University examinations against all the objections which may be brought against them. My purpose is accomplished in attempting to show that examination is the most effective way of enforcing a severe and definite training upon the intellect, and of selecting those for high position who show themselves best able to bear this severe test. It is the popular cry against "Cram" that I have answered, and I will conclude by expressing my belief that any mode of education which enables a candidate to take a leading place in a severe and well-conducted open examination, must be a good system of education. Name it what you like, but it is impossible to deny that it calls forth intellectual, moral, and even physical powers, which are proved by unquestionable experience to fit men for the business of life.

This is what I hold to be Education. We cannot consider it the work of teachers to make philosophers and scholars and geniuses of various sorts: these, like poets, are born, not made. Nor, as I have shown, is it the business of the educator to impress indelibly upon the mind the useful knowledge which is to guide the pupil through life. This would be "Cram" indeed. It is the purpose of education so to exercise the faculties of mind that the infinitely various experience of after-life may be observed and reasoned upon to the best effect. What is popularly condemned as "Cram" is often the best-devised and best-conducted system of training towards this all-important end.[88]

Finally, in the last period of his life Jevons became much interested in the relation of the State to the economic life of the community. On the side of morals and sentiment Jevons was, and always remained, an impassioned individualist. There is a very odd early address of his, delivered to the Manchester Statistical Society in 1869,[89] in which he deplores free hospitals and medical charities of all kinds, which he regarded as undermining the character of the poor (which he seems to have preferred to, and deemed independent of, their health). "I feel bound," he said, "to call in question the policy of the whole of our medical charities, including all free public infirmaries, dispensaries, hospitals, and a large part of the vast amount of private charity. What I mean is that the whole of these charities nourish in the poorest classes a contented sense of dependence on the richer classes for those ordinary requirements of life which they ought to be led to provide for themselves." Perhaps it would brace us and strengthen us if we could feel again those astringent sentiments, and face that vigorous East wind, believing so firmly in the future as to make almost anything tolerable in the present. For the feeling behind this Victorian hardness was grand. "We cannot be supposed," Jevons concludes, "yet to have reached a point at which the public or private charity of one class towards another can be dispensed with, but I do think we ought to look towards such a state of things. True progress will tend to render every class self-reliant and independent."

Nevertheless, considerations of expediency influenced Jevons, as time went on, to move just a little to the Left, though never to nearly the extent that Mill had moved before the end of his life. He had always

[88] Reprinted in *Methods of Social Reform*, p. 99.
[89] Reprinted in *Methods of Social Reform*.

advocated a large public expenditure on education (for this, unlike medical attention apparently, would improve the "characters" of the poor), and on the right kind of museums.[90]   His essay on "Amusements of the People" [91] follows Aristotle in thinking it a public duty to provide good music for universal consumption.   The Hallé orchestra, which he attributed to the presence there of "a large resident, well-cultured German middle-class population," was for him the best thing in Manchester.   In the London of his day, he writes, "one craves sometimes the stirring clang of the trombones, the roll of the drums, the solemn boom of the diapason, and the exciting crescendo of a great orchestra." It is evident that, whatever Jevons felt about the hospitals, he would have acclaimed the B.B.C.   He became, moreover, exceedingly interested in State Trading, as exemplified in the Post Office, and wrote more than once concerning the criteria of policy towards the parcels traffic and telegrams.   The last book published in his lifetime, *The State in Relation to Labour* (1882), takes up a cautious, intermediate position.   "The all-important point," he explains in the preface, "is to explain if possible why, in general, we uphold the rule of *laisser-faire,* and yet in large classes of cases invoke the interference of local or central authorities. . . . The outcome of the inquiry is that we can lay down no hard-and-fast rules, but must treat every case in detail upon its merits."

It may be interesting to put on record the circulation up to the present time of Jevons's publications,[92] apart from the popular text-books already mentioned:

Pure Logic (1863), 1,000.
The Coal Question (1865), 2,000.
The Theory of Political Economy (1871), 7,000.
The Principles of Science (1874), 9,000.
Studies in Deductive Logic (1880), 6,000.
The State in Relation to Labour (1882), 9,000.
Methods of Social Reform (1883), 2,000.
Investigations in Currency and Finance (1884), 2,000.
Principles of Economics (1905), 1,000.[93]

Of the outward facts of his life there is little more to record.   In 1876 he succeeded to the Professorship of Political Economy at Uni-

[90] His essay on *The Use and Abuse of Museums,* reprinted in *Methods of Social Reform,* deserves to be read to-day.

[91] Reprinted in *Methods of Social Reform.*

[92] Kindly supplied to me by Messrs. Macmillan.

[93] The last three of these were published posthumously.

versity College, London.[94] He took a house high up in Hampstead at
the edge of the heath. In 1880 increasing uncertainty of health and a
great preference for writing rather than lecturing caused him to resign
his professorship. He planned to spend three or four years in Switzerland completing his projected *Principles of Economics,* of which a fragment was published posthumously in 1905. On a Sunday morning,
August 13, 1882, he was overcome by faintness while bathing off
Galley Hill, between Bexhill and Hastings, and was drowned. He left
three children, a son and two daughters. His son, Herbert Stanley
Jevons, was, like his father, educated in science—in his case geology
and chemistry—but found his way by natural bent to economics, and
has successively occupied the chairs of economics at Cardiff, Allahabad
and Rangoon. Jevons's wife survived him nearly thirty years until
1910.

Although Jevons died, greatly lamented by his own world, at the
early age of forty-six, I think that his work was done. It was in the
decade of his youth from 1857 to 1865 that he had genius and divine
intuition and a burning sense of vocation. His flame was paler and less
steady at the close.

VII

What sort of man was Jevons in himself? There is no strong personal impression of him which has been recorded, and 54 years after
his death it is not easy to find a definite imprint on the minds of the few
now left who knew him. My belief is that Jevons did not make a strong
impression on his companions at any period of his life. He was, in
modern language, strongly introverted. He worked best alone with
flashes of inner light. He was repelled, as much as he was attracted,
by contact with the outside world. He had from his boyhood unbounded belief in his own powers; but he desired greatly to influence
others whilst being himself uninfluenced by them. He was deeply affectionate towards the members of his family, but not intimate with
them or with anyone. When he was 27, he wrote the following about
his own state of mind at the age of 16:

[94] Miss Collet writes to me: "It was (I believe) through Mill's own views that
Political Economy was never even an optional subject in the University examinations until after graduation in Arts or Science. From 1835 (when McCulloch
retired) to 1853, when Jacob Waley began to lecture, the subject was dropped
at University College. Waley lectured until 1866, when Cairnes succeeded him
[until 1872; then Leonard Courtney 1872–1875; Jevons 1875–1880; Foxwell
1381–1928]."

It was during the year 1851, while living almost unhappily among thoughtless, if not bad companions, in Gower Street—a gloomy house on which I now look with dread—it was then, and when I had got a quiet hour in my small bedroom at the top of the house, that I began to think that I could and ought to do more than others. . . . My reserve was so perfect that I suppose no one had the slightest comprehension of my motives or ends. My father probably knew me but little. I never had any confidential conversation with him. At school and college the success in the classes was the only indication of my powers. All else that I intended or did was within or carefully hidden. The reserved character, as I have often thought, is not pleasant or lovely. But is it not necessary to one such as I? [95]

In Australia he lived almost entirely by himself, and was reluctant to join in the social events of colonial life. In 1857, when he was 22, he wrote home to his sister the following analysis of his own powers:

I have scarcely a spark of imagination and no spark of wit. I have but a poor memory, and consequently can retain only a small portion of learning at any one time, which great numbers of other persons possess. But I am not so much a storehouse of goods as I am a machine for making those goods. Give me a few facts or materials, and I can work them up into a smoothly-arranged and finished fabric of theory, or can turn them out in a shape which is something new. My mind is of the most regular structure, and I have such a strong disposition to classify things as is sometimes almost painful. I also think that if in anything I have a chance of acquiring the power, it is that I have some *originality,* and can strike out new things. This consists not so much in quickness of forming new thoughts or opinions, but in seizing upon one or two of them and developing them into something symmetrical. It is like a kaleidoscope; just put a bent pin in, or any little bit of rubbish, and a perfectly new and symmetrical pattern will be produced.[96]

In 1865, not long before he married, he wrote in his Journal:

At intervals success rewards me deliciously, but at other times it seems but to oppress me with a burden of duty. More and more I feel a lifelong work defined beforehand for me, and its avoidance impossible. Come what will, I cannot but feel that I have faculties which are to be cultivated and developed at any risk. To misuse or neglect them would be treason of the deepest kind. And yet the troubles are not slight which such a high and difficult work brings upon me. One duty, too, seems to clash with others. My idea seems to involve contradictories. I would be loved and loving. But the very studies I have to cultivate absorb my thoughts

[95] *Letters and Journal,* pp. 12, 13 (see also p. 85).
[96] *Letters and Journal,* p. 96.

so that I hardly feel able to be what I would in other ways. And, above all, poverty is sure to be my lot. I cannot aid others as I would wish. Nor in a money-making and loving world is it easy to endure the sense of meanness and want which poverty brings. And if I could endure all this myself, I could not expect nor hardly wish for a wife nor any relative to endure it. Half my feelings and affections, then, must be stifled and disappointed.[97]

After his marriage (his wife had private means) his disposition was not radically changed. He went out very little. He had only a few intimates. Music, which was almost a necessity of life to him,[98] bathing and solitary walks were his favourite relaxations at all times. He was not an easy man to live with, a little irritable towards the interruptions of family life, excessively sensitive to noise, liable to depression and valetudinarianism, without much conversation. But it is recorded that "his hearty laugh was something unique in itself and made everyone the happier who heard it." [99] From an early age he was liable to attacks of liverishness and dyspepsia and constipation, which latterly became so acute as to overshadow everything and interrupt his work, suggesting perhaps some deeper cause.

He was a reluctant and unsuccessful lecturer. "Sometimes I have enjoyed lecturing," he wrote on his retirement from University College, "especially on logic, but for years past I have never entered the lecture room without a feeling probably like that of going to the pillory." [100] The value of his lectures was impaired by his resolution seldom to introduce any of his own ideas but to retail mainly the purest milk of Mill, which he believed to be poison. He never, so far as I know, bred up a worthy pupil; though he was in close touch, at the end of his life, with his two younger contemporaries, Foxwell and Edgeworth.[101] Almost every Sunday when he was in London, Foxwell would call on

[97] *Letters and Journal,* pp. 213–14.

[98] Jevons was an enthusiastic concert-goer who never missed a chance of hearing classical music, an early Wagnerite, an admirer of Berlioz. He had a small organ built into his house at Hampstead.

[99] *Op. cit.,* p. 451.

[100] *Op. cit.,* p. 421.

[101] Also (Miss Collet adds) with Philip Wicksteed. Jevons may have played a significant part in drawing both Wicksteed and Edgeworth to economics. Both had been educated in classics. Edgeworth began his academic work by lecturing on English Language and Literature at Bedford College and on Logic at King's College, and I have no evidence that his interest in economics antedated his contact with Jevons. Wicksteed, Edgeworth and Foxwell may be considered Jevons's offspring, but his contact with all three came some time after they had taken their degrees. The memoir of Jevons in Palgrave's *Dictionary* is by Wicksteed, *q.v.* for W.'s impression of his conversation.

him in Hampstead for a long walk on the Heath; and Edgeworth, who
lived close by, was his frequent companion.   When I talked of Jevons
the other day to Professor Foxwell, recalling these days, "he did not
talk much," he said, "there never was a worse lecturer, the men would
not go to his classes, he worked in flashes and could not finish anything
thoroughly," and then after a pause with a different sort of expression,
"the only point about Jevons was that he was a genius."

A photograph of him in later life, which is prefixed to the *Letters and
Journal,* is familiar. With crinkly beard, curling hair, a broad brow and
square face, full nostrils and a full, somewhat protruding lower lip his
countenance was almost, one might say, of a Jewish cast, as Professor
Foxwell confirms, explicable, doubtless, by his partly Welsh descent,
Jevons being a variant of *Evans.* His complexion was florid, his hair
a darkish brown, and his eyes bluish-grey.   It is a powerful, but not a
brilliant face.   He would pass for a Victorian banker of high standing.
There is also a photograph of him when he was 22 or 23 years old.
This is much more interesting, exceedingly strong, keener, clearer, clean-
shaven, with a straight lean nose, fine eyes and look, and a tangle of
dark unbrushed hair standing back from a high, wide forehead,—a
genius then and not at all a banker.   These two photographs confirm
one's impression that the greatness of Jevons was in his youth.

I have frequently quoted from his Journal, which he kept from 1852,
when he was 17, up to the time of his marriage at the end of 1867.[102]
This Journal is of the highest interest both in itself and for the light
which it casts on his nature.   I wish I could have had access to the
complete text and had not been limited to the extracts published by
his wife in her selection of *Letters and Journal.*   The volumes are believed to be extant in the possession of his children, but their present
whereabouts is uncertain and they are not accessible.   This Journal
received all his confidences and the fruits of his introspection, of his
excessive introspection.   The Journal often, as we have seen, records
depression but also the delight of a creative mind in moments of illumination.   In March 1866, for example, he writes: "As I awoke in the
morning, the sun was shining brightly into my room.   There was a
consciousness on my mind that I was the discoverer of the true logic
of the future.   For a few minutes I felt a delight such as one can seldom
hope to feel."   But he quickly adds: "I remembered only too soon how
unworthy and weak an instrument I was for accomplishing so great a
work, and how hardly could I expect to do it." [103]

[102] At least, there are no extracts from it in the *Letters and Journal* after this
date.

[103] *Letters and Journal,* p. 219.

Hayek

——— on ———

Menger

Carl Menger (1840–1921), the leader of the Austrian school of economics, developed a subjective theory of value in independence from Jevons and Walras. His main work, *Principles of Economics* (1871), was made available in an English translation in 1950. Menger taught at the University of Vienna from 1873 to 1903, and his work inspired both Wieser and Böhm-Bawerk, the two other founders of the Austrian school.

Friedrich August von Hayek (1899–   ), together with Joseph A. Schumpeter (1883–1950; see pp. 734 ff., below), Ludwig von Mises (1881–   ), Gottfried von Haberler (1900–   ), and Fritz Machlup (1902–   ), continued the great traditions of the Austrian school. Hayek was educated at the University of Vienna. He left his native Austria in 1931, and for a period of nearly twenty years was associated with the University of London. Since 1950 he has been teaching at the University of Chicago, joining the other members of the "younger Austrian school" in the United States. Hayek's work, like that of the other Austrians, is characterized by a profound attachment to the tenets of old-time liberalism. His *Road to Serfdom* (1944) has spread his fame widely. In the field of economic theory, Hayek has done outstanding work on capital and on business cycles, being an exponent of the overinvestment theory of the trade cycle. He also has written a number of penetrating studies on the history of social thought, and has edited the works of a number of economists.

THE HISTORY of economics is full of tales of forgotten forerunners, men whose work had no effect and was only rediscovered after their main ideas had been made popular by others, of remarkable coincidences of simultaneous discoveries, and of the peculiar fate of individual books. But there must be few instances, in economics or any other branch of knowledge, where the works of an author who revolutionised the body of an already well-developed science and who has been generally recognised to have done so, have remained so little known as those of Carl Menger. It is difficult to think of a parallel case where a work such as the *Grundsätze* has exercised a lasting and persistent influence but has yet, as a result of purely accidental circumstances, had so extremely restricted a circulation.

There can be no doubt among competent historians that if, during the last sixty years, the Austrian School has occupied an almost unique position in the development of economic science, this is entirely due to the foundations laid by this one man. The reputation of the School in the outside world and the development of its system at important points were due to the efforts of his brilliant followers, Eugen von Böhm-Bawerk and Friedrich von Wieser. But it is not unduly to detract from the merits of these writers to say that its fundamental ideas belong fully and wholly to Carl Menger. If he had not found these principles he might have remained comparatively unknown, might even have shared the fate of the many brilliant men who anticipated him and were forgotten, and almost certainly would for a long time have remained little known outside the countries of the German tongue. But what is common to the members of the Austrian School, what constitutes their peculiarity and provided the foundations for their later contributions is their acceptance of the teaching of Carl Menger.

The independent and practically simultaneous discovery of the principle of marginal utility by William Stanley Jevons, Carl Menger, and Leon Walras is too well known to require retelling. The year 1871,

[This biographical study was written as an Introduction to the Reprint of Menger's *Grundsätze der Volkswirtschaftslehre* which constitutes the first of a series of four Reprints embodying Menger's chief published contributions to Economic Science and which are published by the London School of Economics. Reprinted by permission from *Economica,* November 1934.]

in which both Jevons' *Theory of Political Economy* and Menger's *Grundsätze* appeared, is now generally and with justice regarded as the beginning of the modern period in the development of economics. Jevons had outlined his fundamental ideas nine years earlier in a lecture (published in 1866) which, however, attracted little attention, and Walras began to publish his contribution only in 1874, but the complete independence of the work of the three founders is quite certain. And indeed, although their central positions, the point in their system to which they and their contemporaries naturally attached the greatest importance, are the same, their work is so clearly distinct in general character and background that the most interesting problem is really how so different routes should have led to such similar results.

To understand the intellectual background of the work of Carl Menger, a few words on the general position of economics at that time are required. Although the quarter of a century between about 1848, the date of J. S. Mill's *Principles,* and the emergence of the new school saw in many ways the greatest triumphs of the classical political economy in the applied fields, its foundations, particularly its theory of value, had become more and more discredited. Perhaps the systematic exposition in J. S. Mill's *Principles* itself, in spite or because of his complacent satisfaction about the perfected state of the theory of value, together with his later retractions on other essential points of the doctrine, did as much as anything else to show the deficiencies of the classical system. In any case, critical attacks and attempts at reconstruction multiplied in most countries.

Nowhere, however, had the decline of the classical school of economists been more rapid and complete than in Germany. Under the onslaughts of the Historical School not only were the classical doctrines completely abandoned—they had never taken very firm root in that part of the world—but any attempt at theoretical analysis came to be regarded with deep distrust. This was partly due to methodological considerations. But even more it was due to an intense dislike of the practical conclusions of the classical English School—which stood in the way of the reforming zeal of the new group which prided itself on the name of the "ethical school." In England the progress of economic theory only stagnated. In Germany a second generation of historical economists grew up who had not only never become really acquainted with the one well-developed system of theory that existed, but had also learnt to regard theoretical speculations of any sort as useless if not positively harmful.

The doctrines of the classical school were probably too much discredited to provide a possible basis of reconstruction for those who were still interested in problems of theory. But there were elements in the writings of the German economists of the first half of the century which contained the germs for a possible new development.[1] One of the reasons why the classical doctrines had never firmly established themselves in Germany was that German economists had always remained conscious of certain contradictions inherent in any cost or labour theory of value. Owing, perhaps, partly to the influence of Condillac and other French and Italian authors of the eighteenth century a tradition had been kept alive which refused to separate value entirely from utility. From the early years of the century into the 'fifties and 'sixties a succession of writers, of whom Hermann was probably the outstanding and most influential figure (the wholly successful Gossen remaining unnoticed), tried to combine the ideas of utility and scarcity into an explanation of value, often coming very near to the solution provided by Menger. It is to these speculations, which to the more practical minds of the contemporary English economists must have appeared useless excursions into philosophy, that Menger owed most. A glance through the extensive footnotes in his *Grundsätze,* or the author's index which has been added to the present edition, will show how extraordinarily wide a knowledge he possessed of these German authors and also of the French and Italian writers, and how small a rôle the writers of the classical English school play in comparison.

But while Menger probably surpassed all his fellow-founders of the marginal utility doctrine in the width of his knowledge of the literature—and only from a passionate book collector inspired by the example of the encyclopædic Roscher could one expect a similar knowledge at the early age the *Grundsätze* was written—there are curious gaps in the list of authors to whom he refers which go far to explain the difference of his approach from that of Jevons and Walras.[2] Particularly significant is his apparent ignorance, at the time when he wrote the *Grundsätze,* of the work of Cournot, to whom all the other founders of modern economics, Walras, Marshall, and very possibly

---

[1] The same is largely true of France. Even in England there was a kind of unorthodox tradition, of which the same may be said, but it was completely obscured by the dominant classical school. It is, however, important here because the work of its outstanding representative, Longfield, had through the intermediaryship of Hearn no doubt some influence on Jevons.

[2] It is hardly surprising that he did not know his immediate German predecessor H. H. Gossen, but neither did Jevons or Walras when they first published their ideas. The first book which did justice at all to Gossen's work, F. A. Lange's *Arbeiterfrage* (2nd ed.), appeared in 1870 when Menger's *Grundsätze* was probably already being set up in print.

Jevons,[3] seem to have been directly or indirectly indebted. Even more surprising, however, is the fact that at that time Menger does not seem to have known the work of von Thünen, which one would have expected him to find particularly congenial. While it can be said, therefore, that he worked in an atmosphere distinctly favourable to an analysis on utility lines, he had nothing so definite on which to build a modern theory of price as his fellows in the same field, all of whom came under the influence of Cournot, to which must be added, in the case of Walras, that of Dupuit [4] and, in the case of Marshall, that of von Thünen.

It is an interesting speculation to think what direction the development of Menger's thought would have taken if he had been acquainted with these founders of mathematical analysis. It is a curious fact that, so far as I am aware, he has nowhere commented on the value of mathematics as a tool of economic analysis. There is no reason to assume that he lacked either the technical equipment or the inclination. On the contrary, his interest in the natural sciences is beyond doubt, and a strong bias in favour of their methods is evident throughout his work. And the fact that his brothers, particularly Anton, are known to have been intensely interested in mathematics, and that his son Karl became a noted mathematician, may probably be taken as evidence of a definite mathematical strain in the family. But although he knew later not only the work of Jevons and Walras, but also that of his compatriots Auspitz and Lieben, he does not even refer to the mathematical method in any of his writings on methodology.[5] Must we conclude that he felt rather sceptical about its usefulness?

Among the influences to which Menger must have been subject during the formative period of his thought there is a complete absence of

[3] Dr. Hicks tells me that he has some reason to believe that Lardner's diagrammatic exposition of the theory of monopoly, by which Jevons according to his own testimony was mainly influenced, derives from Cournot. On this point see Dr. Hicks's article on Leon Walras which is to appear in one of the next issues of *Econometrica*. [Reprinted below, pp. 580 ff.—Ed.]

[4] Menger did, however, know the work of Leon Walras's father, A. A. Walras, whom he quotes on p. 54 of the *Grundsätze*.

[5] The only exception to this statement, a review of R. Auspitz and R. Lieben, *Untersuchungen über die Theorie des Preises,* in a daily newspaper (the *Wiener Zeitung* of July 8th, 1889), can hardly be called an exception, as he expressly says that he does not want to comment there on the value of mathematical exposition of economic doctrines. The general tone of the review as well as his objection to the fact that the authors "in his opinion use the mathematical method not only as a means of exposition but as a means of research" confirms the general impression that he did not consider it as particularly useful.

influence of Austrian economists, for the simple reason that, in the earlier part of the nineteenth century in Austria, there were practically no native economists. At the universities where Menger studied, political economy was taught as part of the law curriculum, mostly by economists imported from Germany. And though Menger, like all the later Austrian economists, proceeded to the degree of Doctor of Law, there is no reason to believe that he was really stimulated by his teachers in economics. This, however, leads us to his personal history.

Born on February 28th, 1840, in Neu-Sandec, Galicia, the territory of the present Poland, the son of a lawyer, he came from an old family of Austrian craftsmen, musicians, civil servants and army officers, who had, only a generation before, moved from the German parts of Bohemia to the Eastern provinces. His mother's father,[6] a Bohemian merchant who had made a fortune during the Napoleonic wars, bought a large estate in Western Galicia where Carl Menger spent a great part of his boyhood, and before 1848 still saw the conditions of semi-servitude of the peasants which in this part of Austria had persisted longer than in any part of Europe outside Russia. With his two brothers, Anton, later the well-known writer on law and socialism, author of the *Right to the Whole Produce of Labour,* and Carl's colleague at the faculty of law of the University of Vienna, and Max, in his days a well-known Austrian parliamentarian and writer on social problems, he went to the Universities of Vienna (1859–60) and Prague (1860–3). After taking his doctor's degree at the University of Cracow he devoted himself first to journalism, writing for papers in Lemberg and later in Vienna, on economic questions. After a few years he entered the Civil Service in the press department of the Austrian "Ministerratspräsidium," an office which had always retained a very special position in the Austrian Civil Service and attracted many men of great talent.

Wieser reports that Menger once told him that it was one of his duties to write surveys of the state of the markets for an official newspaper, the *Wiener Zeitung,* and that it was in studying the market reports that he was struck by the glaring contrast between the traditional theories of price and the facts which experienced practical men considered as decisive for the determination of prices. Whether this was

---

[6] Anton Menger, the father of Carl, was the son of another Anton Menger, who came from an old German family that had in 1623 emigrated to Eger in Bohemia, and of Anna *née* Müller. His wife, Caroline, was the daughter of Josef Gerzabek, merchant in Hohenmaut, and of Therese, *née* Kalaus, whose ancestors can be traced in the register of baptism of Hohenmaut back into the 17th and 18th centuries respectively.

really the original cause which led Menger to the study of the determination of prices or whether, which seems more likely, it only gave a definite direction to studies which he had been pursuing since he had left the university, we do not know.   There can be little doubt, however, that during the years intervening between the date when he left the university and the publication of the *Grundsätze* he must have worked intensely on these problems, delaying publication until his system was fully worked out in his mind.[7]

He is said to have once remarked that he wrote the *Grundsätze* in a state of morbid excitement.   This can hardly mean that this book was the product of a sudden inspiration, planned and written in great haste. Few books can have been more carefully planned; rarely has the first exposition of an idea been more painstakingly developed and followed up in all its ramifications.   The slender volume which appeared early in 1871 was intended as a first, introductory part of a comprehensive treatise.   It dealt with the fundamental questions, on which he disagreed with accepted opinion, with the exhaustiveness necessary to satisfy the author that he was building on absolutely firm ground.   The problems treated in this "First, General Part," as it is described on the title page, were the general conditions which led to economic activity, value exchange, price, and money.   From manuscript notes communicated by his son more than fifty years later, in the introduction to the second edition, we know that the second part was to treat "interest, wages, rent, income, credit, and paper money," a third "applied" part the theory of production and commerce, while a fourth part was to discuss criticism of the present economic system and proposals for economic reform.

His main aim, as he says in the preface (p. x, cf. also p. 143n), was a uniform theory of price which would explain all price phenomena and in particular also interest, wages, and rent by one leading idea.   But more than half of the volume is devoted to matters which only prepare the way for that main task—to the concept which gave the new school its special character, i.e. value in its subjective, personal sense.   And even this is not reached before a thorough examination of the main concepts with which economic analysis has to work.

The influence of the earlier German writers with their predilection for somewhat pedantic classifications and long-winded definitions of concepts is here clearly noticeable.   But in Menger's hands the time-honoured "fundamental concepts" of the traditional German textbook

---

[7] The earliest manuscript notes on the theory of value which have been preserved date from the year 1867.

assume new life. Instead of a dry enumeration and definition they become the powerful instrument of an analysis in which every step seems to result with inevitable necessity from the preceding one. And though Menger's exposition still lacks many of the more impressive phrases and elegant formulations of the writings of Böhm-Bawerk and Wieser, it is in substance hardly inferior and in many respects definitely superior to these later works.

It is not the purpose of the present introduction to give a connected outline of Menger's argument. But there are certain less known, somewhat surprising, aspects of his treatment which deserve special mention. The careful initial investigation of the causal relationship between human needs and the means for their satisfaction, which within the first few pages leads him to the now celebrated distinction between goods of the first, second, third and higher orders, and the now equally familiar concept of complementarity between different goods, is typical of the particular attention which, the widespread impression to the contrary notwithstanding, the Austrian School has always given to the technical structure of production—an attention which finds its clearest systematic expression in the elaborate "vor-werttheoretischer Teil" which precedes the discussion of the theory of value in Wieser's late work, the *Theory of Social Economy,* 1914.

Even more remarkable is the prominent rôle which the element of time plays from the very beginning. There is a very general impression that the earlier representatives of modern economics were inclined to neglect this factor. In so far as the originators of the mathematical exposition of modern equilibrium theory are concerned, this impression is probably justified. Not so with Menger. To him economic activity is essentially planning for the future, and his discussion of the period, or rather different periods, to which human forethought extends as regards different wants (see particularly pp. 34–6) has a definitely modern ring.

It is somewhat difficult to believe now that Menger was the first to base the distinction between free and economic goods on the idea of scarcity. But, as he himself says (p. 70n), while the very concept was not known in the English literature, the German authors who had used it before him, and particularly Hermann, had all been trying to base the distinction on the presence or absence of cost in the sense of effort. But, very characteristically, while all of Menger's analysis is grounded on the idea of scarcity, this simple term is nowhere used. "Insufficient quantity" or "das ökonomische Mengenverhältnis" are the very exact but somewhat cumbersome expressions which he uses instead.

It is characteristic of his work as a whole that he attaches more importance to a careful description of a phenomenon than to giving it a short and fitting name. This frequently prevents his exposition from being as effective as might have been wished. But it also protects him against a certain one-sidedness and a tendency towards over-simplification to which a brief formula so easily leads. The classic instance of this is, of course, the fact that Menger did not originate—nor, so far as I know, ever use—the term marginal utility introduced by Wieser, but always explained value by the somewhat clumsy but precise phrase, "the importance which concrete goods, or quantities of goods, receive for us from the fact that we are conscious of being dependent on our disposal over them for the satisfaction of our wants," and describes the magnitude of this value as equal to the importance which attached to the least important satisfaction which is secured by a single unit of the available quantity of the commodity (pp. 87 and 99).

Another, perhaps less important but not insignificant instance of Menger's refusal to condense explanations in a single formula, occurs even earlier in the discussion of the decreasing intensity of individual wants with increasing satisfaction. This physiological fact, which later under the name of "Gossen's law of the satisfaction of wants" was to assume a somewhat disproportionate position in the exposition of the theory of value, and was even hailed by Wieser as Menger's main discovery, takes in Menger's system the more appropriate minor position as one of the factors which enable us to arrange the different individual sensations of want in order of their importance.

On yet another and a more interesting point in connection with the pure theory of subjective value Menger's views are remarkably modern. Although he speaks occasionally of value as measurable, his exposition makes it quite clear that by this he means no more than that the value of any one commodity can be expressed by naming another commodity of equal value. Of the figures which he uses to represent the scales of utility he says expressly that they are not intended to represent the absolute, but only the relative importance of the wants (pp. 163–76), and the very examples he gives when he first introduces them makes it perfectly clear that he thinks of them not as cardinal but as ordinal figures (p. 92).[8]

[8] Further aspects of Menger's treatment of the general theory of value which might be mentioned are his persistent emphasis on the necessity to classify the different commodities on economic rather than technical grounds (cf. pp. 115–17 and 130n), his distinct anticipation of the Böhm-Bawerkian doctrine of the underestimation of future wants (pp. 122 and 127–8), and his careful analysis

Next to the general principle which enabled him to base the explanation of value on utility the most important of Menger's contributions is probably the application of this principle to the case where more than one good is required to secure the satisfaction of any want. It is here that the painstaking analysis of the causal relationship between goods and wants in the opening chapters and the concepts of complementarity and of goods of different orders bears its fruits. Even to-day it is hardly recognised that Menger answered the problem of the distribution of the utility of a final product between the several co-operating commodities of a higher order—the problem of imputation as it was later called by Wieser—by a fairly developed theory of marginal productivity. He distinguishes clearly between the case where the proportions in which two or more factors can be used in the production of any commodity are variable and the case where they are fixed. He answers the problem of imputation in the first case by saying that such quantities of the different factors as can be substituted for each other in order to get the same additional quantity of the product must have equal value, while in the case of fixed proportions he points out that the value of the different factors is determined by their utility in alternative uses (pp. 138–42).

In this first part of his book, which is devoted to the theory of subjective value, and compares well with the later exposition by Wieser, Böhm-Bawerk and others, there is really only one major point on which Menger's exposition leaves a serious gap. A theory of value can hardly be called complete and will certainly never be quite convincing if the rôle that cost of production plays in determining the relative value of different commodities is not explicitly explained. At an early point of his exposition Menger indicates that he sees the problem and promises a later answer. But this promise is never fulfilled. It was left to Wieser to develop what later became known as the principle of opportunity cost or "Wieser's Law," i.e. the principle that the other uses computing for the factors will limit the quantity available for any one line of production in such a way that the value of the product will not fall below the sum of the value which all the factors used in its production obtain in these competing uses.

It has sometimes been suggested that Menger and his school were so pleased with their discovery of the principles governing value in the economy of an individual that they were inclined to apply the same principles in an all too rapid and over-simplified way to the explanation of the process by which the accumulation of capital turns gradually more and more of the originally free factors into scarce goods.

of price. There may be some justification for such a suggestion so far as the works of some of Menger's followers, particularly the younger Wieser, are concerned. But it certainly cannot be said of Menger's own work. His exposition completely conforms to the rule later so much emphasised by Böhm-Bawerk, that any satisfactory explanation of price would have to consist of two distinct and separate stages of which the explanation of subjective value is only the first. It only provides the basis for an explanation of the causes and limits of exchanges between two or more persons. Menger's arrangement in the *Grundsätze* is exemplary in this respect. The chapter on exchange which precedes that on price makes the influence of value in the subjective sense on the objective exchange relationships quite clear without postulating any greater degree of correspondence than is actually justified by the assumptions.

The chapter on price itself, with its careful investigation of how the relative valuations of the individual participants in the exchange themselves will affect the ratios of exchange in the case of an isolated exchange of two individuals, under conditions of monopoly and finally under conditions of competition, is the third and probably the least known of the main contributions of the *Grundsätze*. Yet it is only in reading this chapter that one realises the essential unity of his thought, the clear aim which directs his exposition from the beginning to this crowning achievement.

On the final chapters, which deal with the effects of production for a market, the technical meaning of the term "commodity" (*Ware*) as distinguished from the simple "good," their different degrees of saleability leading up to the introduction and discussion of money, little need be said at this point. The ideas contained here and the fragmentary remarks on capital contained in earlier sections are the only sections of this first work which were developed further in his printed work later on. Although they embody contributions of lasting influence, it was mainly in their later, more elaborate exposition that they became known.

The considerable space devoted here to the discussion of the contents of the *Grundsätze* is justified by the outstanding character of this work among Menger's publications and, indeed, among all the books which have laid the foundations of modern economics. It is, perhaps, appropriate to quote in this connection the judgment of the scholar best qualified to assess the relative merits of the different variants of the modern school, of Knut Wicksell who was the first, and hitherto the most successful, to combine what is best in the teaching of the different groups.

"His fame," he says, "rests on this work and through it his name will go down to posterity, for one can safely say that since Ricardo's *Principles* there has been no book—not even excepting Jevons' brilliant if rather aphoristic achievement and Walras's unfortunately difficult work—which has exercised such great influence on the development of economics as Menger's *Grundsätze.*" [9]

But the immediate reception of the book can hardly be called encouraging. None of the reviewers in the German journals seem to have realised the nature of its main contribution.[10] At home Menger's attempt to obtain, on the strength of this work, a lectureship (*Privatdozentur*) at the University of Vienna succeeded only after some difficulty. He can scarcely have known that, just before he began his lectures, there had just left the University two young men who immediately recognised that his work provided the "Archimedian point," as Wieser called it, by which the existing systems of economic theory could be lifted out of their hinges. Böhm-Bawerk and Wieser, his first and most enthusiastic disciples, were never his direct pupils, and their attempt to popularise Menger's doctrines in the seminars of the leaders of the older historical school, Knies, Roscher, and Hildebrand, was fruitless.[11] But Menger gradually succeeded in gaining considerable influence at home. Soon after his promotion to the rank of *professor extraordinarius* in 1873 he resigned from his position in the prime minister's office, to the great surprise of his chief, Prince Auersperg, who found it difficult to understand that anybody should want to exchange a position with prospects to satisfy the greatest ambition for an academic career.[12] But this did not yet mean Menger's final *adieu* to the world

[9] *Ekonomisk Tidskrift,* 1921, p. 118.

[10] An exception should, perhaps, be made for Hack's review in the *Zeitschrift für die gesamte Staatswissenschaft,* 1872, who not only emphasised the excellence of the book and the novelty of its method of approach, but also pointed out as opposed to Menger that the economically relevant relationship between commodities and wants was not that of cause and effect but one of means and end.

[11] It might not be altogether out of place to correct a wrong impression which may be created by A. Marshall's assertion that between the years 1870 and 1874, when he developed the details of his theoretical position, "Böhm-Bawerk and Wieser were still lads at school or college. . . ." (*Memorials of Alfred Marshall,* p. 417.) Both had left the University together and entered civil service in 1872, and in 1876 were already in a position to expound in reports to Knies's seminar in Heidelberg the main elements of their later contribution.

[12] Menger had at that time already declined the offer of professorships in Karlsruhe (1872), Basel (1873), and a little later also declined an offer of a professorship in the Zürich Polytechnic with prospects to a simultaneous professorship at the University.

of affairs. In 1876 he was appointed one of the tutors to the ill-fated Crown Prince Rudolph, then eighteen years of age, and accompanied him during the next two years on his extensive travels through the greater part of Europe, including England, Scotland, Ireland, France and Germany. After his return he was appointed in 1879 to the chair of political economy in Vienna, and thenceforward he settled down to the secluded and quiet life of the scholar which was to be so characteristic of the second half of his long life.

By this time the doctrines of his first book—apart from a few short reviews of books he had published nothing in the intervening period—were beginning to attract wider attention. Rightly or wrongly, with Jevons and Walras it was the mathematical form rather than the substance of their teaching which appeared to be their main innovation, and which contributed the chief obstacle to their acceptance. But there were no obstacles of this sort to an understanding of Menger's exposition of the new theory of value. During the second decade after the publication of the book, its influence began to extend with great rapidity. At the same time Menger began to acquire considerable reputation as a teacher, and to attract to his lectures and seminars an increasing number of students, many of whom soon became economists of considerable reputation. In addition to those already noted, among the early members of his school his contemporaries Emil Sax and Johann von Komorzynski, and his students Robert Meyer, Robert Zuckerkandl, Gustav Gross, and—at a somewhat later date—H. von Schullern-Schrattenhofen, Richard Reisch and Richard Schüller deserve special mention.

But, while at home a definite school was forming, in Germany, even more than in other foreign countries, economists maintained a hostile attitude. It was at this time that the younger Historical School, under the leadership of Schmoller, was gaining the greatest influence in that country. The *"Volkswirtschaftliche Kongress,"* which had preserved the classical tradition, was superseded by the newly founded *"Verein für Sozialpolitik."* Indeed the teaching of economic theory was more and more excluded from German universities. Thus Menger's work was neglected, not because the German economists thought that he was wrong, but because they considered the kind of analysis he attempted was useless.

Under these conditions it was only natural that Menger should consider it more important to defend the method he had adopted against the claims of the Historical School to possess the only appropriate instrument of research, than to continue the work on the *Grundsätze*. It is to this situation that his second great work, the *Unter-*

suchungen über die Methode der Socialwissenschaften und der politischen Oekonomie insbesondere is due. It is well to remember that in 1875 when Menger started to work on that book, and even in 1883 when it was published, the rich crop of works by his disciples which definitely established the position of the school, had not yet begun to mature, and that he might well have thought that it would be wasted effort to continue while the question of principle was not decided.

In their way the *Untersuchungen* are hardly less an achievement than the *Grundsätze*. As a polemic against the claims of the Historical School to an exclusive right to treat economic problems the book can hardly be surpassed. Whether the merits of its positive exposition of the nature of theoretical analysis can be rated as high is, perhaps, not quite certain. If this were, indeed, its main title to fame there might be something in the suggestion occasionally heard among Menger's admirers that it was unfortunate that he was drawn away from his work on the concrete problems of economics. This is not to mean that what he said on the character of the theoretical or abstract method is not of very great importance or that it had not very great influence. Probably it did more than any other single book to make clear the peculiar character of the scientific method in the social sciences, and it had a very considerable effect on professional "methodologists" among German philosophers. But to me, at any rate, its main interest to the economist in our days seems to lie in the extraordinary insight into the nature of social phenomena which is revealed incidentally in the discussion of problems mentioned to exemplify different methods of approach, and in the light shed by his discussion of the development of the concepts with which the social sciences have to work. Discussions of somewhat obsolete views, as that of the organic or perhaps better physiological interpretation of social phenomena, give him an opportunity for an elucidation of the origin and character of social institutions which might, with advantage, be read by present-day economists and sociologists.

Of the central contentions of the book only one may be singled out for further comment; his emphasis on the necessity of a strictly individualistic or, as he generally says, atomistic method of analysis. It has been said of him by one of his most distinguished followers that "he himself always remained an individualist in the sense of the classical economists. His successors ceased to be so." It is doubtful whether this statement is true of more than one or two instances. But in any case it fails signally to give Menger full credit for the method he actually employed. What with the classical economists had remained something of a mixture between an ethical postulate and a methodological tool, was developed by him systematically in the latter direction. And if emphasis on the subjective element has been fuller and more convincing in the writings of the members of the Austrian School than in those of any other of the founders of modern economics, this is largely due to Menger's brilliant vindication in this book.

Menger had failed to arouse the German economists with his first book. But he could not complain of neglect of his second. The direct attack on what was the only approved doctrine attracted immediate attention and provoked, among other hostile reviews, a magisterial rebuke from Gustav Schmoller, the head of the school—a rebuke couched in a tone more than usually offensive.[13] Menger accepted the challenge and replied in a passionate pamphlet, *Irrthümer des Historismus in der deutschen Nationalökonomie,* written in the form of letters to a friend, in which he ruthlessly demolished Schmoller's position. The pamphlet adds little in substance to the *Untersuchungen.* But it is the best instance of the extraordinary power and brilliance of expression which Menger could achieve when he was engaged, not on building up an academic and complicated argument, but on driving home the points of a straightforward debate.

The encounter between the masters was soon imitated by their disciples. A degree of hostility not often equalled in scientific controversy was created. The crowning offence from the Austrian point of view was given by Schmoller himself who, on the appearance of Menger's pamphlet, took the probably unprecedented step of announcing in his journal that, although he had received a copy of the book for review, he was unable to review it because he had immediately returned it to the author, and reprinting the insulting letter with which the returned copy had been accompanied.

It is necessary to realise fully the passion which this controversy aroused, and what the break with the ruling school in Germany meant to Menger and his followers, if we are to understand why the problem of the adequate methods remained the dominating concern of most of Menger's later life. Schmoller, indeed, went so far as to declare publicly that members of the "abstract" school were unfit to fill a teaching position in a German university, and his influence was quite sufficient to make this equivalent to a complete exclusion of all adherents to Menger's doctrines from academic positions in Germany. Even thirty years after the close of the controversy Germany was still less affected

---

[13] "Zur Methodologie der Staats- und Sozialwissenschaften," in *Jahrbuch für Gesetzgebung, Verwaltung und Volkswirtschaft im deutschen Reich,* 1883. In the reprint of this article in Schmoller's *Zur Litteraturgeschichte der Staats- und Sozialwissenschaften,* 1888, the most offensive passages have been mitigated.

by the new ideas now triumphant elsewhere, than any other important country in the world.

In spite of these attacks, however, in the six years from 1884 to 1889 there appeared in rapid succession the books which finally established the reputation of the Austrian School the world over. Böhm-Bawerk, indeed, had already in 1881 published his small but important study on *Rechte und Verhältnisse vom Standpunkt der wirtschaftlichen Güterlehre,* but it was only with the simultaneous publications of the first part of his work on capital, the *Geschichte und Kritik der Kapitalzinstheorien,* and of Wieser's *Ursprung und Hauptgesetze des wirtschaftlichen Wertes* in 1884 that it became apparent how powerful a support to Menger's doctrines had arisen in this quarter. Of these two works Wieser's was undoubtedly the more important for the further development of Menger's fundamental ideas, since it contained the essential application to the cost phenomenon, now known as Wieser's law of cost, to which reference has already been made. But two years later appeared Böhm-Bawerk's *Grundzüge einer Theorie des wirtschaftlichen Güterwertes* [14] which, although it adds little except by way of casuistic elaboration to the work of Menger and Wieser, by the great lucidity and force of its argument has probably done more than any other single work to popularise the marginal utility doctrine. In the year 1884 two of Menger's immediate pupils, V. Mataja and G. Gross, had published their interesting books on profits, and E. Sax contributed a small but acute study on the question of method in which he supported Menger in his fundamental attitude but criticised him on some points of detail.[15] In 1887 Sax made his main contribution to the development of the Austrian School by the publication of his *Grundlegung der theoretischen Staatswirtschaft,* the first and most exhaustive attempt to apply the marginal utility principle to the problems of public finance, and in the same year another of Menger's early students, Robert Meyer, entered the field with his investigation of the somewhat cognate problem of the nature of income.[16]

But the richest crop was that of the year 1889. In this year were published Böhm-Bawerk's *Positive Theorie des Kapitalzinses,* Wieser's *Natürlicher Wert,* Zuckerkandl's *Zur Theorie des Preises,* Komorzyn-

[14] Originally a series of articles in (Conrad's) *Jahrbücher* it has recently been reprinted as No. 11 of the *Series of Reprints of Scarce Tracts in Economics and Political Science,* published by the London School of Economics (1932).

[15] V. Mataja, *Der Unternehmergewinn,* Vienna, 1884; G. Gross, *Lehre vom Unternehmergewinn,* Leipzig, 1884; E. Sax, *Das Wesen und die Aufgaben der Nationalökonomie,* Vienna, 1884.

[16] Robert Meyer, *Das Wesen des Einkommens,* Berlin, 1887.

ski's *Wert in der isolierten Wirtschaft,* Sax's *Neueste Fortschritte der nationalökonomischen Theorie,* and H. von Schullern-Schrattenhofen's *Untersuchungen über Begriff und Wesen der Grundrente.*[17]

Perhaps the most successful early exposition of the doctrines of the Austrian School in a foreign language was M. Pantaleoni's *Pure Economics* which appeared first in the same year.[18] Of other Italian economists L. Cossa, A. Graziani and G. Mazzola accepted most or all of Menger's doctrines. Similar success attended these doctrines in Holland where the acceptance by the great Dutch economist, N. G. Pierson, of the marginal utility doctrine in his textbook (1884–1889), published later in English under the title *Principles of Economics,* had also considerable influence. In France Ch. Gide, E. Villey, Ch. Secrétan and M. Block spread the new doctrine, and in the United States S. N. Patten and Professor Richard Ely had received it with great sympathy. Even the first edition of A. Marshall's *Principles,* which appeared in 1890, showed a considerably stronger influence of Menger and his group than readers of the later editions of that great work would suspect. And in the next few years Smart and Dr. Bonar, who had already earlier shown their adherence to the school, widely popularised the work of the Austrian School in the English-speaking world.[19] But, and this brings us back to the special position of Menger's work, it was now not so much his writings as those of his pupils which continuously gained in popularity. The main reason for this was simply that Menger's *Grundsätze* had for some time been out of print and difficult to procure, and that Menger refused to permit

[17] In the same year two other Viennese economists, R. Auspitz and R. Lieben, published their *Untersuchungen über die Theorie des Preises,* still one of the most important works of mathematical economics. But although they were strongly influenced by the work of Menger and his group, they build rather on the foundations laid by Cournot and Thünen, Gossen, Jevons and Walras than on the work of their compatriots.

[18] Maffeo Pantaleoni, *Principii di Economia Pura,* Firenze, 1889 (2nd ed. 1894), English translation, London, 1894. An unjust remark in the Italian edition accusing Menger of plagiarism of Cournot, Gossen, Jennings, and Jevons was eliminated in the English edition and Pantaleoni later made amends by editing, with an introduction from his pen, an Italian translation of the *Grundsätze,* cf. C. Menger, *Principii fondamentali di economia pura,* con prefazione di Maffeo Pantaleoni, Imola, 1909 (first published as a supplement to the *Giornale degli Economisti* in 1906 and 1907 without the preface of Pantaleoni). The preface is also reprinted in the Italian translation of the second edition of the *Grundsätze* (to be mentioned below) which was published at Bari, 1925.

[19] Cf. particularly J. Bonar, "The Austrian Economists and Their Views on Value," *Quarterly Journal of Economics,* 1888, and "The Positive Theory of Capital," *ibid.,* 1889.

either a reprint or a translation. He hoped to replace it soon by a much more elaborate "system" of economics and was, in any case, unwilling to have the work republished without considerable revision. But other tasks claimed his prior attention, and for years led to a continual postponement of this plan.

Menger's direct controversy with Schmoller had come to an abrupt end in 1884. But the *Methodenstreit* was carried on by others, and the problems involved continued to claim his main attention. The next occasion which induced him to make a public pronouncement on these questions was the publication, in 1885 and 1886, of a new edition of Schönberg's *Handbuch der politischen Oekonomie,* a collective work in which a number of German economists, most of them not convinced adherents to the Historical School, had combined to produce a systematic exposition of the whole field of political economy. Menger reviewed the work for a Viennese legal journal in an article which also appeared as a separate pamphlet under the title *Zur Kritik der politischen Oekonomie* (1887).[20] Its second half is largely devoted to the discussion of the classification of the different disciplines commonly grouped together under the name of political economy, a theme which, two years later, he treated more exhaustively in another article entitled *Grundzüge einer Klassifikation der Wirtschaftswissenschaften.*[21] In the intervening year, however, he published one of his two further contributions to the substance—as distinguished from the methodology—of economic theory, his important study, *Zur Theorie des Kapitals.*[22]

It is pretty certain that we owe this article to the fact that Menger did not quite agree with the definition of the term capital which was implied in the first, historical part of Böhm-Bawerk's *Capital and Interest.* The discussion is not polemical. Böhm-Bawerk's book is mentioned only to commend it. But its main aim is clearly to rehabilitate the abstract concept of capital as the money value of the property devoted to acquisitive purposes against the Smithian concept of the "produced means of production." His main argument that the distinction of the historical origin of a commodity is irrelevant from

---

[20] The original review article appeared in (Grünhut's) *Zeitschrift für das Privat- und öffentliche Recht der Gegenwart,* Vol. XIV, the separate pamphlet, Vienna, 1887.

[21] See (Conrad's) *Jahrbücher für Nationalökonomie und Statistik,* N.F., Vol. XIX, Jena, 1889.

[22] In the same journal, N.F., Vol. XVII, Jena, 1888. An abridged French translation by Ch. Secrétan appeared in the same year in the *Revue d'Économie Politique* under the title "Contribution à la théorie du capital."

an economic point of view, as well as his emphasis on the necessity of clearly distinguishing between the rent obtained from already existing instruments of production and interest proper, refer to points which, even to-day, have not yet received quite the attention they deserve.

It was at about the same time, in 1889, that Menger was almost persuaded by his friends not to postpone further the publication of a new edition of the *Grundsätze*. But although he actually wrote a new preface to that new edition (excerpts from which have been printed more than thirty years later by his son in the introduction to the actual second edition), nevertheless publication was again postponed. Soon after a new set of publications emerged, which absorbed his main attention and occupied him for the next two years.

Towards the end of the 'eighties the perennial Austrian currency problem had assumed a form where a drastic final reform seemed to become both possible and necessary. In 1878 and 1879 the fall of the price of silver had first brought the depreciated paper currency back to its silver parity and soon afterwards made it necessary to discontinue the free coinage of silver; since then the Austrian paper money had gradually appreciated in terms of silver and fluctuated in terms of gold. The situation during that period—in many respects one of the most interesting in monetary history—was more and more regarded as unsatisfactory, and as the financial position of Austria seemed for the first time for a long period strong enough to promise a period of stability, the Government was generally expected to take matters in hand. Moreover, the treaty concluded with Hungary in 1887 actually provided that a commission should immediately be appointed to discuss the preparatory measures necessary to make the resumption of specie payments possible. After considerable delay, due to the usual political difficulties between the two parts of the dual monarchy, the commission, or rather commissions, one for Austria and one for Hungary, were appointed and met in March 1892, in Vienna and Budapest respectively.

The discussions of the Austrian "Währungs-Enquete-Commission," of which Menger was the most eminent member, are of considerable interest quite apart from the special historical situation with which they had to deal. As the basis of their transactions the Austrian Ministry of Finance had prepared with extraordinary care three voluminous memoranda, which contain probably the most complete collection available of documentary material for a monetary history of the preceding period which has appeared in any publication.[23] Among the members

[23] *Denkschrift über den Gang der Währungsfrage seit dem Jahre* 1867; *Denkschrift über das Papiergeldwesen der österreichisch-ungarischen Monarchie;*

besides Menger there were other well-known economists, such as Sax, Lieben and Mataja, and a number of journalists, bankers and industrialists, such as Benedikt, Hertzka and Taussig, all of whom had a more than ordinary knowledge of monetary problems, while Böhm-Bawerk, then in the Ministry of Finance, was one of the Government representatives and vice-chairman. The task of the commission was not to prepare a report, but to hear and discuss the views of its members on a number of questions put to them by the Government.[24] These questions concerned the basis of the future currency, the retention, in the case of the adoption of the Gold Standard, of the existing silver and paper circulation, the ratio of exchange between the existing paper florin and gold, and the nature of the new unit to be adopted.

Menger's mastery of the problem, no less than his gift of clear exposition, gave him immediately a leading position in the commission and his statement attracted the widest attention. It even achieved what, for an economist, was perhaps the unique distinction of causing a temporary slump on the stock exchange. His contribution consisted not so much in his discussion of the general question of the choice of the standard—here he agreed with practically all the members of the commission that the adoption of the Gold Standard was the only practical course—but in his careful discussion on the practical problems of the exact parity to be chosen and the moment of time to be selected for the transition. It is mainly for his evaluation of these practical difficulties connected with any transition to a new standard of currency, and the survey of the different considerations that have to be taken into account, that his evidence is rightly celebrated. It has extraordinarily topical interest to-day, where similar problems have to be faced by almost all countries.[25]

Statistische Tabellen zur Währungsfrage der österreichisch-ungarischen Monarchie. All published by the k.k. Finanzministerium, Vienna, 1892.

[24] Cf. *Stenographische Protokolle über die vom 8. bis 17. März 1892 abgehaltenen Sitzungen der nach Wien einberufenen Währungs-Enquete-Commission.* Wien, k.k. Hof- und Staatsdruckerei, 1892. Shortly before the commission met Menger had already outlined the main problems in a public lecture, "Von unserer Valuta," which appeared in the *Allgemeine Juristen Zeitung,* Nos. 12 and 13 of the volume for 1892.

[25] It is unfortunately impossible, within the scope of this introduction, to devote to this important episode in currency history the space it deserves because of its close connection with Menger and his school and because of the general interest of the problems which were discussed. It would be well worth a special study and it is very regrettable that no history of the discussions and measures of that period exists. In addition to the official publications mentioned before, the writings of Menger provide the most important material for such a study.

This evidence, the first of a series of contributions to monetary problems, was the final and mature product of several years of concentration on these questions. The results of these were published in rapid succession in the course of the same year—a year during which there appeared a greater number of publications from Menger's hand than at any other period of his life. The results of his investigations into the special problems of Austria appeared as two separate pamphlets. The first, entitled *Beiträge zur Währungsfrage in Oesterreich-Ungarn,* and dealing with the history and the peculiarities of the Austrian currency problem and the general question of the standard to be adopted, is a revised reprint of a series of articles which appeared earlier in the year in Conrad's *Jahrbücher* under a different title.[26] The second, called *Der Uebergang zur Goldwährung. Untersuchungen über die Wertprobleme der österreichisch-ungarischen Valutareform* (Vienna, 1892), treats essentially the technical problems connected with the adoption of a Gold Standard, particularly the choice of the appropriate parity and the factors likely to affect the value of the currency once the transition had been made.

But the same year also saw the publication of a much more general treatment of the problems of money which was not directly concerned with the special question of the day, and which must be ranked as the third and last of Menger's main contributions to economic theory. This was the article on money in volume iii of the first edition of the *Handwörterbuch der Staatswissenschaften* which was then in the process of publication. It was his preoccupation with the extensive investigations carried out in connection with the preparation of this elaborate exposition of the general theory of money, investigations which must have occupied him for the preceding two or three years, which brought it about that the beginning of the discussion of the special Austrian problems found Menger so singularly equipped to deal with them. He had, of course, always been strongly interested in monetary problems. The last chapter of the *Grundsätze* and parts of the *Untersuchungen über die Methode* contain important contributions, particularly on the question of the origin of money. It should also be noted that, among the numerous review articles which Menger used to write for daily newspapers, particularly in his early years, there are two in 1873 which deal in great detail with J. E. Cairnes's *Essays* on the effects of the gold discoveries: in some respects Menger's later views are nearly related to

[26] "Die Valutaregulierung in Oesterreich-Ungarn," (Conrad's) *Jahrbücher für Nationalökonomie und Statistik,* III. F., Vols. III and IV, 1892.

those of Cairnes.[27]   But while Menger's earlier contributions, particularly the introduction of the concepts of the different degrees of "saleability" of commodities as the basis for the understanding of the functions of money, would have secured him an honourable position in the history of monetary doctrines, it was only in this last major publication that he made his main contribution to the central problem of the value of money.   Until the work of Professor Mises twenty years later, the direct continuation of Menger's work, this article remained the main contribution of the "Austrian School" to the theory of money.   It is worth while dwelling a little on the nature of this contribution, for it is a matter on which there is still much misunderstanding.   It is often thought that the Austrian contribution consists only of a somewhat mechanical attempt to apply the marginal utility principle to the problem of the value of money.   But this is not so.   The main Austrian achievement in this field is the consistent application to the theory of money of the peculiar subjective or individualistic approach which, indeed, underlies the marginal utility analysis, but which has a much wider and more universal significance.   Such an achievement springs directly from Menger.   His exposition of the meaning of the different concepts of the value of money, the causes of changes and the possibility of a measurement of this value, as well as his discussion of the factors determining the demand for money, all seem to me to represent a most significant advance beyond the traditional treatment of the quantity theory in terms of aggregates and averages.   And even where, as in the case of his familiar distinction between the "inner" and the "outer" value (*innerer und äusserer Tauschwert*) of money, the actual terms employed are somewhat misleading—the distinction does not, as would appear from the terms, refer to different kinds of value but to the different forces which affect prices—the underlying concept of the problem is extraordinarily modern.

With the publications of the year 1892 [28] the list of Menger's major works which appeared during his lifetime comes to an abrupt end. During the remaining three decades of his life he only published occasional small articles, a complete list of which will be found in the

[27] These articles appeared in the *Wiener Abendpost* (a supplement to the *Wiener Zeitung*) of April 30th and June 19th, 1873.   As is the case with all the early journalistic work of Menger, they are anonymous.

[28] In addition to those already mentioned there appeared in the same year a French article, "La Monnaie Mesure de la Valeur," in the *Revue d'Économie Politique* (Vol. VI) and an English article, "On the Origin of Money," in the *Economic Journal* (Vol. II).

bibliography of his writings at the end of the last volume of the present edition of his collected works. For a few years these publications were still mainly concerned with money. Of these, his lecture on *Das Goldagio und der heutige Stand der Valutareform* (1893), his article on money and coinage in Austria since 1857 in the *Oesterreichische Staatswörterbuch* (1897), and particularly the thoroughly revised edition of his article on money in volume four of the second edition of the *Handwörterbuch der Staatswissenschaften* (1900),[29] ought to be specially mentioned. The latter publications are mainly of the character of reviews, biographical notes or introductions to works published by his pupils. His last published article is an obituary of his disciple Böhm-Bawerk, who died in 1914.

The reason for this apparent inactivity is clear. Menger now wanted to concentrate entirely on the major tasks which he had set himself— the long postponed systematic work on economics, and beyond this a comprehensive treatise on the character and methods of the social sciences in general. It was to the completion of this work that his main energy was devoted and in the late 'nineties he looked forward to a publication in the near future and considerable parts were ready in a definite form. But his interests and the scope of the proposed work continued to expand to wider and wider circles. He found it necessary to go far in the study of other disciplines. Philosophy, psychology and ethnography claimed more and more of his time, and the publication of the work was again and again postponed. In 1903 he went so far as to resign from his chair at the comparatively early age of 63 in order to be able to devote himself entirely to his work.[30] But he was never satisfied and seems to have continued to work on it in the increasing seclusion of his old age until he died in 1921 at the advanced age of 81. An inspection of his manuscript has shown that, at one time, considerable parts of the work must have been ready for publication. But even after his powers had begun to fail he continued to revise and rearrange the manuscripts to such an extent that any attempt to reconstruct this would be a very difficult, if not an impossible task. Some of the material dealing with the subject-matter of the *Grundsätze* and partly intended for a new edition of this work, has been incorporated

[29] The reprint of the same article in Vol. IV of the third edition of the *Handwörterbuch* (1909) contains only small stylistic changes compared with the second edition.

[30] In consequence, almost all the living representatives of the "Austrian School," like Professors H. Mayer, L. von Mises and J. Schumpeter, were not direct pupils of Menger but of Böhm-Bawerk or Wieser.

by his son in a second edition of this work, published in 1923.[31] Much more, however, remains in the form of voluminous but fragmentary and disordered manuscripts, which only the prolonged and patient efforts of a very skilful editor could make accessible. For the present, at any rate, the results of the work of Menger's later years must be regarded as lost.

For one who can hardly claim to have known Carl Menger in person it is a hazardous undertaking to add to this sketch of his scientific career an appreciation of his character and personality. But as so little about him is generally known to the present generation of economists, and since there is no comprehensive literary portrait available,[32] an attempt to piece together some of the impressions recorded by his friends and students, or preserved by the oral tradition in Vienna, may not be altogether out of place. Such impressions naturally relate to the second half of his life, to the period when he had ceased to be in active contact with the world of affairs, and when he had already taken to the quiet and retired life of the scholar, divided only between his teaching and his research.

The impression left on a young man by one of those rare occasions when the almost legendary figure became accessible is well reproduced in the well-known engraving of F. Schmutzer. It is possible, indeed, that one's image of Menger owes as much to this masterly portrait as to memory. The massive, well-modelled head, with the colossal forehead and the strong but clear lines there delineated are not easily forgotten. Tall, with a wealth of hair and full beard, in his prime Menger must have been a man of extraordinarily impressive appearance.

In the years after his retirement it became a tradition that young economists entering upon an academic career undertook the pilgrimage to his home. They would be genially received by Menger among his books and drawn into conversation about the life which he had known so well, and from which he had withdrawn after it had given him all he had wanted. In a detached way he preserved a keen interest in eco-

---

[31] *Grundsätze der Volkswirtschaftslehre* von Carl Menger, Zweite Auflage mit einem Geleitwort von Richard Schüller aus dem Nachlass herausgegeben von Karl Menger, Wien, 1923. A full discussion of the changes and additions made in this edition will be found in F. X. Weiss, "Zur zweiten Auflage von Carl Mengers Grundsätzen," *Zeitschrift für Volkswirtschaft und Sozialpolitik,* N.F., Vol. IV, 1924.

[32] Of shorter sketches those by F. von Wieser in the *Neue österreichische Biographie,* 1923, and by R. Zuckerkandl in the *Zeitschrift für Volkswirtschaft, Sozialpolitik und Verwaltung,* Vol. XIX, 1911, ought to be specially mentioned.

nomics and university life to the end and when, in the later years, failing eyesight had defeated the indefatigable reader, he would expect to be informed by the visitor about the work he had done. In these late years he gave the impression of a man who, after a long active life, continued his pursuits not to carry out any duty or self-imposed task, but for the sheer intellectual pleasure of moving in the element which had become his own. In his later life, perhaps, he conformed somewhat to the popular conception of the scholar who has no contact with real life. But this was not due to any limitation of his outlook. It was the result of a deliberate choice at a mature age and after rich and varied experience.

For Menger had lacked neither the opportunity nor the external signs of distinction to make him a most influential figure in public life, if he had cared. In 1900 he had been made a life member of the upper chamber of the Austrian Parliament. But he did not care sufficiently to take a very active part in its deliberations. To him the world was a subject for study much more than for action, and it was for this reason only that he had intensely enjoyed watching it at close range. In his written work one can search in vain for any expressions of his political views. Actually, he tended to conservatism or liberalism of the old type. He was not without sympathy for the movement for social reform, but social enthusiasm would never interfere with his cold reasoning. In this, as in other respects, he seems to have presented a curious contrast to his more passionate brother Anton.[33] Hence it is

[33] The two brothers were regular members of a group which met in the 'eighties and 'nineties almost daily in a coffee-house opposite the University and which consisted originally mainly of journalists and business men, but later increasingly of Carl Menger's former pupils and students. It was through this circle that, at least until his retirement from the University, he mainly retained contact with, and exercised some influence on, current affairs. The contrast between the two brothers is well described by one of his most distinguished pupils, R. Sieghart. (Cf. the latter's *Die letzten Jahrzehnte einer Grossmacht,* Berlin, 1932, p. 21): "Wahrlich ein seltsames und seltenes Brüderpaar die beiden Menger; Carl, Begründer der österreichischen Schule der Nationalökonomie, Entdecker des wirtschaftspsychologischen Gesetzes vom Grenznutzen, Lehrer des Kronprinzen Rudolf, in den Anfängen seiner Laufbahn auch Journalist, die grosse Welt kennend wenn auch fliehend, seine Wissenschaft revolutionierend, aber als Politiker eher konservativ; auf der anderen Seite Anton, weltfremd, seinem eigenen Fach, dem bürgerlichen Recht und Zivilprozess, bei glänzender Beherrschung der Materie immer mehr abgewandt, dafür zunehmend mit sozialen Problemen und ihrer Lösung durch den Staat befasst, glühend eingenommen von den Fragen des Sozialismus. Carl völlig klar, jederman verständlich, nach Ranke's Art abgeklärt; Anton schwieriger zu verfolgen, aber sozialen Problemen in allen ihren

mainly as one of the most successful teachers at the University that Menger is best remembered by generations of students, and that he has indirectly had enormous influence on Austrian public life.[34] All reports agree in the praise of his transparent lucidity of exposition. The following account of his impression by a young American economist who attended Menger's lectures in the winter 1892–93 may be reproduced here as representative: "Professor Menger carries his fifty-three years lightly enough. In lecturing he rarely uses his notes except to verify a quotation or a date. His ideas seem to come to him as he speaks and are expressed in language so clear and simple, and emphasised with gestures so appropriate, that it is a pleasure to follow him. The student feels that he is being led instead of driven, and when a conclusion is reached it comes into his mind not as something from without, but as the obvious consequence of his own mental process. It is said that those who attend Professor Menger's lectures regularly need no other preparation for their final examination in political economy, and I can readily believe it. I have seldom, if ever, heard a lecturer who possessed the same talent for combining clearness and simplicity of statement with philosophical breadth of view. His lectures are seldom 'over the heads' of his dullest students, and yet always contain instruction for the brightest." [35] All his students retain a particularly vivid memory of the sympathetic and thorough treatment of the history of economic doctrines, and mimeographed copies of his lectures on public finance were still sought after by the student twenty years after he had retired, as the best preparation for the examinations.

His great gifts as a teacher were, however, best shown in his seminar where a select circle of advanced students and many men who had long ago taken their doctor's degree assembled. Sometimes, when practical questions were discussed, the seminar was organised on parliamentary lines with appointed main speakers *pro* and *contra* a measure. More

Erscheinungsformen—im bürgerlichen Recht, in Wirtschaft und Staat—zugewandt. Ich habe von Carl Menger die nationalökonomische Methode gelernt, aber die Probleme, die ich mir stellte, kamen aus Anton Mengers Hand."

[34] The number of men who at one time or another, belonged to the more intimate circle of Menger's pupils and later made a mark in Austrian public life is extraordinarily large. To mention only a few of those who have also contributed some form to the technical literature of economics, the names of K. Adler, St. Bauer, M. Dub, M. Ettinger, M. Garr, V. Graetz, I. von Gruber-Menninger, A. Krasny, G. Kunwald, J. Landesberger, W. Rosenberg, H. Schwarzwald, E. Schwiedland, R. Sieghart, E. Seidler and R. Thurnwald may be added to those mentioned earlier in the text.

[35] H. R. Seager, "Economics at Berlin and Vienna," *Journal of Political Economy*, Vol. I, March, 1893, reprinted in *Labor and Other Essays*, New York, 1931.

frequently, however, a carefully prepared paper by one of the members was the basis of long discussions. Menger left the students to do most of the talking, but he took infinite pains in assisting in the preparations of the papers. Not only would he put his library completely at the disposal of the students, and even bought for them books specially needed, but he would go through the manuscript with them many times, discussing not only the main questions and the organisation of the paper, but even "teaching them elocution and the technique of breathing." [36]

For newcomers it was, at first, difficult to get into closer contact with Menger. But once he had recognised a special talent and received the student into the select circle of the seminar he would spare no pains to help him on with his work. The contact between Menger and his seminar was not confined to academic discussions. He frequently invited the seminar to a Sunday excursion into the country or asked individual students to accompany him on his fishing expeditions. Fishing, in fact, was the only pastime in which he indulged. Even here he approached the subject in the scientific spirit he brought to everything else, trying to master every detail of its technique and to be familiar with its literature.

It would be difficult to think of Menger as having a real passion which was not in some way connected with the dominating purpose of his life, the study of economics. Outside the direct study of his subject, however, there was a further preoccupation hardly less absorbing, the collection and preservation of his library. So far as its economic section is concerned this library must be ranked as one of the three or four greatest libraries ever formed by a private collector. But it comprised by no means only economics, and its collections on ethnography and philosophy were nearly as rich. After his death the greater part of this library, including all economics and ethnography, went to Japan and is now preserved as a separate part of the library of the school of economics in Tokyo. That part of the published catalogue which deals with economics alone contains more than 20,000 entries.[37]

It was not given to Menger to realise the ambition of his later years and to finish the great treatise which, he hoped, would be the crowning achievement of his work. But he had the satisfaction of seeing his great early work bearing the richest fruit, and to the end he retained an intense and never flagging enthusiasm for the chosen object of his

[36] Cf. V. Graetz, "Carl Menger," *Neues Wiener Tagblatt*, February 27th, 1921.

[37] *Katalog der Carl Menger-Bibliothek in der Handelsuniversität Tokio.* Erster Teil. Sozialwissenschaften. Tokio, 1926 (731 pp.).

study. The man who is able to say, as it is reported he once said, that if he had seven sons, they should all study economics, must have been extraordinarily happy in his work. That he had the gift to inspire a similar enthusiasm in his pupils is witnessed by the host of distinguished economists who were proud to call him their master.

Hayek

─── on ───

Wieser

Friedrich von Wieser (1851–1926) was educated at Vienna and at several German universities. He held a teaching position in Prague until he succeeded to Menger's chair at the University of Vienna after the latter's resignation in 1903. Wieser is the author of the only systematic treatise on economics turned out by the founders of the Austrian school, *Social Economics* (1914; English translation 1927). In this work, Wieser proves himself a master of the method of successive approximation, turning from an isolated economic agent to the economy of the household, to the national economy, and to the world economy. Wieser's writings contain further developments of the theory of imputation, that is, of the valuation of producer goods, and to him is due an early version of the concept of opportunity cost. His last work, a penetrating sociological study, *Das Gesetz der Macht* (1926), emphasizes the role of the elite and formulates a "law of small numbers."

WIESER INSPIRED an admiration coming close to worship among all who came under the spell of his powerful personality. Readers of his works cannot fail to be impressed by his human greatness and universality. Those who have never met him in person will appreciate these characteristics more fully when they are shown in the light of all his accomplishments, including those which lie outside the field of economics. I shall try in the following to combine a brief review of Wieser's work in economics with an appraisal of the whole man.

Friedrich von Wieser, an offspring of an old family of Austrian public servants, was born in Vienna on July 10, 1851. His father, a high government employee, had originally intended to become a painter, and Wieser inherited from both parents a pronounced artistic disposition. He grew up in Vienna, and attended, as a class-mate of Böhm-Bawerk, the Schottengymnasium. After graduation at the age of 17 he studied law at the University of Vienna, completing the course at the age of 21.

Wieser's scientific work extends over a period of fifty years. It begins with a report to Professor Knies' seminar in the spring of 1876, when he distinguished himself for the first time, and it ends in June, 1926, when shortly before his death he was at work on the article "Money" for the *Handwörterbuch der Staatswissenschaften*. A straight line can be discerned, which connects the beginning and the end of his career during this half-century, leading eventually to the goal which he had set for himself early in life. This line does not always stand out clearly in the better known of his works, but it nevertheless provides the key to the understanding of his approach to all the problems treated by him. For a fuller understanding we must go back to the early training which he received in the Gymnasium. It was there that he received the decisive stimulus to his later scientific work. In those years Wieser took a deep interest in history.[1] Inspired by his history teacher, and

---

[1] Wieser has himself given an account of his debt to these early impressions, and has told of the later influences which turned him from history to sociology and economics. See his address given on the occasion of the hundredth anniversary of the Schottengymnasium, reprinted in his *Gesammelte Abhandlungen*,

[Translated in abridged form from *Jahrbücher für Nationalökonomie und Statistik*, 1926. By permission.]

by the works of the historian Macaulay, he made plans to study history. Together with Heinrich Friedjung, a fellow-student who later was to become a well-known historian, he tried to master the great mass of historical detail with which he was confronted in school.

Then the events of 1867 occurred, when Austria received a constitution. At the time when Wieser was to begin his university studies, the social group to which his family belonged was filled with vigorous interest in the events of the day. This may have drawn Wieser to the political and social movements and public affairs of the time, and may have been responsible for his decision to study law rather than history.

While a student at the university, Wieser devoted little attention to those disciplines to which later on the main part of his work was dedicated. He was little impressed by Lorenz von Stein's courses in economics. Only the acquaintance with Herbert Spencer's *First Principles,* together with the tremendous influence of Tolstoi's *War and Peace,* turned him definitely away from his youthful attachment to history and led him on to the intensive study of social phenomena. "From now on it was my dream," he tells us, "to write history without names. But, nothing was to become of this either. The most conspicuous social relationships are the economic ones. How could one dare to penetrate more obscure relationships without having first explained these? Economics, however, cannot be understood without an understanding of value. This became my starting point, and soon I found myself drifting on the plank of value theory into the boundless ocean of social phenomena."

History had failed to satisfy Wieser because its methods do not enable the student to gain insight into the laws which govern social phenomena. These Wieser wanted to explore. He wanted to gain insight into the operations of the great impersonal forces in human society, forces to which every individual is subject and which with necessity bring about events desired or predicted by no one. For such investigations a point of departure was not easily found. Eventually, however, Wieser happened to come across a book which showed him the way. Just when leaving the University of Vienna in 1872—together with his fellow-student Böhm-Bawerk, who later became his brother-in-law—he became acquainted with the *Grundsätze der Volkswirtschaftslehre*—principles of economics—of Carl Menger. Menger, then a young lecturer at the University of Vienna, was at that time not personally known to

ed. by F. A. von Hayek, Tübingen, 1929. In briefer form Wieser has sketched his intellectual development in the preface to his *Gesetz der Macht,* Vienna, 1926.

him. Wieser as well as Böhm-Bawerk found in this work the basis for their subsequent studies. These were resumed, first, while in the service of the fiscal administration of Lower Austria, and later, during 1875–1876 and 1876–1877, on a study tour made possible by a traveling fellowship, which brought the two young men in contact with Knies in Heidelberg, Roscher in Leipzig, and Hildebrand in Jena. Both seem to have concentrated soon on those problems which were to become their principal interests in later times and to which they were to contribute work of the highest importance. Their reports given before Knies' seminar in Heidelberg in the spring of 1876 contain basic ideas of the works which they later published. Wieser reported on "The Relation between Cost and Value," [2] Böhm-Bawerk on capital theory.

Wieser's seminar report is interesting in two respects. It demonstrates that Wieser had initiated, at a very early stage, the study of problems to which he later—that is, at least during the first period of his scientific career—was to devote his principal efforts. Furthermore, the seminar report makes it possible to settle definitively the question of the priority of one of the most important doctrines of the modern, subjective theory of value. Usually, Wieser's priority is acknowledged, but rarely in a form implying full recognition since the published works did not seem to establish his priority unequivocally. To make this point clear, it is necessary to anticipate a later phase of Wieser's development. The principal topic discussed in his first printed work,[3] published three years after Böhm-Bawerk's first work, is the same as that of his seminar report. This investigation of the relation between cost and value from the point of view of the subjective theory of value culminates in the interpretation of cost as indirect, or sacrificed utility, that is, as opportunity cost. The interpretation is based on a detailed discussion of the equalization of cost in production. Ever since Pantaleoni, this modernized version of the law of cost is correctly referred to as "Wieser's law" in economic theory.[4] The objection which may be raised against this is based on the fact that Böhm-Bawerk had already introduced the law of cost in complete clearness, although only

[2] First published in his *Gesammelte Abhandlungen* in 1929.

[3] *Ursprung und Hauptgesetze des wirtschaftlichen Wertes,* 1884.

[4] M. Pantaleoni, *Principii di economia pura,* Florence, 1889, pp. 218 ff., English transl. by T. B. Bruce, *Pure Economics,* 1898, pp. 184 ff. L. V. Birck, *The Theory of Marginal Value,* 1922, pp. 320 ff., referred to Wieser's theory of imputation as "Wieser's law," and J. A. Schumpeter, in addition, established "Wieser's principle of continuity" in his *Theory of Economic Development* (first German ed. 1912), transl. by Redvers Opie, 1934, p. 9.

incidentally and at an obscure place.[5] Furthermore, the wide dissemination of the whole new doctrine, including the theory of cost, was largely the result of Böhm-Bawerk's brilliant exposition in a later essay. However, in matters relating to the theory of subjective value—not in matters relating to price—this essay contains, in the main, no more than a review of Menger's and Wieser's doctrines.[6] In the light of all this it is understandable that the impression could be created that the theory of cost, the most important supplementation to Menger's theory of value, was principally or exclusively Böhm-Bawerk's work. In fact, however, there can be hardly any doubt that Böhm-Bawerk, in as much as he needed them for the clear exposition of his own ideas, wanted to relate ideas with which he had been acquainted since the time of his and Wieser's study tour to Germany, without being able to insert a reference to Wieser's still unpublished work.

To be sure, young Wieser's seminar report does by no means contain the precision of expression and conspicuousness of organization characteristic of his later works. But its approach to the problems of value strongly resembles these. Following Menger's solution, most of his successors attempted to solve special problems of value, especially the problem of valuation of producer goods, by applying directly the principle of explanation based on dependent utility, which Menger had established for consumer goods available in fixed quantities. Wieser, however, was not satisfied with the bare application of this formula. Menger's investigations had shown that the value of a good arises from the necessity of choosing a specific use among the many possible uses for a good available only in limited quantities, and that, therefore, it is the human attitude to the problem of utilization of disposable quantities of goods which determines their value. In Wieser's work, human behavior is the point of departure also for the explanation of value in more complex situations, especially in the field of producer goods. From his investigation of the economically required response to certain situations there follows directly his explanation of the mutual relationship between the values of products and of producer goods.

It is not possible to trace in the present context the development of Wieser's ideas in detail. However, a passage from his seminar report may be cited, to supply evidence of the fact that his law of cost is

[5] In a footnote on pp. 105–106 of his *Rechte und Verhältnisse vom Standpunkte der volkswirtschaftlichen Güterlehre,* Innsbruck, 1881. Reprinted in *Gesammelte Schriften,* ed. by F. X. Weiss, Vienna, 1924.

[6] "Grundzüge der Theorie des wirtschaftlichen Güterwertes," *Jahrbücher für Nationalökonomie und Statistik,* 1886, Vol. 13.

already stated there.   He summarizes the relationship between product
values and values of producer goods in these sentences: [7]

> The value of products is always determined by the wants which are
> dependent on them.   These wants are always determined on the basis of
> disposable quantities and needs.   But, instead of a comparison of quanti-
> ties and needs for each type of good, we arrive at the more comprehensive
> comparison of the total needs for products derived from a good of higher
> order [i.e., a producer good], and the total quantity of this good.   The
> value of the producer good is determined by the value of the last product
> which can be produced of the several types of goods, and it is then reflected
> in the values of all other types of goods.   The want which is decisive for
> the value of a product may at first glance be entirely unrelated to these
> types of goods.   It is brought into a relationship to them by the producer
> good, which forms the common link with the complex of its products.

It is not surprising that the group in Heidelberg and the seminar of
one of the founders of the historical school showed little understanding
of Wieser's report.   It is strange, however, that Carl Menger took no
deeper interest in the expansion of his doctrine contained therein when
Wieser showed it to him after his return from the first year of the study
tour.   In any event, he helped Wieser and Böhm-Bawerk to obtain a
renewal of the traveling fellowship for a second year on the basis of
their papers.   Wieser was not discouraged by Menger's lack of interest.
During the next seven years, which he spent in the fiscal administration
of Lower Austria, he continued his studies, and in 1884 he was able to
secure his appointment as lecturer at the University of Vienna, submitting a draft of sections of a book which was published in the same
year.[8]   Again, Menger's attitude was at first reserved, but eventually
he wrote a very favorable report on the book and recommended Wieser
immediately thereafter to the University of Prague, where Wieser was
appointed extraordinary professor of economics in the same year.

Wieser's first book is little known today.   For many years it has
been out of print and hard to obtain.   Although it is superseded by his
later work to a large extent, it had a profound influence on the development of marginal-utility economics, for which it also provided the name.
The subjective theory of value which Menger had developed was only
of limited applicability in the form which he had given to it.   No attempt had been made to apply it to the laws governing the structure
of production, and, in conjunction therewith, to expand it to include the
laws of distribution, the main problem of economic theory.   To be sure,

---

[7] *Gesammelte Abhandlungen*, p. 394.

[8] *Ursprung und Hauptgesetze des wirtschaftlichen Wertes,* Vienna, 1884.

Menger's work contained virtually all elements of this. But the elaboration was lacking, and so was, in spite of the exactness of the presentation, the suggestive formulation of the single doctrines which would have facilitated their wide diffusion. Wieser was the first to introduce such concepts as marginal utility, cognate products, opportunity cost, and imputation, which have become part of the permanent inventory of economic theory. With their help the basic ideas of the subjective theory became more readily intelligible and more widely accepted. Other parts of the book are less known today but are hardly of lesser importance, for example, the introductory section on the scientific significance of language and its concepts, which is highly characteristic of Wieser's way of thinking, the survey of the various explanations of value, and the final remarks on the difference between the valuation of goods by their marginal and by their total utility.

Wieser himself, however, always considered this work, excellent and complete in itself as it was, as a preliminary publication, required by the demands of his academic career. During the first five years of his residence in Prague he continued these studies along the same lines. The form in which he expressed his theories could rarely satisfy his own, highly developed critical sense. It was in fact always the compulsion of external circumstances which induced him to publish his ideas in comprehensive form. His next book, *Natural Value*,[9] is one of the most brilliantly written constructions in the field of economic theory. The immediate occasion of its publication was Wieser's desire to secure the ordinary professorship at Prague, a position to which he was promoted during the same year in which the book was published. *Natural Value* represented the results of thirteen years of intensive work on the problems of economic value, and for the next 25 years it was to contain the definitive formulation of Wieser's views. This book will probably always remain one of the classical works on the subject. Like his first publication, it was devoted to value theory, which it expanded in important points. The principal difference is a new type of approach, also used by Wieser later on in his comprehensive work on economic theory.

Wieser did not attach much value to scientific methodology as special discipline. He rarely occupied himself with the methodological literature, and always regretted that Carl Menger devoted so large a part of his energy to the discussion of methodological problems. He did not believe that methodological studies, separated from the treatment of concrete problems, could advance science, and was convinced that in

---

[9] *Der natürliche Wert*, 1889. English transl. by Ch. A. Malloch, London, 1893.

the proper theoretical treatment of a given subject the suitable method
would emerge. But he did not fail to give an exact account of his own
working procedure, and expressed his opinion of these matters in greater
detail, especially later on in his *Social Economics* and in his review of
Schumpeter's first book.[10]   His discussion of the significance of language and its concepts, as well as of the methods of isolating and idealizing hypothesis and of decreasing abstraction, have been recognized by
specialists in philosophy as standard categories which have given direction to the methodology of the cultural sciences.

In *Natural Value* Wieser made extensive use of the method of isolating and idealizing hypothesis, and on this basis he was able later on
to develop his entire theory of economics. As is well-known, he calls
"natural value" that value which would prevail in a communist society,
assuming complete absence of exchange and a central authority directing the entire economic process. Natural value then would reflect the
social relation between quantity of goods and utility. In a completely
clear and incontestable manner this concept was formulated only later,
in Wieser's *Social Economics,* where the hypothetical datum, on which
the investigation is based, is referred to as "simple economy." The
usefulness of this hypothesis is manifest, however, already in *Natural
Value.* With its help, Wieser is able to deduce the fact of subjective
valuation, fundamental in the explanation of the phenomena of social
exchange relationships—not only in the simple situation confronting
Robinson Crusoe but in all the more complex situations of the social
economy. He succeeds in this without committing the dangerous error
of using the phenomena of the exchange economy, which he wants to
explain, as basis of his explanation. Later on, in his principal economic work, he was to describe the object of his investigation "not as
the meagre household of an isolated economic agent but as an economy
equipped with all the means provided by wealth and technology, an
economy which taxes the thinking mind with all the essential tasks
which economic calculation has to solve." Wieser thus was able to
discuss in detail the significance of economic calculation in the development of production under conditions of advancing technology, and to
formulate rules for the valuation of the various factors of production.
For the first time he enters into a discussion of the peculiar features
attached to the various factors of production from the point of view of
value theory. He also expands the law of cost, as developed by him

[10] Review of *Das Wesen und der Hauptinhalt der theoretischen Nationalökonomie,* in *Jahrbuch für Gesetzgebung, Verwaltung und Volkswirtschaft,* 1911,
Vol. 35.

before, and improves his theory of imputation in such a manner that *Natural Value* has remained the *locus classicus* for this matter to the present day. The basic value theory is supplemented in a decisive fashion, especially with respect to its psychological foundations, when Wieser refers to "Gossen's law of saturation of wants." In a second part, devoted to "Value in the Public Economy," he made a number of suggestions—little utilized up to the present time—for the application of the new value theory to public finance.

With *Natural Value* the first period of Wieser's work in economic theory came to its close. During the subsequent years there followed only two articles, published in English and American periodicals and designed to spread and defend the Austrian theory of value in the English-speaking world.[11] After fifteen years of intensive work devoted to highly difficult problems, a status of exhaustion finally set in, which for many years made the continuation of theoretical studies impossible. While the consequences of overwork compelled him to abstain from the pursuit of his principal interests, Wieser, always an active person, did by no means abandon all scientific and literary efforts. During the nineties he turned to work on problems of economic policy and public finance. As he repeatedly has told, this meant for him relaxation from the heavy theoretical work of the preceding period. In conjunction with this work, he turned to a variety of activities in the public life of Prague. As was true of every group which he entered, he soon held a leading position in the German society of Prague. He had married Marianne Wolf in 1886, and ever after that his house was an important center of German cultural life in Bohemia. His widespread interests brought him into close contact with many scholars and personalities in public life, and his strongly developed artistic disposition made him seek the company of the Prague artists. Last but not least, the Prague period also coincides with the resumption of work in the field of sociological theory.[12]

When Carl Menger resigned from his chair, Wieser was called to the University of Vienna in 1903 to become his successor. The transfer to Vienna took place during a period in which Wieser participated in manifold activities. At that time he was occupied with studies in sociology, politics, and public finance, as well as with newly resumed

---

[11] "The Austrian School and the Theory of Value," *Economic Journal,* 1891; "The Theory of Value (A Reply to Professor Macvane)," *Annals of the American Academy of Political and Social Science,* 1891.

[12] *Ueber die gesellschaftlichen Gewalten,* Prague, 1901. This is an address given by Wieser as rector of the university.

research in economic theory, especially in the field of monetary theory. His Vienna inaugural address, which was devoted to "The Value of Money and its Historical Changes," [13] represented one of the most important achievements of Wieser in a second field of economic theory. It formed the point of departure for highly significant investigations. By applying the basic principle of the subjective theory of value to the problem of the value of money, Wieser provided the key to the solution of the latter problem. This solution was later on successfully expanded by students of Wieser—L. von Mises and F. X. Weiss—and, in conjunction with a parallel development in the English-speaking countries which took place later, it seems today to have become the leading doctrine.

The studies in monetary theory which Wieser published during the first six years in Vienna are the outcome of an expansion of his theoretical system. He continued to work on the perfection of the system during these years, having for long presented it in his lectures in a complete form. Nevertheless it is doubtful whether he would ever have decided to publish this new version in the absence of an especially fortunate occasion. In his own mind he had attained mastery over economic problems, so much so that he felt compelled now to turn to the study of general sociological laws. To him, economic studies had been the highway leading to these investigations. Occupied now with sociological problems, he had published some results of this work,[14] when Max Weber, the great German sociologist, invited him to contribute the volume on economic theory to the *Grundriss der Sozialökonomik,* a huge project of publications in the social sciences in which the most outstanding scholars of the time cooperated. Once more Wieser turned for several years to economic theory. The work on what was to become his principal contribution to economics took much longer than two years—as had originally been the plan—and the manuscript was turned in only reluctantly since Wieser was not completely satisfied with it. However, *Social Economics* [15] is the only comprehensive system of economic theory which the modern, subjective school has produced. Furthermore, and foremost, it probably is the greatest synthetic achievement of current economic theory in general. Since the time of the classical economists there has rarely been written

[13] "Der Geldwert und seine geschichtlichen Veränderungen," *Zeitschrift für Volkswirtschaft,* 1904, Vol. 13.

[14] *Recht und Macht,* Leipzig, 1910.

[15] First German ed., Tübingen, 1914; second ed. 1923. English transl. by A. F. Hinrichs, New York, 1927.

a work such as this, combining a comprehensive theoretical system with a wealth of penetrating insights into the world of economic phenomena. It is not possible in the present context to trace in detail the doctrines presented in this book. Our main task was to follow Wieser's development up to this *magnum opus*, whose content can be assumed as known among economists. A few remarks are in order to characterize the general significance of the book and point out those special features which must be interpreted in the light of Wieser's manner of thinking and working.

On the occasion of Wieser's seventieth birthday, Schumpeter has given in a few sentences so masterly an account of the characteristics of Wieser's work that I cannot think of anything better than to reproduce them here: [16]

> The scholar who enters into Wieser's realm feels at once a new atmosphere. It is as if he were to enter a building which in no way resembles the buildings of our time; whose structure and furnishings are strange to us and not understandable right away—just as there were many scholars who for long did not know what to do with Wieser's work. There is hardly a second author who would owe as little to other writers. Fundamentally, he owes something only to Menger, and to Menger he owes no more than a suggestion. His construction is entirely his own intellectual property, even when he says what already has been said before. There is no mechanical production in the realm of his mind. Every sentence and every formulation carry the mark of original insight. With a sovereign detachment, which we others learned to recognize as his right, he disregards in his work the scientific literature. He is absolutely unable to read fast or to read much. Almost never did he enter into the details of the thought of others. He always kept aloof from professional and, especially, from personal controversies.

It is impossible to express more vividly the characteristic aspects of Wieser's scientific attitude. The existing science was never the object of his work. He never occupied himself with the reconciliation of established doctrines or with the derivation of new statements from the stock of knowledge deposited in these doctrines. Rarely has a theoretical writer differed more profoundly from the generally accepted view of a theorist. In midst of theoretical discussions he was able to keep before his eyes the full reality with all its aspects, and to use his own abstract constructions and those of others only for describing, as completely as possible, a reality with which he always remained in close touch. With his strength thus absorbed, no time was left for the

[16] *Neues Wiener Tagblatt,* July 10, 1921.

penetration and discussion of the thought of others. Compulsion in this direction he considered as a disturbance of his own view of reality. Thus, he went as far as to avoid oral discussions, unless they aimed at the more perfect expression of his own ideas.[17] Never could he be induced to do violence to facts for the sake of greater elegance of the logical construction, and on occasion he was willing to sacrifice greater unity and consistence of thought for the sake of greater realism, even if this could be obtained only by the admission of ideas which were only tenuously related to his construction and not completely worked in.

In this respect his last great contribution to economic science is especially characteristic. In unity of thought and logical consistence it undoubtedly ranks behind Böhm-Bawerk's works. But this is due to the incomparably greater variety of phenomena which are taken into consideration by Wieser, his closer approximation of reality with its abundance of different situations. It is on account of these factors that Wieser is able only to hint at many things without carrying them to their conclusion, and that there appear to be many incompatibilities. As a rounded-out structure, Böhm-Bawerk's system may seem more grandiose to an observer who places the highest value on the strict logical consistence of a system. But Wieser's work is much richer in points of departure for the further development of economic theory, especially in those passages which are often censured as inconsistent.

In *Social Economics* Wieser discussed many new aspects of problems not considered in his earlier writings. Other parts of his doctrine were given definitive perfection. He had dealt extensively in the past of the problems of Book I, the "Theory of the Simple Economy." Here the most important improvement is the insertion of a long section dealing with matters which logically precede the theory of value. In this connection he discusses in detail the theory of production and carries the investigation of the adjustment required in response to different economic situations so far that the solution of the difficult value problems follows by itself. The most important results of the investigation of the structure of production are Wieser's theory of capital and his distinction between reproducible and versatile "cost means of production" and "specific means of production," which cannot be reproduced and are limited to a specific use.[18] In value theory, this distinction pro-

---

[17] Even with Böhm-Bawerk, his brother-in-law, with whose theories his own were conflicting in certain respects, he is said to have never discussed economic questions. There is a report that Böhm-Bawerk on occasion complained that Wieser also failed to pay adequate attention to his, Böhm-Bawerk's, writings.

[18] *Social Economics*, pp. 81 ff.

vides the basis for the very important, but not entirely completed and therefore often misunderstood distinction between different margins of use.

The section dealing with the "Institutions of Exchange" is introduced by an outline of Wieser's sociological theory, which is brought into a close relationship to his economic theory. The most important, and entirely new contribution of the book is, however, Wieser's theory of price. This is now expanded to cover all phenomena of a fully developed market. As the most important and fruitful concepts created in this connection we may mention his "stratification of prices," [19] "market indices," [20] and "monopoloid institutions." [21] Wieser's sovereign insight into complex relationships and his plastic style have unearthed treasures whose utilization will provide abundant work for future generations of economists. The sections on money and credit, which are closely connected with the theory of price and which go far beyond his earlier presentation, are hardly less replete with suggestions and new insight. In the subsequent parts of his book, Wieser gradually approaches the phenomena of the real economy. The more closely he approaches them, the more conspicuous becomes the value of the instrument forged for its explanation in the first parts of the work.

The great work in the *Grundriss der Sozialökonomik* marks the close of Wieser's studies in economics. In this field he had now given his best. The course of events turned his interest to other problems. *Social Economics* had been published a few weeks before the outbreak of the World War of 1914–1918. This explains in part why the expected impact of the book was delayed for long. The tremendous events of the subsequent years directed Wieser's attention irresistibly and definitively to the goal which he had set for himself as a young man: the comprehension of the driving forces behind social events.

During the last two years of the war his scientific and literary work was interrupted by his appointment as minister of commerce. Relieved from official duties after the collapse of Austria, he at once returned to his sociological studies. While continuing other literary activities,[22] he devoted his main efforts to the work which to him meant the crown

[19] *Ibid.*, pp. 186 ff.

[20] *Ibid.*, pp. 173 ff.

[21] *Ibid.*, pp. 220 ff.

[22] Wieser served as a member of the board of editors for the fourth edition of the *Handwörterbuch der Staatswissenschaften*, and was in charge of the Austrian section of the *Economic and Social History of the World War*, sponsored by the Carnegie Endowment for International Peace.

of his life's achievement and in which he wanted to set forth the results of the sociological investigations pursued since his youth. This work was published in 1926, a few months before his death on July 22.[23] On the completion of this book he had labored with great energy, utilizing a number of articles and preparatory studies written during the last few years. The form of exposition raises this favorite child of the great man far above the rank of ordinary scientific literature. Wieser's last book is a fitting demonstration of the general truth that a work which is carried by a great idea assumes the characteristics of a great piece of art. Having as its architect a sovereign master of science, it reaches a towering height above all indispensable detail and becomes related to artistic creation. In this last work, where Wieser shakes off the fetters of specialization and disciplinary methods, his unique personality emerges in all its greatness, combining a universal interest in all fields of culture and art, worldly wisdom and experience, detachment from the affairs of the day, sympathy for the fellow-man, and freedom from narrow nationalism. In him the civilization of old Austria had found its most perfect expression.

[23] *Das Gesetz der Macht,* Vienna, 1926.

Schumpeter
——— on ———
Böhm-Bawerk

Eugen von Böhm-Bawerk (1851–1914), Austrian statesman and economist, is chiefly responsible for the spread of the doctrine of the Austrian school. Böhm-Bawerk attained great reputation during his lifetime, at home as well as abroad, and his works, cited in the essay reproduced here, were early available in English translations. He is remembered for his influential theories of interest and capital, and for his critique of the economics of Karl Marx. Böhm-Bawerk's "time-preference" theory of interest emphasizes the psychological and technical factors which account for the greater urgency of wants for present, as compared with future, goods. It is closely related to his theory of capital, which stresses the element of time in the process of production, and interprets a more "capitalistic" or "roundabout" process of production, facilitated by a fall in interest, as one requiring more time. Böhm-Bawerk's critique of Marx was directed primarily against Marx's utilization of the labor theory of value. It was the first manifestation of the antisocialist attitude of the Austrian group, characteristic also of its younger members (Mises, Hayek).

Joseph A. Schumpeter (see pp. 734 ff., below) here pays a tribute to his teacher Böhm-Bawerk.

THE NAME of Böhm-Bawerk is one of the greatest in the history of economics. He has acquired immortality on account of his fruitful, original ideas, far-reaching constructive power, brilliant way of presentation, outstanding gift of leadership, ever ready preparedness for aggressive and defensive polemics, and all the qualities of character and intellect which are the mark of a teacher in the most exalted sense of this word. The ideas which forever will be connected with his name are as yet not remote enough, are too much surrounded by controversies, to establish in detail which of them are destined to be a lasting component of our science. But his influence is felt among nearly all, and especially among the best, scientific efforts in the field of economics, and it carries the unmistakable mark of the scientific genius, related, in its innermost substance, to the most outstanding intellectual achievements of all time.

Eugen von Böhm-Bawerk was an offspring of a family of civil servants, having been born in Brünn on February 12, 1851, as the son of the vice governor of Moravia. When a young man, his interest turned to science, especially to theoretical physics, in conformity with a mental outlook which aims at exact thinking. However, in response chiefly to external factors, he took up the study of law, thus acquiring a systematic knowledge of economics. Having graduated from the Vienna Schottengymnasium, he studied at the Vienna law faculty. In accordance with Austrian custom, observed especially among the families of public officials, he became an officer in the fiscal administration of lower Austria after he had passed his law examination. Soon he was called into the ministry of finance, where he immediately attracted the attention of his superiors.

Without any hesitation he at once struck root in the field of economic theory, and with a determinate sureness which impressed upon his whole life the unity of a work of art, he created for himself the opportunity for further, more advanced, research. Right after having acquired the doctorate in law in 1875, he was already entirely occupied

[Translated in abridged form from *Neue Oesterreichische Biographie,* Vienna, Amalthea Verlag, 1925. By permission.]

with his own ideas. He went on a study tour in the course of which he visited Heidelberg, Leipzig, and Jena.

In those years economics touched the low ebb of achievement and prestige. It had acquired the character of a science only since the great advance during the first decades of the nineteenth century, which gave precision, foundation, and systematic development to the accomplishments of the eighteenth century. Then the productive impulse died down. Neither Ricardo nor Thünen had successors of equal rank. The legacy deteriorated in the hands of a group of trainbearers. The best of these—and this is true even of John Stuart Mill —had nothing to give but a more or less complete exposition and interpretation of the doctrine of the masters, which was considered as an established system. This development was especially unfortunate because of the tendency to exaggerate the importance of the newly won insight and to apply it directly to the questions of economic and social policy of the time. Economic science appeared to have become inseparably connected with a specific position in economic policy, that is, with old-time economic liberalism. Beset with danger, as this path was, the situation became completely intolerable when the sterile and pedantic doctrinalism of succeeding generations of economists came in conflict with the spirit of an age hostile to economic liberalism.

Economics no longer could satisfy the scientific requirements of the more vigorous minds. The public at large and even the experts considered it as a mere toolbox for liberal argumentation. Scholars turned their interest to the problems of reality rather than to the scientific foundations of economic theory. The younger generation fled from the arid formulae, and few young scholars took the trouble of penetrating more deeply into the inner meaning of the doctrine or made an attempt at its reform. Pronouncing a wholesale condemnation on the "classical system," they turned—especially in Germany— to work in the field of economic history or to social reform. The view became widely recognized that economic science as a system of generally valid truth does not exist, and that such a system at best has to offer a formulation of the politico-economic ideas of its era. This was the intellectual situation which confronted the three men who succeeded in the reconstruction of economic doctrine: Jevons, Menger, and Walras.

Any scientific innovation requires the strength to break the fetters formed by fixed habits of thinking—as was done by these three men. In their case this was infinitely more difficult than is usually true. Many of their fellow-scientists felt no attachment to the old doctrines. This, one might think, could have opened the door to the new doctrines. But since many scholars were inclined to deny, on principle, the possibility of a scientific theory of economic life, their basic attitude to economic theory was negative. This position had served as a point of departure to entirely different fields of interest. Walras, thus, remained a lone thinker to the end of his life. Jevons' struggle was not quite as hard, because in England the interest in economic theory, dulled as it was, had not died. Menger's fate was the result of an accident in the history of science. Immediately after his decisive book was published in 1871, he found two allies, equal in strength, ready to accept his basic principle, and able to defend and develop it with the same vigor: Böhm-Bawerk and Wieser. A constellation of circumstances such as this is extremely rare. It can really be explained only by intellectual affinity and by a sort of self-discovery of what was accepted so readily. The accomplishments of individuals thus were consolidated in a new movement, the so-called Austrian school. Without external aid and connections, and initially in a most precarious position, the weight of its message gradually conquered the scientific world.

Böhm-Bawerk's interest in economic theory was purely scientific. Unlike Marshall, he was not attracted to economics by the desire to obtain an explanation of the social problem. Unlike Marx, he was not driven by the zeal for reformatory action. He wanted to analyze for the sake of analysis, of knowledge, of research itself. He accepted spontaneously Menger's basic thought, which later on he was to round out and defend in a manner in which one defends one's own possession. Combined with this acceptance of Menger's ideas, there appear right away his own fundamental thoughts. They resound already in his first work, which secured him an instructorship in economics at the University of Vienna in 1880 and which was published in a somewhat modified form a year later. This work,[1] having been launched at the time of his study tour, contains apparently only the detail of a very arid chapter. But it treats also of a few interesting methodological problems, and marks the first step in the direction of the problem to which Böhm-Bawerk's life work was to turn, the problem of the economic structure of capitalism. The substance of what he had to say later in mature form seems to have taken shape in these fruitful years, working in him ever since. A mind already formed, who saw his way ahead and knew what he wanted, he met the meagre stimulation which at that time came to him from the outside. In the terminology

---

[1] *Rechte und Verhältnisse vom Standpunkte der volkswirtschaftlichen Güterlehre*, 1881.

of the philosopher Wilhelm Ostwald, he was a "classic" type, and he confirmed Ostwald's theory of the fundamental importance, for the scientist, of the years following upon the termination of physical growth.

With his mental development requiring science as the vocation of his life, the acceptance of a teaching position was the necessary consequence. He went to the University of Innsbruck, where he was promoted to extraordinary professor in 1881 and to full professor in 1884. In Innsbruck he remained from 1880 to 1889. The foundation for his career was laid, the framework of his life established. In these quiet years, which he cherished throughout his entire later life, he completed his scientific work. What came later was only expansion, defense, and improved formulation. We must not overlook an alliance in which this man, so self-reliant in other respects, found an atmosphere of priceless value for his work as scientist and statesman. Like a protective and stimulating power it surrounded his work and provided the basis for the unity and form of his life and achievement. In 1880 he married the sister of his friend, von Wieser, and until his death he enjoyed the happiness of a home as only a warmhearted woman can create it, a style of life in which serenity and interests of all sorts were blended with the established rhythm of the daily work in a happy and stimulating manner.

The doctrines of value and interest form the core of any economic theory. Almost inevitably, the attitude to these two problems determines everything else. They have always been considered the basic problems, and four-fifths of the literature of economic theory consists of investigations and controversies relating to them. Böhm-Bawerk took from Menger the fundamental principle of value theory and, derived therefrom, that of price theory. Here he only had to expand, with the expansion turning primarily into two directions.

Menger's theory of value is applicable in the first place only to those goods which serve directly the satisfaction of human wants. Menger indeed had explained on the basis of the same principle also the formation of the value of all other goods, that is, of goods which do not serve directly the satisfaction of wants but the production of other, want-satisfying goods. While Menger thus derived the value of these goods from the value of the consumer goods, he had not gone beyond the starting point in the elaboration of their value. Critics of Menger's theory of value who recognized it in general insisted right away that it failed to bear light on the manner in which the value of producer goods is established. From this there was only one step to the denial of the possibility of deriving their value from Menger's principle. This step was taken soon, being facilitated by a readily available argument: the productive factors required for the production of a consumer good cooperate in an inseparable combination, and it is, therefore, impossible to attribute to them specific shares in its value. This is the central problem of the so-called theory of imputation, developed by Wieser and Böhm-Bawerk. It was necessary also to expand the principle of price formation, established by Menger, and construct a serviceable theory of price. In this field Böhm-Bawerk was especially successful. His approach to the solution of this problem has remained unshaken to the present time in all its essential points. It is the classical accomplishment of the Vienna school in this realm.

Böhm-Bawerk's investigations in this field were published in the form of a brilliant essay in 1886.[2] He was a tower of strength to the new movement, defending it courageously in many controversies. Among these, that with Heinrich Dietzel of 1890 to 1892 may be mentioned. Intellectually as well as otherwise, this controversy puts him into a favorable light. His polemic never contains the discourteous features which make our controversies so unpleasant. He had early reached a height which compelled him to look down upon most of his colleagues, but he never betrayed with a single word his awareness of this. He always displays in these writings an unruffled respect for his opponent, or, at worst, cool reserve. Never did he permit differences of scientific opinion to disturb personal relationships.

Böhm-Bawerk's theory of interest was exclusively his own contribution, with which his name will always be connected. There is no doubt that it is one of the most magnificent achievements in the history of economic theory. In the process of the capitalistic economy interest plays a role of foremost importance. Moreover, income from interest provides the economic basis for that social group which is most characteristic of this economic system. No wonder then that the picture of the economic process as sketched by the theorist is colored, first of all, by his explanation of interest. The observer's opinion about the nature of interest is bound to influence his socio-political judgment and his general appraisal of the value of capitalism. There are no less than about thirty different theories of interest. Not a single one of these can claim only approximately general recognition. The commonday experience which brings a phenomenon close to the observer does not at all facilitate its theoretical explanation but instead acts as psychological obstacle to scientific investigation.

---

[2] "Grundzüge der Theorie des wirtschaftlichen Güterwertes," *Jahrbücher für Nationalökonomie und Statistik,* Vol. 13, 1886.

Böhm-Bawerk applied to his work responsible and diligent care. This reflected not only his nature but also the situation which confronted him. In the sciences which have attained maturity, especially in physics, the scientist as a rule faces certain problems which are well appreciated by his colleagues. Böhm-Bawerk's task was not just the solution of a scientific problem. Before he could announce his own message, he had, first of all, to teach his readers to see the problem in the right light, to wring from them the assent to the basic points of departure, and to introduce them to the elements of the subject. This he did by first presenting an incredibly diligent and acute analysis of virtually all theories of interest which had been developed before his time. Thereby he produced a critical history of doctrine unexcelled in economic literature, an invaluable tool for the exercise of economic thinking. The publication took place in 1884 in the form of a first volume of his principal work.[3] In 1888 there followed the second volume, the *Positive Theory of Capital*.[4] The tremendous success of the two books was felt only gradually in the economic thinking of our time, in the workshops of the scholars. The influence on disciples, followers, and persons of related views was not limited to mere recognition—on the contrary, these often fought against the innovation with all means. But inevitably they fell under the spell of the personality and the work. Böhm-Bawerk did not achieve the sort of fame which consists of being quoted frequently and which means so little. Instead, he formed the minds and made them think as he thought, so much so that many of the attacks which were directed against him carry the mark of his school. He became one of the great teachers of our science in the most exalted sense of the word. His feel for what was attainable under given circumstances made possible an achievement that is often denied to creative minds. Everything he wrote went into the flesh and blood of that part of our system of theory which is the most alive. But success did not come swiftly. For a long time Böhm-Bawerk ranked after economists whose achievements have grown dim compared with his own. When he started out, there did not exist a circle of like-minded persons. For a long time there was little opportunity for bringing together such a group or for training followers in substantial numbers. The eventual achievement is the more impressive. It came about without a scramble for external

[3] English translation, *Capital and Interest*, by W. Smart, London, 1890. Fourth German ed. 1921.

[4] English translation by W. Smart, London, 1891. Third German ed. 1909–1911.

success, without an appeal to public opinion, without academic politics, but simply by virtue of the written argument, without any of the means which are often indispensable although they conform so badly to the highest ideal of scientific work.

As has been noted, the *Positive Theory of Capital* contains a comprehensive theory of the entire economic process, notwithstanding the title, which seems to indicate a narrower content. Whatever the attitude of future generations may be to this most characteristic product of Böhm-Bawerk's power and to single links in his chain of reasoning—they will always admire its great lines, vigor, and drive. There is no doubt that he aimed at the highest achievement possible in economics, and that what he did achieve represents a peak attained only by few. The comparison with Marx has always been pressed upon me. This may sound strange—but only because Marx' name is immersed by the heat of political passion and because his construction mirrors a different temperament. Marx' name is inseparably connected, first of all, with social movements and political aims which have made him conspicuous and significant to large groups, but which also cover up his scientific achievement. All this is lacking in the case of Böhm-Bawerk. He did not desire to be more than a scientist. Not a single word—none of those words which come so easy in our discipline—is added by him to his purely scientific reasoning. His path is not deluged by social or political waves. His work provides no popular pedestal from which to address the masses. It has no other ornament than its classical form and architecture. Different as the two men, their lives, points of view, and, in so many respects, their works were, as scientists they had substantially the same aim. Both considered interest as the vantage point from which to derive a comprehensive view of the capitalistic economy. Both faced a similar situation with respect to the status of the science of their time, and both were inspired by the recognition of the basic significance of interest. Both took over the elements of value theory from a predecessor: Böhm-Bawerk from Menger, Marx from Ricardo. Both created something whose greatness is manifested by the fact that no counter-argument, as successful as it may be with respect to a concrete point of attack, can detract from the significance of the whole.

From the technical point of view, the essentially new contribution of Böhm-Bawerk's system to economic theory is the mastery of the element of time. By this we do not intend to refer to the fact that the passage of time is accompanied by systematic changes in the economy, that there occurs something in the nature of economic development. Instead, what is meant is the fact that time plays an important role as an element in the normal course of economic affairs, influencing all values, prices, and incomes. It goes without saying that no economist could have ever overlooked this fact. But nobody had known what to do with it, how to find a place for it in the equilibrium systems of the economic magnitudes, and how to derive significant conclusions from it.

Ricardo's treatment is typical in this respect. In the famous first section of his first chapter he makes the attempt to establish his principle of value and price. Then, in the fourth section, he admits that the exchange relationship of two goods, requiring unequal lengths of time for their production, must be different from what the principle of value, as established by him before, would indicate. But he passes over the "why" as well as an explanation of the consequences. Virtually no economic theorist up to Böhm-Bawerk has accomplished anything better. They continued to let this weak point drift, often in a less sincere and clear manner than Ricardo had exhibited. There remained a substantial gap in the economic system.

Böhm-Bawerk was able to fill it with the help of two explanatory facts. In itself, their discovery means as little as, say, the discovery that the movement of falling bodies becomes accelerated. All constructions of pure theory as well as of dramatic art have in common the fact that their factual material tends to be extremely scanty and, as a rule, quite uninteresting. It is the manner in which these meager elements are utilized, and the scope of the explanation achieved with the help of the chain of thoughts based thereon, which account for the value of the theoretical constructions.

It has always been known that a good which is presently available is appreciated more highly than is the same good if it is to be made available, with all possible certainty, at a later time, in a year, for example. The higher appreciation of presently available goods and the lesser appreciation of future wants is one of the two opening wedges which Böhm-Bawerk uses for the admission of the time element to economic theory. The other relates to the length of the process of production. The more time this process is allowed to take, the less does it need to aim directly at the production of the desired final product, and the more complicated can the roundabout ways of production become—taken, for example, in the form of intermediate products and machinery. As the process of production is lengthened, the physical product increases—not just in the same proportion as the length but more than proportionately. The length of the period of production was until Böhm-Bawerk's time regarded as a technological datum, and, hence, as a constant from the point of view of economic theory. Now it is turned into a variable. The economy's stock of consumer goods, whose size permits the taking of roundabout ways of production of different length, becomes a determinant of this variable. It is clear that the length of the period for which the stock of the means of sub- sistence suffices—and, hence, the length of the period of production made possible thereby—depends, in turn, on the amount of claims which must be met out of the stock of consumer goods per unit of time, that is, on the amount of wages and rents. Every possible length of the period of production implies a certain method of production and corresponds to a certain physical product. Any such physical product has, or is expected to have, a certain value and price. Hence, it is clear also that the profitability of all possible methods of produc- tion is uniquely determined by all these magnitudes. If the choice among the various production possibilities is made in accordance with the principle of profit maximization, this establishes unequivocally, after the choice has been made, the value of the claims to the stock of the means of subsistence. This stock, as has been noted, makes possible the chosen method of production. Wages, rents, the amount of capital, the length of the period of production, and the productivity of the method of production are thus quantities which mutually deter- mine each other. All at once the entire economic process appears in a simplicity, clearness, and completeness in which it was never seen before. It is possible to reduce Böhm-Bawerk's theory to a simple system of equations, a step which he failed to take since he was not familiar with higher mathematical analysis. But if this factor is given decisive weight—as is done in theoretical physics—then the conclu- sion is warranted that it was only through Böhm-Bawerk, and, in a somewhat different sense, through Walras, that economics became a science satisfying the requirements of exactness.

The explanation of interest is the most important of the immedi- ately practical results of this approach. Interest is an agio, or pre- mium, placed on the value and price of present consumer goods, especially of the workers' present means of subsistence or of the sums of money which represent these. Interest arises because the possibility of immediate disposal over these goods facilitates the production of larger quantities of the same or of other goods in the future. Interest, thus, is a deduction from other types of income, especially from wage and rent, which is enforced by the valuations of the market. Workers and landowners receive no more than the present value of their productive services, and the increments in value—which are due to the more highly productive methods of production made possible by the passage of time—remain in the hands of the entrepreneur. From him they flow back to the capitalist who has made available to the entrepreneur the means facilitating the application of the more highly productive method of production.   Therefore, workers and landowners do indeed receive the value of the product of their services, but the value is discounted to the present time.   From this the conclusion can be drawn that interest is a feature characteristic of every type of economic system.   The increments in value from which interest flows do not fail to appear, for example, in a socialist society, although there they would not accrue to a private capitalist.

From this also follow the laws governing the amounts of interest, wage, and rent.   Instead of applying his argument to the problem of interest, Böhm-Bawerk could just as well have applied it to wage or rent.   His theory provides the clue for solving all questions of the theory of distribution in a uniform manner, displacing earlier attempts which at best were fragmentary in character.   In his work, the mutual relationship between wage, rent, and interest appears for the first time in an exact form, from which an abundance of specific conclusions can be derived for every concrete instance.   His theory also makes it possible to deduce the law governing the value of the sources of income, especially of land and capital.   In the light of Böhm-Bawerk's doctrine, total wage payments, total interest payments, and the total amount of capital stand in a certain relationship to each other.   Thus, his doctrine provides also the answer to the question to what extent, under given circumstances, the income of the workers can be modified in accordance with the requirements of social policy, and what effect such a modification would have on the economy as a whole.   To this question, his last work is devoted.[5]   Finally, Böhm-Bawerk's system shows for the first time the exact relationship which prevails between the world of valuations and the world of technological data surrounding the process of production.

With the simplest means, and without complicated methods, a great victory was won.   There is, indeed, little to say about Böhm-Bawerk's method.   He was no methodological connoisseur, and did not cherish the methodological controversies which absorb so much space in the literature of economics.   It never occurred to him to insist on the exclusive use of any specific method.   Questions such as the possibility, on principle, of general laws in the field of social science did not weigh on his mind.   He taught method through his practice.

[5] "Macht oder ökonomisches Gesetz," first published in 1914, reprinted in *Gesammelte Schriften,* ed. by F. X. Weiss, 1924–1926.

From now on, his scientific efforts were directed at the expansion, examination, and improvement of the system which he had constructed. They include the essay on *Karl Marx and the Close of His System,* undoubtedly the best critique of Marx which has ever been written.[6] The other publications of the subsequent years were written on the occasion of controversies, and their results were incorporated in the later editions of his main work.

After the great achievement was accomplished, Böhm-Bawerk accepted in 1889 a position in the ministry of finance, a decision eminently in accord with the principles of personal psychological hygiene. The position offered to him was not just that of an economic adviser. He was to fulfill a specific task, the preparation of the draft of the great reform of direct taxation in Austria. This draft became law in 1896, in substance in the form given to it by Böhm-Bawerk. Although his productive impulses now belonged to another field, he held on to his scientific interests. Keeping up with the literature and participating in scientific controversies, he even found time for investigations in his field of specialization, and soon became an important factor in the scientific life of Vienna. A connection with the university was established when he was appointed special lecturer. In 1892 he participated in the founding of a periodical,[7] which he opened up with a beautiful article and in which he published a number of essays. All this did not exhaust the scope of his interests. He was a master of the organization of life. Nothing demonstrates more impressively the strength of his character than the fact that no particular interest, as vivid as it may have been, was permitted to engulf him. Even when facing the most difficult problems of administrative and parliamentary life—for example, when defending government drafts before the parliament—there was nothing that could prevent him from devoting one or two morning hours to scientific work, or a free afternoon to music, or a vacation to his beloved mountains. [During the later course of his government career, Böhm-Bawerk occupied distinguished positions, serving as chairman of an administrative tribunal, and, on three occasions, as minister of finance. During the last years of his life, he returned to teaching, and accepted a full professorship at the University of Vienna. He died on August 27, 1914.—Ed.]

[6] Published in 1896. English translation 1898, new ed. by Paul M. Sweezy, 1949.

[7] "Unsere Aufgaben," *Zeitschrift für Volkswirtschaft, Socialpolitik und Verwaltung,* Vol. 1, pp. 1–10.

Hicks
on
Walras

Léon Walras (1834–1910) firmly established the mathematical method in economics. He was the first to conceive the notion of general economic equilibrium, which, in contrast with the partial-equilibrium approach of Alfred Marshall and other English-speaking economists, became the principal focus of attention of the Lausanne school. Together with Stanley Jevons and Carl Menger, Walras was the founder of the modern, subjective theory of value.

Unable to succeed in his native France, Walras obtained in 1870 a position at what is now the University of Lausanne in Switzerland. He retired from his chair in 1892. Recognition of his path-breaking work came to him only at the end of his life.

Walras' principal works, listed in the following article, are not available in English. The publication of an English translation of the *Éléments* is expected shortly, however.

John R. Hicks (1904–) was educated at Oxford, to which he has returned as teacher after having been affiliated with the London School of Economics and the Universities of Cambridge and Manchester. Hicks' principal work, *Value and Capital* (1939), shows him as an economic theorist of great subtlety. This book is chiefly responsible for the resuscitation of the indifference-curve approach as well as for the growing interest in problems of general economic equilibrium.

I

LIKE JOHN STUART MILL and John Maynard Keynes, Léon Walras [1] was the son of an economist. His father, Auguste Walras, was one of those excellent people (they seem to have existed since very near the dawn of history) who taught the true but unhelpful doctrine that value depends on scarcity (*rareté*); [2] the son followed the father's teaching, but added to it something which lifts it on to another plane of precision. He defined *rareté* as *l'intensité du dernier besoin satisfait par une quantité consommée de marchandise;* [3] scarcity equals marginal utility.

His position with Jevons and Menger as one of the independent discoverers of the Marginal Utility principle is generally regarded as Léon Walras' chief title to fame; and this no doubt justly enough. But anyone who comes a little closer to these writers cannot help feeling a little resentment at the habit of classifying them together, even for the joint receipt of such an honorable title. For each of them made contributions to economics which are peculiarly his own, and it is for these special contributions that they are still worth reading today.

Indeed, the modern reader of Walras' *Éléments d'Économie Politique Pure* is struck by its affinity, not with the work of Jevons or Menger, but with that of Marshall. For a quite considerable part of the way Walras and Marshall go together; and when they separate, it is a difference of interests, rather than of technique, that divides them. While Walras was seeking for the general principles which underlie the working of an exchange economy, Marshall forged an analytical instrument

[1] Born at Évreux, 1834; in 1870, after ten years of journalism, business, and other miscellaneous activities, he became Professor of Political Economy at Lausanne, a position which he held until 1892. His *Éléments d'Économie Politique Pure* appeared in two parts: the theory of exchange in 1874, the theory of production in 1877 (second edition, 1889; 3rd, 1896; 4th, 1900). He died in 1910.

[2] A. A. Walras, *De la nature de la richesse et de l'origine de la valeur* (1832).

[3] *Éléments d'Économie Politique Pure*, p. 76. All references to the *Éléments* will be to the *Édition définitive*, i.e., fourth and subsequent editions.

[Reprinted by permission from *Econometrica*, October 1934.]

capable of easier application to particular problems of history or experience. Yet, since the followers of Walras cannot always afford to be pure philosophers, and Marshallians have their moments of reflection, the two systems have inevitably tended to grow back into one another as the years pass by.

This affinity between two writers of different upbringing and obviously very different mental outlook—their simultaneous development of what was then a very new line of thought—looks at first sight surprising, and one feels almost obliged to explain it by the intrinsic excellence of the path they followed: "it seems no honest heart can stray." Yet in fact there is a clear historical reason for it, one decisive influence we know to have been felt by both. Each of them had read Cournot.

Now although each makes a specific acknowledgement to Cournot, it is in each case couched in very general terms.[4] They each tell us that Cournot showed them how to use the differential calculus in economics, and this may mean much or little. But it is at least striking that certain very significant elements of Cournot's mathematical economics, going far beyond the mere idea of using mathematical methods, appear in Walras and appear in Marshall.

One of these is of course the demand curve itself (which already implies a resolution to treat economic quantities as if they are continuous variables). But more important, and less obvious, is the conception of perfect competition. Cournot's analysis, it will be remembered, passed from Monopoly to Duopoly (or Limited Competition), and from Duopoly to Unlimited Competition, which he defined as a state of affairs in which no single producer is able to influence appreciably the prices of the market. It was this last conception (applied to the theory of exchange value generally) which enabled Walras and Marshall to overcome the difficulties which had baffled Jevons, those difficulties which arise from the differences in the wants of different buyers of a particular commodity.[5] In the hands of Walras, this conception of per-

[4] Walras, *Éléments,* preface, p. viii. Marshall, *Principles,* preface to the first edition, pp. ix–x.

[5] Cf. Jevons' ugly and unsatisfactory device of "trading bodies," which smudges over the distinction between monopoly and competition.

The relation between Jevons' work and that of Cournot is curious. When he wrote the first edition of his *Theory* Jevons had not read Cournot; but he had read Lardner's *Railway Economy,* "which treats certain questions of Political Economy in a highly scientific and mathematical spirit. Thus the relation of the rate of fares to the gross receipts and net profits of a railway company is beautifully demonstrated in pp. 286–293 by means of a diagram. It is proved that the

fect competition was converted into a special technique of using prices as economic parameters. Although of course this technique was used by Marshall as well, its very consistent employment is highly characteristic of Walras' work.

With this equipment, it was fairly easy to give an adequate analysis of the simple exchange of two commodities under competitive conditions. (Cournot had confined himself to the selling of products by producers, and did not examine the logically prior problem.) Accordingly, we find Walras beginning his Éléments in this way (1874), and Marshall following with a substantially equivalent analysis, hidden under the guise of a theory of International Values (1879).[6]

Walras' treatment fails of complete generality in only one respect; the downward slope of the demand curve is not quite so inevitable an assumption as he thought it. But he was well aware that the downward slope of the demand curve does not necessarily imply that the supply curve derived from it is upward sloping. If a person is buying X, and giving Y in exchange, then, if his demand for X becomes inelastic, his supply curve of Y will turn back towards the price-axis. In this case it becomes possible that the demand and supply curves for Y may cut several times; but some of these intersections will be points of unstable equilibrium.

Faced with this difficulty of multiple intersections, Marshall cut the knot by his distinction between the "theory of International Values" and the "theory of Domestic Values." In "International Values," the

maximum profit occurs at the point where the curve of gross receipts becomes parallel to the curve of expenses of conveyance" (Theory of Political Economy, 1st edition, pp. 17–18). Lardner thus plotted total receipts and total costs against price—a peculiar way of putting it, to our ideas; but it is obvious that in so doing he adopted the most direct way possible of expressing the fifth chapter of Cournot's Recherches in geometrical form. Whether this is really what happened, I am unable to say; all that can be said is that it is definitely possible. For at the time Lardner wrote his book (1850) he was living in Paris, and so was Cournot; and there was at least this link between them, that in 1835, three years before he wrote the Recherches, Cournot had translated a book on Mechanics by Lardner into French.

But if we cannot prove the filiation, so much at least is clear: Jevons started from a theory of monopoly substantially identical with Cournot's. Where Walras and Marshall had the advantage over him was in their possession, not only of Cournot's theory of monopoly, but also of his theory of Unlimited Competition.

[6] The Pure Theory of Foreign Trade. There is, I think, no question that Marshall's analysis is quite independent of Walras'. Yet they differ in only two ways: (1) Marshall uses aggregate curves, instead of the simple price-quantity curves used by Walras; (2) Marshall's "Increasing Returns" complication has of course no counterpart in Walras' simpler problem.

possibility of negatively inclined supply curves is serious; but they are unlikely to be particularly important in practice, because the competition of domestic industry generally suffices to keep a country's demand for imports in terms of exports fairly elastic.[7]   In the theory of "Domestic Values," we may take commodities to be usually sold by producers or dealers who have themselves no direct demand for what they sell.   Negatively-inclined supply curves can then only arise from increasing returns.

Apart from the reference to increasing returns (a problem he never seriously examined), this reliance on sale by producers, whose reservation demand is negligible, was Walras' way out also.[8]   But before coming to that point, he widened the problem by a consideration of multiple exchange, where more than two commodities enter into the picture.   In order to treat this question, he supposed one of the n commodities to be chosen as a standard of value (numéraire), in which prices are reckoned, but which is itself subject to no demand other than that which arises from its ordinary properties as a commodity.[9] There thus remained $n - 1$ prices to determine.   From the conditions of given stocks at the commencement of trading, and equalization of the marginal utilities of expenditure in all directions, he derived each individual's demand (or supply) for each commodity.   Then the ordinary equations of supply and demand in each market give the conditions of equilibrium.   They are n in number, but that in the market for the numéraire is superfluous, as it follows from the rest.   There are thus $n - 1$ equations and $n - 1$ unknowns; a set of prices must therefore exist which satisfies the conditions of equilibrium.

Here, for the first time, we have a characteristically Walrasian doctrine.   What is it worth?   On our estimation of it our view of Walras' individual contribution to economics must largely depend.

[7] This is, indeed, to interpret the early Marshall by the late (Money, Credit, and Commerce, pp. 351–352).

[8] Éléments, p. 163.   It may be questioned whether Walras had as much right to it as Marshall (often) had.

[9] "Nous supposons ici les achats et reventes de (A) comme intermédiaire s'effectuant de manière à n'influer en rien sur le prix propre de cette marchandise.   Dans la réalité, les choses se passent tout autrement.   Chaque échangeur a par devers lui un approvisionnement de monnaie en vue de l'échange et, dans ces conditions, l'emploi d'une marchandise comme monnaie, a sur sa valeur une influence que nous étudierons plus loin" (Éléments, p. 156).   Recent economic thought has suffered, I think, by its neglect of this valuable device.   The numéraire is a fanciful notion, perhaps; but it is the only logical way by which we can suppose exchange (or lending) to take place in natura.

Now it is, of course, quite clear that, even when they are applied to this pure problem of exchange, the equations are far too complicated to be of much use in analysing any actual situation. But that is surely not their function. Where they are supremely useful is in elucidating the general way the price-system works, and in giving us a classification of those factors which may be relevant to any particular case. In practice we have to select out of that over-long list those which are most important for each special problem. When that selection is performed, we may get a result which conforms to the simpler scheme employed by Marshall; but on the other hand we may not.

The types of equations used by Walras in determining exchange equilibrium are two; those which express the dependence of the amounts demanded and supplied by particular individuals on the system of market prices, and those which express the equality of demand and supply in particular markets. These two classes stand on very different footings. So far as the first class is concerned, they have become the essential foundation for the whole branch of economics to which they refer. On them is based, and had to be based, all the work in the field of demand and of related goods, which has been carried out by Edgeworth, Pareto, and others. In the process of development Walras' conception of utility has been much refined; but we still work with Walras' equations, however differently we write them.

The second class, which expresses the equation of supply and demand in the different markets, seems much more simple and obvious; yet it has proved much more open to criticism, for it is on this class that the meaning of Walras' system of general equilibrium depends, and by far the most important divergence between Walras and Marshall turns on this point.[10]

Walras' own account of the nature of equilibrium is this. Persons come on to the market with certain stocks of commodities, and certain dispositions to trade ("dispositions à l'enchère") and a particular set of prices is proposed. If at these prices supplies and demands are equal, then there is equilibrium straight away. But if demands and supplies are not equal, prices will be changed until equilibrium is reached.

What, however, Walras does not make really clear is whether any exchanges do or do not actually take place at the prices originally pro-

10 Cf. Edgeworth's review of Walras in *Nature* (1889) and his controversy with Bortkiewicz in the *Revue d'Économie Politique* (1890–91). Also his comment in *Papers,* II, 311.

posed, when those prices are not equilibrium prices.[11]   If there is no actual exchange until the equilibrium prices are reached by bidding, then Walras' argument is beyond reproach on the score of logical consistency, though it may be called unrealistic.   (The market then proceeds under Edgeworth's principle of "recontract," or provisional contract.)   But if such exchanges do take place, then, in general, the final equilibrium prices will be affected by them.

Marshall's way out of this dilemma was to concentrate on a particular market, where he could show that if the marginal utility of one of the commodities exchanged could be treated as constant, then the final rate of interchange would be independent of the path followed to reach it.[12]   But this solution—which is, after all, only a very particular solution—is usually not available in the case of General Equilibrium.

Neither Walras nor Pareto faced up to this difficulty; when we do so, it is impossible to avoid the conclusion that the "Lausanne equations" are of rather less significance than they imagined.   The equations of Walras are not by any means a complete solution of the problem of exchange; but they remain a very significant step towards such a solution.   For Walras' system of prices will be reached, either if contracts are made provisionally or (a more important case) if people come on to the market on successive "days" with the same dispositions to trade, and there is no carry-over of stocks (or a constant carry-over) from one day to the next.   When it is understood in the last sense, the theory of static equilibrium of exchange takes its place as a step towards the development of a complete theory with which future exposition is unlikely to dispense.

II

From the General Equilibrium of Exchange, Walras passed to the General Equilibrium of Production.   For him, as for the Austrians, the problem of production fell into two parts: one relating to the pricing of factors of production, which are only used in combination with one another; the other relating to the rôle of time in production—the theory of capital.

[11] "Les marchés les mieux organisés sous le rapport de la concurrence sont ceux où les ventes et achats se font à la criée, par l'intermédiaire d'agents tels qu' agents de change, courtiers de commerce, crieurs, qui les centralisent, de telle sorte qu'aucun échange ait lieu sans que les conditions en soient annoncées et connues et sans que les vendeurs puissent aller au rabais et les acheteurs à l'enchère" (Éléments, p. 44).   This remains ambiguous.

[12] Marshall, Principles, Book V, Chapter 2; also the Appendix on Barter.

The first of these problems (which corresponds to the Austrian theory of imputation) is really no more than an extension of the theory of value: it studies one particular kind of interrelation of prices. In this field Walras' original work was chiefly confined to a consideration of that problem which from his point of view is the simplest (though the Austrians naturally found it the hardest from their standpoint); the case where the "coefficients of production" are fixed, so that the quantities of all factors needed to produce a unit of each kind of finished product are technically given.

With fixed coefficients, and with perfect competition, the equilibrium prices of the products must depend on the prices of the factors; thus, given the prices of the factors, the whole price-system (of products and factors) can be derived by simple process of addition. But, given this whole price-system, the demands for products and the supply of factors can be determined from the tastes and abilities of the individuals composing the economy. Again, once the demands for the products are determined, the demands for the factors can be technically deduced. We can thus write both the demands for the factors and the supplies of the factors as functions of the set of factor-prices; and determine equilibrium in the factor markets as before. The equilibrium prices in the factor markets now determine the equilibrium prices of the products.

This solution is of course valid only under the assumption of fixed coefficients; but Walras was quite aware that it could easily be extended to the more realistic case of variable coefficients.[13] One cannot help thinking it to be a great pity that he did not trouble to work out this hint, for it would have led directly to the general law of marginal productivity.

---

[13] "Nous supposons, comme on voit, les coefficients . . . déterminés *a priori*. En réalité ils ne le sont pas: on peut employer, dans la confection d'un produit, plus ou moins de tels ou tels services producteurs, par exemple, plus ou moins de rente, à la condition d'y employer moins ou plus de tels ou tels autres services producteurs, par exemple, moins ou plus de profit ou de travail. Les quantités respectives de chacun des services producteurs qui entrent ainsi dans la confection d'une de chacun des produits sont déterminés en même temps que les prix des services producteurs, par la condition que le prix de revient des produits soit minimum" (*Éléments,* p. 212). This passage first appeared in 1877. (The condition of minimum cost follows from that of maximum profit—under conditions of perfect competition.) For Walras' later work on Marginal Productivity, see particularly his "Note sur la réfutation de la Théorie anglaise de fermage de M. Wicksteed," which appeared as an appendix to the third (1896) edition of the *Éléments,* but was subsequently omitted.

Nevertheless, even as it is, this part of Walras' work has great merits. The particular relation which it exhibits has quite general significance, and could hardly have been discovered in any other way than this. Even when the coefficients of production are variable, so that a rise in the price of one particular factor influences the demand for it mainly by encouraging a substitution of other factors within industries, there will still be present this further tendency: that the factors which co-operate with this first factor will find it more profitable to devote themselves to the production of products for which relatively little (or none at all) of the first factor is required.

Again, we have here an excellent illustration of the value of Walras' work for the clearing up of questions of principle—the sort of question which Marshall so frequently left rather confused. Walras' equations give the most exact version that has ever been given of the "opportunity cost" element in value; and at the same time they preserve the essence of the "real cost" principle for which Edgeworth and Marshall contended. They exhibit the supplies of the factors as variable, but as determined by the system of prices in fundamentally the same way as the demands for commodities, with which they are interdependent.

It is hardly necessary, at this date, to discuss at any length that one of Walras' conditions which was so vehemently attacked by Edgeworth [14]—the condition that prices equal costs of production, so that the entrepreneur makes "neither profit nor loss." For this device, in spite of its paradoxical appearance, is nothing else than the reckoning of "normal profits" (the profits which the entrepreneur could earn in other activities) into costs; and similar forms of definition are now adopted for their extreme convenience by many economists who would acknowledge no direct debt to Walras.[15] It may indeed be questioned whether the full implications of this method of statement have been explored—particularly with respect to its application to dynamic conditions. But the device itself needs no defence nowadays.

III

Those parts of Walras' doctrine which we have hitherto considered are on the whole uncontroversial; it is true that they raise difficult problems of interpretation, but no one seems to doubt that in some sense they are valid enough. It is these parts which have passed into

[14] Edgeworth, Papers, I, 25.

[15] E.g., Robinson, Economics of Imperfect Competition; Keynes, Treatise on Money.

the body of economic teaching; and when we want to study them we are inclined to go, not to Walras' own works, but to the rather more elegantly stated versions of his successors, such as Pareto or Wicksell.

Walras' theory of capital, however, has not reached this happy position. By Pareto it was simply ignored; by Wicksell it was attacked.[16] It has therefore not passed into any recognized "Lausanne" tradition, and is liable to be dismissed as something of an aberration. In spite of this, it has its merits; though there can be no question that it needs a good deal of repair in details before it can become a usable theory.

If a reader who is acquainted with the work of Böhm-Bawerk [17] and Wicksell approaches Walras' theory of capital, the first thing which will strike him is that it is purely a theory of fixed capital. Walras begins from a discussion of the capital value of income-yielding goods. He shows that the ratio of capital value to net income yielded (after allowance for depreciation and insurance) must tend to equality for all such goods; otherwise people would sell the more expensive (relatively to yield) and buy the cheaper. Thus there emerges a "rate of net yield" (*taux du revenu net*), which, in equilibrium, must be equal for all capital goods.

How is the "rate of net yield" determined? By the condition that the prices of new capital goods must equal their costs of production. Granted that a certain amount of new saving is coming forward, this saving will give the demand for new capital goods.[18] The saving has then to be divided among the various capital goods that can be produced in such a way as to maximize the rate of net yield.

Substantially, that is Walras' theory; it is a theory, which, if taken literally, is open to very serious objections.

For one thing, as Wicksell pointed out, it determines the rate of interest on the market for new capital; and is therefore apparently inapplicable to stationary conditions, when no net addition to the capital equipment of the community is being made. Further, as Walras

---

16 Wicksell, *Ueber Wert, Kapital und Rente,* pp. 142–3. Barone ("Sopra un libro di Wicksell"—*Giornale degli Economisti,* 1895) replied to some of Wicksell's criticisms, and apparently convinced him that he had overstated his case. Wicksell's comments in his *Lectures* (English edition, I, p. 171) are appreciably milder; while in his late paper "Professor Cassel's Economic System" (reprinted in the English edition of the *Lectures,* p. 236) he takes what I should consider a very balanced view.

17 Walras' theory is of course earlier in date than Böhm-Bawerk's; it was substantially complete by 1877.

18 Savings are of course also a function of the rate of net yield, which now enters into the determination of expenditure on the same footing as the prices of commodities. It must be remembered that savings are expressed in *numéraire.*

would have realized if it had not been for his confusion about the exact meaning of equilibrium,[19] it is only in a stationary state that we can get any sensible sort of equilibrium, so long as people expect the prices of products to remain unchanged in the future (as Walras tacitly assumes they do). This dilemma is fatal to the theory as Walras presents it.

But it is not necessarily fatal to the whole method of approach. For once we assume that the reinvestment of depreciation allowances is not technically given (in the way Walras supposed), but that these funds are reinvested according to the best prospects open for them at the moment of reinvestment; then the "new capital goods" become not only net additions to the capital stock, but also replacements, and the demand for these goods is no longer confined to new savings, but consists of depreciation allowances as well. With this slight extension, Walras' system becomes immune from Wicksell's criticisms; the capital market does not disappear in the stationary state.[20]

Walras did not make this amendment, but its possibility deserves attention; for it shows the essential rightness of his method, which survives the imperfect way in which he used it. Once the amendment is made, Walras' theory of capital becomes as good as Wicksell's, and better than Böhm-Bawerk's. It is still subject to the static limitations within which their theories are also confined, but it is as good a basis for extension in a dynamic direction as theirs—and in some ways it is perhaps better.[21]

IV

Walras' work on the theory of money,[22] and his relatively uninteresting writings on applied Economics, cannot detain us here. It was in

[19] The confusion we discussed above. It gets palpably worse in the later part of Walras' work. See, for example, the rather pathetic passage on pp. 214–215 of the *Éléments*.

[20] It is interesting to observe that, once this amendment is made, the limitation due to Walras' concentration on fixed capital disappears. For the method of reducing fixed capital to circulating, introduced by Jevons and Böhm-Bawerk, works both ways. If a machine is economically identical with a collection of half-finished goods which will be ready at different dates, so is a collection of half-finished goods economically identical with a machine.

[21] The "original factors" of the Austrians, being largely "bygones," are a thorough nuisance in economic dynamics.

[22] See Marget, "Léon Walras and the Cash-Balance Approach to the Problem of the Value of Money" (*Journal of Political Economy*, 1931). In this field Walras did at least make a serious attempt to integrate monetary theory with the rest of economics; he did something to prepare the way for Wicksell.

pure economics that his real interest lay, and the discovery of the conditions of static equilibrium under perfect competition was his central
achievement. Like many pioneers, he was a little vague about the exact
meaning of some of his results, and was perhaps inclined to claim for
them more than they are actually worth. Yet our consciousness of its
limitations should not blind us to the greatness of his achievement.
Static equilibrium is far from being the whole of economics, but it is
an indispensable foundation; and the greater part of that foundation
was laid by Cournot and Walras. There are very few economists who
have contributed so much to the permanent body of established truth
as Walras did.

Comment may be made in conclusion on two qualities of his work
taken as a whole. One is the realization of the unity of economic life
which emerges so forcefully from his pages. Other economists had had
a sense of this unity, but none before had shown it so well. For the
unity which Walras demonstrated is not a unity of resources being
allotted among a single system of ends—the only unity which really
appears in Menger—it is a unity of diverse individual ends reconciled
through the mechanism of the market. Yet this unity is as real as the
other. In a free economic system, under perfect competition,

> thou canst not stir a flower
> Without troubling of a star.

The other great quality of Walras' work to which we may here allude
is its rigorous "methodological individualism." Far better than any
earlier economist—better even than Marshall—he realized that the
only economic explanation of a phenomenon is its reference back to
individual acts of choice. Even he did not emancipate himself entirely
from that sham utilitarianism which was the bane of his contemporaries, and which led them to suppose that the working of the free
market "maximized utility" for the community as a whole.[23] But this
in his work is a mere excrescence, and is easily disregarded. In his central doctrines he held firmly to the true significance of economic subjectivism, and therefore broke with the Labour Theory of Value more
drastically than Marshall, and quite as drastically as the Austrians.[24]
For him individual choice was all-important in its function as explanation; and it is our realization of this which has led us to understand that
it is not, for the economist, necessarily anything more.

[23] Cf. Wicksell's final exposure of this fallacy (*Lectures,* I, pp. 73 ff.).
[24] If he was less conscious of this principle than they were, he wove it even
more tightly into the structure of this theory.

J. M. Clark
— on —
J. B. Clark

John Bates Clark (1847–1938) was the first economic theorist in the United States to attain worldwide reputation. After study at Amherst College and at the Universities of Zürich and Heidelberg, Clark held a number of distinguished teaching positions, being associated with Columbia University for a period of over 25 years. Clark developed independently the notions of marginal utility and marginal productivity, and became the foremost exponent of the marginal productivity theory of distribution. Clark also was an early student of economic dynamics.

John Maurice Clark (1884–   ), son of J. B. Clark and himself an outstanding economist, was educated at Amherst College and Columbia University, where he has been teaching since 1915, succeeding to his father's chair in 1926. J. M. Clark's best-known work in economic theory is his *Economics of Overhead Costs* (1923). A number of his essays have been collected in *Preface to Social Economics* (1936). Clark's work is characterized by a high degree of moderation and common sense, which places him in an intermediary position between out-and-out institutionalists and theorists as well as between the exponents of *laisser-faire* and the advocates of a more active public policy. He has devoted much effort to the development of a concept of "workable competition," and, together with the French economist Albert Aftalion, is credited with having developed the "principle of acceleration" of derived demand.

INTRODUCTION

IT IS with some trepidation that I accept Professor Spiegel's invitation to discuss the work of my father, John Bates Clark, who was the acknowledged leading American creative theorist of the marginal period and group. The reader will naturally expect a sympathetic interpretation—but any constructive thinker has a right to that. And one may discount also the fact that, as is commonly the case, father and son belong to different generations, spanning, in this instance, a period of extraordinarily rapid and unsettling change in ways of thinking. The perplexing thing, I suspect, is a compounding of this with a sympathetic continuity of thought. I may neglect criticisms that seem important to others, because I am content to take particular formulations as points of departure and stages in an unfinished inquiry, and judge that some criticisms will settle themselves, or cease to be live issues, as the inquiry proceeds. Furthermore, where one takes up threads of such an unfinished inquiry and follows them wherever they may lead, the precise point of departure may become blurred. In such a case, how much of one's present impressions of the import of one's predecessor's work is one reading into it in the light of much that has come between; including adaptation to criticisms such as those of Veblen and H. J. Davenport? How far is one warranted in making such adaptations on another's behalf?

BACKGROUND, PERSONAL AND HISTORICAL

John Bates Clark was born in January, 1847, in Providence, Rhode Island, and died in New York City in March, 1938, at the age of ninety-one. The greater part of his economic writing was produced in the last two decades of the nineteenth century and the first decade of the twentieth. We shall ask in a moment what this signifies in terms of historical setting and its influence. He came of a long line of New England Yankees, in whom the puritan tradition had remained strong, while its rigors had been mellowed by time, kindliness, and humor. If a dash of skepticism generated by modern science entered the picture

[Not published before.]

as a liberalizing influence, still the tradition as he reflected it was not open to any suspicion of having trenched on either its religious or its moral capital.

Facts about his ancestors which his later memory selected for recall are symptomatic, not only of his background, but of the tone of his own thought and feeling. These ancestors included farmers, successful merchants turned soldiers "for the duration," a successful physician who turned preacher—in which calling he was apparently less successful—in order that he might serve God more directly. This was John Bates Clark's maternal grandfather; and the grandson on occasion expressed a mild, humorous skepticism as to whether the change really meant better service to the Lord. It meant that his mother grew up as a minister's daughter, with whatever that implied, including economic limitations. Suffice it that he remembered his forebears as men who had some conscience of what they did, and did not hesitate to make personal sacrifices for the greater interest. It seems clear that this, to him, was the decisive meaning of his puritan heritage.

One of his childhood recollections was of attending the celebration of the hundredth birthday of his paternal great-grandfather Daniel Clark, in 1853, probably on the farm he had established after the Revolution, as one of the founders of the now-abandoned village of Plymouth Kingdom, in the hills above Plymouth, Vermont. Thus these two lives spanned the entire history of this country, from the premonitory stirrings that led to independence, to the threshold of the life-and-death struggle with totalitarianism. Other early recollections included the Civil War as seen by a youth in Providence; a depression in which unemployed workers were hired by the city to reclaim land, which became valuable enough to make it a profitable venture; and an incipient insurrection in which the rebels went so far as to place in position a cannon, which they had no serious intent to use, though a real explosion might have been provoked if the authorities had acted stupidly. Such recollections mingled with those of swimming in the Seekonk River, and diving off the bowsprits of anchored sailing vessels.

Of his father, he recalled a neighbor saying: "We've all got faults—all except your father, Johnny—he hasn't got any." Ill health forced his father to give up a dry-goods store. He went into the drafting-room of the Corliss Engine Works, and there gained understanding of the product which enabled him to serve as salesman, advising customers how their needs could best be met. Later still, he moved to Minnesota in search of benefit from a change of climate, and went into a small plow business.

The son, John Bates, had entered Brown University, but when the faculty suffered some losses, he and a friend transferred to Amherst, entering with the class of 1869. Here his course was twice interrupted, once by a relapse of his father's, and the second time by his father's death. During the first interval, the son carried on with the plow business. In that frontier community it was easier to sell plows than to collect for them; and he drove around the state to look after his accounts, deciding how much leniency should properly be granted to country storekeepers whose farmer-customers were having honest difficulties in meeting their bills. After his father's death, the plow business was sold, without loss.

John Bates then finished his course at Amherst, graduating with the class of 1872 and taking highest rank, despite the interruptions in his course. His college friends included Charles R. Garman, later famous as a teacher of philosophy at Amherst, and Anson D. Morse, long professor of history there. It was a serious and stimulating intellectual atmosphere, though teaching was dogmatic, and lacked the intellectual sophistication of the English universities in which his contemporaries, Marshall and Edgeworth, were being nurtured.[1] His mind, while not iconoclastic, was independent, going beyond the text of his instruction; and he already had some germinal ideas for a contribution to economics which impressed President Julius Seelye favorably enough to encourage him to continue his studies in that field.

So he became one of the group of young Americans who studied in Germany, and who later launched the American Economic Association. From 1872 to 1875 he studied, especially at Zürich and Heidelberg, his outstanding professor being Knies. He would appear to have absorbed those features of the German historical school which fitted with his ethical background and which modified, without obliterating, the English classical tendency to regard society as an arithmetic sum of individuals. He conceived society as an organism, but in terms of observable organic relations between the individuals of whom it was composed, rather than of mystical nationalistic entities. His vacations he spent with his mother and sister in the Swiss Alps, which he loved throughout his life.

Returning to this country, he married, in 1875, Myra Smith, also of New England stock transplanted to Minnesota, and joined the faculty of Carleton College. Almost immediately, he was struck down by a critical illness, which left him with permanently reduced working

---

[1] Professor Joseph Dorfman has well depicted this atmosphere, especially in his *Thorstein Veblen and His America*.

strength, but he was able after an absence of two years to resume his duties. Carleton's most brilliant student at the time was Thorstein Veblen, a cultural misfit in Carleton's strait-laced puritan atmosphere, and Clark was able to ease somewhat the obstacles confronting this stormy petrel in his college career. In 1881, after four years of actual teaching at Carleton, he moved to Smith College, then six years old.[2] Here he fell in with the current of Christian socialism then prevalent in the Connecticut Valley—also with Franklin H. Giddings, then a brilliant newspaper man with germinal sociological ideas. While here, he published his first book, *The Philosophy of Wealth,* the materials of which had appeared as articles in the *New Englander* Magazine. With this, his stature as a forward-looking economist was assured.

From Smith he moved to Amherst, where he was in residence two years. During the second year he lectured also at Johns Hopkins, where H. L. Moore studied under him. He then—in 1895—accepted a call to Columbia, where the graduate faculty of political science was being recruited. Here one of his early students was Alvin Johnson, and here appeared his more formal published works in the theory of value and distribution, by which he is now chiefly known among economists, and also his smaller works on the problem of monopoly, which appear to have had some influence on the formative antitrust legislation of 1914. He did popular lecturing at Cooper Union, and was a member of a commission appointed by Governor Hughes to investigate the stock exchanges, suggesting certain constructive reforms. But the activity which ultimately took him out of teaching and writing in economics was the peace movement. He became convinced that the threat of war was the one greatest obstacle to the achievement of man's potentialities for bettering his lot, materially and otherwise. He shunned visionary excesses, but threw in his lot with the "League to Enforce Peace," in which William H. Taft and Elihu Root were prominent and which placed its energies back of the League of Nations. In 1911, he became director of the Division of Economics and History of the Carnegie Endowment for International Peace, the immediate aim of this division being objective studies of war and militarism, internationally conducted. In this he was later succeeded by Professor Shotwell.

[2] The date 1881, given by Dorfman in *The Economic Mind in American Civilization,* Vol. III, p. 189, is based on the Smith College Alumnae Catalogue, and appears more authoritative than the date of 1882, given in an account by Prof. Anson D. Morse, in the Amherst "Olio" of the class of 1896. The latter date was followed in "John Bates Clark: A Memorial," by Prof. Clark's children.

So much of his personal history; what of the America which his work reflects? It was the vigorously-expanding America of the post-Civil-War period, preoccupied with its own affairs, and able, so far, to shrug off the setbacks of intermittent depressions. It included lusty buccaneering, and ominous signs of monopoly; but these did not seem sufficient to vitiate the drive of creative effort which was clearly there. Clark knew that business men were not all saints, nor were they all pirates. In his experience they were prevailingly honest and constructive. With the background which we have already traced, it was perhaps only natural that, in selecting the most basic elements for the keynotes of his deliberately-simplified picture, he should have sketched a society with grave shortcomings, which could nevertheless be cured or sufficiently alleviated for social health, because it had a core, including a moral core, which was sound. Much depends on whether America can justify that faith, in the face of today's more threatening challenge. The outcome is far from secure, and it was perhaps equally natural that Veblen, with his different background and temperament, should reach a more pessimistic conclusion.

One further point. The setting to which an economist now reacts includes not only the conditions and problems of his time, but the tradition of his discipline, which furnishes him the tools with which he attacks his problems. With this tradition a scholar of Clark's temperament was bound, like his great contemporary Alfred Marshall, to maintain continuity of development, branching out on new courses, but building on what had gone before. We shall see that this is what J. B. Clark did.

While the influence of his mature work with his contemporaries was primarily due to the force and coherence of his structure of thought, this was reinforced by an extraordinary capacity to command the affection of those with whom he came in contact, and this in turn was the reflection of his own kindliness of spirit and hospitality of mind. He rarely engaged in controversy; and the chief exception—his interchange with Böhm-Bawerk—bred mutual esteem rather than the opposite. His introduction to the American edition of Rodbertus' *Overproduction and Crises* argued that Rodbertus' ideas should be examined seriously, though he definitely disagreed with them. He was of those who know what they believe, and the reasoned grounds therefor, and he could let his ideas take their chances with others. In his last years, as his powers weakened and the present world grew dim, the one thing that stayed by him most firmly was the faculty of thinking of others ahead of himself.

THE PHILOSOPHY OF WEALTH, 1886

In the *Philosophy of Wealth,* Roscher, Knies, and the Christian socialists are expressly referred to, and the kinship to the latter is
especially evident.[2a] In calling this work "philosophy" and not science,
Clark is presumably following the same considerations that led John
Stuart Mill to include political philosophy in the subtitle of his *Principles of Political Economy.* Actually, however, this volume is a collection of germinal statements in both realms, that of philosophy and
that of science. In it he is more critical than elsewhere of the English
classical economics and of some of the normal processes of business:
specifically, individual self-seeking bargaining apart from competitive
markets, and the concept and practice of unrestricted competition, in
particular as it affects the labor market. He pins more hope than elsewhere on the development of cooperative principles and institutions—
conceived, however, as coming about slowly, *via* successful competition
with the institutions of the competitive system.

Legitimate competition is rivalry subject to moral rules and with a
moral purpose, "rivalry in giving." [3] Actual business practices suffer
from moral dualism. Having roots partly in family or tribal solidarity,
and partly in primitive, unmoral intertribal trading, they still contain
too much of the latter element. Apparently, the seat of the chief moral
depravity is in isolated transactions, not governed by a competitive
market—unproductive shrewd trading. Of this he says: "What is ordinarily termed a good bargain is, morally, a bad bargain," and the credit
business men accord to such successes is misplaced. The pursuit "is
characteristic of the degenerate days of the competitive system." [4] The
medieval gildsmen had a similar idea, frequently requiring a member
who had secured a specially favorable bargain in the purchase of goods
or materials to share it with his fellow-gildsmen. Clark is distinguishing between differential gains from negotiation and from superior productive efficiency in the handling of goods and materials purchased at
the prices generally available, with the implication that it is the latter
and not the former that justify differential gains in business in general.

Another source of discrepancies between private gain and social
product is the existence of inappropriable utilities. This is a highly

---

[2a] This appears in his ethical attitude and in his leaning toward producers' co-
operation as an agency for gradual, but potentially radical, change. This is
distinct from Marxian or political forms of socialism, which he consistently
opposed.

[3] *The Philosophy of Wealth,* pp. 150–155, cf. pp. 45–46.

[4] *Op. cit.,* pp. 159–162.

important germinal idea, which can be found in John Stuart Mill's *Principles of Political Economy,* and has been further developed in A. C. Pigou's *Economics of Welfare.*

On the side of a more conventionally "scientific" value theory, he calls for laying the foundations of economics in a new and more correct conception of human nature (using the term "anthropology") in place of the narrow and one-sided classical concept. And he proceeds to take what he calls a "first sod-crop" from this neglected field, based on self-evident facts, requiring no special research.[5] After this introduction, a present-day reader is bound to be somewhat surprised to find that this sod-crop consists of a germinal statement of marginal-utility theory.[6] The explanation is that it is the self-interested economic man against whom Clark is reacting; and he is setting up—as a first approximation only, be it noted—the man whose motives may contain any mixture of selfish or social interests, but who tries to pursue his ends with rational economy of means, whatever those ends may be. A theory constructed on this basis is still in need of a "new anthropology" to give it more realism. But Clark did introduce conceptions of ethical motivation in sectors of his study where it made more difference than it does in the marginal-utility theory.[7] And this approach did furnish a basis for a theory of value which would make a clean break with the Ricardian labor-cost theory, which had become the basis for the Marxian theory of "surplus value" and corresponding exploitation. The stage was clearly set for such a clean break.

Clark's utility theory is combined with a superficially puzzling statement that, when purchases and sales are made (in a competitive market) it is not individuals, but the social organism, that is setting values on the products. The tangible meaning of this appears to lie in the fact that the individuals' actions are governed by the resultant of the actions of all the others, organized into a "rivalry in giving"; and further, that this resultant serves the ends of the community as a whole.[8] The dilemma of rich and poor is wrestled with, perhaps not wholly successfully. The community is not insensitive to the necessities of the poor, and affords some provision for them; but the more thoroughgoing remedy of socialism would not be as serviceable to the whole as a healthy competitive system.

As already suggested, it is in the labor market that competition appears to least advantage, due to unavoidable inequalities in its impact

[5] *Op. cit.,* pp. 35–36.
[6] *Op. cit.,* pp. 76–88, 91–92.
[7] See especially references to competition as a moral institution, above.
[8] *Op. cit.,* pp. 83–85.

on the two sides to the bargain. Individual competition of workers can give the employer a chance to use the leverage of the unemployed worker to beat down the wages of the others; and competition between employers in the sale of their products can force those who would prefer to pay fair wages to follow the lead of those who beat them down.[9] But labor organization merely raises other problems. "The solidarity of labor on the one hand, and of capital on the other, is the great economic fact of the present day, and this growing solidarity is carrying us rapidly towards . . . a blind struggle which, without arbitration, can only be decided by the crudest force and endurance."[10] "Four systems of industrial organization are now on trial, with a prospect that the fittest will, in the end, survive. If the competitive system in its degenerate state leads to strikes and lockouts, arbitration will survive as between these two. If arbitration concentrates the attention too much on the mere division of the product, profit-sharing may outlive it. If profit-sharing still leaves as subject for dispute the proportion of profits to be given to labor, full cooperation may, in many fields, be the ultimate survivor."[11] "Yet among the systems as such competition should rule, in determining which is the fittest for ultimate survival."[12] The kind of cooperation in which he is interested is that which he identifies with Christian socialism; and he is less interested in the Rochdale system, in which the worker remains an employee and not a member of the enterprise.

One gets a sense that monopoly is felt as a more ominous threat than the abuses of competition. In fact, there is a minor problem in the fact that this book, written before the great trust formations of the turn of the century,[13] seems to paint the monopoly problem in more menacing colors than his later books, written after the movement had gone farther. This may, after all, be natural, starting with a mind of keen awareness, which senses a menacing force in its early stages. The force grows, its methods become less crude, we grow more familiar with it, and find that it somehow does not bring the full calamitous consequences we at first apprehended. Ultimately, the original apprehensions may be fulfilled (probably in forms not wholly expected) unless in the meantime we learn how to domesticate and control the force in question. In Clark's later works, monopoly, while a serious problem,

[9] *Op. cit.,* pp. 133–135, 172.

[10] *Op. cit.,* p. 66.

[11] *Op. cit.,* pp. 186–187.

[12] *Op. cit.,* p. 189.

[13] However, the early abuses connected with the growth of Standard Oil were already attracting attention.

had been analyzed, and potential means of control defined. And even in the earlier work he held that competitive forces could not be wholly extinguished.

The book was eagerly received by the group of young economists who had just organized the Economic Association, and whose attitude was strongly anti-laissez-faire. There had been a move to incorporate a statement of this attitude in the constitution of the Association; but it had been decided instead that the Association should not itself adopt a position on controversial questions, but should afford an open forum for views of all complexions. But the prevailing tone was clear. The *Philosophy of Wealth* was welcomed as a manifesto, critical of unregulated private business and looking hopefully and constructively toward something better, to come through evolutionary change of rather large potential scope.

The question has been raised whether Clark's attitude changed between the writing of this first book and that of his later works of more systematic economic theory. Had the crusader turned conservative? Or was the difference merely the result of passing to a different kind of task; from philosophy to science, from normative speculation to systematic causal analysis? The truth is undoubtedly mixed, but I believe that the second answer contains on the whole more of the truth than the first. Of course, no man who is doing his own thinking as he goes along remains unchanged in all his views for twenty years, and certainly not in the emphasis he places on different aspects of them and the feeling-tone which he feels moved to give to his expression. Furthermore, if the prevailing mood changes, the direction in which it needs to be deflected may change correspondingly. The leader who has incited a radical movement may find it needs more carefully-calculated steering after it is well under way, and the tone of his utterances may change accordingly, though his own views may not have changed.

Perhaps the best way to seek an answer to this question is to turn from Clark's first book to his last distinctly economic publication: the published lecture entitled *Social Justice Without Socialism.*[14] There is the same emphasis on progress, the same acceptance of fair competition as setting valid standards, the same opposition both to monopoly and to socialism, and the same primary importance attached to the issues between capital and labor. Perhaps the chief difference is that, in deal-

---

[14] Published in 1914. During the intervening period, Clark published, among other things, his *Distribution of Wealth,* 1899 (a treatise on static theory of value and distribution); *Essentials of Economic Theory,* 1907 (a summary of statics and a survey of dynamics); and *The Control of Trusts,* 1901, second ed. 1912.

ing with these issues, the later work is content to point to Australasian
and Canadian methods of arbitral adjustment as models, and does not
project its vision beyond these to profit-sharing and producers' co-
operation, which the earlier work had contemplated as long-run evolutionary possibilities. Experience might well account for this; these institutions had not done very well in meeting the competitive test which
the earlier work proposed for them. More directly in evidence is the
fact that in the interim he had formulated his generalized marginal-
productivity theory of distribution, and had satisfied himself that, when
it is working properly, the wage system meets the requirements of economic justice. This would naturally tend to reduce the importance
attached to the search for further means to equity and harmony, such
as copartnership and producers' cooperation.

Despite this real difference, it seems to the present writer that
basically in both these works the same man is speaking, expressing
much the same ethical tone and urge to make the world better, by
evolutionary methods and a temperate interventionism on the part of
government.

FORMAL THEORY OF VALUE AND DISTRIBUTION

From the *Philosophy of Wealth,* Clark turned his main attention to
the development of his systematic structure of marginal theory, which
first appeared in book form in *The Distribution of Wealth* (1899), but
parts of which had been presented as papers and journal articles for a
decade previous. His subject is the theory of value and distribution,
though these are regarded as determined by forces that are integral
parts of the process of production, so that there can be no sharp separation between these problems. He is interested in what happens to
the aggregate of use-values—utilities—and the laws that govern its ap-
portionment among the people who create them. And by the time of
the appearance of the *Distribution of Wealth,* his method of attack had
been maturely formulated. It centered in the division of theory into
statics and dynamics, taking up statics first, and then proceeding to deal
with the complexities of dynamics as departures from the relatively
simple and definable laws of statics.

One key to this method is the conception that it afforded a link to
the methods, and some of the results, of the English classical economists. They sought for the "natural levels" of prices, wages, etc., and
Clark concluded that they were unconsciously seeking static levels—
levels to which actual values would gravitate in a free economy, in the
absence of change and disturbance. As such, their results did not de-

scribe the actual world; but they represented a step in the approach to the endless complexities of reality, and a step too valuable to be discarded. The conclusion was that this step should be made consciously and explicitly, describing a frankly simplified world as an analytical device. Or, in the terms present-day theorists use, he proposed to build a "model" of a complete static economy: fluid, perfectly competitive, free to seek the ultimate equilibrium levels dictated by the controlling factors in force at any given time.

Being a model used as an analytical device, this was quite distinct from the classical concept of a "stationary state" as a goal toward which the actual economy was supposed to be tending historically. Dynamic change was conceived as endless; but at any time there were, in addition to the forces of change, economic forces of gravity which would bring about an equilibrium if they were given the chance to do so. The static model isolated these forces for separate study—necessarily in the realm of the scientific imagination. The forces were not imaginary; they were real. It was only their isolation that was imaginary. Substantially the same theoretical results could probably be secured by conceiving, instead of a static economy, a perfectly and instantaneously fluid one; but this would have forfeited a quality that was important to Clark. Of such a model one could not say that the only imaginary thing about it is the isolation of certain actual forces from certain other actual ones; and this is probably the reason why Clark did not use it, but chose instead to conceive change and progress as stopped, and the equilibrating forces left to operate, some faster and some slower, until the imaginary equilibrium is reached.

This serves to reveal the direction in which these forces are at all times tending to impel the economy, with the qualification that these forces might be acting in one direction over a short period and in a different direction over a longer period.[15] This feature of longer-run and shorter-run normals has, of course, been made familiar by Alfred Marshall. Clark's complete static model, however, represented an extreme case of those "long chains of deduction" which Marshall deliberately avoided, preferring to make his analyses of equilibria more limited, and to check them by comparison with facts more frequently. This is perhaps the chief difference between these two great theorists,

---

[15] *Distribution of Wealth*, p. 428. In discussing the effect of reduced prices in enlarging total effective demand, Clark clearly distinguishes what Hicks has classed as the "income effect" (applicable to commodities of inelastic demand) from the "substitution effect" (connected with elastic demand). See *Essentials of Economic Theory*, pp. 267, 271–275.

their views on the nature and behavior of the economy being essentially similar.

Clark's static state appears to have served three, or possibly four, distinct purposes. Chiefly, perhaps, the behavior of the model served as a first approximation to reality: a point of departure for the allowances and modifications which became necessary as the complexities of reality were introduced bit by bit, these complexities being classified under the all-inclusive head of dynamics. These fell into two main categories: change, and the "frictions" and other resistances which stood in the way of perfect and instantaneous adaptation to changes. Changes included increased population, increased capital, technical progress, changes in economic organization (corporate industry, combination and consolidation, etc.), and changes in consumers' wants. The more general and quantitative aspects of these changes were manageable deductively, by extensions of the static model. But Clark's conception of dynamics extended to matters that required inductive study. And his broadest conception assigned dynamics the limitless task of putting in everything that statics left out. Taken literally, this would cover, for example, the dynamics of human nature, modifying the subjective static equilibrium of marginal-utility theory, and the evolution of institutions of property and contract. These would have more far-reaching impacts than those Clark explicitly developed. His formal dynamics focussed on the five classes of dynamic change previously mentioned, and his static model conceived these five classes of change as stopped, and the economic forces of gravity left to bring about an equilibrium.

Secondly, as a purely analytical instrument, the static state appears to serve to isolate certain causal factors from others, the conclusion being that insofar as the actual economy resembles the static model, this is due to the economic force of gravity, causing things to seek their static levels, and insofar as they differ, the difference is due to the dynamic factors. Thirdly, Clark's standard of what is desirable is made up of the constructively progressive and productive elements of dynamic change, combined with the diffusion of the benefits as pictured in the static model, this diffusion taking place as rapidly as is consistent with giving entrepreneurs a sufficient incentive to adopt improvements. In terms of policy, one conclusion would be that the economy might be made to resemble the static model more closely if changes were slowed down, or if frictions and obstructions were reduced. But incentives to progress were the paramount consideration. Finally, there are indications that Clark at times regarded his statics as representing "the true theory." This would, of course, be exposed to the comment that the choice of a simplified model is not a matter of truth or falsity, but is optional. However, Clark's use of this "true theory" conception would probably turn out to have been in connection with some of his rather rare expressions of dissent from other theories which he regarded as in some respects positively erroneous, and can best be construed in this light.

As already noted, Clark formulated a marginal-utility theory of value, later than Jevons and other originators of such theories, but apparently independently. The materials for such a theory stood ready in the classical economics, which left a challenge in the un-solved problem of the relation between utility and exchange value, and fell back, in Ricardo's case, on a labor theory, which turned into a cost-of-production theory after Ricardo had accepted the idea that labor cost alone does not determine the rates at which things tend to exchange for one another. The classical economics also included the concept of rational weighing of utilities, and the marginal method, the two needing only to be put together to produce a marginal-utility the-ory. The readiness of thinkers to accept such a theory at this time is probably explainable as a result of the use Marx had made of the Ricardian theory, turning it into a theory of exploitation, and leaving liberal economists predisposed to adopt a theory of a basically differ-ent sort.

Under the circumstances, the significant thing about Clark's utility theory consisted of the individual features that distinguished it from others of the same general class. Most distinctive was his conception that commodities are not single utilities, but "bundles" of different utilities, so that individuals, in choosing between different commodities of the same general sort, are valuing, not commodities as wholes, but qualitative differences between them. And different buyers are mar-ginal for different qualitative elements in any given commodity-bundle, the rich setting a value on the most expensive refinements of quality, while people with more modest incomes are marginal valuers of the differences between the lower and cruder grades of the same commod-ity. This is one of the things that lies behind the statement that com-modities are valued by the social organism rather than by individual purchasers.[16] This conception does not seem to have found favor with modern theorists; but it does at least headline a problem which needs to be dealt with, and with which current theory does not appear to deal.

[16] *Distribution of Wealth*, pp. 226, 235–245.

For a "measure of value," as distinct from determinants of the rates at which things exchange, Clark fell back on the marginal disutility of labor as being more nearly homogeneous than utilities; but he does not seem to have put this concept to definite use, nor to have grappled with the problems that would arise in making use of it. He felt the need of it as furnishing something in terms of which values could be added into a social total. But for most purposes, economists seem to use instead the real national income—money income deflated by some kind of index number of prices. In short, they deal with what Ricardo called "riches," rather than value. And this, with all its difficulties and limitations, appears to be a more manageable concept.

Clark's theory of competitive price deserves more attention than it has received, especially the difference between the static and the dynamic forms of the theory. The static model brings about prices that eliminate profits; it assumes "perfect competition," and specifies nearly all the characteristics that are nowadays held necessary to this result, including what would now be called a flat individual-demand curve, but not explicitly including indefinitely-large numbers of competitors.[17] Under dynamic conditions, he held that half a dozen would be enough, if they would not act in concert, and the real requirement was a large enough number to assure that attempts to act in concert would not be successful.[18] This being the case, the question how many are necessary for the static model may be passed over as a rather academic issue: limited numbers are sufficient for the rougher adjustments of actual (dynamic) competitive conditions.

The reasons for this difference may be worth presenting in the present writer's own terms. In the ultimate static equilibrium, costs of production in the different competing enterprises must have been reduced to equality. Then if profits are to be eliminated, producers must have an interest in cutting prices down to *their own costs* as a limit. This will not be the case unless an indefinitely-small price reduction will bring a competitor an indefinitely-large gain in volume of business, relative to his own former volume. This condition can be satisfied in different ways in two different types of market. In a market of the produce-exchange type, where each producer determines his own supply, and supply and demand make the price, a considerable number of producers must be small enough to be able to increase their individual output without perceptibly affecting the price. In a market

[17] *Distribution of Wealth*, pp. 111, 179, 290–291 footnotes, 400, 429; *Essentials of Economic Theory*, pp. 155–156.

[18] *Essentials of Economic Theory*, pp. 201–202.

of quoted prices—more typical of manufacturing—there must be enough producers to make it likely that a price reduction by one will not be instantly met by the others, and its competitive effect neutralized.

But where different producers have different costs of production, there is no question of wiping out all profits. Low-cost producers will make profits at the same prices at which high-cost producers will be losing money. In Clark's scheme, the static norm is the cost of production by the most efficient methods existing at any given time: that is, this is the level to which prices would gravitate if dynamic change ended, but competition impelled producers to imitate the most efficient methods, or drove them out of business if they failed to do so.[19] This imitative process was classed as static, involving no new technical methods. It goes on in a dynamic economy, but never reaches equilibrium, because fresh innovations are continually recreating differences in cost. Hence there are generally producers who can cut below existing prices and still make a profit.[20] For this, there is no need of a "horizontal individual-demand curve," or indefinitely-large numbers.

But this is not all. Under dynamic conditions there is frequent excess capacity, and the added cost of added output is less than total cost per unit. Then producers may have a competitive incentive to cut prices below their own average cost, especially if they can confine the cut to the new business it brings them, or can come somewhere near this result. Then, more or less regardless of numbers of competitors, competition can drive price down to a level that spells bankruptcy for producers in general, and may drive them to some sort of joint action for protection.[21] It was for this reason that Clark deprecated secrecy in prices, since it acted as an entering wedge for cutthroat competition, and without it he thought competition might be more enduring, because more moderate.

This analysis reflected the conditions and problems that were prominent when these theories were formulated. It was later that industrial basing-point pricing, in the form of "Pittsburgh plus," became a prominent issue, and that economists observed that destructive levels

---

[19] *Essentials of Economic Theory,* pp. 263–264. This invites comparison with Marshall's "representative firm." Clark's concept is part of his rigorous static model; Marshall's is closer to actual conditions.

[20] *Op. cit.,* pp. 285–289.

[21] *Control of Trusts,* 2nd ed., 1912, pp. 173–183; *Essentials of Economic Theory,* pp. 413–415.

of competition did not seem actually prevalent; and it was later still that theories of oligopoly and "monopolistic competition" were developed, tending to explain how competition may be limited in its impact without the necessity of collusion.   Clark's theory did not reflect these types of situation; but on the other hand, the type of competitive theory now prevalent does not reflect the elements of his dynamic theory, and is the worse for these omissions.   It seems clear that a well-rounded theory should include both sets of elements.   The modern theory points to the conclusion that imperfect or monopolistic competition always makes prices too high, never too low.   A balanced theory needs to recognize that imperfections may depart from a correct norm in either direction, up or down.

The distinctive features of Clark's treatment of monopoly were his emphasis on the force and importance of potential competition, and on the need of preventing unfair methods of competition, by which he clearly had in mind methods whereby size could assure victory, more or less regardless of whether or not the smaller competitor was as efficient as the larger.[22]   At one time, he envisaged the possibility that potential competition alone might be sufficient, but in his final antitrust policy he recognized the need for active competition also, so that an undue degree of consolidation was included in the things to be prevented, though he still regarded unfair competition as more important than mere size.[23]   The decisive consideration for policy was its effect on progress; and on this score he regarded it as a fact of observation that competition was more favorable than monopoly, though he also recognized the importance of an interval in which an innovator could enjoy a differential advantage.[24]   On this ground he justified patents, though recognizing that they are subject to abuses.   Instantaneous imitation would have less favorable effects than more gradual imitation, both on the incentive to progress and on the adjustments whereby undue displacement of labor might be avoided.[25]   To this latter problem he devoted much attention, holding that, while innovation could not displace labor from the entire economy, it could require labor to shift from industry to industry.

[22] *Control of Trusts,* 2nd ed., pp. 31–38, 83–84, 96–127.

[23] *Essentials of Economic Theory,* pp. 380–381; *Control of Trusts,* 2nd ed., pp. 121, 131–132.

[24] *Distribution of Wealth,* pp. 410–411; *Essentials of Economic Theory,* pp. 359–364.   This principle has been made familiar by Schumpeter.   Clark did not attempt to define the optimum rate of imitation, and resulting diffusion of profits.

[25] *Essentials of Economic Theory,* pp. 259–264.

More basic, perhaps, was Clark's generalized marginal-productivity theory of distribution; and here again it is the distinctive features of his treatment, rather than those it shared with others, which are most important to note. For one thing, it did not contemplate discrepancies between private and social product—possibly as result of the static model in which the general formulation of the theory was developed. Thus he could picture marginal productivity as an addition to total social real income.[26] For another thing, he concentrated on functional distribution: the imputation of shares in the product to the services of the participating factors. He held that this controls personal distribution; and that if the former is satisfactory, the latter will be. In this connection he did not attempt to incorporate into his theory such problems as inheritance, or unequal educational opportunity. And the static model avoids questions of discrepancies between investment-at-cost and capitalized value of future earning power.

Another feature of Clark's treatment is that he deals rather extensively with the difficulties of the basic concepts necessary to a marginal-productivity theory. Labor is a fund of interchangeable units of equal productive power; and capital is a somewhat similar fund of productive goods, normally maintained by reproducing particular instruments and materials as they wear out or are used up. It can move, by investing the replacement fund in different industries, without requiring particular "capital goods" to be moved. Any considerable change in the amount of capital per worker (or per unit of labor) in an industry requires the capital to be put in different forms—for example, substituting power shovels for picks and spades. This process, naturally, takes much time to complete, and is governed by long-term expectations. Perfect attainment could be expected only in the "static state."

This means, for example, that the marginal product of added labor in a plant which, on account of cyclical fluctuations, has unused capacity, is not the basis for a workable scheme of distribution. The necessary adjustments could not take place to any very significant

[26] His first presentation, made from this standpoint, was at a session of the American Economic Association at which Stuart Wood read a paper approaching the same problem *via* the entrepreneur's search for the most economical combination of labor and capital with which to produce a *given* product, labor and capital competing with one another at existing prices charged for their services. Clark regarded these treatments as essentially equivalent in purport. At the time, his own approach gained more acceptance; Wood's would be more congenial to current theoretical trends. In a definitive theory, the two approaches would presumably be complementary. See "The Possibility of a Scientific Law of Wages," American Economic Association, *Publications,* Vol. IV, No. 1, March 1889, pp. 37–69.

extent in response to cyclical fluctuations of the prices of the factors.[27] In Clark's system, short-run changes in the proportions of factors in use depend largely on utilizing "no-rent instruments," or dropping them out of use, or on "no-rent uses" of existing instruments. If this concept had been followed up, in connection with cyclical fluctuations, it might have led to a theory of stand-by capacity, deliberately retained, consisting of instruments which have some value, but which would not be economical for full-time use.

Clark used the term "specific productivity" to emphasize the idea that the increment of product due to a marginal unit of a factor is the product causally attributable to any and every unit of this factor, the units being interchangeable; so that if the units are paid this amount, all labor and all capital each gets what it produces. From this he concluded that distribution on this basis is not robbery, as Marxian socialism contended, but is basically honest. This causal concept, and especially the ethical conclusions, have been subject perhaps to more criticism than any other features of Clark's system; yet he would appear to have regarded them as his most basically-important contribution.

In appraising this clash of views, one must note that Clark did not claim ethical perfection for the system; "honesty" is a more limited concept. But probably the key fact is that his statements are oriented at Marx, and are best construed as an earnest, and not meticulously-qualified, rebuttal of Marxian exploitation theory. Reward to capital is not robbery, but a *quid pro quo* for the productive function of capital. The amount an individual receives depends on the amount and efficiency of productive labor he has performed, or capital he has furnished, and also on conditions. of supply and demand which determine the location of the margin, and which have nothing to do with individual performance or deserving. But under ideally competitive conditions the amount is precisely measured, and this measurement performs a useful service in putting society's productive resources where they will be most productive. To say, as some do, that this is completely devoid of ethical significance, is as unwarranted as it would be to claim that it satisfies all possible ethical standards—a claim no one in his senses would make.

[27] For example, Oskar Lange (*Price Flexibility and Employment,* 1944, pp. 3, 5) has assumed that a reduction in the price of a partially-unemployed factor would increase the employment of that factor, but at the expense of unemployment of other factors (unless further favorable forces enter in) so that it could not in itself eliminate unemployment of all factors. This describes a short-term ("dynamic") adjustment; but the distinction between this and Clark's static equilibrium is somewhat obscured by treating the factors as abstract mathematical quantities.

While Clark's framework of formal theory does not cover such questions as inheritance and educational opportunity, it does recognize numerous hardships and abuses which are treated under "dynamics": for example, monopoly and the milking of corporations by insiders. Progress can displace workers, and he shows concern over the problem, considering how such displacement can be minimized, without blocking progress. But progress is the larger value, benefiting the people as a whole, and returning even to workers whose skills have been devalued some partially-compensating benefits. The chief effect of technological progress under competition, plus an increase in capital per worker, is a diffusion of benefits to consumers and to workers; and the total gain from progress is greater after it has been so diffused than during the interval when the entrepreneur is retaining his share as a differential profit.[28] And few persons object to this kind of reaping where others (chiefly innovating entrepreneurs) have sown. Thus the dominant tone of Clark's treatment, despite recognition of serious evils, is one of optimism. A progressing society can, among other things, afford to do something for its less fortunate members.

Labor organization constitutes an obstacle to automatic achievement of the static distribution, and one which cannot be dismissed as simply as business monopoly, as an unmitigated evil. Clark's ideal is collective bargaining with unions that have no power to limit the supply of labor in any part of the field, or to maintain wages so high as to create unemployment in the trades whose wages have been pushed up. Then wages might approximate a marginal productivity standard. Actually, he seems to see no guarantee that this will happen, though unduly grasping tactics bring some checks, including an increase in non-union mills. (Clark was writing at a time when this safety valve was more generally effective than it is today.) He falls back on arbitration without power to enforce awards, plus an attempt to rid unionism of monopolistic practices that exclude workers from a favored trade into which they would flow if free to do so.

Clark was correct in concluding that, under static conditions, the sum of the marginally-imputed shares would absorb the whole product; but it was left for other economists—Wicksteed and Flux—to produce a mathematically-satisfying demonstration, and definition of the key condition necessary to this result. Put in common-sense terms, it is equivalent to the requirement that an increase in production in an industry, with a harmonious expansion of all factors, shall result in neither increasing nor decreasing unit costs.

[28] *Distribution of Wealth,* p. 410.

There are many more points in Clark's theories that challenge attention, but this paper has exceeded proper length, and must be brought to a close. His most surprisingly far-flung application of his method of analysis is one which applies to the relations between economically developed and undeveloped parts of the world. The ultimate equilibrium he contemplates may well be the longest-run normal in economic theory; and he does not uncover all the problems that would be encountered in carrying migration and export of capital to the lengths that would be required. Perhaps his main purpose here is to put this area of problems on the agenda of theory and to make the reader aware that in concentrating one's analysis on an economy such as the industrially-developed part of the world, one is arbitrarily limiting one's problem, however necessary and legitimate such provisional limitation may be.

There are, in the works here surveyed, certain omissions which are more conspicuous in the perspective of 1952 than they were in the setting in which Clark wrote. There is no active theory of business fluctuations, nor development of their full implications for his theory of value and distribution. There is no treatment of the productivity and perversions of advertising, though the expansion of wants is a basic necessity to his picture of the mechanism of progress. And he falls back at one point on the proposition that supply of some things constitutes demand for others. There is—naturally—no Keynesian economics here. Protectionism is discussed without admitting that a "favorable" balance of trade can in itself be a stimulus to the total economic activity of a country.

All of which amounts to saying that Clark's theoretical pioneering did not anticipate the most characteristic pioneering of thirty to forty years later. It belonged to its generation in the sense in which all such work must so belong. He was one of a group of original thinkers who made the next available advances with the tools and materials at hand, creating systems of value and distribution. The one Clark created had distinctive features, some of which can still repay study.

What may reasonably be asked of the theorists of the current generation is that they integrate their findings with those elements of the thought of the preceding generation which have enduring value, and which they tend to neglect. Toward such an integration, J. B. Clark's works still—roughly a half-century after they were formulated—offer a surprising number of illuminating insights, to any student willing and able to penetrate the barriers of "dated" formulations and grasp the essential thought that lies behind them.

The Growth of
Modern Economics

Bowley
—————————————— on ———
Edgeworth

Francis Y. Edgeworth (1845–1926) held the chair of economics at Oxford while Alfred Marshall was teaching at Cambridge. Edgeworth, who served as the first editor of the
Economic Journal, the publication of the Royal Economic
Society, did outstanding work in mathematical statistics and
economics and in the theory of probability. He was the first
to develop the indifference-curve technique, which Pareto subsequently divested from utilitarian connotations. Edgeworth's
work on indifference- and contract curves may be found in his
Mathematical Psychics (1881); his articles on the theory of
index numbers, international trade, monopoly, and other subjects are collected in his *Papers Relating to Political Economy*
(1925).

Arthur L. Bowley (1869–   ), a distinguished statistician
and economist, was educated at Cambridge, and taught at Reading and at the University of London. Bowley did pioneering
work along many lines of economic statistics. Among his economic work, *The Mathematical Groundwork of Economics*
(1924) stands out.

AMONG THE PIONEERS of econometrics, Francis Ysidro Edgeworth must be given a very high place. Especially important are his contributions with regard to the study of the theory of economics and the theory of statistics by the help of mathematics. For actual measurement he would give place to Jevons, for the theory of measurement to no economist.

With the recent publication of J. M. Keynes's *Essays in Biography*,[1] the facts of Edgeworth's life are familiar. He was born in 1845 at Edgeworthstown, County Longford, Ireland, on the estate where his ancestors established themselves in the sixteenth century—reduced to very small value by the time he inherited it in 1911. His father (1809–1847), who appears to have spent his life in the peripatetic pursuit of knowledge, is described by Thomas Carlyle [2] as he appeared about the year 1836; Maria Edgeworth (1767–1847), the celebrated authoress, well-known in the literary circles of the early nineteenth century, was his aunt. His mother was a Spanish refugee, married after a brief acquaintance in London. One of his great-great-grandfathers was a Huguenot refugee. Francis Ysidro was the youngest of five sons and survived all his brothers. His features suggested his Spanish descent; in his knowledge of French, German, Italian, and Spanish, and in his ready acquaintance with economists of all nations, there is a suggestion of his international origin.

In 1862 he entered at Trinity College, Dublin, where it may be presumed he studied both mathematics and classics. He was never at a loss for a classical quotation. I have found no record of his graduation at Dublin, but in 1867, in his twenty-second year, he went to Oxford, and in 1868 was admitted to Balliol College. In 1869 he was awarded first class honors in Literis Humanioribus, the great school of Philosophy; but he did not actually take his degree (B.A.) till 1873.[3] He

---

[1] Keynes's study of Edgeworth is essentially the same as the obituary that appeared immediately after his death, *Economic Journal*, 1926.

[2] *Life of Sterling*, Part II, Chapter IV.

[3] Subsequently he took the M.A. degree in 1877 (a matter of formality), and at a later date was given an honorary D.C.L. of the University of Durham.

[Reprinted by permission from *Econometrica*, April 1934.]

was admitted to the Bar in 1877. During the ten years after he reached Oxford his interests appear to have been philosophy, ethics and, subsequently, economics. He was immersed in the writings of Bentham and others of the utilitarian school, while in economics he was educated in the works of John Stuart Mill. In this period he probably neglected mathematics, for his mathematical writing indicates a want of systematic training. Though he shows great insight into the principles of mathematics, there is a want of facility and neatness in his handling of problems. Familiar as he was with the work of Laplace, Todhunter, and Clerk Maxwell, he had difficulty in elementary applications. His line of thought is often a little obscure; sometimes he labors the obvious, and at others is so brief as to be difficult to follow. He was always the victim of numerical mistakes and errors in writing and printing. Apparently he settled in London immediately after he left Oxford, and had no definite occupation.

PHILOSOPHY AND THE PHILOSOPHICAL ASPECT OF ECONOMICS

It is evident that in the first part of his life he turned his mind principally to philosophic questions and especially to the relation between ethics and economics. His first known publication is a paper on "New and Old Methods of Ethics" in 1877. He began to interpret utilitarian and economic ideas by mathematical symbols, and very early he must have realized the importance of the conception of probability. The result of this period of study and incubation was the publication of his *Mathematical Psychics* in 1881. The mathematical economics in this book he owes primarily to Cournot, Jevons, and Gossen, something to his great contemporary Marshall; [4] the ethics is developed from Mill and Sidgwick; but the whole conception and treatment are original in the highest degree. It was so original that its importance has been only very gradually realized. The circulation was limited and it was little known; [5] the number of philosophers or economists qualified to understand it was very small, but among them were Jevons and Marshall. The following extracts from *Memorials of Alfred*

[4] Cournot 1801–77, Gossen 1810–58, Jevons 1835–82, Marshall 1842–1924, Edgeworth 1845–1926, Wicksell 1851–1926.

[5] "Three days after Part II was finished, I received and saw for the first time the *Mathematical Psychics* of Professor Edgeworth." Irving Fisher in Preface to *Mathematical Researches in the Theory of Value and Prices,* dated 1892. (The phrase is re-translated from the French edition.)

Marshall, edited by A. C. Pigou, are interesting from many points of view.[6]

Alfred Marshall first became for me a notable name when Jevons [in 1879 or 1880], conversing about mathematical economics, recommended as the latest contribution to that subject the now celebrated papers on the *Pure Theory of Foreign Trade and Domestic Values.* At the same time Jevons highly praised the then recently published *Economics of Industry.* Eagerly studying these writings, I discerned a new power of mathematical reasoning, not only in the Papers bristling with curves and symbols, but also in certain portions of the seemingly simple textbook. With reference to such passages, writing in the year 1881, I characterized the author by a phrase which he himself afterwards acknowledged to be appropriate, "bearing under the garb of literature the armour of mathematics." The phrase might be applied to many passages in the text of the *Principles of Economics.*

J. M. Keynes on Marshall (pp. 25–26):

In 1881 [Marshall], reviewing Edgeworth's *Mathematical Psychics,* after beginning "This book shows clear signs of genius, and is a promise of great things to come," adds "It will be interesting, in particular, to see how far he succeeds in preventing his mathematics from running away with him, and carrying him out of sight of the actual facts of economics."

Perhaps Marshall did not appreciate the path-breaking quality of the book, since he was already averse from the mathematical exposition of economics. The reading of it is at least essential to all who wish to understand the concepts that underlie Edgeworth's later writings, and it is fortunately now easily accessible, since it has been reprinted at the London School of Economics (price 5s.).

PROBABILITY AND STATISTICS

We next find Edgeworth appointed as Lecturer in Logic at King's College, London, in 1880; in 1890 he succeeded Thorold Rogers there as Tooke Professor of Economic Science and Statistics, a chair more noticeable for the distinguished men who have held it than for its emoluments.[7]

Now begins the period of the publications on the theory of probability. In 1883–84, at least six papers appeared in this sphere, of which

[6] P. 66, *Reminiscences* by Professor F. Y. Edgeworth.

[7] The professors have been Thorold Rogers, Edgeworth, Cunningham, Urwick. After the war its annual value was about £50, and it was merged in another professorship, now held by F. A. von Hayek under the original title.

the first was "The Law of Error" (*Phil. Mag.* 1883). While *Mathematical Psychics* laid the foundation and showed part of the construction of the edifice of his economic theory, the paper (only 36 pages) on *Methods of Statistics,* read at the Jubilee Meeting of the Statistical Society in 1885, exhibits at once the whole plan of his statistical work. To use the kind of metaphor in which he delighted, the foundation, based on the work of Laplace, Lexis, and Venn, was laid, the first story was completed, and the framework of the second was partly set up, partly in the process of execution. In the next forty years more stories were added, additional buttresses were erected where the structure was weak, and innumerable decorations within and without added to the amenities of the edifice in the best classical and italianate styles, while secret rooms were provided for initiates. There is little in the subsequent work whose origin cannot be traced through this paper, but, as with *Mathematical Psychics,* it was appreciated by very few, and the development and the use of the important principles which Edgeworth was the first to introduce to English statisticians was left almost entirely to him for many years.

Edgeworth was the philosopher of statistics rather than the practitioner. We may give prominence to two of his main subjects, those in which his point of view differs from most modern statisticians.—Every judgment based on mathematical chance is related to *a priori* probability. There must be some presumption about the field in which the events take place. If an event occurs of which the chance is small, e.g., five successive throws of double-six with a pair of dice, we must choose between the alternatives that the dice were loaded and that an improbable event has taken place. If the difference between the average of two samples is greater than the three times the computed standard deviation, we have the alternatives that the samples were badly selected, that an unusual event has taken place, or that the populations from which they were drawn were essentially different. Or again we may need to assume, as in field samples in agricultural tests, the existence of an underlying normal curve of variation. Edgeworth frequently used the principle of maximum probability and deviations from it—his method of "genuine inverse probability"—but his treatment of it was essentially different from that of Professor R. A. Fisher. I understand the latter to deny the applicability of the conception of *a priori* probability and to make strenuous efforts to evade its use. Edgeworth was convinced that there was always an element of the unknown, that in the end we must fall back on unmeasured experience. But in his hands this did not mean that we could not obtain useful results, for in appropriate cases the influence of the unknown could be reduced to such small dimensions as to leave the result almost unaffected on any reasonable hypothesis. It is not certain, however, that this judgment, based principally on economic statistics, would be applicable to all physical experiments, though he traced it in the theory of atomic motion.

The second subject which Edgeworth developed from a specially distinctive view is the Law of Error. His Law of Great Numbers is usually erroneously classed as one of a species which contains the formulae of Thiele, Charlier, Karl Pearson, and others. It is true that the mathematical expression is very similar, but the fundamental conception is not the appropriateness for representing experimental results, but the determination of a form that would be derived from given hypotheses; the experimental verification is secondary. The hypotheses, based on Laplace's work, are the existence of numerous independent causes and their interplay in producing aggregates or averages. According to the number and strength of these causes, the successive terms of his law of great numbers have greater or less importance. This law is

$$z = e^{-(-\frac{1}{6}!k_1D^3+\frac{1}{4}!k_2D^4-)} \left(e^{-x^2/c^2}/c \sqrt{\pi}\right)$$

where z is the frequency with which a deviation of x from the average of measurements occurs, and c, k_1, k_2, are constants depending on the successive moments of the curve. Qualifications are introduced when the causes are not completely independent and when successive experiments are inter-related. A development to the "method of translation" is made, when the observed quantity is not itself distributed according to the law but is some function of a variable so distributed. The formula is extended also to two or more variables.

It was a favorite theme for Edgeworth that the normal law of error, or its generalized expression, is prevalent in nature and in the subject matter of economics, however much disguised; or, if not in the raw material, then in the play of averages. It is hardly yet realized how nearly normal is the distribution of averages, even when the number of their constituents is small. The law of small numbers is practically indistinguishable from the normal law, unless the numbers are indeed very small. This was pointed out very clearly by Edgeworth. He said, "if the Greeks had been acquainted with the Law of Error, they would have erected an altar to it," presumably alongside that to the Unknown

God. His interest was rather in the fundamental prevalence of the law than in its applicability to the representation of groups; his long series of papers on the Mathematical Representation of Statistical Data (*Statistical Journal,* 1913–18) was, I think, more valuable for its by-products than for its major thesis, and Edgeworth himself expressed doubt of their use. The important applications were in measuring the accuracy of averages, and the significance of the differences between them. His study of fluctuations (*Statistical Journal,* 1885) may be compared with Professor R. A. Fisher's method of variance; the one in a cross table of death-rates in years and districts, the other in a Roman square of agricultural experiments.

A general view of the several facets of Edgeworth's intellectual interests is obtained by studying his work on Index-Numbers of Prices, beginning with his reports to a British Association Committee, 1887–1890. On the statistical side, we find the examination of the merits of various types of averages, of the effect of weights and their small importance in this problem, and of the application of the law of error for determination of precision.[8] On the economic side, there is a very careful and systematic analysis of the quaesitum, the quantity to be measured for particular economic purposes, and of the relation to currency problems. "Beneath the apparent unity of a single question there is discoverable upon a close view a plurality of distinct problems." [9] The logical basis of the investigation is further developed in later papers, especially those which deal with Mr. Correa Walsh's work. It may be recommended to anyone who wishes to do serious work on Index Numbers to read Professor Irving Fisher's *The Making of Index Numbers,* Mr. Walsh's *The Problem of Estimation,* and Edgeworth's series of papers, reports, and reviews. If, in consequence of inability to bring all the views expressed into a coherent body of thought, our aspirant gives up the problem, he will at least have obtained an insight into the psychology of the writers.

In 1892 Edgeworth published his first paper on Correlation. It is idle to try to determine whether he or Professor Karl Pearson can claim priority in arriving at the main ideas which have led to the now well-known methods. Both attacked the problem of joint variation at the point which Galton had reached. Edgeworth gave in 1892 the general

---

[8] "By rejecting the Calculus of Probabilities (Mr. Walsh) has . . . thrown away an instrument necessary for the performance of that measurement" (i.e. of the value of money). *Papers,* II, 376. (Written in 1901.)

[9] *Papers,* I, 199.

formula for multiple correlation in essentially the same form as is now used, viz.,

$$z = Ce^{-1/D \cdot (x_1{}^2 R_{11} + x_2{}^2 R_{22} + \cdots + 2x_1 x_2 R_{12} + \cdots)}$$

where R_{11}, R_{12} $\cdots$ are the minors of the determinant

$$D = \begin{vmatrix} 1 & \rho_{12} & \rho_{13} & \cdot\cdot \\ \rho_{12} & 1 & \rho_{23} & \cdot\cdot \\ \cdot & \cdot & \cdot & \cdot\cdot \\ \cdot & \cdot & \cdot & \cdot\cdot \\ \cdot & \cdot & \cdot & \cdot\cdot \end{vmatrix}$$

Here ρ_{12} is an average of the inverse ratios of an x_1, to that value of x_2 which is most frequently associated with it. This average was more closely investigated and defined in 1893, and an expression for it was obtained which was subsequently identified with Pearson's sum-product formula.

The numerous statistical studies published between 1893 and 1926 are to a very large extent the working out of ideas expressed or latent in the papers already named, with numerous applications to a great variety of problems and with critical and explanatory references to the work of other writers. Throughout the twoscore papers listed for these years runs the thread of the importance of sound fundamental ideas on probability in all mathematical statistics as opposed to purely empirical work. The ground deliberately chosen as central to his position is described in his Presidential Address to the Royal Statistical Society in 1912 "On the Use of the Theory of Probabilities in Statistics Relating to Society."

In writing of Edgeworth's attitude to statistics I feel that I am on fairly safe ground. When, in 1895, I was appointed to lecture on Statistics at the newly founded School of Economics, on Marshall's introduction I wrote to him for advice on the nature and literature of the subject, and he recommended principally Venn's *Logic of Chance,* Todhunter's *History of Probability* and Lexis' *Zur Theorie der Massenerscheinungen,* to which I naturally added his 1885 paper at the Jubilee meeting and his reports on Index-Numbers. From that time till his death I constantly learned from him, worked with him, and met him frequently in London and Oxford. It was with difficulty that I could turn the conversation from the nature of probabilities and the applications of the Law of Error. A trivial anecdote illustrates this. In 1904, a party of economists was bicycling out of Cambridge, and, with some danger to the traffic, Edgeworth began to discuss the method of translation or some similar topic; Professor Cannan drew up alongside and said, "Put on the pace, Bowley, he can't talk mathematics at more than 12 miles an hour."

GENERAL ECONOMICS

In Economics proper, to which I now turn, I cannot claim the same intimacy, and depend rather on the judgment of economists as shown in their quotations from his works, and especially on Pigou's very sympathetic review of Edgeworth's collected papers in the *Economic Journal,* June 1925.

Wherever economic theory called for mathematical treatment Edgeworth's interest was specially aroused, and, though this test by no means admits all the topics he treated, it is of special importance to econometricians.

It is the original analysis in *Mathematical Psychics* that has found the principal place in economic literature, namely the invention or discovery of Indifference Curves and their relation to the Contract Curve. The same analysis was applied in 1893 to the Pure Theory of International Values, and the findings of this study have been incorporated widely in treatment by later authors. Edgeworth did not seek after exceptions or paradoxes for their own sake; but in conscientious analysis he found that accepted rules were only true approximately and within limits. Thus, though convinced that free-trade was the best policy, at least for England, his analysis led to determination of the cases where an import or export duty was in part borne by the foreigner. He was greatly interested in Mr. Bickerdike's view of "incipient taxes" which were advocated as benefiting an importing country, but his final judgment was adverse, as is seen in the concluding sentences of his criticism, which may be quoted in full as typical of his style and outlook.

Thus, the direct use of the theory is likely to be small. But it is to be feared that its abuse will be considerable. It affords to unscrupulous advocates of vulgar Protection a peculiarly specious pretext for introducing the thin edge of the fiscal wedge. Mr. Bickerdike may be compared to a scientist who, by a new analysis, has discovered that strychnine may be administered in small doses with prospect of advantage in one or two more cases than was previously known; the result of this discovery may be to render the drug more easily procurable by those whose intention, or at least whose practice, is not medicinal. It was thus that the "drama of poison" perpetrated in the reign of Louis XIV was initiated by one whose baleful receipt was obtained from Glaser, a chemist of eminence, the discoverer of a new substance.   Let us admire the skill of the analyst, but label the subject of his investigation *Poison*.[10]

From Cournot onwards, it has been recognized that the theory of monopoly demands essentially mathematical treatment.   In this connection we find numerous studies relating to taxation, to railway rates, and other topics.   The possible advantages of monopoly, in every stage from its establishment in one industry to complete socialism, are brought to light, in some cases to be condemned, in others accepted. In particular, Edgeworth discusses the possibility of discrimination, that is, rates or charges differentiated by place or class of customer, which is not inherent in pure competition but may result in net benefit to all concerned.   There is very much that is important in these studies besides the often-quoted proof that in a specially devised and exceptional case a tax on one of two rival commodities may result in a lowering of the price of both.   The mathematical results need for their application statistical data, such as are the proper study of econometricians—for example, questions on whether certain functions are positive or negative—and depend on the actual measurement of their elasticity.

We may agree with Pigou that the papers on the "Application of Probabilities to Economics" (*Economic Journal*, 1910, pp. 286 and 441 *seq.*) are most noticeable, and we may add, most characteristic. One of the earlier sentences in the first paper is "The theory of Probabilities lends to Economics, as to other sciences, certain premises which are evidenced, neither by pure intuition nor by formal induction, but by general impressions and what may be called mathematical common sense."   We can often proceed a considerable distance with certainty by the help of accepted postulates, such that demand in general falls with an increase of price.   Presently the results depend on the neglect of quantities which may be presumed to be small; such results are probably true in the light of general experience of the behavior of continuous functions.   Though no numerical measurement of chance can be obtained, it may be affirmed that the probability of the failure of a theorem is very small.   We may even go further and assume that in the absence of specific information a positive value of a variable is as likely to occur as a negative value, and even this meagre datum may afford definite guidance.   It is to be remarked that in these papers are included not only instances of mathematical chance, but a number of applications of the conception of continuity of functions, where arguments are commonly based on unverified assumptions, not

10 *Papers,* II, 365.

proved to be valid, but held to be reasonable or probable. Closely allied to this is the neglect of quantities presumed to be small.

Though there seems to be a cleavage between the studies on the theory of probability and those on international trade and monopoly, to Edgeworth there was an underlying unity in the fundamental conceptions and in much of the method of Economics and of Statistics; this unity found its expression in the mathematical treatment of both, and his interest was most easily aroused where mathematical ideas were involved, whether in ethics, economics, or statistics. It is in this region of fundamental similarities that we find what is most characteristic of his genius, that which distinguished him from almost all other economists and statisticians.

Neither subjective happiness nor belief can be measured, but indicators can be found in allied measurable quantities. Wealth has a relationship to welfare, belief can be connected with mathematical probability. There are scales of greater and less for incommensurable objects. The utilitarian's ideal of the greatest possible happiness is related to the mathematical economic conception of maximum utility. The best judgment or belief to be obtained from statistical data can be founded on algebraic maxima. From the fundamental expression for maximum utility and maximum probability are derived the detailed equations of exchange on the one side, and such formulae as those for "least squares" on the other, as in Mechanics the principle of minimum potential energy leads to equations of equilibrium. While the foundations are similar, there is also interaction in the developments. Utilitarian ideas are involved in the choice of the "best mean," and probability justifies the conception of the representative firm, of the average man, and of the similarity of groups in relation to utility. In particular in many cases, where the solution of an economic problem depends on the determination of the direction of a curve, *a priori* probability will supply the most plausible answer.

EDITORIAL WORK

In 1891 Edgeworth succeeded Thorold Rogers [11] as Drummond Professor of Political Economy at Oxford and held that chair till he resigned in 1922 and became Emeritus Professor. During the whole of

[11] Thorold Rogers was Professor at Oxford 1862–68 and again from 1888 till his death in 1890. He was Tooke Professor in London from 1859 till 1890, occupying the two chairs simultaneously. Edgeworth gave up the Tooke Professorship on his appointment at Oxford. He was succeeded in London by Dr. W. Cunningham, and at Oxford by D. H. Macgregor in 1922.

this period and till his death in 1926 he was Editor, or one of the Editors, of the *Economic Journal,* the first issue of which was in March 1891.

So far as he had a home it was, according to the time of year, two rooms at Mount Vernon, Hampstead, on the outskirts of and over-looking London, or in his Fellow's room at All Souls College, Oxford. Characteristically he had his own means of transit; from Oxford he bicycled by a route known to his friends as "Edgeworth's way" 30 miles to Great Missenden, whence he took train to Hampstead. Very few of his friends ever penetrated to his sanctum at Oxford—bachelor's rooms, for he never married—very many were entertained by him at All Souls College and at the Savile Club, London. He made no col-lection of books. In London he was to be found working in the rooms of the Statistical Society, and there or at Oxford he studied the books sent to the *Economic Journal* to review. He was also to be met at the sessions of the Statistical Society (President in 1912–14), at the Eco-nomics Society (that used to meet at University College, London where H. S. Foxwell was professor), and at the historic Political Economy Club, to which he was elected in 1891; [12] these three societies meet in regular sequence in the first three weeks of each winter month. He was for many years regular in attendance at the annual meetings of the British Association for the Advancement of Science, being President of the Economic Section in 1889. His name was in the first list of elected members of the British Academy in 1903. Edgeworth was thus the most accessible of the English economists. He usually spent his vacations in the Alps or near Dublin, but otherwise was not a great traveler.

The professional duties at Oxford were during his tenure of office very light. Economics till after his retirement was not a major subject in any "School," and in any case the custom at Oxford is to depend rather on College lecturers and tutors than on professorial teaching. Though he had great influence on many individuals, he did not or-ganize any corporate teaching; the few courses of lectures he gave were not well attended, for indeed he had no faculty for that method of teaching. His work was in fact almost independent of his position at Oxford.

Mr. Keynes has testified to the great importance of his editorial work. It was specially marked in the organization of reviews of books.

---

[12] The first paper he read there was entitled "Under what conditions, if any, is the burden of a customs duty not borne by the consumers of the imported commodity," in 1893. The date is important in connection with his later work on tariff problems.

Though Edgeworth's direct writings turn on a limited number of subjects, his acquaintance with economic theory and with economists was very extensive in place and time and his memory was remarkable. In the reviews written by himself and republished, his encyclopaedic knowledge is as evident as the acuteness of his critical powers; but even these reviews are selective, for he appears to have looked critically at every book that reached the *Journal's* office. A request for a review would be accompanied by some apposite remarks on particular points in the text. Because he never developed a system of economics and never published a book except *Mathematical Psychics,* there is an erroneous impression that his sole interest was in refinements and exceptions, in mathematical curiosa rather than in the broad stream of economic thought; this impression is completely dispelled by reading his volume of reviews. Since nearly the whole edition of his *Papers* has been sold, it is to be hoped that a just view of his range has now been reached by all competent judges.

Readers of Edgeworth's writings [13] are often deterred by what appears to be deliberate obscurantism in the arguments. Many by-paths are followed and left with a quotation from the classics; mathematical curiosa are interspersed with poetry; elaborate metaphors are developed, where one would expect rigid deductions. But if one studies carefully a treatise as a whole, with some knowledge of Edgeworth's general lines of thought, and then reads it a second time, one finds that the whole is coherent, the arguments valid and consecutive, the theme is made clearer and more vivid by the variations. "By steps that are neither violently abrupt nor tediously circuitous, he reaches the heights from which the mutual dependence of all economic quantities can best be contemplated. At those heights too, are observed some curiosities of theory, like Alpine flowers, found only at great altitudes." These words may surely be transferred from his review of a book by another writer and applied to himself.

[13] A nearly complete study of Edgeworth's work can be made from the sources here listed:

Papers Relating to Political Economy. Three volumes. Published on behalf of the Royal Economic Society by Macmillan and Co., 1925.

Review of the above by A. C. Pigou, *Economic Journal,* June 1925.

Mathematical Psychics, 1881, reprinted by the London School of Economics, 1932.

F. Y. Edgeworth's Contributions to Mathematical Statistics. Published as a separate pamphlet by the Royal Statistical Society, 1928. This contains an annotated bibliography of seventy-four papers by him on mathematical statistics.

Demaria
—————— on ——————
Pareto

Vilfredo Pareto (1848–1923), born in Paris as the offspring of Italian nobility, was brought to Italy at the age of 10. He was trained in mathematics and engineering, and became a successful industrialist. Pareto did not turn to economics until he had become a mature man, and in 1893 he succeeded to Walras' chair at the University of Lausanne, continuing the mathematical tradition of that school and its general-equilibrium approach. Pareto is best known for his "law" of income distribution, which indicates that the distribution of income follows a certain pattern which cannot readily be disturbed by measures of public policy. To Pareto is also due the use of the indifference-curve apparatus in the modern fashion, that is, shorn from considerations of utility. The last decade of Pareto's life was devoted to sociological studies. These emphasize the role of elites and of irrational elements in social life, and supplied intellectual ammunition to the oncoming era of Italian fascism.

Giovanni Demaria (1899–   ) was educated at the Universities of Turin and Venice, and has been affiliated with the Bocconi University at Milan since 1934, serving as its rector since 1945. Demaria is a leading economic theorist and editor of the *Giornale degli economisti*.

I

BY A CONSENT which is nearly unanimous, Pareto has been given the honor title, "father of contemporary economic science." In order to appreciate the significance of the work of the great Italian thinker, we must pause for a moment to examine the stage at which economic science had arrived during the third quarter of the past century. At this period, economics abounded with historical interpretations which emphasized certain historical factors, claiming a fundamental character for each of these. This was often done in an arbitrary manner, on the basis of simple intuition, and in complete disregard of theoretical considerations. But during this period the reviewer also meets at every turn quantitative postulates and purely mathematical, that is, exclusively hypothetical, formulations. These were usually expressed in the form of pseudo-universal absolutes, such as the doctrines advanced by English classical economics, and the doctrines of the continental hedonists, which were based on the assumption of personal interest, considered as *causa causarum* of economic activity, of cost as well as of utility.

We do not intend to discuss, in the present context, the original contributions which Pareto made in the realm of historical interpretations, such as his greatly admired *Systèmes socialistes*. However, it seems to us that the scientific appraisal of the position and even the general conceptual limitations of Pareto's original work in economics call for attention to the central point of his sociological system. The equilibrium of economic quantities, in its most general aspects, is interpreted as a historical phenomenon, which is not exclusively economic but political and sociological as well, based, in other words, on meta-economic judgments. From this it follows that the deductive discipline of economics requires postulates and value scales of economic as well as sociological character, and that these in turn need to be supplemented, with the help of the method of successive approximation, by research of the empirical, inductive, statistical, and historical variety. The old-line economic theorists, for the sake of clear exposition and coherent interpretation, had neglected the development of

[Translated from *Revue d'économie politique*, 1949. By permission.]

sociological categories designed to interpret the reality of economic life. It does not suffice, in fact, to speak intuitively of legal institutions, moral beliefs, and sentiments, which dominate the various social spheres, and to say that all this is closely related to the hedonistic springs of action. In order to avoid a uniform and undifferentiated interpretation, it is also necessary to establish a classificatory scheme which embraces these matters. The empirical concepts of history and the no less inductive concepts of the old science of politics must be segregated and then re-aligned in coherent units. Only in this manner can the complete truth be revealed. As Pareto indicated on the occasion of his anniversary at the University of Lausanne in July 1917, these sociological concepts make it possible to attain experimental truth and to find a way out of the impasse to which exclusive reliance on pure economics leads.

The two large volumes of Pareto's *Trattato di sociologia generale* [1] constitute the first contribution to the creation of a system, formed by theorems of mathematical precision, in which the elements of the sociological phenomena are considered by themselves. They also contain, and this concerns economics, a theoretical scheme, unequalled to the present day, for limited competition, oligopoly, and voluntary associations such as industrial combinations and labor unions—configurations which the recent economic theory, especially the English and American, misinterprets rashly in terms of "bargaining strength," "strategies," "minimax," and uncertainty, instead of interpreting them exclusively, as Pareto did, in terms of social causation, "non-logical actions," "derivations," "residues," "combinations," and "persistence of aggregates."

The specific as well as general economic policies pursued by oligopolists, polypolists, and combinations appear undoubtedly as a perpetual search for maximum conditions. Nevertheless, their dynamics, and even their statics, must be brought into close relation to sociological forces, more so, perhaps, than to purely economic forces. From this point of view, it is unfortunate indeed that Pareto's sociological work continues to be badly neglected by the pure economists. They fail to be aware of the hierarchy of sociological and economic values, concentrating their attention, as they do, on purely hedonistic behavior or, at best, limiting themselves to simple historical excursions—whenever they fail to rely exclusively on their precious gift of intuition. No doubt, this part of Pareto's work has a claim to definitiveness. The

[1] Florence, 1916. Translated as *The Mind and Society*, ed. A. Livingston, London and New York, 1935.

fundamental sociological categories which he reveals lead in a rational manner to the economic equilibrium of markets where exchangers are few. They present also characteristics so general that it is difficult to understand how they could have been neglected, in the absence of other investigations of similar profundity or of the formation of sociological rival systems. If they would not exist, it would be necessary to create them. Whatever their qualities, they constitute to this day doctrinal advances of the highest order. It seems indispensable for economists to understand them and to derive from them all conclusions which they are capable of yielding.

After having taken cognizance of the need for sociological expansion of economics along the lines developed by Pareto's genius, we shall now investigate the impetus given by his work to pure and applied economics. In this respect, as we shall see, all his fundamental contributions were published for the first time in the *Giornale degli economisti,* in numerous articles very characteristic for their intellectual strength. These writings were then reformulated in his three radically different books: *Cours d'économie politique* (Lausanne, 1896–1897); *Manuale di economia politica* (Milan, 1906); and *Manuel d'économie politique* (Paris, 1909). The French edition of the *Manuale* differs considerably from the Italian edition in the Mathematical Appendix. A remarkable summary of Pareto's economics is contained in his forty-page article in the *Encyclopédie des sciences mathématiques.*

II

As we have noted, Pareto's economic work made its appearance toward the end of the nineteenth century, at a stage of development of economic science of which the doctrines of the English classicists and the continental hedonists were characteristic. It is well known that these doctrines had arrived at a point at which they had become particular and specific, having turned, in the last analysis, into a mere series of dissociated problems which were integrated in a singularly formal manner. The doctrines of the English classicists had been made comprehensive with the help of a pretentious generalization which presented every economic fact as a phenomenon of absolute cost and the whole of economic facts as a comparative table of absolute costs. The doctrines of the continental hedonists had been made comprehensive with the help of a no less trite panutilitarianism which vested exclusive power of explanation in a neat and subtle theory of utility. These two constructions attach an exaggerated significance to a few economic phenomena, whereas other factors, much more numerous and important, are either relegated to a shadowy existence or cast out altogether from the conceptual framework of the doctrine.

The scientific position of the two doctrines has so often been examined that it would not be interesting to resume the discussion in the present context. It is equally well known that the germ of the concept of general economic equilibrium existed already in the theories of the classical economists and utilitarian authors, and that the first, highly ingenious attempt at the coordination of the classical and utilitarian doctrines was undertaken by Alfred Marshall, dating from the period of his two widely studied works, *The Economics of Industry* (1879), and *Principles of Economics* (1890).[2] But, in reality, there had been no "coordination." The classical doctrine of cost is an empirical universe which denies the utilitarian solution. The hedonistic doctrine itself must also be characterized as a pseudo-logical concept, excluding, as it does, the historical reality of cost. How can one talk of coordination when the problem of the unity of the two explanations claiming universality is resolved by a mere juxtaposition, exclusively empirical, full of precarious casuistry—when it is impossible to say which of the two spheres of judgment is the decisive one?

No doubt, intuition, which infers general conclusions *ex posteriori* on the basis of observed facts, comparing and assembling partial truths, is an artificial construction. Practical, as it is, it nevertheless is a psuedo-concept, leading to a mirage and to deceptive reasoning—as is always true of *a posteriori* rather than theoretical reasoning. This was indeed the path followed by Cournot, Marshall, and Edgeworth, which led to laws—and this is important to note—valid only under the *ceteris paribus* condition, "others being equal."

It was Walras who cast light on the fundamental aspect of economic equilibrium—the mutual dependence of a series of closely aligned relations. As Enrico Barone has pointed out, this construction was not a mere continuation of the first attempts, highly meritorious as they were, of Cournot and Marshall. Instead, it was a veritable jump forward, accomplished in an original and masterly fashion, in the field of pure economics. It is the imperishable merit of Leon Walras—which Pareto in no way shares—of having applied his powerful mind to the development of the framework of the relations of general interdependence. But it is fitting—and this observation is of major impor-

---

[2] This conclusion was drawn, for example, by Umberto Ricci, one of the most distinguished Italian theorists, who contributed to the memorial volume of articles published shortly after Pareto's death. See *Giornale degli economisti,* 1924, No. 1–2. [An English translation of Ricci's article can be found in the *Review of Economic Studies,* October 1933, Vol. 1, No. 1.—Ed.]

tance—to underline the decisive character of the advance of the problem of interdependence due to Pareto's work. The classical economists, and, before them, the authors of fragmentary works written in the course of the seventeenth and eighteenth centuries, had a clear perception of economic interdependence but were unable to visualize it as a whole, even in the form of a rough sketch. To present it as the momentous discovery of Pareto would thus contradict a variety of testimony. It is true indeed that the great Walras was the first to give a demonstration of it in mathematical language and that he incorporated it safely into his own theoretical system. But Pareto, by insisting on the subjective character of interdependence, went farther. And he also may claim technical priority for having presented, for the first time, competitive and purely monopolistic relationships under the same head in an interdependent system, although he overlooked the problem of a larger number of dependent monopolies. But, apart from this, it must be emphasized that Pareto always interpreted his system as a complex of necessarily individual relations. To him, all relations which appear as aggregate today but not from today on—and which lead to the so-called macro-economics—are considered as accidental, ephemeral, and impermanent, only approximately universal or not universal at all.

It is not intended to repeat here what has been said a hundred times about Pareto's work in the histories of economic thought and elsewhere. Instead, we shall try to go beyond the limits of the traditional appraisals of Pareto's work. It seems that nobody has ever observed, or, at least, has paid adequate attention to the fact that Pareto always presents interdependence as a subjective datum, that is, that the activities and value judgments of individuals, not the activities and judgments of the mass, constitute the economic problem. To be sure, numerous economists do not deny this principle, but they believe that in practice they can neglect it with impunity. It suffices to recall only two readily available interpretations, those of Marshall and Walras. In the first edition of his *Principles* Marshall points out that the many subtle points which are required for giving precision to the most general and abstract economic doctrines have only a very limited practical significance.[3] He thereby intended to defend the methodological legitimacy of partial equilibria, of the notions of aggregate demand and supply, and of the representative firm. In the work of the Cambridge school, the idea of general equilibrium ends up in an empirical and approximative formula. If economic analysis progresses in this direc-

[3] Chap. V, 4–7.

tion, it will never emancipate itself from Marshall's empirical and, thus, alogical foundation. Partial equilibria provide insight into detail, useful, no doubt, but unable to open up an exact view of the economic system as a whole: the observer is faced by problems which all are indeterminate. Partial-equilibrium analysis obscures the facts and leads to sophisms and erroneous conclusions. Pareto always considered Marshall a great man, because, "on the basis of a small number of principles, he constructed economic science." This is as far as his admiration went. He immediately emphasizes that "Walras and his school had gone very much farther."

Pareto did not endorse the assumption of constant marginal utility of money, perfectly arbitrary as it is, although convenient and necessary for operations with two-dimensional curves. These times "have passed." In an essay published in 1892 he stated, in connection with arguments based on constant marginal utility of money, and in opposition to Jevons' point of view: "It is peculiar that he made this assumption, since he himself had correctly emphasized the necessity of regarding it as variable. If one considers it as constant, one is unable to deal properly with the most important points of economic science." [4]

Similar observations can be found in an earlier study relating to Auspitz and Lieben's theory of prices: "To start out with an examination of certain aspects, while assuming other economic quantities as constant—this is not merely a question of method. Such a method conforms to the disposition of the human mind; but it is a mistake nevertheless because it promotes the search for a simple expression of phenomena which are so highly complex that one cannot represent them with the help of a curve." [5] It is indeed impossible to draw the curve of the production cost of a commodity on the assumption that equilibrium continues to prevail with respect to other goods. Effects which appear as secondary may be essential; variations of the value of one element may not only modify the value of all unknown quantities but may also change the known quantities in the equations. The dependence among economic quantities is so pronounced that each degree of utility depends upon several quantities. Moreover, in order to carry studies of this sort to their successful conclusion, it is necessary always to observe that the degrees of utility are related to the costs. Thus, the *ceteris paribus* method will never result in an appro-

[4] "Considerazioni sui principi fondamentali dell' economia pura," *Giornale degli economisti,* May, June, August 1892; January and October 1893.

[5] "La teoria de prezzi dei signori Auspitz e Lieben e les osservazioni del professor Walras," *Giornale degli economisti,* 1892.

priate treatment, not even in a coherent treatment, because it never leads to theorems and rigorous corollaries.

It was the highest aim of Pareto's speculation to retrace all relations and correlations among the economic facts, to cast light on the real economic process from its beginning to its end, and to reveal the successive movements which never terminate, which cannot be separated from each other, and which reappear incessantly. In comparison with the thought of Walras, this aim was achieved in an even more complete and masterly fashion.

These are the words with which Pareto honored the memory of Walras shortly after the latter's death:

> Walras' name will endure in science, and his reputation will continuously grow. The evolution which tends to turn political economy into an exact science is not going to be stopped, just as the parallel movements have not been stopped which wrested all modern sciences from empiricism. Once a true science has emerged from literary economics, one will not fail to go back to Walras' work when dating its origin.
>
> The principal merit of this scientist, his very great merit, is based on the study, which he undertook as the first, of a general case of economic equilibrium. Thereby he led economic science on a path which can best be compared with the path opened up to rational mechanics by Lagrange.
>
> Jevons, and later Marshall and Edgeworth, applied mathematics to political economy at the same time as this was done by Walras. But, unlike Walras, these authors did not consider the general hypothesis of economic equilibrium. It is exactly in this case that the application of mathematics becomes useful. If the investigator restricts himself to particular problems, the use of mathematics can lead to interesting results but it cannot cause the science to advance.
>
> General economic equilibrium, on the other hand, casts light upon the great principle of mutual dependence, which requires the use of a special logic, that is, of mathematical logic. In the works of Walras we find the first comprehensive conception of the economic phenomenon, just as the theory of universal attraction entailed, for the first time, a comprehensive conception of the movements of the celestial bodies.[6]

There is, perhaps, no other statement by Pareto which would illustrate better and more succinctly the historical significance of the Walrasian construction. What then is this general hypothesis of economic equilibrium which was studied by Walras for the first time? Pareto surely did not intend to allude to the general assumption of competition, or of constant coefficients of production. Pareto's words, uttered under delicate circumstances, are not of the type employed in a

[6] *Giornale degli economisti*, 1910.

common-place judgment. Having to attach himself to the Walrasian tradition and to emphasize his personal affinity with it, he had to place in bold relief the point where his own system diverged from that of Walras. Everything finds an explanation if we recall what we have noted before: Pareto presents the fact of interdependence as a complex of necessarily individual relations. To be sure, Walras had considered and systematized the individualistic aspect of reality. But he did so with the view of deriving therefrom the aggregative or synthetic categories of total demand, total supply, and total saving, adding up the algebraic sums of the various partial supplies and demands. The Walrasian system does not always rest on the double foundation of individual valuations and individual actions. In certain moments it is based directly on mass actions. It suffices to open up the definitive edition of Walras' *Éléments* to demonstrate this and to appreciate the change brought about by Pareto. At a certain stage of his construction, Walras' work ceases to be theoretical and becomes mere description. Walras does not always recognize that the individual, and his relationships, must invariably remain the primary element. He yields to the mechanism of synthetic functions or synthetic methodological procedures. He considers it legitimate to add up the algebraic sum of the various partial supplies and demands. At this stage, a break, in the nature of a genuine discontinuity, occurs in his system. Before long, the consequences of this were to make themselves felt in the scientific development of the schools of thought which do not belong to the Lausanne group. These were to refer to the high authority of Walras in order to justify systematically what today tends to become a universally fashionable approach to economic science—a fashionable approach but not an essential method.

One can understand the temptation created by the employment of mass categories. The human mind is easily thrown into confusion when confronted by an infinitely complex reality. It feels the spontaneous need for representative schemes which are as simple as possible, that is, synthetic. But what is the result of this? One enters the realm of the deceptive mechanism of synthetic economics, presented at one time in the form of the naive constructions of Moore or Cassel, generated by massive trends which are surreptitiously or openly introduced as assumptions or as *a priori* historical postulates. Similar considerations apply to later developments, such as the "condensed" functions of Keynes and his school, and the functions based on the distinction between wage goods and non-wage goods, elaborated by Pigou and his followers. These constructions are the most formal and the most empirical ones which one can imagine. In a first stage they favor explicative clarification, but they are dialectically erroneous, leading, as they do, to conclusions which are contained in the basic assumptions themselves: within the realm of the hypothesis one moves from the prologue to the epilogue, traversing the whole development from the statement of the problem to its solution. This is true of the hypotheses of extrapolated trends, of algebraic sums, of *ex ante* collective propensities to save and to invest, of discounted profit rates, of the *ex ante* behavior of the interest rate, etc., which lose themselves in precarious casuistry. The march of science eventually comes to a standstill. Science finds itself abandoned to intuition rather than to logic, and confusion results, since only practice, not theory, can determine which of the different hypotheses is the correct one. An irreconcilable opposition arises between the various constructions and potential reality, with the latter continuously and inexorably contradicting the former. True science does not artificially smooth the difficult points in order to resolve them. True science proceeds with the help of pure rather than statistical hypotheses, of hypotheses which do not need to be modified every moment. Pure hypotheses do not need to be changed—otherwise one faces mere pseudo-concepts, arbitrary constructions, sophisms.

Pareto indeed does appreciate the importance of the hypotheses. He recognizes that the conclusions can only be functions of the hypotheses. For this reason his hypotheses are truly universal, being based on the elementary activities of individuals and kept free from historical qualifications. Specific qualifications are provided only in the light of a sociological system. Pareto thus maintains neatly the difference between science and history, insisting that the equilibrium is always and exclusively a complex of relations among individuals. Since contents which are so divers—and lacking in homogeneity, as is the case of individuals, their actions and evaluations—cannot be measured and enumerated, the synthetic categories are not the result of proper reasoning and cannot be universal. In brief, the synthetic categories either serve to express an *a posteriori* synthesis of historical character, or they are intellectual manipulations of reality, helpful, perhaps, in the explanation of reality but without ever shedding the character of arbitrary exteriority.

It is our opinion that the absolute and fundamental character of the individual element, which Pareto places at the basis of his general construction of equilibrium and which he consistently retains, constitutes the major contribution of Paretian scientific speculation. After this contribution was made, it failed to yield all the fruit it is capable of bearing. Only those economists who understand its message will know how to reap this rich harvest. All other theorems discovered by Pareto are only of relatively secondary importance if compared with this foremost and most profound contribution.

III

It is much less difficult now than it was in 1924 to indicate which of Pareto's secondary contributions are the most important ones and how they are to be ranked according to their systematic significance. This is much easier now than it was at the time of Maffeo Pantaleoni, when he refused to indicate the influence of these contributions on subsequent studies. In Pantaleoni's opinion, Pareto's sociological studies represented an alpha, whereas his work in pure economics was in the nature of an omega, bringing a cycle to conclusion and terminating all opportunities for further research aiming at higher generalization. After the passage of a quarter century this judgment seems an inadequate half-truth. Today, mathematical generalization is a sovereign fact, advancing, as it does, irrepressibly in the modern economic literature, which is so rich of controversy rather than of conclusions. At a certain point even the most capable "literary" economists lose heart in the face of so complex a play of economic activities, and feel the spontaneous need for recourse to mathematics, being unable to resign themselves to the historical method with its mere registration of events. Pareto's merit does not rest upon the fact that he expressed himself in the language of mathematics, with the power of one who

sopra gli altri come aquila vola.

There were other powerful minds, Cournot and Edgeworth, for example, who were his equals in the use of mathematics. But, to Pareto, the use of mathematics did not serve exclusively as a means to satisfy the desire to give greater precision to concepts and to delineate the meaning of assumptions with the view of producing a more rigorous demonstration. His use of mathematics was equally inspired by the intention to prove that all economic problems are determinate and determinable. As he put it, "in nature there is no indeterminateness. If we say that a problem is not determinate, then a well-constructed theory must indicate that there was occasion to take into account certain circumstances which were neglected." [7]

[7] *Giornale degli economisti*, 1892.

With respect to the determinateness of economic problems, the proof produced by Walras and Pareto can surely not be considered as definitive. The Walrasian concept of *tâtonnements*—"gropings"— cannot stand up under a rigorous examination since it does not lead to a unique equilibrium position. As the Italian mathematician Gaetano Scorza has shown in a famous polemic with Pareto, there may be more than one equilibrium price even in the case of an exchange of only two quantities between two groups of buyers and sellers.[8] In the case of a larger number of commodities the problem becomes still more complicated. There may be an infinite number of systems of equilibrium prices.

In this connection very difficult problems arise, which in the Paretian analysis are treated with the help of the theory of "closed and open cycles."[9] Aside from an additive constant which determines the unity of measure, an unequivocal correspondence between the quantities of goods combined in the indifference curves and the utilities enjoyed by each individual exists in two cases: (1) when the cycle is closed, that is, when the order of consumption is indifferent, and the pleasure resulting from the incremental consumption of each commodity depends only on the quantity of that commodity; (2) when the pleasure is different, depending on the order of consumption, that is, when the cycle is open. There remains excluded the case of closed cycles when the basic utilities are functions of more than one variable.

Unfortunately, this ingenious theory was met with silence by the contemporary critique.[10] For further penetration into this mysterious realm, the Paretian theory of open and closed cycles does not suffice. A distinction of this type does not adequately exhaust the profundity of the problem. If one has to accept the *consensus auctorum,* it is

[8] *Giornale degli economisti,* 1902.

[9] First developed, in a comprehensive manner, in the *Giornale degli economisti,* July 1906, in response to critical observations by Vito Volterra, same review, April 1906. The matter was taken up again in the Mathematical Appendix to Pareto's *Manuel d'économie politique,* no. 19–21.

[10] Isolated studies may be mentioned, such as those by B. Boninsegni (who treats of the special case when the basic utilities are linear), *Giornale degli economisti,* 1904, and by Sensini, as well as the studies containing reformulations of the integrability conditions by Hotelling, Allen, Wald, Schultz, and Garver. These reproduce solutions known since the time of Lagrange's and Euler's theory of linear and nonlinear differential equations. See also the author's *Principi generali di logica economica,* 2nd ed., Milan, Malfasi, 1948. [For further references, the reader is referred to Paul A. Samuelson, "The Problem of Integrability in Economic Theory," *Economica,* November, 1950.—Ed.]

convenient to take equal account of divergence of opinion. Moreover, the paths should be laid out along which a choice must be made among the infinite number of systems providing solutions and the infinite number of constants and arbitrary integration functions which can be adapted to economic reality. This could be done with the help of certain criteria which satisfy the integrability conditions from the point of view of economic reality. With the form of the basic functions known, one can choose one of the infinite number of positions covered by the functions. In the third place, it seems necessary to abandon certain absolute references if the functions or arbitrary constants are to be determined in advance on the basis of economic reality. This does not mean that one should proceed in accordance with partial equilibrium theory—where the form of the curves is ingeniously presupposed—but, on the contrary, that attention be given to some indisputable empirical truths, the distribution of income, for example; or that an inductive criterion, uncertain as it is, be adopted, consisting of the system of prices as it existed a moment before; or that a relationship be established with the concrete mechanism of price-level determination as controlled by the monetary authorities. The ultimate goal, remote as it may seem, consists of the transformation of problems posed in terms of differential equations into simple algebraic problems.

Whatever the future development of these investigations may be, they will have to resume the basic themes of Pareto's thought. The participants in this dialogue will all stand in the same light, as it were. The public of today, the literary economists, and the exponents of the various partial-equilibrium theories do not have the slightest idea of this dialogue about an issue on which the future of scientific economics depends.

The importance of pure hypotheses has been pointed out in the preceding paragraphs. When these are rigorously defined—as Pareto wanted them to be—and when the integration of the differential equations and the determination of arbitrary constants and functions have finally taken place, the economist of later times will truly be in a position where he can advance to the exploration of the future. He will attain this position when the material for his constructions has become coherent—under the same conditions as those which have enabled the modern scientist to determine thousands of years in advance the movements of the stars and the eclipses on the basis of the law of gravitation. Compared with literary economics and the theories of partial equilibrium—based, to the present, on a series of artifices and on a world of conventions and subterfuges—Pareto's work has broken the path which leads to the proper appreciation of the problem.

IV

The study of the interrelation between demand (or supply), price, and income is equally remarkable among Pareto's relatively secondary contributions. This well-known study takes its origin from the Walrasian system of equations of general equilibrium, and centers around the search for the sign of a double series of partial derivatives. These partial derivatives bring into a precise relationship the small variations of the demand (or of the supply) of different goods, small variations of the income of the exchanger, and small variations of different prices.

At the time of Pareto, everything in this field was still to be accomplished. Although his work left a notable mark, much remains to be done. In any event, Pareto pointed out the direction into which, according to his own prediction, "the economists must move if they aim at the true progress of science." The road laid out by Pareto in 1892, four years before the publication of the *Cours,* was again taken by Slutzky in 1915, and later on has been widely travelled by English and American economists. These applied his method to a number of practical problems, including the statistical derivation of collective demand and supply. Unfortunately there were neglected in their work certain basic objections which can be raised from a heuristic point of view.[11] The theory of the partial derivatives of incomes and prices has for all practical purposes remained at the stage of *cogitationes privatae.* The knowledge of it has, however, spread more widely than is true of the matters discussed in the preceding paragraph, since it has become more widely known in the form of special theories of income and substitution effects and of the multidirectional character of demand and supply.

We shall limit ourselves to a single observation. The theory of partial derivatives concentrates on movements around a point. It would seem desirable to arrive at a complete solution, represented by finite rather than by point variations. This is a problem in dynamics— also studied by Pareto as will be seen shortly.

V

In the Walrasian fortress with its complex of exchanges, consumption, savings, investments, and mutually dependent production, there is one element which was destined to provoke the most profound dis-

---

[11] For a discussion of this matter, which goes beyond the scope of the present context, see the author's *Principi,* pp. 383 ff. [See also Henry Schultz, *The Theory and Measurement of Demand,* Chicago, 1938, pp. 37 ff.—Ed.]

cord with Pareto's speculation. This is the production function, represented by coefficients of production which are axiomatically assumed
as constant. These functions have no roots because they assume
empirically known data—but, on the other hand, these data must be
considered unknown, especially since the dynamic succession can only
be explained in this manner. The difference between theory and reality
is not considerable, however, since the dynamic succession—in the case
of the assumption of an uniformly progressive society—is hardly pronounced. But, in a clearly dynamic situation, the coefficients of production cannot figure among the given data. The idea of passive coefficients of production is untenable in every respect whenever they
constitute active agents in the production function. The theory of
variable coefficients of production constitutes perhaps Pareto's greatest
merit in the field of the representation of the equilibrium of production.

The distinction between constant and variable coefficients of production is fundamental for two reasons.

First, from the point of view of political economy: Pareto was the
first who demonstrated that the coefficients have the same value under
competition and under state socialism. This was done in 1894,[12] fourteen years before the publication of Enrico Barone's famous essay on
this subject.[13] Walras, on the other hand, considered the coefficients
of production as determined in a manner designed to realize minimum
cost. In contrast therewith, Pareto proposes to examine how they
should be determined in order to obtain the maximum of utility for
society, and he studies the relation between the two types of coefficients.
The state should adopt this value as coefficient of production, regardless
of a subsequent redistribution of the goods turned out. When it is
desired to guarantee the workers a certain income irrespective of their
productive contribution, it is preferable to grant them directly a certain
amount of goods, or a certain amount of money taken from other citizens, and thus leave undisturbed the coefficients of production which
assure maximum utility at least cost.

We shall not enter into a detailed critique of Pareto's formulation of
the problem. Objections may be based on the fact that the prices, by
which the coefficients of production are multiplied in order to obtain
the costs, cannot be considered as constants. The unknowns of the
equations of instantaneous exchange undergo variations in conjunction

---

[12] *Giornale degli economisti*, 1894.

[13] [English translation in *Collectivist Economic Planning*, F. A. Hayek, ed.,
London, 1935.—Ed.] The 1908 essay was preceded by the article "Studi sulla dis-
tribuzione," *Giornale degli economisti*, 1896. After two instalments, Barone
discontinued this series of articles, presumably to prepare the 1908 essay.

with the modification of the distribution of goods or money brought about by the public authority. We want to state, nevertheless, that Pareto has posed a true problem of pure economics such as crude observation cannot solve. At the time of Pareto's article, mathematical economics was barely born. Even if his study impresses us as imperfect, as much from the mathematical as from the economic point of view, it nevertheless constitutes one of the very first objective studies. One does not know whether to think more highly of the unruffled calmness of his research, of the mathematical preparation, or of the admirable scientific intuition.

There exists, however, a second reason for the fundamental importance of the distinction between fixed and variable coefficients of production. The coefficients of production which are placed under the sign of the integral representing cost of production, are not independent of the limits of the integrals themselves. This is always true in the case of monopoly, and it is true also in the case of competition, but only for one of the numerous firms in existence—unless the whole question of minimum cost is restricted to the moment when all enterprises attain the equilibrium position, considering only small variations around a point.

These observations confirm the conclusion that it is necessary to solve a system of equations which are not only differential but integro-differential as well as related to the time interval. However, even if the variable coefficients of production are considered from this point of view, the movements occur again around the equilibrium point.

VI

Pareto, like Walras, worked primarily in the realm of statics. He barely touched upon the question of how to elaborate a theoretical apparatus which would approach as closely as possible the concrete phenomena, that is, the question of rational dependencies of the dynamic variety. Pareto recognized this himself: "Enormously much remains to be done in this direction."

Although the present sketch must necessarily be brief, a few references are in order to that part of Pareto's work which contains the equations of dynamic equilibrium.[14]

[14] The relevant references are to the article of 1894, cited before, which later was inserted in the *Cours* of 1896, and, especially, to an article of 1901, likewise published in the *Giornale degli economisti,* which contains the equations of dynamic equilibrium. As has been noted, the first essay, by expressing in terms of derivatives the equations of the variable coefficients of production, diverges

It is true that Pareto's dynamic equations offer only a broad outline. The values of various economic quantities are considered at the time t_1 and then brought into a relationship with the corresponding values at time t_0, the intervening period being very short. The diversity between the two values rests entirely upon the predetermined variation of the coefficients of production. There is implied the assumption of certain innovations, or changes, attributable to outside forces, in the equilibrium of tastes and obstacles. Walras himself had formulated this hypothesis, ascribing the existence of uniformly progressive societies to the variation of the coefficients of production.[15] But Walras had only affirmed that there would be re-equilibrating tendencies as long as the economic quantities had not reached previously established levels. If Pareto's theory would have been restricted in this manner, it would have been rather inconsequential. In the last analysis it would have been reduced to a new form of scholasticism connected with the formulation of certain hypotheses concerning the teleology of the coefficients of production. In effect, the system would not have been dynamic but only static or quasi-static at best, since it would simply contain an explanation of what happens during the time interval. New savings, new capital accumulations, new interest payments, and new production would all have been taken into account, with time considered in physical rather than in dynamic terms. But the essential difficulty would have been passed over with the help of a hypothetical instead of a rational "bridge."

The integration, over time, of the differential equations would simply have been a hypothetical integration, in other words, a science of the possible and virtual, based on certain hypothetical movements arising from the outside.

The real problem, on the other hand, would call for the removal of the indeterminateness which arises from exogenous factors, for the exploration of the roots of these factors. Sooner or later, all problems of pure economics run in this direction. If this decisive turning point is missed, the platform "time" has no significance at all.

In the first paragraph of this study we have come across the problem whether it is possible, by means of a theoretical construction of sociological character, to formulate a theory of these exogenous factors. It was Pareto's idea to develop such a theory through experimentation. He adopted a method of reasoning which had been characteristic of the

from Walras' more primitive procedure. The essay on dynamics is less widely known and its heuristic value less appreciated.

[15] *Éléments d'économie politique pure,* definitive ed., p. 373.

greatest scientists of his time, for example, of Vito Volterra, who had
stated the problem in these terms:

Begin with the formulation of concepts which lend themselves to measurement. Then measure. Then deduce laws. Return from these to the
assumptions, and deduce, with the help of analysis, a science, ideal in
character but rigorously logical. Compare it with reality. Reject or transform the basic assumptions which you have used, if there are contradictions
between the results of the calculation and the real world. Arrive in this
manner at the discovery of new facts and analogies. Then deduce, from
the present status, what has happened in the past and what will happen in
the future. This is a summary, as brief as possible, of the birth and
evolution of a science mathematical in character.[16]

In substance, the "bridge" over time must be constructed with the
help of inductive knowledge. To Pareto, merely hypothetical knowledge has no value, and he brings the experimental part into the fore-
ground of the science. "We do not know," he said, "the rational laws
of movement of the planets, due probably to an infinite number of
causes which only God can know. But we do know that it approximates an elliptical movement." One can approach the economic
phenomena over time in a similar fashion. They, too, are extraordinarily complex, so much so that at a certain point nobody can have
precise knowledge of them. That is why it is necessary to have recourse
to empirical expressions which help to reveal approximative stability
in time and space.

VII

We shall now briefly review Pareto's practical researches. Having
discovered the law of income distribution, and having sharply delineated various types of interpolation, he did much to advance the
experimental part of economics.

Pareto's theory of income distribution is a contribution of such
momentous importance that its author, had he left nothing else behind, could claim rank among the most outstanding masters of human
thought. The curve of "total receipts," as Pareto calls it, virtually is
in the nature of an *a priori* axiom. An abundance of data confirm it.
"When exceptions emerge in the future (as they surely will do sooner
or later), investigations must be undertaken to search for the special
cause responsible for the deviation of the new phenomena from a form

[16] *Giornale degli economisti,* 1901, pp. 442–443.

which so many facts have proved to be the normal one." [17]   If Pareto's law can be considered as pertaining to inductive, quantitative economics, his theoretical results indicate, however, that the mechanism of income distribution forms one of the most important properties of the economic system *vis-à-vis* the budget constraint.

The second contribution is less widely known, although Pareto had devoted much work to this question.   He does not just construct a method of interpolation but of interpolations which are adapted to distinctly different types of oscillations.[18]   With the help of a principle similar to Alembert's, the oscillations are distinguished in accordance with the tangents drawn to the curves.   In a way, this theory is a forerunner of the modern statistical theories of the decomposition of historical series, containing, as it does, their limitations and imperfections. The arbitrary element in the establishment of different points of discontinuity can in part be avoided by the use of a single mathematical criterion, tempered either by *a priori* reasoning aiming at the rational determination of the necessity of maxima and minima and of the length of the various periods, or by unsophisticated historical investigations of the type of Thorp's *Business Annals*.

VIII

Let us return to the topic considered in Section VI.   Nobody can say for sure what the content of the treatise on economic dynamics would have been, which Pareto mentioned so often in his correspondence as well as in public statements,[19] and in which the exogenous factors were to be systematically related to the representation of the equations of dynamic equilibrium.

It may be that Pareto's grandiose construction was stopped by the lack of statistical material of the type which is becoming available only now and to whose collection he gave such a powerful impetus.   It surely is true that the hypothetical "bridge" for dynamic work is better marked today than it was at the time of Pareto.   This is due to the gradual introduction, during the past 25 years, of the Bergsonian concept of

[17] [An able account of Pareto's law is given by Frederick R. Macaulay in Part III, Volume II, of *Income in the United States,* published by the National Bureau of Economic Research in 1922.—Ed.]

[18] Articles in *Giornale degli economisti,* 1892, 1896, 1908; *Journal de la société de statistique de Paris,* 1897; *Rivista Italiana di sociologia,* 1913; *Rivista di scienza bancaria,* 1917.

[19] For example, in the *Rivista di scienza bancaria,* 1917.

evolution,[20] as well as to the investigations of variables and strategic relations through time.

In the light of these investigations, the Paretian method of dynamic abstraction lacks acuity. This criticism does not detract from the honor and recognition which are due to the most illustrious exponent of the Italian school. He considers dynamic abstraction as a mere problem of averages.[21] Today, however, dynamic abstraction has become more specific. The emphasis has become more concrete and more general as well, as witnessed by investigations into the "order of infinitesimals" or by statistical calculations of strategic variables, as done, for example, by J. M. Clark. These studies are still tentative, because, in this realm, the phase of fragmentary equilibria, or, at most, of particular equilibria, has barely been reached. At the moment, these are highly artificial, but they promise more than a merely generic formulation à la Moore. There is agreement that a synthesis must be worked out at the end, and that one or more links must be forged to connect the dynamic partial equilibria obtained from slices of space with economic time. Valuable tools, which can become a lasting component of the alphabet of dynamics, have been made available, at the very first, by Pantaleoni with his dynamic theory of instrumental, complementary, substitute, and joint relations among families of goods and economic agents,[22] then by Keynes and other well-known authors, such as Haberler, with the dynamic theories based on the principle of acceleration and the multiplier.

IX

In the preceding paragraphs we have tried to cast light on the most remarkable parts of Pareto's work. But, side by side with these, there are others which perhaps impressed their author as still more important, at least in view of the length of time which it took to develop them. Nevertheless, these parts do not enable us to separate neatly the

---

[20] We have in mind the "theory of explosion of spontaneous psychological facts," which can claim the right to be cited in dynamics. It deserves recognition as a cardinal point in economic explication, not merely as an accessory criterion. For purposes of demonstration I refer to the various theories relating to the behavior of the modern entrepreneur, developed by Schumpeter and the modern Italian school. Of the latter, little is known abroad.

[21] If one returns to his article "Considerazioni sui principi fondamentali dell' economia pura," *Giornale degli economisti*, 1893, there is barely an indication of the relationship between individual demand (and final degree of utility to the individual) and average demand (and average final degrees).

[22] Course given at the University of Rome, 1903–1904.

Walrasian and Paretian formulations of the problem and to establish
the original character of the latter. We have in mind the arrangement
of the theory of general equilibrium and the theory of the maximum
total utility of a collective entity.

The relationship between the Walrasian and Paretian positions is
very close. Pareto's system of equations is divided into two parts, and
so is that of Walras. The first part treats of instantaneous exchange,
with a complex of given data which in the second part—relating to
capital accumulation and production—figure as many unknowns.
Walras has the same immense conception. Both have pushed the
search for equilibrium positions to the maximum of generality. Pareto's
synthesis is more complete, however, since monopoly and exchange are
considered as one special case of the general theory; since the mathematical argument can be applied equally to societies based on individualism or on socialism; and since the Paretian language utilizes simultaneously a variety of forms of expressions: utility, indifference curves,
and index functions. Such a wealth of vistas and of new perspectives,
added to the gigantic analytical design, constitutes a grandiose spectacle, fascinating to followers and opponents alike. We do not intend
here to pass judgment on Pareto's exposition. We only wish to refer
in passing to the fact that Pareto eliminated psychological analysis from
economics, by rejecting such concepts as the final degree of utility,
rarity, and ophelimity, the corner stones of hedonistic economics, and
by retaining only the pure and simple fact registered by indifference
curves which are derived from experience and which Pareto presents as
an authentic discovery. In our opinion, however, all this is less decisive from the scientific point of view than Pareto believed. In any
event—and this applies equally to the theory of "obstacles" which technology puts in the way of various transformations or which result, for
each individual, from the attitude adopted by his partners—this approach does not raise intrinsically new problems. To Pareto, the theory
of indifference curves was destined to enlarge the world of theory. He
repeatedly found occasion to recommend their application and never
tired in his efforts at their improvement.

In connection with the deduction of the law of demand, he considered as real progress the passing from independent utilities—as formulated already by Dupuit, Gossen, Jevons, Menger, Launhardt, and
Pantaleoni—to complementary utilities—as they can be found also in
the Walrasian equations—and from there to the indifference series, to
the choices among goods, visualized in pairs, and to choices considered
as effects of resistances. From choices he deduced not only the law of
demand but all conditions of economic equilibrium. This procedure

was considered by Pareto as a great advance because it dispensed with the need for knowing whether utility is measurable and for examining total utilities and their partial derivatives. From an analytical point of view, the procedure was entirely new. However, the assumption of known choices is a hypothesis equivalent to the assumption that utility is known. In the theory based on choices, the projections of the indifference curves are considered as known. The other theory, on the other hand, assumes that the pleasure surface is known. In reality, very little is gained in precision, since the empirical knowledge assumed in the two cases remains nearly the same. For this reason the distinction is not as interesting on the practical as on the conceptual level. But, even in the latter realm, the definitions of equilibrium remain identical; only two different ways are selected. Instead of a relation between the intensities of wants there is one between the partial derivatives of the ordinate expressing the equation of choices. The equivalence of the two procedures is sufficiently demonstrated also by the fact that Edgeworth had arrived at the equation of indifference curves by taking knowledge of the pleasure surface as a point of departure. Remaining always on the same conceptual level, there is no obstacle to the formulation of the problem in still other terms, for example, with the help of marginal rates of substitution—as was done by Hicks, using a concept implied by Walras as well as Pareto—or with the help of other concepts such as the Walrasian "transformed utilities" and those which can be derived from certain properties of the determinants. All this does not involve a new idea—unless the new speculation receives a decisive experimental content.

In expressing these thoughts, we do in no way intend to regard the new orientations as rationally unjustified or illegitimate. They illustrate the aptitude of Paretian thought to express the same problem in different formulations. Nobody has had on hand a similar wealth of formulations.

What is the most important conclusion which can be derived from the theory of general equilibrium? In an approximative manner, it was already known in the light of the theory of partial equilibria that a competitive order entails the maximum of total utility for society. Walras had expressed this thought in a general manner, but only in the language of utilities. This procedure could not fail to raise suspicion, operating, as it did, with non-homogeneous quantities. This breach in the Walrasian edifice was repaired in a general manner by Pareto, who multiplied the variations of total ophelimity—pertaining to each individual—by certain coefficients with the view of rendering them homogeneous. In economic equilibrium, the variations of the quantities of goods are multiplied by prices. These products correspond to the relations between the derivative of total utility and marginal utility. In the sociological equilibrium, the Paretian procedure is even more daring. The coefficients in question are determined in the light of an objective goal, such as the prosperity of the collective entity.[23]

Pareto then went on to demonstrate that the problem of the maximum is a problem of production, not of distribution. The variation of a coefficient of production will bring forth increases or reductions of utility for different individuals. When the sum of the increments exceeds the sum of the decrements, it is possible to transfer from the individuals who receive increments such a quantity of goods as is required for the reduction of the decrements to zero, and still have an excess of increments. Society, considered as a whole, thus receives a benefit. In this manner, the search for the value of the coefficient of production guarantees production in such quantities as, if properly redistributed, will assure for each individual maximum utility, expressed as the algebraic sum of the positive and negative utilities.

We do not intend to discuss here whether this procedure is entirely legitimate. Reference has been made to the polemic between Scorza and Pareto, which is of relevance in the present context. Scorza had estimated that the derivatives of total utilities cannot all be positive or negative unless special restrictions prevailed. But even in this case the procedure is not complete, since Pareto's maximum condition can equally be applied to monopoly and imperfect competition.[24] In any event, however, Pareto deserves credit for having arrived, on a road which never was used before, at a new formula, which expresses, imperfectly but in scientific terms, a concept which until his time was discussed only in metaphysics.

X

Pareto belonged to those thinkers who are unable to resign themselves to a single direction in their scientific work. Incessantly he related his own central concepts to a whole world of special studies, covering the vast realm of applied economics. He aimed at the fundamental revision of current principles, traditional concepts, and generally accepted interpretations, with the help of daring speculations which to this day deserve close attention. This applies to the theories

---

[23] This procedure was outlined, for the first time, in the *Giornale degli economisti*, 1913, and was later incorporated in the *Trattato di sociologia generale*.

[24] For a more complete discussion we refer again to our *Principi*, pp. 308 ff.

of circulation in Pareto's writings, to the theory of international trade, and to the inexhaustible historical documentation with which he enriched and supported his theoretical demonstrations. One cannot with advantage neglect his caustic critique of the political and economic regime of his own country as illustrated by the chronicles published by him in the *Giornale degli economisti* and in a number of political dailies. In this critique he is inspired by the principle requiring that all economic activities, public and private, be appraised in the light of experimental logic, abstracting from all idealistic and spiritual premises. In this respect one could correctly speak of a Paretism, that is, of a new pedagogy, a new doctrine of politico-economic education, applied to all interventions of the government in the economic sphere.

Frisch
on
Wicksell

Knut Wicksell (1851–1926) stands out among the Scandinavian school of economists, which includes such men as Gustav Cassel (1866–1945), Eli F. Heckscher (1879–   ), Bertil Ohlin (1899–   ), and Gunnar Myrdal (1898–   ) in Sweden; Ragnar Frisch (1895–   ) in Norway; and Frederik Zeuthen (1888–   ) in Denmark. Inspired by the work of the Austrians and of the Lausanne school, Wicksell developed the marginal productivity theory of distribution, integrating it with the theory of capital and interest. His principal claim to fame rests on his contributions to monetary theory, based on the notion of monetary equilibrium and on the distinction between the actual rate of interest and the "natural" one which would equate the amount of loan capital demanded and that of savings supplied. Wicksell's influence on modern economic thought has been profound and far-reaching. It is noticeable in Hayek's overinvestment theory of the business cycle, with its emphasis on the notions of capital shortage and forced saving, in Schumpeter's theory of economic development, in Frisch's dynamic theory of the business cycle, and in the recent discussion of saving and investment. Moreover, Wicksell's use of mathematics, although often hidden by the literary form of presentation, has set an influential precedent.

Wicksell's principal works are available in English translations: *Interest and Prices* (1936; first published 1898), and *Lectures on Political Economy* (2 vols., 1934; first published 1901–1906).

Ragnar Frisch, associated with the University of Oslo as a student and teacher, is himself a distinguished member of the Scandinavian school and a leading mathematical economist. His appraisal of Wicksell is a model of sustained technical reasoning. Readers unfamiliar with his technique may supplement the study of his essay by one of the articles cited on pp. 655 f., below.

HOMAGE

IN THE *Archiv für Sozialwissenschaft und Sozialpolitik*, 1927, Joseph Schumpeter wrote an introductory article to a paper by Knut Wicksell. Schumpeter's article was written in his incomparable, brilliant style and with the warmth of his fine heart. Nobody who wants to understand Wicksell's greatness must miss this article. The first part of it is in all its brevity so much to the point that it is entirely useless to try to produce anything better by way of introduction to a study of Knut Wicksell. So here it is in translation:

"When the *Archiv* introduces to its readers the last work of Knut Wicksell, it brings, as an exception to its usual policy, a work which has already appeared elsewhere, namely in the *Ekonomisk Tidskrift*, 1925. There are two reasons for this.

"First of all we wanted to honour the Swedish Marshall, and once again see the greatest name in Nordic national economy in our pages. And it is fitting in this case to derogate still more from our usual practice and bestow on the man and his works some words, as his significance in wider circles of colleagues is not yet sufficiently valued, his message not yet exhausted. This is owing to the fact that his character excluded every kind of advertisement, that his amiable modesty left no room for any emphasis on his own contributions, and that he never stressed his powerful originality and never neglected to give the researchers to whom he was attached what was their due. However, it is not only our sense of duty which leads us to render him a justice which he never claimed himself, but also the recognition that scarcely any other of the architects who have laid the foundations of modern analysis, have so much to give us to-day—to give everyone of us who are growing, developing and struggling for new ways and views—as he. This is not only due to his wealth of thought, but also to the traits of his character. As he always thought of the subject only and never of himself and what could serve his own best, he had a style which, indeed, is neither smooth nor simple, but which for that very reason gives us a look into his workshop. We trace the vivid flash of constructive imagination, we see the original formulations, the difficulties and doubts such as they presented themselves

[Not published before.]

to the author. Therefore, he gives us more than the actual result; he teaches research itself and points in every line beyond himself. This is very rare. We perceive most clearly how rare it is when a master shows in detail the machinery of an inquiring mind, as did Ernst Mach concerning mechanics and the theory of heat. For a number of reasons, the most important one being the lack of competent professional criticism, that way of presenting and teaching is nowhere as rare as with us. All the more we must admire and be thankful to the man who, despising any personal success, has been teaching this way. And while considering his lifework, we remember some words that Mach said of Huyghens: 'The remotest generation will know that he was only a human being, but they will also know what kind of a human being he was.'"

Personally, I never met Knut Wicksell. I saw him once when he delivered a lecture in Oslo, but being an unassuming student at the time, I did not have the courage to talk to him. I only remember the appearance of a friendly, obliging, intelligent-looking, elderly gentleman. So my knowledge of his theory came only through his writings. That, however, was a very intense and absorbing form of making his acquaintance. Already from my early student days, I read his writings (in German and Swedish) avidly. And I continued to do so later. There is probably no other economist who has had so much influence on my thinking, at least not in monetary theory. When looking through old notes from lectures I delivered in the Oslo University 1934–35 on modern monetary theories—including besides Wicksell also Lindahl, Myrdal, Marco Fanno, Robertson, Pigou, Keynes, and others—I found that what I did all the time was to classify and treat these theories more or less as so many different ways of formulating Wicksell's fundamental ideas—or of *misunderstanding* them.

When I started my study of Wicksell, I found that his works were not easy reading. Often it was only at the third or fourth reading that I grasped his ideas. Invariably, each new reading made me more and more enthusiastic. Sometimes it happened that I thought I had finally caught him in an inconsistency or in unclear thinking. Every time this happened, it turned out, however, that the error was mine. After a number of such experiences, I reached the conclusion that whenever a person thinks that he has found an inconsistency or a piece of unclear thinking in Wicksell's works, and wants to "correct it," that is only a sure criterion that the person in question has not yet penetrated to the bottom of Wicksell's ideas. The discovery of the fact that Wicksell is, after all, right, will always be a matter only of patience and intelligence on the part of the reader. That conclusion I reached rather early in my study of economics, and later have never had any reason to change it. The impression has been reinforced these days as I have gone through his works anew when writing this paper.

On the economic thinking in the Scandinavian countries the works of Wicksell have had an enormous influence. I think it is correct to say that all living, outstanding economists in these countries have a good knowledge, in many cases a thorough knowledge, of Wicksell's ideas, and have to a large extent applied types of reasoning similar to those of Wicksell.

I don't propose to discuss here the innumerable ways in which Wicksell's ideas and teaching have influenced economic policy. Only one significant fact might be mentioned: Wicksell was usually far ahead of his time in constructive, practical suggestions. One example is the uses that were made of the gold exchange standard and similar systems which he advocated a long, long time ago. Another example in point is the use of the proceeds from export duties for subsidies in order to keep internal prices down. This plan was worked out by Wicksell during World War I.[1] It was not put into effect then, but measures of this sort have in recent years played an important role in the economic policy of Scandinavian countries.

In the following I shall not only give a brief account of the basic points that are to be found explicitly in Wicksell, but also give certain mathematical developments aiming at a condensed synthesis of the main structure of his reasoning in matters of economic theory. I shall confine myself to those parts of the structure, which, as I see it, are the vital ones, leaving all details aside. The essential points, on the other hand, I shall try to cover fairly thoroughly.

1. WICKSELL'S LIFE

Facts about Knut Wicksell's life and works are reported in a number of special papers.[1-14] Suffice it here to give a brief outline.

[1] See Eli Heckscher, p. 82, in *Penningväsenet och penningpolitik*, Stockholm, 1926, with references to Wicksell's work in the question.

[1a] *Lunds Universitets årsberättelse* 1916–17, p. 8.

[2] Oskar Jaeger, "Johan Gustaf Knut Wicksell." *Statsøkonomisk Tidsskrift*, Oslo, 1926.

[3] Bertil Ohlin, "Knut Wicksell (1851–1926)." *Economic Journal*, 1926.

(*Footnotes 4–14 continued on next page*)

THE PERIOD UNTIL 1885

Johan Gustaf Knut Wicksell was born 20 December 1851 in Stockholm. After having passed his first examination (candidatus philosophiæ) in the University of Uppsala in May 1872, he embarked upon extensive postgraduate works with strong emphasis on mathematics. His postgraduate university studies were not very regular—he worked for instance occasionally as a teacher—and thirteen years would elapse before he passed his final university examination (licentiatus philosophiæ) in mathematics in 1885.

Wicksell had come from a religious home, but passed through a religious crisis and became an opponent of the orthodox form of the Christian religion.   His basic attitude in matters of religion is, however, not clear because he never talked about this even with his nearest friends.[15]   One thing, however, is clear.   He had a high moral standing, a great, warm heart, and a deep sympathy for those not

[4] E. Sommarin, "Minnesord över professor Knut Wicksell." *Kungl. Hum. Vetenskapssamfundet,* Lund, 1927.

[5] E. Sommarin, "Förord" to the Swedish 1927 edition of Wicksell's *Förelesningar,* Vol. I.

[6] Joseph Schumpeter, "Zur Einführung der folgenden Arbeit Knut Wicksells." *Archiv für Sozialwissenschaft und Sozialpolitik,* 1927.

[7] E. Sommarin, "Das Lebenswerk von Knut Wicksell." *Zeitschrift für Nationalökonomie,* 1931.

[8] Valfrid Spångberg, "Knut Wicksell och Verdandi." *Verdandi genom femtio år.* Stockholm, 1932.

[9] Johan Åkerman, "Knut Wicksell, a pioneer of econometrics." *Econometrica,* 1933.

[10] Lionel Robbins, "Introduction" to the English edition, 1935, of Wicksell's *Lectures on Political Economy.*

[11] Bertil Ohlin, "Introduction" to the English edition, 1936, of Wicksell's *Interest and Prices.*

[12] Gustav Cassel, "Konkurrensen om Lundaprofessuren" (In *I förnuftets tjänst*), Stockholm, 1940.

[13] Eli Heckscher, "David Davidson." *Minnesteckning foredragen på Vetenskapsakademiens högtidsdag den 31 mars 1951.* (Certain parts also concern Knut Wicksell.)

[13a] [C. G. Uhr, "Knut Wicksell—A Centennial Evaluation." *American Economic Review,* 1951—Ed.]

[14] For the collection of printed source material on Knut Wicksell's life and publications, I am obliged to Mr. Arne Amundsen, research associate at the University Institute of Economics, Oslo.   Mr. Amundsen has also worked out a list of Knut Wicksell's published works, books as well as articles.   The list may be obtained in mimeographed form from the Institute.

[15] Sommarin Ref. 4, p. 22.

living on the sunny side. He was willing to fight for them even though it might mean sacrifices to himself.

As a student he came in contact with a group of radicals, including amongst others the (somewhat older) great poet August Strindberg, the physiologist Hjalmar Öhrvall, and the politician Hjalmar Branting. In the spring term of 1880 he delivered two addresses (on 19 February in a temperance society and on 25 February before an academic public) on poverty, drunkenness, prostitution, and neo-malthusianism. He had witnessed how the unrestricted production of children kept the lower classes in misery, and spoke openly of the remedy: neo-malthusianism. His views and conclusions in this matter also appeared in print. As could be expected a storm of protests arose from conservative quarters. To this Wicksell replied in a booklet (1880).

THE PERIOD 1885–1900

Having passed his final university examination in mathematics in 1885 he was awarded a stipend of the Lorén Foundation. Now his scientific studies in economics developed in full. He went to England, France, Switzerland, Austria, and Germany. The progress of his economic studies and the type of problems and the authors to which he devoted his energy during this period (John Stuart Mill, Böhm-Bawerk, Karl Menger, and others) can be followed from his public speeches and addresses, which in many cases appeared in print afterwards.[16]

At the same time the discussion on neo-malthusianism and the questions connected with it continued. In 1886 and 1887 he gave several talks on this, not only in Sweden, but also in Denmark and Norway. On 16 March 1887 he talked in the radical students' association "Verdandi" that counted many members who have later become prominent in the scientific and political life of Sweden. The association was founded (1882) more or less in protest against the attempts at curtailing the freedom of speech that had followed Wicksell's talks and publications in 1880.[17]

In 1889, at the age of 38, he married the Norwegian Anna Margrethe Kristine Bugge. Wicksell's wife had passed a university examination in Kristiania (now Oslo) in 1886, and she graduated in Law in Lund 1911. She took part in public life, being amongst others a Swedish representative in League of Nations activities.

[16] Sommarin Ref. 4, p. 30. [17] Spångberg Ref. 8, p. 217.

In 1895 Wicksell passed the final university examination in economics and became a doctor of philosophy the same year. It is interesting to note that as late as January 1898 at the age of 46, he wrote:[18] "I hold no teaching post, so that my scientific work is made possible only by special grants. I have in the first place to express my profound gratitude to the administrators of the Lorén Foundation, who for the third time have made me a generous grant. It further gives me particular pleasure to express my respectful appreciation to the Government of Sweden for making me a grant towards this work."

In 1899 he graduated in Law, and the same year became a docent (assistant professor) in Economics and Public Law.

THE PERIOD 1900–1926

In 1901 Wicksell competed with Gustav Cassel for the professorship in Economics and Public Law which had become vacant in Lund after the retirement of Professor G. K. Hamilton.[19] The affair developed in a rather dramatic way. Wicksell's position as an economic scientist was at that time well established and it was quite probable that he would be appointed to the vacant post if the decision was made on the basis of scientific competence alone. That, however, did not seem to be what was going to happen. Conservative quarters did not want to see Wicksell appointed. A chief argument was that a person who had taken such a position regarding neo-malthusianism as Wicksell had, could not be considered fitted for the task of guiding and enlightening others. These quarters therefore worked for the appointment of Cassel. Cassel was scientifically in strong opposition to Wicksell and wanted to have a competent, scientific scrutiny of the points at issue. He wished, of course, very much to see a decision in his own favour, but could not take advantage of any support offered him for other reasons than strictly scientific ones. Therefore, in protest against the kind of arguments that had been used against Wicksell, he withdrew his application, and Wicksell was appointed to fill the vacancy. Even if Wicksell would on the strength of his outstanding scientific contributions have been appointed in any case, Cassel's gesture commands great respect for his scientific integrity and sense of fair play.

In November 1908 Wicksell gave a talk in Stockholm on "The throne, the altar, the sword and the purse." For his forceful, pointed

[18] In the preface to "Geldzins und Güterpreise."
[19] Cassel. Ref. 12, p. 33.

and open way of presenting his views on these things he was sentenced to two months' imprisonment. The terms of his imprisonment cannot have been very severe because some of his well-known writings were produced during this imprisonment.

With the fall term of 1916 he retired from his chair in Lund and moved back to Stockholm for which he had been longing during the professorship years in Lund.[20] His wife had built a home for them on the seaside near Stockholm, about twenty minutes' rail trip from the centre of the town. Wicksell did not like the idea of becoming countryfied and of stagnating. From 1917 he was nearly always present in the meetings of the Stockholm economic society and frequently took part in the discussions, always injecting valuable viewpoints and penetrating theoretical remarks, many of which are preserved in the printed proceedings of the society. He was also busy writing promemoria and articles on monetary questions, but most of all he liked to be in his quiet study at home working on some theoretical problem that appealed to his keen, still unfailingly sharp intelligence. In this way his years passed by, full of activity, until an accidental cold, which unexpectedly developed into pneumonia, ended his life on 3 May 1926.

2. THE THEORY OF CAPITAL AND THE PRODUCTIVITY RATE OF INTEREST

It is unfortunate that Wicksell did not put down his theory of capital in a complete mathematical form. If he had done so, he would have saved his commentators a lot of trouble and helped tremendously to popularize his ideas in our generation. The word popularize here is not a printer's error. We have now—I don't hesitate to say fortunately—reached a stage where the younger generation is very reluctant to use its time and energy on discussions of really complicated points of economic theory unless these points are expressed in rigorous mathematical terms. At the time of Wicksell the situation was entirely different. He simply had to write in a semi-mathematical and literary style if he wanted his writings to be read outside a small group of specialists. It therefore seems worth while to attempt a brief mathematical summary of Wicksell's theory of capital. In presenting such a summary I shall try to reduce the theory to its lowest terms and use a notation which fits in with modern macro-economics.

[20] Sommarin Ref. 4, p. 1.

Wicksell's theory of capital is a theory of the *stationary state* in a society where there are two primary factors of production, land and labour. Suppose that each year there is performed a number of units of services of land equal to x. Out of this total amount a part x_0 is used in such a way that its fruits become immediately available, another part x_1 in such a way that its fruits only become available 1 year hence, still another part x_2 used in such a way that its fruits become available 2 years hence, etc. Similarly for the services of labour (for instance for labour hours) $y_0, y_1, y_2 \cdots$, etc. We then have by definition

$$(2.1) \qquad x = x_0 + x_1 + \cdots + x_n \qquad y = y_0 + y_1 + \cdots + y_n$$

where n is the longest period of delay between an input element and the output element which is attributable to it. The total amount of services of land rendered each year x and of labour done each year y—both constant in a stationary society—are in Wicksell's theory taken as *data* not to be explained.

In this stationary society there will each year emerge a certain amount of finished goods. Wicksell assumes that these goods can be measured in a technical unit. This is equivalent to assuming that only one single kind of good is produced. Let z be the quantity of it that emerges each year. Thus x, y, z all have the denomination "per year."

We assume that z is a technically given production function of the $2n + 2$ input elements $x_0 \cdots x_n, y_0 \cdots y_n$, i.e.,

$$(2.2) \qquad z = f(x_0 \cdots x_n, y_0 \cdots y_n)$$

This means that, if we compare different stationary states and z, $x_0 \cdots x_n, y_0 \cdots y_n$ are the magnitudes belonging to any such state, these magnitudes will always be connected by the relation (2.2) where f is a function whose form is independent of the state considered.

The marginal productivities are denoted

$$(2.3) \qquad f_\tau(x_0 \cdots x_n, y_0 \cdots y_n) = \delta f / \delta x_\tau$$

$$f_{(\tau)}(x_0 \cdots x_n, y_0 \cdots y_n) = \delta f / \delta y_\tau$$

$$(\tau = 0, 1, \cdots, n)$$

The meaning of the phrase "the technical superiority of the roundabout way of production" (Böhm-Bawerk's third ground) can be expressed by certain assumptions about the forms of the functions f_τ and $f_{(\tau)}$. See below.

All the above is purely technical. Now for prices. Let p, q, and P be the prices of land, labour, and the product, respectively, all measured in an arbitrary unit. Wicksell assumes that $P = 1$, that is, all prices are expressed in terms of the good produced. I think, however, that the formulae are more efficiently handled by leaving P as an arbitrary parameter. Wicksell assumes that there exists a possibility of *trade* in the concretizations of land and labour which was performed Θ years ago and then applied in such a form that their fruits would be given off τ years after the services had been rendered ($\Theta = 0, 1 \cdots \tau$; $\tau = 0, 1 \cdots n$). Such concretizations will to-day still have ($\tau - \Theta$) years to go before the finished goods emerge as part of z. If we wanted to, we could handle the problem by considering all these concretizations as separate goods with prices $p_{\tau\Theta}$ and $q_{\tau\Theta}$, respectively, and determine all these prices through equilibrium equations. It is, however, quicker to introduce Wicksell's next assumption immediately. It is to the effect that borrowing operations are possible at an interest rate ρ which is the same for all forms of borrowing. To begin with, nothing is assumed about this rate; it may be positive, negative, or zero. The only assumption at this point is that some rate exists. If this is so and no gain is possible through mere lending and borrowing operations, the prices $p_{\tau\Theta}$ and $q_{\tau\Theta}$ must be correlated in the sense that

$$(2.4) \quad p_{\tau\Theta} = (1 + \rho)^{\Theta} p \qquad q_{\tau\Theta} = (1 + \rho)^{\Theta} q$$

$$(\text{for all } \Theta = 0, 1 \cdots n, \tau = 0, 1 \cdots n)$$

In particular the exchange price of concretizations of land and labour that have no more time to go but are just on the point of giving off their fruits, will be

$$(2.5) \quad p_{\tau\tau} = (1 + \rho)^{\tau} p \qquad q_{\tau\tau} = (1 + \rho)^{\tau} q \qquad (\tau = 0, 1 \cdots n)$$

Now suppose that equilibrium is produced *as if* an entrepreneur each year tries to maximize the entrepreneurial profit

$$(2.6) \quad \pi = Pf(x_0 \cdots x_n, y_0 \cdots y_n) - \sum_{\tau=0}^{n} (p_{\tau\tau} x_\tau + q_{\tau\tau} y_\tau)$$

under constant prices P, $p_{\tau\tau}$, $q_{\tau\tau}$ ($\tau = 0, 1 \cdots n$) and freely variable $x_0 \cdots x_n$, $y_0 \cdots y_n$. There is no contradiction between the assumption that *actually* (2.1) is fulfilled with given x and y, and the assumption that the equilibrium is reached *as if* profit maximization takes place under free variation of $x_0 \cdots x_n$, $y_0 \cdots y_n$. The latter assumption pertains indeed only to the conjectural action of entrepreneurs, not to the final situation produced. Under this conjectural action we must reach a point which is substitutional in the sense that

$$(2.7) \qquad Pf_\tau(x_0 \cdots x_n, y_0 \cdots y_n) = (1 + \rho)^\tau p$$

and

$$Pf_{(\tau)}(x_0 \cdots x_n, y_0 \cdots y_n) = (1 + \rho)^\tau q$$

$$(\tau = 0, 1 \cdots n)$$

The number of variables in the above argument is $(2n + 7)$, namely $(2n + 2)$ for x_τ, y_τ, and 5 for p, q, P, ρ, π. The number of equations are $(2n + 5)$, namely $(2n + 2)$ for (2.7), 2 for (2.1) when x and y are given, and 1 for (2.6). Since one degree of freedom is disposed of by the arbitrary selection of P, there remains one degree of freedom. We may represent it in various ways, for instance by saying that for each given magnitude of ρ all the other variables are determined.

There is, however, another and more fruitful approach, chosen by Wicksell. We may compute *the exchange value of the existent capital stock* and consider this value as representative of the remaining one degree of freedom. That is, for each given magnitude of this value all the other variables, including the interest rate ρ, will be determined. This will give an analysis of the demand side for capital. When this demand is finally compared with the supply of capital as it emerges through the saving in society, the equilibrium position—now including also the value of the capital stock—will be determined.

The exchange value of capital (L. I. 204) [21] is computed as follows. Take the capital stock as it exists at the beginning of any year, and let us—in conformity with the way of reasoning in (5.1)—assume that all the productive services are rendered at the beginning of the year while all the finished product emerges at the end of the year. At the beginning of any year there will then be present τ layers of that kind of land concretizations which have the property that the fruits emerge τ years after the service is performed. Each such layer consists of x_τ units of land service. One of these layers consists of land service just rendered; its exchange value will consequently be px_τ. Another layer consists of land service that was rendered one year ago; its exchange value will consequently be $(1 + \rho)px_\tau$, and so on up to the layer which consists of land service that was rendered $(\tau - 1)$ years ago, and whose fruits will therefore emerge at the end of the year we are now considering. This applies for all $\tau = 1, 2 \cdots n$.

<hr>

[21] References are abbreviated thus: (L. I. 204) means "Lectures," Vol. I, p. 204; (I. P. 101) means "Interest and Prices," p. 101.

Similarly for the work performed. In other words, the exchange value of the capital stock that is present at the beginning of any year is

$$(2.8) \qquad K = \sum_{\tau=1}^{n} \sum_{\theta=0}^{\tau-1} (1 + \rho)^{\theta}(px_\tau + qy_\tau)$$

$$= 1/\rho \sum_{\tau=0(\text{or } 1)}^{n} [(1 + \rho)^\tau - 1](px_\tau + qy_\tau)$$

Wicksell's argument in (L. I. 204) is equivalent to putting $(\theta + 1)$ instead of θ in (2.8). The difference is only a conventional one depending on whether the output is assumed to emerge at the beginning or at the end of the year. The definition (2.8) gives the simplest structure of the formulae, and is in full harmony with the reasoning in (5.1).

K in (2.8) is measured in absolute units—say dollars—so that it will depend on the conventional choice of P. Since all the equations are of the well-known form encountered in static equilibrium theory, all equilibrium prices will simply be proportional to P, and so will K. Our assumption about K may therefore be formulated either by saying that $k = K/P$ is given or by saying that K and P are given, or for brevity by saying that K is given, remembering that P is also given.

The above gives a formal determination of the equilibrium values of the variables for any chosen value of K. To study the structure of the solution we must look into certain relations that can be deduced from the above.

From (2.1), (2.6), and (2.8) follows immediately

$$(2.9) \qquad px + qy + \rho K + \pi = Pz$$

All the terms of (2.9) represent values per unit of time.

From the axiomatic viewpoint (2.9) is a fundamental relation which shows that when the exchange value of capital is computed by (2.8), the difference between the total value of the annual product on the one hand and on the other the sum of the entrepreneurial profit and what is paid annually to the primary factors, land and labour, at the moment when the services of these factors are rendered, is an amount per year equal to one year's interest on the existing capital. This indicates that although capital is not in the technical sense just another factor juxtaposited with the primary factors, but rather a new dimension on each of the primary factors (L. I. 148–150), yet capital has in one particular sense the same position in the problem as the primary factors: it receives a remuneration which forms part of the total value of the product. Incidentally, Wicksell assumes most of the time that the entrepreneurial profit in the equilibrium point is zero. This will always be the case if production follows a pari-passu law, i.e., if the function (2.2) is homogeneous of the first degree. Otherwise the assumption $\pi = 0$ introduces an additional assumption which in general will not be compatible with the other assumptions.[22]

Also from another angle will capital retain a position similar to that of the other factors: We may speak of the marginal productivity with respect to real capital k, dz/dk, calculated under constant x and y (and constant prices and interest rate), and this marginal productivity turns out to be equal to ρ in the equilibrium point. Indeed consider any differential variation $dx_0 \cdots dx_n, dy_0 \cdots dy_n$ compatible with (2.1) under constant x and y, i.e., $\Sigma_\tau dx_\tau = 0$ and $\Sigma_\tau dy_\tau = 0$. For any such variation we have by (2.8) $\rho dK = \Sigma_\tau(1 + \rho)^\tau(pdx_\tau + qdy_\tau)$. On the other hand we have $dz = \Sigma_\tau f_\tau dx_\tau + f_{(\tau)}dy_\tau$; hence in the equilibrium point $Pdz = \Sigma_\tau(1 + \rho)^\tau(pdx_\tau + qdy_\tau) = \rho dK$, so that

$$(2.10) \quad d(Pz)/dK = \rho \quad \text{i.e., } dz/dk = \rho \quad (\text{when } P = \text{const.})$$

This conclusion holds no matter how large π may be in the equilibrium point. We may also prove (2.10) under another set of assumptions, which do not use the equilibrium conditions and are also weaker in other respects. Dividing (2.9) through by P we see indeed immediately that under any variation which leaves ρ and $(px + qy + \pi)/P$ unchanged while (2.9) holds, the result must be the last formula in (2.10).

Thus, if we "apply more capital," i.e., arrange for dK in any of the senses above, we will—*regardless of how this marginal dose of capital is composed*, provided only that it satisfied the conditions specified—always find that the increment in the product reckoned per unit of increment in real capital is equal to the existing rate of interest ρ.

There is still another sense in which capital behaves as a factor of production: The interest rate can be looked upon as the marginal productivity (or more precisely the relative marginal productivity) with respect to waiting. To see this we must define the concept of the *average period of production* $\bar{\tau}$. If it would have been sufficiently accurate to reckon with simple interest, we could have defined $\bar{\tau}$ simply as the weighted arithmetic average of all the individual periods $\tau = 0, 1 \cdots n$. In this case the definition of $\bar{\tau}$ would have been independent of ρ (L. I. 184). Since in fact we have to reckon with compound interest, we must define $\bar{\tau}$ more precisely by saying that

[22] See my paper "Overdeterminateness and optimum equilibrium," *Nordisk Tidsskrift for Teknisk Økonomi*. Copenhagen, 1948.

if the amount $(px + qy + \pi)$ which is paid annually to the primary factors and to the entrepreneurs (if they receive a remuneration at all), increases in value at interest ρ, compounded continuously for this period $\bar{\tau}$, we get the value of the product that emerges annually. In other words the average period of production $\bar{\tau}$ is defined by $(px + qy + \pi)e^{\rho\bar{\tau}} = Pz$, that is

(2.11) $\rho\bar{\tau} = \log \text{nat} \, (Pz) - \log \text{nat} \, (px + qy + \pi)$

Applying to (2.11) a differential variation that leaves ρ and $(px + qy + \pi)$ unchanged we have

(2.12) $\rho = d\log \text{nat} \, (Pz)/d\bar{\tau} = 1/Pz \cdot d(Pz)/d\bar{\tau} = dz/d\bar{\tau} \cdot 1/z$

This is the precise meaning in which the interest rate which exists in the equilibrium point can be looked upon as the (relative) marginal productivity of waiting (L. I. 177 and 184).

Incidentally, if we had defined $\bar{\tau}$ as $K/px + qy + \pi$, we would have obtained $\rho/1 + \rho\tau$ instead of ρ in the left member of (2.12), and if we had defined $\bar{\tau}$ as K/Pz, we would have obtained $\rho/1 - \rho\bar{\tau}$. Both expressions are close to ρ if either ρ or $\bar{\tau}$ is small.

In the equilibrium point we must by (2.7) have

(2.13) $f_\tau(x_0 \cdots x_n, y_0 \cdots y_n) = (1 + \rho)^{\tau - \Theta} f_\Theta(x_0 \cdots x_n, y_0 \cdots y_n)$

(for all τ and Θ)

And similarly for the services of labour. These relations are important for a discussion of the much debated question of whether the equilibrium rate ρ is positive.

Wicksell thinks it will be positive. He is definitely aware of the fact that a proof of this proposition cannot be given simply by referring to the fact that in the equilibrium point we usually have

(2.14) $f_\tau(x_0 \cdots x_n, y_0 \cdots y_n) > f_\Theta(x_0 \cdots x_n, y_0 \cdots y_n)$

when $\tau > \Theta$

And similarly for the services of labour. In order to deduce that the equilibrium point will show a positive ρ, we must build on the existence of the inequality (2.14) taken in the *schedule sense*, that is in the sense that it holds everywhere within a certain domain of the variables involved. Such a formulation of (2.14) is the essence of Böhm-Bawerk's third ground. Wicksell seems to think that the third ground—taken in the schedule sense—is *sufficient* to prove the positivity of the equilibrium interest rate, and that we consequently do not need to evoke Böhm-Bawerk's first ground (less adequate supply of goods in the present than in the future) or his second ground (the undervaluation of future needs). "Thus there remains only the third of Böhm-Bawerk's main reasons" (L. I. 155; see also 150). Let us examine this a little closer.

If we assume technical superiority in a sufficiently strong schedule sense, we can always prove that this superiority is a sufficient condition for the equilibrium ρ to be positive. For instance, if we assume that (2.14) holds identically for all conceivable magnitudes of the variables $x_0 \cdots x_n$, $y_0 \cdots y_n$, we see immediately from (2.13) that ρ must be positive, *wherever* the equilibrium point might fall. But to assume technical superiority in so strong a sense would certainly be going too far. By transferring enough land services from Θ-use (and possibly from other uses) to τ-use ($\tau > \Theta$) it must be possible to press down f_τ and to increase f_Θ to a point where the inequality (2.14) is reversed.

We could weaken the assumption on the technical superiority by considering only those points ($x_0 \cdots x_n$, $y_0 \cdots y_n$) where the individualized marginal productivities satisfy the proportionality conditions

$$(2.15) \quad f_\tau = \alpha(1 + \rho)^\tau \qquad f_{(\tau)} = \beta(1 + \rho)^\tau \qquad (\tau = 0, 1 \cdots n)$$

α, β, ρ being any three numbers, positive, negative, or zero. This would leave us with three degrees of freedom only. If we assumed that (2.14) holds identically over the field defined by (2.15), the positivity of the equilibrium ρ would follow. However, to assume technical superiority in the sense just considered would only weaken the assumption in a very formal way. The fundamental problem would be left: If we throw the elements of the given sum x sufficiently far off into the future, it must be possible to reverse the inequality (2.14) even if we limit ourselves to considering points ($x_0 \cdots x_n$, $y_0 \cdots y_n$) compatible with (2.15) (where no assumption is made about ρ being positive). Numerical examples of this can undoubtedly be constructed.

So, in order to prove that the equilibrium ρ will be positive, it seems that we must fall back on *something that limits the size of* K. We can, for instance, formulate the technical superiority by assuming that (2.14) holds identically in ($x_0 \cdots x_n$, $y_0 \cdots y_n$) within *that* region where (2.1) and (2.7) are fulfilled and where K/P defined by (2.8) has a "reasonable" size. I think that this is, after all, Wicksell's meaning of technical superiority. When this formulation is accepted, a positive equilibrium ρ follows. It seems, however, that it is stretching the terminology a bit to call this set of assumptions a "technical" superiority. We have here assumed so many factors on the *supply side* of "waiting" that we have really used something equivalent at least to Böhm-Bawerk's first and second ground.

This whole question should be analysed further. I believe that when the analysis is carried through in real terms only and the assumptions—for instance Böhm-Bawerk's three grounds—are formulated in so weak a sense that we can adopt them unhesitatingly, then they will not form a set of sufficient conditions for a positive equilibrium rate. The concrete facts which make the occurrence of a zero or a negative interest so unlikely must, in my opinion, rather be sought on the *monetary* side. Under present monetary institutions liquidity may take on such forms that it would require very drastic measures to produce a zero or a negative interest. One would, for instance, have to use monetary notes (and coin) automatically losing in denomination with time.

Assuming that the equilibrium rate ρ is positive, how will it change when we shift our attention from a stationary state with one value of K to another stationary state with a larger value of K (and constant P)? Wicksell says (L. I. 157 and 162) that ρ then will *go down*, which by (2.13) is only another way of saying that the marginal productivity of the long-period uses of land and labour will go down *in relation to* the marginal productivity of the short-period uses. He also claims that the marginal productivities f_0 and $f_{(0)}$ will actually increase and that the uses of land and labour will be shifted in the direction of the longer periods.

In the case where $n = 1$ and the production function expresses a pari-passu law (i.e., is homogeneous of the first degree) these propositions can easily be proved as follows. To simplify we consider only land; the inclusion also of labour would not materially alter the argument. Putting again for brevity $K = kP$, we now have the three equations

$$(2.16) \qquad x_1 f_0(x_0, x_1) = k \qquad x_1 f_1(x_0, x_1) = (1 + \rho)k \qquad x_0 + x_1 = x$$

between the four variables x_0, x_1, ρ, k. From these equations we immediately deduce

$$(2.17) \qquad 1 + \rho = f_1(x - x_1, x_1)/f_0(x - x_1, x_1)$$

The variation from x_1 to $x_1 + dx_1$ (under constant x) produces the variations

$$(2.18) \qquad df_0(x - x_1, x_1) = (f_{01} - f_{00})dx_1$$

and

$$df_1(x - x_1, x_1) = (f_{11} - f_{10})dx_1$$

where $f_{ij} = \delta f_i / \delta x_j$. So long as we are within the region of substitution (i.e., where f_0 and f_1 are positive) and the production law is a pari-passu law, the second order derivatives always have the following signs: f_{00} and f_{11} are negative, f_{01} and f_{10} positive. Thus, if dx_1 is positive, df_0 must necessarily be positive and df_1 negative, from which all the above conclusions follow. In the more general case the proof is not so simple and I have not gone through it rigorously, but it seems probable that Wicksell's conclusions hold in general on reasonable assumptions.

In other words, if we measure K along the horizontal axis and ρ along the vertical axis of a diagram, the curve representing the (ρ, K) relation in the sense just specified will—under constant P and within the domain considered by Wicksell—be a *downward-sloping curve.* This entails, among other things, the fact that the ordinate is a single-valued function of the abscissa and at the same time that the abscissa is a single-valued function of the ordinate.

If we take K as the independent variable, the ordinate read off from the curve indicates the interest rate which would emerge in the production process under the given technical conditions and the given kind of adaptation (profit maximization) and the given constant P when the value of the capital employed is K. This interest rate we may call the *productivity* rate of interest and denote ρ^*. Wicksell does not use any special term or symbol for what I have called the productivity rate. Sometimes he speaks about a natural or a real rate (for instance L. II. 207) as if he should have the ordinate of the above curve in mind, but most of the time his natural, real, or normal rate is handled as an equilibrium concept (compare [6.6] below), so I have found it more convenient to retain a special term for the ordinate of the curve.

It should be noted that Wicksell focussed his attention primarily on the relation between the interest rate and *the existing capital:* ". . . why a given amount of existing social capital gives rise to a certain rate of interest" (L. I. 171). The annual net *addition* to capital, i.e., that concept which we would term net investment and denote I, is a flow concept and must not be confounded with the capital in use K.

When we read Wicksell and consider the context with a willingness to understand, we will never have any real difficulty in understanding whether he thinks of the flow concepts or the stock concepts, but he might not always satisfy our most pedantic claims regarding terminological rigor. My friend and colleague Professor Trygve Haavelmo has insisted strongly on the distinction between flow and stock concepts in connection with Wicksell. I should certainly not have been so careful in my formulation if I had not profited by his remarks.

It is also necessary to distinguish between the demand and supply aspect of these concepts. Saving S is the supply concept corresponding to the demand concept I. The stock concept corresponding to S may be termed capital held and denoted H.

Before proceeding to an application of these concepts in Wicksell's monetary theory, a word must be said about the sense in which investment can be different from saving.

3. HOW CAN INVESTMENT BE DIFFERENT FROM SAVING?

There is no logical difficulty in conceiving of the desired (planned, ex-ante) magnitude of investment as being different from the desired (planned, ex-ante) magnitude of saving, or from actual saving. Nor is there any difficulty in conceiving of a difference between actual investment and actual saving if one of these magnitudes refers to one period of time and the other to another period. The problem concerns the case where investment and saving are both actual (ex-post) figures and refer to the same period.

There is something peculiar about these concepts of actual investment and actual saving, both referring to the same period. Sometimes we find outselves involved in an argument where there seems to be good common sense in assuming that these two magnitudes are different. At other times, equally good common sense would indicate that the two must be equal.

When one has become aware that the problem must be handled from the "ecocirc" (tableau économique) viewpoint, the path of least mental resistance undoubtedly leads to saying that actual investment is by definition always equal to actual saving. I am convinced, however, that this is not the solution we need. To adopt it would mean that we take something important out of the problem. I vividly remember the deception I felt one evening in King's College many years ago when Keynes told me that he had finally decided to make actual investment by definition equal to actual saving. I am sure that this was a step backwards in the "General Theory" as compared with his "Treatise on Money." Keynes' remark: "No one can save without acquiring an asset whether it be cash or a debt or capital-goods" ("General Theory," 1936, p. 81) is in my opinion not to the point. The nature of the asset is essential. It is particularly important in a theory where liquidity is a central theme.

We need a system of concepts which allow both kinds of differences to exist, both an investment-saving difference between two desired or one desired and one actual magnitude, or between magnitudes referring to different periods of time, *and* a difference between two actual magnitudes referring to the same period of time. The first kind of differences will in a sense explain the ultimate "cause" of the movement, the second will explain how that cause in concreto *operates*.

A mechanical analogy will bring out more precisely what I have in mind. Take a U-shaped tube with constant internal diameter, both branches being open in the upper end. When there is liquid in the tube, there will be two columns of fluid connected at the bottom. Let x be the level of the fluid in the left branch, and y that in the right, both measured from the same conventional base. In static equilibrium we must, of course, have $x = y$. Now suppose that a person *desires* to add a certain amount of fluid in the left branch. This desired amount will illustrate the concept of a planned or ex-ante magnitude, and it will be a useful tool when we want to explain the motivations back of what happened on such and such an occasion, but it will not explain the mechanism by which fluid flows from the left to the right branch when the person carries out his intention. To explain *this* it is necessary to use a logical model where the observed actual x at a given point of time may be different from the observed actual y at that same point of time. Without such a model we would not be able to understand what really happens when fluid flows from the left to the right branch and thus re-establishes static equilibrium. On the other hand, if we do use an appropriate model, we can give a very complete and understandable account of what happens. We may for instance explain that a constant inflow per unit of time in the left branch will entail a difference $(x - y)$ which is constant over time, at least approximately if there is no friction in the tubes themselves, but only friction at one point, say in a valve at the bottom, where the two branches communicate. The magnitude of the constant difference $(x - y)$ will depend on how strong the friction in the valve is, and on how heavy the fluid is. An increasing inflow in the left branch will entail a faster increase in x than in y. And so on.

This mechanical analogy may be applied to a great number of economic phenomena. We may for instance let x and y be capital in use and capital held, respectively. Or we may let x and y represent investment and saving per unit of time at any given point of time.

Whether we interpret the analogy one way or the other, there are undoubtedly certain equilibrium situations which it would be natural to characterize by $x = y$, but we would not have perceived the problem sufficiently broadly if we constructed a model where by definition $x = y$ and tried to use this model to explain *what happens* when persons or groups in society try to change the existing invest-ment-saving situation.[23]

To reach a concrete workable definition of the money value of the actual rate of investment per unit of time and the money value of the actual rate of saving per unit of time in such a way that the two may be different, I think we should start by saying that however we finally define these two variables, the difference between them should in one way or the other be connected with the frequently and loosely used concept "credit expansion" or more specially with the concept of an "inflationary credit expansion" produced through the inter-mediary of a special sector, "the banks."

Let K_t be total loans (which in Wicksell's analysis is more or less the same thing as capital in use) [24] and let H_t be total deposits (capital held) at the point of time t. Further let the divided differences (rates of change) be denoted

$$(3.1) \qquad \acute{K}_t = K_t - K_{t-\kappa}/\kappa \qquad \acute{H}_t = H_t - H_{t-\kappa}/\kappa$$

When $\kappa \to 0$, we get derivatives.

Wicksell focusses attention on the *appreciation part* of the change in K_t, that is, the increase in value produced by the mere fact that prices are changing. In modern works on national accounting this aspect of the problem is not considered as explicitly as one could wish. In this respect there is still much to be learned from Wicksell. The following is a suggestion for a system of concepts which may satisfy at the same time the requirements of the theory of the Wick-sellian cumulative process and that of national accounting.

Let P_t be an index of prices such that it can be used for deflating the amount K_t, so that, as before, the ratio $k_t = K_t/P_t$ can be looked upon as the volume of real capital. If K_t is defined simply as loans, k_t would be the deflated value of loans. We have

$$(3.2) \qquad \acute{K}_t = \acute{k}_t P_t + k_{t-\kappa}\acute{P}_t = \acute{k}_t P_{t-\kappa} + k_t \acute{P}_t$$

[23] My friend and colleague Edgard B. Schieldrop, professor of mathematical mechanics at the Oslo University, has at my suggestion worked out a number of equations which can undoubtedly be translated into economic terms. I hope to be able to revert to this on another occasion.

[24] More precisely: the value of circulating real capital.

where

$$(3.3) \qquad \dot{k}_t = k_t - k_{t-\kappa}/\kappa \qquad \dot{P}_t = P_t - P_{t-\kappa}/\kappa$$

When $\kappa \to 0$, we get derivatives and (3.2) becomes the usual formula for the derivative of a product. The following concepts—all reckoned per unit of time—must be distinguished:

$(3.4) \qquad \dot{K}_t =$ increase in the value of capital (investment reckoned inclusive of appreciation on capital)

$(3.5) \qquad \dot{k}_t =$ the volume of real investment

$(3.6) \qquad \dot{k}_t P_t =$ the value of real investment, or shorter investment
$\qquad\qquad\quad = I_t$

$(3.7) \qquad \dot{K}_t/P_t =$ deflated increase in the value of capital

$(3.8) \qquad k_t \dot{P}_t =$ appreciation on capital

When the price index P_t is constant, (3.8) is zero and all the concepts (3.4–7) are practically synonomous. Otherwise they must be kept distinct. I believe that (3.6) comes nearest to expressing "investment per unit of time" in the minds of the majority of those who work on national accounts.

Similar distinctions must be made for the concept capital held = deposits H_t. Let its deflated value be $h_t = H_t/P_t$. Various rates of change can be derived from H_t similar to (3.1–8). In particular saving may be defined $S_t = \dot{h}_t P_t$.

In order that a change in the difference between loans and deposits shall become conceivable, the model must contain some means of storing purchasing power outside of the banks. The most natural way to introduce this possibility is to assume a circulating medium—notes and coin—held by the public, i.e., by "non-banks." Let M be the amount of this circulating medium and $m = M/P$ its deflated value. Assuming that M, K, and H are all measured from conventional origins, we may put

$$(3.9) \qquad\qquad M_t = K_t - H_t$$

hence $\qquad \dot{M}_t = \dot{K}_t - \dot{H}_t \qquad$ and $\qquad m_k = k_t - h_t$

In a concrete case one would have to specify carefully all the items that would come under the headings "loans," "deposits," and "circulating medium," respectively. However complicated the banking system and its operations are, it will always be possible to make the classification in such a way that the definitional equations (3.9) hold. From the above definitions follows

$$(3.10) \qquad I_t - S_t = P_t \dot{m}_t = P_t (d/dt)(M_t/P_t)$$

The formula (3.10) indicates, in my opinion, the way in which we should fundamentally introduce a difference between I_t and S_t.

The above concept $S_t = h_t P_t$ is saving in the restricted sense of including only such values which (through the banking system) *are made available for someone else.* And it is defined exclusive of appreciation, i.e., it expresses the increase in a volume figure (in a deflated figure), this increase being however expressed in monetary units of the current year. An increase in cash holdings is not included in this savings concept. In a broader sense we may consider $(S_t + P_t \dot{m}_t)$ as "saving." This is the value of the increase in the deflated value of *all* reserves whether in the form of deposits or cash holdings. *This* "saving" would by definition be equal to I_t, but this savings concept is not well adapted for a study of how cash holdings are absorbed by the public. For this purpose the appropriate concepts would seem to be I_t and S_t. This is illustrated by the following special cases.

In a model where no cash holdings M_t exist, we will by definition have $I_t = S_t$. This equality will also apply if prices always move *immediately in strict proportion to the amount of cash holdings.* Indeed, if $\dot{m}_t = 0$ for all t, the ratio M_t/P_t would be constant. The existence of a difference between I_t and S_t—that is, the non-proportionality of M_t and P_t—will express a *buffer effect* produced by the cash holdings. In terms of the usual equation of exchange, this effect might be translated as a change in the velocity of circulation of money. The buffer effect is expressed by the difference (3.10). It characterizes the way in which new loans are absorbed by the public. A period of expansion—not necessarily accompanied by rising prices—would be characterized by a positive value of the difference (3.10)—in the mechanical analogy fluid would be driven from the left to the right branch—and a period of contraction would be characterized by a negative value of (3.10). In many cases the average value of (3.10) taken over a year may be small, just as the average difference of level of the fluid in the two branches in the mechanical analogy may be small, but the existence of this small difference may account for the flow of a considerable amount in the course of a year, i.e., a considerable value of $\dot{K}_t$ and of $\dot{H}_t$.

When the above definitions are adopted, the cash holdings should be looked upon as *a draft on the social product,* not—as one would from a purely formal viewpoint—as a draft on the institution that has issued the notes or coin. So far as economic effects in a modern society are concerned, the concept of the note as a draft on the social product is undoubtedly the more relevant. From this viewpoint the notes and coin appear as something half way between real objects and credit instruments. The latter have both a debtor and a creditor —and are indeed nothing but an expression of the relation between these two parties—the former have neither a debtor nor a creditor, but are simply owned by someone. From the social-product viewpoint each note has a creditor—the person who holds it—but no individualized debtor. Having adopted this view on money, we may—to use a term by D. H. Robertson—call the expression (3.10) a "levy" on the public. This levy constitutes the difference between investment and saving.

Two things are essential in order to arrive at a distinction between I and S along the lines here developed: first, that we have segregated one sector, "the banks," to be treated in a special way in the definition of investment and saving; and second, that we have segregated a special kind of objects, namely notes and coin, to be treated in a special way.

If some investment takes place within the enterprises without passing through the banks, one would count this both as investment and saving, and with equal amounts. The same would apply if some of the savings of individuals were invested in real form directly by these individuals. This would follow logically because a given enterprise has not created any "circulating medium" that gets a meaning because of its circulation within this enterprise. And the same would apply to the household of an individual. Equation (3.10) will therefore hold even if I and S are defined as *totals for society*.

If we want to use a model where all transactions are performed by notes and coin alone, we will have to distinguish between two parts of this circulating medium, a "hoarding" part that can, so to speak, be kept out of sight when this is wanted, while the other, "the active part" can be inserted for M in the right member of (3.10). When a part of the circulating medium is transferred from one to the other of these two compartments, there would sometimes emerge a positive and sometimes a negative value of the right member of (3.10). If we introduce "the banks" as a special sector to be treated in a special way from the viewpoint of investment and saving, a distinction between two different parts of the cash holding does not become necessary for the investment-saving definition, although it might of course still be desirable from other viewpoints. It is unessential which one of the above two ways of thinking we accept, provided we arrive at an equation of the form (3.10).

Equation (3.10) must be tied in with the definition of sectorial income (national income if the sector is a nation). Let C be the money value of the sector's consumption per unit of time and, as before, I the money value of the sector's net investment per unit of time, and let A and B denote total exports and imports, respectively, taken in the broadest sense. Finally let G be unilateral transfers (taxes, gifts, etc.) from this sector to the rest of the world, reckoned net, so that G may be positive, negative, or zero. As before, M is the amount of sectorial monetary circulation. Then we have the following hierarchy of income concepts:

(3.11)   Internal income $R^{\text{in}} = C + I$

(3.12)   Disposable income $R^{\text{dis}} = C + I + (A - B)$ ("the internally and externally disposable sector income")

(3.13)   Accruing (released) income $R^{\text{ac}} = R = C + I + (A - B) + G$

(3.14)   Produced income $R^{\text{prod}} = C + S + (A - B) + G$

Since the accruing (released) income will as a rule be the most important income concept to consider, we have for brevity denoted it R without any superscript. Accruing (released) income is the money value of income as it emerges when investment I is reckoned at actual prices at the end of the year, i.e., at prices compatible with the credit expansion that has taken place, if any, while produced income is the money value of income after deducting from the accruing (released) income the amount $(I - S)$, i.e., the "levy" on the public. The difference between accruing (released) income and produced income is the same thing as the difference between the money value of actual investment and that of actual saving, i.e.,

(3.15) $R^{\text{ac}} - R^{\text{prod}} = I - S = P\dot{m} = P(d/dt)(M/P)$

Adopting (3.6) as the definition of investment and, similarly, of saving means that the income concepts (3.11–3.14) are defined exclusive of value appreciation on capital. If we had taken $\dot{K}$ as the definition of investment and $\dot{H}$ as that of saving, the above income concepts would have included value appreciation on capital.

For any individual or any subsector, say No. α, the accruing income R^{α} plus the increase in the loans $\dot{K}^{\alpha}$ to this individual or subsector is the total purchasing power at the individual's or subsector's disposal. It can use this purchasing power for the following six purposes: consume C^{α}, invest at home I^{α}, invest abroad $(A^{\alpha} - B^{\alpha})$, pay unilateral transfers to the rest of the world G^{α}, increase its cash holdings $\dot{M}^{\alpha}$, and increase its deposits $\dot{H}^{\alpha}$. If this equation is summed over all α, and we use (3.9), we get (3.13) where the magnitudes refer to the sector as a whole.

In the sequel the above investment-saving concepts will be applied in expounding Wicksell's theory.

4. CURRENCY THEORY VERSUS BANKING PRINCIPLE

To understand the genesis of Wicksell's monetary theory, one should begin by considering certain other theories which he partly accepts and partly discards.

In one specific sense, Wicksell accepts—as practically every sensible economist would—the quantity theory: "that a large issue of paper currency progressively depreciates in value and thereby raises the prices of all other commodities, calculated in paper money, has been proved too often in history to be open to doubt. Similarly, there are some, though by no means many, examples of a successive withdrawal of paper money rehabilitating its value and causing a fall in commodity prices, in terms of paper money" (L. II. 170).

All this is simple. The essence of Wicksell's problem is something different, namely how *bank credit to the public*, either in the form of notes or of fictitious deposits, will affect prices. On this point we should consider in particular the currency theory, whose principle exponent was Ricardo, and the banking principle defended by Tooke.

In a nutshell, Ricardo's views can be expressed by saying that "the banks possess, by the granting of credit, and especially by the issue of notes, an unlimited power to increase the circulating medium, and therefore to raise commodity prices" (L. II. 171). In this process, the interest rate plays, according to Ricardo, an important role. The height of the interest rate will be causally connected with the increase or decrease in circulating medium, not with the existing amount of it. A liberal issuance of bank credits in the form of notes or fictitious deposits would tend to produce an easy money market, and this easiness would lower the interest rates. Viewed from the other side, this low interest rate would, under ordinary circumstances, be the means by which the banks could make the public absorb the enlarged amount of circulating medium. This easiness of the money market would be maintained as long as, and no longer than, the outflow of new circulating medium took place. As soon as the outflow had ceased and the increased circulating medium had produced its effects on prices, the easy money market would be gone, and the money rate would move up again to its former height. In other words, the low money rate represented so to speak the position of a valve through which the new circulating medium flowed into the system. A changed position of the valve and a changed strength of the flow would, more or less, be the same thing.

Wicksell accepted the essence of this conclusion: ". . . Ricardo rightly insists that a fall in money interest can only take place so long as the surfeit of money has not led to a corresponding increase in prices. As soon as this occurs, there no longer exists any surfeit of money, relative to the requirements of turnover" (L. II. 179). But Wicksell is dissatisfied with the *analysis* which led Ricardo to his conclusions. In Wicksell's opinion, Ricardo was too narrowly concerned with the "high price of bullion" aspect of the problem (L. II. 176) and did not distinguish sufficiently sharply between internal commodity prices and the external premium on gold. He thinks Ricardo's proof on this point is all too slender (L. II. 177). On the whole, he holds that Ricardo does not go sufficiently deeply into the *mechanism* which connects rising prices and the issuance of bank credit. It is precisely on this point that Wicksell thinks his own contribution will be illuminating.

Tooke—in opposition to Ricardo—holds the view that "the volume of exchange media is never the cause, but on the contrary, always the effect, of fluctuations in prices and of the requirements of turnover for the medium of exchange" (L. II. 173). Tooke's view on this point could perhaps be characterized as the "small-coin view." Everybody will, of course, agree that the level of commodity prices is not (to any sensible degree) affected by the amount of pennies and other small coins in circulation. Under ordinary circumstances, the need for these types of circulating media will be *determined by* the existing level of commodity prices (and by trading habits). Any attempt to force a larger amount of pennies and small coins on the public, would simply result in a flow of these denominations back to the banks. Tooke's view is that the issuance of bank credit has a similar effect on prices. The commodity prices are determined by speculation, taking account of production costs and specific factors in the market. In general, there is no speculation in the commodity markets based on easy bank credit and a low interest rate.

To this Wicksell remarked that "Tooke has . . . confused two essentially different phenomena" (L. II. 184), namely, speculation in goods owing to political events, failure of harvest, etc., and the regular element of speculation that enters into current business transactions under capitalistic production. In the first case, the interest rate is an element of minor importance—on this point Tooke is correct—but in the second case, the interest rate is of paramount importance, and it acts precisely in the way which Wicksell himself wanted to explain.

Thus, to sum up, Wicksell admits the correctness of important elements both in the currency theory and in the banking principle, but he considers neither as giving a satisfactory *systematic analysis* of the mechanism which connects bank credit, interest rate and prices. This analysis is furnished by his own "positive solution."

5. PRELIMINARY EXPOSITION OF WICKSELL'S MONETARY THEORY

The main line of Wicksell's argument in his monetary theory is concerned with what would happen if the primary factors of production—land and labour—remained constant in real-terms equilibrium, while certain constellations within the *monetary* system changed. The evolution to which this would give rise is the famous Wicksellian cumulative process which manifests itself as a mere *price movement*. The underlying real-terms equilibrium, which in the monetary theory is assumed constant, is explained fully in that part of his theory which in his lectures was treated in volume I (compare Section 2 above). Wicksell was, of course, well aware of the fact that the evolution of the monetary factors actually influences also the underlying real factors, and in his monetary theory he makes frequent remarks on this. But they remain as side remarks. To quote but one example: ". . . It is, of course, not impossible for the rise in prices to be counteracted to a certain extent by an increase in production, for example if previously there had been unemployment, or if higher wages had induced longer working hours, or even by the increasing roundaboutness which is undoubtedly invoked by a fall in interest rates, even if it occurs artificially. But all these are secondary considerations" (L. II. 195).

The essential fact which, according to Wicksell, distinguishes the monetary market mechanism from the market mechanism of a real good, he explains as follows: "The movement and equilibrium of actual money prices represent a fundamentally different phenomenon, above all in a fully developed credit system, from those of *relative* prices. The latter might perhaps be compared with the mechanical system which satisfies the conditions of *stable* equilibrium, for instance a pendulum. Every movement away from the position of equilibrium sets forces into operation—on a scale that increases with the extent of the movement—which tend to restore the system to its original position, and actually succeed in doing so, though some oscillations may intervene. The analogous picture for *money* prices should rather be some easily movable object, such as a cylinder, which rests on a horizontal plane in so-called *neutral* equilibrium" (I. P. 100–101).

The mechanism by which this effect is produced, is explained in "Interest and Prices" (pp. 136–141) and later in his "Lectures." The reasoning in "Interest and Prices" can most effectively be translated into an accounting system. See table (5.1). The assumption here is that no addition is made to the stock of fixed capital goods. For simplicity, the production of consumption goods (by means of a stock of capital goods and an inventory of consumption goods) is assumed to take place in cycles of one year's duration. Wicksell considers the four groups or parties indicated in table (5.1).

TABLE (5.1). TRANSACTIONS IN A SOCIETY CONSISTING OF THE FOUR WICKSELLIAN GROUPS

		Cash Transactions								Loans	Deposits
		Entrepreneurs		Landlords and Workers		Capitalist-Commodity Dealers		Banks			
Transactions at the beginning of the year	(1)	K							K	K	
	(2)		K'	K'							
	(3)				K'	K'					
	(4)		K''			K''					
	(5)						K	K			K
Transactions at the end of the year	(6)					ρK			ρK		0
	(7)					K			K		0
	(8)	$(1+\rho)K$					$(1+\rho)K$			0	
	(9)		$(1+\rho)K$					$(1+\rho)K$		0	
Grand total		$(2+\rho)K$	$(2+\rho)K$	K'	K'	$(2+\rho)K$	$(2+\rho)K$	$(2+\rho)K$	$(2+\rho)K$		

The *entrepreneurs* own fixed capital goods, but have otherwise no capital of their own. At the beginning of the year, they borrow from the banks an amount K (line 1), which they immediately, that is to say, at the beginning of the year, pay out in two sums, K' and K'' where $K' + K'' = K$, as follows: K' (line 2) is paid in advance to the *landlords and workers* in remuneration for the services they will render in the year's production. These services are used by the entrepreneurs to repair and renew (but not more than renew) the fixed capital goods which the entrepreneurs own, and also used to produce the year's consumption for society as a whole. The consumption goods emerge as finished products at the end of the year. The sum K' received by the landlords and workers from the entrepreneurs at the beginning of the year is immediately used by them (line 3) for buying from the capitalist-commodity dealers all the consumption goods which the landlords and workers need for the whole year. The sum K'' (line 4) is paid out by the entrepreneurs at the beginning of the year to buy from the capitalist-commodity dealers the consumption goods which the entrepreneurs need for the whole year.

The *capitalist-commodity dealers* are pure rentiers. At the beginning of the year they hold for one moment their whole fortune—which is $(1 + \rho)K$—in real form, namely as an inventory of all the consumption goods which are used in society as a whole for one year. At the beginning of the year, the rentiers immediately sell for an amount K' to the landlords and workers (line 3) and for an amount K'' to the entrepreneurs (line 4) and keep for themselves (not shown) an amount ρK to be consumed in the course of the year. Having done that, the capitalist-commodity dealers immediately deposit the proceeds of the sales, that is, the amount $K = K' + K''$, in the banks. It is unessential how we imagine that the various payments around new year are performed. It may be done by an instantaneous use of cash (notes), or by drafts on the banks, or by clearing in the banks, the account of one party being credited at the same time as the account of another party is debited with the same amount.

The *banks* receive at the beginning of the year a deposit K from the capitalist-commodity dealers, and lend this sum immediately to the entrepreneurs. The interest to be paid on the loan granted to the entrepreneurs is to be the same as that paid on the deposits made by the capitalist-commodity dealers.

At the end of the year, the following transactions take place. First, the entrepreneurs sell to the capitalist-commodity dealers as much of the year's production of consumption goods as is necessary in order to pay off the entrepreneurs' debt to the banks as of the end of the year. This debt is equal to K plus the interest ρK. In other words, the entrepreneurs are assumed to sell commodity goods for a total amount of $(1 + \rho)K$.

Let C be the value of total net output at current prices, that is, the value of the consumption goods that emerge annually in the productive process directed by the entrepreneurs. This value need not be exactly equal to the value $(1 + \rho)K$ of the consumption goods which the entrepreneurs must sell in order to cover exactly their debts to the banks as of the end of the year. In order to describe the difference we may define a coefficient $\bar{p}$ by the equation

$$(5.2) \qquad\qquad (1 + \bar{p})K = C$$

All prices are assumed given and constant during the year. The coefficient $\bar{p}$ may provisionally be taken as the definition of the natural (or normal) rate of interest.

Wicksell considers the difference $(1 + \bar{p})K - (1 + \rho)K = (\bar{p} - \rho)K$. When this difference is positive he visualizes it as consisting of a stock of consumption goods which the entrepreneurs *need not sell*, but may put aside for themselves: ". . . and laying them on one side for the consumption of the coming year" (I. P. 142).

Thus, the total value of consumption goods which the entrepreneurs receive annually (after the first year) as remuneration for their taking part in the economic activity can be looked upon as consisting of two parts: K'' and $(\bar{p} - \rho)K$. The former is a "normal" part, and the latter is a "surplus" which is positive or negative accordingly as the natural rate of interest is larger than or less than the market rate.

The existence of such a surplus will exert a profound influence on the course of affairs. Take for instance the case where it is positive: "If entrepreneurs continue, year after year, perhaps, to realise some surplus profit of this kind, the result can only be to set up a tendency for an expansion of their activities. I emphasize once again that so far it is purely a question of a *tendency*. An *actual* expansion of production is quite impossible, for it would necessitate an increase in the supply of real factors of production . . . such changes . . . we need not consider . . . at this point" (I. P. 143). That is to say, *if* prices remained constant, the entrepreneurs *would*, at least after some time, discover that they realized an unusually large profit, and so would, amongst them, start a scramble for expansion. Since in real terms there could not be any expansion, the *bidding of the entrepreneurs* would push prices up. This bidding and driving up of prices would necessitate larger bank credit (on this point Wicksell comes very close to a Tooke-ian reasoning) and these credits would be available: "In our ideal state every payment, and consequently every loan, is accomplished by means of cheques or giro facilities. . . . No matter what amount of money may be demanded from the banks, that is the amount which they are in a position to lend" (I. P. 110). The price movement would spread—as a first approximation roughly proportionally—over all sectors of the economy. In other words, all the real factors would be maintained exactly as they are assumed in table (5.1). *But there would be a proportional increase of K, K', K'',* while $\bar{p}$ and ρ, and consequently also the difference $(\bar{p} - \rho)$ remained constant. So long as the increase in K, K', and K'' is proportional, nothing would be disturbed in the balancing of the accounts of the table (5.1). In other words, *the same argument* regarding the scramble for expansion under constant real factors, leading to a price inflation, could be *constantly repeated*. This is in essence the famous Wicksellian cumulative process. Any possible side effects on the underlying real situation could only take place within rather narrow limits, and would not be cumulative because the natural resources are not unlimited as is the potential bank credit. The above argument would work both ways, that is, both under an inflation and under a deflation.

So, the whole development depends on the difference between $\bar{p}$ and ρ. The market rate ρ can be changed more or less at will through a decision of the banks. For the natural rate $\bar{p}$, the situation is entirely different. As is seen from (5.2), this rate will depend only on the ratio C/K, which, on the assumptions accepted, is a *technical* datum. In other words, the natural rate $\bar{p}$ cannot be changed except as the result of a change in the underlying real factors. When we ask for the "cause" of the price inflation, it is, therefore, plausible to express it by saying that the market rate of interest "is kept too low."

This whole argument depends obviously on the possibility of segregating out a part of the entrepreneurs' annual consumption, which can be considered a "surplus" part, and therefore will create the incentive to expand entrepreneurial activity. Since this is a crucial part of the argument, it should be considered a little closer. What precisely is the criterion on which a part of the remuneration to the entrepreneurs can be segregated out as a "surplus" distinct from the "normal" part of the remuneration? Are not the entrepreneurs at liberty to draw the line of demarcation arbitrarily? If the answer is yes, the whole theory would really amount to saying that prices move up whenever the entrepreneurs happen to be in a mood to make them move up, and vice versa.

This apparent indeterminacy of the price tendency can be expressed in terms of the elements of table (5.1), by saying that any example of the form (5.1) which leads to a difference between the natural rate and the market rate, can, within the framework of Wicksell's ideas, be replaced by another where no such difference exists. To see that such a transformation is possible, we note that the set-up has four degrees of freedom which we may represent, say, by the parameters

K, K', C and ρ. Suppose that these four numbers are given. Using these data, let us transfer the activity which consists of simply *possessing* an amount $(\bar{p} - \rho)K$ of consumption goods, from the group "entrepreneurs" to the group "capitalist-commodity dealers," and maintain all the rest of the example. This, certainly, would not be contrary to Wicksell's way of reasoning in this matter. It would, indeed, seem to be the only reasonable thing to do when the capitalists are defined the way they are in Wicksell's reasoning here. This transfer would mean that we retain the original magnitudes K', C and ρ, while replacing K by $\bar{K}$ and determining this $\bar{K}$ by the condition that all the consumption goods produced are sold by the entrepreneurs in order to pay off their debts with the banks at the end of the year; i.e., we would have $C = (1 + \bar{p})K = (1 + \rho)\bar{K}$.

This gives $\bar{K} = \dfrac{1 + \bar{p}}{1 + \rho} K = \left(1 + \dfrac{\bar{p} - \rho}{1 + \rho}\right) K$. The new example thus constructed would be of the same form as (5.1), with K replaced by $\bar{K}$, and K'' by $K'' + (\bar{K} - K)$, while K' and C would be unchanged. The new natural rate would by (5.2) be equal to ρ; i.e., the entrepreneurial "surplus" profit would now have disappeared.

The solution of the puzzle is that Wicksell has an additional consideration which gives an independent determination not only of K', but also of K'', so that a transformation of the above kind is excluded (and only proportional changes of K, K' and K''—for instance those that occur during an inflation or a deflation—are permitted). Indeed, on the "normal" part of the entrepreneurial profit Wicksell says: ". . . he (the entrepreneur) . . . obtains the same return for the trouble of conducting his business as he would have obtained for conducting similar business on behalf of others, for instance of a company" (I. P. 140). In other words, the "surplus" profit that starts the scramble for expansion emerges when the entrepreneur, who carries on business on his own account, realizes a *higher* remuneration for his own services and for that of the fixed capital goods which he possesses than he *could have* obtained by taking a salaried job and letting out on hire his fixed capital goods.

In the subsequent section I shall attempt to put the concept of the natural rate into a broader perspective and connect it with the other parts of Wicksell's theory.

6. SYNTHESIS BETWEEN CAPITAL THEORY AND MONETARY THEORY

In his capital theory Wicksell discusses the effects produced by a *change* in real capital, a "change" being interpreted as the shifting of our attention from one stationary situation to another. In his monetary theory, on the contrary, he assumes in essence a *constant* real capital. It is by no means easy to see how these two lines of thought gear into each other. And yet, there is an intimate connection between the two parts of the theory.

To bring out this connection we must have recourse to a "roundabout" way of reasoning. We must consider more closely what I called the productivity rate of interest (end of Section 2). This should not be taken as synonomous with what Wicksell calls the natural or normal or real rate nor with what he calls the market rate. It is only a parameter by which we so to speak *temporarily add one dimension to the problem*. This device elucidates, in my opinion, the whole problem. The reasoning about the Wicksellian cumulative process and the meaning of the concepts natural, normal, or real rate will then follow consistently—and indeed in a rather obvious way—by a consideration of a special case obtained by an additional assumption which again takes out one degree of freedom. When the theory is formulated in this way, it becomes, as I see it, immune to the special kind of criticism that has been directed against it by Lindahl, Myrdal, and Ohlin.[25]

In fig. (6.1) let the productivity rate ρ^* be measured on the vertical axis and the volume of real capital in use $k = K/P$ on the horizontal axis. This real value k is the same thing as the value of capital K when we put $P = 1$, i.e., when we measure value in terms of the product. In other words k is exactly the concept which Wicksell uses in his theory of capital. This volume k at any given point of time is a technical datum which is defined independently of the market rate. Indeed, the magnitudes $x_0 \cdots x_n$, $y_0 \cdots y_n$ of Section 2 are technical variables defined without any reference to a rate of interest. Similarly for the production function (2.2). Suppose that we are in a point $(x_0 \cdots x_n, y_0 \cdots y_n)$ belonging to the field (2.15) where α, β, ρ are any numbers. This is a necessary condition for the point to be in real term equilibrium. The value of the parameter ρ in this point as determined by (2.13) is the productivity rate of interest. Thus, in any point $(x_0 \cdots x_n, y_0 \cdots y_n)$ belonging to the field (2.15) the productivity rate is a technical datum. And so are p and q. Inserting these values in (2.8), we get K, and hence $k = K/P$, which is independent of P. In other words, in any point $(x_0 \cdots x_n, y_0 \cdots y_n)$ belonging to the field (2.15) the volume k of real capital is a technical datum, independent of the market rate. I am convinced that this is a true rendering of the essence of Wicksell's thought. It is not

---

[25] Summarized by Ohlin in his Introduction to *Interest and Prices*, 1936, p. xvii.

necessary to build the definition of k on an existing market rate.
And even if we wanted to let the market rate influence the definition
of k in some way, we might still arrive at two different concepts
ρ^* and ρ.

Draw—as defined at the end of Section 2—the down-sloping curve
that connects ρ^* and k. Let $k = F_k(\rho^*)$ be the function that expresses

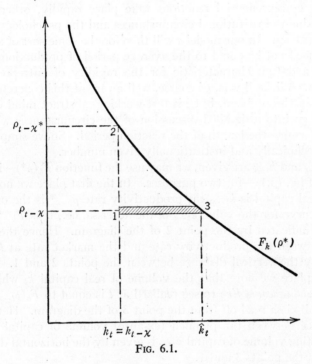

FIG. 6.1.

how k depends on ρ^* along this curve, and let $F_k^{-1}(k)$ be its inverse.
The relative prices p and q of the input elements are determined by
k and will therefore in general change with k along the curve. On the
vertical axis of fig. (6.1) we also measure the market rate of interest ρ.

The curve of fig. (6.1), which was originally—in Section 2—defined
as a static curve expressing a comparison between stationary alternatives, may also help to explain certain *changes over time*, provided we
add some convention on the *rapidity* with which things might move.

Consider two points of time t and $t - \kappa$ separated by an interval
of time κ, which we may call the entrepreneurial *reaction period*. This
means that the situation at $t - \kappa$—characterized by the market rate
$\rho_{t-\kappa}$ and the volume of real capital $k_{t-\kappa}$—will determine the plans of
the entrepreneurs for t. If we retain the assumption of the abstract

example (5.1), we may imagine that the production is split up into separate periods of length κ, so that the productive services of land and labour are performed at the beginning of each such period while the product falls due at the end of the period. In this case the reaction period will be exactly equal to the period of production. In reality the whole process is, of course, of a more continuous sort: Certain entrepreneurial reactions take place rapidly, others more slowly, due to institutional circumstances and the psychology of the entrepreneurs. In our model κ will therefore be some sort of average which need not be equal to the average period of production, but is simply a datum characteristic for the rapidity of entrepreneurial reaction. Wicksell was, of course, well aware of this concrete background of the problem, but his fast-working, abstract mind did not stop to go into a detailed discussion of the circumstances which in fact determine the length of the reaction period. So we simply take κ as a technically and institutionally given number.

If $\rho_{t-\kappa}$ and $k_{t-\kappa}$ are given, we may use the function $F_k(\rho^*)$—i.e., the curve of fig. (6.1)—for two purposes. In the first place we note that when real capital is $k_{t-\kappa}$, the productivity rate $\rho_{t-\kappa}{}^*$ is the ordinate of the curve for the value $k_{t-\kappa}$ of the abscissa, i.e., it is $F_k^{-1}(k_{t-\kappa})$. This is indicated by the point 2 of the diagram. Hence the difference between the productivity rate and the market rate at $t - \kappa$ is given by the vertical distance between the points 2 and 1. In the second place we note that the volume of real capital $\hat{k}_t$ which the entrepreneur *would like* to see realized at t is equal to $F_k(\rho_{t-\kappa})$, that is, the abscissa read off from the point 3 of the diagram. Hence the difference between the planned (ex-ante) volume of capital $\hat{k}_t$ and the existing volume of capital $k_{t-\kappa}$ is given by the horizontal distance between the points 3 and 1.

This being so, what will happen if the situation at $t - \kappa$ is given by the two numbers $\rho_{t-\kappa}$ and $k_{t-\kappa}$? According to the basic assumptions indicated in Section 5 the entrepreneurs will through the banking system be in a position to command the nominal (money) capital K_t which they need for carrying out their plans, but they might *not* be in a position to control the actual magnitude k_t of the volume of real capital at t. This is crucial for the whole reasoning. Wicksell assumes $k_t = k_{t-\kappa}$, but that is not an essential part of the argument. What is essential at this point is only to take the actual volume of capital k_t which will be realized at t as some given magnitude. The development of prices—that is, of the *general price level* of the goods which form the product of the production process, i.e., the price P of the volume z defined in Section 4—can now be determined. Indeed, let $P_{t-\kappa}$ and P_t be these price levels at $t - \kappa$ and t, respectively, and let us for the time being assume that the entrepreneurs do *not* take account of anticipated price changes. They will then want to employ at t a nominal (money) capital equal to $P_{t-\kappa}F_k(\rho_{t-\kappa})$, and will by assumption actually employ it. That is,

$$(6.3) \qquad K_t = P_{t-\kappa}F_k(\rho_{t-\kappa}) \qquad \text{i.e., } k_t P_t = P_{t-\kappa}F_k(\rho_{t-\kappa})$$

One should note the fundamental logical difference between $\hat{k}_t = F_k(\rho_{t-\kappa})$ and $K_t = P_{t-\kappa}F_k(\rho_{t-\kappa})$. The difference is more than just a transformation from a volume figure into a value figure. The former is an ex-ante figure and the latter an ex-post figure. From (6.3) follows immediately

$$(6.4) \qquad P_t - P_{t-\kappa}/\kappa P_{t-\kappa} = F_k(\rho_{t-\kappa}) - k_t/\kappa k_t$$

The divided difference to the left in (6.4) is the relative rate of change of the general price level over the interval κ (for $\kappa \to 0$ we get the logarithmic derivative d lognat P_t/dt). The expression to the right in (6.4) is obtained graphically from fig. (6.1). Consider the point 1 with ordinate $\rho_{t-\kappa}$ and abscissa k_t (which now need not be equal to $k_{t-\kappa}$), and also consider point 3. The numerator in the right member of (6.4) is the horizontal distance between the points 3 and 1 (positive in the example), and the denominator is equal to κ times the abscissa of the point 1. In other words the ratio which the numerator of (6.4) bears to the denominator *is directly and easily read off from the graph*, apart from the factor κ. The smaller the factor κ, under a given shape of the curve in (6.1), the larger will be the relative rate of change of the price level. This is only an expression for the obvious fact that the price level will move all the faster the quicker the entrepreneurs react. A finite rate of change of the price level is due to a non-zero reaction period of the entrepreneurs.

The above gives already a first part of the more elaborate theory of the cumulative process. Assuming that the actual volume of real capital at t (the abscissa of the point 1 in fig. (6.1) is *given*, we can say that the general price level will *increase* when the market rate is below the productivity rate that corresponds to the given volume of capital, and that it will *decrease* in the opposite case. And we can further say that the price level will move all the faster the greater the difference between the market rate and the productivity rate (the greater the vertical distance between the points 2 and 1). These conclusions follow immediately from a mere inspection of fig. (6.1) provided the curve is sloping down (which was one of the main results of the analysis of Section 2).

The above analysis uses *two* data: a given market rate and a given volume of capital. This is the sense in which we may call the analysis two-dimensional. So long as only the shape of the curve in fig. (6.1) is given, the point $(\rho_{t-\kappa}, k_t)$ may fall anywhere in the diagram. To reach the final formulation of the theory of the cumulative process we must add a new datum, namely a schedule expressing the supply of capital, i.e., the willingness of the public to wait. First assume that there are no cash holdings and that $F_h(\rho_t)$ is a function that indicates the real (deflated) value of capital held h_t, i.e., of deposits, which the public wants to maintain when the market rate is ρ_t (the interest on deposits and that on loans are assumed equal). In other words $F_h(\rho_t)$ is a *reserve-preference* schedule for the public (when there are no cash-holdings). In this connection we do not discuss the other factors (income, etc.) on which F_h might depend.

It is assumed that the public at any time is in a position actually to make the deposits it wants to make, so that actual deposits H_t measured in current monetary units are at any time equal to $H_t = P_t F_h(\rho_t)$. Let the upward-sloping dotted curve of fig. (6.2) represent the shape of the function $F_h(\rho_t)$—the supply curve for the volume of (the deflated value of) deposits, the ordinate of the curve being ρ_t and the abscissa the value of the function $F_h(\rho_t)$. Wicksell assumes that $F_h(\rho_t)$ is an *increasing* function of the market rate ρ: "A high rate of interest encourages saving" (L. II. 113). In fig. (6.2) we have indicated the curve rather steep because h might not be very strongly influenced by ρ. The whole argument leading up to the Wicksellian cumulative process can be applied even though $F_h(\rho_t)$ is independent of ρ_t (the curve a vertical line). If there are no cash holdings, we must by (3.9) have $k_t = h_t$, so that $k_t = F_h(\rho_t)$. Any actually realized (ρ_t, k_t) point, such as 1, must therefore lie on the supply curve. In other words, having introduced this curve we are now confronted with a one-dimensional analysis of points along this curve. By (6.4) this gives

(6.5) $P_t - P_{t-\kappa}/\kappa P$

$$= F_k(\rho_{t-\kappa}) - F_h(\rho_t)/\kappa F_h(\rho_t) \qquad \text{(when } M_t = 0)$$

The right member of this formula only depends on the number κ, on the market rates at t and $t - \kappa$ and on the shapes of the two curves in fig. (6.2). If $\rho_{t-\kappa} = \rho_t$, the ratio expressed by the right member of (6.5) is obtained by drawing a horizontal line indicating the level of the market rate and expressing the horizontal distance between the points 1 and 3 as a fraction of the abscissa of point 1. This ratio divided by κ will give the actual relative rate of change of the price level over the interval between $t - \kappa$ and t.

The analysis of how the price change is determined can be further simplified. Indeed, when the time interval κ and the shapes of the two curves of fig. (6.2) are given, we may compute the ratio in question for each level ρ of the market rate (assumed the same in $t - \kappa$

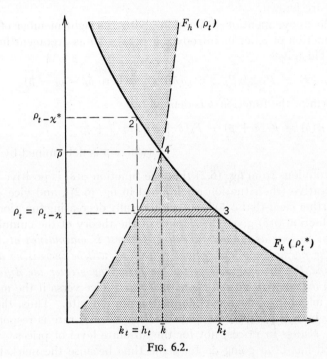

FIG. 6.2.

and t). The shape of the function of ρ thus defined is uniquely determined and may be considered only as another form of our data on the behavior of the entrepreneurs and the public.

From fig. (6.2) it is obvious that the value of this function *passes from positive to negative* when ρ passes a specific value $\bar{\rho}$ which is uniquely determined by the shapes of the two curves. This value $\bar{\rho}$ is the root of the equation

$$(6.6) \qquad F_k(\bar{\rho}) = F_h(\bar{\rho})$$

The root of this equation—in fig. (6.2) the ordinate of the point 4— is the *natural*, or if we like, the *normal* rate of interest. It is ". . . the rate of interest which would be determined by supply and demand if no use were made of money and all lending were effected in the form of real capital goods" (I. P. 102). Or shorter: "The rate of interest at which *the demand for loan capital and the supply of savings* exactly agree" (L. II. 193). Thus, while the market rate may be observed directly in the market place, the natural or normal rate is only the root of an equation. It is, however, in principle just as realistic as the market rate and may be computed when the shapes of the two curves are known.

In the above-mentioned function giving the right member of (6.5) as a function of ρ, let us introduce $\delta = (\rho - \bar{p})$ as argument instead of ρ. This gives

(6.7) $P_t - P_{t-\kappa}/\kappa P_{t-\kappa} = \phi(\delta_t)$ (where $\delta_t = \rho_t - \bar{p}$)

The form of the function ϕ is defined by

(6.8) $\phi(\delta) = F_k(\delta + \bar{p}) - F_h(\delta + \bar{p})/\kappa F_h(\delta + \bar{p})$

(where $\bar{p}$ is determined by [6.6])

It is obvious from fig. (6.2) that the function $\phi(\delta)$ is positive when δ is negative (the situation exemplified in fig. [6.2]), and vice versa. It is further clear that $\phi(\delta)$ is a monotonically decreasing function of δ. This function $\phi(\delta)$ gives the essence of the theory of the cumulative process: *So long as the market rate of interest is maintained at a level below the normal rate, the general price level will be increasing all the time, and the increase will be all the faster the greater the difference between the market rate and the normal rate.* Vice versa if the market rate is maintained at a level above the normal rate. Thus, the difference between the market rate and the normal rate is responsible for the *change* in prices, not for the absolute level of prices. If an inflation has been going on for some time because the market rate has been lower than the normal rate, the price level will be brought to a *standstill*, but will not be brought back to its previous state if the market rate is made equal to the normal rate (L. II. 196).

In my opinion this conclusion points out something of great importance in a free competitive economy. This is not the place to discuss the modifications necessary in an economy which is more or less directly controlled. Nor do I propose to discuss *how low* the market rate would have to be if it should under exceptional circumstances in a free economy (for instance in the depression of 1930 in U. S.) be able to turn a tide of deflation. It might then possibly have to be negative.

The equilibrium point where $\rho = \bar{p}$ has several interesting properties. When we speak of the "interest rate" at this point, it does not matter whether we think of the market rate ρ, the productivity rate

ρ^* or the normal rate $\bar{\rho}$ because all these concepts are here equal. And when we speak of "capital" at this point, it does not matter whether we think of the volume of capital which the entrepreneurs would like to employ $\hat{k}_t$ or that which they actually employ k_t. When the market rate deviates from $\bar{\rho}$, we may from fig. (6.2) and the preceding formula derive a great number of concrete practical interpretations on which I need not dwell here.

The argument can easily be generalized to the case where ρ_t and $\rho_{t-\kappa}$ may be different. If they are, the points 1 and 3 would be at different levels, 1 at the level $\rho_{t-\kappa}$ and 3 at the level ρ_t. For instance if $\rho_{t-\kappa}$ is below the normal rate the ensuing increase in the price level may be *somewhat* reduced by raising ρ_t—perhaps even above $\bar{\rho}$—but this compensating effect would not be very great if the F_h curve is steep. If this curve is vertical, ρ_t is without influence, only $\rho_{t-\kappa}$ will then effect the ratio (6.5).

If cash holdings exist, we let as before $F_h(\rho_t)$ denote the preference schedule for (the deflated value of) deposits and introduce a new function $F_m(\rho_t)$ expressing the preference schedule for (the deflated value of) cash holdings, so that $F_{hm}(\rho_t) = F_h(\rho_t) + F_m(\rho_t)$ will be a total reserve preference function of the public. Assuming that nothing prevents the public from maintaining at any time the cash holdings they like, we see by (3.9) that the real (deflated) value of actual loans will be $k_t = F_{hm}(\rho_t)$. Inserting this for k_t in (6.4) we get

$$(6.9) \quad P_t - P_{t-\kappa}/\kappa P_{t-\kappa} = F_k(\rho_{t-\kappa}) - F_{hm}(\rho_t)/\kappa F_{hm}(\rho_t)$$

(in the general case)

Essentially this leads to the same sort of theory as in fig. (6.2) only with a different meaning of the supply curve. In any case the essence of Wicksell's explanation of the relative price change is the *difference* between a demand and a supply magnitude.

Both these magnitudes in Wicksell's theory represent a *stock* concept. We shall now look into a circumstance which at first sight seems rather surprising, namely that the relative price change can also be expressed in several ways as a ratio whose numerator is a difference between certain *flow concepts*, which in essence are rates of change with respect to time of the nominal values of the magnitudes in the numerators of (6.5) and (6.9).

From the first expression in (3.2) we get $\dot{K}_t - \dot{k}_t P_t = k_{t-\kappa}\dot{P}_t$, hence by (3.6) $k_{t-\kappa}\dot{P}_t = \dot{K}_t - I_t$, or by (3.10) $k_{t-\kappa}\dot{P}_t = \dot{K}_t - (S_t + \dot{m}_t P_t)$. That is,

$$(6.10) \quad P_t - P_{t-\kappa}/\kappa P_{t-\kappa} = \dot{K}_t - (S_t + \dot{m}_t P_t)/K_{t-\kappa}$$

$$= \dot{K}_t - I_t/K_{t-\kappa} \quad \text{(in the general case)}$$

If the cash holdings are not identically zero, we may make a further transformation. In (6.10) we insert for I_t the expression $\dot{k}_t P_t = (\dot{h}_t + \dot{m}_t)P_t = \dot{H}_t - h_{t-\kappa}\dot{P}_t + \dot{m}_t P_t$, and carry the term with $\dot{P}_t$ over to the left. When $M_{t-\kappa} \neq 0$, this gives

$$(6.11) \quad P_t - P_{t-\kappa}/\kappa P_{t-\kappa} = \dot{K}_t - (\dot{H}_t + \dot{m}_t P_t)/K_{t-\kappa} - H_{t-\kappa}$$

$$= \dot{M}_t - \dot{m}_{t-\kappa}/M_{t-\kappa} \qquad (\text{if } M_{t-\kappa} \neq 0)$$

If there is no buffer effect, that is, if $\dot{m}_t = 0$ for all t, an obvious simplification takes place in the formulae (6.10–11). The first numerator to the right in (6.10) then becomes $\dot{K}_t - S_t$, and that in (6.11) $\dot{K}_t - \dot{H}_t$.

In (6.10–11) the relative price increase is expressed in various ways as a fraction whose numerator is the difference not between two stock concepts as in (6.9), but between two flow concepts. At the same time the factor κ in the denominator has disappeared. The numerator in the first expression to the right in (6.10) is the difference between *investment*, reckoned inclusive of appreciation on capital in use, and *saving*, reckoned exclusive of appreciation on the reserves but embracing all reserves, both deposits and cash holdings. The numerator in the last expression in (6.10) is the difference between investment, reckoned inclusive of appreciation on capital in use, and investment, reckoned exclusive of such appreciation. Similarly the numerator of the second expression in (6.11) is the difference between investment, reckoned inclusive of appreciation on capital in use, and saving, reckoned inclusive of appreciation for the deposits part and exclusive of appreciation for the cash holdings part.

In the argument leading up to (6.5)—or more generally up to (6.9)—and further to (6.10–11) we have, with Wicksell, assumed that a complete renewal of the capital stock takes place within the time interval considered, and that therefore the "general" price level P_t is also the price level of the goods of which the capital stock is made up. Compare the example (5.1). This, of course, is a strong simplification. In a further development of the analysis along these lines one would want to consider separately the value of gross annual investment J (defined as $J = I + D$, where D is annual depreciation on capital). This would lead amongst others to an explicit distinction between the price of capital goods and that of consumption goods, but I shall not follow up this line of thought here.

Any of the numerators to the right in (6.10) may be looked upon as a definition of an "inflationary credit expansion." For instance, in a case where all three terms in the first equation in (3.2) are positive, we may look upon $\dot{K}_t$ as total credit expansion or, if we like, as investment in a broad sense, including appreciation on capital. This investment we may say is financed *in part* by actual saving $\dot{k}_t P_t$ (including in this expression both S_t and $\dot{m}_t P_t$) and *in part* by the "inflationary credit expansion" $(\dot{K}_t - \dot{k}_t P_t)$. Since the latter expression is the same as $k_{t-\kappa} \dot{P}_t$ (which leads to [6.10]), we see how the inflationary credit expansion causes the price level to rise. When Wicksell speaks about "credit as between man and man" (L. II. 193), I think he simply means such credit operation that does *not* give any chance for producing an "inflationary credit expansion" because it does not pass through the banks. On the subsequent page (L. II. 194) he explains the elastic credit supply through the banks.

Since all the ratios (6.10–11) are by definition identically equal to (6.5), or more generally to (6.9), we may, if we so choose, consider the motivations expressed by the right members of (6.5) or (6.9) *equally as motivations concerning* the ratios (6.10–11), and we could, if we wanted to, develop the whole theory by starting from a consideration of the difference in the numerators in any of these ratios. Therefore, there is no contradiction between the facts expressed by (6.10–11) and Wicksell's reasoning on the stock concepts in (6.6) and (6.9). In the above analysis both aspects of the problem—that relating to the stock concepts and that relating to the flow concepts —are brought out in one coherent system of concepts and notations.

7. A DYNAMIC THEORY OF THE BUSINESS CYCLE

A cumulative process may start any time and continue for a considerable period because the normal rate may be changed for a great number of causes, technical and otherwise while ". . . the banks never alter their interest rates unless they are induced to do so by the force of outside circumstances" (L. II. 204). Such circumstances will eventually emerge for institutional and other reasons. Thus there exists a tendency for the market rate to gravitate towards the normal rate, but this tendency only comes about through the price movement. In a period of expansion the price movement will (à la banking principle) increase the need for cash holdings by the public and thereby put a strain on the banks. This conception of the price movement as the vehiculum for forcing the market rate in line with the normal rate is a major point in Wicksell's reasoning: ". . . there exists . . . no other connection between the two than the *variations in commodity prices* caused by the difference between them. And this link is elastic, just like the spiral springs often fitted between the body of a coach and the axles" (L. II. 206).

To bring out the manner in which these various factors act and react on each other during an upswing, a turning phase and the subsequent downswing, according to Wicksell's ideas, it will be well to use a simple dynamic model which admittedly disregards many concrete details, also many details discussed by Wicksell, but in return brings out clearly the main structure of the argument.

If we should incorporate (6.7) as it stands—with a finite κ—into a dynamic theory, we would be led to mixed difference and differential equations of an extremely complicated nature. Such an analysis will, however, not be necessary for the present purpose as we only aim at a rough description of the course of affairs. We simply replace the *average* rate of change of P over the interval κ, which is written in the left member of (6.7) by the *instantaneous* rate at t. Introducing for brevity $Q_t = \text{lognat } P_t$, the equation (6.7) will then take the form

$$(7.1) \qquad \dot{Q}_t = \phi(\delta_t) \qquad \text{where } \dot{Q}_t = dQ_t/dt$$

The effect of the finite number κ will still be present because it affects the form of the function ϕ in the right member of (7.1). The larger κ, the smaller ϕ. Compare (6.8). Since $\phi(\delta)$ is a monotonically decreasing function of δ and positive for $\delta < 0$, negative for $\delta > 0$, we may as a rough linear approximation put $\phi(\delta) = -\beta\delta$, where β is a positive constant, all the smaller the larger κ. This gives

$$(7.2) \qquad \dot{Q}_t = -\beta\delta_t \qquad (\beta \text{ a positive constant})$$

In the course of a cycle the attitude of entrepreneurs as well as that of the public will change. In particular it will change through *anticipations*. Wicksell considers them very explicitly. Here it will be sufficient to take account of how the *price changes* themselves affect the anticipations and thereby the behaviour and preferences of the individuals: "The upward movement of prices will in some measure 'create its own draught.' When prices have been rising steadily for some time, entrepreneurs will begin to reckon on the basis not merely of the prices already attained, but of a further rise in prices . . ." (I. P. 96). "Indeed, if the rise in prices itself gives birth to exaggerated hopes of future gains, as often happens, the demand for bank credit may far exceed the normal . . ." (L. II. 207).

We can express this by saying that the functions F_k and F_h (or more generally F_{hm}) depend explicitly on the rate of change of prices and that consequently also $\bar{\rho}$ depends on this rate. This does not necessarily mean that we must assume the form of the function ϕ to the right in (7.1)—and β in (7.2)—to depend explicitly on the price change. Indeed an important part of the anticipation effects produced by price change is already taken care of when we say that the normal rate $\bar{p}$ depends on the price change. Let us suppose that this is sufficiently accurate, so that we can still assume in the right member of (7.1) a given function ϕ of constant form and depending only on the single variable δ_t. As an example of such a situation consider the case where the entrepreneurs as well as the public are motivated by interest in real terms instead of in nominal terms. They will then consider a nominal market rate ρ as equivalent to a real-terms interest rate of $(\rho - \dot{Q})$. In other words, at the market rate ρ there would now be a demand for real capital equal to $F_k(\rho - \dot{Q})$ and a supply of real deposits equal to $F_h(\rho - \dot{Q})$, where F_k and F_h are the functions previously considered. In other words, the supply and demand curves in fig. (6.2) would simply get *an equal vertical shift* which means that the root of the new equation (6.6)—or more generally of the equation with F_{hm} instead of F_h—would simply be $\bar{p}_t = \bar{p}_0 + \dot{Q}$ where $\bar{p}_0$ is the root of the original equation. This is an example of a case where we would still have (7.1) with a function ϕ depending only on the one variable $\delta_t = \rho_t - \bar{p}_t$. More generally let us put

$$(7.3) \quad \bar{p}_t = \bar{p}_0 + \gamma \dot{Q}_t + \lambda Q_t \quad \text{(where } \bar{p}_0, \gamma, \lambda \text{ are constants)}$$

and let us assume that this transformation is sufficient to take care of the anticipations so that we still have an equation of the form (7.1). The above example shows that a value of γ in the neighbourhood of 1 might not be too unrealistic. The inclusion of a term with Q_t besides $\dot{Q}_t$ in (7.3) can be looked upon more as a means of producing a shift in phase of the time variable part of ρ_t (as one would by aggregating, with weights, a sine function and its derivative) than as a means of introducing the effect of a *partial* variation of Q_t under constant $\dot{Q}_t$.

Now for the other factors that change cyclically. In the strictly monetary part of the theory Wicksell assumes constant output and constant real capital, but in his special comments on the business cycle (L. II. 209) he very much stresses the real factors, recognizing however also the importance of money (L. II. 210). All in all I think it is correct to say that his attitude is that the essence of the problem resides more in the interplay of the factors than in any one of them taken separately.

To incorporate total output in this interplay, it will for the present purpose suffice simply to use the well-established fact that total output and prices, roughly speaking, *move together* in the cycle. We might express this by assuming

(7.4) $\dot{z}_t/z_t = \mu(\dot{P}_t/P_t)$,

i.e., $\dot{z}_t/z_t = \mu\dot{Q}_t$ (μ a positive constant)

In Wicksell's theory the velocity of circulation of money V is conceived of in such a manner that $Pz = MV$ becomes the equation of exchange. For the velocity V as thus defined it would seem reasonable in our simplified model to assume a relation similar to that of (7.4).

(7.5) $\dot{V}_t/V_t = \nu(\dot{P}_t/P_t)$,

i.e., $\dot{V}_t/V_t = \nu\dot{Q}_t$ (ν a positive constant)

Finally we may condense Wicksell's argument about the behaviour of the banking authorities into a relation between the *acceleration* of δ_t, i.e., $\ddot{\delta}_t$, and the increase in the cash holdings of the public. This increase is indeed in Wicksell's theory the main element which puts a strain on the liquidity situation of the banks and thus finally produces a motivation for an adjustment of the market rate. In the first approximation we may express it by putting

(7.6) $\ddot{\delta}_t = \Theta(\dot{M}_t/M_t)$ (Θ a positive constant)

The coefficient Θ in (7.6) must be positive because it is a positive increase in the cash holdings of the public that produces the incentive for the banks to raise the market rate.

From the above equations we get by simple substitutions

(7.7) $\ddot{\delta}_t = -\alpha^2\delta_t$ where $\alpha^2 = \beta\Theta(1 + \mu - \nu)$

The meaning of the coefficients in (7.7) is such that it is realistic to assume $1 + \mu - \nu > 0$, hence the time shape of δ_t is

(7.8) $\delta_t = -A \cos(a + \alpha t)$

the amplitude A and the phase a being determined by initial conditions which may be given conventionally.

From (7.7) is seen that the cycle is all the *shorter:*

1. The larger β, i.e., the stronger the price effect of the difference between market rate and normal rate (in particular: all the shorter the shorter the reaction period κ).

2. The larger Θ, i.e., the stronger the banking authorities react on a tightening of the liquidity situation.

3. The larger μ, i.e., the more elastic the reaction in total output is.

4. The smaller ν, i.e., the more constant the velocity of circulation of money is.

Inserting (7.8) into (7.2) we get

(7.9) $\quad \dot{Q}_t = \beta A \cos (a + \alpha t) \qquad Q_t = \beta A/\alpha \sin (a + \alpha t) + \text{const}$

Carrying this into (7.3) and again using (7.8) we get after some reduction

(7.10) $\quad \bar{p}_t = A \sqrt{\alpha^2\gamma^2 + \lambda^2} \sin (a' + \alpha t) + \text{const}$

(7.11) $\quad \rho_t = A \sqrt{\alpha^2(\gamma - 1/\beta)^2 + \lambda^2} \sin (a'' + \alpha t) + \text{const}$

The phase relations of a' and a'' to a are given by

(7.12) $\quad tg(a' - a) = \alpha\gamma/\lambda \qquad tg(a'' - a) = \alpha(\gamma - 1/\beta)/\lambda$

If by convention the square root in (7.10–11) is taken positive, the angle $(a' - a)$ is to be taken in the first quadrant and $(a'' - a)$ in the first or fourth quadrant.

These phase relations are interesting. Indeed the three time series $\bar{p}_t$, Q_t, ρ_t may be taken as characterizing the same three groups of phenomenon as the famous Harvard A, B, C-curves: A = speculation, i.e., industrial stock prices, etc., leading the movement; B = cost of living index and production, moving in the middle of the cycle; and C = interest rate, lagging behind. From the Wicksellian viewpoint $\bar{p}_t$ is undoubtedly the nearest we can come to an expression for speculation: The entrepreneurs look to $\bar{p}_t$ to find motivation for what to do next, and this determines the course of prices. On the other hand the market rate is pulled towards $\bar{p}_t$. Q_t represents the B-curves and ρ_t the C-curves. The nature of the A, B, C lags and a rough estimate of how they depend on the structural coefficients of the system are brought out by the above simplified model: from (7.12) follows that $\bar{p}_t$ must always lead over Q_t. And Q_t will lead over ρ_t when $\gamma < 1/\beta$. This inequality will certainly prevail when the movement of prices does not exert an exceptionally strong influence on the anticipations of the entrepreneurs and of the public, and the entrepreneurs are not extremely quick in demanding the new loans which a high level of the productivity rate may warrant (κ not too small). Since it is an empirical fact that the market rate will usually lag behind the price level (about one-eighth of a period), it seems reasonable to conclude that the two conditions just mentioned are fulfilled in reality.

The above extremely simplified account of the cyclical behaviour of prices, interest rate, and output proceeds on the assumption that there is no friction or similar phenomena which will eventually dampen the oscillations. In reality such dampening factors are, of course, present, and a fundamental problem arises of what is the source of energy that *maintains* the oscillations.

On this point we find what, in my opinion, is one of the most profound contributions of Wicksell: The source of energy that maintains the oscillations is to be found in the fact that the human population is *increasing* and that the technical progress does not proceed in perfect *simultaneity* with the population increase. The population increase proceeds fairly smoothly, but technical progress is distributed irregularly in time, and this very irregularity, paradoxical as it may seem, is just the explanation of why the observed, approximately regular economic fluctuations are maintained.

In a meeting of the "Nationalekonomiske Föreningen" on 27 March 1924 (where Professor Harald Westergård had delivered an address on Economic Barometers) Wicksell took part in the discussion, and the following precious words from him are conserved in print (Nationalekonomiske Föreningens Forhandlinger, 1924, p. 86. Published in *Ekonomisk Tidskrift*): "I beg to be excused for bringing in an old thought I have had, but for which I have nowhere found any response. I can't drop the idea, however, because I cannot find that it has been disproved. In my opinion there is one particular fact in the human economy which by necessity must produce a disturbance in it. It cannot proceed evenly from one year to another so long as there is an increase in population. The increase in population, which goes on all the time, does not only require that the new men get employed like the old, nor is it enough that capital accumulation goes on at the same rate as the increase in population, but it requires in addition—because the large factor nature is unchanged —that there are all the time introduced new methods of production, that is, technical progress goes on. The question then is if this technical progress can proceed according to a curve that increases as smoothly as the curve of the increasing population. It is difficult to escape the conclusion that here there must be a certain lack of harmony. The technical progress will either come a little before or a little after the increase in population. In the former case there ought to be an increase and in the latter case temporarily a decrease in the standard of living. This cause in itself is, of course, all too irregular to produce a true periodicity, even if we do not go very far in our requirements to regularity. It may be, however, that there is something else which is responsible for the periodicity, namely the structure of the human society itself. The difference between technical progress and human wants causes a jerk in the organism, and this jerk is transformed into a wave proceeding in a certain rhythm because of the structure of the human society itself. It takes for instance a certain time before one summons courage after having passed through economic disasters, etc. I have many times used the analogy that if one hits a rocking horse with a hammer, the blows may fall quite irregularly and still the movement of the rocking horse be more or less regular because of its own form."

These words, in all their brevity, give a fairly complete statement, I think, of the basic principles of the theory of erratic shocks which have come to mean so much in modern economic theory. They form so to speak the final link in the long chain of Wicksell's thoughts that lead all the way from the ultra-simple, abstract assumptions concerning the fundamentals of capital theory, through the somewhat less abstract theory of the cumulative process to a conception of the full-fledged modern society in its progressing and swinging form.

Robbins
———————— on ————————
Wicksteed

Of Philip H. Wicksteed (1844–1927) a contemporary once said that he could hold his own with more specialists, each on his own ground, than any man in England. A classical scholar, mathematician, Unitarian minister, and successful extension lecturer, Wicksteed's principal contribution to economics is his *Common Sense of Political Economy* (1910), a monumental presentation of marginal-utility economics which blends in unique fashion the thought of Jevons with that of the Austrians and the Lausanne school. Wicksteed is also remembered as the man who in a famous controversy with George Bernard Shaw was successful in turning Shaw away from the crude labor theory of value.

Lionel Robbins (1898–   ) is one of the ablest defenders of the free-market economy among contemporary economists. Robbins was educated at the University of London, where he has been teaching since 1929. He is the author of the leading treatise on economic method, *An Essay on the Nature and Significance of Economic Science* (1932). His work reflects the tradition of the Cambridge school as well as the influence of the Austrians.

PHILIP HENRY WICKSTEED, the author of the *Common Sense of Political Economy,* was one of the most remarkable intellectual figures of the half-century which has just passed. He was a leading member of the unitarian ministry. He was one of the foremost mediæval scholars of his time. He was an economist of international reputation. He was a savant who made contributions of permanent value to highly technical branches of knowledge. He was a teacher who, without vulgarisation, succeeded in making intelligible to many the main significance of the various fields of learning in which he moved. There can be few men who have so successfully combined such a wide range of intellectual pursuits with such conspicuous excellence in each of them.

The main facts of his external career are soon told.[1] The variety of Wicksteed's experience lay in the world of thought rather than in the world of action. He was born in October, 1844, at Leeds in Yorkshire. His father, Charles Wicksteed, was a unitarian minister, and on completing his undergraduate studies at University College, London, he himself decided to enter that ministry. In 1874, he was appointed successor to James Martineau at Little Portland Street Chapel, and in this position for the next twenty years he played a leading part in unitarian circles in London. But, from a very early date, his activities had begun to extend beyond this rather limited sphere. His philosophical interests led him to Dante and the Middle Ages. His interest in ethics and sociology led him to Economics. He had a genius for teaching and he became one of the most successful of the early University Extension lecturers. In 1897, his theology having become more and more unorthodox and his literary and philosophical preoccupations having become more and more pressing, he resigned his position at Little Port-

[1] For a full account of Wicksteed's life and literary achievements see C. H. Herford, *Philip Henry Wicksteed, His Life and Work.* In preparing this Introduction, I have drawn liberally on a chapter on Wicksteed's economic writings, which I contributed to that work. But I have expanded it considerably and in certain places where, in the light of further reflection or information, it seemed desirable, I have slightly altered the emphasis.

[Reprinted by permission from Robbins' introduction to Wicksteed's *Common Sense of Political Economy,* London, George Routledge and Sons, 1933.]

land Street and henceforward supported himself and his family by
lecturing and by writing.   In this period he produced the *Common
Sense of Political Economy* and many of his most important works on
the Middle Ages. He died of an obstruction in the throat on March
18th, 1927. It is characteristic of his whole life-work that until two
days before his death he was engaged in the dictation of a translation
of Aristotle.

According to Dr. Herford, Wicksteed's interest in economic problems
was first aroused by a perusal of Henry George's *Progress and Poverty*.
But, unlike so many who have been stirred by that powerful but essentially ignorant manifesto, he was moved, not merely to propaganda, but
to further inquiry. He embarked upon an examination of the meaning
of economic phenomena in the large. All his life he retained a sympathy for the idea of land nationalisation, although the reasons by
which he justified this attitude, and the practical measures he was willing to support, differed *toto cœlo* from the arguments and measures
usually associated with that cause.[2]   But the main significance of his
early acquaintance with this movement was, not that it led him to believe in the desirability of public bodies acquiring, out of the proceeds
of taxation, certain forms of landed property, but that, in the course of
the inquiries thus initiated, he was led to the study of Jevons.

By the beginning of the 'eighties, the Jevonian innovations in pure
Economics were beginning to emerge from their initial obscurity.   They
had received favourable notice abroad; and, at home, in spite of Cairnes'

---

[2] See the very cautious paper on *Land Nationalisation* read before the Political
and Economic Circle of the National Liberal Club. "It is indeed impossible,"
he wrote, "that we should follow out Henry George's delightfully simple plan of
seizing the land straight away and leaving the landlords to find their compensation
in the happier order of society in which they would find themselves living. Land
has been freely recognised as private property for generations past.   It has
changed hands backwards and forwards; and even if a great deal of it has been
stolen within the historic memory of man, the thieves have long ago sold out
under the direct sanction of the community and gone to their reward. We cannot make social reform a mere game of hunt-the-slipper, and ask the last man
who passed on the article to help us in seizing and despoiling the man to whom
he has just passed it.   And if we pay him compensation, then we must either
raise money at once out of the present generation; that is to say, we must call
upon the possessors of wealth of every kind to endow the State by a huge act of
self-renunciation—a call to which it is to be feared they will not respond—or
else we must borrow the money with which to buy out the landlords, and saddle
ourselves with a debt which may for many years absorb the whole revenue we
derive from the land." Wicksteed's hope seems to have been that land should
gradually be acquired by the State out of the proceeds of taxation and that
there might be enacted certain modifications in the law regarding property rights
in minerals discovered in the future.

hostility and Marshall's cold water, they were beginning to attract the attention of the educated public. From his first acquaintance with them, Wicksteed seems to have realised their immense force and revolutionary significance. In order to be in a position to understand them to the full, he supplemented his own mathematical training by taking lessons in the differential calculus. A copy of the second edition of the *Theory of Political Economy,* which was purchased by Wicksteed in 1882, is in the possession of the present writer; the marginal annotations on almost every page show how profoundly and extensively he had meditated on its doctrines. In the utility theory of value, which was Jevons's main contribution, he discovered a foundation on which could be built a system of economic analysis, more far-reaching in its scope and more exact in its detailed development than any that had yet been possible.[3]

Wicksteed's first contribution to theoretical Economics was an application of the Jevonian analysis to the criticism of the Marxian theory of value—an article on *Das Kapital* which appeared in the socialist journal, *To-Day,* in October, 1884. The article is not merely a criticism; it is an independent exposition of the new theory which carries it further forward and, on more than one point, adds important new corollaries. The Labour Theory is shown to be false. The cases which it appears to explain are explained more convincingly as special instances of a more comprehensive theory. "A coat is not worth eight times as much as a hat to the community because it takes eight times as long to make it. . . . The community is willing to devote eight times as long to the making of a coat because it will be worth eight times as much to it."[4] It was the first scientific criticism of Marx's theory—written years before Böhm-Bawerk's or Pareto's—and in some respects it remains the most decisive. The argument is developed with the ease and certainty of a man who is completely sure of himself, not because of any self-deception or premature synthesis, but because he has mastered the essential material. Mr. George Bernard Shaw, at that time a Marxian Socialist, made a controversial reply; but as Mr. Shaw, who, as he has subsequently related,[5] was eventually persuaded by Wicksteed that he was wrong, would be the first to admit, the significance of his reply lay not so much in what it itself contained, but rather in the fact

[3] See the preface to the *Common Sense* (pp. xxxi, xxxii) and the articles on Jevons, contributed to *Palgrave's Dictionary of Political Economy* and *The Economic Journal* (pp. 801–813 of the 1933 edition of the *Common Sense,* edited by Lionel Robbins).

[4] *Common Sense,* 1933, p. 718.

[5] *Times,* March 25th, 1927.

that it elicited further elucidations of Jevons.[6] It is, perhaps, worth noting that Wicksteed's rejoinder contains one of the earliest recognitions of the relative nature of the concepts invoked by the utility theory of value.

In 1888, Wicksteed began to venture on more constructive exposition. In that year he published his *Alphabet of Economic Science*—an attempt to restate and to elaborate positively the central guiding principles of the theory he had learnt from Jevons. The book is avowedly an introduction. Forty pages of careful mathematical illustration of the notion of limiting rates preface the attempt to apply this notion to the explanation of exchange values, and copious and minute illustrations accompany every step in the subsequent argument. In the history of theory, the book is, perhaps, chiefly notable for its introduction of the term "marginal utility"—a rendering of the Austrian *Grenz-nutzen* —as a substitute for the Jevonian "final utility," which, for obvious reasons, had tended to lead to confusions. But the book is not merely of historical interest. It still preserves considerable pedagogic value. Much as has been written on the subject with which it deals since that date—not least by Wicksteed himself—it still remains one of the best available introductions to the subject with which it deals. Other introductions may be easier to read and perhaps more entertaining to the student; but none is more calculated to give him real grasp and comprehension. In broad outline, of course, nothing can be simpler than the general notion of diminishing marginal utility. But in closer application to the problems of price determination, the notion is apt to prove elusive, at least to the non-mathematician; and more than one economist of standing has been betrayed into grotesque misconstructions. It is the great merit of Wicksteed's work that, starting from a point at which no knowledge of the calculus is assumed in his readers, he succeeds in expounding the theory with such minuteness and precision, that misconstructions of this sort should be impossible for anyone who has read it with normal attention.[7]

The book was an immediate success among economists. With one stride, Wicksteed had secured a place in that esoteric circle whose pro-

[6] "The Jevonian Criticism of Marx: A Rejoinder" (*Common Sense*, 1933, pp. 731–733).

[7] Some of the main propositions of the *Alphabet,* and of a paper subsequently contributed to the *Quarterly Journal of Economics*—"On Certain Passages in Jevons's Theory of Political Economy" (*Common Sense*, 1933, pp. 734–754)— were subsequently restated in articles for the first edition of *Palgrave's Dictionary.* See articles under the general heading "Elementary Mathematical Economics," "Dimensions of Economic Quantities," "Degree of Utility," "Final Degree of Utility" (*Common Sense*, 1933, pp. 755–765).

nouncements on pure theory command international attention. It was referred to approvingly by Edgeworth; and the great Pareto, most ferocious of critics, most uncompromising guardian of the sanctities of pure theory, gave it a prominent place in the bibliography of works on *"Economie pure"* which appeared in Part I of his *Cours*. With the general public, however, it was not such a success. The severity of its exposition and the uncompromising treatment of difficulties were inimical to its prospects of popularity. It is the one introduction to mathematical economics for non-mathematicians which really does what it promises—conduct its reader by arguments comprehensible to those with no previous knowledge of the calculus to a point at which the central propositions which involve acquaintance with that technique are thoroughly intelligible. But the non-mathematicians who have used it are still lamentably few in number.

The preface to the *Alphabet* had promised that, if it proved to meet a want among students of economics, it should be followed by similar introductions to other branches of the science. This plan seems to have been abandoned. For the next work was one which by no stretch of language could be described as introductory or simple. This was the celebrated *Essay on the Co-ordination of the Laws of Distribution,* published in 1894.[8]

By the beginning of the 'nineties, the centre of gravity in theoretical Economics had shifted from the narrow problem of commodity value to the wider problem of distribution or, as it is sometimes called, the pricing of the factors of production. Jevons and his fellow-innovators abroad had suggested a theory which, as a first approximation, might be held to elucidate the prices which could be secured for "ultimate commodities." But the further problem to decide in what proportions the prices were "distributed" between the different factors co-operating in the production of these commodities had not yet reached a satisfactory solution.[9] It was this problem which the *Essay* was designed

[8] This work has recently been republished as No. 12 in the London School of Economics Series of Reprints of Scarce Tracts in Economics and Political Science.

[9] The nature of the problem was clearly indicated by Menger in his *Grundsätze* in 1871, though the solution he suggested was subsequently shown to be unsatisfactory. Walras' equations of production in 1876 provided a solution which was valid under certain special assumptions and Wieser in his *Ursprung und Hauptgesetze des wirtschaftlichen Wertes* (1884) and *Natürlicher Wert* (1889) indicated certain indispensable conditions of a general solution. But it was not until the 'nineties that the marginal productivity theory in its general form was systematically expounded and discussed. As a solution to particular problems, of course, it is as old as Ricardo and Longfield and von Thünen.

to solve.   The solution offered was what has come to be known as the marginal productivity theory of distribution.   If the product to be distributed is P, then, to use Wicksteed's own statement, "the ratio of participation in the product on which any factor K can insist . . . will be dp/dk per unit, and its total share will be $dp/dk \cdot K$." [10]

By the time the *Essay* was published, the idea that the notion of marginal productivity might play a part in the explanation of the pricing of the factors of production was becoming widely accepted among the more advanced economists.   Just as, at the beginning of the 'seventies, the utility theory of value had occurred simultaneously to Jevons, Walras and Menger, so, at the beginning of the 'nineties, the productivity theory of distribution was "in the air" and different variants had been put forward by J. B. Clark and others.   The same cannot be said, however, of the main proposition of the *Essay;* namely, that if each factor is rewarded according to its marginal productivity, the sum of the remunerations of the separate factors will exactly exhaust the product: in other words, that the marginal productivity analysis is a *sufficient* explanation of distribution in this sense.   This bold generalisation has always been associated with the argument of the *Essay,* and it is true to say that, even at the present day, it remains the subject of lively controversy.[11]   In later years, Wicksteed himself, as the result of criticism by Edgeworth and Pareto, became dissatisfied with his own demonstration, declared it to have been a premature synthesis and, in the *Common Sense of Political Economy,* announced it to be finally withdrawn.   The grounds of his dissatisfaction, however, were technical and mathematical; it would be wrong to suppose—as has sometimes been the case—that he renounced the productivity analysis in general. Certainly the solution offered in its place in the *Common Sense of Political Economy* does not differ so noticeably from that of the *Essay* as to suggest that the earlier version was to be regarded as wholly mis-

[10] *Op. cit.,* p. 9.

[11] See Hicks, *The Theory of Wages,* Mathematical Appendix (*i*) (pp. 233–239), and also "Marginal Productivity and the Principle of Variation," *Economica,* Feb., 1932, pp. 79–89.   In these essays, it seems to me that Mr. Hicks has gone a long way towards a final resolution of this long-debated problem.   It is significant that, in the syllabus of a course of lectures given in 1905 (pp. 849–862, *Common Sense,* 1933), *i.e. after* the appearance of the criticisms by Pareto and Edgeworth, to which he refers in his apparent recantation (see p. 373n., *Common Sense,* 1933), Wicksteed continues to use the general formula of the *Essay.*   This is, surely, strong presumptive evidence that Wicksteed did not regard these criticisms as invalidating the general marginal productivity theory and that his acknowledgment that the solution was "erroneous" merely referred to the form in which the mathematical argument had been developed.

leading. In fact, as Mr. Hicks has recently pointed out, a very trifling modification is all that is needed to make the theorem logically watertight. Wicksteed's proposition was not untrue; the only criticism to which it is exposed is that its demonstration was incomplete. It was not so exhaustive as its author at first supposed. This is not a very grave defect in a new theory: we are none of us so near the goal as we believe ourselves to be.

For sixteen years after the appearance of the *Essay,* Wicksteed published little on economic theory. A couple of reviews in the *Economic Journal*—on Jevons's *Principles* in 1905 and on Pareto's *Manual* in 1906—constitute the sum of his published utterances. But all this time, his mind was revolving the terms of a synthesis wider than anything he had hitherto attempted, and in 1910 he published his *magnum opus* in this field—the *Common Sense of Political Economy.*

It is not easy in a short space to give an adequate idea of this work. The title conveys less than nothing; indeed, never was a work of this kind more unfortunately named. It is not "common sense" in the ordinary sense of the term, and it is not *political* economy. It is, on the contrary, the most exhaustive non-mathematical exposition of the technical and philosophical complications of the so-called *marginal* theory of pure Economics, which has appeared in any language. The chief work with which it can be compared in this respect is Wieser's *Theorie der Gesellschaftlichen Wirtschaft;* but even Wieser, like Marshall and other authors of "systems," really covers a much wider area and does not enter into nearly the same degree of detail.[12]

The aim of the book was twofold. On the one hand, it attempted a systematic exposition of the utility theory of value such that any reader commencing from no previous knowledge of economic analysis would be in a position to achieve "an intimate comprehension of the commercial and industrial world." On the other, it involved an attempt to "convince professed students of Political Economy that any special or unusual features in the system thus constructed are not to be regarded as daring innovations or as heresies, but are already strictly involved and often explicitly recognised in the best economic thought and teaching of recent years."[13] As usual, Wicksteed made no claims to originality. Indeed, he refrained from making claims which might

---

[12] Another work which may be mentioned in this connection is Sulzer, *Die wirtschaftlichen Grundgesetze* (Zürich, 1895). This remarkable book seems almost wholly to have escaped attention but, in many respects, it ranks with Wicksteed's as the forerunner of a school of thought which has come into prominence only in the last few years.

[13] See *Common Sense,* 1933, p. 2.

very well have been made. But he did definitely hope that his work
would compel recognition of the degree to which Economics had been
changed by the discussions of the last forty years.

"I believe," he said, "that the reconstruction contemplated by Jevons has
been carried to a far more advanced point than is generally realised even
by those who are themselves accomplishing it. Adhesion to the traditional
terminology, methods of arrangement and classification, has disguised the
revolution that has taken place. The new temple, so to speak, has been
built up behind the old walls, and the old shell has been so piously preserved and respected that the very builders have often supposed themselves
to be merely repairing and strengthening the ancient works, and are hardly
aware of the extent to which they have raised an independent edifice. I
shall try to show in this book that the time has come for a frank recognition
of these facts." [14]

The book is divided into three parts. In the first comes a systematic
exposition of the marginal analysis. This is introduced by an extensive
analysis of the economics of household administration, in which the
principles of what the Germans call *Naturalwirtschaft* are exhaustively
examined. This is followed by a minute explanation of the notions of
margins and limiting rates of expenditure, unparalleled in the whole
literature of modern economic theory for clarity and precision. "Nowhere," said the late Professor Allyn Young in reviewing the book for
the *American Economic Review,* "is there so clear a (non-mathematical) explanation of the meaning of marginal significance, or so effective
a refutation of those writers who have thought that the existence of
indivisible goods puts insurmountable obstacles in the way of the marginal analysis." [15] The analysis then opens out to include the phenomena of money and exchange. The implications of the Economic
Nexus in the *Verkehrswirtschaft* are expounded. Markets, Earnings,
Interest, are systematically examined and, finally, at a great height, the
interrelations of distribution and cost of production are made the basis
for an exhibition of the concept of economic equilibrium in its widest
possible sense.

The second part of the book, which is described as "Excursive and
Critical," consists of a series of special studies of more technical problems of analysis. The notions of the diagrammatic representations of
margins and total utility are investigated with a precision and minuteness which provides a significant contrast to the cursory treatment usually afforded these matters even in respectable textbooks. There follow

[14] *Common Sense,* 1933, p. 2.
[15] *American Economic Review,* 1911, pp. 78–80.

special studies of the supply curve and markets, and an examination of the concepts of increasing and diminishing returns and their relation to the theory of rent, in which some of the subsidiary propositions of the *Essay on the Co-ordination of the Laws of Distribution* are expounded and developed. Finally, in Part Three, the general system of analysis elaborated in the earlier chapters is applied to the elucidation of certain practical problems—Housing, Unemployment, Redistribution of Wealth, Taxation, Land Nationalisation, Socialism, and so on. The treatment here is less detailed, more discursive than before, the Lucretian passage which prefaces this part of the book suggesting perfectly its intention:

> But this faint spoor suffices for an alert mind: so that thou thyself may'st come at all the rest. For just as hounds, when once they have found the true track, full often search out with their nostrils the lair of the mountain-roaming quarry, hidden though it be with foliage, even so may'st thou, in such things as these, see for thyself one thing after another, work thyself into the secret hiding-places and thence drag out the truth.

The book was the culmination of Wicksteed's life work in this branch of knowledge. Into it he poured all the subtlety and persuasiveness, all the literary charm, of which he was capable. It is a masterpiece of systematic exposition. It is the most complete statement of the implicit philosophy of economic analysis which has been published in our day. It has sometimes been complained that it is too long, that in places the detail of the argument becomes tiring; but, in fact, it is just this exhaustiveness which constitutes one of its main recommendations as a treatise. It explains small points and it refuses to gloss over difficulties. It is true that it makes no concessions to the kind of reader who has been brought up on the modern "Outline." You cannot "get the heart out" of Wicksteed in a couple of hours' reading. It is a work which must be read slowly, conned over diligently—in short, treated with the respect with which any work of careful intellectual architecture must be treated if it is to yield the enlightenment and æsthetic satisfaction which it is capable of yielding. Walter Pater once said very truly that in all great art there is something which small minds find insipid. A failure to sit through the *Common Sense* is a pretty sure sign of intellectual smallness.

The *Common Sense* was the last of Wicksteed's books on Economics. But in 1913 he was elected President of Section F of the British Association and he chose for the subject of his presidential address "The Scope and Method of Political Economy in the Light of the 'Marginal' Theory of Value and Distribution." This address is probably the best statement in short compass of Wicksteed's main contribution to Economic Science.[16]   There is nothing in it which is not already stated in the *Common Sense*.   But by very reason of the necessity for concision the outline is clearer, the contrasts more vividly pointed.   There has never been a better explanation of the methodological significance of the subjective theory of value, nor a more uncompromising rejection of much that still passes for orthodox Economics.   It is nearly twenty years since Wicksteed demonstrated to the British Association the true nature of the supply curve.   To-day the majority of economists would accept his demonstration as irrefutable.   Yet since the war, there has appeared a great mass of literature on the cost question which, for all the awareness it displays of the essential problem at issue, might for the most part have been the same if Wicksteed had never written.[17]   None the less, few things can be more certain than that until the propositions which Wicksteed stressed in this paper are incorporated into the general body of cost analysis, the whole controversy will continue to present an appearance of paradox and unreality—an intellectual backwater, full no doubt of strange fish and queer animalculæ, but lacking that relation to the main stream of general equilibrium theory which alone can give it real significance.[18]

Wicksteed's place in the history of economic thought is beside the place occupied by Jevons and the Austrians.   The main stream of eco-

[16] Towards the end of his life, Wicksteed made yet one further statement of his views in the short article on Final Utility in the second edition of *Palgrave's Dictionary* (see *Common Sense*, 1933, pp. 797–800).   The propositions are so compressed and general that the nuances of expression may well escape notice.   But to readers already acquainted with the main body of Wicksteed's work it is full of interesting suggestions.

[17] The conspicuous exception is Knight, "Some Fallacies in the Interpretation of Social Cost" (*Quarterly Journal of Economics,* 1924, pp. 582 *et seq.*).   It is no accident that Professor Knight is able at once to steer through a great fog of unreality to the essential solution of the problem under discussion.

[18] It is, perhaps, worth stressing the point that the objection here implied is not to partial equilibrium analysis as such, but to partial equilibrium analysis unrelated to the general theory of equilibrium.   It may be quite true that the general theory of equilibrium by itself is often too abstract and general for useful application.   But it is equally true—and it is a thing which has often been forgotten in recent discussions—that partial equilibrium analysis unaccompanied by a continual awareness of the propositions of general equilibrium theory is almost certain to be misleading.   It may be asserted without fear of serious contradiction that most of the confusion in the recent cost controversy has sprung from the attempt to make the constructions of partial equilibrium analysis carry more than they can legitimately bear.   Cp. Knight, "A Suggestion for Simplifying the Statement of the General Theory of Price," *Journal of Political Economy,* Vol. XXXVI, pp. 353–370.

nomic speculation in this country in the last forty years has come *via* Marshall from the classics. This is not to say that the work which derives from Marshall any longer has any very intimate relation with the work of Ricardo and his contemporaries. Quite the contrary, indeed; a very good case could be made out for the view that, with all their differences, the systems which seem to make the clearer break with the past are, in fact, nearer in spirit to the classical system than those which have preserved more closely the classical terminology and apparatus. The judgment relates merely to origins. In intention at any rate Marshall's position was essentially revisionist. He came not to destroy, but—as he thought—to fulfil the work of the classics. Wicksteed, on the other hand, was one of those who, with Jevons and Menger, thought that "able but wrong-headed man David Ricardo" had "shunted the car of Economic Science on to a wrong line, a line on which it was further urged towards confusion by his equally able and wrong-headed admirer John Stuart Mill"; and that complete reconstruction was necessary. He was not a revisionist, but a revolutionary. I have cited already the passage from the preface to the *Common Sense* in which he says that the time has come to recognise that modern Economics is not a reconstruction of the old, but a new and independent edifice. The same point of view is very strongly presented in his review of Sir Sydney Chapman's *Political Economy*.[19]

The difference is to some extent one of emphasis and conception of theory rather than in the substance of theory itself. But, none the less, it modifies materially the presentation of theory by the representatives of the Schools concerned. In spite of considerable agreement on many analytical principles, there is a world of difference between the "look" of Marshall's *Principles* and Wicksteed's *Common Sense of Political Economy* or Wieser's *Theorie der Gesellschaftlichen Wirtschaft*. The difference shows itself most clearly, perhaps, in the use made of the fundamental notion of Marginal Utility. For Jevons, Menger and their followers the discovery of the Concept of Marginal Utility meant essentially the revolutionising of the main corpus of analytical economics. In their hands the concept of marginal utility became an instrument whereby the whole statement of the theory of economic equilibrium was altered. The innovation started in the sphere of the theory of exchange. But it was speedily developed and applied to the theories of production and distribution. From 1871 to the present day, the whole development of Economics in these quarters has been a steady

[19] *Common Sense*, 1933, pp. 818–822.

process of refinement and extension of the application of this concept.[20] This was not so for Marshall; still less for his followers. For Marshall and the Marshallians, marginal utility plays a minor part in the main body of equilibrium theory. It is an embellishment to the theory of the market. If one wants to explain why the demand curve slopes downwards, well, the Law of Diminishing Marginal Utility may be invoked, if you like that sort of thing. It is a ritual to be repeated before the real performance commences. The main substance of Marshall's theory of value and distribution relates to costs—in the first instance to money costs, but in the last analysis to a conception of real costs coming directly from Adam Smith and Ricardo.[21] The Law of Diminishing Marginal Utility becomes of significance for Marshall and his followers only when they pass from considerations of equilibrium to considerations of welfare. It is in the shadow world of consumers' surplus and the constructions based upon that concept that marginal utility assumes for them its main significance. The law is essentially a tool, not of equilibrium analysis, but of "Welfare Economics." [22]

Such differences are, perhaps, in part, differences of the focus of attention. But there can be little doubt that behind them lie certain differences in the central core of theory. This is especially noticeable in the theory of costs. As is well known, Marshall and (up to a recent date) most of his followers insisted that costs, in the last analysis, were something real and absolute—a conception independent of utility. Wicksteed and the Austrians, on the other hand, denied that they were anything but foregone alternatives. Wieser's Law of Costs becomes— as Wicksteed so magnificently demonstrated—the key-stone, as it were,

[20] See the article, "Grenznutzen," by Dr. P. Rosenstein-Rodan, in the *Handwörterbuch der Staatswissenschaften,* 4 aufl.

[21] It can legitimately be argued, I think, that, in this respect, Marshall was more Ricardian than Ricardo. By the end of his life, Ricardo was certainly far away from a real cost theory of value. It is an interesting circumstance that, in spite of Marshall's continual reiteration of the significance of the time factor, he makes little or no attempt to develop Ricardo's path-breaking treatment of this question (see *e.g.* the Letters to McCulloch, p. 71). For developments of this sort, we have to go not to Marshall, but to Jevons, to Böhm-Bawerk, and to Wicksell.

[22] It is interesting to observe that the assumption of inter-personal comparisons of wants and desires, on which "Welfare Economics" is based, was decisively rejected by Wicksteed as early as 1888. "There is another truth which must never be lost sight of on peril of a total misconception of all the results we may arrive at in our investigations; and that is that by no possibility can desires or wants, even for one and the same thing, which exist in *different minds* be measured against one another or reduced to a common measure" (*Alphabet of Economic Science,* p. 68).

of the whole edifice of the Subjective Theory of Value.[23] No doubt, in part, this difference of theory was due to a difference of ultimate assumptions concerning the nature of the conditions of economic equilibrium.[24] But in part it was due to an ultimate difference of opinion concerning what psychological comparisons were *relevant* in the determination of any equilibrium. So far as this was the case, time has decided in favour of the revolutionaries. The conception of real costs as displaced alternatives is now accepted by the majority of theoretical economists, but, as I have suggested already, we are still a long way from making it part and parcel of our daily speculations on those problems to which it is most relevant.

The influences which shaped Wicksteed's thought were not confined to Jevons and the earlier Austrians. Himself no mean exponent of the mathematical method, he was deeply influenced by the work of those who carried the application of mathematical methods furthest—by the work of Walras and Pareto. Reviewing the *Manual* of the latter in 1905,[25] he hailed it as "a work which is likely to modify and stimulate economic thought to an extent quite disproportionate to the number of its readers. It will probably be understood by few, but everyone who understands it will be influenced by it." The *Common Sense of Political Economy,* written in the years immediately following this review, bears witness everywhere to the extent to which Wicksteed himself had been affected. It is interesting in this respect to compare the theory of the *Common Sense* with the theory of the *Alphabet.* Superficially, the two theories are the same; and no doubt they do belong to the same family. But a closer inspection will reveal important points of difference. The *Alphabet* starts from the idea of the rate at which total utility is increasing; the *Common Sense* from the positions on the relative scale of preferences which marginal units of different commodities occupy. In the *Alphabet,* in spite of the earlier recognition of the relativity of the utility concept, utility is treated as if it were something absolute and measurable. In the *Common Sense,* the sole relevance of *relative* utility is emphasised and the idea of *measurability* tends to give place to the idea of *order.* In the *Alphabet,* the analysis is definitely "one-thing-at-a-time." In the *Common Sense,* the emphasis on the com-

---

[23] *Common Sense,* 1933, pp. 359 ff. See also Mayer, "Friedrich Wieser, Zum Gedächtnis" (*Zeitschrift für Volkswirtschaft und Sozialpolitik,* N.F., Bd. 5, p. 636).

[24] I have tried to exhibit this difference of assumption between Marshall and the Austrians elsewhere. See my article "On a Certain Ambiguity in the Conception of Stationary Equilibrium" (*Economic Journal,* 1930, pp. 194–214).

[25] *Common Sense,* 1933, pp. 814–818.

plementarity of utilities and the simultaneity of the determination of
all values is continuous. And so one could go on. There is no feature
of the presentation which does not bear evidence of reformulation and
improvement.

In all this, the influence of Pareto is very strongly discernible. But
it would be a great mistake to regard Wicksteed as a mere expositor of
other people's theories. He was much more than that. He was an
independent and original thinker. He adopted many of the constructions of Pareto but, as with the other theories by which he was influenced, he developed them further and combined them into a system
which was essentially his own. Wicksteed's approach is by no means
the same as Pareto's. His analysis of the conditions of equilibrium is
much less an end in itself, much more a tool with which to explain the
tendencies of any given situation. He was much more concerned with
economic phenomena as a process in time, much less with its momentary end-products. In all this, he is to be regarded not so much as a
follower of Pareto, but as a forerunner of another line of development.
The closest affinities to the doctrines of the *Common Sense* are to be
found not in the work of Zawadski, Moret or Pietri Tonelli but in the
work of Mayer, Schönfeld, and Rosenstein-Rodan.

Apart, however, from his services as exponent of the general theory
of equilibrium, there are certain particular contributions for which
Wicksteed will always be remembered. I have discussed already his
studies in the theory of distribution. Whatever the ultimate decision
as to the truth or falsehood of the particular theorem which he advanced with regard to the adequacy of the productivity analysis, there
can be no doubt that economists owe him a high debt of gratitude for
having focussed attention on this aspect of the problem. It is not
always those who are finally right who make the greatest contribution
to progress.

A second contribution which must always be associated with his
name is his famous demonstration of the reversibility of the market
supply curve. The general proposition that the reservation prices of
sellers are, in the ultimate analysis, demands, was one which he continually reiterated with varying shades of emphasis. "What about the
supply price that usually figures as a determinant of price, co-ordinate
with the demand curve?" he asked in the address to the British Association in 1913, to which I have already alluded.

I say it boldly and baldly: there is no such thing. When we are speaking
of a marketable commodity, what is usually called the supply curve is, in

reality, the demand curve of those who possess the commodity, for it shows the exact place which every successive unit of the commodity occupies in their relative scale of estimation. The so-called supply curve is, therefore, simply a part of the total demand curve. . . . The separating out of this portion of the demand curve and reversing it in the diagram is a process which has its meaning and its legitimate function . . . but is wholly irrelevant to the determination of price.[26]

It is safe to say that no one who has followed through his beautiful diagrammatic analysis of this proposition, and realised its wider implication that *all* psychological variables can be exhibited as phenomena of demand acting on fixed stocks—either of products or factors or time or human capacity—will deny that the whole of the analysis of economic equilibrium has received thereby a transforming elucidation.

Finally, in the realm of technical contributions, we must notice his analysis of the relation between the marginal productivity theory of distribution and the Ricardian theory of rent. The discovery that the rent analysis of the classics is the productivity analysis with, as Edgeworth put it, the relation between dose and patient reversed, was, of course, not peculiar to Wicksteed. By one of those singular coincidences which seem to characterise the progress of our science, the idea seems to have occurred almost simultaneously to at least three writers in the early 'nineties—Wicksteed himself, J. B. Clark, and the much-neglected H. M. Thompson, author of *The Theory of Wages*.[27] But of the demonstrations of this proposition, Wicksteed's was incomparably the most precise and convincing; and, at the present day, a teacher who wishes to convince some recalcitrant student of the truth of this doctrine cannot do better than refer him to the classic formulation which is to be found in Book II, Chapters V and VI, of the *Common Sense of Political Economy*.[28]

But apart from these technical contributions and far transcending them in general importance come Wicksteed's elucidations of the methodological implications of the subjective theory of value—particularly those discussions of what he called the "economic relationship,"

[26] For a very elegant demonstration of this last possibility in relation to the problem of hours of labour, see Wicksell, *Vorlesungen*, Bd. I, p. 159.

[27] See *Co-ordination of the Laws of Distribution*, pp. 18–20; J. B. Clark, "Distribution as Determined by a Law of Rent," *Quarterly Journal of Economics*, 1891, pp. 289 *et seq.;* Thompson, *The Theory of Wages*, Chapter IV, *passim.*

[28] *Common Sense*, 1933, pp. 527–574. See also the article from *Palgrave's Dictionary of Political Economy*—"Economics and Psychology" (*Common Sense*, 1933, pp. 766–771).

which are to be found in that chapter of the *Common Sense* entitled "Business and the Economic Nexus." [29]   This, if I read him correctly, was the feature of his work to which he himself attached greatest importance, and it is for this above all that he deserves to be remembered.   Before Wicksteed wrote, it was still possible for intelligent men to give countenance to the belief that the whole structure of Economics depends upon the assumption of a world of economic men, each actuated by egocentric or hedonistic motives.   For anyone who has read the *Common Sense,* the expression of such a view is no longer consistent with intellectual honesty.   Wicksteed shattered this misconception once and for all.   Yet, curiously enough, no aspect of his thought has been more completely neglected.   The reason is not far to seek. In England, at any rate, the average economist, secure in the tradition of an analysis which has proved its worth in practice, is apt to be impatient of inquiries which linger on implications and modes of conception.   The man in the street, egged on by the inexpert practitioners of other branches of the social sciences, may reproach him for an ingrained materialism and an assumption of a simplicity of motive unwarranted by the complexity of the situation to be analysed.   But such reproaches leave him indifferent.   He knows in his bones that they are unjust.   He knows that, unlike his traducers, he is in possession of analytical instruments which do genuinely elucidate the understanding of complicated social relationships, and he regards with impatience those semi-metaphysical inquiries which harp on ultimate assumptions. The instinct, no doubt, is a healthy one and has saved us from the torrents of logomachy which at times have threatened entirely to submerge economic analysis elsewhere.   None the less, not all inquiries of this sort are sterile, and it may be contended, I think, that those which have been based on the subjective theory of value [30] have thrown the whole corpus of economic science into an entirely new light—a light in which Economics is seen to be a discussion not of the nature of certain *kinds* of behaviour arbitrarily separated off from all others, but of a certain *aspect* of behaviour viewed as a whole.   It is perhaps too early to evaluate the individual contributions to this stream of thought, for the movement is by no means exhausted, but when its final history comes to be written, I think it will be found that Wicksteed's exhaustive

[29] *Common Sense,* 1933, pp. 158–211.

[30] See especially Mises, "Vom Weg der subjektivistischen Wertlehre" (*Schriften des Vereins für Sozialpolitik,* 183/1, pp. 76–93) and "Soziologie und Geschichte" (*Archiv für Sozialwissenschaft und Sozialpolitik,* Bd. 61, pp. 465–512); also Strigl, *Die ökonomischen Kategorien und die Organisation der Wirtschaft.*

examination of the "economic relationship," and his insistence that there can be no logical dividing line between the operations of the market and other forms of rational action, are by no means among the least important or the least original.[31]

[31] In my *Essay on the Nature and Significance of Economic Science* I have endeavoured to bring out some of the implications of this part of Wicksteed's teaching.

Viner

on

Marshall

Alfred Marshall (1842–1924), the founder of the Cambridge school of neoclassical economics, held the chair of political economy at Cambridge from 1885 to 1908, succeeding the blind economist Henry Fawcett, a follower of Mill. Marshall, in turn, was succeeded by his pupil, A. C. Pigou. Pigou retired in 1943, and this distinguished chair is now held by Dennis H. Robertson, the leading exponent of the Cambridge school in the field of monetary theory.

Alfred Marshall is best known for his *Principles of Economics* (1890). Since the publication of this work, no other original book in economics has encompassed the entire theoretical thought of its time. Marshall reportedly developed marginal analysis before Jevons' *Principles* and independently of him, but an overly cautious attitude, the opposite of that of Jevons, made him postpone the publication of his findings.

Marshall was a master of partial-equilibrium analysis, with demand and supply supplemented by many new tools of analysis. His profound influence is in part due to his sense of continuity, which made him de-emphasize the novelty of his own contributions, linking them with the thought of the classics. Correspondingly, Marshall's theory of value embraces both cost and utility as explanatory principles. Again, his method was mathematical in substance, but he repeatedly warned against methodological abuses which would turn the tool into an end in itself.

(On Viner, see above, p. 201.)

MALTHUS ONCE said, with reference to Senior's lectures on population, that "it was among the disadvantages of public lectures, that the lecturer sometimes thought he was called upon to say something new, where there was nothing new to be said." Malthus, it may be ventured, would have been willing to concede that he had contributed substantially to placing Senior in that position by having himself previously said most of what was worth saying about population. Asked to speak to the Association on Marshall as part of the celebration of the fiftieth anniversary of the publication of his *Principles,* I find myself very much in the position Malthus thought Senior was in.

My own plight I attribute mainly to four factors: First, so much of what knowledge I may have about Marshall has been gained through the years from the late Dr. Taussig's writings, teaching, and conversation that I can no longer separate what I have learned for myself from what I have derived from him. Secondly, the fifty years and more of published commentary on Marshall's *Principles* have made it difficult to find fresh cause for praise or complaint. Third, the admirable *Memorials of Alfred Marshall,* 1925, edited by Pigou, and containing penetrating and enlightening contributions by Keynes, Edgeworth, and Pigou on the relation of Marshall's personality and social philosophy to his economics, has so thoroughly exploited the biographical data available even to insiders that not much scope is left to those who had never seen nor heard Marshall in the flesh nor had an opportunity to draw on the rich fund of oral Cambridge tradition. What would be ordinarily a substitute, published letters, are also unavailable except for the few published in the *Memorials.* Finally, Mr. Schumpeter has kindly made available to me in advance a generous-sized abstract of his paper on the pure theory aspects of Marshall's *Principles,* with the consequence that I cannot easily, without resort to plagiarism, fill out what I can find to say within my own assignment by encroachment on his.

If, then, what I say should sound unduly familiar and commonplace, solace must be sought in the also familiar and commonplace reflection that on the subject of Marshall what is new is highly unlikely at this

[Reprinted by permission from *American Economic Review,* Vol. 31, No. 2, June 1941.]

late date also to be both true and significant. I will deal in turn with the influence on Marshall's economics of his political views, of his moral philosophy, and of some of his methodological predilections.

I

Marshall was in many respects a highly representative late Victorian intellectual. He was a Victorian "liberal" in his general orientation toward social problems, as probably also in the narrower partisan sense. English economics was throughout the nineteenth century intimately bound up with English politics, and throughout the century English economists had, probably without any important exception, political affiliations or preferences which influenced and were influenced by their economic doctrines. It is possible to ascertain with some degree of assurance the political affiliations of the earlier economists from their economic writings, but this requires an examination of their position with respect to issues which, though of minor importance for economics, sharply divided the various political groupings. On the major economic issues of the nineteenth century which were also important political issues, notably, foreign trade policy, the treatment of the poor, and the economic rôle of the state, there was much overlapping of position as between the political parties, at least during the first half of the century. By the middle of the century all the political parties as parties had accepted, or had ceased to contest, the free trade doctrine which stemmed from Adam Smith and which all the major economists except Malthus enthusiastically supported. By the late 1830's there was opposition only from one wing of the Tories and from the extreme radicals to the principle of confining relief to the able-bodied poor on the basis of "less eligibility"; that is, of granting it only in such unattractive form that the incentives to industry, thrift, and prudential control of the birthrate should not be undermined, a principle developed with almost complete agreement by the classical economists on the strength of Smithian individualism, Benthamite-Malthusian population theory, and the Malthusian-Ricardian law of diminishing returns, plus in all probability a large dose of unconscious puritanism. The period from 1800 to 1850 was, whatever party was in power, fairly consistently a period of piecemeal legislative repeal, item by item, of the mass of legislation restrictive of domestic freedom of enterprise which had survived on the statute books from the mercantilist period, and this trend also was aided and abetted by all the classical economists from the Benthamites, at one extreme, to the most conservative Whigs, like Malthus and Senior, at the other.

On the major political issues of the first half of the century, therefore, while there might be a question as to whether the classical economists were determining the historical trend, or merely riding it, it is clear that they were not fighting it. It can now be seen, if it was not then possible to do so, that what conflict there then was between legislators and economists turned for the most part on the pace, and not on the general direction, of the legislative activity.

Even the Tory party, whose basic political philosophy seemed to be that all institutions were evil when new and irreproachable when aged, was moving, though slowly, reluctantly, and with misgivings and internal dissension, on the paths mapped out for it by the anti-Tory economists. It is in fact a paradox in the history of the relations of economics and politics in early nineteenth century England that the one political movement of importance which the historians most unitedly ascribe to the influence of the economists, the advocacy of extreme *laissez-faire* by the Manchester School, was the only one which the leading economists felt impelled expressly to denounce as going counter to, or at least beyond, the teachings of political economy. In so far as the dogmatic *laissez-faire* position of the Manchester School found in its own day, aside from the tariff question, any adherents among the ranks of economists, these were Continental or American economists. John Stuart Mill, Senior, Cairnes, McCulloch, Torrens, Longfield, the only English economists of note of the period, all sharply dissociated themselves from some at least of the doctrines of the Manchester School and denied its pretensions to support from the "principles of political economy." The classical economists did espouse *laissez-faire,* but a *laissez-faire* avowedly subject to qualification and requiring specific justification in each case of potential application.

The Manchester School, in any case, had but a brief period of power. The growing information—and exaggeration—about working and living conditions in the factory towns, the steadily increasing political power of the working classes even under the restricted suffrage of the Reform Act of 1832, and the widespread humanitarian reaction against the doctrine of governmental impotence to remedy unmerited distress, made support of governmental inaction as a policy increasingly dangerous politically to any party which committed itself too strongly to it. With the establishment by the second Reform Act of 1867 of very nearly complete adult male suffrage, it became necessary for both the aristocratic Conservative or Tory party and the by-now predominantly middle-class Liberal party, if either were to gain or retain power as against the other, and if a third and "subversive" working-class party, as strong as or stronger than they, was not to come into being, to woo the working classes by support of a policy of wider governmental activity in relief of distress and poverty. Social reform through legislation thereafter became respectable political doctrine for both parties, and reform legislation in fact obtained active support alternately or simultaneously from both major parties during the remainder of the century.

During the period of Marshall's youth, John Stuart Mill was the only economist of great public eminence, and Mill, who in his own youth had been one of the original Benthamites, had in his intellectual development absorbed something from almost every major humanitarian and utopian current of his time while managing substantially to retain most of the form and much of the substance of the sterner doctrines of the Bentham-James Mill-Ricardo circle under whose discipline he had been brought up to a too-precocious maturity. With his too-catholic blending of the dour individualism and the unrelenting *a priori* political democracy of the classical school, the utopianism of the Owenites and the St. Simonians, the patriarchal humanitarianism of Wordsworth and Coleridge, and the new misgivings as to the workings of political democracy and social equalitarianism in actual practice as revealed in the United States, John Stuart Mill was the connecting link with respect to political presuppositions for Marshall, as for many later economists in England (and also in the United States), between the classical school of the 1820's and the late-Victorian neoclassical economics. It is substantially true that from the 1870's on all English economic *theorists* of any note were, although with varying degrees of certitude and enthusiasm, political liberals of the John Stuart Mill type. It incidentally seems also to be substantially true that all the English economic *historians* of note were conservative, imperialist, anti-democratic, in their political tendencies, or else went far beyond the liberals in their advocacy of radical social and economic reforms.

The data available on Marshall's political opinions are scanty and scattered. They suffice, however, to support the following summary of the substance and content of his political liberalism as being probably correct as far as it goes:

(1) Marshall was a believer in political democracy, meaning by it essentially universal (male) suffrage, decisions reached by free discussion and by majority vote, and an electorate educated at public expense. In the Benthamite tradition, he held these beliefs not on natural rights grounds, but on the utilitarian ground that they were essential for good government.

(2) Marshall was an individualist in most of the many senses of the term. His ultimate criterion for appraising the social value of any policy was the nature of its probable impact upon the character and well-being of *individuals*. His appraisals of policies and trends were always in terms of what they did for individuals, singly or in groups, and never in terms of their contribution to the prestige or power of an idealized "state" distinguishable from its people. His hope for social progress rested primarily on the capacity for industry, thrift, enterprise, voluntary coöperation, and "economic chivalry," of enlightened individuals, and he had limited, though some, faith in the possibilities of betterment through restrictive or coercive legislation or through the direct exercise of governmental enterprise in the economic field.

(3) Marshall also was essentially a political equalitarian in the Bentham-J. S. Mill sense. He not only wished every (male) adult to count as one and only as one in the machinery of political democracy, but he believed, with the English classical school, that in so far as there were significant differences in the capacities and the economic status of the different social classes these class differences were for the most part not due to biological differences in innate capacity or character as between individuals but were due instead to environmental differences, to inequality of opportunity: "the poverty of the poor [was] the chief cause of that weakness and inefficiency which are the cause of their poverty." [1]

(4) Basically, Marshall's political doctrines carried the hallmark also of Victorian complacency and gentility. While he recognized the problem of poverty as a major one, he never revealed any doubt that it could be substantially resolved within the limits of British parliamentary democracy and of a free enterprise economy. He was impatient alike with theories of economic history which treated economic and social progress as if it was in any sense inevitable or automatic, and with pessimistic theories which treated it as impossible, or as impossible without revolutionary political changes. He was confident that if only there were sufficient goodwill ("economic chivalry") and economic understanding substantial progress would in fact occur, and he evidently had faith in the effectiveness of sound moral preaching to produce the goodwill and of sound Cambridge economics to produce the understanding. The progress he sought, moreover, was not to be merely a matter of more goods, but of access to and liking for a more leisurely and more refined life for *all* the people, so that even hod-carriers could

[1] "The Present Position of Economics" (1885), in A. C. Pigou, ed., *Memorials of Alfred Marshall* (London, Macmillan, 1925), p. 155.

be gentlemen. The stamp of these political doctrines is perceptible throughout his economic writings.

II

Marshall is said by his biographers to have come to economics from ethics. But his early interest in ethics arose out of his search for a guide to his conscience rather than from an intellectual interest in the metaphysical aspects of moral philosophy. In his younger days at Cambridge as student and teacher the conflict waged hot between utilitarian and idealistic theories of ethics, but there is no evidence that Marshall ever took real interest in this controversy or believed that it had immediate significance for his economics. It would be more accurate, I think, on the basis of the available evidence, to say that Marshall came to economics from his morals, from his zeal to make a contribution to the social betterment of man. Of the many passages in his writings which reveal Marshall's conviction that it is the duty of educated men to strive for the improvement of social conditions, and that a sound and moralized economics is a valuable instrument to this end, and his self-dedication to economics in this spirit, the following are representative:

Is there not a great fund of conscientiousness and unselfishness latent in the breasts of men, both rich and poor, which could be called out if the problems of life were set before them in the right way, and which would cause misery and poverty rapidly to diminish? [2]

It will be my most cherished ambition, my highest endeavour, to do what with my poor ability and my limited strength I may, to increase the numbers of those, whom Cambridge, the great mother of strong men, sends out into the world with cool heads but warm hearts, willing to give some at least of their best powers to grappling with the social suffering around them; resolved not to rest content till they have done what in them lies to discover how far it is possible to open up to all the material means of a refined and noble life. [3]

. . . I have devoted myself for the last twenty-five years to the problem of poverty, and . . . very little of my work has been devoted to any inquiry which does not bear on that. [4]

[2] Lecture by Marshall (1883) quoted in "In Memoriam: Alfred Marshall," by Pigou, *op. cit.,* p. 83.

[3] "The Present Position of Economics" (1885), *ibid.,* p. 174.

[4] Alfred Marshall, "Minutes of Evidence taken before the Royal Commission on the Aged Poor, June 5, 1893," *Official Papers* (London, Macmillan for the Royal Economic Society, 1926), p. 205.

I see no grounds for questioning either Marshall's complete sincerity in this connection, or the conformity of his life as a whole—which of course does not mean the whole of his life in every detail—to his announced principles. The moral earnestness with which Marshall regarded the rôle of economics and his own rôle as an economist was thoroughly Victorian, was altogether in keeping with the spirit of his times in liberal educated circles. If, in so far as simple formulae ever have validity when applied to the thought of a generation, late eighteenth century thought can be said to have reflected enlightenment without zeal, light without warmth, and our present-day world to exhibit zeal without enlightenment, heat without light, then it may be remembered that the late Victorian age in which Marshall reached maturity was the age of "sweetness *and* light," of reason tempered—some would say alloyed—by pity.

There are genuine differences in tone here between the Benthamite economists of the 1820's and Marshall. In one of the passages I have cited, Marshall spoke of the need for "cool heads but warm hearts." Bentham and his followers laid more stress on the dangers than on the benefits which might result from warmheartedness. The Benthamites had, as much as Marshall, dedicated their lives to the betterment of the conditions of the mass of mankind, and Marshall, like the Benthamites, believed that charity and goodwill unguided and unrestrained by "sound" general principles could do more harm than good. But Bentham's circle believed that acquaintance with sound principles was more urgently needed than goodwill. In Marshall's case this does not seem to be true, for Marshall seems on the whole to have been more fearful of too little stress on the heart than of too little exercise of the mind. There is a passage in Marshall's writings which is interesting not only because of its bearing on this point but also because it is the only passage in all of Marshall's writings in which I have been able to detect the slightest taint of humor—and even here it may well have been unconscious:

> G. Possibilities of Discrimination
> [between worthy and unworthy]
>
> . . . .
>
> 9. Patience in bearing other people's
> sufferings is as clear a duty as patience
> in bearing one's own, but it may be
> carried too far.[5]

[5] "Royal Commission on the Aged Poor (1893). Memorandum and Evidence offered to the Commissioners by Professor Alfred Marshall. (i) Preliminary Memorandum. *A*. Preliminary Statement." *Ibid.*, pp. 202–3.

John Stuart Mill was here again the connecting link between the Benthamites and Marshall. Under the influence largely of Wordsworth, he had reacted against his father's and Bentham's social philosophy as unduly cold and hard, and as lacking the moderating element obtainable from giving a larger rôle to "feeling." Mill introduced into the main line of English economic thought the sentimentality, the heart-throbbing, which Bentham, James Mill, Ricardo, McCulloch, Malthus, and Senior had carefully avoided. John Stuart Mill had thus made it more difficult for the humanitarians and the tear-evoking novelists to accuse the economists of having made it possible to freeze one's heart and yet live at peace with one's conscience. When Bagehot wrote, in a not wholly facetious vein, that "no real Englishman in his secret soul was ever sorry for the death of a political economist; he is much more likely to be sorry for his life," it was not economists like J. S. Mill or Marshall whom he had in mind. In any case, once Marshall had become the leading British economist it ceased to be a common charge against economics that "it dries up the hearts and the imaginations of the most who meddle with it" (Miss Lucy Aikin), or that all that it asked of men "is that they should harden their hearts" (Robert Southey); and the question whether humane men could be devotees of the dismal science had ceased to be a live one.

While it could be argued that these were more largely differences in mode of expression as between the Benthamites and Marshall, corresponding merely to changes in verbal style, than differences in substance, it seems clear that Marshall's lesser willingness to be patient about the immediate woes of the poor led him actively to seek means of reconciliation between advocacy of relief of distress on humanitarian grounds and adherence to the Benthamite principle that it was urgent to preserve unimpaired by excessive charity the capacity for and the will to practice self-help on the part of the poor. To take one instance: the classical economists, in appraising the claims of the aged poor to generous relief, held that, as old age was a foreseeable contingency, in general provision for it should be regarded as an individual responsibility. They drew no distinction between absence of reserves for old age due to expenditures on gin, on the one hand, and to expenditures on the education, nutrition and health of children, on the other. Marshall expressly refused to follow them on this point:

Too much stress is often laid both from the ethical and from the economical point of view on those forms of thrift which result in material provision for sickness and old age, in comparison with those forms which benefit the coming generation.

This is greatly due to the influence exerted on the administrators of poor-relief and charity by the economic and social philosophy of the early years of this century.[6]

When Marshall spoke of the task of economics to search for methods of opening up to all "the material means of a refined and noble life," he again used language which the Benthamites would not have found to their taste. Bentham would have spoken instead in terms of making available greater provision for the poor, without setting limits as to the amount to be desired of such increase in provision or inquiring as to its contribution to the refinement or ennobling of the life of the poor, provided only it contributed to their happiness. To Bentham, or so he claimed at least, "pushpin was equal to poetry" if they produced equal quantities of happiness, and he and his followers carefully avoided resort to any criterion for appraisal of the use which men made of their resources except its effect on their own, or their neighbors', or their children's happiness.

Here again John Stuart Mill was the connecting link between the strict utilitarianism of the early classical school, on the one hand, and the Victorian stress on refinement and nobility of Marshall, on the other hand; for Mill had diluted the Benthamite doctrine by insisting that over and above the purely quantitative differences between utilities there was a hierarchy of higher-and-lower, nobler-and-less-noble utilities which should be taken into account. Whatever may be the merits of this issue, and it is one on which there still seems to be as much room for inconclusive debate as there was when it was first raised, for Marshall the choice in favor of Mill as against Bentham was a convenient one. It not only put him in accord with the dominant ethical thought in the Cambridge of his time, but it also enabled him to retain an evangelistical note in his economics even after he had on intellectual grounds eliminated it from his theology.

Marshall, however, never explicitly discussed these ethical issues, and in fact sought deliberately to avoid being entrapped into open discussion thereof and into formal statement of his position by using as colorless and irenic terms as were available to express the ethical implications and presuppositions of his economics. Without surrendering or completely concealing his position, he thus succeeded fairly well in escaping the necessity of ever having to defend it.

[6] *Ibid.*, p. 202.

III

Marshall came to economics also from mathematics. Educated at Cambridge, noted for its emphasis on the educational and disciplinary value of rigorous training in mathematics, he attained high distinction in that field as a student. He taught mathematics before he taught economics. He had not only distinct aptitude but also great liking for mathematical forms of reasoning. It is clear, however, that he had grave mistrust of the consequences of unrestrained employment of formal mathematics in economic analysis. One factor in this distrust was probably a lurking puritan suspicion of the morality of any highly pleasurable activity: the formulation and solution of economic problems in mathematical, and especially graphical, terms yielded him so much intellectual and aesthetic delight that it for that reason alone became somewhat suspect to him as a worthy occupation. Mathematics, and especially graphs, were Marshall's fleshpots, and if he frequently succumbed to their lure it was not without struggle with his conscience. It can also be said for Marshall that when he did succumb he not only frequently warned his readers not to take his mathematical adventures too seriously but shielded them from the young and the susceptible by confining them to footnotes and appendices where, as he rightly anticipated, only the hardened sinners already beyond further corruption would prolongedly gaze. Marshall also was anxious for a wide audience, and the fact that the bulk of his potential readers were both unable and unwilling to read economics in mathematical form no doubt was an additional consideration.

But Marshall had other and presumably better reasons for misgivings as to the effect on economics of the extensive use of mathematics. First, the mathematical approach required rigorous abstraction, whereas Marshall thought that the economist must strive to account for the concrete. Secondly, although this may not be wholly a different consideration, Marshall believed that economics must become more complicated and more biological in character, whereas mathematical economics tended toward excessive simplification and sought its prototype rather in mechanics than in biology.

Marshall from the first had a live sense of the complexity and variability of the interrelations between economic phenomena, and of the biological rather than mechanical nature of these interrelations. During his early years at Cambridge, as student and as teacher, the influence of Darwin and of Huxley was strong. Cambridge was becoming a center for distinguished work in the biological sciences, challenging in intellectual prestige to some extent the traditional academic aristocracies of theology, philosophy, the classics, and mathematics and the physical sciences. While I know of no evidence that Marshall was ever a serious student of biology, and I have been unable to find that there was any personal intimacy between Marshall and the distinguished Cambridge biologists, physiologists, pathologists, psychologists, and so forth of his time, biological ideas were then very much in the air, and could be absorbed without special effort. In any case, Marshall saw in biological rather than in mechanical modes of thought the most suitable instruments of economic analysis. ". . . in the later stages of economics, when we are approaching nearly to the conditions of life, biological analogies are to be preferred to mechanical, other things being equal. . . . The Mecca of the economist is economic biology rather than economic dynamics." [7]

The biological sciences have in fact proved least tractable of all the natural sciences to abstract mathematical analysis, for largely the same reasons, I suppose, which in all probability led Marshall, and others, to see but a limited scope for the fruitful use of mathematics in economic theory: (1) great complexity of the problems; (2) significant variables too great in number for their separate analysis and yet not great enough in number to make reliance upon technical probability theory without specific analysis of particular variables a safe procedure; (3) the absence of reversibility in the interactions of variables; (4) the restricted scope for completely controlled experiment; (5) the absence of that complete indifference of the investigator to the material with which he is working and to the nature of his results which is the only reliable guarantee of scientific objectivity which we can have.

Devotees of the mathematical approach to economic problems frequently claim for that approach that the alternative non-symbolic method, or the "literary method" as they too generously put it, is too imprecise and clumsy a tool for the exposition in all their complexity of the relationships between economic variables, with the implication that it is the complexity of economic problems, rather than their simplicity, which establishes a necessary and fruitful field for the use of mathematics. Marshall, both in his formal writings and in his letters of warning to his disciples against overindulgence in mathematics, seems to me to have taken exactly the reverse view, although not in so many words; namely: that non-symbolic language and simple statistical methods alone had the elasticity to deal with the infinite detail and variability of concrete economic phenomena; that resort to mathe-

[7] "Distribution and Exchange" (1898), *Memorials,* pp. 317–18.

matics, unless confined to a preliminary stage of economic investigation, involved a greater degree of surrender of this elasticity than it was wise to accept; and that only the relatively simple propositions in economics could be expressed in mathematical form, and even then only at the cost of artificial and often serious further simplification. It must have been the complexities of the biological as distinguished from the mechanical aspects of economic problems which Marshall had in mind, for I cannot see how he could have intended to deny that, whatever the degree of complexity of the mechanical type economic problems may involve, they can be handled better with than without the aid of mathematics.

There was still another element leading Marshall to cry down the value of the mathematical method. Marshall, at least in his frequent moralizing moods, placed no high value on economic analysis as a good in itself, as a cultural pursuit or a substitute for chess. Writing to Edgeworth in 1902, he said:

In my view "theory" is essential. No one gets any real grip of economic problems unless he will work at it. But I conceive no more calamitous notion than that abstract, or general, or "theoretical" economics was "economics" proper. It seems to me an essential but a very small part of economics proper: and by itself sometimes even—well, not a very good occupation of time.[8]

From this and other passages it can be inferred that Marshall, believing as he did that it was "pure theory" which lent itself most fully to mathematical exposition, that for economics to be a serviceable instrument of human betterment it must be extended to include consideration of the concrete detail not readily or at all amenable to abstract mathematical treatment, and that the attraction of mathematics led some economists to neglect the concrete detail and to confine themselves to pure theorizing, minimized the usefulness of mathematics to economics in order to check the tendency toward what he regarded as undue abstraction.[9]

I am no mathematician myself, and I try always to remember and to profit from Edgeworth's merited reproof to an Italian economist who

---

[8] Letter by Marshall to Professor F. Y. Edgeworth (1902), *ibid.*, p. 437.

[9] *Cf.* J. M. Keynes, "Alfred Marshall, 1842–1924," *ibid.*, p. 37: ". . . Marshall was too anxious to do good. He had an inclination to undervalue those intellectual parts of the subject which were not *directly* connected with human wellbeing or the condition of the working classes or the like, although *indirectly* they might be of the utmost importance, and to feel that when he was pursuing them he was not occupying himself with the Highest. . . . When his intellect chased diagrams and Foreign Trade and Money, there was an evangelical moraliser of an imp somewhere inside him, that was so ill-advised as to disapprove."

had had the temerity to question the usefulness of Edgeworth's application of the mathematical method to taxation problems: "The withers of the mathematician are not wrung by these commonplaces. The use of the method is not necessarily attended with an exaggeration of its importance. The inability to use it is not a qualification for appreciating its usefulness." Professional mathematicians have assured me, moreover, that the uninitiated can have no conception of the feats which can be performed by the aid of the elastic, the precise, the versatile, and the delicate apparatus of the modern higher mathematics. Although they have also upon occasion suggested to me that economists are pressing it to perform false miracles, I venture no disclaimer, therefore, of whatever general or specific claims for their method mathematical economists may make, provided they are confined to mathematical claims beyond my understanding or ability to test. But non-mathematical economists with an inferiority-complex—which today includes, I feel certain, very nearly all non-mathematical economists—may be pardoned, perhaps, if they derive a modest measure of unsanctified joy from the spectacle of the great Marshall, a pioneer in mathematical economics himself, disparaging the use of mathematics in economics, and counting as wasted effort the mastery of any other economist's mathematical symbols. If, as seems doubtful, Marshall's warnings served to dissuade any budding Cambridge economic geniuses with aptitude for mathematics from acquiring an abundant command of its techniques, they no doubt served economics ill rather than well. But if they helped to check the descent of economics to the status of an unwanted foundling on mathematics' doorstep, they did render a useful service.

If Marshall's puritan conscience led him to disparage the method from which he undoubtedly derived the greatest intellectual excitement and joy, even that over-scrupulous conscience occasionally took a holiday. Marshall recognized that the instruments for a general ethical calculus were lacking, but he claimed that the institution of money provided an adequate basis for calculations of *economic* satisfaction and sacrifice: "The pure science of Ethics halts for lack of a system of measurement of efforts, sacrifices, desires, etc., fit for her wide purposes. But the pure science of Political Economy has found a system that will subserve her narrower aims." [10]

Marshall was well aware and repeatedly acknowledged that the monetary unit represented substantially different quantities of satisfaction and of sacrifice for rich and for poor, respectively. It would

[10] "Mr. Mill's Theory of Value" (1876), *ibid.*, p. 126.

seem that this was an insuperable barrier to the use of market prices as a measurement of such satisfaction and sacrifice as between different persons, and that, with his acceptance of the problem of poverty as the major problem for economics, Marshall would have felt obliged to recognize that even for a calculus of economic happiness no satisfactory instruments of measurement were available. His zeal for quasi-quantitative analysis and for reaching value-judgments overcame, however, his other scruples, and he adopted an analytical procedure which operated to distract attention from the necessity of making full allowance for the inequality in the distribution of wealth and income in reaching such value-judgments. In a passage in his *Principles* which has not escaped unfavorable notice by others, Marshall offered what must be regarded as a glaringly weak defense of this procedure:

> On the whole, . . . it happens that by far the greater number of the events with which economics deals affect in about equal proportions all the different classes of society; so that if the money measures of the happiness caused by two events are equal, there is not in general any very great difference between the amounts of the happiness in the two cases.[11]

Marshall was here setting up a screen between himself and his readers, on the one hand, and the problem of poverty on the other, in order to be free to engage, without too sharp pangs of conscience, in what was for himself a delectable intellectual activity. This was not Marshall at his best, however, nor even the normal Marshall, and there have been few of us who have made conscience be our guide as to subjects of investigation and methods of analysis as steadily and as consistently as did Marshall.

I do not regard it as part of my function to render a definite appraisal of Marshall as man or as economist. In any case, those aspects of Marshall's work with which I have dealt are not really matters for appraisal, and narration and description are all that is called for. That Marshall was a great figure, one of the greatest, in the history of our discipline, and that without being by any means flawless he nevertheless fully earned his status, I would strongly argue if I knew of sufficient dissent from significant quarters and on significant grounds to give any point to such argument.

But Marshall is now long dead, and the rule "De mortuis non nisi bonum" is a required rule of morals or of good manners only for men very recently dead. There would be no point therefore in treating Marshall, whether the man or his work, with special tenderness or

11 Alfred Marshall, *Principles of Economics,* 6th ed., p. 131.

reserve. He had, beyond doubt, his weaknesses on both counts, including some with which he may have infected his followers, so that we regard them as points of strength. I am sure also that even his virtues are not to be admired by us to the point of slavish imitation. Each generation should—and will—work out its own economics, borrowing from, reacting from, improving upon, retrograding from, that of the preceding generation. Marshall's economics is now distinctly that of a generation which is past, and is increasingly *not* that of our own. For one thing, it is essentially the economics of a society assumed to be free and to have its economic affairs conducted by free individuals. Freedom, whether of the economic system as such, or of individuals, has over a large part of the earth's surface either never existed or been suppressed. The appropriate economics of the day is, moreover, the economics of war and preparation for or against war, *Wehrwirtschaft,* and Marshall here has only very limited guidance to offer.

It was a characteristic of Victorian, including Marshallian, public utterances that they typically ended on a double note, of assurance, on the one hand, of continuance into the future of all the well-established institutions and cherished values of the Victorian Age, and of promise, on the other hand, of continued betterment of the social conditions of mankind. Both the Victorian complacency with respect to the present and the Victorian optimism with respect to future progress are now utterly inappropriate. As a social philosopher, Marshall is not yet merely a period piece. If he should become so in the near future, it would properly be a matter for concern, but not for surprise.

Haberler
——— on ———
Schumpeter

Joseph A. Schumpeter (1883–1950), educated at Vienna and a pupil of Böhm-Bawerk, abandoned a distinguished teaching career in Europe during the thirties and came to the United States. He taught at Harvard from 1932 to his death, and in 1948 served as president of the American Economic Association, the first foreign-born economist to attain this distinction.

Throughout his works, Schumpeter is concerned with the operations of the capitalist system, with emphasis placed on the strategic role of the entrepreneur, whose innovations push economic development forward. Innovations also stand in the center of Schumpeter's theory of business cycles. Emotionally, Schumpeter was deeply attached to the institutions of capitalism, and he viewed with alarm the rise of anticapitalist forces, engendered, in his opinion, by the very success of capitalism. Schumpeter was a brilliant writer, interested also in the history of economic thought, and he wrote a number of fascinating essays on other great economists.

Gottfried von Haberler (1900–   ) was a long-time associate of Schumpeter. Educated at Vienna, like Schumpeter, Haberler now teaches at Harvard. His principal works are *Theory of International Trade* (1935), and *Prosperity and Depression* (1937).

J OSEPH A. SCHUMPETER [1] was one of the great economists of all time. His claim to that rare title—remember Keynes's famous dictum that "good economists are the rarest of birds"—rests as much on the fact that he was much more than an economist as on his achievements in the economic field itself. He himself used to say that an economist who is not also a mathematician, a statistician, and most of all a historian is not properly qualified for his profession. He was all these and more besides: he had an encyclopaedic knowledge not only of the history of economic doctrines, which was one of his special fields, but also of the history of economic facts and institutions and of general political and social history. He had not received professional training in mathematics, and the manipulation of numbers and of algebra did not come to him easily; but he acquired a great mathematical knowledge and could follow and effectively expound what even among mathematical economists is regarded as complicated mathematical analysis. He was not an expert statistical technician, but he had a profound understanding of the logic and limitations of statistical inference and kept abreast of new methods and of statistical source materials. All his life he was deeply interested in the theory of social relations and social philosophy and made important contributions to sociology and to social and political philosophy.

In some of these fields he had his superiors. There are in economics more refined and versatile mathematical theorists, there are more resourceful statisticians, and economic historians who know more about certain periods and certain subjects than he did. But as a master of all branches of economics and as a universal scholar, Schumpeter held a unique position among contemporary economists.

Schumpeter was not only a great scholar and original thinker, but he was also a strong, colorful, and exceedingly complex personality. A quite unusual capacity for understanding the minds and views of

[1] I am grateful to a number of people for help and information, among them Professors A. Gerschenkron and E. H. Chamberlin, Mrs. T. Stolper, and Drs. F. Somary, H. Staehle, and Heinrich Höfflinger.

[Reprinted by permission of the publishers, in abridged form, from *The Quarterly Journal of Economics,* Volume LXIV, #3, August 1950, Cambridge, Mass.: Harvard University Press, 1950.]

others, a strong touch of irony, which, at times, seemed to verge on cynicism, and a wonderful sense of humor were combined with deep moral convictions, absolute devotion to his friends, and intense likes and aversions. But his dislike of certain kinds of people was controlled by his kindheartedness and generosity. He was especially considerate to his students, and those who confided in him and sought his advice could always be sure of getting his help and counsel. Indeed, he spent a disproportionate amount of time, tutoring and helping students— those of limited as well as of superior ability.

He was an effective and dramatic speaker, a master of the spoken as well as of the written word, and his lectures and addresses were always stimulating, had usually some new idea and striking formulation, and were never stale or dull. No wonder that he was a tremendously inspiring teacher.

Schumpeter died from a cerebral haemorrhage in his sleep on January 8, 1950, one month before his sixty-seventh birthday.

I. CHILDHOOD AND UNIVERSITY, 1883–1906

Jozsi (pronounced Yoshi), as he was called at home and by his friends, was born at Triesch in the Austrian province of Moravia (now Czechoslovakia) on February 8, 1883, the only child of the cloth manufacturer (Tuchfabrikant) Alois Schumpeter and his wife Johanna. Jozsi's mother was born at Wiener-Neustadt, an industrial town thirty miles south of Vienna, on June 9, 1861, the daughter of a physician, Dr. Julius Grüner, by his marriage with Julie Wydra. Little is known of the ancestry of Schumpeter's parents; but so much is certain: that he was the product of a typically Austrian mixture of several of the many nationalities that lived in the Austro-Hungarian monarchy.[1a]

In 1901, Schumpeter registered as a student in the Faculty of Law at the University of Vienna, and in 1906 the degree of *Doctor utriusque juris* (doctor of law—literally: doctor of each of the two laws, viz., of Roman law and canon law) was conferred upon him. In Vienna, as in most continental universities, economics was (and still is) taught in the Faculty of Law, and for the law degree, courses and a compre-

---

[1a] According to one theory, the name Schumpeter is of Italian origin, being a German corruption of Giampietro. Schumpeter's dark features, which he had inherited from his father, lend some support to this hypothesis. But I was unable to obtain reliable confirmation.

hensive examination in economics and political science were (and still are) required.[2]

At the beginning of the century Vienna was a great center of economic learning. Menger had, however, withdrawn from active work in the University (including his celebrated seminar) before Schumpeter's time, although he did not resign his chair until 1903 when Wieser became his successor. Thus Schumpeter was not a student of Menger, and according to reliable reports met him only once or twice.

His first serious work in economics seems to have been done in what we would now call a statistical research seminar conducted by the eminent economic historian and statistician, K. Th. v. Inama-Sternegg,[3] in conjunction with Franz v. Juraschek.[4] Other seminars he attended were those of F. v. Wieser and of E. v. Philippovich where he seems to have reported on the beginnings of his *Dogmengeschichte*. When Böhm-Bawerk resigned as Minister of Finance in 1904, he returned to academic life as professor in the University of Vienna, and conducted in 1905 and 1906 a famous seminar, in which Schumpeter was an active participant. Other prominent members were Ludwig v. Mises and Felix Somary, his lifelong friend. It was made lively and at times stormy by the participation of a group of young Marxists who later became theoretical and political leaders in the Austrian and German Social Democratic parties. There was Otto Bauer, the brilliant theorist, dialectician, and intellectual leader of the Austrian socialists after 1918, who seems to have been mainly responsible for Schumpeter's appointment as Minister of Finance of the Austrian Republic in 1919. There was Rudolf Hilferding, the author of the famous book *Das Finanzkapital* and twice Minister of Finance of the German Republic.[5] Another member was Emil Lederer, later Professor in Heidelberg and Berlin, who in 1934 became Alvin Johnson's main collaborator in the foundation of the Graduate Faculty at the New School for Social Research in New York. Schumpeter and Lederer were friends throughout the latter's life, and he seems to have been on good terms with Hilferding.

[2] Since 1920, a special degree in political science, *Doctor rerum politicarum*, including economics, has been available. But it has not become very popular.

[3] See the biographical note on Inama-Sternegg by another eminent economic historian, Alfons Dopsch, in *Encyclopaedia of the Social Sciences*, Vol. VII.

[4] Inama was director of the Austrian Central Statistical office and was succeeded by Juraschek.

[5] See P. M. Sweezy's introduction to Rudolph Hilferding, *Böhm-Bawerk's Criticism of Marx* (New York: A. M. Kelley, 1949). This is Hilferding's reply to Böhm-Bawerk's *Karl Marx and the Close of His System*.

Schumpeter's profound knowledge of Marxian theory and his intimate familiarity with the continental socialist movement as well as with the psychology of the socialist leaders, which lent color and freshness to a long series of articles culminating in his book, *Capitalism, Socialism and Democracy* (see especially Part V, "A Historical Sketch of Socialist Parties"), originated in those seminar meetings.

A member of that seminar told the author of the present essay that in the heated debates between Böhm-Bawerk and the Marxists, Schumpeter attracted general attention through his cool, scientific detachment. The seemingly playful manner in which he took part in the discussion, an attitude which was strongly pronounced in his early writings (especially in his first book, *Wesen und Hauptinhalt der theoretischen Nationalökonomie*) and which never left him entirely, was evidently mistaken by many for a lack of seriousness or an artificial mannerism. Böhm-Bawerk, however, with whom Schumpeter had close personal connections, at once recognized his talents, and was instrumental in securing Schumpeter's *Habilitation* (i.e., granting the *venia legendi,* the right to lecture) in the University of Vienna in 1909 and his appointment to the chair of political economy in the University of Czernowitz in the same year. It must be mentioned, however, that the greatest Austrian economist of his generation never was offered a chair in his *Alma Mater Vindobonensis,* although there were many opportunities before he finally left his native country in 1925.

II. EARLY ACADEMIC CAREER, 1906–18

After graduation in 1906, Schumpeter went to England for a stay of several months, mainly in London, but with occasional visits to Cambridge and Oxford, where he paid his respects to Marshall and Edgeworth. In 1907, he married Miss Gladys Ricarde Seaver, daughter of a high dignitary of the Church of England,[6] and in the same year the Schumpeters went to Egypt. The preface to his first book bears the date line "Kairo, March 2, 1908." Late in 1908 or early 1909, they returned to Vienna, and in the autumn he started his work as Professor in Czernowitz, the capital of Bukowina, the easternmost province of Austria, which was after 1918 included in Rumania, in 1939 annexed by Russia, in 1941 retransferred to Rumania, and is now a part of Russia.

[6] At the outbreak of the war in 1914, his wife was visiting in England. She did not return to Austria, and in 1920 the marriage was dissolved by mutual consent.

Apparently Czernowitz was eastern indeed, and Schumpeter's Harvard colleagues were later entertained by stories of extracurricular activities that might well have come out of the Arabian Nights. The two years in Czernowitz seem to have been very happy ones, and the university, where the academic careers of many young Austrian scholars started, was by no means without intellectual stimulation. Eugen Ehrlich, the well-known founder of the sociological theory of jurisprudence, whose book, *Fundamental Principles of the Sociology of Law,* was published in an English translation by the Harvard University Press, was Schumpeter's colleague. So was another eminent jurist, Georg Petschek, who in 1939 came as research associate to the Harvard Law School.

In 1911, Schumpeter was called to the University of Graz, the capital of the Austrian province of Styria, 150 miles south of Vienna. He was appointed by Imperial Rescript ("Zufolge Allerhöchster Entschliessung") against the vote of the faculty which had proposed some local nonentity. He was the youngest full professor in the faculty and, being the only economist in the university and having been put in charge of economic instruction at the *Technische Hochschule* as well, he had at first a very heavy teaching schedule ranging over the whole field of economics, including public finance. Despite all that, he managed to offer interesting special courses on such subjects as economic democracy and the problem of the social classes.

In the stuffy provincial atmosphere of Graz, which had none of the oriental lures of Czernowitz, he never felt happy and at home. But Graz was only a three hours' train ride from Vienna, and in later years he went there whenever possible. The academic year 1913–14 Schumpeter spent in New York at Columbia University, as Austrian exchange professor. He gave a course in theory, one in social classes, and a seminar. In March 1914, he received the honorary degree of Litt.D. from Columbia,[7] and returned to Austria just before the outbreak of the war. He left Graz late in 1918, but remained a member of the faculty until 1921.

Schumpeter's scientific output during the years between his graduation from the University in 1906 and the end of the First World War was stupendous, especially if one considers that during that period he lived in five different places with as many different cultures, located in four countries on three continents, and that according to reports he made full use of the many opportunities to enjoy life which prewar

[7] He also received an honorary Doctor of Laws in 1939 from the University of Sofia, Bulgaria.

Vienna and London, not to speak of Cairo and Czernowitz, offered in abundance.

In 1906 appeared his first major article "Über die mathematische Methode der theoretischen Ökonomie"; in 1908, when he was barely twenty-five years old, he published his first great book, *Wesen und Hauptinhalt der theoretischen Nationalökonomie;* and in 1912 his celebrated *Theorie der wirtschaftlichen Entwicklung.*[8] These two volumes immediately established his preeminence in the field of economic theory. "He never was a beginner" (Spiethoff in his beautiful obituary of Schumpeter in *Kyklos,* 1950). When he was thirty, he wrote a history of his science: *Epochen der Dogmen- und Methodengeschichte*[9] is a profound and mature piece of work which, however, only the expert can fully appreciate.

A sort of supplement to his *Dogmengeschichte* is the booklet, which discusses the past and future of the social sciences.[10] Having grown out of a lecture in Czernowitz in 1911, this essay is shorter and uses less heavy scholarly equipment than the *Dogmengeschichte.* It deals with economics and sociology in their relation to philosophy and history, but contains also interesting remarks on technical economic questions which foreshadow later developments. On page 125, for example, Schumpeter calls for empirical, "especially statistical," studies with a view to determining the shape of "demand curves." In addition to these books, every year there flowed from his pen a stream of important articles, some of them of considerable length, as well as innumerable book reviews.

His business cycle theory was first fully expounded in the *Theory of Economic Development,* but the article on economic crises in 1910 already gave an outline of what was to come, and in the preface to the *Theory of Economic Development* Schumpeter stated that he had conceived the fundamental ideas as early as 1905. His famous theory of interest was clearly sketched in his first book, although fully developed in the second. The first book also contains interesting thoughts on the theory of saving, which recurred later in the book on *Business Cycles.* "Saving is not a function of income."[11] He holds

[8] Translated into English by Redvers Opie under the title *Theory of Economic Development* (Cambridge, Mass.: Harvard University Press, 1934). Hereafter the book will be referred to by its English title.

[9] In *Grundriss der Sozialökonomik,* Vol. I, Tübingen, 1914 (second impression, 1924), 106 large pages.

[10] *Vergangenheit und Zukunft der Sozialwissenschaften,* Munich, 1915, 140 small pages.

[11] *Wesen,* p. 308.

that people quickly get used to higher income and do not really save more when their income rises.[12]

Schumpeter's basic sociological views, too, which were first published in 1927 in a lengthy paper [13] and were later elaborated in his *Capitalism, Socialism and Democracy*, seem to have crystallized at an early date. In a prefatory note to his 1927 article, he states that "the fundamental idea originated in 1910 and was first propounded in a series of popular lectures on 'State and Society' in Czernowitz during the winter 1910–11." [14] Similarly, many of his views on socialism, with which the Anglo-American public became first acquainted through his widely read book on socialism in 1942, found clear expression as early as 1918 in the brochure *Die Krise des Steuerstaats*, in 1919 in his brilliant essay *Zur Soziologie der Imperialismen*,[15] and in two exceedingly interesting and sparkling articles on socialism in England and in our country.[16]

Apart from the specific content, Schumpeter's very first publications display several features which are characteristic of all his work. There is, first, the great liking for the mathematical method in economics. It remained undiminished throughout his life, but it did not imply a neglect or underestimation of the importance of historical knowledge and research for the study of economics. On the contrary, he used to say that in case he had to give up either his historical or mathematical training, he would abandon the latter rather than the former.

His enthusiasm for the mathematical method was in contrast to the small use he made of it. In that respect, he was the exact opposite

[12] He even maintains that more saving is done in lower and middle income brackets than in the very high ones (*ibid.*). Few will accept this statement, but it must be emphasized that he defines income *exclusive* of dynamic entrepreneurial profits. That is, I think, also the clue to his distinction between saving (out of income) and *not-spending*. This distinction which is made in *Business Cycles* (Vol. I, p. 75 ff.) can already be found in his first book (*Wesen*, p. 309). The matter is a little obscure, but it seems that these dynamic profits are treated as capital gains and thus are not part of income. They are, at any rate, the almost exclusive source (apart from forced saving through inflation) of the financing of investment and of capital formation.

[13] "Die sozialen Klassen im ethnisch homogenen Milieu," *Archiv für Sozialwissenschaft*, Vol. LVII (1927), pp. 1–67.

[14] At Graz, Columbia, and later in Bonn he gave a course of lectures on social classes.

[15] *Archiv für Sozialwissenschaft*, Vol. XLVI, pp. 1–39, 275–310 (also issued as a pamphlet).

[16] "Der Sozialismus in England und bei uns," *Der Österreichische Volkswirt*, December 13 and 20, 1924.

of Marshall: while Marshall had a mathematical bent of mind and mathematical training, and while his theoretical achievements would have been impossible without the use of mathematics, "he never gave full credit to the faithful ally" [mathematics] and "hid the tool that had done the work." [17]   Schumpeter did not have an essentially mathematical mind but he extolled the use of mathematics, and his enthusiasm stimulated scores of students to utilize and to perfect mathematical methods of analysis in economics.   But more important is that his earliest writings reveal two qualities which were so characteristic of the man and the scholar: his ideas and style of expression are highly original and supremely independent of his scientific environment.

By the time he left the university, he had read and studied a vast amount of economic literature, classical and modern, especially in English.[18]   He was greatly impressed by, and highly admired, the work of Walras, the younger.   In the preface to his first book, he said that Walras and Wieser, who was one of his professors, were the two economists to whom he felt closest.   But while Wieser was hardly mentioned in his later work (although he wrote a beautiful though brief obituary),[19] he kept his high regard for Walras.   In his appraisal of Marshall's *Principles* (1941), he calls Walras "the greatest of all theorists," [20] and in his preface to the Japanese translation of the *Theory of Economic Development* (1937) he said that "as an economist" he owed more to Walras "than to any other influence." [21]

Schumpeter is usually regarded as a member of the Austrian school. The fact is, however, that as a man and as a scholar he was from the beginning a citizen of the world.   He never liked to identify himself with any nationality, group, or school.   What he said of Menger holds of Schumpeter himself: "He was nobody's pupil."   This complete intellectual independence is already apparent in his earliest writings. Concretely, they show little specifically "Austrian" influence.[22]   There

[17] Schumpeter, "Marshall's Principles: Semi-Centennial Appraisal," *American Economic Review,* Vol. XXXI (June 1941), p. 240.

[18] See especially the article on the mathematical method in economics, 1906. His first book followed consciously the then current fashion (which he later gave up) of English and American books of dispensing with bibliographical footnotes almost entirely.   But his great knowledge of the literature is clear from the text and other publications.

[19] *Economic Journal,* June 1927, pp. 328–330.

[20] *Loc. cit.,* p. 239.

[21] Page 2.

[22] It is entirely to the credit of the scientific milieu and a tribute to the great scholars who acted in it that it stimulated the growth of independent thinkers.

is, it is true, a chapter on imputation in the *Wesen und Hauptinhalt* (and a long supplementary article on it appeared a year later), and his theory of cost may be termed "Austrian," but in most other respects his views were not those prevailing in Vienna at that time. Schumpeter refused to take sides in the *Methodenstreit* between Menger and Schmoller, although the skirmishing was still going on and the air was still full of the smoke of battle. The mathematical method was not very popular in Vienna.[23] Still less popular was the behavioristic attitude which he adopted in his first book and his rejection of the so-called "psychological method" and the use of "introspection." Wieser was especially critical of Schumpeter on that point.[24] It is worth noting that Schumpeter changed his views in this respect later on. In his theory classes at Harvard and in conversations he often argued on "psychological grounds," using introspection in favor of cardinal utility or, occasionally, even for the possibility of interindividual comparison of utility.[25]

Schumpeter undoubtedly was influenced by Böhm-Bawerk's capital theory, and used the concept of roundabout methods of production in his theory of economic development. But he gave it a special dynamic slant and his interest theory is entirely different from the Böhm-Bawerkian.[26]

[23] Wieser especially did not like it. Böhm-Bawerk probably did not object, for he had a clear, mathematical mind himself, although unfortunately no mathematical training whatsoever. There were, of course, the two outsiders, *Auspitz* and *Lieben*, whose *Untersuchungen über die Theorie des Preises* (Vienna, 1889) was an outstanding contribution to mathematical economics. But there is no evidence that Schumpeter was especially influenced by them, although he was fully familiar with their work.

[24] See his review article "Das Wesen und der Hauptinhalt der theoretischen Nationalökonomie, Kritische Glossen," in *Jahrbuch für Gesetzgebung, Verwaltung und Volkswirtschaft im Deutschen Reich*, Vol. XXXV, Leipzig, 1911. Reprinted in F. v. Wieser, *Gesammelte Abhandlungen*, ed. F. A. Hayek (Tübingen, 1929).

[25] Lest anybody think this to be an obsolete and settled issue, I should like to quote from a recent work of one of the most eminent mathematicians and philosophers of our time: "Scientists would be wrong to ignore the fact that theoretical construction is not the only approach to the phenomena of life; another way, that of understanding from within (interpretation), is open to us. . . . Of myself, of my own acts of perception, thought, feeling and doing, I have a direct knowledge. . . . This inner awareness of myself is the basis for the understanding of my fellow-men whom I meet and acknowledge as beings of my own kind, with whom I communicate. . . ." Hermann Weyl, *Philosophy of Mathematics and the Natural Sciences* (English ed., Princeton, 1949), p. 283.

[26] See Böhm-Bawerk's long criticism, "Eine 'dynamische' Theorie des Kapitalzinses," *Zeitschrift für Volkswirtschaft, Sozialpolitik und Verwaltung*, Vol. XXII, 1913. In the same volume is a reply by Schumpeter and a rejoinder

The great intellectual independence of environmental influences, the absolute refusal to be swayed by current fashions in science and politics, the complete freedom of mind, all this (paradoxically combined with a quite unusual capacity of understanding other people's views—witness his biographical essays) was strikingly characteristic. People who did not know Schumpeter well frequently thought that this was nothing more than a passion to contradict, to take the opposite view, often intensified by an almost perverse pleasure in being unpopular and standing alone. It is true, he enjoyed *épater les bourgeois* and especially *épater les épateurs des bourgeois* (so he managed to shock and antagonize Philistines on the right and on the left at the same time), and he was quite capable occasionally of defending for argument's sake a position in which he did not believe. *L'art pour l'art* in discussions was by no means foreign to him. But he did not really relish being in a minority all the time. His independence was not a pose. One could truly say of him what Nietzsche said about Schopenhauer:

> Seht ihn nur an—
> Niemandem war er untertan.[27]

III. FORAY INTO STATESMANSHIP AND BUSINESS, 1919–24

Most of Schumpeter's life was wholly devoted to thinking, teaching and writing, although he was never merely a bookish sort of person. He always took a lively interest in public and world affairs, felt intensely about, and never hesitated to express emphatic opinions on, current political issues. But it was only during the brief period from the end of the First World War to 1924 that he was actively engaged first in political life and then in business.

During the war he made no secret of his pacifist, pro-Western (especially pro-British) [28] and anti-German attitude. In the pamphlet on the crisis of the tax state,[29] instead of adopting the official phraseol-

by Böhm-Bawerk. Böhm-Bawerk's article is reprinted in E. v. Böhm-Bawerk, *Kleinere Abhandlungen über Kapital und Zins* (ed. F. X. Weiss, Vienna, 1926). The exchange with Böhm-Bawerk covers 120 pages and is one of the great controversies in our science.

[27] Friedrich Nietzsche, *Werke,* Vol. V (Leipzig: Alfred Kröner Verlag 1930), p. 501.

[28] This attitude is most clearly revealed in his "Soziologie der Imperialismen" which appeared in 1919 but must have been written during the war.

[29] *Die Krise des Steuerstaats.* An enlarged version of a lecture, Graz, 1918. *Steuerstaat* is a state that relies on taxes for its revenue in contrast to the state in a socialist society which receives the bulk of its revenue from the income of

ogy and speaking of "the heroic fight for freedom and survival" or something like that, he referred to the war as that "bloody madness" which was "devastating Europe." Having good connections with the high aristocracy from his college days in the Theresianum, he seems to have been involved in the abortive attempt on the part of Emperor Karl and the court circle to arrange for a separate peace between Austria and the Western powers.

After the armistice the German socialist government set up a socialization commission in Berlin with the purpose of studying and preparing for the nationalization of industries. The head of the commission was Karl Kautsky, and Hilferding and Lederer, Schumpeter's acquaintances from university days, were prominent members. He received a call to join the commission, and spent two or three months late in 1918 and early in 1919 in Berlin. The work seems to have consisted in holding something like seminar discussions on the subject of socialization and other economic problems.

Schumpeter's membership in the *Sozialisierungskommission* has often been taken as proof of his socialist convictions. This is incorrect. The *Sozialisierungskommission* was not entirely composed of socialists, as the following passage from F. W. Bruck [30] shows: "So the '*Sozialisierungskommission*' was established in 1918 to which politicians and economists of various shades belonged. Among them were . . . some outspoken socialist theoreticians such as Kautsky, Lederer and Hilferding, and people of liberal standards like Franke and Vogelstein. This committee sometimes co-opted other men of high reputation as thinkers and practical men; in this way Professor Schumpeter joined the commission. . . ."

Schumpeter's attitude was revealed by his answer to the question, put to him by a young economist, of how he, who had extolled the role of the entrepreneur and the efficiency of the private enterprise system,[31] could be connected with the socialization commission: "If somebody wants to commit suicide, it is a good thing if a doctor is present."

On February 16, 1919, the first republican parliament was elected in Austria. The strictly Marxist socialists (official title: Social Democrats) emerged as the largest party and a coalition government of the socialists and the so-called Christian Social party (a Catholic con-

nationalized industries. Thus the *Steuerstaat* is the fiscal complement to the free enterprise, capitalist economy.

[30] *Social and Economic History of Germany from William II to Hitler* (Oxford University Press, 1938), p. 155.

[31] In *Die Krise des Steuerstaats*.

servative party) was formed with Dr. Karl Renner, a right wing socialist, as head.[32] Neither of the two political parties was eager to take
responsibility for the almost insoluble and politically unrewarding task
of grappling with Austria's finances. So they agreed to let a nonpoli-
tical expert try his hand at that hopeless and unpopular job. (In this
respect, too, history repeated itself after World War II.) Otto Bauer,
who was Secretary for Foreign Affairs in the Renner government,
proposed Schumpeter for the position of *Staatssekretär für Finanzen*.
On March 15, Schumpeter moved to the magnificent baroque palace
built by Eugène of Savoy, one of Austria's greatest statesmen, where
his teacher Böhm-Bawerk had held the same office under more favorable circumstances; he resigned from the Ministry of Finance on
October 17, 1919.[33]

About two years after he left the government, Schumpeter became
president of the Biedermann Bank, a small but old and highly respected
private banking house. The bank did not long survive the stabilization
crisis. It went bankrupt in 1924, and since it was one of the first banks
to fail and many people lost money—during the following years Austrians had to get used to bank failures, in fact hardly a single bank
escaped that fate—the collapse of the Biedermann Bank came as a
great shock and put its president in a difficult position. Unlike most
other bankers, he did not save any part of his personal fortune in the
crash and even managed in subsequent years to repay his personal
debts out of his earnings.

He decided to return to academic life and accepted an invitation
to be a guest professor in Japan. But when soon after he received
an invitation from the Prussian Ministry of Education to a chair at
the University of Bonn, which had become vacant by the retirement
of Heinrich Dietzel, the eminent liberal economist, he went there instead. In his later years he never forgot that it had been a Japanese
and a German university that offered him the opportunity to resume
the quiet life of a scholar. His sentimental attachment to both countries and his sharp reaction to chauvinistic wholesale condemnation

[32] The same coalition has again been in power since 1945, the only difference
being that the Catholic party has changed its name to People's party, and the
Social Democrats to Socialist party. In 1946 Dr. Renner became president of
the second Austrian Republic.

[33] It was traditional for theoretical economists in Austria to take part in
practical affairs. Menger took a lively interest in public issues and was highly
influential in bringing about the Austrian currency reform in the 1890's which
culminated in the adoption of the gold standard; Böhm-Bawerk was senior
official in the Treasury and three times Minister of Finance; Wieser was Minister
of Commerce.

of the German and Japanese peoples and their culture during the Second World War had one of its roots in that experience.

Before he left Vienna, he married a charming and beautiful Viennese girl, Annie Reisinger, of humble origin, to whose schooling he had contributed for several years. This marriage was entirely happy, but very brief. His wife died in 1926 in childbirth in Bonn. Her death and that of his mother (also in 1926), to whom he had been greatly devoted, came as a terrible shock, and after that time a streak of resignation and pessimism was unmistakable in his character.

IV. ACADEMIC LIFE IN BONN AND HARVARD, 1925–50

The move to Bonn constituted a complete break with his past life in more than one respect. As a typical member of the old Austrian (pre-1914) society, Schumpeter had never been a friend and admirer of Germany. In spite of that he soon felt at home in the scholarly and cultured atmosphere of the old university town on the Rhine. He formed a new set of lasting and intimate friendships. That does not mean that he forgot his old friends. But he never visited his native country again. I do not think the motive was resentment or wounded pride. It was rather the logical consequence of his resolve to give up all ambition to play a role in politics and business and to devote himself entirely to scholarship.

The change from Bonn to Harvard was less abrupt. He taught in Harvard during the academic year 1927–28, and again during the autumn term of 1930. But after he resigned from Bonn and went to Harvard permanently in 1932, he never revisited Germany although he spent the next three summers (until 1935) in Europe.

The first years at Harvard he lived with F. W. Taussig. In 1937 he married Elizabeth Boody, a descendant of an old New England family and an economist in her own right. As time went on, he leaned more and more on her devotion and wise counsel in all practical matters. Without her loving and understanding care, he could not have achieved as much as he did.

The scholarly achievements of his Harvard years are most impressive indeed. There is first the great two volume work *Business Cycles* (1939), which is better described by its subtitle, "A Theoretical, Historical, and Statistical Analysis of the Capitalist Process." It is a monument to theoretical acumen, truly encyclopaedic erudition, painstaking scholarship, and perseverance. The main ideas, which are those of his *Theory of Economic Development,* as well as the general scope of the work, are well known and need not be indicated here. But what is not generally known, and perhaps sounds improbable, is that, apart from some clerical assistance, he wrote the book single-handed. The fact is that, although he was a very sociable man and appreciated the necessity and usefulness of scientific teamwork, Schumpeter was always a lone wolf in his scientific work. Everything he published he wrote out in longhand, and for a long time, having no secretary, he had even to write his letters in his own hand.

But he always had the rare and priceless talent—Böhm-Bawerk called it a "gift of God," [34] adding that it could be a dangerous gift—of easy and quick expression. He could read and absorb new ideas and facts with amazing speed, and he never found it difficult in writing or speaking to find the right word or phrase from a tremendous vocabulary in both German and English. In fact, he used the English language with a verve and pungency that few could equal. However, in the short-run the reception of the business cycle book was disappointing. The reasons are not hard to understand. The book is not well arranged and is not easy to read. It is written in a heavy and often involved style with no concessions to the reader or to current fads. It appeared at the beginning of the war at a time when the wave of Keynesianism and depression economics was at its very height. But apart from these unfavorable external circumstances, it is the kind of book which takes considerable time to exert its full influence.

The next book, *Capitalism, Socialism and Democracy,* was (for a serious book, not a textbook) a great popular success. It has appeared in several editions,[35] and was translated into at least five foreign languages. It was written within a year or two and the author regarded it as nothing more than a *parergon*.

During the last years Schumpeter had been working on a great history of economic analysis. The manuscript is almost finished and will be published by Mrs. Schumpeter in two volumes under the title, *History of Economic Analysis.*

Apart from these books, he wrote many articles, among them the historical and biographical masterpieces on Taussig, Marshall, Keynes, Fisher, Pareto, and Mitchell (in that order). These essays, together with earlier ones on Walras, Menger, and Böhm-Bawerk and the essay on Marx in Part I of *Capitalism, Socialism and Democracy,* will be

[34] See his criticism of Schumpeter's theory of interest in *Zeitschrift für Volkswirtschaft* (Vienna, 1913), Vol. XXII, p. 61.

[35] New York: Harper and Bros. first ed., 1942; second revised ed., 1947; third enlarged ed. with a new chapter, 1950. There have also been three editions in England (London, Allen & Unwin).

published soon under the title *Ten Great Economists: From Marx to Keynes,* by the Oxford University Press.

During all his Harvard years (excepting two sabbatical terms which he spent working in his home in Taconic), Schumpeter carried a full teaching load, and, especially during the earlier part of the period, organized and attended all sorts of special discussion groups and seminars. He always felt that the official minimum teaching assignment in the university was too heavy to permit professors adequate time for research and writing, and strongly urged its reduction. But he himself usually taught much more than the official minimum. That again was typical: he preached wine for others but drank water himself.

Schumpeter was the most cooperative and considerate colleague anyone could imagine. He was always ready to offer his help, to serve on a committee, or to substitute for an indisposed colleague in a lecture or seminar, and was most reluctant and apologetic in asking for similar favors. His standards concerning the dignity and social status of university professors and scholars were of the highest order, and he often complained that, in most American universities and in American society at large, scholars did not enjoy the social status they ought to have and were overburdened with administrative duties. He nevertheless did his full part, along with the youngest instructors, in performing menial chores, such as foreign language examinations. He never behaved like a prima donna, although he was often regarded as one, especially by outsiders.

His teaching program consisted of a full course in advanced theory which he offered every year. Every other year or so he would offer a half course in business cycles and one in the history of economic doctrines, and now and then a half course in money and banking. In recent years he gave regularly a half course in socialism and social movements. The content of all these courses would be varied from year to year, but they all suffered from one defect: by listening to Schumpeter's lectures and studying his reading assignments and suggestions, students could have never found out that he himself had ever written anything on those subjects.

V. SCHUMPETER'S CONTRIBUTION TO ECONOMICS

The time for a complete and detailed appraisal of Schumpeter's scientific achievements and of his place in the history of economics has not yet arrived. Full appreciation of a work of such magnitude and complexity requires greater time distance for proper perspective, especially inasmuch as his last great book, the *History of Economic Analysis,* which promises to be in itself a major event in the history of economic thought, is not yet available. The following remarks are therefore nothing more than a preliminary sketch.

In the opening pages of his revealing biography of Böhm-Bawerk,[36] he points out that Böhm-Bawerk's entire scientific work is one thoroughly integrated whole. Practically everything Böhm-Bawerk wrote was directed towards the well-defined goal of working out his model of the capitalist economy. Also his numerous and endless controversies were devoted to the sole purpose of clarifying and supporting Böhm-Bawerk's own theoretical structure.[37] "He knew exactly what he wanted in science and in life, which one can say of but few men, and therefore it is easy to review his work." [38]

Schumpeter's own work is much more difficult to describe, and his place in modern economics not easy to define. There are several reasons for this. It is true that Schumpeter, like Böhm-Bawerk and most great social scientists (Edgeworth might perhaps be regarded as an exception), had a broad over-all picture of the socio-economic process, a "vision" as Schumpeter used to call it which, like the plot in a good drama, gives unity to his work. His "grand design," the contours of which can already be discerned in his first book (*Wesen und Hauptinhalt,* 1908), found its full expression in his *Theory of Economic Development* (1912) and was lavishly, sometimes labori-

---

[36] "Das wissenschaftliche Lebenswerk Eugen von Böhm-Bawerks," *Zeitschrift für Volkswirtschaft, Verwaltung und Sozialpolitik,* Vol. XXIII (1914), Vienna. The title of this lengthy essay (73 pages) does not do justice to the content. It is not confined to an appraisal of Böhm-Bawerk's scientific work, but contains also a brilliant description and analysis of the great economist's personality with many penetrating observations on what might be called the economics and psychology of economic theorizing. This is probably the most revealing of Schumpeter's biographical essays. It is written with much feeling and shows the close personal and scientific relation with Böhm-Bawerk. In view of that, it seems appropriate in an appraisal of Schumpeter's work to devote some space to a comparison of his system with that of Böhm-Bawerk, especially since in most points here considered, Böhm-Bawerk's views are representative not only of Austrian but of Walrasian and Marshallian economics as well.

[37] Böhm-Bawerk's criticisms and polemics were always polite and urbane in tone as well as truly scientific and constructive in content. He criticized not for criticism's sake but in order to test and defend *The Positive Theory of Capital* against other views. That holds fully also of his Marx critique ("Karl Marx and the Close of His System") which, as Schumpeter said, "will never cease, as far as the theoretical content of the Marxian system goes, to be *the* Marx critique" (*loc. cit.,* p. 474).

[38] Schumpeter, *loc. cit.,* p. 457.

ously worked out, illustrated, and tested in his *Business Cycles* and further elaborated in his *Capitalism, Socialism and Democracy*. It is much more complex than that of Böhm-Bawerk and other neoclassical economists.

In the first place, while Böhm-Bawerk's model (also that of Walras but not that of Marshall) is essentially static,[39] Schumpeter's model is dynamic in nature. It is not dynamic in the sense of modern sequence analysis; it is not "micro-dynamics," the word "micro" being here used not in the sense of dealing with the behavior of the smallest economic units (household and firm) as contrasted with aggregate quantities (national income, consumption, investment). In this latter sense, Schumpeter *is* a "micro-theorist," at least as far as his methodological credo is concerned. He was always suspicious of aggregates and averages—"beware of averages," he said in his very first paper—and he often urged that economic analysis should be based on the theory of household and firm. But in his "theoretical practice," he was, it seems to me, as other economists who hold similar views, unable to avoid the use of aggregates and averages. The word "micro" is here used in the sense of being concerned with minor, unimportant fluctuations. Schumpeter's theory was not micro-dynamics as exemplified by modern post-Keynesian multiplier-acceleration models, and the like. He was quite familiar with those models. He highly appreciated the mathematical ingenuity which goes into their construction, discussed them in considerable detail in his classes,[40] and was willing to make limited use of them for the explanation of minor oscillations around the great waves of economic development,[41] but he felt that they are just as incapable of explaining the great economic rhythm as the ripples caused by high winds on the surface of the sea are incapable of influencing the great rhythm of the tide.

Schumpeter's dynamic mechanism is driven by more powerful forces than the vagaries of the propensity to consume and the acceleration principle. The nature of these forces (technological and organizational innovations, entrepreneurial activity, and the credit mechanism which enables the dynamic innovator to draw productive resources

[39] This may sound strange because Böhm-Bawerk stresses the time element so much. But one can deal with the time factor by means of the method of comparative statics. That is what Böhm-Bawerk did.

[40] See also *Business Cycles*, Vol. I, Chapter IV.

[41] From conversation and remarks in classes it appears that he was ready to accept an inventory mechanism *à la* Abramowitz and Metzler as explanation for the short cycle (Kitchin cycle).

from the static "circular flow" economy) are too well known to make detailed discussion necessary.[42]

In the preface to the Japanese Edition of his *Theory of Economic Development* he says:

. . . When in my beginnings I studied the Walrasian conception and the Walrasian technique . . . I discovered not only that it is rigorously static in character . . . but also that it is applicable only to a stationary process. These two things must not be confused. A static theory . . . can be useful in the investigation of any kind of reality, however disequilibrated it may be. A stationary process, however, is a process which *actually* does not change of its own initiative, but merely reproduces constant rates of real income as it flows along in time. If it changes at all, it does so under the influence of events which are external to itself, such as natural catastrophes, wars, and so on. Walras would have admitted this. He would have said (and as a matter of fact, he did say it to me the only time I had the opportunity to converse with him) that . . . economic life is essentially passive and merely adapts itself to the natural and social influences which may be acting on it, so that the theory of a stationary process constitutes really the whole of theoretical economics. . . . I felt very strongly that this was wrong, and that there was a source of energy within the economic system which would of itself disrupt . . . equilibrium. If this is so, then there must be a purely economic theory of economic change which does not merely rely on external factors. . . . It is such a theory that I have tried to build and I believe . . . that it contributes something to the understanding . . . of the capitalist world and explains a number of phenomena . . . more satisfactorily than . . . either the Walrasian or Marshallian apparatus.[43]

I have strong doubts that the sharp distinction between disequilibrating forces working from within the economic system and those operating on the economic system from the outside contributes anything to the understanding of economic development. But the concrete mechanism of economic change, as described and analyzed by Schumpeter, undoubtedly constitutes a great advance over traditional neoclassical economics.

In these respects he felt himself to be, and actually was, closer to Marx than to Walras, Böhm-Bawerk and, even more, than to Keynes.[44]

[42] These things have been often discussed. There is now available the excellent and convenient study by R. V. Clemence and Francis S. Doody, *The Schumpeterian System* (Cambridge, Mass., 1950).

[43] Pages 2 and 3.

[44] In this preface to the Japanese edition of the *Theory of Economic Development,* he mentioned that it was *not* clear to him at the outset "what to the reader will perhaps be obvious at once, namely, that this idea and this aim [to construct

Indeed, all his life he was attracted by the grandeur of the Marxian system, although he was by no means an uncritical admirer of Marx and, in recent years, he scornfully disapproved of what he derisively referred to as "the Keynesianization of Marx," that is of the attempts at interpreting Marx in terms of the Keynesian system; this he regarded as a complete emasculation of the Marxian system. There are two other characteristics of Schumpeter's system which seem to put him closer to Marx than to Walras, Böhm-Bawerk, and Marshall. These are, first, the important role assigned to social relationships and to the institutional framework (as against "purely economic" factors) and second, the historical slant and intent of his theory.

These differences between Schumpeter on the one hand and Böhm-Bawerk and other "pure" economists on the other are, however, only a matter of degree. He had no sympathy whatever for the vague, almost metaphysical "collectivism" of which there is so much in Marxist writings. By this I mean "the special and exclusive outlook upon the whole of social life" claimed by the Marxists—an outlook which postulates social forces that operate on and influence individual behavior and are somehow independent of the totality of individual actions.[45] Schumpeter always adhered to what he called "methodological individualism," [46] i.e., the principle that social phenomena and forces must be defined and interpreted in terms of interrelations and interactions, often of great complexity, between individuals and their subjective motivations.

According to Schumpeter, Böhm-Bawerk's theory—and here again Böhm-Bawerk stands for modern theoretical economics—is not "unsocial," but the "sociological framework" is only "lightly indicated." [47]

a theory of economic development which relies on forces internal to the economic system] are exactly the same that underlie the economic teaching of Marx" (p. 3).

[45] See, for example, Sweezy's edition of Böhm-Bawerk and Hilferding (*loc. cit.*), especially Sweezy's introduction, pp. xx–xxii, and Hilferding, Chap. III, "The Subjectivist Outlook" (p. 184 ff.), where the "social and unhistorical" standpoint of Marx is contrasted with the "unsocial and unhistorical" standpoint of Böhm-Bawerk and of orthodox theory in general. Marxism inherited this social metaphysics from German idealistic philosophy (Hegel), and it shares it with systems like that of Othmar Spann, who derives it from the same source. I know that the Marxists as well as Spann would deny violently and indignantly that their views have anything in common with one another, although they originate from the same source. This illustrates the truth of the observation that there is nowhere so much hatred as between members of the same family.

[46] See the lengthy discussion in *Wesen und Hauptinhalt,* Part I, Chap. VI, "Der methodologische Individualismus."

[47] See Schumpeter's biographical essay on Böhm-Bawerk, *loc. cit.,* p. 489. In Marshall's work the social framework is more fully elaborated than in Walras' or in Böhm-Bawerk's writings.

It should be observed that Böhm-Bawerk sharply distinguishes between the individual household economy (Robinson Crusoe economy), the competitive price economy, and the centrally planned (socialist) economy.[48]   It is true, however, that Böhm-Bawerk and other marginalists are largely concerned with analyzing economic relationships which hold wherever men apply scarce resources to unlimited wants, irrespective of the particular social organization of society.   Schumpeter did not deny that there are such all-embracing regularities, but he was of the opinion that they are of more limited validity than traditional economic theories assume.   In that sense his theory is more "social," i.e., it differentiates more according to the social framework than that of Böhm-Bawerk and other modern theorists.

The difference comes to a head in connection with the problem of interest, capital accumulation, and the business cycle.   In the *Theory of Economic Development* and in his famous controversy with Böhm-Bawerk on the rate of interest,[49] Schumpeter argued that the rate of interest is institutionally and dynamically determined.   There would be no interest either in a stationary or semistationary price economy nor in a centrally planned (socialist or single household) economy (whether stationary or progressive), while according to Böhm-Bawerk, the rate of interest is a basic economic category, independent of the concrete social and institutional arrangements. In this particular respect most economists, including many modern socialists, would side with Böhm-Bawerk, holding that as a calculating or accounting category (though not as a distributive share) the rate of interest has a place also in the socialist economy.[50]

It should not be overlooked that Schumpeter's contribution to interest theory is not confined to the somewhat questionable proposition that in a stationary state the rate of interest would be zero.   He might well have admitted that there must be a positive rate of interest in a

[48] There is a chapter on interest in the socialist economy in his *Positive Theory of Capital*.   There is also the important article "Macht oder ökonomisches Gesetz?" (*Zeitschrift für Volkswirtschaft,* Vol. XXIII, Vienna, 1914, reprinted in *Gesamte Schriften,* Vol. I, ed. F. X. Weiss) which deals with the problem of the extent to which economic laws can be interfered with by government action.

[49] *Zeitschrift für Volkswirtschaft,* Vol. XXII, 1913.

[50] Keynes's interest theory is superficially similar to Schumpeter's inasmuch as he conceives of the rate of interest as a purely psycho-monetary phenomenon. But his position on this issue is basically ambiguous and contradictory.   As is so often the case, one has to distinguish between Keynes's formalized system and a confusing though suggestive welter of surrounding remarks, which contains much that goes not only beyond but also contradicts the liquidity theory of interest of his formalized system.

stationary state, but insisted that the interest rates which we find in practice are raised above the stationary level by the dynamic forces described in his theory.

The controversy concerning the rate of interest is, however, only one facet of the whole problem. The difference between Schumpeter's scheme of things and that of Böhm-Bawerk (and Böhm-Bawerk here stands again for a large part of neoclassical economics), goes deeper; it concerns the whole conception of the process of capital accumulation and economic progress. Let me briefly indicate the difference.

According to Böhm-Bawerk and most other modern economists (including especially F. H. Knight) [51] the process of capital accumulation is essentially, or at least potentially, smooth and continuous. People save and savings are invested. Thus the capital stock grows and output increases. In addition, the production function changes, new methods and processes are invented all the time, and output increases for that reason too. These writers recognize, of course, that the process of economic development through capital accumulation and advances in technological knowledge is often interrupted. The business cycle and the recurrence of economic depressions are not ignored. But these phenomena are regarded as inessential deviations, due to monetary disturbances and the like—disturbances that could be avoided or at least reduced to insignificant proportions by appropriate policies.

Schumpeter would not deny that some progress can be realized in a smooth and orderly fashion by continuous accumulation of capital and gradual improvement of technology. But he thinks it could not amount to much. The really big changes which shape the course of economic development are not made, cannot be made, gradually and continuously; they must be forced upon the stationary, circular flow economy in intermittent pushes. The business cycle (at least the major cycle), which for many other theorists is the result either of monetary surface phenomena (avoidable aberrations of monetary policy [Mises, Hayek]) or of lags and frictions (Hawtrey) or of the vagaries of multiplier and acceleration principle and the like, becomes in Schumpeter's theory an integral part of the process of economic development in the capitalist system. The complicated mechanism which produces this result and its constituent parts, the path-breaking role of the innovator-entrepreneur and of the host of imitators who

[51] I hope Professor Knight will not object to being grouped with Böhm-Bawerk. His objections to the concept of a period of production and the like seem to me of minor importance in the present context.

follow suit, the function of productive credit inflation and forced saving succeeded by autodeflation and all the rest, is well known. Capitalism for Schumpeter becomes, thus, a narrower concept than for Böhm-Bawerk and most neoclassical economists. It is not synonymous with an individualistic price economy and still less with an economy which uses capital on a large scale; it is a very special type of price economy, namely, that one which is so organized that the indicated rhythmic mechanism can operate. ". . . Capitalism is defined by three features . . . : private ownership of the physical means of production; private profits and private responsibility for losses; and the creation of means of payments—bank notes and deposits—by private banks. The first two features suffice to define private enterprise. But no concept of capitalism can be satisfactory without including the set of typically capitalistic phenomena covered by the third." [52]

The complicated interaction of social and economic forces reappears again, on a higher level as it were, in the theory of the socio-political disintegration of capitalism as fully elaborated in his *Capitalism, Socialism and Democracy*, although clearly foreshadowed in earlier writings. Schumpeter finds that economically speaking the capitalist system has served the human race very well indeed. It has raised the volume of output and standard of living tremendously. Glaring inequalities of income could easily be removed without serious impairment of the productivity of the economic machine. He saw no economic reason why capitalism should not continue to function with equal success in the future. But, at the same time, he was convinced that capitalism was doomed, because by its very success it is bound to destroy its own supporting and protecting social structures. This piece of social dynamics is not widely accepted, nor does it seem to be a necessary consequence of the rest of Schumpeter's theoretical structure. But it throws into high relief the great complexity and the close interrelations of economic and social forces that are so characteristic of Schumpeter's work.

It was said above that Schumpeter's theory is more historical than that of Böhm-Bawerk and of most other modern economists. Schumpeter was always deeply interested in historical problems and a strong supporter of the historical method of understanding social and economic phenomena. He had historical feeling and perspective, and a tremendous historical knowledge. Many of his writings had a historical slant. His *Wesen und Hauptinhalt* (1908) and *Theory of Economic*

[52] "Capitalism in the Postwar World," in *Postwar Economic Problems*, ed. by S. E. Harris (New York, 1943), p. 113.

Development (1912) are, however, entirely unhistorical, although the theory expounded in the latter book is the basis of later historical interpretations. Schumpeter was, however, not a "historicist" in the sense in which Hegel and Marx [53] were, that is to say, he did not enunciate sweeping historical laws, although he evidently played with the idea of predetermined historical evolution, and was much intrigued by Marx's historical construction. But his devotion to exact methods and rigid scientific discipline did not permit him to go far in the direction of historico-philosophical speculation. He found much truth in the "materialistic interpretation" of history. Economic factors go a long way to explain the course of history,[54] but not all the way: an acceptable "philosophy of history" must "leave adequate room for the quality of leading personnel and in the special case at hand [he was speaking of Bolshevist Russia] for the quality of the leading individual," namely, Stalin.[55]

This is, then, in bare outline Schumpeter's socio-economic world picture, an exceedingly complex structure indeed. The basic ideas were conceived at a very early time, but much of his work throughout his life was spent in elaborating details, making adjustments here and there, and testing his theory against the facts of history; but unlike Böhm-Bawerk he did not defend his theory in extensive polemics.[56] Moreover (again unlike Böhm-Bawerk, whose self-denial and moderation in that respect he had praised so highly), Schumpeter permitted himself the luxury of spending much effort in fields and on

[53] For a penetrating analysis and criticism of historicism, see Karl Popper's three highly instructive articles, "The Poverty of Historicism" (*Economica*, 1944–45), and his book, *The Open Society and Its Enemies*, especially Vol. II, *The High Tide of Prophecy: Hegel and Marx* (London, 1945; 2nd rev. ed., Princeton, 1950).

[54] Interesting remarks can be found in his essay "Sozialistische Möglichkeiten von heute" (1920), where it is argued that political revolutions always follow after economic revolutions, never precede them—admitting, however, that the Russian case is an exception, a statement that recurs in his *Capitalism, Socialism and Democracy*.

[55] *Capitalism, Socialism and Democracy*, 2nd ed., p. 399.

[56] Schumpeter did not believe in the usefulness of polemical discussion. Typical are the following remarks in his article on Sombart ("Sombarts Dritter Band," i.e., third volume of *Der moderne Kapitalismus, Schmoller's Jahrbuch*, Vol. LI, 1927). "The fight about methodology [the *Methodenstreit* initiated between Menger and Schmoller] is obsolete, although there is occasional inclination to fight rearguard actions. . . . Science has got over that, not by fighting out epistemological issues and by subsequent conversion of both sides to a common creed, but in this manner that practical work on concrete problems proceeded in the way indicated by the nature of the task on hand" (p. 350).

subjects that were not at all, or only loosely, connected with his main work. In fact, there is no branch of economics in which he was not deeply interested and well versed, and few to which he has not made important contributions.

Static theory was covered by his first book and by many articles, especially in his earlier period. To the theory of money he made an important contribution in his celebrated paper "Das Sozialprodukt und die Rechenpfennige" (1917) and elsewhere. In its dynamic aspects the theory of money, credit and banking is, of course, an integral part of his theory of economic development and as such found extensive treatment in numerous writings. There are two long chapters on "Money, Credit, and Business Cycles" in the forthcoming *History of Economic Analysis*. There are, furthermore, his sociological studies, mainly in the essays on the theory of social classes (1927) and imperialism (1919) and in his *Capitalism, Socialism and Democracy* (1942), which are, it is true, closely connected with his basic model, but go far beyond it in several directions. And above all, there are his biographical essays and his extensive studies in the history of economic thought culminating in the posthumous *History of Economic Analysis*. Once more, unlike Böhm-Bawerk, he deals not only with those aspects of the work of other economists and of other theoretical systems which have a direct or indirect bearing on his own structure, but tries to understand them, men as well as theories, in their totality.

The wide range and complexity of Schumpeter's scientific work reflects accurately the universality and complexity of his mind. He begins the preface of his first book with the quotation "Alles verstehen, heisst alles verzeihen"—"Tout comprendre c'est tout pardonner." This adage is indeed a clue to his mind. He understood every theory, every standpoint, every method, and found in each something true and useful, realizing clearly, at the same time, their defects and limitations. He was extremely open-minded, saw all sides of every question without being eclectic, that is to say, without trying to reconcile the irreconcilable, or merely to assemble unconnected and uncoordinated theorems and facts.

Let me illustrate by a few examples. He was deeply interested in pure static theory and was a real connoisseur of mathematical refinements in that area, a "theoretical *gourmet*" as he himself put it, He was, nevertheless, fully aware of the limitations, or what he thought were the limitations, of static theory and was very critical of what he regarded as uncritical applications, e.g., those typically made of the theory of monopoly and monopolistic competition in the area of welfare economics. He was enraptured by the econometric method, but again became quite impatient with certain econometric analyses of the trade cycle.[57] He had a very high opinion of the productive power of capitalism and an ingrained dislike for socialism. At the same time, he was not blind to what he thought were the cultural drawbacks of capitalism and went out of his way to prove that socialism could work and was compatible with democracy.[58]

The complexity, diversity, and universality of Schumpeter's mind is the key to a proper understanding of the man and his work. It explains a certain lack of systematic arrangement and neatness in his writings which became more pronounced in later years and is especially evident in his book on *Business Cycles,* where he tried to deal with the capitalist process in all its complexity. The great wealth of ideas which constantly streamed through his mind, and his acute awareness of all sides of every question, and of the limitations of each standpoint and method, made it very hard for him to present his views on any subject neatly and systematically. He was not always able fully to integrate his ideas, and he easily gave the impression of being undecided about important issues or even contradictory. He was fully aware of these shortcomings in his presentations and envied those writers who, because they held simpler views, were not troubled by such difficulties.

His somewhat involved literary style which can be perhaps best described as "baroque" gives adequate expression to the complex structure of his mind. It is characterized by long sentences, numerous

[57] See his contribution to the National Bureau Conference on Business Cycles, November 1949.

[58] Schumpeter was, however, never a socialist, if by that word we designate those who *advocate* socialism, which is in Schumpeter's own words "an institutional arrangement that vests the management of the productive process with some public authority." ("Capitalism in the Postwar World," *loc. cit.,* p. 113.) It would not be necessary to dwell upon this fact, which should be obvious to any reader of Schumpeter's book on socialism, if it were not also a fact that frequently the opposite assertion is made. For example, the editor of the German translation of *Capitalism, Socialism and Democracy* says in his introduction: "Schumpeter ist Sozialist" and a little later again refers to him as "that socialist"! (Professor Edgar Salin, in "Einleitung" to *Kapitalismus, Sozialismus und Demokratie,* Bern; A. Francke, 1946, p. 8.)
It is true that Schumpeter was pessimistic with respect to capitalism's chances of survival. But he did not say that socialism was inevitable. In the preface to the second edition of his *Capitalism, Socialism and Democracy,* he defends himself against the reproach of "defeatism" (p. 11). To call him a socialist is like calling Cassandra a Greek partisan because she prophesied the fall of Troy!

qualifying phrases, qualifications of qualifications, casuistic distinctions of meanings. These qualities of his style are especially pronounced, as one would expect, in his German writings, because the German language offers more freedom for complicated constructions.[59]

VI. WHY IS THERE NO "SCHUMPETER SCHOOL"?

I have often asked myself the question and have heard it raised by others, why there are no Schumpeterians in the sense in which there are Keynesians, or even Böhm-Bawerkians and Marshallians, not to mention Marxians. Schumpeter had many ardent admirers and scores of devoted students. Wherever he taught he attracted the cream of the student body, and literally hundreds of economists in all lands have been profoundly influenced by his teaching and writing. But there is no Schumpeter school.

It would be tempting to explain this in terms of external circumstances: Schumpeter was born in a less fortunate part of the world than Keynes, a comparison with whom is especially instructive because he (1883–1946) was Schumpeter's exact contemporary. Schumpeter's real fatherland, the Austro-Hungarian monarchy, disintegrated while he was still in the beginning of his scientific career. The new Austria did not offer him an opportunity for academic success; in Germany he arrived on the eve of a horrible revolution, which did not leave him enough time to take root; and seven or eight of the eighteen years in the quiet haven of Harvard were largely lost, as far as the formation of a school was concerned, through the emotional and intellectual disturbances incident to war and preparations for war. This may sound plausible. But I do not think it is the real explanation. Whatever the influences of the external course of his life on his character and personality—and they must have been considerable—the basic, internal structure of Schumpeter's mind and work offers a better explanation for the fact that he did not found a school.

Schumpeter's universality and open-mindedness and the complexity of his system made the crystallization of a Schumpeter school difficult. *Tout comprendre c'est tout pardonner* is not a powerful rallying cry. What he said of Marshall—that "unlike Mill, he would never have said that some problem or other was settled for all time to come and there

[59] On the stylistic traditions of the German scientific language see the interesting remarks by H. H. Gerth and C. W. Mills in their preface to the translation of Max Weber's *Essays in Sociology* (New York: Oxford University Press, 1946, pp. 5 and 6).

was nothing about it that called for further explanation either by himself or another writer" [60]—holds fully of Schumpeter himself. "I never wish to say anything definitive; if I have a function it is to open doors, not to close them"—he said in the informal farewell address to his students in Bonn.[61] He was, thus, prevented by a self-imposed injunction from constructing a neat simplified version of his theory as Keynes did.[62] The construction of such a simplified system is evidently necessary for the formation of a compact group of disciples. But above all, unlike Marshall and Keynes, Schumpeter was constitutionally unable "to give his readers exactly what they craved—a message which was both high-minded and comforting—and at the same time to answer to the call of his conscience." [63] He did not and could not, like Marshall, "cheerfully sympathize, from a warm heart, with the ideals of socialism, and patronizingly talk down to socialists from a cool head." [64] With him it was rather the other way round; he disliked intensely the ideals of the socialists but found much truth in their teaching. Again, he was unlike Marshall and Keynes in that it *was* "primarily intellectual curiosity" that "brought [Schumpeter] into the economist's camp. He was [*not*] driven to it from ethical speculations by a generous impulse to help in the great task of alleviating the misery and degradation . . . among the . . . poor." [65]

To summarize: The main reason why no Schumpeter school developed is that Schumpeter was neither a reformer nor an enthusiastic partisan of capitalism, socialism, planning, or any other "ism"; he was a scholar and an intellectual. It is hardly a compliment to economics as a science, but it seems to me to be a fact that nonscientific factors play such an important role in the formation of economic schools. In the purely scientific sphere Schumpeter's open-mindedness and universality, the lack of fighting spirit for any particular approach, the fact that he

[60] "Alfred Marshall's *Principles*," *American Economic Review*, June 1941, p. 237.

[61] A typescript of that speech is in the possession of Wolfgang Stolper, who kindly showed it to me.

[62] There is good reason to believe that Keynes did this quite consciously, in order to get the immediate action which the situation in his opinion demanded, although he never took the simplified Keynesianism—"vulgär Keynesianism," to use the technical Marxian phrase (which should not be translated as "vulgar")— quite so seriously and uncritically as do many of his followers.

[63] See Schumpeter, "Alfred Marshall's *Principles*," *loc. cit.*, p. 244.

[64] *Ibid.*

[65] *Ibid.*, p. 239. The quotation, referring in the original to Marshall, has been reversed above, in order to apply to Schumpeter.

found something useful and acceptable in almost every theory and method helped to prevent development of a Schumpeter school.[66]

Schumpeter himself was conscious of all this. In his farewell address to his students in Bonn he said: "I have never tried to bring about a Schumpeter school. There is none and it ought not to exist. . . . Economics is not a philosophy but a science. Hence there should be no 'schools' in our field. . . . Many people feel irritated by this attitude. For in Germany alone there are half a dozen economists who regard themselves as heads of such 'schools,' as fighters for absolute light against absolute darkness. But there is no use combating that sort of thing. One should not fight what life is going to eliminate anyway. Unlike politics and business, immediate success should not matter in science. . . . I for my part accept the judgment of future generations."

This was his philosophy in these respects. But he would have been less human than he was, if his feelings had been as austere and resigned as his philosophy. In fact, he was far from unreceptive to external success and popularity; and, although he rarely showed it, he often suffered from lack of response and appreciation. He was a good laugher and could enjoy exuberantly a stimulating conversation, a good story, a brilliant joke, but he was fundamentally not a happy man. And at the bottom of his unhappiness and resignation was, I believe, the cleavage between his high and austere ideals on the one hand and his human feelings and impulses on the other.[67] Again, he was aware of this, and he envied those who—like the utilitarians and Victorians, like Marshall and Keynes—are not plagued by an unbridgeable gulf between their ideals and their emotions, who manage "at the same time to answer the call of their conscience" and to be "comforting" to themselves and to others.

[66] It could also be argued that the times were not propitious for a popular success of his theories, because the heydey of capitalism or at least of that phase of capitalism which Schumpeter describes had passed when the *Theory of Economic Development* appeared. This, however, seems to me questionable. During the nineteen-twenties, capitalism was still very much alive almost everywhere—at least *ex visu* of the twenties, if not in the light of what happened later, which nobody foresaw at the time. In the United States capitalism is vigorous even at this time. At any rate, I prefer the more subjective explanation given in the text.

[67] There were also other, partly external, factors in the situation. On these compare Arthur Smithies' subtle and understanding analysis of Schumpeter's personality in the forthcoming *American Economic Review* for September 1950.

Samuelson

─────────── on ───────

Keynes

John Maynard Keynes (1883–1946) was educated at Eton and Cambridge. A British statesman, financier, and protector of the arts, his great contribution to economics includes a theory of the determination of the level of national income. The national income, Keynes insists, may find its equilibrium level below that which would correspond to full employment. With Keynes's work, the micro-economics of the individual consumer, the individual firm, and the single commodity or service became supplemented by the aggregative macro-economics of the national income and the level of employment. Keynes's principal publication, *The General Theory of Employment, Interest, and Money* (1936), also shows him as a master of prose, as do his brilliant biographical pieces and other writings. A biography, *The Life of John Maynard Keynes,* was published by R. F. Harrod in 1951.

Paul Anthony Samuelson (1915–   ) was educated at Chicago and Harvard, and now teaches at the Massachusetts Institute of Technology. Samuelson is a leading economic theorist, whose *Foundations of Economic Analysis* (1947) contains explorations of dynamic economics as well as contributions to the theory of employment, production, distribution, and value. Samuelson was the first recipient of the John Bates Clark medal, conferred on him by the American Economic Association in 1947.

THE DEATH of Lord Keynes will undoubtedly afford the occasion for numerous attempts to appraise the character of the man and his contribution to economic thought. The personal details of his life and antecedents will very properly receive extensive notice elsewhere.

It is perhaps not too soon to venture upon a brief and tentative appraisal of Keynes's lasting impact upon the development of modern economic analysis. And it is all the more fitting to do so now that his major work has just completed the first decade of its very long life.

THE IMPACT OF THE GENERAL THEORY

I have always considered it a priceless advantage to have been born as an economist prior to 1936 and to have received a thorough grounding in classical economics. It is quite impossible for modern students to realize the full effect of what has been advisably called "The Keynesian Revolution" [1] upon those of us brought up in the orthodox tradition. What beginners today often regard as trite and obvious was to us puzzling, novel, and heretical.

To have been born as an economist before 1936 was a boon—yes. But not to have been born too long before!

> Bliss was it in that dawn to be alive,
> But to be young was very heaven!

The *General Theory* caught most economists under the age of 35 with the unexpected virulence of a disease first attacking and decimating an isolated tribe of South Sea islanders. Economists beyond 50 turned out to be quite immune to the ailment. With time, most economists in-between began to run the fever, often without knowing or admitting their condition.

I must confess that my own first reaction to the *General Theory* was not at all like that of Keats on first looking into Chapman's Homer.

---

[1] I owe much in what follows to discussions with my former student, Dr. Lawrence R. Klein, whose rewarding study shortly to be published by The Macmillan Company bears the above title. [*The Keynesian Revolution*, 1947.—Ed.]

[Reprinted by permission from *Econometrica*, July 1946.]

No silent watcher, I, upon a peak in Darien. My rebellion against its pretensions would have been complete except for an uneasy realization that I did not at all understand what it was about. And I think I am giving away no secrets when I solemnly aver—upon the basis of vivid personal recollection—that no one else in Cambridge, Massachusetts, really knew what it was about for some 12 to 18 months after its publication. Indeed, until the appearance of the mathematical models of Meade, Lange, Hicks, and Harrod there is reason to believe that Keynes himself did not truly understand his own analysis.

Fashion always plays an important role in economic science; new concepts become the *mode* and then are *passé*. A cynic might even be tempted to speculate as to whether academic discussion is itself equilibrating: whether assertion, reply, and rejoinder do not represent an oscillating divergent series, in which—to quote Frank Knight's characterization of sociology—"bad talk drives out good."

In this case, gradually and against heavy resistance, the realization grew that the new analysis of *effective demand* associated with the *General Theory* was not to prove such a passing fad, that here indeed was part of "the wave of the future." This impression was confirmed by the rapidity with which English economists, other than those at Cambridge, took up the new Gospel: e.g., Harrod, Meade, and others at Oxford; and still more surprisingly, the young blades at the *London School* like Kaldor, Lerner, and Hicks, who threw off their Hayekian garments and joined in the swim.

In this country it was pretty much the same story. Obviously, exactly the same words cannot be used to describe the analysis of income determination of, say, Lange, Hart, Harris, Ellis, Hansen, Bissell, Haberler, Slichter, J. M. Clark, or myself. And yet the Keynesian taint is unmistakably there upon every one of us. (I hasten to add—as who does not?—that I am not myself a Keynesian, although some of my best friends are.)

Instead of burning out like a fad, today ten years after its birth the *General Theory* is still gaining adherents and appears to be in business to stay. Many economists who are most vehement in criticism of the specific Keynesian policies—which must always be carefully distinguished from the scientific analysis associated with his name—will never again be the same after passing through his hands.[2]

It has been wisely said that only in terms of a modern theory of effective demand can one understand and defend the so-called "classi-

[2] For a striking example of the effect of the Keynesian analysis upon a great classical thinker, compare the fructiferous recent writings of Professor Pigou with his earlier *Theory of Unemployment*.

cal" theory of unemployment. It is perhaps not without additional significance in appraising the long-run prospects of the Keynesian theories that no individual who has once embraced the modern analysis has—as far as I am aware—later returned to the older theories. And in universities where graduate students are exposed to the old and new income analysis, I am told that it is often only too clear which way the wind blows.

Finally, and perhaps most important from the long-run standpoint, the Keynesian analysis has begun to filter down into the elementary textbooks; and as everybody knows once an idea gets into these, however bad it may be, it becomes practically immortal.

THE GENERAL THEORY ITSELF

Thus far, I have been discussing the new doctrines without regard to their content or merits, as if they were a religion and nothing else. True, we find a Gospel, Scriptures, a Prophet, Disciples, Apostles, Epigoni, and even a Duality; and if there is no Apostolic Succession, there is at least an Apostolic Benediction. But by now the joke has worn thin, and is in any case irrelevant.

The modern saving-investment theory of income determination did not directly displace the old latent belief in Say's Law of Markets (according to which only "frictions" could give rise to unemployment and overproduction). Events of the years following 1929 destroyed the previous economic synthesis. The economists' belief in the orthodox synthesis was not overthrown, but had simply atrophied: it was not as though one's soul had faced a showdown as to the existence of the Deity and that faith was unthroned, or even that one had awakened in the morning to find that belief had flown away in the night; rather it was realized with a sense of belated recognition that one no longer had faith, that one had been living without faith for a long time, and that what after all was the difference?

The nature of the world did not suddenly change one black October day in 1929 so that a new theory became mandatory. Even in their day, the older theories were incomplete and inadequate: in 1815, in 1844, 1893, and 1920. I venture to believe that the 18th and 19th centuries take on a new aspect when looked back upon from the modern perspective; that a new dimension has been added to the rereading of the Mercantilists, Thornton, Malthus, Ricardo, Tooke, David Wells, Marshall, and Wicksell.

Of course, the Great Depression of the Thirties was not the first to reveal the untenability of the classical synthesis. The classical philosophy always had its ups and downs along with the great swings of business activity. Each time it had come back. But now for the first time, it was confronted by a competing system—a well-reasoned body of thought containing among other things as many equations as unknowns. In short, like itself, a synthesis; and one which could swallow the classical system as a special case.

A new *system*, that is what requires emphasis. Classical economics could withstand isolated criticism. Theorists can always resist facts; for facts are hard to establish and are always changing anyway, and *ceteris paribus* can be made to absorb a good deal of punishment. Inevitably, at the earliest opportunity, the mind slips back into the old grooves of thought since analysis is utterly impossible without a frame of reference, a way of thinking about things, or in short a theory.[3]

Herein lies the secret of the *General Theory*. It is a badly written book, poorly organized; any layman who, beguiled by the author's previous reputation, bought the book was cheated of his 5 shillings. It is not well suited for classroom use.[4] It is arrogant, bad-tempered, polemical, and not overly-generous in its acknowledgments. It abounds in mares' nests and confusions: involuntary unemployment, wage units, the equality of savings and investment, the timing of the multiplier, interactions of marginal efficiency upon the rate of interest, forced savings, own rates of interest, and many others. In it the Keynesian system stands out indistinctly, as if the author were hardly aware of its existence or cognizant of its properties; and certainly he is at his worst when expounding its relations to its predecessors. Flashes of insight and intuition intersperse tedious algebra. An awkward definition suddenly gives way to an unforgettable cadenza. When it finally is mastered, we find its analysis to be obvious and at the same time new. In short, it is a work of genius.

It is not unlikely that future historians of economic thought will conclude that the very obscurity and polemical character of the *General Theory* ultimately served to maximize its long-run influence. Possibly such an analyst will place it in the first rank of theoretical classics along with the work of Smith, Cournot, and Walras. Certainly, these four

---

[3] This tendency holds true of everybody, including the businessman and the politician, the only difference being that practical men think in terms of highly simplified (and often contradictory) theories. It even holds true of a literary economist who would tremble at the sight of a mathematical symbol.

[4] The dual and confused theory of Keynes and his followers concerning the "equality of savings and investment" unfortunately ruled out the possibility of a pedagogically clear exposition of the theory in terms of schedules of savings and investment determining income.

books together encompass most of what is vital in the field of economic theory; and only the first is by any standards easy reading or even accessible to the intelligent layman.

In any case, it bears repeating that the *General Theory* is an obscure book so that would-be anti-Keynesians must assume their position largely on credit unless they are willing to put in a great deal of work and run the risk of seduction in the process. The *General Theory* resembles the random notes over a period of years of a gifted man who in his youth gained the whip hand over his publishers by virtue of the acclaim and fortune resulting from the success of his *Economic Consequences of the Peace*.

Like Joyce's *Finnegans Wake,* the *General Theory* is much in need of a companion volume providing a "skeleton key" and guide to its contents: warning the young and innocent away from Book I (especially the difficult Chapter 3) and on to Books III, IV, and VI. Certainly in its present state, the book does not get itself read from one year to another even by the sympathetic teacher and scholar.

Too much regret should not be attached to the fact that all hope must now be abandoned of an improved second edition, since it is the first edition which would in any case have assumed the stature of a classic. We may still paste into our copies of the *General Theory* certain subsequent Keynesian additions, most particularly, the famous chapter in *How to Pay for the War* which first outlined the modern theory of the inflationary process.

This last item helps to dispose of the fallacious belief that Keynesian economics is good "depression economics" and only that. Actually, the Keynesian system is indispensable to an understanding of conditions of overeffective demand and secular exhilaration; so much so that one anti-Keynesian has argued in print that *only* in times of a great war boom do such concepts as the marginal propensity to consume have validity. Perhaps, therefore, it would be more nearly correct to aver the reverse: that certain economists are Keynesian fellow travellers only in boom times, falling off the band wagon in depression.

If space permitted, it would be instructive to contrast the analysis of inflation during the Napoleonic and First World War periods with that of the recent War and correlate this with Keynes's influence. Thus, the "inflationary gap" concept,[5] recently so popular, seems to

[5] This "neo-Austrian" demand analysis of inflation has, if anything, been overdone in the present writer's opinion; there is reason to suspect that the relaxations of price controls during a period of *insufficient* general demand might still be followed by a considerable, self-sustaining rise in prices.

have been first used around the Spring of 1941 in a speech by the British Chancellor of Exchequer, a speech thought to have been the product of Keynes himself.

No author can complete a survey of Keynesian economics without indulging in that favorite indoor guessing game: Wherein lies the essential contribution of the *General Theory* and its distinguishing characteristic from the classical writings? Some consider its novelty to lie in the treatment of the *demand for money,* in its liquidity-preference emphasis. Others single out the treatment of *expectations.*

I cannot agree. According to recent trends of thought, the interest rate is less important than Keynes himself believed; therefore, *liquidity preference* (which itself explains part of the lack of importance of the interest rate, but only part) cannot be of such crucial significance. As for expectations, the *General Theory* is brilliant in calling attention to their importance and in suggesting many of the central features of uncertainty and speculation. It paves the way for a theory of expectations, but it hardly provides one.

I myself believe the broad significance of the *General Theory* to be in the fact that it provides a relatively realistic, complete system for analyzing the level of effective demand and its fluctuations. More narrowly, I conceive the heart of its contribution to be in that subset of its equations which relate to the propensity to consume and to saving in relation to offsets-to-saving. In addition to linking saving explicitly to income, there is an equally important denial of the implicit "classical" axiom that motivated investment is *indefinitely expansible or contractible,* so that whatever people *try* to save will always be fully invested. It is not important whether we deny this by reason of expectations, interest-rate rigidity, investment inelasticity with respect to over-all price changes and the interest rate, capital or investment satiation, secular factors of a technological and political nature, or what have you. But it is vital for business-cycle analysis that we do assume definite amounts of investment which are highly variable over time in response to a myriad of exogenous and endogenous factors, *and which are not automatically equilibrated to full-employment saving levels by any internal efficacious economic process.*

With respect to the level of total purchasing power and employment, Keynes denies that there is an *Invisible Hand* channeling the self-centered action of each individual to the social optimum. This is the sum and substance of his heresy. Again and again through his writings there is to be found the figure of speech that what is needed are certain "rules of the road" and governmental actions, which will benefit everybody but which nobody by himself is motivated to establish or follow.

Left to themselves during depression, people will try to save and only end up lowering society's level of capital formation and saving; during an inflation, apparent self-interest leads everyone to action which only aggravates the malignant upward spiral.

Such a philosophy is profoundly capitalistic in its nature. Its policies are offered "as the only practical means of avoiding the destruction of existing economic forms in their entirety and as the condition of the successful functioning of individual initiative."

From a perusal of Keynes's writing, I can find no evidence that words like these resemble the opportunistic lip-service paid in much recent social legislation to individual freedom and private enterprise. The following quotations show how far from a radical was this urbane and cosmopolitan provincial English liberal:

How can I accept [the communistic] doctrine which sets up as its bible, above and beyond criticism, an obsolete economic textbook which I know to be not only scientifically erroneous but without interest or application for the modern world? How can I adopt a creed which, preferring the mud to the fish, exalts the boorish proletariat above the bourgeois and intelligentsia who, with all their faults, are the quality of life and surely carry the seeds of all human advancement. Even if we need a religion, how can we find it in the turbid rubbish of the Red bookshops? It is hard for an educated, decent, intelligent son of Western Europe to find his ideals here, unless he has first suffered some strange and horrid process of conversion which has changed all his values. . . .

So, now that the deeds are done and there is no going back, I should like to give Russia her chance; to help and not to hinder. For how much rather, even after allowing for everything, if I were a Russian, would I contribute my quota of activity to Soviet Russia than to Tsarist Russia.[6]

Nothing that I can find in Keynes's later writings shows any significant changes in his underlying philosophy. As a result of the Great Depression, he becomes increasingly impatient with what he regards as the stupidity of businessmen who do not realize how much their views toward reform harm their own true long-run interests. But that is all.

With respect to international cooperation and autonomy of national policies, Keynes did undergo some changes in belief. The depression accentuated his post-World-War-I pessimism concerning the advisability of England or any other country's leaving itself to the mercy of the international gold standard. But in the last half dozen years, he began

6 J. M. Keynes, *Essays in Persuasion,* 1932, pp. 300 and 311. [New edition, London, Rupert Hart-Davis, 1951.—Ed.]

to pin his hopes on intelligent, concerted, multilateral cooperation, with, however, the important proviso that each nation should rarely be forced to adjust her economy by *deflationary* means.

PORTRAIT OF THE SCIENTIST

There is no danger that historians of thought will fail to devote attention to all the matters already discussed. Science, like capital, grows by accretion and each scientist's offering at the altar blooms forever. The personal characteristics of the scientist can only be captured while memories are still fresh; and only then, in all honesty, are they of maximum interest and relevance.

In my opinion, nothing in Keynes's previous life or work really quite prepares us for the *General Theory*. In many ways his career may serve as a model and prescription for a youth who aspires to be an economist. First, he was born into an able academic family which breathed in an atmosphere of economics; his father was a distinguished scholar, but not so brilliant as to overshadow and stunt his son's growth.

He early became interested in the philosophical basis of probability theory, thus establishing his reputation young in the technical fields of mathematics and logic. The *Indian Currency and Finance* book and assiduous service as Assistant Editor and Editor of the *Economic Journal* certified to his "solidity" and scholarly craftsmanship. His early reviews in the *Economic Journal* of Fisher, Hobson, Mises, and of Bagehot's collected works gave hints of the brilliance of his later literary style. The hiatus of the next few years in his scientific output is adequately explained by his service in the Treasury during the First World War.

The first extreme departure from an academic career comes, of course, with the Byronic success of the *Economic Consequences of the Peace,* which made him a world celebrity whose very visits to the Continent did not go unnoticed on the foreign exchange markets. As successful head of an insurance company and Bursar of King's College, he met the practical men of affairs on their own ground and won the reputation of being an economist who knew how to make money. All this was capped by a solid two-volume *Treatise on Money,* replete with historical accounts of the Mycenean monetary system, and the rest. Being a patron of the ballet and theater, a member of the "Bloomsbury Set" of Virginia Woolf and Lytton Strachey, a Governor of the Bank of England, and peer of the realm simply put the finishing gilt on his portrait.

Why then do I say that the *General Theory* still comes as a surprise? Because in all of these there is a sequence and pattern, and no one step occasions real astonishment. The *General Theory*, however, is a mutant notwithstanding Keynes's own expressed belief that it represents a "natural evolution" in his own line of thought. Let me turn, therefore, to his intellectual development.

As far back as in his 1911 review of Irving Fisher's *Purchasing Power of Money*,[7] Keynes expresses dissatisfaction with a mechanical Quantity Theory of money, but we have no evidence that he would have replaced it with anything more novel than a Cambridge cash-balance approach, amplified by a more detailed treatment of the discount rate. All this, as he would be the first to insist, was very much in the Marshallian oral tradition, and represents a view not very different from that of, say, Hawtrey.

Early in life he keenly realized the obstacles to deflation in a modern capitalistic country and the grief which this process entailed. In consequence of this intuition he came out roundly against going back to the prewar gold parity. Others held the same view: Rist in France, Cassel in Sweden, *et al*. He was not alone in his insistence, from the present fashionable point of view vastly exaggerated, that central-bank discount policy might stabilize business activity; again, compare the position of Gustav Cassel. Despite the auspicious sentence concerning savings and investment in its preface, the *Tract on Monetary Reform* on its analytical side goes little beyond a quantity-theory explanation of inflation; while its policy proposals for a nationally-managed currency and fluctuating exchange are only distinguished for their political novelty and persuasiveness.

In all of these, there is a consistency of pattern. And in retrospect it is only fair to say that he was on the whole right. Yet this brief account does not present the whole story. In many places, he was wrong. Perhaps a pamphleteer should be judged shot-gun rather than rifle fashion, by his absolute hits regardless of misses; still one must note that even when most wrong, he is often most confident and sure of himself.

The *Economic Consequences of the Peace* proceeds from beginning to end on a single premise which history has proved to be false or debatable. Again, he unleashed with a flourish the Malthusian bogey of overpopulation at a time when England and the Western European world were undergoing a population revolution in the opposite direc-

---

[7] *Economic Journal,* Vol. 21, September, 1911, pp. 392–398. This is a characteristically "unfair" and unfavorable review, to be compared with Marshall's review of Jevons, which Keynes's biography of Marshall tries weakly to justify.

tion. In his controversy with Sir William Beveridge on the terms of trade between industry and agriculture, besides being wrong in principle and interpretation, he revealed his characteristic weakness for presenting a few hasty, but suggestive, statistics. If it can be said that he was right in his reparations-transfer controversy with Ohlin, it is in part for the wrong reasons—reasons which in terms of his later system are seen to be classical as compared to the arguments of Ohlin. Again, at different times he has presented arguments to demonstrate that foreign investment is (1) deflationary, and (2) stimulating to the home economy, without appearing on either occasion to be aware of the opposing arguments.

None of these are of vital importance, but they help to give the flavor of the man. He has been at once soundboard, amplifier, and initiator of contemporary viewpoints, whose strength and weakness lay in his intuition, audaciousness, and changeability. Current quips concerning the latter trait are rather exaggerated, but they are not without provocation. It is quite in keeping with this portrait to be reminded that in the early '20's, before he had an inkling of the *General Theory,* or even the *Treatise,* he scolded Edwin Cannan in no uncertain terms for not recognizing the importance and novelty of modern beliefs as compared to old-fashioned—I might almost have said "classical"—theories.

Where a scientist is concerned it is not inappropriate, even in a eulogy, to replace the ordinary dictum *nihil nisi bonum* by the criterion *nihil nisi verum.* In all candor, therefore, it is necessary to point out certain limitations—one might almost say weaknesses were they not so intrinsically linked with his genius—in Keynes's thought.

Perhaps because he was exposed to economics too young, or perhaps because he arrived at maturity in the stultifying backwash of Marshall's influence upon economic theory—for whatever reason, Keynes seems never to have had any genuine interest in pure economic theory. It is remarkable that so active a brain would have failed to make any contribution to value theory; and yet except for his discussion of index numbers in Volume I of the *Treatise* and for a few remarks concerning "user cost," which are novel at best only in terminology and emphasis, he seems to have left no mark on pure value theory.[8]

[8] Indeed only in connection with Frank P. Ramsey's "A Mathematical Theory of Saving" (*Economic Journal,* Vol. 38, December, 1928, pp. 542–559) does he show interest in an esoteric theoretical problem; there he gave a rather intricate interpretation in words of a calculus-of-variations differential-equation condition of equilibrium. His reasoning is all the more brilliant—and I say this seriously!— because it is mathematically unrigorous, if not wrong. The importance which Keynes attached to this article is actually exaggerated and can be accounted for

Just as there is internal evidence in the *Treatise on Probability* that he early tired of somewhat frustrating basic philosophic speculation, so he seems to have early tired of theory. He gladly "exchanged the tormenting exercises of the foundations of thought and of psychology, where the mind tries to catch its own tail, for the delightful paths of our own most agreeable branch of the moral sciences, in which theory and fact, intuitive imagination and practical judgment, are blended in a manner comfortable to the human intellect." [9]

In view of his basic antipathy to economic theory, it is all the more wonder therefore that he was able to write a biography of Alfred Marshall, which Professor Schumpeter has termed not only one of the best treatments of a Master by a Pupil but one of the best biographies ever written.[10] Never were two temperaments more different than that of the two men, and we can be sure that the repressed Victorianism and "popish" personal mannerisms which Keynes found so worthy of reverence in a Master and Father would have been hardly tolerable in a contemporary.

From Marshall's early influence, no doubt, stems Keynes's antipathy toward the use of mathematical symbols, an antipathy which already appears, surprisingly considering its technical subject, in the early pages of the *Treatise on Probability*. In view of the fact that mathematical economists were later to make some of the most important contributions to Keynesian economics, his comments on them in the *General Theory* and in the Marshall and Edgeworth biographies merit rereading.[11]

Moreover, there is reason to believe that Keynes's thinking remained fuzzy on one important analytical matter throughout all his days: the relationship between "identity" and functional (or equilibrium-schedule) equality; between "virtual" and observable movements; between causality and concomitance; between tautology and hypothesis. Somewhere, I believe in the 1923 *Tract,* he already falls into the same analytic confusion with respect to the identity of supply and demand for

only in terms of his paternal feeling toward Ramsey, and his own participation in the solution of the problem.

[9] *Essays in Biography,* 1933, pp. 249–250. [New edition, London, Rupert Hart-Davis, 1951.—Ed.]

[10] Keynes's discussion of Marshall's monetary theory is much better than his treatment of Marshall's contribution to theory.

[11] Keynes's critical review of Tinbergen's econometric business-cycle study for the League of Nations reveals that Keynes did not really have the necessary technical knowledge to understand what he was criticizing. How else are we to interpret such remarks as his assertion that a linear system can never develop oscillations?

foreign exchange which was later to be his stumbling-block with respect to the identity of saving and investment.

Perhaps he was always too busy with the affairs of the world to be able to devote sufficient time for repeated thinking through of certain basic problems. Certainly he was too busy to verify references ("a vain pursuit"). His famous remark that he never learned anything from reading German which he didn't already know would be greeted with incredulity in almost any other science than economics.[12] What he really meant was that his was one of those original minds which never accepts a thing as true and important unless he has already thought it through for himself. Despite his very considerable erudition in certain aspects of the history of thought, there was probably never a more ahistorical scholar than Keynes.

Finally, to fill in the last little touch in this incomplete portrait of an engaging spirit, I should like to present a characteristic quotation from Keynes:

> In writing a book of this kind the author must, if he is to put his point of view clearly, pretend sometimes to a little more conviction than he feels. He must give his own argument a chance, so to speak, nor be too ready to depress its vitality with a wet cloud of doubt.

Is this from the *General Theory*? No. From the *Treatise on Money* or the *Tract*? No, no. Even when writing on so technical a subject as probability, the essential make-up of the man comes through so that no literary detective can fail to spot his spoor.

THE ROAD TO THE GENERAL THEORY

It was not unnatural for such a man as I have described to wish as he approached fifty to bring together, perhaps as a crowning life work, his intuitions concerning money. Thus the *Treatise* was born. Much of the first volume is substantial and creditable, though hardly exciting. But the Fundamental Equations which he and the world considered the really novel contribution of the *Treatise* are nothing but a detour and blind alley.

The second volume is most valuable of all, but it is so because of the intuitions there expressed concerning bullishness, bearishness, etc., and

---

[12] Around 1911–1915, he was the principal reviewer of German books for *E.J.;* also he must have read—at least he claimed to have—innumerable German works on probability. That he could not speak German with any fluency is well attested by those who heard him once open an English lecture to a German audience with a brief apology in German.

even these might have been prevented from coming into being by too literal an attempt to squeeze them into the mold of the Fundamental Equations. Fortunately, Keynes was not sufficiently systematic to carry out such a program.

Before the *Treatise* was completed, its author had already tired of it. Sir Isaac Newton held up publication of his theory for twenty years because of a small discrepancy in numerical calculation. Darwin hoarded his theories for decades in order to collect ever more facts. Not so with our hero: let the presses roll and throw off the grievous weight of a book unborn! Especially since a world falling to pieces is ripe to drop Pollyanna and take up with Cassandra on the rebound.

Perhaps not being systematic proved his salvation. A long line of heretics testifies that he is not the first to have tried to weld intuition into a satisfactory, unified theory; not the first to have shot his bolt and failed. But few have escaped from the attempt with their intuitions intact and unmarred. In an inexact subject like economics, concepts are not (psychologically) neutral. Decisions based upon ignorance or the equiprobability of the unknown are not invariant under transformation of coordinates or translation of concepts. Simply to define a concept is to reify it, to breathe life in it, to create a predisposition in favor of its constancy; *vide* the falling rate of profit and the organic composition of capital, the velocity of circulation of money, the propensity to consume, and the discrepancy between saving and investment.

The danger may be illustrated by a particular instance. Shrewd Edwin Cannan in characteristic salty prose throughout the first World War "protested." [13] At first his insights were sharp and incisive, his judgments on the whole correct. But in the summer of 1917, to "escape from an almost unbearable personal sorrow," he undertook to set forth a *systematic* exposition of the theory of money. The transformation of Cinderella's coach at the stroke of twelve is not more sudden than the change in the quality of his thought. Here, I am not so much interested in the fact that his voice becomes shrill, his policies on the whole in retrospect bad—as in the fact that his intuitions were perverted and blunted by his analysis, almost in an irrecoverable way! Not so with Keynes. His constitution was able to throw off the *Treatise* and its Fundamental Equations.

While Keynes did much for the Great Depression, it is no less true that the Great Depression did much for him. It provided challenge, drama, experimental confirmation. He entered it the sort of man who might be expected to embrace the *General Theory* if it were ex-

[13] E. Cannan, *An Economist's Protest,* 1927.

plained to him. From the previous record, one cannot say more. Before it was over, he had emerged with the prize in hand, the system of thought for which he will be remembered.

Right now I do not intend to speculate in detail on the thought-process leading up to this work, but only to throw out a few hints. In the 1929 pamphlet, *Can Lloyd George Do It?*, written with H. D. Henderson, Keynes set up important hypotheses concerning the effects of public works and investment. It remained for R. F. Kahn, that elusive figure who hides in the preface of Cambridge books, to provide the substantiation in his justly famous 1931 *Economic Journal* article, "The Relation of Home Investment to Unemployment." Quite naturally the "multiplier" comes in for most attention; which is in a way too bad since the concept often seems like nothing but a cheap-Jack way of getting something for nothing and appears to carry with it a spurious numerical accuracy.

But behind lies the vitally important consumption function: giving the propensity to consume in terms of income; or looked at from the opposite side, specifying the propensity to save. With investment given, as a constant or in the schedule sense, we are in a position to set up the simplest determinate system of underemployment equilibrium—by a "Keynesian savings-investment-income cross" not formally different from the "Marshallian supply-demand-price cross."

Immediately everything falls into place: the recognition that the *attempt* to save may lower income and actual *realized* saving; the fact that a net autonomous increase in investment, foreign balance, government expenditure, consumption will result in increased income *greater* than itself, etc., etc.

Other milestones on the road to Damascus, in addition to the Lloyd George pamphlet and the Kahn article, were Keynes's testimony before the Macmillan committee [14] and his University of Chicago Harris Foundation lectures on unemployment in the summer of 1931. In these lectures, Keynes has not quite liberated himself from the terminology of the *Treatise* (*vide* his emphasis on "profits"); but the notion of the level of income as being in equilibrium at a low level because of the

---

[14] Young economists who disbelieve in the novelty of the Keynesian analysis on the ground that no sensible person could ever have thought differently might with profit read Hawtrey's testimony before the Macmillan Committee, contrasting it with the Kahn article and comparing it with Tooke's famous demonstration in his *History of Prices*, Volume I, that government war expenditures as such cannot possibly cause inflation—*because what the government spends would have been spent anyway, except to the extent of "new money" created.*

necessity for savings to be equated to a depressed level of investment is worked out in detail.

From here to the *Means to Prosperity* (1933) is but a step; and from the latter to the *General Theory* but another step. From hindsight and from the standpoint of policy recommendations, each such step is small and in a sense inevitable; but from the standpoint of having stumbled upon and formulated a new system of analysis, each represents a tremendous stride.

But now I shall have to desist. My panegyric must come to an end with two conflicting quotations from the protean Lord Keynes between which the Jury must decide:

> In the long run we are all dead.

> . . . the ideas of economists and political philosophers, both when they are right and when they are wrong, are more powerful than is commonly understood. Indeed, the world is ruled by little else. Practical men, who believe themselves to be quite exempt from any intellectual influences, are usually the slaves of some defunct economist. Madmen in authority, who hear voices in the air, are distilling their frenzy from some academic scribbler of a few years back. I am sure that the power of vested interests is vastly exaggerated compared with the gradual encroachment of ideas . . . soon or late, it is ideas, not vested interests, which are dangerous for good or evil.[15]

[15] *General Theory*, pp. 383–384.

Colin Clark

─── on ───

Pigou

Arthur Cecil Pigou (1877–   ) was educated at Cambridge, where he succeeded in Marshall's chair in 1908. Pigou's claim to fame is based, first of all, on his work in the field of welfare economics, which he, with Pareto, may be said to have founded. Pigou's work marks a new phase in the history of economics, with emphasis shifting from "happiness" to "welfare." Pigou's welfare criteria are the size, distribution, and stability of the national income, and the widespread use of the national-income concept in modern economics is in part due to the precedent set by him. After the passing of Lord Keynes, Pigou came to be considered the greatest living economist by many thoughtful students of economics.

Colin Clark (1905–   ) was educated at Oxford and taught at Cambridge until 1937, when he emigrated to Australia, where he now heads the Bureau of Industry in Queensland. Clark's early training was in the field of chemistry. He is an ingenious user of statistics, and his work in the field of national income and in operational economics generally has made him the leading contemporary exponent of what once was known as "political arithmetic." Clark's best-known works are *The Conditions of Economic Progress* (1940), and *The Economics of 1960* (1942).

I T IS RARE for relations between teacher and pupil to be so close as they were between Marshall and Pigou, or for a Professor to teach so faithfully, thoroughly and persistently the doctrines of his predecessor.

When Marshall was forming his ideas in the 1870's Economics as we now know it hardly existed. It would be an interesting task for some student of ideas to analyse the influence which John Stuart Mill had upon Marshall—not of course directly, but through Sidgwick and other intermediaries.

Slowly and carefully Marshall assembled his *Principles,* which to this day leave an unmistakable stamp upon the thinking of all those who have been influenced by them. Perhaps Keynes came nearest to expressing the inexpressible when he wrote, in 1922, that it was not the purpose of Economics to furnish a settled body of conclusions but "an apparatus of the mind, a technique of thinking."

Pigou, as an under-graduate, studied mathematics, as Marshall had before him. I do not know whether its position can be challenged now, but I think it can be said without any fear of contradiction that, at the beginning of the century, Cambridge certainly led the world in the rigour and profundity of its mathematical training. Formal instruction in Economics was only just beginning at that time, and Pigou assimilated what under-graduate teaching was available as a sort of afterthought to his mathematical degree. Pigou then undertook the preparation of a post-graduate research thesis. Like many another research student after him, he recalls, he had proposals for a thesis which would re-constitute the whole of economic theory as then known. Marshall refused these proposals and required of him a detailed factual study of "Industrial Disputes"—Their Causes and Consequences." Before long Pigou was very grateful for this decision. It brought a realistic influence into his economic thinking and we can trace its effects for many years afterwards.

On one recent occasion, however, Pigou expressed some dissatisfaction with his up-bringing—blaming not Marshall but himself. The one subject which he really thoroughly understood, he told his audience, was mountain climbing (a pursuit to which he has devoted all his avail-

[Not published before.]

able leisure throughout his lifetime). From the many books published on this subject, he said, there was little difficulty in picking out those which were essentially compilations of the writings of others; and those written by men who really *knew* the mountains which were their subject. It was likewise, he feared, with many books on economics. And so, in conclusion, he warned his audience that they should "while you are still young and your minds are still plastic, do what I myself have conspicuously failed to do" and spend as much time as they could in workshops, farms, mines, ships, and other places where actual economic events occur, and get "the feel" of them.

Marshall retired from the Professorship at Cambridge in 1908 and Pigou was appointed his successor while still, by all the standards of that time, extraordinarily young. Pigou produced his *magnum opus* only four years after his appointment to the Professorship, where Marshall took several decades. *Wealth and Welfare*, published in 1912, the product of an extraordinary concentration of thought, certainly opened a new chapter in economic science. The book has been many times reprinted under its new title *Economics of Welfare*, and some sections have been split off to be re-written as separate books. But in this remarkable treatise, written comparatively early in life, are set out many of the most important of Pigou's contributions to economic thought.

Throughout his teaching career (he held the Professorship until 1943) Pigou devoted most of his attention and emphasis to the pure unchanged Marshallian doctrine, and tended to under-emphasise his own additions thereto. In spite of this modesty which many would regard as excessive, there were, in the earlier years, pedantic Marshallians who resented Pigou's ideas and writings.

Using Marshall's theoretical concepts and methods of reasoning, Pigou applied himself to the fundamental problems of economic action. Unqualified *laissez-faire* was questioned by John Stuart Mill; by the time of Marshall definite qualifications to the *laissez-faire* doctrine had been established, though, to the minds of most contemporary observers, these constituted only unimportant exceptions. *Wealth and Welfare*, in one of its aspects, may be described as a systematic and ordered enquiry into all the cases where Public Authorities may be justified in intervening in the workings of the economic system. In his presentation of his theory of welfare economics, Professor Pigou emphasises many points of departure from Marshall's analysis.

Unlike Cannan who expressly stipulates that the kind of welfare with which economics is associated is that which is derived from material sources—*material* in the sense of being purchasable by money,

Pigou's welfare economics, based as it is upon utility theory, is derived from the theory of ethics known as *Utilitarianism*. It was generally considered that Utilitarianism had long been inadequate as a theory of ethics when Pigou subjected it to the exhaustive treatment witnessed in *The Economics of Welfare*. He accepted ethical Utilitarianism insofar as he treated economics as subordinate to ethics, thereby escaping the errors of most of the nineteenth century economists who claimed the absolute validity of Utilitarianism for economic conclusions. He contends that man's object is not wealth as such, but a much broader concept—"welfare." The welfare of an individual is the sum total of the satisfactions he experiences, and the sum total of the welfare of individuals constitutes the welfare of society. This is indeed the doctrine as expounded by Bentham. Recognising that welfare was a "thing of very wide range" he found it necessary to limit the subject matter. This he did by defining economic welfare as that portion of social welfare measurable in money. ("Hence, the range of our inquiry becomes restricted to that part of social welfare that can be brought directly or indirectly into relation with the measuring-rod of money"— *The Economics of Welfare,* Second Edition, p. 11.[1])

Professor Pigou goes on to explain (p. 31), "Generally speaking, economic causes act upon the economic welfare of any country, not directly, but through the making and using of that objective counterpart of economic welfare which economists call the national dividend or national income." Thus it may be observed that he defines economic welfare subjectively but speaks of national dividend as "that part of the objective income of the community . . . which can be measured in money. The two concepts, economic welfare and the national dividend, are thus co-ordinate. . . ." Here Pigou has again resorted to Marshall and incorporated his definitions of the national dividend— the flow of goods and services annually produced after maintaining capital intact.[2]

It is still too early to say how much of this analysis will survive the disappearance of Benthamite Utilitarianism as a basis. Benthamism was shaky even in the nineteenth century, and by now, it must be conceded, almost all of its ideas will have to be abandoned.

---

[1] London, Macmillan and Company, 1924. By permission of the publishers.

[2] A note of caution should be sounded here. From the subjective level of analysis whereby the value of net additions to capital is derived from the expected level of income and not *vice versa,* this concept of maintaining intact the existing stock of capital by making good the wear and tear of such goods is rendered quite inadequate. No provision for depreciation due to obsolescence arising out of changes in technique, etc., is made by this procedure.

The primary problem to which Professor Pigou has devoted his attention concerns the relationship between the economic interests of individuals on the one hand, and of the community of which such individuals are members, on the other. Further, he is concerned with the extent to which, and the conditions under which, the pursuance of the economic interests of individuals will occasion an improvement in the economic conditions of the community. He has, therefore, taken as his norm the desirability of maximising economic welfare and has laid down important criteria of economic desirability. The assumption that each individual tries to maximise his own satisfaction is an essential feature of the utility theory of welfare economics. This assumption underlies the theory of consumers' demand as expounded by Marshall and modified firstly by Pigou and latterly by Hicks and Knight. For Marshall, utility meant "capacity to give satisfaction"—the price a rational man was prepared to pay for a commodity was supposed to measure the satisfaction he expected to receive from it. This definition of utility obviously takes the economist into the realms which properly belong to the psychologist. A person may not buy a commodity to get satisfaction; his reason for buying it may be, in part at any rate, connected with desire for authority or social status.

Thus the welfare, or utility, or satisfaction which we get from a commodity is not (to state the issue in more modern terminology) solely a question of our rate of consumption of that commodity, and of other commodities; it may also depend, to a considerable extent, upon whether or not that commodity is being consumed by certain other persons. Pigou used to give a telling illustration of this principle in his lectures by a reference to the social custom of wearing top hats at funerals (now completely vanished, but serving for lecture purposes until as late as the 1920's). One received satisfaction from wearing one's top hat at a funeral (I believe the wearing of top hats at weddings also occasionally served for purposes of illustration) if the other men present were also wearing them. But to be the only man so attired made one conspicuous and a source of embarrassment to one's friends.

Notice the modest and unassuming manner of life which is taken as the background for this illustration. How easy it would be, in the contemporary world, to find examples proving the opposite, where a garment or other object of consumption does not give satisfaction unless it does render its user conspicuous, and embarrass his or her friends?

Professor Pigou recognised also the fact that the satisfaction expected from the purchase of a commodity and the satisfaction actually obtained from that purchase are two different things. A mistake may have been made—also unforeseen contingencies may have occurred—

so that actual satisfaction may diverge from desired satisfaction. Pigou therefore treated utility as "desire" for a commodity: he employs the term "desiredness." ". . . we are entitled to use the comparative amounts of money which a person is prepared to offer for two different things as a test of the comparative satisfactions which these things will yield to him, only on condition that the ratio between the intensities of desire that he feels for the two is equal to the ratio between the amounts of satisfaction which their possession will yield to him" (p. 23). . . . "For the most general purposes of economic analysis, therefore, not much harm is likely to be done by the current practice of regarding money demand price indifferently as the measure of a desire and as the measure of the satisfaction felt when the desired thing is obtained" (p. 24).

On this assumption, the individual is supposed to spend his money in such a way as to obtain the same amount of satisfaction from the various goods and services on which the marginal unit of money might be spent.[3] It follows therefore that the individual adjusts the marginal utilities of such goods and services in direct proportionality to their prices. Hence, given the relevant prices and the principle of diminishing marginal utility, it is possible to determine the pattern of expenditure of the individual. This analysis, however, differs from the indifference curve analysis of consumers' behaviour insofar as utility in the former is a cardinal concept, whereas the latter concept of utility is entirely an ordinal one.

However, Professor Pigou emphasises an important exception to the above generalisation because of people's attitude toward the future insofar as present pleasures or satisfactions are preferable to future pleasures or satisfactions even when their magnitudes are similar and there exists no doubt as to their certainty. This, he argues, provides a "far-reaching economic disharmony. For it implies that people distribute their resources between the present, the near future, and the remote future on the basis of a wholly irrational preference" (p. 25). Pigou believes that economic welfare could be increased by a discriminatory taxation in favour of saving; that the "State should protect the interests of the future *in some degree* against the effects of our irrational discounting, and of our preference for ourselves over our descendants" (p. 29).

[3] It should be noted that Pigou has also taken over from Marshall the practice of assuming that the marginal utility of money is the same for different individuals so that quantities of satisfaction are proportionate to the quantities of money.

That each individual behaves in such a way as to maximise his utility was a necessary condition of attaining the maximum aggregate utility which could be obtained from a given set of factors of production.

Perhaps the greatest divergence from the Marshallian technique is made by Pigou in his displacement of Marshall's "Surplus Analysis" (which is confined to "chunks of economic welfare") by a marginal analysis which is primarily concerned with balancing the advantages and disadvantages of very small variations in output in different industries. He finds no use whatever for any type of measure which involves the use of surpluses and measures the economic welfare of the community indirectly by measuring the physical national dividend valued at appropriate prices. Marshall, it will be remembered, tried to overcome the difficulties of measuring surpluses by devoting attention to changes in the surpluses of specific goods whilst assuming the surpluses from other goods to be constant.

As to the maximisation of the production of wealth, this will occur if productive resources are so distributed that the net social yield to a marginal unit is equal to all uses. "Since, *ex hypothesi,* there is only one arrangement of resources that will make the values of the marginal net products equal in all uses, this arrangement is necessarily the one that makes the national dividend . . . a maximum" (p. 121).

It is into the framework of this "maximum" that Pigou works his celebrated cases of divergences between the private and social products. The social net product, Pigou defines (p. 151) as "the aggregate contribution made to the national dividend," and the private net product as "the contribution (which may be either greater or less than the above) that is capable of being sold and the proceeds added to the earnings of the person responsible for the unit of investment."

The first class of divergence is connected with the separation between tenancy and ownership of certain durable instruments of production. Pigou points out that "over a wide field some part of the investment designed to improve durable instruments of production is often made by persons other than their owners. Whenever this happens, some divergence between the private and social net product of this investment is liable to occur, and is larger or smaller in extent according to the terms of the contract between lessor and lessee" (p. 152). This class of divergence is usually associated with wasteful forms of tenancy wherein the terms of the contract do not provide for adequate compensation to the lessee for the maintenance and improvements made during his tenure, and consequently a farmer, towards the end of his tenancy, "in his natural and undisguised endeavour to get back as much of his capital as possible, takes so much out of the land that, for some

years, the yield is markedly diminished. . . . Another important field
in which it is present is that of 'concessions' to gas companies, electric
light companies and so forth. An arrangement, under which the plant
of a concessionaire company passes ultimately, without compensation,
into the hands of the town chartering it, corresponds exactly to the
system of land leases without provision for compensation for tenants'
improvements" (p. 154).

The second class of divergence is usually associated with the "smoky
chimney" concept, where the production of a commodity gives rise to
incidental (uncharged) services or (uncompensated) dis-services to a
party who is neither producer nor consumer but who merely happens
to be in the vicinity of the place of production.

The final and most important case of divergence is that in which
Pigou maintains that the marginal social product of the resources employed in an industry with decreasing supply price is greater than their
marginal private product so that the output of such an industry is less
than the optimum amount. This argument is based on a distinction
made, on the one hand, from the two standpoints of the supply price
of a commodity; the supply price from the standpoint of the community
and from the standpoint of the industry, whilst, on the other hand, the
further distinctions between the supply price of a commodity from the
standpoint of the industry and the supply price of the "equilibrium
firm." Pigou uses the supply price of the equilibrium firm as the
reciprocal of the marginal social product whilst the supply price from
the standpoint of industry represents the reciprocal of the marginal private product used in that industry. Consequently, where the supply
price from the industry is less than the supply price of the equilibrium
firm, as is the case in an increasing returns industry, Professor Pigou
concludes that the marginal social product is greater than the marginal
private product. It will be seen then that this argument amounts to
much the same thing as the celebrated proposal of Marshall to sub-
sidise increasing returns industry—that the economic welfare of the
community can be increased by subsidising the increasing returns
industries.

However, Pigou is normally concerned with an economic system
which is fairly competitive. Thus there would be an automatic equali-
sation of the marginal private products in all industries and very little
variation between the marginal private and the marginal social products.
Consequently, the optimum output in each industry can be attained by
equating its marginal private product to its marginal social product by
a tax or a subsidy. That is to say, he proposes free enterprise where
decreasing or constant returns in industry prevail, but considers inter-

vention necessary in the case of increasing returns. Because free enterprise will not cause increasing returns industries to develop as quickly as is socially desirable, he proposes a tax and subsidy but is not averse, it appears, to nationalisation (as in the United Kingdom) or regulated monopolies (as in U. S. A.). It is not certain that he would approve of oligopolies regulated only by difficulty of new-comers entering an imperfect market which is the present-day condition of much British and American industry: this tends to give a distribution of productive resources which is highly arbitrary and probably far removed from the social optimum.

It is hard to over-emphasise the importance of this latter concept. Though originally propounded by Marshall, to whom Pigou gives all the credit, yet it is in Pigou's work that we find the elaboration and definiteness which establish it as an important new economic principle. In effect, industry subject to constant and diminishing returns should be left entirely to free enterprise; in all industries where increasing returns prevail to any important extent, there is a *prima facie* case for Public Authorities, not necessarily to intervene, but at any rate to keep the situation under close review and be prepared to intervene if occasion demands.

This important topic, for some unexplained reason, was left almost alone by subsequent writers. The first to actively resuscitate it and emphasise its importance seems to have been Professor Lerner.

However, during the intervening period, a good deal of quiet theoretical work on the difficult problems arising out of the existence of Increasing Returns was done by Professor Robertson. In such industries, as we would now put it, marginal cost may be below average cost over an important range of output. Under these circumstances, Professor Robertson pointed out, the tendency to monopolistic or cartellised organisation of industry becomes very strong. The case for public supervision and regulation is certainly strengthened thereby.

Application of these principles, which seem to be obviously true, would cause a revolution in the administrative world (in the U. S. A. also, not merely in Great Britain). The industries which are clearly working under conditions of constant or diminishing returns are agriculture, building and mining. Under a rational economic policy all attempts at control or regulation of these industries would cease. There would be no more rent controls, no more attempts at Government provision of housing, no more guaranteed prices for farm products. To allow the gales of competition to blow at full blast—in the case of agriculture, internationally as well as internally—would yield the maximum social advantage.

But while the economic planners should be compelled to let go their prey in these fields, they will have to be called on to attack much larger game which, at present they often do not have the courage to face, i.e., the really powerful monopolies and cartels in the leading Increasing Returns industries.

Casting our minds back to Adam Smith's time we should reflect that the world in which he lived was one in which almost all industries were carried on under conditions of decreasing returns, and that his *laissez-faire* conclusions were therefore valid. He does in fact specify a few exceptional activities which might be considered to be of an Increasing Returns nature, and thinks that action by Public Authority might be justified therein.

Whereas Marshall assumed a diminishing marginal utility of money income, Pigou considered diminishing utility as applicable only to real income. This raises the problem of comparison of real incomes of individuals.

As I wrote in *Conditions of Economic Progress,*[4]

Comparisons of economic welfare between one community and another, one economic group and another, and between one time and another, are the very framework of economic science. Anything which can be done to promote the scope and improve the technique of such comparisons is of fundamental importance. Certain modern theoretical economists have gone so far as to say that it is impossible to compare the level of income between two communities or between two individuals, or even between the same individual at different times; in other words, they deny the existence of an objectively measurable economic welfare (and incidentally provide themselves with a magnificent excuse for avoiding any study whatever of realistic and quantitative economics). Exponents of this view do not realise what an intellectual anarchy they will let loose if their theories are adopted. Deprive economics of the concept of welfare and what have you left? Nothing: except possibly the theory of the trade cycle, where all values may be capable of expression in money terms without the intro-duction of the concept of welfare. Even in this case you might be left in great doubts as to whether even the trade-cycle problem is worth solving.

There is a good deal of rather ignorant sophistication on this subject nowadays, but most of those who indulge in these views turn out in fact never to have read the relevant passages in *Economics of Welfare*. In a brilliant piece of logical reasoning it is there clearly shown that economic welfare can be compared between times and places, and that the best comparison, under conditions prevailing in the actual world, can be made

[4] Second edition, pp. 16–18. London, Macmillan and Company, 1951. By permission of the publishers.

by use of a so-called "Fisher" index number (though by right of simultaneous discovery, it might well be called a Pigou-Fisher index).

To compare for instance the real value of $0.795 produced per hour
worked in U. S. A. in 1929, and 1.28 Rm., or $0.305 at par of exchange,
produced per hour worked in Germany in the same year, we must take
account of the actual quantities of goods and services produced, or, in
other words, what the money will buy. The average American over that
period spent his income in a certain way, purchasing certain quantities of
goods and services. If he had gone to Germany and had set out to purchase exactly the same goods and services, he would have found that they
were 0.9 per cent cheaper in the aggregate than in his own country. The
German with his income purchased certain goods and services, by no
means in the same proportion as the American. He spent much less of
his income on motor cars and rent, and much more on food. The German going to America and purchasing the goods and services which he
was accustomed to consume would find that they were 19.8 per cent
dearer. In comparing the real value of incomes in the two countries we
must therefore allow something between 19.8 and 0.9 per cent for the
difference in purchasing power of money. The ideal formula gives us the
result that the comparative real income per head can be obtained from the
geometrical mean of these two ratios, or

$$\frac{\text{Average real income in America}}{\text{Average real income in Germany}}$$

$$= \frac{\text{Average money income in America}}{\text{Average money income in Germany}}$$

$$\times \sqrt{\frac{\text{Cost of American goods at German prices}}{\text{Cost of German goods at American prices}}}$$

$$= \frac{0.795}{0.305} \times \sqrt{\frac{0.991}{1.198}}$$

The ratio is seen to be 2.37 as against the 2.60 which we obtained from
a crude comparison of money incomes.

By the application of this and other index numbers we can make comparisons of economic welfare of different times, places and groups of
people without in any case having to use any more elaborate formulae
than the one given above. In some cases even simpler comparisons will,
in the present state of knowledge, be all that are worth while attempting.

Pigou produced more fruitful work during the 1920's. At the beginning of the decade he was a Member of a Royal Commission on
Income Tax, and was one of the signatories of a complex and comprehensive report, in the light of which a number of changes were made in

British Income Tax Law. After some years of further thought he published his book, *A Study in Public Finance,* in 1928. This book will not be of great value to the ordinary student of the subject. It does not give the descriptive background and the ordered array of facts which the ordinary student needs. But for the thinker charged with any important responsibility for action in this field, this book is obligatory reading. Its fundamental point is that our present taxation systems unduly discriminate against saving, and therefore, in the long run, leave us enjoying much less economic welfare than we might have had. He makes a cautious approach to the idea that businesses should be tax exempt on all funds re-invested. At this point, reading between the lines of the book, you can see him beginning a long fencing match with an invisible opponent—perhaps his old friend Lord Stamp, who had been Chairman of the Board of Inland Revenue at the time of the Royal Commission? Are businesses to be exempted only if they re-invest their savings in their own business or if they have purchased other assets also? If this exemption is to be given to companies is it fair to deny it to individual traders, or indeed to men making savings out of their salaries or wages? These administrative and social problems Pigou declines to discuss, and the question lapses. Again, there is an inexplicable interval of time before other writers begin to take up this fundamentally important question.

Of equal importance about this time was the publication of *Industrial Fluctuations* in 1926—likewise a section of *Wealth and Welfare* now transformed into a complete book. We have had so much trade cycle theory in the last twenty-five years that we may fail to realise that it must have started somewhere. Before Pigou wrote this book, there was remarkably little in the field. Professor Robertson had written a pioneering work, of an empirical and tentative nature, as early as 1914. Aftalion in France was a brilliant worker born, we might say, before his due time. Pigou was much influenced by his work and gives him the fullest recognition.

Industrial Fluctuations, unlike some of Pigou's other books, is based upon a most careful ordering of all the statistical facts available at that time, and upon some brilliantly correct generalisations.

During the last two decades Pigou has made several important contributions to the theory of unemployment. With Keynes he had, at the time, numerous differences. During the last year the whole issue between himself and Keynes has been clearly, fairly and generously set out in a very short and easily read book of lectures. In this he makes it clear (it was not quite clear twenty years ago) that he concedes the most important point in Keynes's doctrine, namely, that the economic system as a whole is not self-regulating, and may, under certain circumstances, get into a state of under-employment which may persist indefinitely.

Many of the contemporary misunderstandings between Pigou and Keynes arose from the fact that Keynes's theory essentially turned on money out-lays and money wages, whereas Pigou always preferred to think in terms of real product, real consumption and real wage.

Pigou treats the subject of unemployment mainly in mathematical form offering "a simplified model of the economic world rather than that world itself in its full completeness" (*The Theory of Unemployment*, Preface, p. vi).[5] Despite his own warning that "great violence is being done to realities," Pigou persists in investigating the general problem of employment as a whole by the use of such simplified models. "Whether and in what degree a study of simplified models throws light on problems of real life can only be decided by trial. After, not before, trial has been made, will come the time to pass judgment" (*Employment and Equilibrium*, p. 4).[6]

In the latter treatise a model is constructed from which are abstracted many of the vagaries and complications of real life but which nevertheless allows for the full influence of the basic factors of the problem. The model adequately provides for the examination of the conditions determining "short-period flow-equilibrium." Six major assumptions are made throughout the study, namely, a closed economic system; perfect homogeneity of labour; the stock of fixed capital consists of a large number of precisely similar structures; the obsolescence of fixed capital is ignored; complete mobility of labour, both as to locality and occupation, which implies the same money wage rates ruling throughout the economy; and, finally, money wages are used exclusively in buying consumption goods. Since Pigou starts from much the same types of assumptions about reality as Keynes did, it is not surprising that much the same result is obtained despite the difference in method.

In testimony before the Macmillan Committee in 1930 Professor Pigou attributed unemployment to interference with the "free working of economic forces" and to wage rates being "out of adjustment with the general conditions of demand." Here Pigou insisted that his analysis was on the "real" and not the "money" level and Keynes, who was a member of the questioning Committee, tried without success to get Pigou to shift from the "real" to a "money" analysis.

[5] London, Macmillan and Company, 1933. By permission of the publishers.
[6] London, Macmillan and Company, 1941. By permission of the publishers.

He says (*The Theory of Unemployment,* Preface, p. v), "It is possible to study the problem of unemployment either from the money end or from what I shall call, in contrast, the real end. The two studies, if made complete and carried through correctly, must necessarily come to the same thing, their analyses meeting in the middle. There can, therefore, be no question of the one way of approach being right and the other wrong. Both are right, and both can be used with profit." Because of the attention economists had concentrated upon the money end about this time, Pigou considered that this resulted in the overstressing of the role that money played in normal times. He therefore chose to write *The Theory of Unemployment* from the real end and so bring back into perspective "very important factors of a non-monetary character," dealing with the monetary factor at a fairly late stage (*ibid.*). In *Economics in Practice* (1935) he continued to emphasise the "real" as against the "monetary" analysis.

In *The Theory of Unemployment* Professor Pigou attacks the problem of unemployment by the use of the marginal productivity theory in conjunction with a slight modification of "The Old Classical Wages Fund Theory." To him the volume of employment is dependent upon the two fundamental factors: the real rates of wages for which work people stipulate, and the shape of the real demand function for labour. Throughout the investigation he employs "wage goods" as the standard of comparison of real wages with other values. Wage goods are the goods on which wages are spent, and consequently comprise the real remuneration of the work people. The measurement of an aggregate of wage goods, it is explained, depends on a system of weighting in an index number.

Preliminary inquiry is made into the "differences, or variations, in quantity of labour demanded that are associated with given differences, or variations, in the rates of real wages for which work people stipulate, *when the relevant real demand functions for labour are given"* (p. 33).

Assuming, as he does, conditions of competition, the investigations really commence with the short-period principle, that in any centre "the quantity of labour demanded there at any given rate of real wage is such that the value in terms of wage-goods of its marginal net product (i.e., of the difference made to the total physical yield of the marginal man with the help of existing equipment) approximates to that rate of wage *plus* the rate of employers' contribution to sickness and unemployment insurance" (p. 41).

Pigou divides industries into two categories, those "engaged in making wage-goods at home and in making exports, the sale of which creates claims to wage-goods abroad," i.e., wage-goods industries, and other industries or non-wage-goods industries. The demand for labour in the wage-goods industries depends on the labour productivity function in such a manner that the marginal net product of a unit of labour must be equal to the real wage per unit stipulated for. Now, from p. 90, the volume of employment in non-wage-goods industries is a function of the volume of employment in the wage-goods industries.

As may be seen, therefore, from p. 143, wage-goods form the basic foundation on which Pigou constructs his theory. "When the real rate of wage stipulated for is given, the quantity of labour demanded in the aggregate of all industries varies, and can only vary, in precise proportion to the quantity of wage-goods available for, and devoted to, the payment of wages."

The section entitled "Monetary Factors Affecting Variations in the Level of the Real Demand Function for Labour" contains a proposal for a standard monetary system defined as "One so constructed that, for all sorts of movements in the real demand function for labour or in real ratio of wages, whether they last for a long time or a short, the aggregate money income is increased or diminished by precisely the difference made to the number of work people (or other factors of production) at work multiplied by the original rate of money wages" (pp. 205–206).

Pigou does not put forward the standard monetary system as the basis of an ideal monetary policy. He intends it to be used as a criterion to distinguish between ordinary monetary disturbances and non-monetary disturbances. For him, disturbances involving a departure from the standard monetary system are monetary ones.

Professor Pigou holds the principal weapon for maintaining the standard system to be the discount rate and open market policy of the Central Bank. But in times of deep depression the expedient of public loan expenditures should also be used. "In those circumstances attempts to uphold the standard monetary system, so long as reliance is placed on purely monetary defences, are bound to fail. If, however, at the same time that the banking system keeps money cheap, the Government adopts a policy of public works, the risk of failure is greatly reduced" (p. 213).

Pigou concludes that "the factor that determines the long-run relation between the real wage-rate stipulated for and the real demand function is best described in a general way as wage policy . . . policy designed to produce, or, it may be, producing more or less by accident, certain sorts of relation, in all or some centres of production, between wage rates and the state of demand. . . . There is reason to believe, however, that the goal at which wage policy aims is sometimes, in some centres of production at all events, a wage rate substantially higher than the rate which, if adopted everywhere, would yield nil unemployment" (p. 253).

Notes of this sort may convey some outline of Pigou's doctrines, but no commentator, however skilled, can really succeed in conveying Pigou's personality—the marvellous concentration of mind and perfection of reasoning, the quiet but penetrating criticism, the modest and retiring manner, the genuine love for his students.

Index

Abramovitz, Moses, 437, 751
Acceleration principle, 592, 647, 751, 755
Accounting, 398
Accumulation of capital, 324–325
Adamson, Robert, 474, 478, 482, 488
Addison, Joseph, 199
Adler, Georg, 321–322
Adler, K., 551
Adler, Max, 318–319
Aftalion, Albert, 592
Aggregation, 633, 637, 751, 763
Agriculture, 48, 56–58, 83–109, 483
Aikin, Lucy, 726
Åkerman, J., 656
Alembert, Jean Lerond d', 56
Alembert's principle, 646
Allen, R. G. D., 639
Allocation of resources, 785–787
American Economic Association, 595, 601
Amundsen, Arne, 656
Anarchism, 272, 289–290
Anderson, James, 141, 163, 166, 464
Annuities, 27
Apologetic character of economics, 230, 237, 239, 329
Applied economics, 370, 403
Arbitration, 600, 602, 611
Aristotle, 3–15, 28, 59, 367
Arnd, Karl, 104
Artificers, Statute of, 33
Ashley, W. J., 178
Assumptions in economics, 66, 72, 637
Athens, 3–15
Auspitz, R., 530, 542, 634, 743
Austrian school, 80, 134, 363, 510, 547, 652, 700, 710–713, 742–743, 750, 768
    Böhm-Bawerk, 568–579

Austrian school, Menger, 526–553
    Wieser, 554–567
Avarice, 21–30

Babbage, Charles, 147, 499
Bacon, Francis, 37, 189, 196, 372
Bagehot, Walter, 515, 726, 771
Bain, Alexander, 276
Balance, of trade, 38, 56
    of payments, 52
Banking, 22–30, 56, 169–171
    principle, 676–678
Bargaining power, 139, 599–600, 630
Barker, Sir Ernest, 206
Barone, Enrico, 72, 589, 632, 642
Barter, 472, 479
Basing point, 607
Bastable, C. F., 466
Bastiat, Frédéric, 226–240
Bauer, Otto, 737
Becher, Johann Joachim, 36
Beer, M., 83
Behaviorism, 743
Bentham, Jeremy, 41, 150, 253, 276–277, 323, 389, 394, 396–398, 428, 490, 617, 720–727, 782
    appraised by Mill, 184–200
    appraised by Viner, 201–225
Bergson, Henri, 646–647
Bernouilli, Daniel, 464
Berry, Arthur, 466
Bertrand, J., 463, 471–472
Besant, Annie, 152
Beveridge, William, 506, 773
Bickerdike, C. F., 623
Bimetallism, 53–55
Biology, 385–395, 728–730
Birck, L. V., 557
Birth control, 149, 152, 204, 657
Bissell, Richard, 765

Bitterman, Henry J., 131–132
Blackstone, Sir William, 188
Blanc, Louis, 229, 266–267
Blanqui, J. A., 105, 247, 372
Block, M., 542
Bloomsbury set, 771
Bodin, Jean, 39, 376
Böhm-Bawerk, E. v., 127, 183, 314, 321–322, 526–527, 533–537, 541, 543, 545, 548, 555, 557–559, 565, 589, 590, 597, 657, 660, 665–667, 703, 712, 734, 737–738, 746, 748, 750–758, 760
    appraised by Schumpeter, 568–579
Boisguilbert, Pierre, 107
Bonar, James, 142, 154, 181, 542
    on Malthus, 144–149
Boninsegni, B., 639
Booth, Charles, 346
Bortkiewicz, L. von, 585
Bosanquet, Charles, 162
Bowley, Arthur L., appraisal of Edgeworth, 615–627
Bradlaugh, Charles, 152
Branting, Hjalmar, 657
Bray, John Francis, 130, 133, 269, 271, 289, 291–294
British socialism, 269–296
Brougham, H. P., 286, 289, 291, 295
Bruck, F. W., 745
Bubble Act, 35
Buchanan, David, 105
Bücher, Karl, 410
Buckle, H. T., 368
Bullion Report, 162–163
Bullionists, 31–41
Bulwer-Lytton, Edward, 216
Burns, Arthur F., appraisal of Mitchell, 413–442
Burns, John, 342
Büsch, A. F., 365
Business cycles, 144, 156, 399, 413–442, 491, 497–506, 526, 609–610, 652, 693–699, 734, 747–748, 751, 754–755, 759, 769, 774, 790–792

Cairnes, J. E., 49, 52–53, 121, 225, 510, 522, 546, 702, 721
    appraisal of Bastiat, 226–240
Calculus, differential, 175, 582, 703
    utilitarian, 184–200, 207–211

Calvin, J., and Calvinism, 20, 28, 254
Cambridge school of economics, 156, 718
Camden, Lord, 188
Cameralists, 31–41, 365
Candlestick makers, petition of, 226–228
Cannan, Edwin, 28, 142, 287, 497, 623, 773, 776, 781
Canning, George, 246
Cantillon, Richard, 42–60, 64, 136, 517
Capital, 91, 101–109, 127, 134–143, 153, 176–177, 287–289, 320, 324–326, 451–453, 458, 481, 483, 501, 508, 510, 526, 543, 609–610, 652, 754–755
    Böhm-Bawerk, 568, 572–578, 743–744
    Walras, 586–590
    Wicksell, 659–669, 683–693
    Wieser, 565
Capital levy, 169
Capital shortage, 652
Capitalism, 101–109, 320, 734, 750–759, 762, 770, 772
    defined, 756
Carey, Henry, 483
Carlyle, Thomas, 144, 148, 198, 215, 311, 616
Carrington, R. C., 503
Cash-balance approach, 772
Cassel, Gustav, 589, 636, 652, 656, 658, 772
Catchings, W., 131
Causal relations, 65
Census, 147, 149
Central banking, 772, 793
Cernuschi, Henri, 53
Ceteris paribus, 66, 632, 634–635
Chamberlin, E. H., 734
Chapman, Sidney, 711
Chaptal de Chanteloup, J. A. C., 246
Charity, 19–30, 41, 49, 520, 726–727
Charlier, C. V. L., 620
Chartists, 295, 310
Chevalier, Michel, 247, 499
Child, Sir Josiah, 38–39, 48, 372
Child labor, 264
Choice, 591
Chrematistics, 262

Christian ethics, and economics, 16–30, 41
Christian socialism, 598, 600
Circular flow, 83, 752
Circulating capital, 101, 136, 176, 590
Circulation, 40, 93–109
Clark, Colin, on Pigou, 779–794
Clark, John Bates, 381, 388, 398, 706, 715, 763
  appraised by J. M. Clark, 592–612
Clark, John Maurice, 415–416, 437, 647, 765
  on J. B. Clark, 592–612
Clarke, Daniel, 148
Class, 260–261, 278–279, 409–411
Class struggle, 313, 318–320, 410–411
Classical economics, 112–249, 368, 528, 570, 598, 602–603, 631–633, 711, 721, 767
  Bastiat, 226–240
  Bentham, 184–225
  Malthus, 144–157
  Mill, 201–225
  Ricardo, 158–183
  Say, 241–249
  Smith, 113–143
Clemence, R. V., 752
Closed and open cycles, 639
Cobbett, William, 150, 271
Cobden, Richard, 225, 227
Coefficients of production, 587, 635, 642–643
Cognate products, 560
Colbert, Jean-Baptiste, 33, 35, 41, 84–85, 245–246
Cole, G. D. H., appraisal of Owen, 297–312
Cole, Margaret, 297
Coleridge, Samuel Taylor, 153–154, 216, 219, 722
Collective action, 406
Collective bargaining, 407
Collet, C. E., 515–516, 522, 524
Colonial system, 35
Colonization, 275
Colquhoun, Patrick, 278–279, 282, 292
Combination laws, 287, 308
Commodity-value of labor, 101–109
Common law, 407

Commons, John R., 378
  appraised by Perlman, 403–412
Communal property, 3–15, 18–19
Communism, 3–15, 18–19, 69–71, 272, 277, 280–281, 283, 292–293, 303, 770
Communist Manifesto, 267
Comparative advantage, 158
Competition, 109, 139–140, 222–224, 261, 263, 266, 277, 284, 302, 304, 463–464, 582, 591–592, 598–601, 605–608, 610, 630
Complementary goods, 464, 533, 647
Comte, Auguste, 215, 221, 295
Condillac, E. B. de, 53, 529
Condorcet, Marquis de, 152
Conservation, 493–497
Considérant, V. P., 229
Constant, Benjamin, 256
Constant coefficients of production, 587, 635, 642–643
Constant marginal utility of money, 634
Constant returns, 175
Consumer and consumption, 279, 466–467, 604, 611, 769–770, 777
  cooperation, 303
  loans, 22–30
  rent, 467
  surplus, 785
Contract curve, 615, 623
Convertibility of paper money, 162, 164
Cooper, Thomas, 286
Cooperation, 184, 270, 273, 281, 294, 297–312, 343, 346, 350, 598, 600
Corn laws, 493
Correlation analysis, 621–622
Cosmopolitanism, 241, 246
Cossa, L., 542
Cost of production, 86–109, 175–183, 235, 462–464, 510, 557–559, 606–607, 710, 712, 718
Cournot, Antoine Augustin, 116, 182, 419, 453–454, 476, 509, 512–513, 529–530, 542, 582–583, 591, 617, 624, 632, 638, 767
  appraised by Fisher, 458–469
Courtney, Leonard, 522
Cozens-Hardy, H. H., 515

Credit, 22–30, 79–80
  expansion, 671, 676–678, 756
  Wicksell, 652–699
Croce, Benedetto, 62
Crusoe, Robinson, 335, 365, 480, 561, 754
Cumulative process, 678
Cunningham, William, 32, 618, 625
Currency theory, 676–678

Daire, Eugène, 56
Darwin, Charles, 122, 147, 150–151, 317–321, 327–328, 385–395, 402, 492, 728, 776
Darwin, George, 511
Davanzati, Bernardo, 39, 77–78
Davenant, Charles, 39, 50, 52, 59, 372
Davenport, H. J., 378, 391, 439, 593
Davidson, D., 656
Deflation, 771–772
Demand, and income, 641
  and supply, 74–80, 144, 156, 175–183, 458, 462–463, 471–472, 582–585, 606, 641, 712, 714–715, 766, 777
  effective, 144, 156, 765, 769
  elasticity, 75
  for money, 769
  price, 180
  Say's law, 241, 258–268
  statistical demand curve, 641, 740
Demaria, Giovanni, appraisal of Pareto, 628–651
Democracy, 205, 215, 722
Depletion of resources, 493–497
Depreciation of exchange, 161–163
Depression, 144, 156, 326, 399, 766, 769
Depression economics, 768
Determinateness of equilibrium, 472, 638–639, 644
Determinism, 304, 757
Development, economic, 158, 166, 175–176, 317–321, 331, 484, 493–497, 603–604, 611–612, 646–647, 652, 698, 734, 751–755
Dewey, John, 415–416
Diagrams, 509
Dialectic materialism, 313, 317–321
Diderot, Denis, 56

Dietzel, Heinrich, 573, 746
Differential, calculus, 175, 582, 703
  rent, 141, 158, 163
  wages, 118–122
Diminishing returns, 144, 175, 464, 720, 786–788
Diminishing utility, 77, 80, 116, 475, 712
Dismal science, 144, 148
Distribution and distribution theory, 93–99, 113–143, 248, 261, 264, 277, 279, 281, 284–285, 287–290, 292, 322–323, 331, 451–453, 559–560, 592, 602, 609–612, 628, 645–646, 652, 705–706, 715
Disutility, 180, 475, 508, 606
Division of labor, 113–114, 396, 399
Doherty, John, 308
Doody, Francis S., 752
Dopsch, A., 737
Dorfman, Joseph, 378, 383, 392, 428, 595
Douglas, Mrs. Stair, 219
Douglas, Paul H., on Adam Smith, 113–143
Dublin, Louis I., 136
Duchâtel, Tanneguy, 247
Dühring, Eugen, 372
Dunbar, C. F., 174
Duns Scotus, 19
Duopoly, 458, 463, 465, 582
Dupuit, Jules, 116, 464, 509, 512, 530
Dynamics and statics, 65–67, 455, 590–592, 602–611, 630, 641–647, 652, 751–758, 763

Econometrics, 616, 759, 774
Economic historians, 722
Economic man, 716
Economic laws, 72
Économistes. See Physiocrats
Economists, influence of, 778
Edgeworth, F. Y., 52, 223, 225, 392, 463, 465, 467, 490, 514, 524–525, 585–586, 588, 595, 632, 635, 638, 705–706, 715, 719, 730, 750
  appraised by Bowley, 615–627
Edgeworth, Maria, 616
Education, 301–302, 353, 521
Effective demand, 144, 156, 765, 769

Ehrenberg, Richard, 453
Ehrlich, Eugen, 739
Einaudi, Luigi, 61–82
Elasticity of demand, 75
Ellis, Howard, 765
Ely, Richard T., 542
Emigration, 151
Empiricism, 157, 222, 366, 413–442, 448, 637
Encyclopédistes, 56–57, 62
Engels, Friedrich, 295, 313, 317–319, 374
English socialism, 269–296
Engrossing, 23
Entrepreneur, 42, 64, 241, 288, 472, 480, 588, 609, 734, 751, 755
Épinay, Madame d', 62
Equality, 75–76, 134, 263, 279–281, 723
Equations, system of, 577, 584–586, 640, 648–650, 769
Equilibrium, 65–67, 69, 75, 455, 471–474, 479, 533, 580, 590–591, 603, 625, 628–652, 678–679, 710, 714, 763, 777
Ethics, 3, 16–30, 41, 116–117, 193–200, 207, 229–233, 599, 610, 617, 723–725, 727, 731, 761, 782
Euler, L., 639
Evans, G. Heberton, 437
Evolution, 150–151, 317–321, 385–395, 646–647
Exchange, 173–183, 231, 244, 471–472, 582–586
    foreign, 28, 40, 53–54, 161–163, 461–462, 774–775
    value, 114–117, 165, 173–183, 233–240, 242–249
Expectations, 769
Exploitation, 599, 610

Fabian Society, 296, 297, 341–359, 403–405, 409
Factor price, 480–481, 535, 554, 557–559, 561, 572–573, 586–588, 659–669, 705–706
Factory legislation, 270, 305–306
Fair price, 22–30
Falling profit rate, 139

Fanno, Marco, 654
Fascism, 628
Fashion, 76
Fatalism, 260
Fawcett, Henry, 495, 718
Fay, C. R., on Malthus, 144–145, 149–153
Felicific calculus, 184–200, 207–211
Feudalism, 16–30, 32, 106–109
Feuerbach, L. A., 317
Final degree of utility, 178–181, 509, 704
Firth, Raymond W., 225
Fisher, Irving, 287, 617, 621, 748, 771–772, 789
    on Cournot, 458–469
Fisher, R. A., 619, 621
Fixed capital, 101, 176, 590
Fixed price, 22–30
Flux, A. W., 611
Fontenay, R. de, 230
Forbonnais, F. Véron de, 58
Forced saving, 205, 652
Forecasting, 495
Foreign exchange, 28, 40, 53–54, 161–163, 461–462, 774–775
Fortrey, Samuel, 40
Foster, W. T., 131
Fourier, F. M. C., 247–248, 263, 281, 295
Foxwell, H. S., 130, 316, 488, 490, 511–514, 517, 522, 524–525, 626
    on Ricardian socialists, 269–296
Franklin, Benjamin, 210
Free goods, 115, 533
Free trade, 36, 41, 63, 91–92, 158, 163–164, 169, 203, 226–228, 246, 267–268, 465–466, 623–624, 720
Freedom of enterprise, 720, 770
Freedom of entry, 787
French origin of economics, 59–60
Frictions, 604, 755, 766
Friedjung, Heinrich, 556
Frisch, Ragnar, on Wicksell, 652–699
Functional analysis, 454–455, 460
Fundamental equations, 775–776
Furniss, E. S., 140
Future goods, 28, 80, 534, 568, 572–578, 659–669

Galiani, Ferdinando, 42, 61–82, 365
Galton, Sir Francis, 122, 392, 621
Ganzoni, Eduard, 63
Garman, Charles R., 595
Garnier, Joseph, 474
Garver, Raymond, 639
Gay, Edwin F., 429
General equilibrium, 580, 628–651, 710, 714
Geoffrin, Marie Thérèse, 62
George, Henry, 296, 702
    appraised by Hobson, 329–340
Gerschenkron, A., 734
Gerth, H., 760
Giddings, Franklin H., 596
Gide, Charles, 542
Giffen, Robert, 492
Gilbart, J. W., 499
Gladstone, W. E., 496
Godwin, William, 153–154, 271–277, 304
Gold, 39, 52–54, 161–164, 495, 499–500
    exchange standard, 655
    standard, 545–546
Goldscheid, Rudolf, 321
Goldsmith, Oliver, 199
Gompers, Samuel, 411
Goods, free, 115, 533
    future, 28, 80, 534, 568, 572–578, 659–669
Goschen, Viscount, 53
Gossen, Hermann Heinrich, 64, 76, 78, 116, 453, 464, 509, 512, 529, 534, 562, 617
    appraised by Walras, 470–488
Government, and business, 63, 81, 113, 211–214, 241, 263–264, 770, 781, 784, 787
    debt, 168–169
    spending, 777
Gratian, 18, 20
Gray, Asa, 389
Gray, John, 130–133, 269, 271, 278–279, 281–285, 292
Graziani, A., 542
Great Depression, 766
Greatest-happiness principle, 195, 207
Greek economics, 3–15
Greenbacks, 417–420

Gregory, T. E., 140, 171, 497
Grimm, Friedrich Melchior, 62
Gross, Gustav, 538, 541
Guilds, 34, 264, 371

Haavelmo, Trygve, 669
Haberler, Gottfried von, 526, 647, 765
    on Schumpeter, 734–762
Hadley, A. T., 462
Hales, John, 37
Halévy, Élie, 211, 213
    on Sismondi, 253–268
Hall, Charles, 269, 271, 273–276, 279
Halley, Edmund, 50, 52, 59
Hamilton, G. K., 658
Hamilton, Sir William, 210
Hansen, Alvin, 765
Happiness, 195, 205, 207, 625, 779
Harmony of interests, 41, 211–212, 229–231, 262, 784–785
Harrington, James, 206, 372
Harris, Joseph, 57, 115–116
Harris, Seymour, 765
Harrod, R. F., 763, 765
Hart, A. G., 765
Hartley, David, 192, 218
Hawtrey, R. G., 755, 772, 777
Hayek, F. A., 64, 72, 216, 568, 618, 642, 652, 743, 755, 765
    on Menger, 526–553
    on Wieser, 554–567
Hearn, W. E., 529
Heckscher, Eli F., 652, 655–656
    on mercantilism, 31–41
Hedonism, 184–200, 207–211, 320, 508, 648, 716
Hegel, G. W. F., 315, 317–321, 327–328, 365, 401, 753, 757
Helvetius, Claude Adrien, 211, 304
Henderson, Hubert, 777
Herford, C. H., 701–702
Hermann, F. B. W., 529, 533
Herschel, John, 496
Herschel, William, 503
Hicks, J. R., 530, 649, 706–707, 765, 783
    on Walras, 580–591
Higgs, Henry, 42
Hildebrand, Bruno, 64, 363, 366, 537, 556

Hilferding, Rudolph, 318, 737, 745, 753
Hill, William, 416
Himes, Norman E., 152, 204
Hinrichs, A. F., 563
Historians, economic, 722
Historical laws, 757
Historical school of economics, 73, 148, 528, 538–539
List, 241
Roscher, 363–377
Schmoller, 363
History of economics, 366, 372–373, 740
Hobbes, Thomas, 41, 123, 206, 222, 372
Hobson, John A., 771
on George, 329–340
Hodgskin, Thomas, 130–131, 269, 271, 285–291
Höfflinger, H., 734
Holbach, Baron d', 62, 304
Hollander, J. H., 171, 183
Holyoake, G. J., 275
Hotelling, H., 639
Hours of work, 264
Hughes, Charles E., 596
Hultgren, Thor, 437
Hume, David, 36, 43–44, 47, 56, 122, 143, 186–187, 209, 379–380, 382
Hume, Joseph, 287
Huskisson, William, 246
Hutcheson, Francis, 115
Hutton, R. H., 491, 515
Huyghens, Christian, 654
Huxley, Thomas H., 43, 345, 728

Ideal state of Plato, 3–15
Immigration, 151
Imperialism, 741, 744
Import bounties, 465
Imputation, 535, 554, 557–560, 562, 572–573, 587
Inama-Sternegg, K. Th. v., 737
Incentives, 20–30, 139–141, 190–192, 207–211, 216–221, 385–395, 604, 716
Incidence of taxes, 143, 158, 167
Income, 541, 740
and demand, 641

Income, distribution, 628, 645–646
tax, 789–790
Increasing returns, 175, 583–584, 786–788
Index numbers, 428–429, 499, 502, 615, 621–622, 788–789
Indifference curve, 458, 580, 615, 623, 639, 648–649, 651
Individualism, 241, 245, 270, 272, 338, 591, 720, 722
methodological, 633, 636–637, 753
Induction in economics, 156
"Industrial," 281
Industrial reserve army, 324–328
Industrial Revolution, 299, 311
Industry versus agriculture, 84–109
Infant industries, 38
Inflation, 205, 417–422, 756, 768
gap, 768
Wicksell, 652–699
Inheritance, taxation of, 204
Innovation, 608, 652, 734, 751, 755
Instantaneous adjustments, 66
Institution, defined, 403, 406
Institutional economics, 73, 592
Commons, 403–412
Mitchell, 413–442
Veblen, 378–402
Insurance, 204
Integrability, 639–640
Interdependence of economic phenomena, 65–66, 633
Interest, 78–80, 128–143, 182, 231, 451–452, 457–458, 481, 508, 652, 676, 754–755, 769
Böhm-Bawerk, 568, 572–578
morality, 22–30
pure, 27
Schumpeter, 743–744
Wicksell, 652–699
International trade, 158, 468, 615, 623–624. See also Free trade; Protection
International unit, 788–789
Interpersonal comparisons, 712, 732, 784, 788
Introspection, 743
Investigational economics, 403
Investment, 176–177, 501, 652, 669–676, 755

Investment and saving, 669–676, 767–
    770, 772, 777–778
Invisible hand, 769
Irish origin of economics, 59–60
Iron law of wages, 288
Italian origin of economics, 62

Jaeger, Oskar, 655
James, William, 389, 393–394
Jefferson, Thomas, 121
Jenkin, Fleeming, 464, 508–509
Jevons, Herbert Stanley, 182, 490,
    497, 506, 508, 522
Jevons, William Stanley, 64, 76, 116,
    128, 178–183, 210, 225, 278, 345,
    394, 460–461, 464, 468–469, 473–
    474, 476–478, 481–482, 488, 527–
    530, 537–538, 542, 570–571, 580–
    582, 590, 605, 616–618, 634, 700,
    702–713, 718, 772
  appraised by Keynes, 489–525
  appraised by Marshall, 178–183
  on Cantillon, 42–60
Johnson, Alvin, 596, 737
Johnson, Dr. Samuel, 188
Joint stock company, 35
Jones, Richard, 104, 222
Joseph, H. W. B., 127
Joyce, James, 768
Juraschek, F. v., 737
Just price, 22–30

Kahn, R. F., 777
Kaldor, N., 765
Kautsky, Karl, 101, 745
Kautz, Julius, 474
Keynes, John Maynard, 424, 581, 588,
    616, 618, 626, 636, 647, 654,
    669, 719, 730, 734, 748, 751–754,
    760–762, 780, 790
  appraised by Samuelson, 763–778
  on Jevons, 489–525
  on Malthus, 144–145, 153–157
Kimball, Janet, 132
King, Gregory, 52, 59
King's College, London, 618
Klein, Lawrence R., 764
Knies, Karl, 64, 363, 366, 537, 555–
    556, 595, 598
Knight, Frank H., 710, 755, 765, 783

Komorzynski, Johann von, 538, 541
Krünitz, J. G., 365
Kuznets, Simon, 437

Labor, 48, 93–109, 451–453, 609–610
  division of, 113–114
  economics, 403–412
  legislation, 264, 270, 305–306, 341–
    359
  market, 598–600
  pain, 236, 475
  supply, 139–141
  theory of value, 21, 49–51, 57–58,
    101–109, 113–143, 158, 165–166,
    173–183, 269–296, 313, 321–328,
    529, 568, 591, 599, 700, 703
  unions, see Unions
Laboulaye, E. de, 483
Labour Party, 341, 343, 404
Lagrange, J. L., 639
Laisser faire, 35–36, 39–41, 63, 109,
    113, 184, 211–214, 224, 226, 239,
    244, 277, 279, 294, 521, 592,
    601, 721, 781
Lalor, John, 286
Land, 48, 51, 56–58, 236–240, 274–
    275, 482–485, 702
  physiocrats, 83–109
  reform, 158
  tenure, 222
Lange, F. A., 474, 529
Lange, Oskar, 765
Langton, W., 55
Laplace, P. S. de, 617, 619
Lardner, D., 530, 582–583
Large-scale industry, 109
Laspeyres, Etienne, 36
Lassalle, Ferdinand, 278, 295–296
Laughlin, J. L., 378, 382, 416–417
Launhardt, W., 472
Lausanne school, 580, 628, 652, 700
  Pareto, 628–651
  Walras, 580–591
Lavergne, Léonce de, 56
Lavoisier, Antoine Laurent, 59
Law, John, 40, 45, 56, 115
Laws, economic, 72
  of demand and supply, 181
  of diminishing returns, 175
  of error, 620–622

Laws, of great numbers, 620
of markets, 241, 258–268, 766
of nature, 24, 41, 67–68
of small numbers, 554
Lederer, Emil, 737, 745
Legal institutions, 407–408
Leibniz, G. W. von, 373
Leopardi, Giacomo, 65
Lerner, A. P., 765
Lerner, Max, 378
Leroux, Pierre, 229
Levasseur, P. E., 371
Levy on capital, 169
Lewis, G. C., 224
Lexis, W., 619, 622
Liberalism, 64, 225–226, 526, 550, 570, 720, 722, 770
Lieben, R., 530, 542, 545, 634, 743
Lindahl, Erik, 654
Liquidity preference, 754, 769
List, Friedrich, 38, 365–366
on Say, 241–249
Lloyd, William Forster, 76
Location theory, 445, 457
Locke, John, 39–40, 48, 50, 59, 115–116, 121, 128, 285, 330, 372
Loeb, Jacques, 392
London School of Economics, 341, 347, 353
Longfield, Mountifort, 529, 705, 721
Lotka, A. J., 136
Lovett, William, 206
Lowenthal, Esther, 130
Luther, Martin, 21

Macaulay, Frederick R., 437, 646
Macaulay, Thomas Babington, 148, 206, 215, 517, 556
McCulloch, John Ramsay, 43–44, 125–126, 130, 133, 173, 221, 499–500, 522, 712, 721, 726
on Ricardo, 158–172
Macgregor, D. H., 625
Mach, Ernst, 654
Machiavelli, Niccolò, 65, 367
Machlup, Fritz, 526
Macleod, Henry Dunning, 44, 55, 182
Macmillan, Alexander, 496
Macmillan Committee, 777, 791
Macro-economics, 633, 751, 763

Malthus, Thomas Robert, 51, 113, 136, 139, 142, 163, 171, 174, 177, 204, 221, 259, 274–275, 277, 294, 377, 387, 450, 490, 493–494, 514, 719–720, 766, 772
appraised by Bonar, Fay, and Keynes, 144–157
Managed currency, 772
Manchester school, 224, 311, 721
Mandeville, Bernard, 41, 210
Mansfield, Lord, 188
Marget, A., 590
Marginal analysis, Austrian school, 526–579
Böhm-Bawerk, 568–579
Clark, 592–612
Gossen, 470–488
Jevons, 489–525
Marshall, 718–733
Menger, 526–553
Thünen, 456
Walras, 580–591
Wicksteed, 700–717
Wieser, 554–567
Marginal cost, 464
Marginal demand price, 179
Marginal productivity, 456, 587, 592, 602, 609–611, 652, 705–706, 715, 792
Marginal utility, 61, 76–80, 115, 175, 508, 534, 560, 581, 592, 599, 605, 704, 711–712
Markets, law of, 241, 258–268, 766
Marshall, Alfred, 64, 75–76, 148–149, 158, 225, 269, 396–398, 424, 453–454, 463, 490, 509–512, 516, 529–530, 537, 542, 571, 580–588, 591, 595, 597, 603, 607, 615–618, 622, 632–635, 652, 703, 707, 711–712, 722, 742, 748, 750, 752–753, 760–762, 766, 772–774, 777, 780–788
appraised by Viner, 718–733
on Ricardo, 173–183
Marshall, Mary, 511
Martineau, Harriet, 152–153
Martineau, James, 701
Marx, Karl, 21, 64, 117–118, 125–128, 130, 133, 154, 177, 204, 267, 269, 274, 278, 285–286, 288,

291–292, 294–296, 303–304, 333, 345, 374, 401–405, 409–410, 568, 571, 575, 579, 605, 610, 703, 737–738, 748, 750, 752–753, 757, 760–761
appraised by Veblen, 313–328
on the physiocrats, 100–109
Masson, David, 219
Mataja, V., 541, 545
Materialist conception of history, 303, 313, 317–321, 757
Mathematics and mathematical economics, 175, 179, 210–211, 445, 530, 577, 703
Cournot and Fisher, 458–469
Edgeworth, 615–627
Frisch and Wicksell, 652–699
Gossen, 470–488
Jevons, 489–525
Keynes, 774
Marshall, 718–733
Pareto, 628–651
Schumpeter, 740–742
Thünen, 451, 454, 456
Walras, 580–591
Maurice, Frederick, 215–216
Maxima and minima, 472, 475, 480, 591, 625, 646, 648–650, 783–785
Maxwell, James Clerk, 617
Mayer, Hans, 548, 713–714
Mazzola, G., 542
Meade, J. E., 765
Measurement, 616
Medieval economic thought, 3, 16–30
Meeker, Royal, 428
Mendel, G. J., 392
Menger, Anton, 130, 270–271, 316, 530–531, 550–551
Menger, Carl, 64, 76, 182, 464, 556, 558–559, 562, 570–573, 575, 580–581, 591, 657, 705–706, 711, 737, 742–743, 746, 748, 757
appraised by Hayek, 526–553
Menger, Karl, 530, 549
Menger, Max, 531
Mercantilism, 17, 63–64, 84–85, 105, 139–140, 243, 246, 263, 766
appraised by Heckscher, 31–42
Mercier, de la Rivière, 99
Method, Böhm-Bawerk, 578

Method, Cantillon, 64
Galiani, 62, 64–75
historical, 363–377
Marshall, 728–732
mathematical, 458–469
Menger, 538–540
Mill, 222–223
Mitchell, 417–418
of approximation, 67, 69, 455, 554
Ricardo, 277–278
Ricardo and Malthus, 174
Ricardo and Smith, 259–260
Schumpeter, 752–754
Thünen, 448
Veblen, 378–402
Wieser, 560–561, 564–565
Methodenstreit, 363, 743, 757
Methodism, 253
Metzler, Lloyd, 751
Meyer, Robert, 538, 541
Micro-economics, 751, 763
Middle ages, economic thought, 3, 16–30, 32–41
Migration, 151
Minimax, 630
Mill, James, 130, 133, 152, 163, 172, 187, 205–206, 208, 215–216, 218, 258, 286, 295, 726
Mill, John Stuart, 38, 49, 113, 121, 138–139, 147, 149, 158, 181, 208, 215, 226, 232, 281, 295–296, 331, 336, 345, 396, 398, 489–490, 497, 513–516, 528, 570, 581, 598–599, 617, 657, 711, 718, 721, 723, 726–727, 731, 780–781
appraised by Viner, 201–225
on Bentham, 184–200
Millar, John, 285
Miller, Adolph, 416
Mills, C. W., 760
Mills, F. C., 437
Mills, John, 504
Milton, John, 148
Mirabeau, Marquis de, 99, 103, 106
Mises, Ludwig von, 526, 547–548, 563, 568, 716, 737, 755, 771
Mitchell, Wesley C., 209, 211, 748
appraised by Burns, 413–442
on Veblen, 378–402

Money, 22–30, 32–33, 39, 59, 70–72, 78–80, 205, 283, 438, 671, 772, 784, 793
  Cambridge school, 718
  Cantillon, 52
  Keynes, 769, 775–776
  marginal utility of, 634
  market, 22–30
  Menger, 544–547
  Mitchell, 417–420
  monetary equilibrium, 652
  Ricardo, 161–163
  Schumpeter, 758
  value of, 164, 181
  Veblen, 396–398
  Walras, 590
  Wicksell, 652, 676–693
Monopolistic competition, 758
Monopoly, 23, 141, 143, 164, 204, 223, 275, 419, 445, 462, 464, 600–601, 608, 611, 615, 624, 650, 758, 787
Monroe, A. E., 42
Moore, H. L., 596, 636, 647
Moral arithmetic, 209–210
Moret, J., 714
Morse, Anson D., 595
Motives, economic, 20–30, 139–141, 190–192, 207–211, 216–221, 385–395, 604, 716
Multiple equilibrium, 639
Multiplier, 647, 751, 755, 777
Mun, Thomas, 37, 39–40, 48, 372
Myrdal, Gunnar, 652, 654

National Bureau of Economic Research, 413–414, 427, 429–433
National income, 430, 466–467, 674–675, 763, 779, 782
Nationalism, 241, 244–245. *See also* Protection
Nationality of economics, 59–60
Nationalization of land, 274, 329–340, 482–485, 702
Natural harmony, 211–212
Natural law, 24, 41, 67–68, 365–366, 376
Natural rate of interest, 652
Natural resources, 493–497
Natural rights, 231, 315, 722

Natural science, 498
Natural selection, 150–151, 319, 385–388
Natural value, 177, 560–562
Natural wage, 451–454
Nature, 63, 66, 68
Navigation laws, 35, 245
Necker, Jacques, 62, 365
Neoclassical economics, 718
Neo-malthusianism, 657–658
Net product, 83–109
New Austrian school, 526
New Harmony, 308
New School for Social Research, 737
Newmarch, William, 499
Newton, Sir Isaac, 53–55, 59, 461, 776
Nicolini, Fausto, 62
Noncompeting groups, 121, 226
Normal profit, 588
Normal value, 175
Normative character of economics, 230–232
North, Sir Dudley, 372
Numéraire, 584, 589

Ogilvie, William, 271, 275
Ohlin, Bertil, 652, 655–656, 773
Öhrvall, Hjalmar, 657
Oligopoly, 458, 462, 465, 582, 630, 787
Ollerenshaw, J. C., 504
Oppenheimer, Franz, 321, 324
Opportunity cost, 535, 554, 557, 588
Optimum situations, 648–650, 783, 785–787
Optimum size of farms, 457
Origin, national, of economics, 59–60
Oscillations, 646, 698
Ostwald, Wilhelm, 572
Overdeterminateness, 664
Overinvestment, 652
Overpopulation. *See* Population
Overproduction, 264, 266, 326, 766, 769
Oversaving, 329
Oversupply, 156
Owen, Robert, 130, 263, 271, 274, 276–277, 281–285, 293, 295, 518, 722

Owen, Robert, appraised by Cole, 297–312
Owen, Robert Dale, 152, 282, 291
Oxford, 625

Pain-and-pleasure calculus, 184–200, 207–211, 216–221
Paine, Thomas, 154, 232, 239, 271, 275
Paley, William, 156, 216
Palgrave, Inglis, 55, 492
Pantaleoni, M., 542, 557, 638, 647
Paper money, 40, 162, 164, 283
Pare, William, 280
Pareto, Vilfredo, 69, 458–459, 463, 468, 585, 589, 615, 703, 705–707, 713–714, 748, 779
    appraised by Demaria, 628–651
    law of, 628, 645–646
Particular equilibrium, 580, 633–634, 647, 710, 718
Patents, 608
Pater, Walter, 709
Patten, S. N., 542
Payments, balance of, 52
Pearson, Karl, 122, 392, 620–622
Peel, Sir Robert, 164, 168
Period of production, 659–669
Perlman, Selig, appraisal of Commons, 403–412
Pessimism, 259
Petition of the candlestick makers, 226–228
Petschek, Georg, 739
Petty, Sir William, 38–41, 47–48, 50–52, 58–59, 372, 492
Philippovich, E. v., 737
Philosophic radicals, 147, 184, 203–204
Philosophy, and economics, 3–30
    utilitarian, 184–200
Physicians. See Hall; Mandeville; Oppenheimer; Petty; Quesnay
Physiocrats, 32, 51, 56, 63–64, 67–68, 142, 230, 242, 289
    appraised by Marx, 100–109
    appraised by Smith, 83–99
Pierson, G. N., 542
Pietri-Tonelli, A. de, 714

Pigou, A. C., 145, 454, 599, 618, 623–624, 627, 636, 654, 718–719, 724, 765
    appraised by Colin Clark, 779–794
Place, Francis, 152, 286–287
Planning, 754
Plato, 3–15, 62, 276
Playfair, William, 498
Pleasure-and-pain calculus, 184–200, 207–211, 216–221
Plenty versus power, 37
Political arithmetic, 779
Political democracy, 205, 215, 722
Politics and economics, 3, 65, 67
Poor laws and poverty, 19, 147, 150–152, 203, 275, 284, 290, 306, 334, 343, 354, 599, 720, 723, 726–727
Popper, Karl, 757
Population and population theory, 38, 51–52, 63, 81, 136–138, 144, 157, 259, 274–275, 327–328, 493–494, 497, 604, 698, 720, 772
Positive character of economics, 229–232
Postlethwayt, Malachy, 58
Poverty. See Poor laws
Precious metals, 39, 52–54, 59
Price, Richard, 210
Price, discrimination, 624
    fixing, 22–30
    just, 22–30
    movements, 500–501, 669–678
    theory, 471–472, 479, 532
        Böhm-Bawerk, 573
        Clark, 606
        Galiani, 74–80
        Ricardo, 173–183
        Smith, 114–117
        Wieser, 566
Priestley, Joseph, 210
Prime cost, 176
Probability theory, 615, 617–625, 771, 774
Production, 480–481, 586–588
    cooperatives, 309
    function, 642–643
    See also Cost of production
Productive forces, 241, 244–245
Productivity, 56–57, 83–109, 142, 242–243, 278–279, 285, 327, 668

Professorship of political economy, first, 148–149

Profit, 18–30, 79, 86–109, 126–143, 177, 288, 336, 588, 600, 608, 777
sharing, 600

Progress, 149, 274, 317–321, 331, 484, 493–497, 603–604, 611–612, 646–647, 652, 698, 734, 751–753

Propensity, to consume, 768–770, 777
to save, 740–741

Property, 3–15, 18–19, 128–129, 134, 141, 204, 224, 231, 266–267, 272–274, 289–291, 293, 327, 329–340, 407, 482, 702

Protection, 38–39, 92, 169, 226–228, 241, 267–268, 465–466, 468, 612, 623–624

Proudhon, P. J., 229, 266–267, 294

Psychology, 385–395

Public debts, 168–169, 480

Public finance, 541, 562, 790

Public health, 520

Puritanism, 720. *See also* Calvin

Quantity theory of money, 417–419, 767, 772

Quesnay, François, 48, 51, 56–57, 59, 83–109, 142

Quetelet, Adolphe, 147

Radicals, philosophic, 147, 184, 203–204

Rae, John (1796–1872), 464

Rae, John (1845–1915), 113

Raleigh, Sir Walter, 372

Ramsey, Frank P., 773–774

Ranke, Leopold von, 374

Rathbone, Eleanor, 136

Read, Samuel, 286

Real cost, 588, 712

Recontracting, 586

Reform bills, 185, 308, 721

Reid, Thomas, 210

Reisch, Richard, 538

Religion and economic life, 16–30, 41, 600

Renner, Karl, 746

Rent, 86–109, 128–143, 147, 158, 163, 165–166, 331–340, 482–485, 544, 578, 715

Reparations, 773

Representative firm, 607

Reproduction cost, 101–109

Residual share, 143, 336

Returns, 175, 464, 583–584

Ricardian socialists, 114, 128–133, 150
appraised by Foxwell, 269–296

Ricardo, David, 49, 64, 108, 113, 115, 117–118, 124–128, 130, 133, 135, 139, 141, 148, 154, 205, 215–216, 221, 237–238, 248, 259, 277–278, 286, 288, 292, 307, 316, 323, 331, 336, 345, 365, 377, 388, 419, 464, 482, 514, 537, 570, 575–576, 599, 605–606, 676, 705, 711–712, 715, 720–721, 726, 766
appraised by McCulloch, 158–172
appraised by Marshall, 173–183

Ricci, Umberto, 632

Rice, Stuart, 415

Rist, Charles, 772

Robbins, Lionel, 510, 656
on Wicksteed, 700–717

Robertson, D. H., 654, 674, 718

Robinson, Joan, 588

Rochdale pioneers, 303, 600

Rodbertus, Karl Johann, 177, 597

Rogers, Thorold, 371, 503, 618–619, 625

Root, Elihu, 596

Rorty, Malcolm, 429

Roscher, Wilhelm, 64, 450, 474, 529, 537, 556, 598
appraised by Schmoller, 363–377

Roscoe, William, 490–491

Rosenstein-Rodan, P., 712, 714

Rossi, P., 247

Roundabout process of production, 568, 576–577

Rousseau, Jean Jacques, 62, 72, 232

Royal Society, 492

Royal Statistical Society, 147

Ruskin, John, 117, 144, 311, 329

St. Antonino, 16–30

St. Thomas Aquinas, 16–30

Saint-Simon, C. H. de, 215–216, 247, 263, 281, 295, 722

Salin, Edgar, 759

Samuelson, P. A., 639
  on Keynes, 763–778
Savigny, F. K. von, 367
Saving, 589, 652, 669–676, 740–741,
  755, 773, 784, 790
  and investment, 669–676, 767–770,
  772, 777–778
Sax, Emil, 538, 541–542, 545
Say, Jean Baptiste, 180, 229, 257, 372
  appraised by List, 241–249
  law of, 241, 258–268, 766
Say, Louis, 243
Scandinavian school of economics,
  652, 655
Scarcity, 25, 74–80, 533
Schaeffle, Albert, 316
Schelling, F. W. J., 365
Schieldrop, E. B., 671
Schmoller, Gustav, 32, 410, 538–540,
  743, 757
  on Roscher, 353–377
Schneider, Erich, on Thünen, 445–457
Scholastic thought and economics, 3,
  16–30
Schönfeld, L., 714
Schüller, Richard, 538, 549
Schullern-Schrattenhofen, H. von, 538,
  542
Schultz, Henry, 639, 641
Schumacher, H., 447, 453
Schumpeter, J. A., 526, 548, 557, 564,
  608, 647, 652–653, 656, 719, 774
  appraised by Haberler, 734–762
  on Böhm-Bawerk, 568–579
Schuster, Arthur, 503
Scorza, G., 639, 650
Scripture and economic thought, 16–
  30
Seager, H. R., 551
Seasonal fluctuations, 498–500
Secrétan, Charles, 477, 485, 542–543
Secular movements of prices, 500–501
Sedgwick, Adam, 216
Seelye, Julius, 595
Selection, natural, 150–151, 319, 385–
  388
Self-interest, 230, 244
Seligman, Edwin R. A., 32, 317
Senior, Nassau, 149, 224, 514, 719–
  721, 726

Sensini, G., 639
Sentimentality, 726, 761
Serra, Antonio, 39
Sewall, H. R., 116
Shaw, G. B., 700, 703
Shelley, Percy Bysshe, 153–155
Shotwell, J. T., 596
Sidgwick, Henry, 149, 225, 617, 780
Sieghart, R., 550
Silberner, Edmund, 205
Silver, 39, 52–54, 59
Single tax, 83, 108, 329–340
Sismondi, Simonde de, 294
  appraised by Halévy, 253–268
Skelton, O. D., 127
Slichter, Sumner, 765
Slutzky, E., 641
Small holdings, 264
Smart, W., 542, 574
Smith, Adam, 21, 32, 36, 39–40, 42–
  43, 48, 50, 60, 63–64, 68, 100–
  101, 105, 149, 161, 165, 174,
  202–203, 212, 221, 223, 229,
  241–247, 254–268, 271, 281, 285,
  289, 294, 323, 331, 365, 372,
  377, 396, 399, 514, 543, 712,
  720, 767, 788
  appraised by Douglas, 113–143
  on the physiocrats, 83–99
Smith, Sydney, 148
Smithies, Arthur, 762
Social justice, 272
Social legislation, 341–359
Social net product, 785–787
Social reform, 144, 146, 203–204,
  570
Social security, 204, 264
Socialism, 128–133, 150, 158, 184,
  204, 224, 228–229, 233–240, 247–
  248, 253–359, 598, 601, 610, 759
  British, 341–359
  Christian, 598, 600
  of the chair, 363
  Ricardian, 114, 128–133, 150, 269–
  296
  utopian, 722
Socialization, 224
Sociology, 628–631, 637, 765
Socrates, 3–15
Somary, F., 734, 737

Sombart, Werner, 757
Sommarin, E., 656–657
Southey, Robert, 726
Spångberg, Valfrid, 656–657
Spann, Othmar, 753
Specialization, 113–114, 396, 399
Specific productivity, 610
Spence, Thomas, 271
Spencer, Herbert, 292, 345, 556
Spiegel, H. W., 593
Spiethoff, A., 740
Spitalfields weavers, 280
Sraffa, Piero, 205
Staehle, H., 734
Staël, Madame de, 256
Stamp, Josiah, 790
Statics. *See* Dynamics and statics
Stationary state, 138, 590, 603, 660
Statistical demand curve, 641, 740
Statistics, 147, 149, 214, 245, 374, 365,
    413–442, 493–518, 615–616, 618–
    623, 779
Stein, Lorenz v., 556
Stein, Ludwig, 318
Stephen, Leslie, 311
Sterling, John, 215–216
Steuart, Sir James, 104, 106
Stolper, T., 734
Stolper, W., 761
Stone, I. N., 429
Strachey, Lytton, 771
Strigl, R. von, 716
Strikes, 600
Strindberg, August, 657
Structure of production, 533, 568,
    576–577
Subjectivism, 591, 633
Subsidies, 655, 786–787
Subsistence wage, 135–136, 144, 158,
    326
Substitution, 78, 647, 649
Substitution effect, 641
Sulzer, G., 707
Sunspots, 503–506
Supply, 74–80, 156, 175–183, 510,
    583–584, 766
    and demand, 777
    of capital, 143
    of labor, 139–141

Supply, price, 180
    reversibility of curve, 714–715
Surplus and surplus value, 83–109,
    125, 128–133, 142, 269–296, 313,
    321–328, 484, 599
Sweezy, Paul M., 737, 753

Tableau économique, 68, 83, 93–99
Taft, William H., 596
Tariff, 33, 92, 465–466, 468
Taussig, F. W., 201, 719, 747–748
Tawney, R. H., 205–206, 225, 253
    on medieval economic thought, 16–
    30
    on the Webbs, 341–359
Taxation, 83, 108, 143, 158, 167, 169,
    329, 331, 464, 623–624, 784,
    787, 790
Taylor, J. E., 491
Technological progress, 149, 264, 604,
    611, 698
Thaer, A. D., 447
Theological utilitarianism, 219
Thiele, T. N., 620
Thompson, H. M., 715
Thompson, William, 130–131, 133,
    150, 269, 271, 273, 276–281, 285,
    289, 292–293, 295, 316
Thornton, Henry, 766
Thorp, Willard L., 437, 646
Thünen, J. H. von, 464, 509, 513, 530,
    542, 570, 705
    appraised by Schneider, 445–457
Time, element of, 66, 176–177, 183,
    533, 568, 572–578, 586–588, 644–
    645, 751
    preference, 118, 568, 572–578
Tinbergen, J., 774
Todhunter, Isaac, 617, 622
Tolstoi, Leo, 556
Tooke, Thomas, 677, 681, 766, 777
Tooke Professorship, 618
Torrens, Robert, 214, 224, 721
Trade, balance, 38, 56
    terms, 773
    unions, 264, 270, 288, 390, 292–
    293, 308–310, 343, 348–359, 404,
    406–411, 600, 611, 630
Trading bodies, 179–180, 582
Transfer problem, 773

Turgot, Robert-Jacques, 83–109, 365
Twiss, Travers, 372

Uhr, C. G., 656
Uncertainty, 630
Underconsumption, 253–268, 326
Unearned increment, 329–340
Unemployment, 39, 49, 144, 151, 156, 262, 264, 325–328, 763, 766, 769, 777, 790–792
Unfair competition, 608
Unions, 264, 270, 288, 290, 292–293, 308–310, 343, 348–359, 404, 406–411, 600, 611, 630
Unity of economic life, 591
University College, London, 522
Urwick, E. J., 618
Use value, 114–117
User cost, 773
Usury, 22–30, 188
Utilitarianism, 184–225, 253, 316, 320, 323, 394, 591, 617, 625, 648, 716, 722, 782
Utility, 74–80, 113–117, 173–183, 277, 460–461, 470–488, 506–511, 529–530, 534, 648–649, 651, 703–704, 712–713, 718, 727, 783–785
of money, 784
Utopian socialists, 146, 247–248, 263, 272, 297–312, 722

Value, 57–58, 101–109, 113–143, 147, 158, 214
Austrian school, 526–579
Bastiat, 231–240
Cantillon, 49–51
Cournot, 460–465
Galiani, 74–80
Gossen, 475
Jevons, 506–511
Marshall, 718–733
of money, 164, 181, 500
Ricardo, 173–183
Smith, 113–143
surplus, 269–296
use and exchange, 114–117, 165, 262
See also Labor, theory of value
Vanderlint, Jacob, 291

Vauban, Seigneur Sébastien le Prestre de, 59
Vaughan, Rice, 48
Veblen, Thorstein, 329, 404–405, 415–416, 439, 593, 596
appraised by Mitchell, 378–402
on Marx, 313–328
Venn, T. J., 619, 622
Verein für Sozialpolitik, 363, 538
Vico, Giambattista, 62, 68
Villeneuve-Bargemont, A. de, 266, 372
Villermé, L. R., 266
Villey, E., 542
Viner, Jacob, on Bentham and Mill, 201–225
on Marshall, 718–733
Vogelstein, Th., 745
Voltaire, François Marie Arouet, 62, 186
Volterra, V., 639, 645

Waentig, H., 455
Wages, 18–19, 21, 38, 48–49, 57, 86–109, 113, 127–143, 158, 165, 176–177, 269–296, 321–326, 451–453, 457, 578, 610–611, 792–794
differences, 118–122
fund, 134, 292, 510, 792
goods, 636, 792–793
Waiting, 177
Wald, A., 639
Waley, Jacob, 515, 522
Walker, Francis, 224, 336
Wallace, Alfred Russell, 150–151
Wallas, Graham, 286
Walras, A. A., 530, 542, 581
Walras, Léon, 69, 182, 460, 464, 468, 509, 527–529, 537–538, 542, 570–571, 577, 628, 632–636, 639, 641, 644, 648–649, 705–706, 713, 742, 748, 750–753, 767
appraised by Hicks, 580–591
on Gossen, 470–488
Walsh, C. M., 122, 621
Wants, 534–535
War economics, 81–82, 168–169, 768
Warfare between man and nature, 63, 68
Waterhouse, Theodore, 515
Wealth, 39–40, 48, 55, 242–243

Webb, Beatrice and Sidney, 143, 184, 403–406
  appraised by Tawney, 341–359
Weber, Ernst Heinrich, 116
Weber, Max, 564, 760
Weiss, F. X., 549, 558, 563, 744, 754
Wells, David, 766
Whateley, Richard, 491
Whewell, William, 219
Whitaker, A. C., 122
Whitbread, Samuel, 154
Wicksell, Knut, 536, 589–591, 712, 715, 766
  appraised by Frisch, 652–699
Wicksteed, Philip, 116, 524, 611
  appraised by Robbins, 700–717
Wieser, F. von, 122, 124, 183, 428, 526–527, 531, 533–537, 541, 548–549, 571, 573, 705, 707, 711, 713, 737, 742–743, 746
  appraised by Hayek, 554–567
Wieser's law, 535, 557, 712
Wilson, Thomas, 24

Wolman, Leo, 437
Wood, Stuart, 609
Woolf, Virginia, 771
Wordsworth, William, 215–216, 722, 726
Workable competition, 592
Welfare economics, 598–599, 650, 712, 758–759, 779–794
Weller, Émil, 58
West, Edward, 141, 163
Westergård, Harald, 698
Weyl, Hermann, 743
Working hours, 264
Wright, Francis, 282
Wyclif, 25

Young, Allyn, 708
Young, Arthur, 140
Younger Austrian school, 526
Yule, G. U., 506

Zawadski, W., 714
Zeuthen, Frederik, 652
Zuckerkandl, Robert, 538, 541, 549